PSYCHOLOGY OF TERRORISM

Key Readings in Social Psychology

General Editor: ARIE W. KRUGLANSKI, University of Maryland at College Park

The aim of this series is to make available to senior undergraduate and graduate students key articles in each area of social psychology in an attractive, user-friendly format. Many professors want to encourage their students to engage directly with research in their fields, yet this can often be daunting for students coming to detailed study of a topic for the first time. Moreover, declining library budgets mean that articles are not always readily available, and course packs can be expensive and time-consuming to produce. **Key Readings in Social Psychology** aims to address this need by providing comprehensive volumes, each one of which will be edited by a senior and active researcher in the field. Articles will be carefully chosen to illustrate the way the field has developed historically as well as current issues and research directions. Each volume will have a similar structure to include:

- an overview chapter, as well as introduction to sections and articles
- questions for class discussion
- annotated bibliographies
- full author and subject indexes

Published Titles

The Self in Social Psychology	Roy F. Baumeister
Stereotypes and Prejudice	Charles Stangor
Motivational Science: Social and Personality Perspectives	E. Tory Higgins and Arie W. Kruglanski
Emotions in Social Psychology	W. Gerrod Parrott
Social Psychology and Human Sexuality	Roy F. Baumeister
Intergroup Relations	Michael A. Hogg and Dominic Abrams
The Social Psychology of Organizational Behavior	Leigh L. Thompson
Social Psychology: A General Reader	Arie W. Kruglanski and E. Tory Higgins
Social Psychology of Health	Peter Salovey and Alexander J. Rothman
The Interface of Social and Clinical Psychology	Robin M. Kowalski and Mark R. Leary
Political Psychology	John T. Jost and James Sidanius
Close Relationships	Harry T. Reis and Caryl Rusbult
Social Neuroscience	John T. Cacioppo and Gary G. Berntson
Social Cognition	David L. Hamilton
Small Groups	John M. Levine and Richard L. Moreland
Social Comparison Theories	Diederik A. Stapel and Hart Blanton
Attitudes: Their Structure, Function, and Consequences	Russell H. Fazio and Richard E. Petty
Psychology of Terrorism: Classic and Contemporary Insights	Jeff Victoroff and Arie W. Kruglanski

For continually updated information about published and forthcoming titles in the Key Readings in Social Psychology series, please visit: **www.keyreadings.com**

PSYCHOLOGY OF TERRORISM
Key Readings

Classic and
Contemporary Insights

Edited by

Jeff Victoroff
University of Southern California
Keck School of Medicine, USA

Arie W. Kruglanski
University of Maryland at College Park, USA

Ψ **Psychology Press**
Taylor & Francis Group
NEW YORK AND HOVE

Published in 2009
by Psychology Press
270 Madison Avenue
New York, NY 10016
www.psypress.com

Published in Great Britain
by Psychology Press
27 Church Road
Hove, East Sussex BN3 2FA
www.psypress.com

Psychology Press is an imprint of the Taylor & Francis Group, an informa business

Typeset in Times by RefineCatch Limited, Bungay, Suffolk, UK
Printed in the USA by Sheridan Books, Inc. on acid-free paper
Paperback cover design by Hybert Design
Paperback cover: "Eyes Behind the Mask" image by Alan Crosthwaite; "War Headlines" image © iStockphoto.com/
Nicholas Belton

10 9 8 7 6 5 4 3 2 1

Library of Congress Cataloging in Publication Data
A catalog record for this book is available from the Library of Congress.

ISBN 978–1–84169–464–1 (hbk)
ISBN 978–1–84169–465–8 (pbk)

Contents

About the Editors   x

Preface   xi
  Jeff Victoroff and Arie W. Kruglanski

Editors' Note   xiii

Acknowledgments   xiv

Introduction   1
  Jeff Victoroff and Arie W. Kruglanski

SECTION I
What is Terrorism and How Can Psychology Explain It?   3

READING 1
Individual Terror: Concept and Typology   9
  Ze'ev Iviansky

READING 2
Understanding Terrorist Behavior: The Limits and Opportunities of Psychological Inquiry   23
  Walter Reich

READING 3
The Psychology of Terrorism: "Syndrome" versus "Tool" Perspectives   35
  Arie W. Kruglanski and Shira Fishman

READING 4

The Mind of the Terrorist: A Review and Critique of
Psychological Approaches   55

Jeff Victoroff

SECTION II

Why Would One Want to Become a Terrorist?
Terrorists' Personality and Motivation   87

READING 5

Cheshire-Cat Logic: The Recurring Theme of Terrorist Abnormality
in Psychological Research   95

Andrew Silke

READING 6

The Terrorists in Their Own Words: Interviews with 35 Incarcerated
Middle Eastern Terrorists   109

Jerrold M. Post, Ehud Sprinzak, and Laurita M. Denny

READING 7

Palestinian Suicide Terrorism in the Second Intifada:
Motivations and Organizational Aspects   119

Assaf Moghadam

READING 8

Genesis of Suicide Terrorism   145

Scott Atran

READING 9

The Strategic Logic of Suicide Terrorism   157

Robert A. Pape

READING 10

Altruism and Fatalism: The Characteristics of Palestinian
Suicide Terrorists   185

Ami Pedahzur, Arie Perliger, and Leonard Weinberg

SECTION III

Why Would One Want to Become a Terrorist?
Possible Economic or Political Origins of Terrorism   195

READING 11

Does Poverty Cause Terrorism?   201

Alan B. Krueger and Jitka Maleckova

READING 12

Does Democracy Promote or Reduce Transnational
Terrorist Incidents?   211

Quan Li

READING 13

Who Are the Terrorists? Analyzing Changes in Sociological Profile
among Members of ETA   227

Fernando Reinares

SECTION IV

Why Would Terrorists Enjoy Wide Popular Support?   247

READING 14

Social Dominance and Social Identity in Lebanon:
Implications for Support of Violence Against the West   253

Shana Levin, P. J. Henry, Felicia Pratto, and Jim Sidanius

READING 15

Arab Attributions for the Attack on America:
The Case of Lebanese Subelites   269

Jim Sidanius, P. J. Henry, Felicia Pratto, and Shana Levin

READING 16

Mortality Salience, Martyrdom, and Military Might:
The Great Satan Versus the Axis of Evil   281

Tom Pyszczynski, Abdolhossein Abdollahi, Sheldon Solomon, Jeff Greenberg,
Florette Cohen, and David Weise

SECTION V
How Does One Become a Terrorist? Social and Psychological
Factors in Terrorism   299

READING 17
Recruitment Processes in Clandestine Political Organizations:
Italian Left-Wing Terrorism   307
Donatella della Porta

READING 18
The Psychopolitical Formation of Extreme Left Terrorism in a
Democracy: The Case of the Weathermen   317
Ehud Sprinzak

READING 19
Social Psychology of Terrorist Groups   331
Clark R. McCauley and Mary E. Segal

READING 20
Social Psychological Aspects of Political Terrorism   347
Ariel Merari and Nehemia Friedland

READING 21
Understanding Terror Networks   361
Marc Sageman

SECTION VI
Is Terrorism Rational? A Logical Perspective   367

READING 22
The Logic of Terrorism: Terrorist Behavior as a Product of
Strategic Choice   371
Martha Crenshaw

READING 23
A Theoretical Analysis of Transnational Terrorism   383
Todd Sandler, John T. Tschirhart, and Jon Cauley

SECTION VII
Is Terrorism Evil? 405

READING 24
Justifications and Means: The Moral Dimension of
State-Sponsored Terrorism 409
Grant Wardlaw

READING 25
Islam's "Neglected Duty" 419
Mark Juergensmeyer

SECTION VIII
How Can Terrorism Be Overcome? 435

READING 26
Soft Power and the Psychology of Suicide Bombing 441
Scott Atran

READING 27
Do Targeted Assassinations Work? A Multivariate Analysis
of Israel's Controversial Tactic during Al-Aqsa Uprising 445
Mohammed M. Hafez and Joseph M. Hatfield

READING 28
What Happened to Suicide Bombings in Israel? Insights from a
Terror Stock Model 467
Edward H. Kaplan, Alex Mintz, Shaul Mishal, and Claudio Samban

Author Index 477
Subject Index 486

About the Editors

Jeff Victoroff began his career in academic medicine. After training in Neurology and Psychiatry at Harvard and a fellowship in Neurobehavior at UCLA, he joined the faculty of the University of Southern California Keck School of Medicine. His initial research focused on neurodegeneration and on the reasons for aggression seen in patients with neurological disorders. After 9/11 he made a dramatic change in his research career to study the deep causes of human aggression, including both individual and collective violence, from a transdisciplinary perspective.

Arie W. Kruglanski is a Distinguished University Professor at the University of Maryland and one of the most cited researchers in Social Psychology. His interests have centered on the psychology of judgment and knowledge formation, as well as on the processes of group decision making, goal formation and implementation. He has served as Editor of the *Journal of Personality and Social Psychology: Attitudes and Social Cognition* and the *Personality and Social Psychology Bulletin*. Among other distinctions, he has received the Donald T. Campbell Award for Distinguished Scientific Contribution to Social Psychology, the Humboldt Foundation Life Achievement Award (Forschungpreis), and the NIMH Research Scientist Award Ko5. His publications include over 180 scientific literature articles, chapters, and books on social personality psychology.

He is Editor of two Psychology Press series—*Key Readings in Social Psychology* and *Principles of Social Psychology*—and co-editor of a series of upper-level texts called *Frontiers of Social Psychology*.

Preface

The specter of terrorism (whether international or domestic) is casting its dark shadow these days on the future of orderly societies, threatening cataclysmic events in which staggering numbers of people will lose their lives and world economies will be dealt shattering blows. Remembrance of the horrors of 9/11/01 in Manhattan, 3/11/04 in Madrid, and 7/7/05 in London conveys in vivid images the vulnerability of even the most powerful of today's nations to sneak attacks by fanatics willing to sacrifice their lives for a cause they believe is right and just.

The phenomenon of modern international terrorism is not new, yet even though it is over 100 years old the scope of its menace has continued to grow. Whereas the 19th century Russian anarchists practiced terrorism through the assassination of public figures, subsequent terrorist waves added tactics to the arsenal of fear-inducing tools at the terrorists' disposal. Hijacking of planes, kidnapping (and occasional beheading) of hostages, release of poison gas, suicide bombings, or use of improvised explosive devices are just some of the terrible methods now available to all those who feel that their grievances (whether real or imagined) warrant the infliction on their perceived malefactors of the most ruthless and horrific of punishments. The greatest current fear, of course, is that terrorists will lay their hands on nuclear, chemical, and/or biological weapons that would bring the threat they represent to the dreaded next level.

Substate terrorism is a form of psychological warfare. Its intent is to frighten the targeted populations into panic and disorder that will presumably translate into pressure on their respective governments to yield to terrorists' demands and reach accommodations that advance the terrorists' causes. Psychology plays a role at the other end as well. It relates to states of mind under which individuals have no qualms about killing innocent civilians while getting themselves killed as well, and to psychological processes that bring about such extraordinary states of mind. Indeed, no thorough understanding of terrorism is possible without psychological insights into its workings both at its *source* (the psyche of the terrorist perpetrators) and at its *targets* (the psyche of those exposed to the terrorist threat).

Psychological analyses of modern terrorism have been available in the social science literature at least since the late 1960s and the 1970s, a time when a wave of terrorist attacks at different parts of the globe catapulted the topic to the top of the world's agenda. Scholars from many social science disciplines have earnestly attempted to understand the mind of the terrorist. In the present volume we have tried to convey valuable psychological insights into terrorism by sampling what to us and to other experts appear to constitute the most informative treatments of this topic.

Our selection of articles for this volume followed a systematic, multistage process. We first contacted 26 recognized authorities on the psychology of terrorism representing the overlapping academic worlds of psychology, social science, and political science. We asked for their short-lists—the best papers they had ever read on the psychology of terrorism. We then examined the lists and identified papers that kept coming up in various scholars' recommendations. And of course we exercised our own best judgment as to what are the most informative and readable contributions of the lot. Next we submitted a list of 38 fine papers to Psychology Press and they took their turn in soliciting expert feedback. The ratings of those reviewers helped us winnow down the 38 to 28 papers that arguably comprise the essence of achievement in the field to date. Deliberately, these offerings include all-time classics as well as novel contributions discussing the "here and now" of terrorism. They represent psychologically relevant perspectives derived from diverse social science disciplines and they address a wide range of terrorist groups differing on multiple dimensions (ideological background; time and geographical location of activity). Such variety should, hopefully, afford the readers a general perspective on the psychology of terrorism and what its different instances share in common and how they differ.

We then organized the 28 papers we selected into themes that made sense to us and that organize the discourse about the psychology of terrorism around several meaningful issues. These themes inevitably overlap. In the human species, individual and social psychology are naturally intertwined. Readers may well find intriguing information vital to one theme in papers that have been sorted into a different thematic batch. But overall, we hope that you, dear readers, will find our organizing scheme helpful. It is, therefore, with pleasure and anticipation that we offer this collection of readings on the psychology of terrorism to the many students from diverse social science disciplines who may find the topic intriguing, the psychological approach to it valuable, and the deep lessons indispensable in our long-term struggle for peace and against violent extremism.

Jeff Victoroff
Arie W. Kruglanski

Editors' Note

This volume represents the thought and labor of a large and very special cohort. After 9/11, scholars and practitioners of all stripes were struggling to educate themselves about the phenomenon of terrorism—struggling to answer questions from family and friends and colleagues and sometime leaders—how could anyone do such things? Yet the truly expert analyses of the psychology of terrorism are widely scattered across journals and books and time. Pulling together the best writings in a single volume was an obvious duty. But choosing the best writings required consultation with a large number of renowned authorities in order to assure that the final offering would represent an expert consensus.

Therefore, we are deeply indebted to the following scholars, without whose thoughtful advice this book could never have been prepared: Yonah Alexander, Nicole Argo, Scott Atran, Mia Bloom, Ronald Crelinsten, Martha Crenshaw, Mark Dechesne, Christine Fair, Dipak Gupta, Mohhamed Hafez, Art Kendall, Gary LaFree, Jitka Maleckova, Ariel Merari, Jerrold Post, Ami Pedahzur, Ian Reader, Martin Rudner, Magnus Ranstorp, David Rapaport, Marc Sageman, Todd Sandler, and Jessica Stern. We would like to extend a very special thanks to John Horgan and to Rogelio Alonso, whose responses to our queries yielded literal treasure troves of ideas.

We also wish to thank psychologist Janice Adelman, whose ongoing support, careful analysis, and critical thinking enriched the entire process. And, as ever, we are immensely grateful to our wonderful wives, Alla and Hannah, whose support and advice (and tolerance!) makes life worth living.

Acknowledgments

The editors and publisher are grateful to the following for permission to reproduce the articles in this book:

Reading 1: Iviansky, Z. (1977). Individual Terror: Concept and Typology. *Journal of Contemporary History*, *12*, 43–63. Copyright © 1977, reprinted by permission of Sage.

Reading 2: Reich, W. (1998). Understanding terrorist behavior: The limits and opportunities of psychological inquiry. In W. Reich (Ed.), *Origins of Terrorism: Psychologies, Ideologies, Theologies, States of Mind* (pp. 261–280). Washington, DC: The Woodrow Wilson Center Press. Copyright © 1998.

Reading 3: Kruglanksi, A. W., & Fishman, S. (2006). The Psychology of Terrorism: "Syndrome" Versus "Tool" Perspectives. *Terrorism and Political Violence*, *18*, 193–215. Published by Taylor & Francis Group.

Reading 4: Victoroff, J. (2005). The mind of the terrorist: A review and critique of psychological approaches. *Journal of Conflict Resolution*, *49*, 3–42. Copyright © 2005, reprinted by permission of Sage Publications.

Reading 5: Silke, A. (1998). Cheshire-cat logic: The recurring theme of terrorist abnormality in psychological research. *Psychology, Crime and Law*, *4*, 51–69. Published by Taylor & Francis Group.

Reading 6: Post, J. M., Sprinzak, E., & Denny, L. M. (2003). The terrorists in their own words: Interviews with 35 incarcerated Middle Eastern terrorists. *Terrorism and Political Violence*, *15*, 171–184. Published by Taylor & Francis Group.

Reading 7: Moghadam, A. (2003). Palestinian suicide terrorism in the second intifada: Motivations and organizational aspects. *Studies in Conflict and Terrorism*, *26*, 65–92. Published by Taylor & Francis Group.

Reading 8: Atran, S. (2003). Genesis of suicide terrorism. *Science*, *299*, 1534–1539. Reprinted with permission from AAAS.

Reading 9: Pape, R. A. (2003). The Strategic Logic of Suicide Terrorism. *American Political Science Review*, *97*, 343–361. Copyright © The American Political Science Association, published by Cambridge University Press, reproduced with permission.

Reading 10: Pedahzur, A., Perliger, A., & Weinberg, L. (2003). Altruism and fatalism: The characteristics of Palestinian suicide terrorists. *Deviant Behavior*, *24*, 405–423. Published by Taylor & Francis Group.

Reading 11: Krueger, A. B., & Maleckova, J. (2002). The economics and the education of suicide bombers: Does poverty cause terrorism? *The New Republic Online* [posted June 20, 2002]. Published by The New Republic.

Reading 12: Li, Q. (2005). Does democracy promote or reduce transnational terrorist incidents? *Journal of Conflict Resolution*, *49*, 278–297. Copyright © 2005, reprinted by permission of Sage Publications.

Reading 13: Reinares, F. (2004). Who are the terrorists? Analyzing changes in sociological profile among members of ETA. *Studies in Conflict and Terrorism*, *27*, 465–488. Published by Taylor & Francis Group.

Reading 14: Levin, S., Henry, P. J., Pratto, F., & Sidanius, J. (2003). Social dominance and social identity in Lebanon: Implications for support of violence against the West. *Group Processes and Intergroup Relations*, *6*, 353–368. Copyright © 2003, reprinted by permission of Sage.

Reading 15: Sidanius, J., Henry, P. J., Pratto, F., & Levin, S. (2004). Arab attributions for the attack on America: The case of Lebanese subelites. *Journal of Cross-Cultural Psychology*, *35*, 403–416. Copyright © 2004, reprinted by permission of Sage Publications.

Reading 16: Pyszczynski, T., Abdollahi, A., Solomon, S., Greenberg, J., Cohen, F., & Weise, D. (2006). Mortality salience, martyrdom, and military might: The Great Satan versus the axis of evil. *Personality and Social Psychology Bulletin*, *32*, 525–537. Copyright © 2006, reprinted by permission of Sage Publications.

Reading 17: della Porta, D. (1988). Recruitment processes in clandestine political organizations: Italian leftwing terrorism. In S. Tarrow, B. Klandermans & H. Kriesi (Eds.), *From Structure to Action* (pp. 155–169). New York: JAI Press Inc. Reprinted with permission.

Reading 18: Sprinzak, E. (1998). The psychopolitical formation of extreme left terrorism in a democracy: The case of the Weathermen. In W. Reich (Ed.), *Origins of Terrorism: Psychologies, Ideologies, Theologies, States of Mind* (pp. 65–85). Washington, DC: The Woodrow Wilson Center Press. Copyright © 1998.

Reading 19: McCauley, C. R., & Segal, M. E. (1987). Social psychology of terrorist groups. In C. A. Hendrick (Ed.), *Group Processes and Intergroup Relations* (pp. 231–256). Newbury Park, CA: Sage Publications. Copyright © 1987, reprinted by permission of Sage.

Reading 20: Merari, A., & Friedland, N. (1985). Social psychological aspects of political terrorism. In S. Oskamp (Ed.), *International Conflict and National Public Policy Issues* (pp. 185–205). Beverly Hills, CA: Sage Publications. Copyright © 1985.

Reading 21: Sageman, M. (2005). Understanding terror networks. *International Journal of Emergency Mental Health*, *7*, 5–8. Published by Chevron Publishing Corporation.

Reading 22: Crenshaw, M. (1998). The logic of terrorism: Terrorist behavior as a product of strategic choice. In W. Reich (Ed.), *Origins of Terrorism: Psychologies, Ideologies, Theologies, States of Mind* (pp. 7–24). Washington, DC: The Woodrow Wilson Center Press. Copyright © 1998.

Reading 23: Sandler, T., Tschirhart, J. T., Cauley, J. (1983). A theoretical analysis of transnational terrorism. *The American Political Science Review*, *77*, 36–54. Copyright © The American Political Science Association, published by Cambridge University Press, reproduced with permission.

Reading 24: Wardlaw, G. (1989). Justifications and means: The moral dimension of state-sponsored terrorism. In D. C. Rapoport & Y. Alexander (Eds.), *The Morality of Terrorism*. New York: Columbia University Press. Copyright © 1989.

Reading 25: Juergensmeyer, M. (2000). Islam's neglected duty. In M. Juergensmeyer, *Terror in the Mind of God: The Global Rise of Religious Violence* (pp. 60–83). Berkeley & Los Angeles, CA: University of California Press. Copyright © 2000.

Reading 26: Atran, S. (2004). Soft power and the psychology of suicide bombing. *Terrorism Monitor*, *2*(11), 1–3 [June 3, 2004]. www.jamestown.org. Published by The Jamestown Foundation.

Reading 27: Hafez, M. M., & Hatfield, J. M. (2006). Do targeted assassinations work? A Multivariate analysis of Israel's controversial tactic during Al-Aqsa uprising. *Studies in Conflict and Terrorism*, *29*, 359–382. Published by Taylor & Francis Group.

Reading 28: Kaplan, E. H., Mintz, A., Mishal, S., & Samban, C. (2005). What happened to suicide bombings in Israel? Insights from a terror stock model. *Studies in Conflict and Terrorism*, *28*, 225–235. Published by Taylor & Francis Group.

Introduction

Jeff Victoroff and Arie W. Kruglanski

Terrorism is applied psychology. It is literally the application of knowledge about others' minds—knowing what others are likely to dread—to guide the behavior of some aggressors in a conflict. Despite the many definitions that have been offered, a few elements common to this type of aggression have percolated to the surface of terrorism scholarship and won some degree of consensus: Terrorism means attacks on non-combatants to cause fear and to advance a political aim. Thus terrorism only exists because humans are endowed by evolution with a theory of mind: We think and feel, we plot and we fear, and we base our social actions on the assumption that other humans do too. We know what would make us so afraid that we might change our behavior, and we assume that similar things would make others so afraid that they would change their behaviors. Terrorists use that assumption—apply that psychology—to guide their violent plans and acts. Thus the *psychology of terrorism* is the essence of terrorism. It is terrorism's reason for being, and, sometimes, it is terrorism's reason for succeeding.

Yet the psychology of terrorism might also be regarded as a set of fascinating, interlocking pieces of the puzzle of conflict psychology: the psychology of groups who regard one another as threats and who deal with that feeling in different ways; the psychology of intergroup enmity, which is both a cause and an effect of political violence; the psychology of dehumanizing the other, which permits

one to overcome natural inhibitions against violence and to hurt or kill; the psychology of the members of a group who support extreme forms of violence against another group; the interesting psychology of that small subset of people who join politically violent organizations; the psychology of those who actually plan or commit the attacks on non-combatants; the psychology of the effectiveness of fear in changing group behavior (whether or not the change is the one desired by the terrorist); the psychology of outrage at attacks on civilians, and how it may lead to counterresponses that the terrorists did not want or expect; the psychology of individual traumatized victims, acquaintances of victims, and other individuals who fear becoming victims; and the psychology of leaders of targeted groups, whose temperament may play a key role in the terrorists' ultimate success or failure in provoking policy change.

As suggested in the Preface, this collection of readings is thematically organized around several fundamental questions one may want to raise about the psychology of terrorism. The first section (*What is Terrorism and How Can Psychology Explain It?*) addresses the elemental question of what the phenomenon of terrorism consists of and what it is that psychology needs to explain to illuminate this phenomenon. Sections II and III (*Why Would One Want to Become a Terrorist?*) both delve into the reasons and causes that may prompt individuals to make the fateful leap from radical ideas to radical actions. Section II deals with factors related to the *person* (specifically, an individual's personality and motivation) and Section III addresses factors related to the *situation* (specifically, economic and political features potentially conducive to terrorism). Section IV (*Why Would Terrorists Enjoy Wide Popular Support?*) asks about communal support for terrorism, a factor that appears to be critically important for the persistence of many terrorist groups. Section V (*How Does One Become a Terrorist?*) addresses the process of becoming a terrorist. Section VI (*Is Terrorism Rational?*) inquires into the logic of terrorism, whether such a logic even exists, and what its features might be. Section VII (*Is Terrorism Evil?*) raises the moral issue on many people's minds: whether the atrocities perpetrated by terrorists invariably earn them the label of evil and immoral beings. Finally, Section VIII (*How Can Terrorism Be Overcome?*) addresses the pressing pragmatic issue: Given the heterogeneity of its drivers, the multiplicity of its manifestations, and the immensity of its potential threat—and perhaps capitalizing on the insights of social psychology—how might terrorism be overcome?

Each section is preceded by a general introduction that frames the articles in their proper context. Each reading is further preceded by editors' comments and several discussion questions intended to focus the reader's attention on the key issues raised by the specific offering. Taken as a whole, this compilation is intended to represent the best of the best—the state of the art—and the most comprehensive and engaging single volume summary of the psychology of terrorism.

SECTION I

What is Terrorism and How Can Psychology Explain It?

Terrorism is of central concern these days to human societies the world over and it poses considerable challenges to foreign policies, military strategies, and immigration philosophies of numerous nations. The vulnerability to terrorist attacks of major systems essential to the functioning of organized states (e.g., the transportation system, the water system, the health system, the power system, the monetary system) is immense, particularly in light of terrorists' inestimable potential to acquire chemical, nuclear, or biological weapons and use them to wreak untold damage on the workings of orderly communities. Given the number, diversity, and spread of terrorists' potential targets, full-proof protection may seem impossible in terms of the sheer amount of human resources this may require and the untold economic costs it may exact. Yet the entire effort would be superfluous if it were possible to confront the problem at its source (rather than at its target) and convince terrorists to abandon their pernicious enterprise. It is here that psychology comes in, for in essence terrorism is a form of human behavior that should conform to general psychological laws and principles. But how can terrorism be psychologically understood? And what is terrorism anyway? Several articles in the present section address these issues from different disciplinary perspectives. Ze'ev Iviansky (a historian), in an article in 1977 (Reading 1), depicts the ideological beliefs of 19th century anarchists and their attitudes toward terrorism. According to Iviansky, anarchist terrorism "is not accompanied by the prospect of victory or not even the desire for victory. It is a suicidal act that defies morality and society, motivated by a pining for the future kingdom of freedom, equality and justice." It is an example of what has become known as "individual terror," expressing the emphasis that "terrorist activity, despite the fundamental ideological motivation, was always individual." Writing 20 years later Walter Reich (Reading 2) notes the considerable variety of terrorisms over the course of human history and warns against the dangers of overgeneralization and reductionism in approaching terrorism. Kruglanski and Fishman (Reading 3) juxtapose two distinct psychologies of terrorism, one that views it as a psychological syndrome characterized by unique properties and one that views it as a tool that any individual or group might use under appropriate circumstances. Finally, Jeff Victoroff (Reading 4) notes the abundance of theory and speculation about the psychology of terrorism and the paucity of controlled empirical research that bears on these conceptual analyses. In all, the readings in this section provide a sampling of the kinds of problems that a compelling psychological analysis of terrorism must confront.

Reading 1—Iviansky (1977). Individual Terror: Concept and Typology

Editors' Comments

A major issue faced by those who wish to understand terrorism as a psychological phenomenon is whether it is a unique phenomenon, distinct from other types of political violence. The author answers this affirmatively, arguing that the modern terrorism is qualitatively different from prior such forms of violence in terms of the role the terrorists assign to themselves, to society, and to their deed. In a fascinating account, Iviansky expounds the early ideas underlying 19th century anarchism, including its central notion of "propaganda by the deed." This article reviews initial arguments for the efficacy of terrorism, the logic behind its impersonal nature, its choice of targets, and the psychological commonalities underlying distinct types of terrorism (such as anarchism, social revolution, and nationalism). This is an important introduction to modern terrorism, its ideology, and its early manifestations.

Discussion Questions

1. Why does 19th century terrorism merit the label of "individual terror"?
2. What did terrorist ideologues understand by the notion of "propaganda by the deed"?
3. What common characteristics were shared by terrorism-perpetrated anarchists, social revolutionaries, and nationalists?

Suggested Readings

Hoffman, B. (1998). *Inside terrorism*. New York: Columbia University Press.
Rapoport, D. C. (2004). Modern terror: The four waves. In A. K. Cronin & J. M. Ludes (Eds.), *Attacking terrorism: Elements of a grand strategy* (pp. 46–73). Washington, DC: Georgetown University Press.

Reading 2—Reich (1998). Understanding Terrorist Behavior: The Limits and Opportunities of Psychological Inquiry

Editors' Comments

In this important overview the author identifies some preliminary considerations that, in his opinion, should constrain the psychological study of terrorism. The foremost such constraint is the variety of terrorist acts that may defy the application of general psychological principles (but see the opposite view expressed by Iviansky in Reading 1). This chapter provides a thumb-nail history of terrorism across the ages, starting with the Jewish Zealots and the *Sicarii* of the 1st century AD, and all through the heterogeneous terrorist groups that sprung up in the second half of the 20th century and are still active today. The author also warns against the attempt to locate a root cause of terrorism that may constitute both a sufficient and a necessary condition for terrorism to appear. Thus, he is critical of attempts to trace terrorism to possible biochemical causes or psychopathological factors, or indeed to a specific personality structure. Instead, it is suggested that terrorism may be understood in terms of its subjective rationality and the rewards that joining a terrorist organization may offer to individuals in specific circumstances. The chapter ends with suggestions for further research on terrorism, including state-sponsored terrorism that may fuel reciprocal substate terrorism.

Discussion Questions

1. Does the heterogeneity of groups and individuals who have perpetrated terrorism make it impossible to identify general psychological principles that apply to terrorism? If so, why? If not, why not?
2. Reich is critical of the reduction of terrorism to biological, psychopathological, or personality factors. Does that mean that these factors are necessarily irrelevant to terrorism as a phenomenon?
3. Why, in your opinion, is it necessary or desirable for students of present-day terrorism to be aware of the history of terrorism?

Suggested Readings

Arblaster, A. (1977). Terrorism: Myths, meaning and morals. *Political Studies*, 25, 413–424.
Hubbard, D. G. (1978). Terrorism and protest. *Legal Medical Quarterly*, 2, 188–197.
Rapoport, D. (1998). Sacred terror: A contemporary example from Islam. In W. Reich (Ed.), *Origins of terrorism: Psychologies, ideologies, theologies, states of mind* (pp. 103–130). Washington, DC: Woodrow Wilson Center Press.

Reading 3—Kruglanski and Fishman (2006). The Psychology of Terrorism: "Syndrome" versus "Tool" Perspectives

Editors' Comments

This paper distinguishes between two psychological approaches to the study of terrorism that the authors label the "syndrome" versus "tool" approaches. The "syndrome" approach views terrorism as a uniform phenomenon with unique psychological markers at levels of personality, situation (e.g., related to poverty or political oppression), and the social group. The "tool" approach, in contrast, regards terrorism as a tool in an asymmetric warfare that any group or individual can potentially use. The tool perspective suggests conditions under which a group may desist from the use of terrorism, namely if an alternative tool or means to the group's goal appeared available. Moreover, it suggests that the tendency to employ terrorism as a tool may be undermined if that tool appeared to be incompatible with the group's or its members' alternative objectives (e.g., derived from moral values or individualistic concerns). The tool perspective does not imply the irrelevance of biological, personality, situational, or group-related factors to the practice of terrorism. Rather than considering such factors as root causes, the tool perspective approaches them as potential contributing factors that might strengthen an individual's tendency to buy into a terrorism-justifying ideology that views political violence as an efficient and morally warranted tool for attainment of the terrorists' ideological objectives.

Discussion Questions

1. What criticisms can be leveled against the "syndrome" conception of terrorism?
2. What is the nature of the distinction between root causes and contributing factors?
3. What advantages for counterterrorism efforts are offered by the "tool" perspective on terrorism?

Suggested Readings

Horgan, J. (2003). Leaving terrorism behind: An individual perspective. In A. Silke (Ed.), *Terrorists, victims and society: Psychological perspectives on terrorism and its consequences* (pp. 3–27). Chichester, UK: John Wiley & Sons.

Marsella, A. (2003). Reflections on international terrorism: Issues, concepts and directions. In F. Moghaddam & A. Marsella (Eds.), *Understanding terrorism: Psychosocial roots, consequences and interventions*. Washington, DC: American Psychological Association.

Schmid, A., & Jongman, A. J. (1988). *Political terrorism*. Amsterdam: North Holland Publishing.

Reading 4—Victoroff (2005). The Mind of the Terrorist: A Review and Critique of Psychological Approaches

Editors' Comments

This paper reviews the major theories and empirical studies on the topic of the psychology of terrorism. Research is summarized regarding sociological and demographic characteristics of terrorists and critically evaluates research concerning personality traits alleged to characterize terrorists. This article first compares psychopathological theories that explain terrorism as a symptom of Axis I psychological disorders or as a result of sociopathic traits, as contrasted with the polar opposite approach, rational choice theories such as strategic choice theory or game theory, which conceptualize terrorism as a predictable, logical way to achieve a desired goal. Little evidence to date supports the psychopathological theories, and while rational choice approaches afford some useful *post hoc* explanations, they cannot explain why only very few individuals among many sharing the same political grievances or ideological positions make the leap to terrorism. The paper next reviews a number of sociological theories, including social learning theory, the frustration–aggression hypothesis, relative deprivation theory, oppression theory, cultural theory (of collectivism versus individualism), and social identity theory. Among the older psychoanalytically oriented theories are narcissism, paranoia, and absolutist theory. Finally, non-psychoanalytic psychological theories of terrorism are examined, including cognitive theories, novelty-seeking theory, humiliation–revenge theory, and theories of group process. This paper illuminates the large number of psychological concepts that have been brought to bear on the phenomenon of terrorism, points out the limitations and challenges that this bewildering diversity of notions presents for a coherent understanding of the phenomenon, and urges that it is high time for rigorous empirical research.

Discussion Questions

1. Given the extant empirical research on psychological factors in terrorism, what kind of research is presently needed to advance our understanding of the phenomenon?
2. In what sense is terrorism "rational," and in what sense is it not?
3. Given the diverse theoretical frameworks brought to bear on the explanation of terrorism, what general statements can be made about the likely role of personality factors, social processes, and situational circumstances that may foster terrorism?

Suggested Readings

Alexander, Y. (2002). *Palestinian religious terrorism: Hamas and Islamic Jihad*. Ardsley, NY: Transnational Publishers.

Badey, T. J. (1998). Defining international terrorism: A pragmatic approach. *Terrorism and Political Violence*, *10*, 90–100.

Friedland, N. (1992). Becoming a terrorist: Social and individual antecedents. In L. Howard (Ed.), *Terrorism: Roots, impact, responses* (pp. 81–93). New York: Praeger.

Friedland, N., & Merari, A. (1985). The psychological impact of terrorism: A double-edged sword. *Political Psychology*, *6*, 591–604.

READING 1

Individual Terror: Concept and Typology

Ze'ev Iviansky

Revolutionary terrorism ('individual terror') has been of central importance in recent history, receiving widespread publicity. Yet in historical research and political science, it has remained a virtual no-man's land. Indeed, it has as yet not even been adequately defined.[1]

The first question confronting the student of terrorist events since the end of the nineteenth century is whether or not we are dealing with a phenomenon possessing its own special features. Is this a new form of revolutionary violence? Or perhaps merely the continuation of ancient political assassination, somewhat perfected – something in the nature of 'systematic assassination', which is differentiated from traditional political assassination in being, as Felix Gross puts it, 'a political method, a tactic guided by a strategy?'[2]

It will be argued here that political terror as practised in the modern world is qualitatively new – a phenomenon essentially distinct from political assassination, as practised in the ancient and early modern eras. The modern terrorist not only uses methods different in kind from the political assassin, but also has a different view of his role, of society, and of the significance of his act.

The immediate roots of 'individual terror' lie in the late nineteenth century, when its manifestations were not isolated incidents, but a continuous wave of new revolutionary violence with its own ebb and flow, which lasted until the outbreak of the first world war and the Russian Revolution. One act of

'individual terror' – the assassination of Archduke Francis Ferdinand at Sarajevo – started the 'Great War'; another, Dora Kaplan's attempt on the life of Lenin (30 August 1918), gave the pretext for the 'Red Terror'[3] – a period of uninterrupted anarchistic terror in Europe and the United States, terrorist warfare in Russia, and struggles for national liberation, using terror, in Ireland, Poland, the Balkans and India.

'Individual terror' is one of the manifestations of the modern age of violence, a symptom and expression of the great changes taking place in the spheres of social stratification, government, technology, ideology and revolutionary activity. It is a new phenomenon with specific features; its systematic character does not distinguish it from classical political assassination, but its different complex of ideological motives and goals involving the eternal 'twins' of means and ends.

One of the striking features of the term 'individual terror' is that it was neither coined nor adopted by the movements that propagated it or had recourse to this form of violence. Anarchism professed belief in 'propaganda by the deed.' The revolutionary syndicalists who derived their inspiration from its other manifestations called it *reprise individuelle* (individual expropriation) or 'direct action.' The programme of the executive committee of the Russian Narodnaya Volya Party (1879) speaks of 'destructive and terroristic activity.' N. Morozov, the leading theoretician of Narodnaya

9

Volya's terrorism, at first calls the method, which he establishes on strategic and ideological foundations, 'neo-partisan warfare', and later, 'terroristic warfare', because this was the 'expression adopted by the people.' The fighting organization of the Polish Socialist Party (PPS), which, under the leadership of Josef Pilsudski, had recourse to terror, termed the method 'the armed deed' [Czynzbrojny]. In India, the wave of terrorist activity which swept the country at the beginning of this century was known as 'the Russian method.'

The term 'individual terror' developed in the course of the later controversy between the Social Revolutionaries (SRs) and the Mensheviks and Bolsheviks (SDs) in Russia, both of the latter opposing terror on principle. In other words, it was coined by those who *opposed* terror in order to expose the contrast between the struggle they were advocating, i.e. the class struggle, and that of the SRs, which they presented as a struggle of the individual or of individuals.

The term coined by the opponents of terrorism was adopted later by some of its proponents for a number of reasons. Firstly, the term suited, in principle, the emphasis that devotees of the method placed on the personality, on the individual and his historical achievement – on the heroes in history. It emphasized the fact that terrorist activity, despite the fundamental ideological motivation, was always individual. Any blow aimed at shaking the establishment, the regime, the state or the foreign conqueror was always realized through individual acts of violence. Moreover, the disappearance of the movements which originally advocated and employed this method, and the victory of their opponents, who had invented the term, made its use almost inevitable.

Modern terror began with the slogan 'propaganda by the deed', advocated in the declaration of the delegates of the Italian Federation of the Anarchist International of 3 December 1876:

> The Italian Federation believes that the insurrectionary deed, which is designed to promote the principles of socialism by actions, is the most efficient means of propaganda and the one most capable of breaking through to the deepest social

strata, and of attracting the most vital forces of humanity to the struggle of the Internationale.[4]

On 5 August 1877, Paul Brousse, one of the early activists and ideologists of anarchism (but who quickly abandoned it) offered his interpretation of the slogan 'propaganda by the deed' as a method intended 'to show them [the weary and inert masses] that which they were unable to read, to teach them socialism in practice, to make it visible, tangible, concrete.' Even if the instigators of 'propaganda by the deed' were to be defeated, Brousse argued, 'it does not matter; the idea will march on, will put on flesh and sinews, and live in the eyes and on the faces of the people, who will shout for joy as it passes.'[5]

Peter Kropotkin, on the other hand, who, years later, concluded that it was impossible to demolish with a few kilograms of dynamite, historical structures erected over thousands of years, wrote:

> By actions which compel general attention, the new idea seeps into people's minds and wins converts. One such act may, in a few days, make more propaganda than thousands of pamphlets. Above all, it awakens the spirit of revolt; it breeds daring . . . Soon it becomes apparent that the established order does not have the strength often supposed. One courageous act has sufficed to upset in a few days the entire governmental machinery, to make the colossus tremble . . . The people observe that the monster is not so terrible as they thought . . . hope is born in their hearts.[6]

At that point, Kropotkin claims, the existing regime puts up desperate resistance: 'The government persists; it is savage in its repressions.' And this in turn 'provokes new acts of revolt, individual and collective, it drives the rebels to heroism.'[7]

As interpreted by the anarchists who espoused it, the slogan 'propaganda by the deed' refers to acts of violence which will demonstrate revolution in a tangible way, i.e. arouse and excite, elucidate and explain. The terrorist act itself becomes a manifesto; neither the removal of tyrants, opponents or enemies, nor the seizure of power is the declared aim of this violence, but protest and confrontation. It is the 'pulling of the trigger' of revolution, as Chalmers Johnson put it; it is an act that may release and set in motion the forces of insurrection and the revolutionary potential of the masses.

The programme of the executive committee of the Narodnaya Volya Party calls for 'destructive and terroristic activity.' It states (paragraph 2, section d):

> Terroristic activity consists of the destruction of the most harmful persons in the government, the protection of the Party from spies, and the punishment of official lawlessness and violence in all the more prominent and important cases where it is manifested. The aim of such activity is to break down the prestige of government, to furnish continuous proof of the possibility of pursuing a contest with the government, to raise in that way the revolutionary spirit in the people, and finally, to form a body suited and accustomed to warfare.[8]

The aim of terrorist activity, which in this case is but another form of 'propaganda by the deed', is to shatter the myth of the magic of governmental power, to fan faith and ardour among members of the organization and the people. It was to be an 'excitative element', as it was called by a subsequent generation of Russian terrorists, and to build up the strength and experience of the people in the struggle. The assassination of individuals is, henceforth, a means of indirectly achieving strategic and ideological ends.

Seventy years later, the newspaper of *Lehi* (Freedom Fighters for Israel), who also advocated 'individual terror', was to proclaim in one of its first issues:

> There was a time when the question of terror was hotly debated in the land of revolutions, Russia . . . The period of those debates has long since receded into the past . . . An argument can arise only from an incorrect presentation of the question. If the question is: is it possible to start a revolution or to bring about liberation by means of terror? the answer is: No! If the question is: do these actions help to bring revolution and liberation nearer? the answer is: Yes! . . . Firstly, terror is, for us, part of contemporary political warfare and it plays a very large role. In language which will be heard throughout the world, even by our

> wretched brothers beyond the borders of this land, it is proof of our war against the occupier . . . It is not aimed at persons, but at representatives, and is therefore effective. And if it also shakes the population out of its complacency, so much the better. Thus, and for no other reason, the battle for liberation will commence.[9]

Modern technological developments have provided a determined minority with new sources of strength and with a sense of power. It is a striking fact that the outbreak of individual terror followed closely on the heels of the invention of dynamite. The era of dynamite began in May 1862 when Alfred Nobel succeeded in detonating nitroglycerine under water.[10] Further progress in the use of explosives was made in 1875, with the invention of a nitroglycerine and nitrocellulose compound known as gelignite. By 1876, news of the invention of dynamite had been welcomed by militant anarchists and revolutionaries in Russia as the harbinger of a new era in the struggle to change the social and world order. Almost the entire revolutionary movement in Russia turned to terrorism, largely due to the lure of dynamite. From 1879 gelignite was used for all attempted assassinations of Narodnaya Volya members. The use of dynamite was not merely of technical significance, as noted by Mikhail Frolenko, a member of the executive committee of the Narodnaya Volya Party who personally took part in many of the assassination attempts. In his memoirs, he relates a debate in the executive committee of the party, when it was suggested that the attempt on Alexander II's life should be carried out using the old, conventional weapon, an accurate pistol. This weapon was more easily available and cheaper than dynamite; and furthermore had a greater chance of success. The possibility was flatly rejected for one simple reason: 'This assassination would not have created the same impression; it would have been interpreted as an ordinary murder, and would not have expressed a new stage in the revolutionary movement.'[11]

In terrorism's selection of the objects of violence, the impersonal aspect was intensified as the method took root and spread. Accordingly, hostages were taken and murdered, and targets for destruction and death indiscriminately selected. In

1903, Vladimir Burtsev, who eventually became one of the hunters of the provocateurs and their operatives and the unmasker of Azev, and who unceasingly insisted upon the necessity of not ignoring moral considerations when resorting to terror, published in London a pamphlet titled *To Arms*. In it, he appealed for a study of the 'art of war', which had reached a high level of perfection and development, because this knowledge was in many cases likely 'to ensure victory and prevent the defeat of the organization'. He emphasized that 'during the struggle [the revolutionaries should] think of victory rather than how, in [their] magnanimity, [they] are to secure the support of the bourgeoisie.' Aiming at the renewal of the terrorist struggle, he advocated the seizure of hostages from among the 'favourites' of the bourgeoisie and the authorities, in order to redeem the prisoners and the wounded from among the people. 'The taking of hostages', he wrote, 'is the only way we have of making the enemy treat the people as a belligerent party; he who devotes himself to the cause of the revolution, cannot but subject himself to its stern laws.'[12]

The impersonal aspect is intensified by the use of weapons made available by modern technology. Through technology, dangerous destructive powers can fall into the hands of a determined revolutionary minority, and eventually into the not over-fastidious hands of any criminal group. It also presents revolutionaries with the possibility of striking at the nerve centres of modern society, at its sources of energy and production, its transportation and communication systems (for example, terrorist attacks on airlines).

August Vaillant, the anarchist assailant who, on 9 December 1893, hurled a bomb into the chamber of the House of Representatives at the Palais Bourbon in Paris, declared: 'The more they are deaf, the more your voice must thunder out so that they will understand you.'[13]

In the anarchist myth of dynamite, the new weapon was presented as a modern revolutionary 'alchemy' and as a compensation for many evils: for humiliation and weakness, for discrimination and frustration, for anger at social exploitation and injustice. Johann Most, the anarchist apostle of dynamite, extolled in the pages of *Freiheit* (1880) the revolutionary use of the new weapon, explaining that it was within the power of dynamite to destroy the capitalist regime just as it had been within the power of gunpowder and the rifle to wipe feudalism from the face of the earth.[14]

A year before the Haymarket affair in Chicago in 1886, Albert Parsons, one of those condemned to death for his part in the catastrophe, and one of the anarchist movement's martyrs, declared in the columns of his newspaper:

> Dynamite: of all the good stuffs, that is the stuff! . . . In giving dynamite to the downtrodden millions of the globe, science has done its best work. Thedear stuff can be carried in the pocket without danger, while it is a formidable weapon against any force of militia, police or detectives that may want to stifle the cry for justice that goes forth from the plundered slaves.[15]

Before being led away to execution, Parsons declared: 'Dynamite comes as the emancipator of man from the domination and enslavement of his fellow men . . . it is democratic, it makes everyone equal . . . it is a peacemaker.'[16]

The use of dynamite exercised a decisive influence on the formation of the method of terrorist warfare in Russia and on the crucial importance attached to its slogan, the 'blow at the centre.' It is not at all surprising that one of the outstanding leaders of the SRs and its theoretician, Chernov, declared in 1909 at the Fifth Conference of the SRs:

> We must not allow routine to set in here. Terror is a form of military combat, a form of war, and as in war, any state whose military tactics are outdated exposes itself to failure. So too in internal war . . . in the war of terror, we must master modern techniques of warfare . . . Terror will be terror in the true sense of the word only if it represents the revolutionary implementation of the achievements of the most advanced technical sciences at any given moment.[17]

And indeed, at that very moment, the provocateur Azev was proposing to the party a grandiose scheme for using an airplane to bomb the Czar's Winter Palace.

In all the manifestos on anarchist terrorism, and also in its later permutations, according to the syndicalist slogan *action directe*, the vulnerability of the establishment at its sources of power and along its communication lines is discussed. These become, henceforth, tempting targets for indiscriminate blows, and give an additional dimension to the impersonal aspect of the method.

In the sphere of the socio-political struggle too, the 'blow at the centre' was nourished by the premise that the centre, i.e., the Czar or the political leadership, is the weakest link in the existing order, its Achilles' heel. Alexander Mikhailov, one of the central figures and remarkable characters of the Narodnaya Volya Party, wrote in his last letter from prison to friends:

'The victories and the successes have done their work. They have uncovered the vulnerability of royalty . . . Just one more mighty blow. It is necessary to send but two more heads rolling and you have won. Absolutism will become untenable (no one will dare any more risk his neck on the scaffold that awaits tsars and absolute rulers . . .)'[18]

No longer is the head of the ruler the ultimate target of the terrorist; the centre is henceforth that target. The specific quality of 'individual terror', in general, rests on a new motivation and strategic conception, whose distinguishing marks are varying designations of goals and enemies, the impersonality with which they are determined, and the blurred distinction between guilt and reprisal. (For propaganda purposes the argument of personal guilt is often emphasized, but this is not the reason for action, nor is reprisal its objective.) Those to be judged and destroyed are not public figures or rulers, but the social order in its entirety, the economic establishment, the absolutist or foreign rule. The modern age as the broad background to the appearance of this revolutionary violence, the new complex of motivations and aims, the resort to the latest technological devices, the revolutionary who accepts anonymity as the prerequisite for action – these are the main justifications for treating 'individual terror' as a distinctive phenomenon and as a new stage in revolutionary violence and strategy.

Therefore, 'individual terror' maybe defined as a system of modern revolutionary violence aimed at leading personalities in the government or the Establishment (or any other human targets). The motivation is not necessarily personal but rather ideological or strategic. This method differs from traditional political conspiracy assassination, in that it is, in essence, not directed at individuals who are considered stumbling-blocks to the seizure of power or sworn enemies of the organization, but rather against the foreign conqueror, the social order, or the Establishment embodied in these individuals. Infliction of personal injury is intended to weaken or destroy regimes, but, paradoxically, one of the clearest manifestations of modern 'individual terror' is its impersonal character. It seeks to sow disorder and panic, to undermine and jeopardize the security of rulers and regimes, and to serve as the spearhead of revolution by stirring up the masses with exemplary deeds and the creation of revolutionary cadres trained to further the struggle.

In the same measure, one of the typical manifestations of modern revolutionary terror is that, as the political and economic regime becomes more established, thereby losing its personal link with the masses, so the blows of 'individual terror' become more cruel and arbitrary. As a modern phenomenon, revolutionary terror has become total, like the totalitarian means of oppression and annihilation, the concentration camps, the bombing of urban populations and the indiscriminate consequences of the atomic bomb.

It is no doubt true that there are three different types of terrorism in the modern era, each with its own ideology and modes of action – those associated with anarchism, with the social revolution, and with national liberation. But seen in a broader historical perspective, the differences are clearly overshadowed by the fundamental features they have in common.

A wave of anarchist assassination attempts occurred simultaneously in Germany, Italy and Spain in 1878, and spread to France and the United States in the 1890s. To be a monarch, concluded Umberto I of Italy, after two attempts on his life, is

practical advantage over a revolution of the masses; and, finally, the fear of the horrors inherent in the elemental nature of a revolution and uprising of the masses.

One of the most important programmatic pamphlets of the Narodnaya Volya Party during the short period of its activity commencing in 1880, is a work by Nikolai Morozov, a member of the executive committee. It presents the thesis of a permanent terrorist revolution. Morozov was in no doubt that tyranny would be obliterated by means of terror. Because of its secrecy, the element of surprise and the strength of loyalty, terror is 'a war of strength against strength, of equals; a war of bravery against oppression, science and learning against the bayonet and the gallows.' It endows individuals with the 'strength of the mighty, to perform deeds which are almost beyond the power of mortals. Never was there in history so convenient a situation for a revolutionary party and such successful methods of fighting'.[30]

However, with the suppression of tyranny, there is always the danger that a new tyranny will arise. In order to obviate this, it is necessary to keep the weapon of terror in readiness: to challenge any future tyranny, new elite terrorist groups will rise up 'to destroy the tyranny in a series of political assassinations' against individuals who are the backbone of the regime.

Accordingly, the vision of a future without tyranny is one of permanent political, individual terror precluding the possibility of another tyranny arising. 'This terror' writes Morozov, 'has good chances for the future, but only if it bases itself on an idea and not a splinter group; an idea cannot be destroyed but isolated fighters can.' The 'terrorist revolution' or the 'neo-partisan struggle', as he formulated it in earlier articles, is a 'realization of the revolution in the present.'

In that same year, a pamphlet entitled *Terrorism and Routine*, by V. Tarnovsky, proclaimed the terrorist revolution to be the most moral and effective alternative to the blood-drenched revolutions of the masses with their high toll of victims. This revolution, Tarnovsky argued, is to be seen as the application of science to the art of revolution. It is a revolution which 'reduces the people's sufferings to a minimum', avoids bloodshed and many thousands of innocent victims.[31]

Later, in 1886, Lev Shternberg presented terror as 'the way of realizing the aims with the least number of victims and in the shortest possible time.' It is, in Shternberg's words, the last resort of a party that cannot join in open battle with the might of modern government, and it is the confirmed weapon of the revolutionary intelligentsia.[32]

In this type of 'individual terror', characterized by its organizational framework, and by the presence of the elite of the revolutionary intelligentsia, the approach is still abstract and impersonal. The aim is to shatter and undermine the 'absolutist state', give history a push, destroy the myth of power (e.g. the Czar's charisma), and to disseminate an idea and a state of mind by deeds. The feverish intensity of its activities is governed by the illusion of the ultimate blow. Individual political assassination is of only secondary importance: such acts are the means to the ideological ends.

The factor common to anarchist terror and terrorist warfare in the cause of social revolution is the belief in striking at the regime by eliminating its leading figures. In a third type of 'individual terror', there is terrorist warfare in the cause of national liberation from foreign rule, the professed aim being to sow disorder and undermine the prestige of the alien power, so indicating the movement's determination to carry the struggle to a successful conclusion. The clearest examples are provided by the national liberation movements in Poland, Ireland and the Balkans at the turn of the century.

In the case of Poland, terror was conceived as the 'armed deed', the only possible act in the historical circumstances. The *Czyn zbrojny* was the alternative to the trauma of the open uprisings which had been rooted. It can be distinguished from Russian 'terrorist warfare' not only by its different goal – liberation from a foreign oppressor – but also by its methods. In Poland, terror erupted under pressure from the masses; the proletarian element predominating. It concentrated on acts of sabotage and on clashes with the foreign rulers and their local collaborators. Neither the removal of a governor nor the destruction or plundering of an institution was the end and purpose of the struggle; its object was rather to strike a blow at the structure of the foreign regime, to weaken it.[33] So too, in Ireland and the Balkans, terror, in the cause of national liberation, sought to release the stranglehold of the foreign oppressor by acts of sabotage designed to cause the collapse of the government.

From this standpoint, the terror associated with national liberation bears some similarity to partisan warfare. It is, however, unlike partisan warfare, in that its goal is not territorial conquest or the capture of bases for partisan operations. Insofar as there is a desire for conquest, it is aimed at the conquest of the souls and gaining the support of the masses. Here too, the abstract end purpose predominates.

There is a further distinction between this and partisan warfare, in that terrorist warfare is organized on a long-term basis: just as in strategic terms there is no desire for conquered territory, so too the spiritual aspect is oriented towards future generations, the gesture, the challenge of history, the duty to die for the future – these are the crucial elements.

This is also the reason for the vast differences in the morale. Thus the element of sacrifice and the 'day of the shadow of death' is so important. Victor Serge, recalls in his memoirs a mood of collective suicide of the Illégalistes.[34] Hence, the importance of the proud bearing at the gallows, the last letter to friends, history and future generations. In the eyes of many terrorists, the whole purpose of their life and death is nothing but a last will and testament for generations to come.

Another expression of this can be found in the desire to eliminate any individual or personal imprint. Many perished under false names: the use of a pseudonym was an expression of liberation from all private and individual attachments. Anonymity is also conspicuous in the publications of the anarchists and of the Russian terrorist movement. Not merely a conspiratorial measure, it is an expression of a state of mind, of that same impersonalism engraved on the whole of 'individual terror.' Ivan Turgenev gave it literary expression in his novel, *On the Eve*, which was dedicated to

Sofia Perovskaya, daughter of the Czarist governor-general, who went to the scaffold with Zhelyabov.

The 'Revolutionary's Catechism' states that the revolutionary must cut himself off from all individual attachments, obligations, sympathies and memories. He is nothing but revolutionary 'capital.' Moreover, he is a man whose fate is sealed. He is merely an agent and a number. The opening words of this pamphlet state: 'The revolutionary is a lost man: he has no interests of his own, no cause of his own, no feelings, no habits, no belongings, he does not even have a name.'

Reviewing the growth and development of terror, Russia being the outstanding example, we discern that what was initially a defensive arm within the framework of the 'Land and Freedom Party' became the arm of disorganization, which set itself the object of undermining the state and the structure of authority. This finally became its predominant activity, characteristically expressed in the feverish intensity of Narodnaya Volya's 'striking at the centre.'

In this process of escalation one can distinguish a complex of particular, concrete goals:

1. Terror as retaliation for the arbitrary nature of tyrannical rule and its infringement on the rules of human conduct.
2. Terror as the judgment of the people, with its ability to respond to the miscarriage of justice with an alternative justice, by punishing the judges and their lords, or by rescuing and releasing by force those who have fallen into their net.
3. Terrorist activity, the invisible organization and the 'executive committee' which henceforward conceal an additional authority, independent, competitive and oppositional, within the absolutist state, the foreign government or the ruling establishment.
4. Wherever a system of checks and balances against arbitrariness and absolutism, exploitation and oppression, is lacking, terror is called upon to play this role, both by virtue of the limitation which the terrorist act places on tyranny, and by virtue of intimidation and warning.

5. By means of protest, this weapon of the few becomes, according to this conception, the expression and embodiment of the protest of the masses. Wherever protest is forbidden, terror becomes the only possible way to express it. It is coupled with the concept of 'the people's justice.' The terrorist organization also tries to present itself as a court of justice whose legitimacy is equal to that of the courts of the tyrannical and arbitrary government.

6. It becomes a means of 'propaganda by the deed', by exploiting the above elements, and also by means of the underground press, the platform of the court room, the example of self-sacrifice and the show of strength when dealing blows at the centre. Modern means of communication, in particular the press (like radio and television today), reverberate its message around the world and thereby lend it weight.

7. According to this conception, the secrecy, flexibility and manoeuverability of a small band of determined and brave men can undermine the 'wall' of military and police might, and breach it, revealing its weak points by sowing insecurity, disorder and fear. The significance of terror is, after all, in spreading alarm.

8. It claims, therefore, to imprison the omnipotent rulers in their own palaces, to undermine and disrupt the governmental machinery, to inflict a blow on the morale of subordinates and, as a result, to shatter their prestige and authority, but also to arouse and excite the indifferent and wavering masses. In the terminology of terror this is the excitative role.

These are the elements of defence and undermining. The terrorist organization contends that, by means of consistent terror, using the most advanced technology, it is capable of undermining the state, and the government, and of establishing within them the nucleus of revolutionary power, ready to act when the time is ripe.

However, there is an additional element in all the manifestations of 'individual terror.' The main goal of 'individual terror' is to prevent compromise. And therein lies its greatest success. Terrorism tends to be most widespread in situations where a crucial political move is imminent, and at times of political chaos. It is against this background that the anarchist explosion and the terrorist struggles in their various forms emerged.

Terrorism's distinctive avoidance or rejection of compromise, stabilization or agreement can be seen as its most substantial and conspicuous achievement from yet another point of view. Under certain historical conditions, as was the case in Russia, Ireland and Poland, it became the starting-point of revolution or national liberation. Russian social democracy, for example, developed as a result of the controversy over terror, and in conflict with it. The Russian revolution emerged from this crucible. 'In the prime of their youth', writes Lenin in his *What is to be Done*, 'almost all of them [the future revolutionaries] knelt reverently before the heroes of terror; abstention from the bewitching spell of this heroic tradition required a hard struggle.'[35] The terrorist struggle in Russia paved the way for the revolution, by preventing compromise and stabilization. It did not turn out to be an alternative to revolution. The vision expounded by Morozov of a permanent terrorist struggle, as a limitation and constraint on present and future tyrannies, was exaggerated and unfounded. The Russian terrorists failed to see that terror paves the way not only to revolution, but also to a much mightier and greater terror: the counter-terror of the totalitarian state, of concentration and extermination camps. This is one of its dialectical and tragic developments, and it is a lesson which must be faced by our generation.

The great danger for the future is the atom bomb falling into the hands of terrorists. The evolution of 'individual terror' in the modern age, with its abstract and lofty aims, translated into indiscriminate, blind and arbitrary blows, and the increasing vulnerability of the modern world to attacks at its numerous vital spots are turning this danger into a nightmare of earth-shattering consequences.

In his memoirs, Morozov recalls an instructive conversation with the author of *Underground Russia*, Stepniak Kravchinsky (one of the first to embark on the path of terror, though he objected to it as a method): the former says to his friend: 'I have given much thought to the ways of armed struggle, all those popular uprisings, barricades, clashes between the masses and the armed forces and terrifyingly cruel armies. How many thousands of people perish in vain, how many broken hearts remain after they have perished . . . Isn't it better to adopt the David and Goliath or Wilhelm Tell method?' To this Kravchinsky replied: 'The danger is that after a crown of laurels has been woven for Wilhelm Tell, there will be scores of feeble-minded imitators, capable of indiscriminately shooting at the "enemies of humanity", and thus his method will become so sullied that you yourself will be ashamed of it.'[36]

NOTES

1. Research into the phenomenon of terrorism has been minimal. 'There is very little foundation-backed research in the US and almost none in Britain or in Europe generally,' writes Paul Wilkinson in Political Terrorism (London, 1974), adding that such research remains as yet 'an unheeded cri de coeur' (29–31). Noting the same conspicuous absence in their study The Politics of Assassination (Englewood Cliffs, N.J. 1970), Murray Clark Havens, Carl Leiden and Karl M. Schmitt remark that 'virtually no systematic research has been made on assassination' (p. xi).
2. Felix Gross, Violence in Politics (The Hague 1972), 1. In his characterization of individual terror (12–22), Gross stresses its political and centralistic traits, thus excluding anarchist assassination. See also his rather clumsy classification of individual terror into five major strategic types: (a) individual; (b) random; (c) random focussed; (d) mass terror; (e) dynastic assassination.
3. After this attempt, Stalin and Voroshilov cabled Lenin from the Tsaritsyn front: 'The Military Council of the North Caucasian War Sector . . . replies to this vile underhand attack by the organization of open, mass, systematic terror against the bourgeoisie and its agents.' (J. Stalin, Sochinenya, IV, 128, cited in E.H. Carr, The Bolshevik Revolution [Harmondsworth, 1966], 175). On this occasion, Zinoviev declared: 'The bourgeoisie kill separate individuals, but we kill whole classes' (cited by Smilg Benario, 'Na Sovetskoi Sluzhbie' in Arkhiv Russkoi Revolucji, III [Berlin 1921], 150).
4. J. Guillaume, ed., L'Internationale, Documents et Souvenirs 1864–1887, IV (Paris 1910), 114.
5. Ibid., 225–27.
6. Peter Kropotkin, 'The Spirit of Revolt' in Revolutionary Pamphlets (New York 1968), 35–43.
7. Ibid.
8. 'Programma Ispolnitelnovo Komiteta' in Literatura Socialno Revolucjonnoi Partji 'Narodnoj Voli' (Paris 1905), 165. It should be pointed out that this paragraph is a direct development of the reference to terrorism in the programmes of the 'Land and Freedom' organization (from which the 'People's Will Party' emerged). In 1876–77 the draft programme was titled 'Agitation by the Deed'; in May 1878 it was re-titled 'Disorganization of the State.'
9. 'Terror' in Hechazit [The Front], no. 2, 1943 in Fighters for the Freedom of Israel, Collected Works, I (Tel Aviv 1956), 141–44 (in Hebrew).
10. The first criminal use of nitroglycerine took place in 1865 when V. King Tompson, a resident of Brooklyn, New York, insured a cargo on the German steamship Moselle for a large sum of money. Just before its embarkation, King planted an explosive device of nitroglycerine on board. The bomb exploded too soon and killed the assailant together with the crew. In all, twenty-eight people were killed and 200 injured. See Nicolas Halasz, Nobel – A Biography (London 1960), 50–51. On the history of dynamite see also Eric Bergensen, Alfred Nobel: The Man and His Work (London 1962); and H. Schück and R. Sohlman, The Life of Alfred Nobel (London 1929). In the latter source, the authors claim that Alfred Nobel cherished a deep sympathy for Russian radicals, up to his last days. See 127 and 181.
11. M. Frolenko, 'Nachalo Narodnichestva' in Katorga i Ssylka, no. 24 (1936), 22.
12. V. Burtsev, K Oruzhyu (London 1903), 4–9.
13. Henry Varenne, De Ravachol à Caserio (Paris 1895), 119.
14. See Robert Hunter, Violence and the Labour Movement (London 1916), 66–68.
15. See Alarm, 21 February 1885, in L. Adamic, Dynamite: The Story of Class Violence in America (New York 1934), 47.
16. See H. David, History of the Haymarket Affair (New York 1936), 343.
17. See A. Spiridovich, Histoire du Terrorisme Russe, 1886–1917 (Paris 1930), 587–88.
18. A.P. Pribyleva Korba and V.N. Figner, A.D. Michailov (Leningrad 1925), 208 (Letter dated 15 February 1882).
19. 'Sono gli incerti del mastiere' – King Umberto's remark to General Ponzio Vaglia after the second assassination attempt on his life (22 April 1897) failed. See Ernest Alfred Vizetelly, The Anarchists: Their Faith and Their Record, Including Sidelights on the Royal and other Personages who have been Assassinated (London 1911), 214.
20. Cesare Lombroso pointed out the suicidal aspect at the height of terrorist activity in the early twentieth century. See Les Anarchistes (Paris n.d.), 93 et seq.
21. Emma Goldman, 'The Psychology of Political Violence' in Anarchism and other Essays (New York 1910), 113 and 114.
22. Victor Serge, Memoirs of a Revolutionary, 1901–1904 (London 1963), 1 et seq.

23. Manfred Hildermeier, 'Zur Sozialstruktur der Führungs-
gruppen und zur terroristischen Kampfsmethode der
Sozialrevolutionären Partei Russlands 1917' in Jahr-
bücher für Geschichte Osteuropas Vol. 20 no. 4, December 1972, 540.
24. See L. Adamic, Dynamite, 349 et seq. Gerald Brennan,
The Spanish Labyrinth (Cambridge, Mass. 1943), 70.
25. See Paul Avrich, The Russian Anarchists (Princeton
1971), 65 (from a 1907 letter by Vladimir Striga
[Lapidus]).
26. In the December 1907 issue of The Indian Sociologist,
Shyami Krishna Varma, one of the initiators and leaders
of this movement, writes:

It seems that any agitation in India must be carried on
secretly and that the only methods which can bring
the English government to its senses are the Russian
methods vigorously and incessantly applied.

One of the outstanding leaders of the Congress Party, Bal
Gangadhar Tilak, went out of his way to praise dynamite
and the bomb. In an article published in his newspaper in
1908 (which caused the closure of the paper and Tilak's
arrest), he writes:

The manufacture and possession of arms can be prevented by law and police supervision, but the same
cannot be said of the bomb. It resembles more a
magical charm than a visible object manufactured in
a factory . . . No law possesses the power to keep the
knowledge of the manufacture of bombs from those
that are bent upon using them. (Quoted in Ram
Gopal, How India Struggled for Freedom [Bombay
1467], 191 and 192.)

In the Punjab alone in 1914, some 5,000 people were
tried for treason. Five hundred were sentenced to death
and executed, while 800 were sentenced to life imprisonment, and about 500 were banished to a slow death on
'Devils Islands' (the Andaman Islands). Ten thousand
were detained without trial. These numbers surpass comparable figures in Russia during the years of revolutionary
terror. On the extent of the use of the terrorist method in
India, see Gopal, op. cit., 224–31.

On the importance of terror in the liberation of India,
see also Valentine Chirol, Indian Unrest (London 1910):
'They have of all Indians been the most slavish imitators
of the West as represented at any rate by the Irish Fenians
and the Russian anarchists . . . The use of the bomb has
become the common property of revolutionists all over
the world' (146).

The affair of one of the leaders of the terrorist movements in India is described in D.K.V. Savarkar, A Study of
the Evolution of Indian Nationalism (London 1967); and
in the comprehensive book by Vidya Sagar Anand,
Dhananjay Keer Veer Savarkar (London 1967).

27. 'Podgotovitelnaya Rabota Partii' in Revolucjonnoje

Narodnichestvo 70-ch godov, II, edited by S.S. Volk
(Moscow 1965), 175–84.
28. Incidentally, at the same trial, Josef Pilsudski was also
sentenced; his brother, Bronislaw, was given life
imprisonment, but the sentence was commuted to fifteen
years.
29. 'Programma Terroristicheskoj Frakcji Partji Narodnaya
Volya' In Zhizn Kak Fakel, edited by A.I. Ivanski (Moscow 1966), 294–303.
30. N. Morozov, 'Terroristicheskaya Bor'ba' (London [but
Geneva], n.d. [but 1880]) (English translation in Felix
Gross, Violence in Politics, pp. 102 et seq.
31. V. Tarnovsky [Gerasim Romanenko], Terrorizm i Routina
(London [but Geneva], 1880).
32. Lev Shternberg, Politicheski Terror v Rossii, Hectograph
ed., 1884 (copy in Institute for Social History,
Amsterdam).
33. In a lecture delivered in 1910, the future Marshal Josef
Pilsudski concludes: 'The principal service of the militant
organization was to save the idea of an armed movement
which would have been completely lost without its struggle' (Jozef Pilsudski, Pisma-Mowy-Rozkazy [Collected
Works] III [Warsaw 1930], 22, cited in Joseph Pilsudski,
The Memories of a Polish Revolutionary and Soldier
[London 1931], 175).

He also states: 'Terrorism seemed to the rank and file
the only thinkable system of physical struggle with the
enemy; the influence of Russia was evident.' (Pisma-
Mowy-Rozkazy, op. cit., 5; the statement is omitted from
the English version).

Pilsudski's biographer, Pobog-Malinowski, adds: 'It
was also clearly understood that it [terrorism] will not
bring about victory. There was nevertheless no one who
could imagine any other possible method of struggle.'
The general mood of these militants was 'that their task
was to labour for the future, while they themselves will
not live to enter into the promised land' (W. Pobog-
Malinowski, Jozef Pilsudski [1901–1908] II [Warsaw
1935], 228–29).

In a letter written before he left to take part in the hold-
up of the mail train at Bezdany, a railway station on the
River Niemen, on 26 September 1908 – the only militant
action in which he personally participated – Pilsudski
explained the ideas that inspired him during this period.
Since this letter was also intended 'as a political testament
in case he did not return,' his explanations are all the more
valuable:

I only beg you not to make of me 'A good officer' or
'a dreamer and sentimentalist', that is, a man of self-
sacrifice, stretched upon the cross of humanity, or
something of that sort. I was that to a certain degree
in the days of exalted and cloudy youth; now it is
past, never to return. That dreaming and being cruci-
fied distressed me in our intelligentsia; it is weak and
helpless. I am helpless. I am fighting and will die,
only because I cannot live in this latrine which our

life amounts to. It offends me, as a man with dignity above that of a slave. Let children play at growing flowers, socialism or Polonism, or anything else they like in this atmosphere of a latrine, not even of a watercloset! I can't. That's not sentimentalism, not dreaming, not the clap-trap of social evolution or anything of that sort; it is simply being a man. I want to conquer; without a fight, and a fight with the gloves off, I am not even a babbler, but simply a beast submitting to stick and whip. I think you understand me. It is not despair, not immolation which guides me, but the desire to conquer, to prepare victory.

My final idea, which I have never yet expounded, is the necessity in our circumstances of turning every party, and above all the socialists, into an organ of physical force; an organ, to describe it in terms odious to our 'Humanitarians' (hysterical girls who can't bear to hear glass scraped, but let you spit in their faces), of superior brute strength. I wanted to work out this idea in my actions during the last few years, and promised myself to achieve it or to die. I have already achieved a good deal in this direction, but too little to be able to rest on my laurels and occupy myself seriously with the immediate preparation for the fight, and now I am staking everything on one card. I have been called a noble socialist; I am a man of whom even his enemies do not publicly say foul things; a man, then, who has been of some little service in the general culture of the nation, and I wish to underline with my own person this bitter, this very

bitter truth, that in a nation which does not know how to fight for itself, which withdraws every time someone strikes it in the face, men must even die in actions which are not lofty, beautiful and great. (See Memories, 160–61).

This extraordinary letter was addressed to a Jewish friend and party comrade and not to Ignacy Daszynski, as stated in the English edition (Memories, above), nor to an 'unknown' person, as stated in the official Polish edition (Pisma-Mowy-Rozkazy, op. cit., II, 309).

34. One of the well-known poems by Avraham Shtern, murdered leader of Lehi (Israel Freedom Fighters), gives expression to this mood in the following line:

And we shall believe in the day of the shadow of death
A time when the rifle will sing its battle-song
We shall wrestle with God and death
And welcome Zion's redeemer.
We shall welcome him. Our blood will be
A red carpet on the streets
And upon this carpet – our brains
Like white roses.

35. Incidentally, Krupskaya, Lenin's wife, remarks in her memoirs that this passage is autobiographical. See N. Krupskaya, Memories of Lenin (New York 1970), 45.
36. N. Morozov, Povest' Moei Zhizni (Moscow 1947), II, 149–50.

READING 2

Understanding Terrorist Behavior: The Limits and Opportunities of Psychological Inquiry

Walter Reich

Several aspects of terrorism seem susceptible to psychological inquiry—the effects of terrorism on its victims, for example, and the behaviors of both terrorists and authorities during hostage negotiations. But the aspect of terrorism that seems most susceptible of all to such inquiry—that, for better or worse, almost begs for it—is the psychology of the terrorists themselves: their developments, motivations, personalities, decision-making patterns, behaviors in groups, and, some would argue, psychopathologies. Certainly, the public has turned to psychiatrists and psychologists regularly, particularly after witnessing especially violent terrorist acts, to explain this aspect of terrorist behavior; and psychiatrists and psychologists, just as regularly, have rushed to give explanations, sometimes without even being asked.

But susceptible as terrorists' motivations and personalities may be, in principle, to psychological inquiry, such inquiry, in practice, is regularly beset by problems that, in devious but powerful ways, limit, undermine, or even vitiate it—problems that, in the main, stem from too exclusive a focus on psychology itself or too narrow a definition of it. This chapter focuses on some of those problems and, when possible, suggests ways in which they can be avoided or overcome.

Overgeneralization

Persons and groups have carried out terrorist acts for at least two thousand years. During that considerable span of human experience, such acts have been carried out by an enormously varied range of persons with an enormously varied range of beliefs in order to achieve an enormously varied range of ends—including, in the case of at least one terrorist group, as I note later, no end at all. Even if we are careful to include in our historical catalogue of terrorist acts only those that satisfy one contemporary, restrictive definition of the term—let's choose, for our purposes here, the State Department's definition, which, in recent years, has been "premeditated, politically-motivated violence perpetrated against noncombatant targets by subnational groups or clandestine state agents, normally intended to influence an audience"—the list we can produce is breathtaking in its variety and scope. Given this variety and scope, it would be foolish to believe that many psychological principles can be adduced that apply to and explain all of the entries on the list.

To be sure, terrorism is not nearly so broad and universal a phenomenon as, say, violence or war—phenomena that occur under such astonishingly varied circumstances and for such astonishingly varied reasons that few would even dream of offering a single, overarching psychological theory to explain them all. Still, terrorism is so varied and complex a phenomenon that it should give pause to anyone whose aim it is to understand it—or, to be more precise, whose aim it is to understand the many different terrorisms that the deceptively singular term covers.

Yet psychological accounts of terrorism are replete with explanations that ignore or blur the variety and the complexity.[1] Blanket statements, some of which will be cited later, tend to be made that attribute certain characteristics to "terrorists" with the implication that all terrorists, of whatever variety, possess them. In part, it is a problem of semantics: It is always hard for writers to remind readers that only one particular group of terrorists is being discussed and not all of them through recorded history. But that is probably too generous an explanation for this penchant for psychological overgeneralization about terrorism. Too often overgeneralization is a product of loose and weak thinking, a disregard for the need for evidence, and the habit, unfortunately endemic in so many areas of psychological discourse, of having a single idea and applying it to everything.

Even the briefest review of the history of terrorism reveals how varied and complex a phenomenon it is, and therefore how futile it is to attribute simple, global, and general psychological characteristics to all terrorists and all terrorisms.

Some of the earliest terrorist campaigns were carried out in an arena that has seen so many of them in recent years, the zone now known as the Middle East. Perhaps the most striking of these campaigns was the one carried out by two Jewish groups during the first century A.D., the Zealots and the Sicarii. Their primary goal was to inspire popular insurrection among Judea's Jews against its Roman occupiers, an insurrection that would result not in a compromise with the occupiers but in total rebellion. A second purpose, perhaps no less assiduously pursued, was to cleanse Jewish religious institutions and society of persons too closely aligned with Roman and Hellenistic ways. The method used by the Sicarii, or daggermen, was assassination. As Josephus describes it:

> The Sicarii committed murders in broad daylight in the heart of Jerusalem. The holy days were their special seasons when they would mingle with the crowd carrying short daggers concealed under their clothing with which they stabbed their enemies. Thus, when they fell, the murderers joined in cries of indignation, and through this plausible behavior, were never discovered. The first assassinated was Jonathan, the high-priest. After his death there were numerous daily murders. The panic created was more alarming than the calamity itself; nearly everyone, as on the battlefield, hourly expected death. Men kept watch at a distance on their enemies and would not trust even their friends when they approached.[2]

The goals of the Zealots and of the Sicarii were clearly political—they wanted an end to Roman subjugation—and depended on the belief that extraordinary actions were necessary in order to rouse a passive or corrupted populace. But their goals were also religious, and depended on the belief that such actions not only were justified on religious grounds but would even bring on divine intervention.

Another early terrorist movement in the Middle East, that of the Assassins, also had political goals, but these were ultimately designed to serve primarily religious ends. Active from the eleventh through the thirteenth century A.D., the Assassins, whose origins were in Shia Islam, believed that Islam had been corrupted; and, also using daggers,

[1] See H. A. Cooper, "What Is a Terrorist: A Psychological Perspective," *Legal Medical Quarterly* 1 (1977): 16–32; H. H. A. Cooper, "Psychopath as Terrorist: A Psychological Perspective," *Legal Medical Quarterly* 2 (1978): 188–97.

[2] Josephus, *The Jewish War*, in *Works* (London: Heinemann [Loeb Classical Library], 1926), quoted in David C. Rapoport, "Fear and Trembling: Terrorism in Three Religious Traditions," *American Political Science Review* 78, no. 2 (1984): 658–77. On the Zealots and Sicarii, see also S. J. D. Cohn, *Josephus in Galilee and Rome* (Leiden: Brill, 1979); David C. Rapoport, "Introduction: Religious Terror," in *The Morality of Terrorism: Religious and Secular Justification*, edited by David C. Rapoport and Yonah Alexander (New York: Pergamon, 1982); and M. Smith, "Zealots and Sicarii: Their Origins and Relations," *Harvard Theological Review* 64 (1971): 1–19.

they assassinated Muslim leaders who, they believed, represented and propagated that corruption. They sought not only the death of their enemies but also the publicity that the assassinations excited—publicity that, they hoped, would result in attention to their cause, recognition that it was just, and the bringing about of a new, cleansed, and revitalized theological and social order.[3]

The era of modern terrorism is usually said to have begun in the nineteenth century with the rise, in Russia, of the *Narodnaya Volya* (People's Will). In 1879, that party's program spoke of "destructive and terroristic activity," and its methods, which involved assassination of Tsarist officials in the hope of provoking Russian society into revolution, were opposed by later Russian revolutionaries, particularly the Bolsheviks, who believed that revolution could be attained successfully not by "individual terror" carried out by a small elite of intellectuals but by class struggle carried out by the masses. Such individual terror came to be called "propaganda by the deed"[4]—that is, the method, using extreme acts, by which the masses would be stirred not only to understand the depth of their subjugation but also the vulnerability of the authorities. As Peter Kropotkin puts it:

By actions which compel general attention, the new idea seeps into people's minds and wins converts. One such act may, in a few days, make more propaganda than thousands of pamphlets. Above all, it awakens the spirit of revolt; it breeds daring. . . . Soon it becomes apparent that the established order does not have the strength often supposed. One courageous act has sufficed to upset in a few days the entire governmental machinery, to make the colossus tremble. . . . The

people observe that the monster is not so terrible as they thought . . . hope is born in their hearts.[5]

But repression, such a terrorist hopes, is born in the hearts of the authorities. They react fiercely, Kropotkin predicts; the masses suffer terribly, become enraged, and respond with revolution.

For many anarchists, terror itself was an end; indeed, one anarchist group in Russia during the revolution of 1905–7 advocated *bezmotivniy terror* (unmotivated terror).[6] For anarchists, the invention of dynamite introduced an era of exciting destructive possibilities in which individuals could be, in their actions, as powerful as governments. Some anarchists advocated violence aimed not just at authorities but also at the general public, particularly those parts of it, such as the bourgeoisie, who could be identified as supporting the existing order merely because they profited from it. "There are no innocents," Emile Henry, the young French anarchist, said at his trial for throwing a bomb into the Café Terminus.

For the early Russian revolutionaries who advocated terror, however, it was to be carried out with discrimination and with clear purposes in mind. Authorities were the targets, not ordinary citizens. But even then the method had to be justified. And the justification was that the authorities' monopoly on power gave the revolutionaries no other choice, and that, in overturning mass tyranny, which was responsible for mass deaths, assassinations were actually life-saving and moral. Such terrorists, usually intellectuals, spent a great deal of time worrying about, and seeking justifications for, the moral dilemmas provoked by the method they had adopted.

During the early part of this century, as revolutionary, ideological terrorism grew strong, so did terrorism aimed at nationalist ends. Such terrorism developed great prominence in Ireland, but it was also evident in the Balkans, Armenia and

[3] See Rapoport, "Fear and Trembling," 658–77. See also Bernard Lewis, *The Assassins: A Radical Sect in Islam* (London: Weidenfeld and Nicholson, 1967).

[4] This term was probably first used in the declaration of the Italian Federation of the Anarchist International of 3 December 1876. See Ze'ev Iviansky, "Individual Terror: Concept and Typology," *Journal of Contemporary History* 12 (1977): 43–63.

[5] Peter Kropotkin, "The Spirit of Revolt," in *Revolutionary Pamphlets* (New York, 1968), 35–43, quoted in Iviansky, "Individual Terror," 43–63.

[6] See Walter Reich, "Serbsky and Czarist Dissidents," *Archives of General Psychiatry* 40 (1983): 697–8.

elsewhere. Between the wars, especially in the 1920s, right-wing terrorism, particularly by the Nazis and the Italian Fascists, was used to intimidate enemies and create publicity; a number of right-wing groups in Eastern Europe devolved into little more than criminal gangs.

After World War II, guerrilla warfare related to decolonization predominated, although terrorism occurred in a number of areas; for example, it was used by the Irgun and the Stern Gang in mandate Palestine. But in the 1960s and 1970s terrorism of several varieties once again became a frequent occurrence in a number of geographic zones. In Western Europe and Latin America it was, and remains, heavily left wing; one 1986 communiqué by a Belgian left-wing terrorist group, the Fighting Communist Cells, restated, for the thousandth time, and in the same apocalyptic, incendiary language used in previous ideological iterations, such terrorism's goal: the resumption of combat so that "the spark sets the plain ablaze, so that the class struggle burns down history."[7] Elsewhere, nationalist-separatist terrorism was prominent among the Palestinians, Basques, Armenians, Croatians, Sikhs, Tamils, and others. And the IRA continued its campaign against the British, now the oldest terrorist campaign in the world. Recently, in the 1980s, terrorism in the name of another cause, religion, reemerged with particular force and ardor in the Middle East, primarily in Lebanon and Iran, with its special characteristics and justifications, thus bringing the history of terrorism full circle to its beginnings in that convulsed corner of the world.

Certainly, a number of themes and characteristics are shared by many of the terrorist groups and movements mentioned in this short history; the goals of achieving terror and publicity for the cause are shared by nearly all of them. But one searches with difficulty and probably in vain, for psychological qualities that are shared by all or nearly all of the terrorists and terrorist groups mentioned here. The constellation of psychological qualities

that may characterize West European terrorists, such as the Red Army Faction of West Germany, Direct Action of France, and the Red Brigades of Italy, is probably quite different from the ones that characterize or characterized, say, the followers of Abu Nidal or the members of the Palestinian Front for the Liberation of Palestine, the Armenian ASALA, the Basque ETA, the Shi'ite groups, the Croats, or even the leftist terrorists in Latin America, such as the Tupamaros of Uruguay, the Shining Path of Peru, the Montoneros of Argentina, or the M-19 of Colombia. Indeed, even within the United States, the qualities that may have characterized the Weatherman group were no doubt different from the ones that characterized the black members of the Symbionese Liberation Army. And regarding fundamental attitudes toward one of the central facets of terrorism—violence—different terrorist groups, even those that have shared the "left wing" designation, have, across the decades, varied enormously. Thus, the *Narodnaya Volya* tortured themselves about the snuffing out of any life, even that of a hated government official, whereas modern-day leftist terrorists, as well as most others both now and in the past, have managed to justify easily almost any killings, even of the most indubitably innocent souls.

Moreover, the terrorist groups themselves shift in character. Some terrorist groups that were once on the right have ended up on the left, and vice versa; and most are, in fact, mixtures of types, such as leftist nationalists, rightist nationalists, religious nationalists, and so on. In terrorism, there are many mixed and borderline conditions.[8]

The lesson that the psychological researcher must draw from the long history of the terrorist enterprise, and especially from its variety and complexity, applies not only to the study of individual terrorists but also to the study of the terrorist groups themselves. Like individual terrorists, the groups to which they belong, and ultimately the

---

[7] James M. Markham, "Terrorists Put Benign Belgium Under Mental Siege," *New York Times*, 6 February 1986, p. A-2.

[8] For an extended and rich discussion of the many varieties of terrorism and of the ways in which various terrorist movements have undergone radical changes over time, see Walter Laqueur, *The Age of Terrorism* (Boston: Little, Brown, 1987).

communities from which those groups arise, are not necessarily alike in their psychological characteristics, even if they share certain goals or orientations.

Religiously oriented nationalist terrorists, for example, are driven by forces and shaped by circumstances that are usually specific to particular religious or nationalist experiences—experiences that lend powerfully determining characteristics to those particular groups. Why else have some nationalities with deep feelings of having been wronged by history or by other nationalities, such as the Palestinians, Basques, Armenians, and Croatians, given rise to groups that carry out terrorism in order to right those wrongs, whereas other nationalities that have been wronged, such as the Germans who were displaced from Eastern Europe after World War II and many other nationalities that lost parts of their homeland or were never permitted a homeland, have not? And why have some terrorist movements persisted in their efforts for decades whereas others have not?

Clearly, differences in the political circumstances surrounding those groups, as well as in the responses given to their grievances and actions, have played important roles in determining the nature, momentum, and success of their terrorist efforts. But no less important have been the particular characteristics of terrorist groups themselves. However similar such groups may be, they are usually, in significant ways, also very different; and, as in the cases of individual terrorists, the differences are probably at least as telling as the similarities.

Reductionism

Closely related to the problem of overgeneralization is the problem of reductionism: Just as it is easy, and usually unjustified, to attribute specific characteristics to a wide range of terrorists and terrorist groups, so it is easy, and usually unjustified, to attribute all or much of terrorist behavior to one or another specific cause. Yet this has often been done, and occasionally it still is.

In the 1870s, as terrorism was gaining strength

not only in Russia but also in Italy, Cesare Lombroso, who believed that criminality in general was a congenital condition, attributed terrorist behavior, and in particular bomb throwing, to pellagra and other vitamin deficiencies. At the same time, other authorities examined the connection between terrorism and barometric pressure, moon phases, alcoholism, droughts, and cranial measurements.[9]

A century later, some authors have returned to biological causes to explain terrorist violence. David G. Hubbard, a psychiatrist, has suggested that there may be a connection between inner-ear vestibular function and terrorism.[10] He has also suggested that terrorism may be partly a result of the levels of certain chemicals in the brains of terrorists, specifically norepinephrine, acetylcholine, and endorphins.[11] Paul Mandel, a biochemist at the Center for Neurochemistry in Strasbourg, having studied the inhibitory effects of gamma-aminobutyric acid (GABA) and serotonin on violence in rats, extrapolated his findings to terrorism. He suggested recently, in a newspaper interview, that emotional self-stimulation can lower brain serotonin levels so as to promote the violence associated with religious fanaticism, and that the Ayatollah Khomeini "suppressed his GABA and serotonin levels through religious excitation . . . and now there's no inhibition." According to the newspaper, Mandel believes that the ayatollah would have benefited from drug treatment.[12]

---

[9] Cesare Lombroso and R. Laschi, *Le Crime Politique et les Révolutions* (Paris, 1982), passim. The ideas of Lombroso regarding the physical causes of terrorism, as well as those of others, are discussed in Laqueur, *Age of terrorism*, 151.

[10] David G. Hubbard, "Terrorism and Protest," *Legal Medical Quarterly* 2 (1978): 188–97.

[11] David G. Hubbard, "The Psychodynamics of Terrorism," in *International Violence*, edited by Y. Alexander and T. Adeniran (New York: Praeger, 1983), 45–53. For research on the relationship between dopamine, norepinephrine, acetylcholine, and aggression in animals, see Louis J. West, "Studies of Aggression in Animals and Man," *Psychopharmacology Bulletin* 13 (1977): 14–25.

[12] Quoted in Jon Franklin, "Criminality Is Linked to Brain Chemistry Imbalances," *Baltimore Evening Sun*, 30 July 1984. For both animal and human studies on the relationship

Presumably, not only would the ayatollah have benefited if he had taken drugs, but so would Iraq, Kuwait, the whole Persian Gulf, the thousands of Iranian Revolutionary Guards reportedly blown up while holding their plastic keys to Paradise, and, not least, the Western hostages who fell into the hands of the Iranian-inspired Hizballah in Lebanon.

Less reductionistic but still problematic efforts have been made to attribute much of terrorism to mental illness—efforts reviewed by Corrado.[13] Two authors, for example, have expressed the view that terrorists are psychopaths.[14] Certainly, terrorist groups reside at the fringes of the societies they inhabit, and it stands to reason that those groups might preferentially attract persons with various mental illnesses so that the proportion of their membership that is made up of the mentally ill might be higher than that proportion in the general population. It seems clear, however, that the proportion is not strikingly high, and that terrorists do not, in general, suffer from mental illnesses either of a psychotic or other type.[15] To be sure, Ferracuti and Bruno, in studying the prevalence of mental illness among Italian terrorists during the 1970s, found more am members of right-wing groups than among members of left-wing groups;[16] but even among those terrorists, psychopathology does not appear to be the primary source of terrorist motivation or activity.

Nor does that constellation of characteristics long sought but still not found, the "terrorist personality," appear to account for terrorist behavior; indeed, it almost certainly does not exist. The most exhaustive interview studies of terrorists ever carried out, sponsored by the West German Ministry of the Interior and involving 227 left-wing West German terrorists and 23 right-wing extremists, revealed a number of patterns in the personal histories of the subjects that seemed significantly more common among them than among other West Germans of their age—patterns such as the loss, at an early age, of one or both parents, severe conflicts with authorities, and frequent episodes of school and work failures.[17] But other patterns—in particular, two personality constellations, one consisting of extreme dependence on the terrorist group, extroversion, parasitic lifestyle, and stimulus seeking and the other consisting of hostility, suspiciousness, aggressiveness, and self-defensiveness—also are described in the study[18] and are difficult to compare with the patterns for other persons of the same age who live at society's edge.

In any case, these patterns of individual history or personality, even if they could be demonstrated to be characteristic of these particular kinds of

---

between GABA, serotonin, and aggression in both animals and human beings, see Gerald L. Brown and Frederick K. Goodwin, "Human Aggression—A Biological Perspective," in *Unmasking the Psychopath*, edited by W. H. Reid et al. (New York: W. W. Norton, 1986); Gerald L. Brown, Frederick K. Goodwin, and William E. Bunney, Jr., "Human Aggression and Suicide: Their Relationship to Neuropsychiatric Diagnosis and Serotonin Metabolism," in *Serotonin in Biological Psychiatry*, edited by B. T. Ho et al. (New York: Raven Press, 1982), 287–307.

[13] R. R. Corrado, "A Critique of the Mental Disorder Perspective of Political Terrorism," *International Journal of Law and Psychiatry* 4 (1981): 293–310. Heskin has come to this conclusion also regarding IRA terrorists; see K. Heskin, *Northern Ireland: A Psychological Analysis* (New York: Columbia University Press, 1980).

[14] See Cooper, "What Is a Terrorist," 16–32, and K. I. Pearce, "Police Negotiations," *Canadian Psychiatric Association Journal* 22 (1977): 171–4.

[15] W. Rasch, "Psychological Dimensions of Political Terrorism in the Federal Republic of Germany," *International Journal of Law and Psychiatry* 2 (1979): 79–85.

[16] F. Ferracuti and F. Bruno, "Italy: A Systems Perspective," in *Aggression in Global Perspective*, edited by A. P. Goldstein and M. H. Segall (Elmsford, N.Y.: Pergamon, 1983).

[17] G. Schmidtchen, "Terroristische Karrieren: Soziologische Analyse anhand von Fahn-dungsunterlagen und Prozessakten" ["Terrorist Careers: Sociological Analysis Based on Investigation and Trial Documents"], in *Analysen zum Terrorismus [Analysis of Terrorism]*, edited by H. Jäger, G. Schmidtchen, and L. Süllwold (Opladen: Westdeutscher Verlag, 1981), vol. 2, *Lebenslauf-Analysen [Biographical Analysis]*.

[18] Süllwold, "Stationen in der Entwicklung von Terroristen: Psychologische Aspekte Biographischer Daten" [Stages in the Development of Terrorists: Psychological Aspects of Biographical Data], in *Analysen zum Terrorismus*, edited by Jäger, Schmidtchen, and Süllwold, vol. 2.

terrorists—a demonstration that has not been accomplished—are unlikely to be characteristic of other terrorists from other groups. The paths to a life of terrorism appear to be quite different in different societies and different types of groups. If any "terrorist personality" reliably could be found among West German leftists, it probably would be very different from the typical personalities (if such typical personalities were in fact to exist) of Middle Eastern terrorists of the nationalist or religious sort, and even different from leftist terrorists in Latin America.

Other attempts at attributing terrorist behaviors, in some blanket way, to particular psychological mechanisms, processes, or characteristics also seem to be without foundation. It is unlikely, for example, as Corrado has noted, that "narcissism" explains the terrorism of even a small number of ideologically radical groups,[19] or that the death wish does, either.[20]

Even attempts to explain, on the basis of one or another motivation, certain very stylized, specific terrorist acts by specific populations in specific places—in particular, suicide car bombings by Shi'ites against Israelis in southern Lebanon—ultimately have been shown to be wrong, or only partly true. To be sure, some of those bombers probably were quite ready to blow themselves up in a holy act of explosive, Paradise-seeking martyrdom. But in the case of at least one such about-to-be suicide car bomber, a sixteen-year-old Shi'ite from Beirut's southern suburbs who was apprehended by the Israelis just before he was about to drive the lethal car that had been prepared for him, the motivation was not religious. Rather, he was coerced by officials of the Shi'ite militia, who used threats against his family. The last thing the secular boy wanted to do, it turns out, was to kill

himself—either for Allah or for anyone or anything else.[21]

Inadequate Appreciation of the Palpable and Psychic Rewards of Belonging to Terrorist Groups

Just as there is a psychology of needs, so there is a psychology of rewards. Certainly, a life of terrorism can satisfy needs such as support and approval from other members of the terrorist group, opportunities for violence, lashing out against the world of one's parents, and many others of which most of us would not be proud.

But there are other things that a life of terrorism can provide that, although they may also be things of which most of us would not be proud, may play a significant role in the decision of some terrorists to join terrorist groups—things such as power, prestige, privilege, and even wealth. These things, described pungently in an essay by Conor Cruise O'Brien,[22] are attractive to young people from impoverished backgrounds—backgrounds of the sort that are common in many zones of terrorist conflict, such as the Middle East and Northern Ireland—and together serve as a powerful impetus for many of these people to join terrorist groups. They are especially accessible to terrorists in cultures that have a long and persistent revolutionary tradition—cultures in which terrorist traditions have popular roots.

And the rewards of joining can be enormously satisfying. In some groups, terrorism can provide a route for advancement, an opportunity for glamour and excitement, a chance at world renown, a way of demonstrating one's courage, and even a way of accumulating wealth.[23] No small advantages, these,

[19] See Christopher Lasch, *The Culture of Narcissism* (New York: W. W. Norton, 1979), 154, and Gustave Morf, *Terror in Quebec: Case Studies of the F.L.Q.* (Toronto: Clarke, Irwin, 1970), 107, quoted in R. R. Corrado, "A Critique," 293–310.

[20] See Cooper, "What Is a Terrorist," 16–32, and "Psychopath as Terrorist," 253–62.

[21] Thomas J. Friedman, "Boy Says Lebanese Recruited Him as Car Bomber," *New York Times*, 14 April 1985, p. 1. For a general discussion of the motivations of suicide bombers, see Chapter 10 in this volume.

[22] Conor Cruise O'Brien, "Thinking About Terrorism," *Atlantic Monthly* (June 1986), 62–6.

[23] The annual budgets of a number of terrorist organizations now exceed the budgets of some small states. According to

and almost totally unstudied by researchers seeking to understand why terrorists become terrorists, and why they continue to do what they do.

Psychologizing Motivations that are Understandable Enough when Discussed in Everyday Language

"Hatred," "revulsion," "revenge"—these terms characterize precisely the feelings and motivations of many terrorists. Somehow, they seem too human for psychiatrists and psychologists to use in scientific discourse. But used they should be. Using them brings us closer to the psychological states of many terrorists, and to what they want, than using the milder terms with which we may feel more comfortable, such as "anger" or "frustration"— terms that convey a lesser sense of some terrorists' moods and convictions.[24]

These nonprofessional but accurate descriptive terms should be used in psychiatric discourse because they are true, and because they can help explain, in some cases, the continuation of terrorism even after significant demands have been satisfied. Terrorists' frustration may be lessened by such achievements, but the hatred, the revulsion, and especially the desire for revenge may not. Therefore, these motivations may continue to spur the terrorist enterprise even after many demands have been satisfied.

Even psychiatrists and psychologists accustomed to professional language should, in this very human arena, use the most powerfully human terms. The words we use in discussing a subject affect the way in which we think about it. If we use words like "hatred," "revulsion," and "revenge" rather than "anger," "opposition," and "desire for political change," we may better understand the

---

Laqueur (*The Age of Terrorism*, 102), in 1975 the annual budget of Fatah was $150 million to $200 million (in 1980 dollars), with other Palestinian factions gathering their own millions; the IRA's budget was, in the same year, $1 million to $3 million; and the budgets of each of several South American groups, raised from the sales of illicit drugs, were $50 million to $150 million in 1985. With such sums changing hands in clandestine ways, significant amounts are bound to reach the pockets of people at least as interested in comforts as in selfless causes. Even George Ibrahim Abdullah, the Christian Lebanese terrorist for whose release from a French prison his friends and relatives engineered a wave of Paris bombings in September 1986, devolved, according to his neighbors in the Lebanese village of Qobayat, from a nationalist idealist into a fighter not for a cause but for wealth. Referring to Abdullah's group, one neighbor told a reporter, "They were once idealists and now they do it all for money." See Nora Boustany, "The Christian Village That Spawned the Paris Bombers," *Washington Post*, 26 October 1986. On the tendency that develops among some terrorists to accumulate precisely the material goods whose accumulation they despise in others, see Michael Baumann, *Terror or love: Bommi Baumann's Own Story of His Life as a West German Urban Guerrilla* (New York: Grove Press, 1979), p. 104.

[24] For examples of what appear to be hatred, revulsion, and revenge as the primary goals of various terrorist groups and acts, see Thomas L. Friedman, "Armed and Dangerous: A Mideast Consumed by the Politics of Revenge," *New York Times*, 5 January 1986, sec 4, p. 1, about Abu Nidal and some other Palestinian groups.

In the case of Abu Nidal and his organization, Jerrold Post's thesis that "the cause is not the cause" seems apt. (See Chapter 2 in this volume.) According to this thesis, the official, political goals of the organization, as publicized as they may be, are less important than the goal of maintaining the existence of the terrorist organization itself. Post's thesis is strengthened, I think, by an appreciation of the central roles that such feelings as hatred and revenge have come to play in the ethos of some terrorist groups—roles that have displaced, and even rendered irrelevant, most of the original nationalist ones. However, whereas Abu Nidal might not stop terrorism even if the Palestinians were to achieve a state that displaced not only all of Israel but also every other country in the Middle East, most terrorist groups probably ultimately could be satisfied enough by the achievement of their goals to stop their terrorism, despite their current feelings of hatred and vengefulness— although what they might consider satisfactory achievements may require from their adversaries comprises that, for them, would add up to nothing less than political or national suicide. Thus, feelings of hatred and desire for revenge are shared by many terrorists, and these feelings probably increase the difficulty the terrorists may have, for other reasons, in stopping their terrorism. For a small percentage of these terrorists, however, those feelings probably constitute the residue of the nationalist and idealist goals for which they adopted a life of terrorism in the first place.

For a specific example of terrorist actions that appeared to observers to be explicable only in terms of a logic of hatred, revenge, and the need to commit violence, see Don Podesta, "Terror for Terror's Sake: Motive Missing in Egyptair Hijacking," *Washington Post*, 1 December 1985, p. A-l.

kinds of responses that need to be constructed to contend with the impulse and reality of terrorism.

Our own impulses—the preference for compromise, say, and for reason—may produce pallid rejoinders to demands that are, in many cases, apocalyptic. The language we use in discussing and examining terrorist groups should reflect with fidelity the reality of their members' inner lives and provide us with a realistic sense of which responses, in which cases, might be effective in reducing terrorism, and which might not.

Ignoring Rational Reasons for Choosing a Terrorist Strategy

Many terrorist groups routinely offer strategic, logical reasons to explain their use of terrorism; and many people who study terrorism just as routinely prefer to believe that those reasons are only covers for the real reasons, which must derive solely or primarily from deep needs. Sometimes they do—but rarely solely, and sometimes not even primarily.

Numerous declarations and memoirs by terrorists going back to the nineteenth century provide rationales for the adoption of terrorist strategies, such as the assertion that terrorism is an efficient revolutionary method, and perhaps the only one, that can be used by a weak force against a powerful regime.[25] Many of these rationales are summarized by Martha Crenshaw in Chapter 1 of this volume

and elsewhere.[26] In general, it should be remembered that, although these rationales are the rationales of terrorists, and although what they often rationalize is acts of indiscriminate murder, the rationales may make strategic sense. To the extent that they do, psychological research should not ignore them. Strategic logic can spur actions no less powerfully than emotional logic.

Inaccessibility to Direct Research on Terrorists

Many terrorists believe, for good reason, that any attempt to explain their motivations in psychological terms diminishes the validity of their ideas, their actions, and their beings. If they are serious in their commitment to their causes and have no illusions that they can convert to their views the researcher who asks to meet with them—a researcher who is likely to be seen as a representative of the government, society, or class against which they have organized their actions—they are likely to refuse to meet with that researcher, even if they are languishing in prison with nothing else to do. Agreement to meet with a psychiatrist or psychologist is more likely to occur when the terrorists have already begun to have doubts about their decision to adopt a terrorist career; and, in such cases, the information provided, as rich as it may be, inevitably affected by the change in psychological orientation.

Ignoring State Terrorism and the Destructive Acts of Western Governments

Critics, especially critics on the political left, object to terrorist studies in part on the grounds that they tend to ignore (for reasons of ideological convenience, they often argue) the kind of terrorism

[25] See, for example, the following documents and works: Peter Kropotkin, "Programma Ispolnitel'novo Komiteta" [Program of the Executive Committee], in *Literatura Sot-sial'no Revolutsionnoi Partii "Norodnoi Voli" [Literature of "The People's Will" Social Revolutionary Party]* (Paris, 1905); Nikolai Morozov, *Terroristicheskaya Bor'ba [The Terrorist Struggle]* (London, 1880); Michel Confino, *Violence dans la Violence* (Paris: F. Maspero, 1973); Carlos Marighella, *Mini Manual of the Urban Guerilla* (London, 1971); Menachem Begin, *The Revolt* (Los Angeles: Nash, 1972); Leila Kadi, *Basic Political Documents of the Armed Palestinian Resistance Movement* (Beirut: Palestine Liberation Organization Research Center, *1969*): and Charles Foley (ed.), *Memoirs of General Grivas* (London: Longman's, 1964).

[26] See Martha Crenshaw, "The Logic of Terrorism," Chapter 1 of this volume, and "The Strategic Development of Terrorism," a paper prepared for delivery at the 1985 annual meeting of the American Political Science Association, New Orleans.

that has produced more destruction than any other: the terrorism carried out by states against their own people. These critics often argue that terrorism researchers have insufficient sympathies for the sources of most modem terrorist movements—the aspirations of the poor and the oppressed to shake off the yoke of colonial or capitalist rule or to end the occupation of their homelands by nations or peoples or governments that are supported by Western colonial interests.

As a result of this lack of sympathy, those critics argue, terrorism specialists tend to see terrorism in purely negative terms. In addition, the critics argue, because the terrorism researchers are generally members of Western societies, they are inclined to support the regimes and types of polities—namely, liberal democracies—that are the targets of so many terrorist groups, and fail to see the ways in which those regimes oppress certain minorities, classes, or national groups or support other countries that do so. Such oppression, the critics argue, constitutes a form of terrorism, a terrorism that is often far worse in its effects, scope, and ruthlessness than the acts of the substate terrorists.[27]

These arguments cannot be dismissed outright. State terrorism has certainly been the most potent and destructive form of terrorism the world has seen: Nazi Germany and the Soviet Union, to name the two regimes that have engaged in it most egregiously, have indeed amassed deaths that a near eternity of conventional substate terrorist actions could not hope to accomplish. Whether substate terrorist actions have become the focus of terrorism specialists because of an ideological preference for Western values and interests and whether such a preference distorts the effort to understand terrorism in psychological terms are, however, different matters.

For some terrorism specialists, including some who concern themselves with the psychology of terrorism, Western interests and concerns probably

are paramount. This may be due, in part, to the fact that most of these specialists are Westerners themselves, as well as to the fact that they are well acquainted with the ravages that substate terrorism has caused. In addition, some of these specialists have been employed by their governments in the military, the police, or the foreign-affairs bureaucracies, or have worked as consultants to these organizations. In those roles they have had, as their primary responsibility, the theoretical or operational task of combating terrorist activities—a responsibility whose exercise is not promoted by the readiness to feel empathy for terrorist aspirations, whether of the revolutionary or the third-world variety.

Many researchers interested in the psychology of terrorism, however, appear to be genuinely interested in terrorism as a human activity—as a product of individual and group motivation, thinking, and interaction. Although capable of recognizing, and even having empathy for, terrorist needs and feelings, most of them also recognize the human toll exacted by those needs and feelings as they are expressed through terrorist behavior. They are accustomed to working with individuals and groups, and so find it natural to work with substate terrorists. But they tend to feel unprepared—as a result of a lack of theory and experience, rather than ideological bias—to deal with the psychologies of leaders and nations that carry out terrorism against their own or other peoples or that are accused by one or another terrorist group, or by people sympathetic to those groups, of doing so.

In the main, the kinds of actions carried out by terrorist individuals and groups differ in character, strategy, scope, and motivation from the kinds of actions carried out by states against persons or populations who oppose, or are considered undesirable by, those states. The nature of terrorist behavior, and perhaps also the nature of the moral and psychological questions raised by that behavior, differs in the cases of state and substate terrorism and requires different methods of analysis.

The complaint that terrorism specialists, including those who study the psychology of terrorism, have a selective preference for studying one kind of

[27] A vigorously argued formulation of much of this position is contained in a 1977 review of eleven books on terrorism by Anthony Arblaster, "Terrorism: Myths, Meaning and Morals." *Political Studies 25*, no. 3 (1977): 413–24.

terrorism rather than another is not utterly without merit. But that criticism does not necessarily render impossible the valid study of the one, and it does not facilitate the successful study of the other.

Suggestions for Research

In the light of these problems, as well as the evolving nature of terrorism in our time, what should researchers do who wish to study the psychology of terrorism? Which issues should they keep dearly in mind, and which questions should they ask? A few suggestions come to mind:

1. Certainly, researchers should remember that terrorism is varied and complex and that terrorists should not be discussed as if they all have the same motivations, aims, and forms of behavior. It is precisely because it is so easy to overgeneralize and to engage in psychological reductionism that researchers should take special care to identify the individuals and groups whose behaviors they are studying, limit their explanations to those individuals and groups, define the circumstances under which those explanations are valid, and not suggest that their explanations explain more than they do.

2. A strong acquaintance with the history of terrorism seems especially important for researchers in this field; it is important for them to appreciate not only the great breadth of terrorist experience but also the analogues of modern attitudes that existed in previous times. The power of history to teach by analogy has been well demonstrated by two researchers at the Rand Corporation who examined the fascination that terrorists of a hundred years ago had for the new and powerful material called dynamite, the advantages they saw in it, the ways in which they rationalized its use, and the ways in which they did, in fact, use it.[28] These researchers'

goal was to consider whether terrorists' experience with dynamite, which was a superexplosive a hundred years ago, might teach us anything about the ways in which terrorists today might seek to use contemporary superexplosives—that is, nuclear ones—or other means of mass killings, such as chemical and biological weapons. They concluded that we do, in fact, have something to learn from history in this case and that millenarian terrorists consumed by a desire for revenge are probably the ones who would be most likely to use nuclear devices if they could obtain them. The study was a good and judicious use of history as a tool of analysis; more such studies are worth doing.

3. Studying the rewards of the terrorist life would add an important perspective to our understanding of terrorist motivations. The achievement of status and comfort is an attractive goal in all sectors of society, both in the West and in the East, and both in industrialized and in third-world societies. This also seems to provide powerful motivation in terrorist groups, and it deserves deeper examination.

4. Direct research on terrorists is difficult but valuable. Whenever it is possible, it should be attempted. When it is not possible, and certainly in historical cases, attention should be paid to the words that terrorists issue—memoirs, pronouncements, rationales. Although these words may be self-serving, that does not mean that they are not also, in some significant way, revealing.

5. The psychology of state terrorists is worth examining no less than is the psychology of substate terrorists. If knowledge of the latter is sketchy, knowledge of the former is even more so. People who carry out state terrorism tend to be even less available to direct study than people who carry out substate terrorism. Still, enough is available in the form of documents and witnesses to offer a substantial basis for fruitful research.

6. In any study of group psychology, it is important to consider the nature of the group and the connections between it and the larger community of sympathy from which it arises; it

---

[28] David Ronfeldt and William Sater, "The Mindsets of High-Technology Terrorists: Future Implications Form an Historical Analog," *Rand Note N-1610-SL*, prepared for Sandia Laboratories (Santa Monica, Calif.: Rand Corporation, March 1981).

makes a difference if that community is large and supports the terrorist enterprise or if it is small and unrepresentative of the larger population in whose name the terrorists claim to struggle—a population that, in fact, rejects both the terrorists and their struggle.

7. One of the chief dangers of terrorism is the destructive potential of the responses it may precipitate. In nineteenth-century terrorist writings, provocation was identified as a goal of revolutionary terrorist acts: Provoke the government to institute repressions and the population will see just how repressive and worthy of removal that government is. In this age of international terrorism, in which the United States, a superpower with nuclear weapons, is frequently targeted by groups supported by various states, some of which may, in turn, be supported by the Soviet Union, the dangers of escalation and, ultimately, large-scale death are, if remote, nevertheless serious. It may be of some value to examine just how rationally terrorists and their state sponsors think about the international consequences of their actions, and just how rationally the leaders of large countries that are the targets of terrorist actions think about the consequences of their countermeasures.

8. Why do some radical oppositionist groups become terrorist while others, under the same or similar circumstances, continue to pursue essentially peaceful means to achieve their goals? To be sure, political and strategic arguments can be adduced that show why terrorism is an effective strategy. But it is rarely the only strategy that can be pursued. What circumstances in the environment of oppositionist, not-yet-terrorist groups, or within the groups themselves, give the members of such groups the sense, at some point, that terrorism is the only possible—indeed, the necessary—choice? What role, if any, do governments play in provoking or promoting that sense? If they do play such a role, is there anything they can or should do to act in some other way so that the initial, fateful step from radical opposition to terrorism—a step examined by Ehud Sprinzak in Chapter 5 of this volume—is not taken?

9. Finally, what induces terrorists to discard their terrorist careers, if not the ideologies that spawned and sustained those careers? The experience of the Italian "penitents," described by Franco Ferracuti in Chapter 4 of this volume, is instructive; but too little is understood about this phenomenon, and more study of it would be well justified.

Being alert to these issues and asking these questions would lead to a better psychological understanding of terrorist behavior. Most important for psychological researchers is the need to remember that terrorism is a complicated, diverse, and multidetermined phenomenon that resists simple definition, undermines all efforts at objectivity, forces upon all researchers moral riddles of confounding complexity, and is as challenging to our intellectual efforts to understand it as it is to our collective efforts to control it. It is an example and product of human interaction gone awry and is worth studying and understanding in the human terms that befit it: as conflict, struggle, passion, drama, myth, history, reality, and, not least, psychology.

The Psychology of Terrorism: "Syndrome" versus "Tool" Perspectives

Arie W. Kruglanski[1] and Shira Fishman

Two psychological perspectives on terrorism are distinguished, approaching it as a "syndrome" and as a "tool," respectively. According to the "syndrome" view, terrorism represents a psychologically meaningful construct with identifiable characteristics on individual and group levels of analysis. According to the "tool" perspective, terrorism represents a strategic instrument that any party in a conflict with another may use. Research thus far has found little support for the "syndrome" view. Terrorists do not seem to be characterized by a unique set of psychological traits or pathologies. Nor has research uncovered any particular "root causes" of terrorism. The vast heterogeneity of terrorism's users is consistent with the "tool" view, affording an analysis of terrorism in terms of means-ends psychology. The "tool" view implies conditions under which potential perpetrators may find terrorism more or less appealing, hence offering guidance for the "war on terrorism."

Few would disagree that terrorism is the scourge of our times. Though hardly a new phenomenon, its development and proliferation in the latter part of the twentieth century have turned it into a

Arie W. Kruglanski is Distinguished University Professor in Psychology at the University of Maryland, College Park, and a co-director of START, National Center for the Study of Terrorism and the Response to Terrorism. He is a social psychologist with research interests in belief formation, motivation and group processes.

Shira Fishman is a doctoral student in social psychology at the University of Maryland, College Park. Her interests include self-regulation, and the interface of social and psychopathological processes.

Address correspondence to Arie W. Kruglanski, Psychology Department, University of Maryland, College Park, MD 20742. E-mail: arie@psyc.umd.edu formidable menace, threatening human lives worldwide and bent on unraveling the economic and political orders of contemporary societies.

Social scientists' interest in the problem has been growing steadily, paralleling the growth and proliferation of terrorism itself. An unprecedented impetus to this research was lent by the tragic events of September 11, 2001 in New York and Washington, with significant "boosters" of the Madrid March 11, 2004 and the London July 7, 2005 bombings. Currently, considerable efforts in the U.S. and abroad are being expended on studying diverse aspects of terrorism in quest of a solid, empirically based knowledge into its workings on which effective countermeasures could be based. Psychological science plays an essential part in this enterprise.

Psychologists' interest in the study of terrorism is not surprising. Terrorism, after all, is a behavioral phenomenon governed by human agency. Individuals must *decide* to execute a terrorist act and be *motivated* enough to perpetrate the carnage, often to the point of taking their own lives in the process. Terrorists' acts of self-immolation and their indiscriminate killings of innocent civilians strike one as horrific and bizarre. They simply cry out for a psychological explanation.

How can terrorists bring themselves to perpetrate the horrors that they do? *Why* do they hate us so much? *Are* they mentally disturbed? *Do* they have a death wish? *Were* they driven to their heinous deeds by sheer desperation? Are *we* to blame? These questions on many people's minds pose a challenge to psychology as a field of science, with a great deal of importance riding on the answers.

It is possible to distinguish two contrasting psychological approaches to terrorism, presently labeled as the *syndrome* versus *tool* perspectives. By "syndrome," we mean a conception of terrorism as a monolithic entity, a meaningful psychological construct with identifiable properties. This approach resembles the "medical model" of psychopathology in portraying terrorism as a kind of "disease" with a definite etiology, developmental trajectory, and consequences. It implies that "ter-

rorists" should be demarcated from non-terrorists by their *internal* psychological make-up, that is, their personality traits, motivations, and socialization history. It suggests that a generic "terrorist group" should turn out to have a distinct organizational structure and evolutionary sequence. It implies that "terrorism" should be found to emanate from a set of *external* "root causes" (e.g., poverty, poor education, or political oppression). Above all, it suggests that one could generalize one's insights about a given terrorist group to all others. Carrying out such reasoning to its logical conclusion implies, for example, that the way the Weathermen organization in the U.S. progressed through various crisis stages culminating in full blown political violence[2] or the way the Red Brigades terrorism in Italy was dismantled through the Italian "repentance laws"[3] will have important lessons for understanding other brands of terrorism, e.g., the Salafi terrorism currently menacing the West, various South American terrorist groups, or the ancient Zealots of the first century A.D.

The "tool" approach is rooted in the psychology of goal-means relations.[4] It assumes rather little about the uniform psychological properties of terrorists or their organizations. Instead, it views terrorism as a *means to an end*, a tactic of warfare that anyone could use. It suggests that, like the rocket launcher, the tank, or the AK-47 assault rifle, terrorism may be employed by non-state militias, state-sponsored armies, even lone perpetrators. Rather than adopting a "bottom-up" approach seeking to psychologically characterize certain terrorist groups, in the hope that this would generalize to other terrorist groups, it takes a "top down" perspective based on a conceptual distinction between *terrorists* (potentially *any* social entity or actor) and *terrorism* as a means to an end. The "psychology" here is very different from that of the "syndrome" approach. It is a psychology of means employment.[5] Its major concern is the conditions under which an individual or a group would opt for a given course of action versus its possible alternatives, given these actors' objectives.

Terrorism as a Syndrome

The Terrorist Personality

Even though the anti-colonial wave of terrorism was clear in its implication that "one man's terrorist is another man's freedom fighter," and hence, that the search for a uniform, psychologically meaningful "terrorist syndrome" is unlikely to be fruitful, the search for such a personality has not abated. John Horgan, in a review of terrorist personality literature, points out that as late as 1981, a review of the literature on terrorism and mental disorders found that psychopathy was the feature most commonly associated with terrorists.[6] Andrew Silke concurs. In his words, "in the early 1970s . . . it was widely believed that terrorists suffered from personality disorders and that there would be an exceptionally high number of clinical psychopaths, narcissists and paranoids in the ranks of the average terrorist group."[7] Similar beliefs continue to this day to permeate psychological thought on terrorism. Thus, following the events of September 11, 2001, Walter Laqueur wrote that "all terrorists believe in conspiracies by the powerful, hostile forces and suffer from some form of delusion and persecution mania . . . The element of . . . madness plays an important role" in terrorism.[8]

Yet, the systematic quest for a unique terrorist personality has yielded few encouraging results. Painstaking empirical research conducted on the German Red Army Faction (the Baader Meinhof Gang), the Italian Red Army Brigades, the Basque ETA, and various Palestinian organizations did not reveal anything particularly striking about the psychological make-up of members of terrorist organizations.[9] As Clark McCauley eloquently put it:

> The results of these investigations take several feet of shelf space, but are easy to summarize. The terrorists did not differ from the comparison group of non-terrorists in any substantial way; in particular, the terrorists did not show higher rates of any kind of psychopathology. . . . Indeed terrorism would be a trivial problem if only those with some kind of psychopathology could be terrorists. Rather we have to face the fact that normal people can be terrorists, that we are ourselves capable of

terrorist acts under some circumstances. This fact is already implied in recognizing that military and police forces involved in state terrorism are all too capable of killing non-combatants. Few would suggest that the broad range of soldiers and policemen involved in such killing must all be suffering some kind of psychopathology.[10]

John Horgan expressed a similar view, writing that, "despite their attractiveness (via the simplicity any potential results would imply), personality traits are useless as predictors for understanding why people become terrorists."[11] As we shall argue later, however, personality traits are not necessarily irrelevant to terrorism even though they may not constitute the unique psychological determinants of terrorism.

"Root Causes" of Terrorism?

If no internal personality factors, then perhaps external "root causes" may form the unique psychological determinants of terrorism. Major such suggested "root causes" have been socioeconomic status, age, and education along with frustration, relative deprivation, and religious faith. According to Marc Sageman, the "root causes" approach suffers from the "fundamental issue of specificity."[12] Although many people may be exposed to the same hardships in life or share similar backgrounds, very few of them actually become terrorists. Thus, none of the suggested factors can be expected to constitute both the necessary and the sufficient causes of terrorism.

Consistent with this notion, a number of large-scale empirical studies have found no relationship between poverty and terrorism, both at the level of the individual terrorists and at the aggregate level of their country of origin.[13] Sageman's research on the Salafi jihad movement uncovered that its leadership and its largest membership cluster had come mostly from the upper and middle classes.[14] Robert Pape's recent study of suicide bombers' demographic profile indicated that only seventeen percent in their midst were unemployed or part of the lower classes, considerably less than their fair share representation in their societies, of which they make up about one-third overall.[15]

considerations of group dynamics, along with those concerning the "terrorist personality" and the "root causes" of terrorism, combine to suggest that a quest for the terrorist syndrome could be a "will-of-the-wisp."

Discarding the notion of terrorism as a psychological syndrome raises the question of what the psychology of terrorism might consist of, after all. The answer would seem to require that we first clarify what exactly is meant by "terrorism" as a category. Unfortunately, the conceptual picture in this department is rather murky.

Defining Terrorism

Alex Schmid and Albert Jongman, in their comprehensive volume *Political Terrorism*, list no less than 109 definitions of terrorism, and they do not even pretend to be exhaustive.[40] Why is it so difficult to agree on a definition? A major hardship stems from the fact that the term "terrorism" is highly pejorative these days, evoking the motivation to distinguish it from forms of aggression that one wishes to condone.[41] Consider a recent definition of terrorism by the U.S. Department of State. It asserts that " 'terrorism' is a premeditated, politically motivated violence (conducted in times of peace) perpetrated against noncombatant targets by sub-national groups or clandestine state agents, usually intended to influence an audience to advance political ends."

This allows one to demarcate terrorism from (a) state originated violence at times of war (e.g., the bombings of German or Japanese cities during WWII), (b) incidental killings of noncombatants (so-called "collateral damage"), and (c) underground resistance to occupation. One cannot but wonder whether this definition of terrorism and many others has been shaped by the desire to set it apart from forms of violence that one's own nation or its allies were engaged in, and that one wished to defend as legitimate and moral. Indeed, one person's terrorist is another person's freedom fighter, an inevitable consequence of allowing one's *motivations* to dictate one's *definitions*.[42] As a case in point, Khalil Shikaki's public opinion poll of

December 21, 2003 found that 98.1 percent of the Palestinian's surveyed *agreed or strongly* agreed that, "the killing of 29 Palestinians in Hebron by Baruch Goldstein at al Ibrahimi Mosque in 1994" constitutes terrorism, whereas 82.3 percent of the same respondents *disagreed or strongly disagreed* that, "the killing of 21 Israeli youths by a Palestinian who exploded himself at the Tel Aviv Dolphinarium" constitutes terrorism.[43]

One way out of this quandary is to define terrorism in terms of a core element explicit or implicit in nearly all the definitions: the strategic use of terror for the advancement of one's objectives. In this vein, R. P. Hoffman proposed that "terrorism is a purposeful human political activity . . . directed toward the creation of a general climate of fear and . . . designed to influence in ways desired by the protagonist, other human beings, and through them, some course of events."[44] Similarly, Anthony Marsella argued that all definitions include the idea that terrorism is "the use of force of violence by individuals or groups that is directed toward civilian populations and intended to instill fear as a means of coercing individuals or groups to change their political or social positions."[45] Bruce Hoffman proposed that "terrorism [is] the deliberate creation and exploitation of fear through violence or the threat of violence in the pursuit of political change."[46] Boaz Ganor suggested that "the terrorists' primary aim is to create fear within the target population."[47] Finally, Caleb Carr stated that "terrorism . . . is simply the contemporary name given to the modern permutation of warfare deliberately waged against civilians with the purpose of destroying their will [presumably via terror] to support either leaders or policies that the agents of such violence find objectionable."[48] Carr fully realized that his definition "draws no distinction between conventional military and unconventional paramilitary forces." Yet to him, this, precisely, was the point, because:

> Anyone who asserts that a particular armed force or unit or individual that deliberately targets civilians in the pursuit of a political goal is for some reason not an exponent of terrorism has no genuine interest in defining and eliminating this savage phenomenon, but is rather concerned with

excusing the behavior of the nation or faction for whom he or she feels sympathy.[49]

Terrorism as a Tool

The latter approach represents a shift from a syndrome perspective on terrorism to a view of terrorism as a tool, deployed for whatever purpose. In this vein Shibley Telhami criticized the "syndrome" views inherent in "the global war on terrorism as if [it were] a movement, an ideology or a political coalition, with little differentiation between cases." Instead, he proposed to view "terrorism . . . as an *instrument*, not a movement; as an immoral means employed by groups some of which have just causes, some of which do not."[50]

The "tool" view of terrorism as a utilitarian use of fear requires the coming to terms with the fact that in recent history numerous organized states actually perpetrated "terrorism." Rudolph J. Rummel estimates that during the twentieth century, 169,000,000 people were killed by the activities of governments, including 130,000,000 killed by people's own governments. The remaining 39,000,000 are the estimates of civilians killed by enemy forces during various wars. In the preponderance of those cases, "killing by government" was carried out in order to break the enemy morale and hence, to advance the state's objectives.[51] This, of course, is quintessentially "terroristic." It is striking in this context that according to Rummel, merely 518,000 civilians were killed in the twentieth century by non-state groups of which genuine "terrorists" (e.g., as opposed to guerilla fighters) are only a part. This amounts to less than half of a percentage point of civilians whose demise was brought about by state power. As McCauley observed: "State terrorism was not only first, it continues to be more dangerous."[52]

Rounding off this discussion of terrorism's users is the realization that *isolated individuals* too can, and have, employed this tactic. Ted Kaczynski, the ill-famed "Unabomber," used terrorism in pristine isolation. Erik Rudolph, the Atlanta bomber, appears to have been a "lone gunman," relatively speaking.[53] John Muhammad and Lee Malvo

induced terror for their pecuniary purpose in a pairwise formation.

Implications of the "Tool" View

The Moral Dimension

A major implication of the "tool" view of terrorism has concerned its presumed moral unacceptability, warranting a total "war on terrorism" aimed at eradicating it in all of its shapes and forms. Telhami expressed it clearly: "The argument against terrorism is essentially moral: To dissuade others from using such tactics, one has to speak with moral authority . . . The ends no matter how worthy cannot justify the means . . . The deliberate attack on civilian targets is unacceptable under any circumstances."[54] Carr similarly branded terrorism as "murderous," "brutal," and "savage," on an equal plane with such morally reprehensible activities as genocide, piracy, and slavery.[55] Much like Telhami, Carr could see "no circumstances under which [terrorism is] excusable."[56] He ultimately argued for the use of an unremitting force against terrorism, amply justified by the essential *immorality* of the phenomenon and its *evil* nature.

Moral Dilemmas

But the "end does not justify the means" doctrine, though intuitively appealing, turns out to be troublesome on both moral and psychological grounds. For strictly speaking, it is *precisely* the end that justifies a means—what else? Why else would one get into a car and *drive* (the means) if not to *get somewhere* (the end)? Why else would one *maintain a diet* (the means) if not for *one's health or appearance* (the end)? At least in its literal sense then, the "end does not justify the means" statement seems inaccurate.

A more nuanced interpretation of this phrase, however, *is* reasonable. Its intent is that a *given end* does not justify the means *if* the latter undermined another important goal. For instance, advancing "freedom from oppression" may not appear to warrant the means of "targeting civilians" because this undermines the superior end of "preserving human life." That makes sense. But what if the undermined end was *less* important than the end advanced? For instance, would one *lie* to save a child's life? Would one steal from the rich to give to the poor? Both latter cases exemplify Lawrence Kohlberg's moral dilemmas in which an activity, (e.g., lying, stealing) detrimental to one goal (such as that of honesty), may serve a superior end (the saving of a life, alleviation of suffering). In fact, Kohlberg regards the decision to lie or steal under these circumstances a more evolved form of morality than a rigid adherence to the compromised objective.[57]

In essence, whether an end justifies a means depends on a moral calculus: an end may justify terrorism if it exceeded in its moral significance the end obstructed by terrorism, but it may not justify terrorism if the opposite held true. It is in precisely those terms that in August 1945, Harry Truman justified the use of the A and H bombs on Hiroshima and Nagasaki. Ending the war and saving countless American and Japanese lives was more important than the preservation of the fewer lives the bombing would claim. Numerous Americans agreed. In short, rather than in black and white, morality often comes in shades of gray.

The moral calculus implicit in the "end justifying means" issue is not just a matter of arm-chair philosophizing. It has substantial implications for the "war on terrorism." First, even though we may regard terrorism as atrocious, the terrorists and their supporters may feel morally justified in their activities if they deemed the ends advanced by terrorism superior to the ends forestalled. As a case in point, in a recent work, Anat Barko interviewed the launchers of Palestinian suicide bombers in Israeli security prisons and found that moral justifications constituted a dominant explanatory category of their actions.[58]

Secondly, under the appropriate circumstances, the counterterrorists too may sacrifice (what to them appear) the less important in favor of more important objectives. Thus, in the war against terrorism, military forces often risk inflicting "collateral damage" and killing innocent civilians because they deem such risks unavoidable. Thirdly,

the fight against terrorism *itself* might appear morally unjustifiable if the end it promised to achieve (e.g., elimination of a terrorist group at a far corner of the globe fighting a just cause against a ruthless and corrupt dictatorship) threatened to hinder one's own foreign policy priorities (e.g., the spreading of democracy or the protection of civil liberties). In this connection, David Rapoport noted that:

> Despite its pre-eminent status as a victim, Cold War concerns led the U.S. sometimes to ignore its stated distaste for terror. In Nicaragua, Angola, and elsewhere the U.S. supported terrorist activity, an indication of how difficult it was to forgo a purpose deemed worthwhile even when deplorable tactics had to be used.[59]

It is arguably for these reasons that international coalitions, forged to fight terrorism, may be fragile. Thus in the 1890s, the so-called "Golden Age of Assassination," a consensus emerged to fight terrorism through international police cooperation and improved border control. The underlying sentiment of this agreement is expressed poignantly in the following pronouncement by Theodore Roosevelt against anarchist terrorism (that with slight changes of terminology might well be misattributed to George W. Bush): "Anarchy is a crime against the whole human race, and all mankind should band together against the Anarchist. His crimes should be made a crime against the law of all nations declared by treaties among all civilized powers."[60] Yet:

> The consensus lasted three years only. The U.S. refused to send a representative to a St. Petersburg signing ceremony for a German/Russian sponsored protocol to meet these objectives. In a second chapter of this story, the Americans refused to adhere to it even when asked to do so later. They feared that an extensive involvement in European politics might be required. . . . Italy refused, too, for a very different . . . concern. If Anarchists were returned to their original countries, Italy's domestic troubles might be worse than its international ones.[61]

In other words, a concerted and unrelenting counterterrorist effort may not only require considerable investments but might clash at times with the political and morally inspired interests of members of the international community, who may, therefore, support it only by word, rather than by deed, if that.

The Psychological Dimension

In an important sense, whether one views terrorism as moral or immoral is a matter of deciding which end is more important (that advanced or that hindered by terrorism). This is often a matter of subjective perception driven by psychological factors. Research has uncovered a phenomenon of "focalism" whereby increasing the subjective focus on a given objective leads to the suppression of alternative objectives.[62] Increasing the perceived importance of ends, assumed to be served by terrorism (e.g., a defense of one's religion, freedom from oppression), may psychologically inhibit and dwarf the perceived importance of other incompatible ends (protection of innocents, peaceful co-existence with one's neighbors). In the same way, a focus on security (substantially intensified in the wake of the 9/11/01 attacks in the U.S., the 3/11/04 attacks in Madrid, and the 7/7/05 attacks in London) may jeopardize other important concerns, such as individual rights or good foreign relations. Psychological considerations thus add a layer of complexity to deciding the "end justifying means" issue in the context of fighting terrorism.

Global War on Terrorism

All of which suggests that the "global war on terrorism" concept may need to be reassessed. First, it seems unrealistic. Because anybody can, has, and potentially will, use the "fear factor" in an attempt to advance their important objectives—taking seriously the fight against all "terrorism" could mean a fight on too many fronts and against too many adversaries. Secondly, because of the moral complexities involved, we need to choose our battles carefully and focus on terrorists whose defeat is truly worth the price. This means replacing the indiscriminant globalism of our struggle with focused specificity. In contrast to a general "war on terrorism," it suggests restricting the struggle to

specific groups that use terrorism. In words of the 9/11 commission: "the enemy is not just 'terrorism,' some generic evil. This vagueness blurs the strategy. The catastrophic threat at this moment in history is more specific."[63]

The Psychology of Means Employment and the Use of Terrorism

The Terrorism Tool

By now, early into the twenty-first century, "terrorism" boasts a rich inventory of tactical techniques, honed by years of terrorist experience, recorded in terrorist manuals, available on the Internet and caught up with cutting-edge technologies. Whereas the nineteenth century Anarchists aimed to induce terror through the gunning down of public figures, subsequent terrorist movements enlarged the repertory of violent moves to include plane hijackings, kidnapping and/or hostage taking, beheading, suicide bombings, car bombings, and poisonous gassings. The greatest current fear is the potential future use by terrorists of Weapons of Mass Destruction (WMD), which might bring the terrorist threat to the dreaded next level.[64] Today's terrorism has immediate access to the mass media and, hence, to the spreading of its message and instruction in its techniques to billions of people worldwide. According to Betty Pfefferbaum, "media coverage is an essential weapon of terrorists . . . [used] to convey their message; to gain recognition of their cause, demands and grievances; and to spread fear and anxiety."[65] For all the foregoing reasons, terrorism these days constitutes a highly appealing and accessible "tool," a means of carrying out a variety of belligerent activities against potential targets.

Launching Terrorism

Psychologically speaking, the launching of terrorism on the part of some perpetrators requires a deliberate decision, rooted in the belief that spreading fear in a targeted population will advance their objectives.[66] Indeed, the proponents of terrorism and its ideologues have been at pains to provide elaborate rationales for the efficacy of terrorism. A well-known rationale, offered by the Russian anarchists of the late nineteenth century and echoed by the leftist terrorists of the 1970s and 1980s, was that terrorism would reveal the state's impotence and provoke it to excessive counter-measures contrary to its stated values, thereby unmasking its hypocrisy and paving the way to a revolution. A similar logic appeared in Carlos Marighella's mini-manual for the urban guerilla and was cited by left-wing terrorists in Europe and South America. A different rationale for the efficacy of terrorism, grounded in the presumed weakness and degeneracy of the West, was articulated by Sayyed Hassan Nasserallah in his "spider web" theory about the mere appearance, but not the reality, of Western (Israeli) potency.[67] A similar justification was offered by Osama bin Laden, who in a 2003 sermon stated:

> America is a great power possessed of tremendous military might and a wide-ranging economy, but all this is built on an unstable foundation which can be targeted, with special attention to its obvious weak spots. If America is hit in one hundredth of these weak spots, it will stumble, wither away and relinquish world leadership.[68]

The Legitimation of Terrorism

Because of its extreme nature involving the killing of innocents and a likely (if not certain) self-destruction in the process, the use of terrorism requires not only instrumental but also moral justification that would lend it legitimacy above and beyond its instrumentality as a means. Such justification has typically rested on lofty collectivistic ideologies involving justice to the "people," freedom from oppression, service to God, or retribution for crimes against one's nation. For instance, Osama bin Laden in a 1997 interview with CNN had this to say in justifying a jihad against America:

> We declared jihad against the United States because the U.S. government is unjust, criminal and tyrannical. It has committed acts that are extremely unjust, hideous and criminal . . . The

mention of the U.S. reminds us before everything else of those innocent children who were dis-membered, their heads and arms cut off . . . This U.S. government abandoned even humanitarian feelings by these hideous crimes.[69]

Similarly inflammatory language appears in incitements to terrorism by other ideologues of various ilks. In summary, because terrorism undermines such important objectives as staying alive and preserving the lives of innocent fellow human beings—its launching requires a justification via superordinate ends whose importance exceeds even such commonly cherished purposes. In the terminology of means-ends psychology, the use of the terrorism tool requires the demonstration that in this case the end does justify the means and that the carrying out of attacks against civilians does not undermine one's objective of living up to the ideals of moral decency and of the preservation of ethical values.

The Place of Ideology

As implied above, the use of terrorism (on the part of organizations or individuals) requires a belief system supporting terrorism. Such a belief system contains notions whereby terrorism is (a) instrumental to the attainment of the actors' objectives, and (b) justifiable on moral grounds, and hence compatible with these actors' ethics. Such a belief system may be grounded in a variety of different ideologies, including religious faith, as well as ethno-nationalist and socialist ideologies.[70] Individuals' traits, motivations, and psychological states (e.g., brought about by oppression, poverty, or relative deprivation) may dispose them to embrace such terrorism-justifying ideology to a greater or a lesser extent. In that sense, those factors may constitute psychological contributing factors to terrorism. Furthermore, these factors are interchangeable, and hence none may claim to constitute the root cause of terrorism. What seems psychologically necessary for the embracement of terrorism is a justificatory system, that is, an ideology claiming terrorism to constitute an effective and acceptable tool given the actors' objectives.

Discouraging Terrorism

The above analysis of the means (or "tool") conception of terrorism has implications for strategies to discourage terrorism. Consistent with the present notions, this may require persuading the perpetrator that (a) this particular means is ineffectual in reference to the actors' objectives, (b) that there exist alternative, more effective means to the actors' ends, and (c) that terrorism constitutes a hindrance to the attainment of other important objectives.

Though schematically simple, implementation of these strategies is anything but, in fact. A major difficulty is that events are subject to construal, often biased by motivations. For instance, throughout much of the second intifada, close to eighty percent of the Palestinian population supported the use of terror tactics (e.g., suicide bombings) against the Israelis, believing this to be an effective tool in their struggle.[71] It is not that motivations imbue judgments directly; rather, they may work through the recruitment of supportive arguments for the desired position. As noted earlier, extreme Islamists have maintained that the West is weak and corrupt; hence, it will crumble under pressure sooner or later.[72] This credo immunizes its believers against present setbacks, viewed as temporary stumbling blocks on the way to an ultimate victory. The Crusader state, re-conquered by the Muslims after centuries, often is invoked as a parallel to contemporary jihad in showing proof of success.[73] In short, proof is in the "eye of the beholder," and it is often shaped by motivation.

Multifinality

Terrorism also might be difficult to give up because, besides its presumed advancement of the perpetrators' *ideological* (political, religious, ethno-nationalistic) objectives, it affords the *emotional* satisfaction of watching the enemy suffer, which boosts one's sense of potency and prowess. In that sense, terrorism is "multi-purpose" or "multi-final," compounding its appeal.[74] From this perspective, such policies as "ethnic profiling," "targeted assassinations" or the inadvertent "col-

lateral damage" inflicted during anti-terrorist campaigns might backfire by fueling the rage of the terrorists and their supporters, hence amplifying the emotional goal of vengeance against the enemy.[75] A recent empirical analysis suggests that "targeted hits" by the Israeli forces boosted the estimated recruitment to the "terrorist stock," presumably due to the Palestinians' motivation to revenge the fallen comrades. Whereas "targeted hits" do hurt (a repeated demand by Palestinian negotiators was that the Israelis desist from employing this particular strategy) and may arguably decrease the perception that terrorism is effective (due to the organizational disruptions that the elimination of leaders may create), they concomitantly increase the appeal of terrorism by inflating the intensity of the emotional goal it may serve. In this regard, the research found that the arrests of terrorism suspects (i.e., a less inflammatory means) tended to reduce (rather than inflate) the "terrorist stock" and hence, to lower the incidence of Palestinian terrorism.[76]

Feasibility of Alternatives to Terrorism

Whereas additional *goals* (such as revenge) may increase terrorism's appeal, availability of alternative *means* to the terrorism's goal may decrease it. For instance, following the election of Mahmud Abbas to the presidency of the Palestinian authority, representing a renewed chance to revive the peace process (i.e., an alternative means to ending the Israeli occupation), support for suicide attacks among the Palestinians dipped to an all-time low in seven years, reaching a mere twenty-nine percent, according to the Palestinian pollster Khalil Shikaki.[77]

Nonetheless, fifty-seven percent of the respondents opposed the steps taken by the Palestinian Authority to punish the launchers of suicide attacks. As Shikaki summarized it: "Public opposition to a crackdown on those who commit violence against Israelis might reflect the belief that the peace process has not yet been revived. . . . The public seeks to maintain the option of returning to violence if diplomacy fails."[78]

from their broad population bases, but from political entities such as states whose interests are seen as compatible with the terrorist activities in specific instances. For instance, in the 1930s Italy and Hungary were believed to provide material support to Balkan terrorists; during the Cold War, the Soviet Union extended consistent support to anti-colonialist terrorist organizations; Greece extended support to a Cypriot terrorist organization (EOKA); Arab states supported the anti-French Algerian FLN; Syria, Iraq, and Libya extended state support to Palestinian terrorists. See Gurr (see note 35 above), 97; Robert Hager, Jr. and David A. Lake, "Balancing Empires: Competitive Decolonization in International Politics," *Security Studies* 9 (Spring 2000): 108–148; David C. Rapoport, "Modern Terror: The Four Waves," in Audrey K. Cronin and James M. Ludes, eds., *Attacking Terrorism: Elements of a Grand Strategy* (Washington, D.C.: Georgetown University Press, 2004), 46–73.

37. Khalil Shikaki, Palestinian Center for Policy and Survey Research, 2005, http://www.pcpsr.org/index.html.
38. Bruce Hoffman, *Inside Terrorism* (New York: Columbia University Press, 1998).
39. Reuven Paz, "Who Wants to Email Al-Qaeda?" PRISM Series of Global Jihad (July 2004), http://www.e-prism.org/images/PRISM_no_2_vol_2_-_Who_Wants_to_Email_Al-Qaeda.pdf.
40. Alex P. Schmid and Albert J. Jongman, *Political Terrorism* (Amsterdam: North Holland Publishing, 1988).
41. Historically, this has not been always the case. For instance, in 1878, Vera Zasulich, upon wounding a Russian police commander, threw her weapon to the floor proclaiming "I am a terrorist not a criminal," Rapoport (see note 36 above).
42. Rapoport comments on how Menachem Begin defined members of his Irgun as "freedom fighters" rather than terrorists, a coinage that was widely adopted in the U.N. debates, for example. See John Dugard, "International Terrorism and the Just War," in David C. Rapoport and Yonah Alexander, eds., *The Morality of Terrorism* (New York; Columbia University Press, 1989), 77–98. Governments, on the other hand, began to refer to all violent rebels as "terrorists." In this day and age, the suicide bombers in Iraq and elsewhere are variously referred to in the media as "terrorists," "militants" or "insurgents," Rapoport (see note 36 above), 46–73.
43. Khalil Shikaki, Palestinian Survey Research (Dec 2001) at http://www.pcpsr.org/survey/polls/2001/p3a.html.
44. R. P. Hoffman, "Terrorism: A Universal Definition," (Ph.D. diss.), Claremont Graduate School, 1984.
45. Anthony Marsella, "Reflections on International Terrorism: Issues, Concepts and Directions," in Fathali Moghaddam and Anthony Marsella, eds., *Understanding Terrorism: Psychological Roots, Consequences and Interventions* (Washington, D.C.: American Psychological Association, 2004), 16.
46. Hoffman (see note 38 above), 43.
47. Boaz Ganor, "Terrorism as a Strategy of Psychological Warfare," *Journal of Aggression, Maltreatment and Trauma* 9 (2005): 33–43.
48. Caleb Carr, *The Lessons of Terror: A History of Warfare Against Civilians* (New York: Random House, 2002), 6–7.
49. Ibid.
50. Shibley Telhami, *The Stakes: America in the Middle East* (Boulder, CO: Westview Press, 2004), 15.
51. Rudolph J. Rummel, *Death by Government* (New Brunswick, NJ: Transaction Publishers, 1996).
52. McCauley (see note 10 above), 34.
53. Ehud Sprinzak, "The Lone Gunman," *Foreign Policy* 127 (Nov/Dec 2001): 72–74.
54. Telhami (see note 50 above), 16–17.
55. Carr (see note 48 above).
56. Ibid, 24.
57. Lawrence Kohlberg, *The Psychology of Moral Development: Essays on Moral Development* 1 (San Francisco: Harper & Row, 1984).
58. Anat Barko, "On the Way to Paradise: The World of Suicide Bombers and Their Launchers," Yedioth Ahronoth, Sifrei Chemed (2004).
59. Rapoport (see note 36 above), 58.
60. As cited in Richard B. Jensen, "The United States, International Policing, and the War Against Anarchist Terrorism 1900–1914," *Terrorism and Political Violence* 13 (Spring 2001): 5–46.
61. Rapoport (see note 36 above), 52.
62. David Dunning, "Prediction: The Inside View," in Arie W. Kruglanski and Tory Higgins, eds., *Social Psychology: A Handbook of Basic Principles, 2nd edition* (New York: Guilford Press, in press); James Y. Shah, Arie W. Kruglanski, and Ronald Friedman, "Goal Systems Theory: Integrating the Cognitive and Motivational Aspects of Self-regulation," in Steven Spencer and Steven Fein, eds., *Motivated Social Perception: The Ontario Symposium* 9 (Mahwah, NJ: Lawrence Earlbaum Associates, 2003), 247–275.
63. National Commission on Terrorist Attacks Upon the United States, *The 9/11 Commission Report* (New York: Norton 2004), 362.
64. Glenn E. Schweitzer and Carole C. Dorsch, *SuperTerrorism: Assassins, Mobsters and Weapons of Mass Destruction* (New York: Plenum, 1998).
65. Betty Pfefferbaum, "Victims of Terrorism and the Media," in Andrew Silke ed., *Terrorists, Victims and Society: Psychological Perspectives on Terrorism and Its Consequences* (West Sussex, England: John Wiley & Sons, 2003), 177.
66. Martha Crenshaw, "Questions to be Answered, Research to be Done, Knowledge to be Applied," in Walter Reich, ed., *Origins of Terrorism: Psychologies, Ideologies, Theologies, States of Mind* (Washington, D.C.: Woodrow Wilson Center Press, 1990/1998), 247–260.
67. Ian Buruma and Avishai Margalit, *Occidentalism: The*

West in the Eyes of its Enemies (New York: Penguin, 2004).

68. As cited in David Ignatius, "Winning a Battle of Wills," *The Washington Post* (13 July 2005), A21.

69. "Interview with Osama Bin Laden," CNN News, March 1997 at http://news.findlaw.com/hdocs/docs/binladen/binladenintvw-cnn.pdf.

70. Pape (see note 15 above).

71. Khalil Shikaki, Palestinian Survey Research, March 2005, http://www.pcpsr.org/survey/polls/2005/p15a.html.

72. Buruma and Margalit (see note 67 above).

73. Carole Hillenbrand, *The Crusades: Islamic Perspectives* (Chicago, IL: Fitzroy Dearborn Publishers, 1999).

74. Kruglanski, "Goal Systems," (see note 4 above).

75. Atran (see note 13 above).

76. Edward Kaplan, Alex Mintz, Shaul Mishal, and C. Samban, "What Happened to Suicide Bombings in Israel? Insights From a Terror Stock Model," (Unpublished manuscript, Yale University, 2005).

77. Shikaki, (see note 72 above).

78. Ibid.

79. Ferracuti (see note 3 above), 64.

80. Shikaki (see note 71 above).

81. James DeNardo, *Power in Numbers: The Political Strategy of Protest and Rebellion* (Princeton, NJ; Princeton University Press, 1985).

82. Arie W. Kruglanski and Agnieszka Golec, "Individual Motivations, The Group Process and Organizational Strategies in Suicide Terrorism," in Eva M. Meyersson Milgrom, ed., *Suicide Missions and the Market for Martyrs: A Multidisciplinary Approach* (Princeton, NJ: Princeton University Press, in press).

83. Rohan Gunaratna, *Inside Al Qaeda: Global Network of Terror* (New York: Columbia University Press, 2002), 93.

84. For example, on Oct. 13, 2005, in ceremony sponsored by Abu Mazen, the President of the Palestinian Authority, one million dollars was distributed to families of Palestinian terrorists, http://www.intelligence.org.il/eng/eng_n/al_ansar_e.htm#; Stern (see note 13 above), 54; Sageman (see note 12 above), 99–135.

85. Sageman (see note 12 above), 182.

86. Gunaratna (see note 83 above), 19.

87. Shikaki (see note 71 above).

88. Walter Reich, "Understanding Terrorist Behavior: The Limits and Opportunities of Psychological Inquiry," in Walter Reich, ed., *Origins of Terrorism: Psychologies, Ideologies, Theologies, States of Mind* (Washington, D.C.: Woodrow Wilson Center Press, 1990/1998), 261–280.

89. Gollwitzer and Bargh (see note 4 above); Kruglanski, "Goal Systems" (see note 4 above).

The Mind of the Terrorist: A Review and Critique of Psychological Approaches

Jeff Victoroff *

This article reviews the state of the art of available theories and data regarding the psychology of terrorism. Data and theoretical material were gathered from the world's unclassified literature. Multiple theories and some demographic data have been published, but very few controlled empirical studies have been conducted investigating the psychological bases of terrorism. The field is largely characterized by theoretical speculation based on subjective interpretation of anecdotal observations. Moreover, most studies and theories fail to take into account the great heterogeneity of terrorists. Many practical, conceptual, and psychological barriers have slowed progress in this important field. Nonetheless, even at this early stage of terrorism studies, preliminary reports suggest that modifiable social and psychological factors contribute to the genesis of the terrorist mind-set. Psychological scholarship could possibly mitigate the risk of catastrophic attack by initiating the long overdue scientific study of terrorist mentalities.

Terrorism has surely existed since before the dawn of recorded history (Merari and Friedland 1985). Human nature has not changed. However, three interlocking trends have significantly changed the nature and degree of the threat: the globalization of commerce, travel, and information transfer,

*Department of Neurology and Psychiatry, University of Southern California School of Medicine.
Author's note: This work was supported in part by a grant from the Freya Foundation for Brain, Behavior, and Society. I gratefully acknowledge critical reviews of this manuscript by Jessica Stern and Todd Sandler. It represents a revision of a lecture first presented at the annual meeting of the American Neuropsychiatric Association, San Diego, California, March 2002. Address reprint requests to victorof@usc.edu.

which puts economic disparities and ideological competition in sharp relief and facilitates cooperative aggression by far-flung but like-minded conspirators; the ascent of religious fundamentalism as an aggrieved competitor with the market-economic, democratic, and secular trends of modernity; and the privatization of weapons of mass destruction, putting the potential of macro-terrorist acts into the hands of small groups or even individuals (Hoffman 1998; Laqueur 1999; Enders and Sandler 2000). September 11, 2001, is one result—and probably a warning of events to come (Gunaratna 2002). It perhaps would not be an exaggeration to state that these fast-evolving trends together constitute a clear and present danger to the security of civilization (Stern 1999).

It would seem appropriate for the scholarly disciplines of psychology and psychiatry to bring their intellectual resources to bear on the political problem of terrorism, a problem that—stripped to the basics—is one of atypical human behavior. Apart from a drive for truth, political psychological theory advises that the better a target group understands the roots of the terrorist mind-set, the better that group may develop policies to effectively manage the risk (Wardlaw 1989; Clayton, Barlow, and Ballif-Spanvill 1998). Despite the compelling need for such an understanding, many theoretical and practical impediments have delayed, and perhaps even derailed, the objective scientific psychological study of terrorism (Reich 1998; Horgan 2003). Indeed, the following question must be asked: to what degree are leading psychological theories of terrorism supported by valid concepts and objective research? A comprehensive review of the literature suggests that a lack of systematic scholarly investigation has left policy makers to design counterterrorism strategies without the benefit of facts regarding the origin of terrorist behavior—or, worse, guided by theoretical presumptions couched as facts. Investigating the terrorist mind may be a necessary first step toward actualizing modern political psychology's potential for uncovering the bases of terrorist aggression and designing an optimum counterterrorism policy.

Information for this article was derived from a review of the unclassified literature on psychosocial aspects of terrorism, including peer-reviewed articles, books and book chapters, news reports, and personal communications with terrorism experts. Scholarly articles were identified by a search for the term *terrorism* in the following databases: PsychINFO (1887–2003), Sociological Abstracts (1974–2003), Medline (1966–2003), and Lexis-Nexis Academic Universe (1980–2003), as well as from bibliographies of the identified articles. This article critically reviews published theories of the psychological bases of terrorism, reviews the psychosocial data describing terrorists, defines the limits of and impediments to inquiry in this field, and offers a preliminary political-psychological classification of terrorism.

Definition and Dimensions of Terrorist Behavior

Schmid (1983) compiled 109 academic definitions of terrorism, suggesting that there are roughly as many available definitions as there are published experts in the field. The lack of consensus is to some extent inescapable, given the heterogeneity of terrorist behaviors, the variety of declared or assumed motivations, and the question of point of view, a.k.a., the "one man's terrorist is another man's freedom fighter" problem (Jenkins 1982; Hoffman 1998). Nonetheless, two common elements are usually found in contemporary definitions: (1) that terrorism involves aggression against noncombatants and (2) that the terrorist action in itself is not expected by its perpetrator to accomplish a political goal but instead to influence a target audience and change that audience's behavior in a way that will serve the interests of the terrorist (Badey 1998; Laqueur 1999).

The typology of terrorism is complex and controversial since actors can be characterized across multiple variables. Schultz (1980) proposed seven such variables—causes, environment, goals, strategy, means, organization, and participation—that might be specified for revolutionary versus subrevolutionary terrorism. Post (2004) usefully divided political substate terrorism into (1) social revolutionary terrorism, (2) right-wing terrorism, (3) nationalist-separatist terrorism, (4) religious extremist terrorism, and (5) single-issue (e.g., animal rights) terrorism, proposing that each type tends to be associated with its own social-psychological dynamics. A more comprehensive typology is shown in Table 4.1, listing variables subject to analysis and classifications within those variables.

Any such typology must be considered a heuristic compendium of ideal types, and classes should not necessarily be construed as dichotomous. For example, while many instances of collective violence unequivocally meet the criteria for state terrorism (e.g., the gassing of Iraqi civilians in Halabja), the distinction between state and substate terrorism can be blurred, as in the case of pro-government paramilitary death squads in South Africa or Columbia (Hoffman 1998; Stern 1999). It is an open question whether a particular type of mind is disproportionately associated with a given political category of terrorism. Yet another challenge to any psychological inquiry into the "mind of the terrorist" is that terrorist groups typically exhibit hierarchical organization, with various *roles* assumed within each level of that hierarchy (see Figure 4.1). Each position on such a matrix may attract individuals with different predispositions who perhaps play their roles because of profoundly different psychological factors. One might postulate, for example, that some leaders are more likely to be self-imagined idealists or altruists, others are driven by messianic delusions, others by ethnic or religious animus, and others by entrepreneurial ambitions—a point that seems clear when we intuit, for example, the differences of psychic attributes likely separating the three convicted terrorist leaders Shoko Asahara, Abu Nidal, and Nelson Mandela. Of course, roles may blur depending on the type of the group and its size. Nonetheless, since individuals of different temperaments might play extremely different parts in a terrorist group, any empirical study claiming to characterize "the psychology of terrorists" might be very misleading if it fails to stratify its findings according to level and role.

Most important for a psychological analysis, it seems reasonable that there may be heterogeneity in the temperaments, ideologies, thought processes, and cognitive capacities of terrorists *within* political categories, hierarchical levels, and roles (Taylor and Ryan 1988; Reich 1998). Thus, it is essential to acknowledge from the outset that any effort to uncover the "terrorist mind" will more likely result in uncovering a spectrum of terrorist minds.

Psychosocial Data Describing Terrorists

Demographic studies from the 1960s and 1970s constructed a profile of the typical terrorist as a well-educated single male in his mid-twenties from

TABLE 4.1. Dimensions of Terrorism

Variable	Classification
Perpetrator number	Individual vs. group
Sponsorship	State vs. substate vs. individual
Relation to authority	Anti-state/anti-establishment/separatist vs. pro-state/pro-establishment
Locale	Intrastate vs. transnational
Military status	Civilian vs. paramilitary or military
Spiritual motivation	Secular vs. religious
Financial motivation	Idealistic vs. entrepreneurial
Political ideology	Leftist/socialist vs. rightist/fascist vs. anarchist
Hierarchical role	Sponsor vs. leader versus middle management vs. follower
Willingness to die	Suicidal vs. nonsuicidal
Target	Property (including data) vs. individuals vs. masses of people
Methodology	Bombing, assassination, kidnapping/hostage taking, mass poisoning, rape, other (e.g., bioterrorism, cyberterrorism)

bombers, failed suicide bombers, or trainers, and offers no specific demographic, socioeconomic, or psychological data (Hassan 2001; Atran 2003). (Some of these data will be incorporated into a forthcoming book [N. Hassan, personal communication, 2004].) Barber (1999) conducted the most extensive study of psychological factors possibly associated with Islamic political violence. His report is based on data from the Palestinian Family Study, a project involving 6,923 ninth-grade students in the West Bank and Gaza. Aggressivity and mood were measured with the Child Behavior Checklist (Achenbach and Edelbrock 1987), "family values" were measured by one question regarding the importance that respondents placed on getting married and having a family, and participation in the intifada of 1987–1993 was measured by the yes/no response to a single question: "Before the withdrawal of Israeli troops from the Gaza Strip and Jericho, did you ever distribute leaflets, protect someone from Israeli soldiers or police, march or demonstrate against the occupation, and throw stones at Israeli soldiers?" A yes answer to this question was positively associated with depression, aggression, and family values. Unfortunately, this question does not allow discrimination between violent and nonviolent political participation, undermining conclusions one might draw from this ambitious study regarding the predictive value of psychological factors for Islamic insurgent aggression.

Overview of Psychological Theories

Attempts to account for the behavior of terrorists fall into two general categories: top-down approaches that seek the seeds of terrorism in political, social, economic, or even evolutionary circumstances and bottom-up approaches that explore the characteristics of individuals and groups that turn to terrorism (e.g., Wieviorka 1993, 2004). These approaches are not mutually exclusive. In fact, approaches such as rational choice theory and relative deprivation/oppression theory combine these points of view, considering interactions between circumstances and actors. While acknow-

ledging the importance of top-down analyses and ultimate causes, this article focuses primarily on bottom-up approaches and proximal causes in substate terrorism. The principal approaches are organized into groups for the sake of clarity. However, it will become apparent that conceptual overlap exists between theories within and between groups. It will also become apparent that a particular fundamental conceptual framework—such as psychoanalysis—may inform diverse theories and that the same theory may be championed from different conceptual frameworks. For example, group theory has psychoanalytic and nonpsychoanalytic champions. Theories of terrorism also vary in the extent to which they consider psychological differences between terrorists playing different roles (e.g., leaders vs. followers), whether terrorists are regarded as psychologically homogeneous or heterogeneous, and whether subtypes of terrorism are associated with subtypes of terrorists.

Psychopathological Theory

At one end of the spectrum is the popular opinion that terrorists must be insane or psychopathic (Hacker 1976; Cooper 1977; Pearce 1977; Taylor 1988). Here a distinction must be made: modern Western psychiatry identifies adult behavioral disorders according to a multiaxial classification scheme in which Axis I refers to the major clinical illnesses—those such as schizophrenia or major depression—while Axis II refers to personality disorders—such as antisocial personality disorder (APD) (American Psychiatric Association 2000). APD is the current term for a pattern of remorseless disregard for the rights of others that was called *psychopathy* up until the mid-1950s and *sociopathy* thereafter. *Psychosis* refers to a loss of reality testing observed primarily in a subgroup of Axis I disorders (e.g., schizophrenia) but is *not* expected in Axis II disorders such as APD. *Insanity* is not a behavioral science term but a legal term that *usually* implies psychosis, although its definition is subject to significant jurisdictional variance (Resnick and Noffsinger 2004). Hence, a psychotic or "insane" person is so mentally disordered as to not know right from wrong, while a sociopath knows right from wrong and chooses wrong for selfish reasons without pangs of conscience.

In regard to Axis I clinical disorders among terrorists, very little research has been done involving comprehensive psychiatric examination, and no properly controlled research is found in the open literature. However, the conclusion—at least on the basis of uncontrolled empirical psychological studies of left-wing German militants, members of the Algerian Front de Libération Nationale (FLN), members of the Provisional Irish Republican Army (PIRA), and Hezbollah—has been that terrorists do not usually exhibit what we refer to as Axis I or even Axis II psychiatric disorders (Crenshaw 1981; Jäger, Schmidtchen, and Süllwold 1981; Heskin 1984; Merari 1998). German psychiatrist Wilfred Rasch (1979) examined eleven terrorist suspects, including members of the Baader-Meinhof group, and reported on a Federal Police study of another forty persons wanted as terrorists, finding no evidence of mental illness in any respondent. Post, Sprinzak, and Denny (2003; also see Post and Gold 2002) also found no Axis I disorders on psychiatric evaluations of twenty-one secular and fourteen radical Islamic Middle Eastern terrorists. As criminologist Franco Ferracuti (1982) suggested more than two decades ago, and as has been supported by subsequent reports (Reich 1998; Silke 1998; Horgan 2003), while terrorist groups are sometimes led by insane individuals, and while a few terrorist acts might be attributed to unequivocally insane persons, terrorists rarely meet psychiatric criteria for insanity.

Rather, most of the literature attributing clinical mental disorder to terrorists speaks of the remorseless personality type, psychopathy or sociopathy (Taylor 1988). Cooper (1977, 1978), for example, states that terrorists, like psychopaths, are ruthless "outlaws" and "outcasts" who adhere to an anomalous scheme of values out of tune with that of the rest of society and that there is a "near identity of this fundamental characteristic in both the psychopath and the terrorist." Pearce (1977) stated that terrorists were sociopaths acting antisocially due to "superego lacunae," meaning gaps in self-

monitoring; he supports his conclusion partly on the basis of tattoos found on one terrorist.

The claim of sociopathy, advanced without evidence from any empirical study, raises the important question of whether terrorism is usually antisocial or prosocial behavior. It makes a common kind of sense that individuals who harm innocents are antisocial. Those who reject and attack their own society, such as the German student who joined the 1970s Red Army Faction or the Christian-to-Muslim convert who joins a modern radical Islamic cell, stand against their own and might be regarded as antisocial. Yet several lines of reasoning tend to discredit the simplistic claim that antisociality is typical or even common among terrorists. First, extensive evidence supports the observation that, far from being outcasts, terrorists are often regarded by their in-group as heroic freedom fighters. As Post (2004) points out, nationalist-separatist terrorists must be distinguished from revolutionary terrorists in this regard since the former are typically regarded as risking their lives for social welfare, while the latter attack their society of origin. That is, the Basque student who joins the ETA, the Chechen "black widow" who terrorizes a Moscow theater, or the Liberation Tigers of Tamil Ealem (LTTE) suicide bomber all use terrorism to fight on behalf of their in-group. The Irishman who joins the PIRA or the Middle Eastern student who joins an Islamic radical group, depending on his specific nation and province, may enjoy considerable popular support and conscientiously serve his society in a prosocial way. Ironically, therefore, with respect to in-groups of identity, certain types of terrorism often represent prosocial behavior. Second, evidence exists from the quantitative literature that the actions of terrorists, even those who fail and die, might benefit their kin and social group (Azam forthcoming). Further evidence of the prosociality of some terrorists comes from the empirical work of Italian sociologist Donatella della Porta (1988): among 1,214 Italian militants, 351 (45.6 percent) enjoyed personal ties with eight or more group members before joining a terrorist organization. This raises the question of how large one's group of identity must be to consider collaboration prosocial, but it at least suggests that recruitment often involves a network of shared social values. Pedahzur, Perliger, and Weinberg (2003) examined this issue from the perspective of Durkheim, who distinguished altruistic suicide—suicide in the service of society—from egoistic and anomic suicide. Based on the observation that 80 Palestinian suicide terrorists from 1973 to 2002 exhibited a higher rate of religious education, membership in fundamentalist organizations, and repeat terrorist acts compared with nonsuicidal terrorists, these authors proposed that they were probably acting from altruistic motives. Indeed, this is the essence of the concept of *istishad*, selfless death in the service of Allah (Post, Sprinzak, and Denny 2003; see also Sageman 2004). It is obviously conceptually inadequate to judge antisociality from the perspective of the targeted out-group, yet it is premature to conclude that *most* members of ethnic, religious, or national-separatist terrorist groups exhibit prosociality based on these limited reports. Some antisocial individuals perhaps use the moral cover of group affiliation to disguise their aggressive and remorseless drives. However, pending data to the contrary, it seems plausible that many terrorists act in a prosocial manner, both believing themselves to be serving society and judged by their in-group to be acting in its interest. (It is a separate question to ask whether they subjectively adopt the moral position that Corrado [1981] labeled "misplaced idealism.") Thus, Ferracuti's (1982) formulation regarding the relationship between insanity and terrorism might equally apply to the relationship between sociopathy and terrorism: sociopaths may sometimes be among the terrorists, but terrorists are not, by virtue of their political violence, necessarily sociopaths. Intuitively, one might expect different personality traits among antisocial and prosocial terrorists. This speculation requires further study.

Rational Choice Theory

If most terrorists do not meet diagnostic criteria for a major mental illness or for sociopathy, must one conclude that they are rational? This raises the question of the explanatory power of rational choice theory—the theory that terrorist action derives from a conscious, rational, calculated decision to take this particular type of action as the optimum strategy to accomplish a sociopolitical goal (Sandler, Tschirhart, and Cauley 1983; Sandler and Lapan 1988; Crenshaw 1992; Wilson 2000). A distinction should be made between rational—or strategic—choice theory and other individual or group psychological theories of terrorism. The latter try to explain why people are inclined toward a type or style of behavior (e.g., to be a terrorist), while rational choice theory, derived from economics, assumes this behavioral proclivity as a given and attempts to explain how changes in policy—the rules of the "game" that is played between terrorists and governments—might predictably alter behavior. Since rational choice theory considers both policy and individual behavioral responses to policy, it combines the top-down and bottom-up approaches.

Game theory, based on this "assumption of rationality" in strategic choice formulations, has been used to analyze and predict political behavior since the seminal work of Deutsch in the 1950s (Deutsch 1954; Deutsch and Krause 1962; Milburn and Watman 1981; Machina et al. 1989). Empirical support for game theory comes from experiments in which volunteers play against rivals in games such as the prisoner's dilemma, sometimes to win a payoff such as points, sometimes to avoid costs such as loss of face or electric shocks (von Neumann and Morgenstern 1947; Deutsch 1954; Borah 1963; Rapoport and Chammah 1968). Sandler and Arce (2003) listed six strengths of modern game theory for revealing quantifiable factors theoretically underlying the behavior of terrorists and targeted governments: game theory (1) captures the interdependent nature of such interactions, (2) helps discover the strategic implications when each side acts according to its best guess about how the other side thinks, (3) incorporates the impact of threats and promises from each side, (4) takes advantage of the observation that "players" tend to maximize goals subject to constraints, (5) helps predict outcomes in bargaining over demands, and (6) acknowledges the impact of uncertainty—

incomplete information—on all the above. They cite the example of the shift away from skyjackings to kidnappings after the installation of metal detectors at airports in 1973 as evidence of a predictable and rational response to new constraints.

Political scientist Martha Crenshaw (2000) has cautioned that the ostensible goal of terrorists often appears so unlikely to be achieved by the chosen action that it is difficult to support an overarching rationalist theory of terrorism. Furthermore, the outrageous inhumanity of attacks on innocent civilians challenges the commonplace understanding of "rational" behavior. Given questions about incoherent motivations, ghastly means, and political inefficacy of terrorism, some scholars have proposed that the typical terrorist is not simply a "rational actor" in the strict Weberian sense (Brannan, Eslerm, and Anders Strindberg 2001). On the other hand, historical evidence suggests that terrorism is sometimes a practical, low-cost strategy through which subordinate groups leverage their power to successfully achieve their ends (Sandler and Enders 2004). Indeed, modern history is replete with examples of successful substate political violence: Irgun's bombings were a major factor in securing the independence of Eretz Israel from the British; terrorism by the Irish Republican Army (IRA) precipitated accommodations leading to the Irish Free State; Shi'ite Muslim terrorists provided key assistance in the ouster of the Shah of Iran; Hezbollah's suicide bombing campaign of 1983–1985 directly led to the American, French, and Israeli withdrawal and establishment of a Shi'a-controlled society in major parts of Lebanon; and the African National Congress (ANC) used terrorism as part of its remarkably successful strategy to overthrow the apartheid government of South Africa. More recently, al Qaeda's brutal transnational campaign, including the mass murders at New York's World Trade Center in 2001, may have not only rapidly advanced Usama bin Laden's stated goal of removing the large U.S. military presence from Saudi Arabia but also served as an extremely potent recruiting tool (Laqueur 1987; Hoffman 1998, 1999; Whittaker 2001). Thus, historical precedents support many terrorists'

expectations of success, so the theory of strategic choice must not be discounted on the grounds that terrorism's goals are uniformly improbable. Game-theoretical approaches are also sophisticated enough to recognize that the "winnings" that satisfy terrorists may not be their overt anti-government goals but less obvious goals such as martyrdom, which may not only serve as an end in itself but also yield unexpected benefits to the terrorist's offspring that exceed the "opportunity cost" of an educated life lost prematurely (Brooks 2002; Azam forthcoming). Moreover, game theory has yielded evidence of counterintuitive but important predictions such as the possibility that government investments in deterrence might waste resources or even produce paradoxical increases in threats (Sandler and Arce 2003).

Strategic choice theory potentially offers vital insights into the potential payoff of terrorist versus government actions. By uncovering otherwise cryptic benefits, this approach may help explain otherwise enigmatic behaviors. Insofar as humans evolved to function as sophisticated calculators of risks and benefits, and insofar as groups function collectively to actualize the will of their members, one can make quantitative predictions regarding the theoretical circumstances under which terrorist behavior serves group and individual interests. Such microeconomic analyses may help in calculating the likely outcome of different policy options, such as hardening targets, calculating concessions, or performing retaliatory strikes (Sandler and Lapan 1988; Lee 1988; Brophy-Baermann and Conybeare 1994; Sandler and Arce 2003; Sandler and Enders 2004). But the following question remains: what are the limitations, or even potential pitfalls, of the game-theoretical approach?

Evidence suggests that very few individuals who rationally believe that terrorism may advance their cause ever become terrorists (Schbley 2000). This is conceivably related to the discovery that 85 percent of World War II infantrymen facing the enemy failed to pull the triggers of their weapons, despite the urgent rational benefits (Grossman 1995). In other words, even obvious strategic benefits may not compel humans to violence, an arguably irrational result of modern culture. And some terrorists (e.g., "lone wolf" terrorist Theodore Kaczynski) commit violence due to unequivocally irrational motives (in his case, paranoid schizophrenia). Thus, the rare and idiosyncratic decision to become a terrorist cannot be explained by rational choice theory. Yet it is inappropriate to criticize this theory because it fails to explain why only a tiny minority of individuals turns to terrorism; it does not try to. It focuses instead on what members of this rare group are likely to do under various conditions.

Two other criticisms of rational choice theory may be more compelling. First, rational choice theory claims predictive power for future events, extrapolating both from laboratory experiments of the behavior of nonterrorists playing non-naturalistic games and from post hoc analysis of real-world incidents. But as Wieviorka (1993, 57) observed, this kind of strategic analysis weighs "questions of resources and power relationships . . . as if the principles underlying their actions had been established once and for all, and as if the effects of violence were predictable and measurable" (see also Wieviorka 2004). The uncertainty of the principles of terrorist-government interaction adds to the uncertainty of the facts known by the players since, as the early work in game theory illustrates, a slight change in the "rules" may yield opposite behavioral results (von Neumann and Morgenstern 1947; Milburn and Watman 1981; Machina et al. 1989). Refinements in the understanding of terrorist-government engagements based on increasingly sophisticated event analysis and classification should reduce this element of uncertainty and strengthen the predictive validity of this approach.

Second, it may be dangerous to assume that a profile of a "typical player" will predict an actual terrorist's responses. As Merari (2002, 4) has said, "In a perfectly rational system, the basic idea of deterrence is to deliver a clear, credible message to the opponent that the cost of pursuing a certain course of behavior outweighs its benefits. In reality, however, this simple formula rarely, if ever, works according to expectations." The most likely explanation for such unanticipated consequences is simply that the immense plasticity and individual variability of the human central nervous system often generate idiosyncratic and individualistic responses that defy predictions not only because of incomplete information held by the actor but also because of impulsivity, faulty cognition, and emotional processes that overrule adaptive choices. Writing the applicable game-theoretical equation becomes ever more challenging as imponderable variables are added to accommodate individual emotional peculiarities of terrorists, victims, and governments: the lure of bravado and romance of risk, the self-destructive urge for "success" in likely failure with or without the utility of martyrdom, the Svengali-like influence of charismatic leaders on either side whose followers march in maladaptive columns, the power of rage to better reason, the blindness of ambition, the illogic of spite, or the frenzy of revenge all may contribute to the stochastic occurrence of surprising scenarios. Moreover, the lack of an empirically validated typology of terrorist variants complicates writing optimum theorems for subtypes of players who may exhibit very different behavioral proclivities (Bowen et al. 1985; Friedland and Merari 1985; Merari 2002). Nonetheless, no behavioral theory is expected to accommodate all examples; the law of large numbers by itself guarantees some failures of prediction. It would be sufficiently valuable if rational choice calculations predicted a higher proportion of terrorist behaviors than did nonquantitative methods or reliably predicted responses in some subtype of engagements. Merari's (2002) strong claim that terrorist behaviors "rarely, if ever" follow such predictions is the key question. Further empirical work should be able to resolve that debate.

I would propose that rational choice analysis is a powerful tool for discovering theoretically valid and surprisingly counterintuitive forces that probably influence terrorist and government behaviors. Game theory may also prove invaluable in predicting likely changes in the *base rate* (the rate predicted in rational actor simulations) of behaviors of an idealized terrorist in response to concessions or deterrents. However, rational choice theories cannot predict idiosyncratic responses. Policy recommendations that predict deterrence of terrorist acts are only as valuable as their capacity to anticipate the extraordinary variability and adaptability of humans.

Moreover, at present, rational choice theory does not explain why a very few individuals, among hundreds of thousands in virtually identical political positions, become terrorists. As Crozier (1960, 9) suggested, "Men do not necessarily rebel merely because their conditions of life are intolerable: it takes a rebel to rebel." Individual factors must be at work. Temperaments vary. Human frontal lobe cortical planning based on rational calculation of costs and benefits is forever subject to limbic tyranny. Passion often trumps rationality, behaviors may deviate significantly from the predicted base rate, and understanding the mind of the terrorist—with or without prediction of future behavior—requires investigations beyond the realm of game theory.

If neither insanity/sociopathy nor rational choice can fully account for the genesis of terrorist behaviors, what alternative psychological explanations seem most plausible? As Crenshaw (1986, 386) stated, even though terrorism does not result from a specific psychopathological condition, that is not to say that "the political decision to join a terrorist organization is not influenced or, in some cases, even determined by subconscious or latent psychological motives." In other words, although terrorists rarely exhibit psychological *disorders*, they may exhibit identifiable psychological *traits* or may have been influenced by identifiable social factors. Political scientists, sociologists, psychologists, and psychiatrists have offered diverse opinions regarding the degree to which the roots of terrorist aggression are innate versus acquired, the product of psychodynamic versus social forces, or the product of individual versus group forces. The most frequently cited theories can be divided into sociological theories, psychoanalytic approaches to individual psychology, nonpsychoanalytic psychological approaches to individual psychology, and theories of group process.

Sociological Theories

Social Learning Theory

Bandura's (1973, 1998) social learning theory of aggression suggests that violence follows observation and imitation of an aggressive model, and a variant of this theory has been invoked to explain terrorist behaviors not as the consequence of innate aggressivity but of cognitive "reconstrual" of moral imperatives. Teenagers living in hotbeds of political strife may directly witness terrorist behaviors and seek to imitate them or, even more commonly, learn from their culture's public glorification of terrorists—for example, the "martyr posters" lining the streets of Shi'a regions of Lebanon and Palestinian refugee camps or the songs celebrating the exploits of the PIRA (Crenshaw 1992; Taylor and Quayle 1994; Kelly and Rieber 1995). Social learning of the acceptability of terrorist violence may also take a didactic form, as in the teaching of an extremist form of jihad in many Pakistani and Palestinian *madrasas*—religious schools for young Muslim boys. Madrasas have existed since the time of Muhammad, but the recent worldwide resurgence of Islamic fundamentalism has led to an increase in their numbers and possibly in the violence of their message (Armstrong 2000; Marshall and Danizewski 2001; Kepel 2002; Atran 2003). Evidence suggests that a minority of prominent transnational Muslim terrorists were educated in madrasas (Sageman 2004; Anonymous 2004). This, however, does not exclude the possibility that widespread education of this type influences even nonattendees via cultural diffusion.

Terrorist didactic learning also occurs via the dissemination of terrorist philosophy and methodology in communiqués, audiovisual tapes, compact disks, books, and Web sites. The most influential historical example may be the widely translated 1969 "Mini-Manual" or "Handbook of Urban Guerilla Warfare" by Brazilian terrorist Carlos Marighella (1971; also see Saper 1988), which, among other practical advice, suggests that readers learn to pilot a plane. The charter of the Islamic Resistance Movement (Harakat Al-Muqawama Al-Islamiya [Hamas]) represents a more recent example; article 15 of this document emphasizes the importance of teaching jihad: "We must imprint on the minds of generations of Muslims that the Palestinian problem is a religious one . . . I indeed wish to go to war for the sake of Allah! I will assault and kill, assault and kill, assault and kill" (Alexander 2002, 57). It seems plausible that didactic teaching or social learning may influence some young people toward terrorism. However, the social learning/cognitive restructuring model fails to explain why only a small minority among the hundreds of thousands of students educated for jihad in madrasas, the millions exposed to extremist publications, and the tens of millions exposed to public glorification of terrorists have become terrorists. As Taylor and Quayle (1994, 32) put it, "Not everyone from those communities, although subject to those same or similar influences, becomes a terrorist" (see also Sageman 2004). Therefore, while social learning probably helps animate the small minority who turns to political violence, this theory fails to explain why *these* particular individuals become terrorists. Other factors must be sought.

Frustration-Aggression Hypothesis

This raises the question of how politically motivated people reach the point of no return at which their potential energy is converted into violent action. The frustration-aggression (FA) hypothesis—one outcome of an interdisciplinary collaboration by political and social scientists at Yale University to better understand the violence observed in early twentieth-century Europe—has often been cited, attributing the final expression of the terrorist impulse to desperation in the face of oppression (Dollard et al. 1939; Friedland 1992). Political psychologist John Chowing Davies (1973, 251) has even stated, "Violence is *always* a response to frustration" (emphasis added). The FA hypothesis is included here as a sociological theory, although the original intent of Dollard et al. (1939) was also to account for individual behavior; thus, terrorist violence of either groups or individuals might be explained by this theory.

However, the application of this theory to terrorism studies has been criticized on several grounds:

millions of people live in frustrating circumstances but never turn to terrorism, many terrorists do not belong to the desperate classes whose frustration they claim to be expressing, and terrorism does not uniformly appear to be an act of last resort by those who have exhausted alternate approaches (Billig 1976; Merari and Friedland 1985; Laqueur 1987; Friedland 1992; Sidanius and Pratto 1999). The leftist terrorism of 1970s Europe, for example, was primarily perpetrated by members of privileged classes, and state-sponsored terrorism can hardly be attributed to the oppression of the government by its victims. Frustration, therefore, may plausibly play some part in the genesis of some political violence, but the FA hypothesis is not by itself sufficient to explain terrorism.

Relative Deprivation Theory

It has also been proposed that economic disparities cause terrorism. This claim underlies Gurr's (1970) theory of relative deprivation—that rebellions come to be when people cannot bear the misery of their lot. As Schmid (1983) observed, Gurr's theory derives more from psychoanalysis than from empirical sociology and is conceptually born of the FA hypothesis. Irrespective of these psychiatric roots, multiple writers have claimed a sociological link between poverty and terrorism (Schmid 1983; Harmon 2000; Hasisi and Pedahzur 2000; Krueger and Maleckova 2002). More recently, increasing differences between the material welfare of the haves and have-nots have been postulated to provoke a new era of political violence that will accelerate as globalization not only creates new foci of poverty but facilitates communication between those who perceive themselves to be globalization's victims (Maya, Lander, and Ungar 2002). One possibility is that either absolute deprivation or relative economic disparity ignites terrorist sentiments, especially among members of an oppressed underclass.

The major European revolutions of the eighteenth through the early twentieth centuries were probably provoked, at least in part, by class disparities. From the French to the Russian revolutions, have-nots indisputably became major participants in political violence (Zamoyski 1999). On the other hand, as noted above, the left-wing terrorists of the 1960s to 1970s were not usually impoverished; indeed, they were sometimes accused of belonging to an idle middle class that expropriated the misery of a different class to serve their own goals. So, although poverty may play a role in some political violence, relative deprivation is neither necessary nor sufficient to explain revolutionary terrorism. Evidence also exists that right-wing extremism occurs independent of economic status. Canetti and Pedahzur (2002), for example, reported that right-wing extremist sentiments were unrelated to socioeconomic variables among 1,247 Israeli university students.

Krueger and Maleckova's (2002) previously cited important work with Palestinians does not support a simple poverty-causes-terrorism conclusion. However, their analysis is based on socioeconomic background, not on socioeconomic *prospects*. Given the 70 percent adult unemployment rate in Gaza, the gross domestic product of less than $1,000 throughout the Palestinian Territories, the severely constrained economic opportunities despite educational achievement due to the unresolved Israeli-Palestinian conflict, and the cultural importance of the male breadwinner role, it is premature to rule out the possibility that diminished economic *prospects* have helped provoke Palestinian terrorism (Bennet 2004). Furthermore, nationalist-separatist and many religious fundamentalist terrorists tend to enjoy the support of their communities. In such cases, terrorism may be a prosocial activity ostensibly undertaken on behalf of all classes. If the *entire* in-group (that of the political actor) faces economic disparities relative to an out-group (that of the privileged target), participation in political violence would not be expected to be an economic class phenomenon but a group-of-identity phenomenon. Further research will be necessary to determine the relationship between class of origin, economic expectations, individual factors, and terrorism.

Oppression Theory

Multiple authors, from sociologists to revolutionaries, contend that oppression provokes political violence (Fanon 1965; Whitaker 1972; Schmid 1983). Particularly in the case of nationalist-separatist or ethnic-sectarian terrorism (e.g., ETA, PIRA, Hamas), actors often cite the injustice of their treatment by governments that rob them of identity, dignity, security, and freedom as the motive for their joining a terrorist group (Crenshaw 1986; Taylor and Quayle 1994; Post, Sprinzak, and Denny 2003). Since it is difficult to measure oppression itself—a sociopolitical relationship subject to point of view—and since the impact of oppression may be felt subjectively to greater or lesser degrees by individuals within a community at risk, *perceived* oppression may be the proper cognitive-emotional variable to examine as a potential risk factor for terrorism. There are innumerable scales and instruments for assessing perceived prejudice and discrimination (e.g., McNeilly et al. 1996; Utsey and Ponterotto 1996; Neto 2001; Loo et al. 2001; Murry et al. 2001; Duckitt et al. 2002). However, virtually all of these are specifically designed to address the experience of a single group—in most cases, African Americans. None of them measures the life-and-liberty-threatening dominion of one group over another implied by the psychopolitical concept of oppression. In fact, an extensive review of multiple databases reveals that no general psychological instrument has yet been validated and published for the study of perceived oppression. As a result, no persuasive empirical evidence is available supporting the much-cited hypothesis that oppression or its perception drives the behavior of terrorists.

Even if perceived oppression could be shown to breed terrorism, it would never be a sufficient explanation. As Silke (2003, 33) said so well, "Very few individuals of aggrieved minorities go on to become active terrorists. The question has always been, why did these particular individuals engage in terrorism when most of their compatriots did not?" Sociological theories, like rational choice approaches, do not answer this question.

selflessness. Both of these forms of infantile retreat are hypothesized to mobilize the expression of the desire to destroy the source of the injury (i.e., narcissistic rage). This rage is, in essence, rage against the damaged self, projected onto the target of the terrorist's animus, as if the target were the source of the intolerable feelings the terrorist has about himself (Crayton 1983; Akhtar 1999). According to Risto Fried (1982), the target or victim is treated as a "discardable object," which psychoanalyst Richard Pearlstein cited as evidence that terrorism is a "spectacularly vivid example of narcissistic object manipulation."

The theory of terrorist narcissism is consistent with many reports regarding the pathologically dependent psychology of cult adherents, but it is perhaps more pertinent that it fits with empirical observations of both Hubbard (1971) and el Sarraj (2002) that terrorists, far from being the aggressive psychopaths of public imagination, are often timid, emotionally damaged adolescents—those who have suffered ego injuries such as parental rejection that delay or prevent full achievement of adult identity—who seem to be in search of affiliation and meaning. In this respect, narcissism and identity theory overlap. Potential support for the importance of narcissism comes from Gustave Morf's (1970) clinical examinations conducted with prisoners held as members of the Front for the Liberation of Quebec (FLQ). Morf reported that these individuals exhibited narcissistic traits, wishing to put themselves at the center of the universe, but did not fulfill the criteria for a full-blown narcissistic personality disorder. He further concluded that a "permissive society" was responsible for their narcissism. However, he used no standardized psychological instruments, reported no statistical data, and used no control group. Like Sageman's (2004) previously cited exegesis of ten terrorist biographies, the conclusions regarding narcissism are impressionistic, not empirical. As a result, it remains undetermined whether the prevalence of narcissistic traits among terrorists exceeds the prevalence in the general population. And other authorities have objected that narcissism is unlikely to explain terrorism in even a small number of groups (Corrado 1981; Reich 1998). Again,

the intuitively plausible scenario of identity deficit with narcissistic rage in the developmental path to terrorism has yet to be supported by scientific study.

Paranoia theory

George Washington University psychiatrist Jerrold M. Post is unequivocally among the principal contributors to political psychological theories of terrorism. Post (1998, 2004) offers a comprehensive, psychoanalytically based formulation of terrorist behaviors—one that includes an explanation for the terrorist's capacity for murder: echoing Kohut (1972, 1978), he posits that the salient feature of terrorist psychology is projection, an infantile defense that assigns intolerable internal feelings to an external object when an individual who has grown up with a damaged self-concept idealizes the good self and splits out the bad self. This projection is proposed to be the root of an adult persistence of the infantile phase that Melanie Klein called the "paranoid-schizoid position" (Robins and Post 1997). While not overtly psychotic, the paranoid position nonetheless inflames the terrorist with suspicions that justify bloody acts of "self-defense" against his victims: "the zeal of the torturer, the alacrity of the killer, represents his eagerness to destroy the devalued and disowned part of the self" (Robins and Post 1997, 146). Post's paranoia theory offers a developmental model that explains not only why only a minority of individuals with political grievances turns to terrorism but also why terrorists kill those who do not appear to constitute an imminent threat.

Post (1998, 2004) bases his theory in part on an interpretation of the findings of the German psychological team that interviewed 250 radicals from the 1970s—mostly left-wing revolutionaries (Jäger, Schmidtchen, and Süllwold 1981; Böllinger 1981). Unfortunately, despite the earnest ambitions of that major study, no formal measurements of paranoia were used, there was little effort to stratify according to hierarchical level and role, there were no controls, and extrapolations from this subtype of terrorists to other political categories may be inappropriate. It seems plausible, for example, that the student radical of the 1970s who adopted a flagrantly antisocial revolutionary ideology is more likely to have exhibited some kind of psychological atypicality than is the typical Palestinian extremist or Sunni Iraqi insurgent who chooses behavior widely supported within his community. A scientifically weak but plausible criticism of the paranoia theory is provided by Sageman's (2004) finding that nine of ten Muslim terrorist biographies revealed no evidence of paranoia. Yet the most important criticism of such psychoanalytical theories is that it is impossible to test any hypothesis that attributes covert adult psychodynamic forces to covert psychosexual processes postulated to have occurred decades before, in infancy. Paranoia theory, like narcissism theory, remains an intriguing albeit impressionistic psychoanalytic interpretation that might, after controlled research using validated measures of paranoia, someday be shown to explain some instances of this very heterogeneous adult behavior.

Absolutist/apocalyptic theory

Harvard psychiatrist Robert J. Lifton is another important contributor. Lifton's (2000) major recent contribution is an account of the Aum Shinrikyo cult and other apocalyptic groups that envision mass destruction as a path toward replacing the corrupt world with a pure new social order. Apocalyptic groups typically exhibit absolutist moral polarization, idealization of a messianic figure, and impaired reality testing, imagining vast conspiracies of evil such as a "world shadow government" of Jews. Lifton's insights—that absolutist/totalist moral thinking helps motivate terrorism via its seductive appeal to young adults with weak identities and that terrorists defend themselves from normal emotional responses to violence through denial, psychic numbing, or isolation of affect—both fit with psychoanalytic theory. Although neither absolutism nor isolation of affect by themselves offers an *animus belli* or explains the specific impulse to harm innocents, it seems plausible to predict that irrational violence against the "other" would be precipitated when pathological defenses lead to black-and-white thinking about the out-

group combined with paranoia about in-group annihilation. This is consistent with the proposal of Devine and Rafalko (1982) to the effect that, paradoxically, terrorists are often uncompromising moralists who see the world in starkly polar terms.

Lifton's (2000) absolutist approach to terrorism represents a compelling combination of psychoanalytic developmental theory with a theory of atypical cognitive style. However, the evidence offered to support this theory consists of a subjective, theory-driven interpretation of unstructured interviews with a few individuals who may not be representative, and the postulated existentialist despair, irrational fantasies of worldwide dominion, and pathologically dependent group behavior of apocalyptic cults led by messianic leaders seem to characterize only a small minority of terrorist actions. One must still explain the majority.

The great strengths of psychoanalytic interpretations of terrorism are their acknowledgment that individual developmental factors beginning in early childhood probably influence adult behavioral proclivities, their recognition of the enormous power of the unconscious to influence conscious thought, and their observation that covert psychodynamic forces of groups may subsume individuality. The great weakness is their lack of falsifiability. Psychoanalysis has been largely abandoned among modern psychiatrists precisely because it rejects the scientific method, asking that adherents accept its propositions as received wisdom. This is not by any means to deny that early childhood, unconscious processes, and group dynamics may be key factors in the genesis of terrorism. However, psychoanalytic claims regarding pseudophysical intrapsychic dynamics tied to presumptive stages of sexuality cannot be confirmed according to the modern methods of social and behavioral science. A less ideological and more empirical psychodynamic model that nonetheless considers the crucial role of the unconscious—tested, for example, via controlled research examining whether a stratified subgroup of terrorists exhibit elevated scores on validated measures of maternal rejection, self-absorption, or paranoia—

Humiliation-revenge theory

Humiliation—and the consequent internal pressure for revenge—is another psychological factor that has been hypothesized to drive terrorist violence (Juergensmeyer 2000). Revenge for humiliation by an oppressor is, in fact, an ancient cultural tradition with direct links to the current violence in the Middle East. The oppression of the early Christians, embodied in the image of Christ on the cross, was part of the inspiration for the apocalyptic movement in Christianity that culminated in the First Crusade (Armstrong 2001). A cycle of oppression and humiliation, followed by violent action in the name of liberation, characterizes the subsequent history of the Middle East. Palestinian psychiatrist Eyad el Sarraj (2002) has specifically observed that humiliation is an important factor motivating young suicide bombers. Dr. Abdul Aziz Rantisi, the late political leader of Hamas, confirmed this notion in a statement published three years before his death via targeted killing by the Israeli Defense Forces: "To die in this way is better than to die daily in frustration and humiliation" (Juergensmeyer 2000, 187). Several other authorities also propose that humiliation, either by parents in early childhood or by political oppressors later in life, can provoke terrorism, but no quantitative research has yet explored this hypothesis (Crayton 1983; Volkan 1997; Stern 2003). Whether considered from the psychoanalytic point of view as an inevitable dynamic consequence of narcissistic injury or from the nonpsychoanalytic point of view as a painful social stressor, humiliation seems plausible as the root of an urge to retaliate against political entities that are perceived to be responsible.

The concept that feelings of humiliation or being taken advantage of gives rise to a passion for revenge is very familiar in forensic psychiatry and criminology and probably contributes to many nonpolitical murders (Miller 1993; Brooks, Thomas, and Droppleman 1996; Schlesinger 2000; Meloy 2001). Note that revenge, in itself, should not be regarded as antisocial behavior but as a normal and potentially useful activity. Jurisprudence formalizes this feature of social contracts, emphasizing retribution in part as deterrence, and polities have used vengeance for misdeeds to maintain their integrity at least since the Trojan War. Indeed, revenge is an emotion that is probably deeply rooted in the adaptive instinct to punish transgressors who violate the contracts of social species; hence, it is a motivator that often serves not only the goals of a vengeful individual but also the goals of his group (Clutton-Brock and Parker 1995). In this sense, revenge is often prosocial and sometimes—if the vengeance taker (e.g., Achilles or suicide bombers) stands to suffer and his group to gain—even altruistic. In a recent study combining psychological with functional neuroimaging studies in humans, de Quervain et al. (2004) showed that individuals punish social transgressors even when it is quite costly to the punisher, and they reported evidence that this altruistic behavior was driven by deep subcortical brain activity that may have overruled the more rational cortex. Knutson (2004) highlights the self-defeating and emotionally driven nature of vengeance demonstrated by this study, stating that these findings "chip yet another sliver from the rational model of economic man." While this science intriguingly helps to explain how revenge might motivate terrorists and perhaps governments to commit murderous behaviors without likely strategic benefits, no questionnaire data or measurements of subjective humiliation, desire for revenge, or emotional satisfaction after retribution in terrorists or ex-terrorists have yet been published. This plausible theory awaits better substantiation.

Theories of Group Process

Most published psychological theories explain terrorism as the product of group psychology within idiosyncratic subcultures that coalesce in reaction to circumstances they perceive as intolerable (Taylor and Ryan 1988; Friedland 1992; Hoffman 1998; Merari 1998; Levine 1999; Post 2004; Sageman 2004). Membership in a terrorist organization offers disciples a heady liquor of a well-defined personal role, a righteous purpose, the opportunity for revenge for perceived humiliations, and the lifting of constraints on the expression of otherwise prohibited behaviors—freeing the member from personal responsibility for attacks on outgroups (Hacker 1983; Taylor and Ryan 1988; Weinberg and Eubank 1994; Stern 1999). Group forces, including ideological indoctrination, repetitive training, and peer pressures, have been hypothesized to influence the group's violence, whether or not individual members were predisposed to such behavior (Crenshaw 1992; Clayton, Barlow, and Ballif-Spanvill 1998). This may occur because collective identity subsumes individual identity. As Post, Sprinzak, and Denny (2003, 176) put it, "An overarching sense of the collective consumes the individual. This fusion with the group seems to provide the necessary justification for their actions with an attendant loss of felt responsibility." This description of the submersion of individuality is very reminiscent of Eric Hoffer's (1951, 128) statement that people who plunge into mass movements "are fashioned into incomplete and dependent human beings even when they have within themselves the making of self-sufficient entities." Withdrawal from the mainstream may increase the potency of collective thought: based on a semi-quantitative review of life histories of more than 1,500 Italian and German militants, greater isolation is associated with greater separation from social reality (della Porta 1992).

The principal debate among those discussing group versus individual factors in political violence centers on whether group dynamics are sufficient in and of themselves to turn an average person into a terrorist or whether individual history and personality must be considered as well. Sageman, one strong proponent of the group hypothesis, goes so far as to say that "it's a group phenomenon. To search for individual characteristics . . . will lead you to a dead end" (Rotella 2004, A3). However, Sageman's psychiatric assessments of Islamic mujahedin were exclusively based on secondary sources that did not include any objective behavioral data, so his conclusion seems premature. Rasch (1979, 82) observed that the dynamics of living in a terrorist group tends to alienate one from others but that "the starting point and personal needs existing at

the time of entry into the terrorist group are very different for the different terrorists." This claim of initial psychological heterogeneity followed by group-induced homogenization appears sensible, but it requires empirical verification. Consistent with this theory, Friedland (1992) postulated that terrorism is not purely a group phenomenon but is obviously the result of an *interaction* between social processes and individual dispositions. However, he proposes three conditions under which individual proclivity to violence is a relatively minor factor in the group's terrorist turning: (1) deprivation is intense, (2) the group has ideologized its discontent, and (3) the group is cohesive and clearly differentiated from the out-group. He gives the example of the Palestinians, whose special circumstances drive individuals with no special propensity to violence to undertake terrorist acts. This formulation seems plausible on its surface. However, one still must account for the fact that, while most Palestinians support suicide bombing, a very small minority does it. Furthermore, no published studies support the proposition that these three conditions increase group dynamic success in driving nonviolent persons to political violence. Unless and until systematic research is conducted making in-depth psychological comparisons between terrorists and matched controls from identical political circumstances and estimating premembership and postmembership willingness to harm innocents, one cannot meaningfully quantify the relative influence of individual and group factors.

Limits and Impediments to Behavioral Science Research on Terrorism

Psychiatrist Walter Reich (1998, 262) has warned that "psychological accounts of terrorism are replete with explanations that ignore or blur the variety and complexity . . . a product of loose and weak thinking, a disregard for the need for evidence, and the habit, unfortunately endemic in so many areas of psychological discourse, of having a single idea and applying it to everything." Reich's strong caveat against overgeneralization and reductionism is a vital counter to the potpourri of psychological theories promulgated by terrorism scholars. In this, he supports Corrado's (1981) critical review of the mental disorders approach to political terrorism; Corrado states that a terrorist personality probably does not exist and that efforts to psychopathologize this type of aggression are rooted in biased theory, not in unbiased data.

Caveats against overgeneralization and unwarranted medicalization of terrorist behaviors are logical and important. Yet it seems reasonable to seek a middle ground between the reductionist position that proposes a single psychology of terrorism and the nihilist position that denies any explicit psychology of terrorism. That is, until a rigorous effort is made to investigate the null hypothesis via the collection of empirical evidence, it is premature to conclude that there are no distinguishing psychological characteristics among the tiny minority of individuals who are willing to send a terrifying political message to a target audience by attacking innocent noncombatants.

Why has the behavioral science community so far failed to amass a persuasive body of evidence in this domain? Multiple practical and theoretical impediments have delayed the scientific psychological study of terrorism. Most of the practical barriers are obvious. For example, terrorism research may involve expensive and inconvenient travel to politically unstable regions, is potentially dangerous, and raises ethical issues that may challenge institutional review boards (e.g., Wieviorka 1995; Brannan, Eslerm, and Anders Strindberg 2001). These issues may explain why journalists, rather than academics, have published a substantial proportion of the available literature reporting behavioral observations of terrorists. Active terrorists may have little motivation to cooperate with behavioral assessment, and inactive terrorists may no longer exhibit the psychology of interest (Reich 1998). Language barriers—including the lack of expert translations of high-quality psychological instruments—frustrate collection of data. Authorities may deny scholars access to incarcerated terrorists because of security concerns and the perception that such assessments are not pertinent to counterterrorism.

A theoretical issue that seriously limits the utility of interviews with specific terrorists or groups is the fact that, contrary to some published hypotheses, terrorism is not a unitary behavior (Crenshaw 1986; Laqueur 1987; Haroun 1999). As a result, theories that attempt to generalize and reduce the psychology of terrorism begin with a premise that is inconsistent with the available observations, and studies based on such theories will produce results with limited predictive value since they conflate data from mixed populations. Classifying terrorism according to probable homogeneous psychological subtypes that are "at least descriptive, inclusive, discrete, endowed with forecasting or prognostic value, policy-generating, possibly etiological, and theoretically grounded," as advised by Ferracuti (1982, 132), may be an indispensable preliminary step to designing research projects and interpreting data (Wilson 2000). Moreover, as Crenshaw (1986, 384–85) urged, "the analysis of terrorism deals with the intersection of psychological predispositions (which may be derived as much from prior experience and socialization as from psychological traits emerging from early childhood and infancy) and the external environment." A complete understanding of the psychology of terrorism, therefore, will require the difficult investigation of the *dynamics of that intersection*, in concert with an understanding of the forces of group dynamics and a quantitative analyses of events, a challenge demanding an interdisciplinary perspective beyond the borders of parochial regimes.

Funding has long been a problem, with limited federal support (Jenkins 1983). In 2004, the U.S. Homeland Security Department (DHS) published a Broad Agency Announcement soliciting proposals for a university-based Homeland Security Center for Behavioral and Social Aspects of Terrorism and Counter-terrorism, to be funded at $4 million per year for three years (U.S. Department of Homeland Security 2004). On one hand, this is a historic first, the largest grant ever offered to support research on this vital issue. On the other hand, the amount involved represents a very small proportion of the DHS research budget of more than $500 million per year (Brumfiel 2003) and a paltry part of the U.S. defense budget. The announcement

with diminished executive function may be less predictable. Those with subnormal cognitive flexibility may be less adaptable and more irrational in bargaining. Those with atypical temperaments—who are driven by an excessive need for self-affirmation, hatred, vengefulness, or self-destructiveness—may behave more erratically. Improved modeling of markers of psychological subtypes may enhance the prediction of terrorist behaviors.

4. Accepting that terrorists are heterogeneous, four traits may possibly be characteristics of "typical" terrorists who lead or follow in sub-state groups:

   a. High affective valence regarding an ideological issue
   b. A personal stake—such as strongly perceived oppression, humiliation, or persecution; an extraordinary need for identity, glory, or vengeance; or a drive for expression of intrinsic aggressivity—that distinguishes him or her from the vast majority of those who fulfill characteristic a
   c. Low cognitive flexibility, low tolerance for ambiguity, and elevated tendency toward attribution error
   d. A capacity to suppress both instinctive and learned moral constraints against harming innocents, whether due to intrinsic or acquired factors, individual or group forces—probably influenced by a, b, and c

These four characteristics seem plausible based on the above summary of research. They are testable hypotheses proposed for further study.

5. It seems plausible that the culture of origin differentiates, to some degree, expected individual and group dynamics. However, group theory would predict that the internal psychodynamics of a terrorist group is influenced as much by the specific personality of its leader and the temperaments of its followers as according to any systematic difference according to politically types (e.g., nationalist/separatist vs. religious).

6. The current thrust of strategic choice studies focuses on predicting the behavior of committed terrorists. For the purposes of long-term security policy formulation, an increased emphasis should be placed on early prevention, that is, on the analysis of the interaction between those psychological, cultural, economic, and political factors that influence uncommitted but impressionable young people to turn toward terrorism.

7. A balance must be achieved between the benefits of secrecy and the urgent need to advance knowledge in this field. Restricted access to data will slow scholarly progress with unknown consequences to national and international security. A review of the ultimate impact of this issue at the highest levels of security policy may be required to optimize this balance and overcome potentially counterproductive barriers.

8. Scholars must be willing to attempt research that brings them into direct contact with active terrorists, recently active terrorists, or those at risk for becoming terrorists. Noncoercive recruitment, voluntary participation, and informed consent are essential.

9. A major investment is required to advance the field of the behavioral and social aspects of terrorism. Meaningful research is likely to be interdisciplinary, empirical, controlled, ethical, conducted across levels of analysis, and directed at root causes and modifiable risk factors along the entire chain of causality from historical forces to childhood influences to the moment of a terrorist act. Since the best experts in any discipline are inevitably scattered geographically, rather than depending on a single center of excellence, funding commensurate with the magnitude of the threat should be available on a competitive basis to serious scholars wherever they work through independent science supporters such as the National Science Foundation or the Department of Defense.

The problem is to ask questions the answers to which are most likely to make a difference for security, to prioritize research within the remarkable spectrum of possible investigations, and to develop practical projects. For example, is the carrot of perceived concern for victims of disenfranchisement or the stick of high-altitude bombing a better investment in reducing the psychological forces nurturing the next generation of potential terrorists? What observable behavioral traits distinguish terrorist groups or leaders who would be likely to back away from aggression if their grievances were addressed by negotiation, as opposed to traits distinguishing groups that can only be deterred by force? Is the social influence of fundamentalist madrasas associated with a measurable increase in the likelihood of adult terrorist behavior? If so, could support for alternative, culturally valued education help impressionable young people find more productive foci for their high emotional energy? Do economic prospects and a sense of personal hope reduce the lure of terrorism? If so, what socioeconomic or psychological factors modify that association, and what cost-benefit formula is applicable? Do psychological traits of leaders of target nations drive policies that mitigate or exacerbate the threat? Answers to these and similar questions may be part of the key to avoiding catastrophic violence in the twenty-first century.

REFERENCES

Achenbach, T. M., and C. Edelbrock. 1987. *Manual for the youth self-report and profile*. Burlington: University of Vermont, Department of Psychiatry.

Akhtar, S. 1999. The psychodynamic dimension of terrorism. *Psychiatric Annals* 29:350–5.

Alexander, Y. 2002. *Palestinian religious terrorism: Hamas and Islamic Jihad*. Ardsley, NY: Transnational Publishers.

American Psychiatric Association. 2000. *Diagnostic and statistical manual of mental disorders*. 4th ed., text revision. Washington, DC: American Psychiatric Association.

Anonymous. 2004. *The 9/11 Commission report: Final report of the national commission on terrorist attacks upon the United States*. New York: Norton.

Armstrong, K. 2000. *Islam*. New York: The Modern Library.

———. 2001. *Holy war: The Crusades and their impact on today's world*. New York: Anchor.

Atran, S. 2003. Genesis of suicide terrorism. *Science* 299:1534–9.

Azam, J.-P. Forthcoming. Suicide-bombing as intergenerational investment. *Public Choice*.

Badey, T. J. 1998. Defining international terrorism: A pragmatic approach. *Terrorism and Political Violence* 10:90–107.

Bandura, A. 1973. *Aggression: A social learning analysis*. New York: Prentice Hall.

———. 1998. Mechanisms of moral disengagement. In *Origins of terrorism: Psychologies, ideologies, theologies, states of mind*, edited by W. Reich, 161–92. Washington, DC: Woodrow Wilson Center Press.

Barber, B. K. 1999. Political violence, family relations, and Palestinian youth functioning. *Journal of Adolescent Research* 14:206–30.

Begin, M. 1977. *The revolt: Story of the Irgun*. Jerusalem: Steimatzky's Agency.

Bennet, J. 2004. In chaos, Palestinians struggle for way out. *New York Times*, July 15, 1, 10–11.

Billig, M. 1976. *Social psychology and intergroup relations*. London: Academic Press.

Böllinger, L. 1981. Die entwicklung zu terroristischem handeln als psychosozialer prozess: begegnungen mit beteiligten. In *Analyzen zum terrorismus 2: Lebenslaufanalysen*, edited by H. Jäger, G. Schmidtchen, and L. Süllwold. Darmstadt, Germany: DeutscherVerlag.

Borah, L. A. 1963. The effects of threat in bargaining: Critical and experimental analysis. *Journal of Abnormal and Social Psychology* 66:37–44.

Bowen, R., Y. Alexander, R. Cox, M. Crenshaw, and D. Rapoport. 1985. Colby College conference report. *Terrorism: An International Journal* 8:79–112.

Brannan, D. W., P. F. Eslerm, and N. T. Anders Strindberg. 2001. Talking to "terrorists": Towards an independent analytic framework for the study of violent substate activism. *Studies in Conflict and Terrorism* 24:3–24.

Brooks, A., S. Thomas, and P. Droppleman. 1996. From frustration to red fury: A description of work-related anger in male registered nurses. *Nursing Forum* 31:4–15.

Brooks, D. 2002. The culture of martyrdom: How suicide bombing became not just a means but an end. *The Atlantic Monthly* 289:18–20.

Brophy-Baermann, B., and J. A. C. Conybeare. 1994. Retaliating against terrorism: Rational expectations and the optimality of rules versus discretions. *American Journal of Political Science* 38:196–210.

Brumfiel, G. 2003. Research mired in homeland security delays. *Nature* 424:986.

Bryant, E. T., M. L. Scott, C. J. Golden, and C. D. Tori. 1984. Neuropsychological deficits, learning disability, and violent behavior. *Journal of Consulting and Clinical Psychology* 52:323–4.

Budner, S. 1962. Intolerance of ambiguity as a personality variable. *Journal of Personality* 30:29–50.

Canetti, D., and A. Pedahzur. 2002. The effects of contextual and psychological variables on extreme right-wing sentiments. *Social Behavior and Personality* 30:317–34.

Carey, B. 2002. Method without madness? *Los Angeles Times*, July 7, 1.

Clark, R. 1983. Patterns in the lives of ETA members. *Terrorism* 6:423–54.

Clayton, C. J., S. H. Barlow, and B. Ballif-Spanvill. 1998. Principles of group violence with a focus on terrorism. In *Collective violence*, edited by H. V. Hall and L. C.

Whitaker, 277–311. Boca Raton, FL: CRC Press.

Clutton-Brock, T. H., and G. A. Parker. 1995. Punishment in animal societies. *Nature* 373:209–16.

Cooper, H. H. A. 1977. What is a terrorist: A psychological perspective. *Legal Medical Quarterly* 1:16–32.

——. 1978. Psychopath as terrorist: A psychological perspective. *Legal Medical Quarterly* 2:253–62.

Corrado, R. R. 1981. A critique of the mental disorder perspective of political terrorism. *International Journal of Law and Psychiatry* 4:293–310.

Crayton, J. W. 1983. Terrorism and the psychology of the self. In *Perspectives on terrorism*, edited by L. Z. Freedman and Y. Alexander, 33–41. Wilmington, DE: Scholarly Resources, Inc.

Crenshaw, M. 1981. The causes of terrorism. *Comparative Politics* 13:379–99.

——. 1986. The psychology of political terrorism. In *Political psychology*, edited by M. G. Hermann, 379–413. San Francisco: Jossey-Bass.

——. 1992. How terrorists think: What psychology can contribute to understanding terrorism. In *Terrorism: Roots, impact, responses*, edited by L. Howard. New York: Praeger.

——. 2000. The psychology of terrorism: An agenda for the 21st century. *Political Psychology* 21:405–20.

Crozier, B. 1960. *The rebels. A study of post war insurrections*. London: Chatto & Windus.

Dahl, R. E. 2004. Adolescent brain development: A period of vulnerabilities and opportunities. *Annals of the New York Academy of Sciences* 1021:1–22.

Davies, J. C. 1973. Aggression, violence, revolution and war. In *Handbook of political psychology*, edited by J. N. Knutsen, 234–60. San Francisco: Jossey-Bass.

della Porta, D. 1988. Recruitment processes in clandestine political organizations: Italian left-wing terrorism. *International Social Movement Research* 1:155–69.

——. 1992. Political socialization in left-wing underground organizations: Biographies of Italian and German militants. *International Social Movement Research* 4:259–90.

DeMause, L. 1986. The real target wasn't terrorism. *Journal of Psychohistory* 13:413–26.

de Quervain, D. J. -F., U. Fischbacher, V. Treyer, M. Schellhammer, U. Buck, and E. Fehr. 2004. The neural basis for altruistic punishment. *Science* 305:1254–8.

Deutsch, K. W. 1954. Game theory and politics. *Canadian Journal of Economics and Political Science* 20:76–83.

Deutsch, K. W., and R. M. Krause. 1962. Studies of interpersonal bargaining. *Journal of Conflict Resolution* 6:52–76.

Devine, P. E., and R. J. Rafalko. 1982. On terror. *Annals of the American Academy of Political & Social Science* 463:39–53.

Dollard, J., L. W. Doob, N. E. Miller, W. Mowrer, and R. R. Sears. 1939. *Frustration and aggression*. New Haven, CT: Yale University Press.

Duckitt, J., C. Wagner, I. du Plessis, and I. Birum. 2002. The psychological bases of ideology and prejudice: Testing a dual process model. *Journal of Personality and Social Psychology* 83:75–93.

el Sarraj, E. 2002. [Televised interview]. *CBS News*, April 4.

Enders, W., and T. Sandler. 2000. Is transnational terrorism becoming more threatening? A time series investigation. *Journal of Conflict Resolution* 44:307–32.

Erikson, E. 1959. *Identity and the life cycle*, 171. Psychological Issues Monograph 1. New York: International University Press.

Ernst, M., S. J. Grant, E. D. London, C. S. Contorreggi, A. S. Kimes, and L. Spurgeon. 2003. Decision making in adolescents with behavior disorders and adults with substance abuse. *American Journal of Psychiatry* 160:33–40.

Fanon, F. 1965. *The wretched of the earth*. New York: Pelican. Reprint of *Les damnes de la terre* (Paris, 1961).

Ferracuti, F. 1982. A sociopsychiatric interpretation of terrorism. *Annals of the American Academy of Political and Social Science* 463:129–40.

Ferracuti, F., and F. Bruno. 1981. Psychiatric aspects of terrorism in Italy. In *The mad, the bad and the different: Essays in honor of Simon Dinitz*, edited by I. L. Barak-Glantz and C. R. Huff. Lexington, MA: Lexington Books.

Freud, S. 1953–1974. Thoughts for the times on war and death. In *Standard edition of the complete psychological works of Sigmund Freud*, vol. 14, edited by J. Strachey. London: Hogarth

Fried, R. 1982. The psychology of the terrorist. In *Terrorism and beyond: An international conference on terrorism and low-level conflict*, edited by B. M. Jenkins. Santa Monica, CA: RAND.

Friedland, N. 1992. Becoming a terrorist: Social and individual antecedents. In *Terrorism: Roots, impact, responses*, edited by L. Howard. New York: Praeger.

Friedland, N., and A. Merari. 1985. The psychological impact of terrorism: A double-edged sword. *Political Psychology* 6:591–604.

Gabbard, G. O. 2000. Psychoanalysis. In *Kaplan and Sadock's comprehensive textbook of psychiatry*, 7th ed., edited by B. J. Sadock and V. A. Sadock, 563–607. Philadelphia: Lippincott Williams & Wilkins.

Gazzaniga, M. S., ed. 2000. *The new cognitive neurosciences*. 2nd ed. Cambridge, MA: MIT Press.

Grossman, D. 1995. *On killing: The psychological cost of learning to kill in war and society*. Boston: Little, Brown.

Gunaratna, G. 2002. *Inside Al Qaeda: Global network of terror*. New York: Columbia University Press.

Gurr, T. 1970. *Why men rebel*. Princeton, NJ: Princeton University Press.

Hacker, F. J. 1976. *Crusaders, criminals, crazies: Terror and terrorism in our time*. New York: Norton.

——. 1983. Dialectic interrelationships of personal and political factors in terrorism. In *Perspectives on terrorism*, edited by L. Z. Freedman and Y. Alexander, 19–31. Wilmington, DE: Scholarly Resources, Inc.

Handler, J. S. 1990. Socioeconomic profile of an American terrorist: 1960s and 1970s. *Terrorism* 13:195–213.

Harmon, C. C. 2000. *Terrorism today*. London: Frank Cass.

terrorism and emphasizes the strategic purpose underlying the phenomenon, which, to him, is to coerce modern liberal democracies to make territorial concessions. Finally, Pedahzur et al. (Reading 10) examine the motivations of Palestinian suicide bombers to conclude that these correspond to both types of suicide identified by Durkheim in his classic work, namely altruistic suicide committed for the benefit of one's society and fatalistic suicide derived from individuals' sense of hopelessness and personal crisis. The challenge for the reader is to compare and contrast these valuable insights into terrorists' motivation in order to develop a broader perspective on the motivational factors most likely to underlie terrorism and to examine whether one might weave these disparate insights into a uniform conceptual framework.

Reading 5—Silke (1998). Cheshire-Cat Logic: The Recurring Theme of Terrorist Abnormality in Psychological Research

Editors' Comments

To an average member of a Western society, acts of terrorism may seem irrational and bizarre. What good might be accomplished, it is often asked, by a massive killing of innocent civilians and by annihilating oneself in the process, as may often be the case. Such cruelty and callousness may seem so far from the normal modes of behavior as to beg for a psychopathological explanation. Indeed, the extreme acts of violence and self-destruction that terrorists exhibit call to mind psychopathic killers, serial murderers, or deranged sadists, the likes of which fill the institutions for the criminally insane. It is not surprising, therefore, that the hypothesis of terrorists' psychopathology was so readily adopted—on the basis of such fragmentary data—by early theorists of terrorist behavior. Silke explains why several psychological problems such as narcissism and antisocial and paranoid personality disorders caught the fancy of psychological theorists seeking to understand terrorist behavior and criticizes the quality of evidence adduced in support of the notion that terrorists suffer from these alleged disorders. He also criticizes the logic of inferring psychopathology not from well-established psychological diagnostic instruments but from the unproven assumption that all terrorists *must* be psychologically disturbed—and therefore that they are.

Discussion Questions

1. What exactly is wrong with what Silke refers to as Cheshire-Cat logic?
2. What policy implications may follow from the notion that terrorists are irrational and emotionally disturbed?
3. What kind of evidence is brought to support the claims linking terrorism and psychopathology? Conversely, has Silke presented convincing empirical evidence that terrorists do *not* suffer from atypical psychological traits? How might this question better be resolved?
4. If psychopathology is inadequate to explain terrorism, is it irrelevant to terrorism? What can then explain terrorists' behavior?

Suggested Readings

Corrado, R. R. (1981). A critique of the mental disorder perspective of political terrorism. *International Journal of Law and Psychiatry, 4*, 293–309.

Post, J. M. (1998). Terrorist psycho-logic: Terrorist behaviour as a product of psychological forces. In W. Reich (Ed.), *Origins of terrorism: Psychologies, ideologies, theologies, states of mind* (pp. 25–40). Washington, DC: Woodrow Wilson Center Press.

Rasch, W. (1979). Psychological dimensions of political terrorism in the Federal Republic of Germany. *International Journal of Law and Psychiatry, 2*, 79–85.

Reading 6—Post, Sprinzak, & Denny (2003). The Terrorists in Their Own Words: Interviews with 35 Incarcerated Middle Eastern Terrorists

Editors' Comments

In this paper Post, Sprinzak, and Denny describe semi-structured interviews they conducted with 35 incarcerated Palestinian terrorists representing Hamas, Islamic Jihad, Hizballah, and Fatah. The authors' conclusion is that the social environment of youth was a major influence on joining a terrorist organization. The peer group appeared to have been of greater influence than the home environment in determining whether an individual would join a given organization, although the home upbringing seemed to influence whether the individual would join a secular (Fatah) or a religious organization (Hamas, Islamic Jihad, or Hizballah). It is also the case that individuals' entry into the organization was typically through personal friendships and contacts with existing members. In this sense, "who you know" seems to precede "what you know" (i.e., adopting the terrorism-justifying ideology). The authors emphasize the fusion of the individuals' goals and identity with the organization's goals and identity. Members of both the secular and the religious organizations believed in the necessity and efficacy of martyrdom in advancing their group's objectives. Finally, of considerable interest, imprisonment for terrorism seemed to enhance their commitment to their organizations through interaction with their fellow prisoners.

Discussion Questions

1. What, in your opinion, were the main psychological insights of the Post, Sprinzak, and Denny research?
2. How do their findings square with the notion of prison sentence as a severe punishment meant to deter the perpetrators from repeating their crimes?
3. Why did members of the militant Palestinian organizations subjugate their personal goals to the collective goals of the organization?

Discussion Questions

1. In what sense is suicide bombing a rational choice for terrorist organizations?
2. Is there a sense in which suicide bombing is also "rational" from the individual's perspective?
3. According to Atran, which policies may work or not work in reducing the incidence of suicidal terrorism?

Suggested Readings

Gambetta, D. (2005). *Making sense of suicide missions*. Oxford: Oxford University Press.
Hafez, M. M. (2006). Rationality, culture and structure in the making of suicide bombers: A preliminary theoretical synthesis and illustrative case study. *Studies in Conflict and Terrorism, 29*, 165–185.
Hoffman, B. (1998). *Inside terrorism*. New York: Columbia University Press.

Reading 9—Pape (2003). The Strategic Logic of Suicide Terrorism

Editors' Comments

In this paper, Robert Pape reports an empirically based analysis of the logic of suicidal terrorism. In agreement with Atran, he proposes that suicide terrorism is rational at the organizational level in that it constitutes an effective tactic that has forced liberal democracies such as the USA, France, Israel, or Italy to make territorial concessions to terrorist organizations. He also agrees with Atran that many suicide attackers may be irrational or fanatical, but the organizations have learned that it pays. Of particular interest, Pape suggests that suicidal terrorism has its limits. Specifically, suicide terrorism may make target nations surrender modest goals but it is unlikely to compel states to abandon important interests related to physical security or national wealth. In terms of the policy implications of this analysis, Pape comes down on the side of measures designed to reduce the perpetrators' ability to carry out suicide attacks, by investing "significant resources in border defenses and other means of homeland security."

Discussion Questions

1. What, according to Pape (as well as Atran), constitutes rationality on the individual level?
2. Though Pape and Atran agree that suicide terrorism makes sense (i.e., is rational) at the organizational level, but not on the individual level, the two writers draw entirely different policy conclusions from their analysis. What is the nature of these differences, and how, if at all, can they be reconciled?

3. What accounts for the coercive power of suicide attacks to force concessions from the targeted parties?

Suggested Readings

Crenshaw, M. (1981). The causes of terrorism. *Comparative Politics*, *13*, 397–399.
George, A. (1972). *Limits of coercive diplomacy*. Boston, MA: Little, Brown.
Pape, R. (1997). Why economic sanctions do not work. *International Security*, *22*, 90–136.

Reading 10—Pedahzur, Perliger, & Weinberg (2003). Altruism and Fatalism: The Characteristics of Palestinian Suicide Terrorists

Editors' Comments

Whereas the papers by Atran and Pape focus on the organizational logic of suicide terrorism, the paper by Pedahzur, Perliger, and Weinberg addresses the underlying motivations of individuals that increase their readiness to volunteer or be recruited for acts of suicidal terrorism. Of interest, the present authors' point of departure is the notion of suicide itself. Specifically, they invoke Durkheim's classic notion of altruistic suicide, which occurs when a person commits the act for the sake of her or his ingroup in which he/she feels deeply integrated. Pedahzur et al. juxtapose this type of suicide with Durkheim's fatalistic suicide stemming from situations of hopelessness "that result from continuous political and economic oppression." Pedahzur and colleagues apply the distinction between altruistic and fatalistic suicide to the problem of suicidal terrorism by Palestinians in recent years. Of greatest interest, perhaps, Pedahzur et al. suggest the possibility that, in the case of Palestinian society, suicide terrorism is both fatalistic and altruistic—that is, it involves both types of motivation. The authors derive a number of hypotheses from notions of altruistic versus fatalistic suicides and test them against event data obtained from an open data source (*Ha'aretz*, a major Israeli newspaper).

Discussion Questions

1. Pedahzur et al. suggest that in Palestinian suicide attacks both altruistic and fatalistic motives likely play a part. How might the two motivations interact?
2. In what ways does the Pedahzur et al. paper provide additional insights into the phenomenon of Palestinian suicide terrorism beyond previously available knowledge?
3. How do the various hypotheses proposed by Pedahzur et al. follow from the notions of altruistic and fatalistic types of suicide? That is, what underlying logic leads from these notions to the hypotheses?

Suggested Readings

Kruglanski, A. W., Chen, X., Dechesne, M., Fishman, S., & Orehek, E. (in press). Fully committtted: Suicide bombers' motivation and the quest for personal significance. *Political Psychology*.

Merari, A. (1998). The readiness to die and kill. In W. Reich (Ed.), *Origins of terrorism: Psychologies, ideologies, theologies, states of mind* (pp. 192–207). Washington, DC: Woodrow Wilson Center Press.

Sprinzak, E. (2000). Rational fanatics. *Foreign Policy*, *120*, 66–73.

Cheshire-Cat Logic: The Recurring Theme of Terrorist Abnormality in Psychological Research

Andrew Silke*

Using an encounter from Alice In Wonderland as a metaphor, this article examines the long-running attempt to apply a psychopathology label to terrorists. The disorders of greatest interest to researchers (antisocial, narcissistic and paranoid personality disorders), are described in order to highlight their attraction for theorists. A review of evidence follows. The critique finds that the findings supporting the pathology model are rare and generally of poor quality. In contrast, the evidence suggesting terrorist normality is both more plentiful and of better quality. However, in response to a failure to find any major psychopathology, a trend has emerged which asserts that terrorists possess many of the traits of pathological personalities but do not possess the actual clinical disorders. This development has effectively tainted terrorists with a pathology aura, without offering any way to easily test or refute the accusations.

"In that direction," the Cat said, waving its right paw round, "lives a Hatter: and in that direction," waving the other paw. "lives a March Hare. Visit either you like: they're both mad."

"But I don't want to go among mad people," Alice remarked.

"Oh, you ca'n't help that," said the Cat: "we're all mad here. I'm mad. You're mad."

"How do you know I'm mad?" said Alice.

"You must be," said the Cat, "or you wouldn't have come here."

(Carroll, 1865)

*Department of Applied Psychology, University College Cork, Western Road, Cork City, Ireland. E-mail: a.silke@ucc.ie

Extreme violence has always seemed to have had a special ability to bias our perceptions of the perpetrator's psychology. In the immediate aftermath of World War II, an Allied psychologist examined the Rorschach scores of 16 captured Nazi leaders, including the scores of Hermann Goering and Rudolf Hess. The psychologist concluded that the Rorschach results showed the individuals were *"hostile, violent, and concerned with death, that they needed status, and that they lacked any real human feeling."* This matched perfectly with the public expectation of what such men would be like. However, years later, these same scores were inserted among a selection of scores belonging to normal, healthy subjects. The mix was then given to a panel of experts who were unable to distinguish the Nazi scores from the rest, and found nothing whatsoever to support the earlier derogatory diagnosis (Dworetzky, 1988, p. 440).

This is an example of what I call Cheshire-Cat logic. Alice's first encounter with the Cheshire-Cat is one of the most memorable scenes of Lewis Carroll's book. The cat believes only mad people could inhabit Wonderland, so consequently anyone you meet there, *must* be mad. Attribution theory has shown that we tend to view our own behaviour as stemming from situational or environmental forces, but that we see the behaviour of other people as stemming from internal forces, such as stable personality traits (Eisen, 1979; Quattrone, 1982). Cheshire-Cat thinking can be considered a form of attribution error where observers develop expectations about an individual's personality based on what the individual does or, as in Alice's case, where the individual is located. Perhaps no study better demonstrates such a process in action than Rosenhan's (1973) classic work on the staff of psychiatric hospitals.

The major finding of the study was that the staff failed entirely to detect the presence of normal individuals among the psychiatric patient population. A central theme was how in many instances the staff "profoundly misinterpreted" normal behaviour, so that it would fit in with preconceived expectations they had of the patient's supposed psychopathology.

Such Cheshire-Cat perceptions can be seen in the way terrorists are perceived in our society. Terrorism is a topic which provokes extreme perceptions, perceptions which spill easily into considerations of the actors behind the violence. Terrorist violence is so unusual and runs so contrary to the accepted standards of society, that it seems to suggest psychological anomaly. The often extreme callousness and brutality of terrorist acts leaves it difficult for commentators to remain objective when considering the motivations and personalities of the terrorists. Misconceptions and prejudices born in the wake of the amorality of terrorist acts—the wanton destruction of property and the suffering of victims—if pervasive enough will go on to influence the policies used to combat terrorism and can have a powerful influence on official attitudes on how to deal with terrorists. Adopting misguided policies, for example by refusing to negotiate in the belief that terrorists cannot be expected to respond reasonably to conciliatory approaches, can needlessly prolong campaigns of violence and exacerbate the search for acceptable solutions.

While many terrorism researchers contend that terrorist psychopathology is a dead issue, resolved over a decade ago, the reality is that it has continued to survive as a resilient source of inspiration on which to base theories. That terrorists are somehow psychologically different from the rest of the population has become an underlying assumption of much, if not most, psychological research on terrorists in the past 30 years. As Schmid and Jongman (1988) noted, "The chief assumption underlying many psychological 'theories' . . . is that the terrorist is in one way or the other not normal and that the insights from psychology and psychiatry are adequate keys to understanding."

In an early review of evidence, Corrado (1981) found virtually no data to support the view that terrorists were in some way psychologically abnormal and plenty of evidence to suggest just the opposite. Nevertheless, modern authors (e.g. Johnson and Feldmann, 1992) continue to formulate hypotheses based on the same unsubstantiated models Corrado disparaged years previously. Has then, new evidence emerged to warrant the enduring interest in terrorist psychopathology?

The simple answer to this question is no, but then again the paucity of work that has been done on the individual psychology of terrorists means that recent evidence of any kind is rare. Modern research efforts are being channelled—productively—into a group and organisational focus (e.g. Post, 1987a; Crenshaw, 1990). Combined with these more accessible avenues of research, most general books on terrorism agree with Corrado that one "cannot accept the comforting and unchallenging assumption that equates [terrorist] behaviour with mental illness" (Taylor and Quayle, 1994, p. 189). Most serious researchers in the field at least nominally agree with the position that terrorists are essentially normal individuals.

However, there is some dissension in the ranks. Respected theorists such as Wilkinson (1977) and Laqueur (1977) have made generalisations about terrorists that indicate a perception of them as being abnormal. Other theorists such as Post (1987b) and Pearlstein (1991), are more forthright about their beliefs and have built explanations of terrorists around models of abnormal personalities.

With regard to criminal behaviour in general, it is worthwhile to note that some authors (e.g. Raine, 1993) believe that a psychopathological model has enormous explanatory power. Certainly, as far as violent criminals are concerned there does seem to be more than a little justification to believe this to be the case (Hodgins, 1995). In the past decade, psychopathy in particular has attracted enormous interest as an explanation of persistent crime and violence (Hare, 1996). While such interest may be of value in considering "ordinary decent" criminals, its usefulness with regard to terrorists is far less certain. While government agencies may be quick to view terrorists as simply violent criminals, very few researchers would share this perception (Schmid and Jongman, 1988).

However, ambiguities about who exactly is a terrorist and who is not, have helped to spread the government-style perception into wider society. There is still no precise and agreed definition of terrorism, and some have concluded mordantly that "it is unlikely that any definition will ever be generally agreed upon" (Shafritz, Gibbons and Scott, 1991). A refreshingly concise definition is provided by Martha Crenshaw, probably the most prominent psychologist involved in terrorism research, when she described terrorism as "a particular style of political violence, involving attacks on a small number of victims in order to influence a wider audience" (Crenshaw, 1992). The claims as to what kind of behaviour fits into this definition vary enormously[1] but the focus of this paper is very much that of 'insurgent' terrorism. Insurgent terrorism is essentially a strategy of the weak, adopted "by groups with little numerical, physical or direct political power in order to effect political or social change" (Friedland, 1992).

In practical terms, 'insurgent' terrorists are members of small covert groups engaged in an organised campaign of violence. This violence is often extreme and frequently indiscriminate. The terrorists themselves tend to live isolated and stressful lives and enjoy varying levels of wider support. Nationalist/separatist groups such as the IRA or ETA have a considerable degree of support from their ethnic groups, where new recruits are relatively easy to find. The ideological groups such as the Red Army Faction or the Italian Red Brigades have a much more limited support base and more difficulty in finding dedicated recruits.

However, even 'popular' terrorist groups represent only a violent and extreme minority within what is still a minority section of the larger society. While terrorists, especially the larger ethnic groups such as the IRA, may be largely tolerated within their communities, the number of individuals actively involved in the campaign of violence is always relatively low. Ultimately, very few individuals of aggrieved minorities go on to become active terrorists. The question has always been, why did these particular individuals engage in terrorism when most of their compatriots did not?

---

[1] Interested readers are referred to Silke (1996) for a recent account of the definitional debate.

The Cheshire-Cat Theory of Terrorists

A concern with this recurring question perhaps explains why theorists have persistently returned to the concept of psychological abnormality as a basis on which to build an understanding of terrorists. One example of the resilience of such thinking is provided by Hassel, who in 1977 proposed a typology of terrorists based on psychopathology. Fifteen years later, Johnson and Feldmann (1992) drew upon this profile when developing their own model, which again saw terrorists as essentially possessing pathological personalities.

The new version described terrorist leaders as being "*fanatical*" and as having "*a paranoid and narcissistic pathology.*" The paranoid personality was not reserved for leaders alone, but was also claimed to be a frequent hallmark of other members. Individuals who actually carried out attacks, possessed an additional "*underlying antisocial matrix.*" Finally, it was noted that most members of terrorist groups possessed what DSM-II referred to as the "*inadequate personality.*"[2]

Such typologies have persistently cropped up in the research literature. Time and again, the importance of one personality type or another has been stressed and linked to certain individuals or roles within terrorist groups. Turco (1987) noted that this mode of thinking was particularly rampant in the reasoning of law enforcement agencies, who unerringly focused in on the psychopathic personality. Their claim was, and generally still is, that psychopaths are the foot soldiers of terrorist groups, providing the core around which the group is built.

However, it is not simply clinically naive police officials who have devoted much effort in espousing terrorist pathology, a steady flow of researchers have proposed similar, if somewhat more sophisticated models. For example, Suellwold (1981) proposed that there were two personality types particularly attracted to terrorism. The first displayed the characteristics of the narcissistic personality, while the second could be described as the typical paranoid personality.

Suellwold's typology provided the basis for a more complex model developed by Turco in 1987. Turco saw the following personality types as relevant:

(1) the inadequate personality with an excessive, exaggerated demand and "grand play";

(2) the antisocial personality with a criminal outlook and direct rational expectations;

(3) the paranoid with bizarre demands, frequent religious overtones and underlying homosexual conflicts; and

(4) the hypomaniac or depressive as whom one must consider a "suicide to be." (Turco, 1987)

The temptation to view terrorism in terms of abnormality, particularly such forms of it as the antisocial, narcissistic and paranoid personality types becomes very understandable once one realises how appropriately terrorists can be viewed in these terms. The repeated attempts to portray terrorists in terms of abnormal personalities is not simply the result of academic observers succumbing to the popular myth of the terrorist as madman (though that may have some role). Rather, observers cannot but fail to notice the striking parallels between the two.

The Terrorist as Psychopath

Corrado (1981) carried out one of the first reviews of the effort to view terrorists as psychologically

---

[2] It is interesting to note that while Johnson and Feldmann's work was completed in the 1990s, their model did not look to the available DSM-III-R for reference but instead drew on older DSM editions. The reader will find that the early editions of DSM are quoted extensively in this article. The reason for this is ultimately a disheartening one. The peak period of activity in researching the abnormality of terrorists occurred in the late 70s and early 80s when DSM-II and DSM-III were in use. Not surprisingly, researchers drew upon those editions to hypothesise about terrorist personalities. The more recent research and theorising, such as Johnson and Feldmann's, has cemented itself around the earlier work, in the process taking on board the older DSM terms and definitions. To better illustrate these theorists' reasoning the same older versions are used in this article.

abnormal. In his critique, Corrado gave particular emphasis to the personality disorder of sociopathy or psychopathy (now known as the *antisocial personality*). He noted that this was "the most prominent mental disorder linked to political terrorism and terrorism in general."

He quotes Pearce (1977), a strong advocate of terrorist sociopathy, to illustrate how the terrorist was viewed. Pearce regarded the terrorist as "an aggressive psychopath, who has espoused some particular cause because extremist causes can provide an external focal point for all the things that have gone wrong in his life."

The following describes the coping style of the typical antisocial personality, and illustrates very effectively why this pathology holds such attraction for theorists:

> They are driven by a desire to dominate and humiliate others, to wreck vengeance upon those whom they see as having mistreated them . . .

> People are used as means to an end, often subordinated and demeaned so that they can vindicate themselves for the grievances, misery, and humiliation they experienced in the past. By provoking fear and intimidating others, they seek to undo the lowly caste into which they feel they were thrust in childhood. Their search for power, therefore, is not benign; it springs from a deep well of hate and the desire for retribution and vindication. (Millon, 1981)

The parallels between this description of the antisocial personality and anyone engaged in terrorism are striking. The terrorist is challenging the dominant forces in society with violence, attempting to replace the established power structure with one of their own choosing. There is a disregard for life, to the extent that totally innocent individuals may be callously used, for example, taken as hostages or deliberately targeted in random attacks.

The media rarely goes beyond the sociopath in any discussion of terrorist abnormality, but among academics other disorders are a source of considerable interest. Pre-eminent among these lesser known pathologies is the narcissistic personality disorder.

The Terrorist as Narcissist

There is a strong relationship between the antisocial personality and the narcissistic personality. Millon (1981, p. 157) noted broad clinical similarities between the narcissist and the psychopath, and that both types focused angrily on maintaining their independence. For these personalities, ". . . self-determination is a protective manoeuvre; it is a means of countering, with their own power and prestige, the hostility, deception, and victimization they anticipate from others."

Such strong similarities with the antisocial personality underlie the attraction the narcissistic personality has for those speculating about terrorists, and researchers have focused on this disorder with considerable energy. Both Lasch (1979) and Pearlstein (1991) have said that a narcissistic disorder lies at the heart of the terrorist personality, and others, such as Post (1987b) and Suellwold (1981), have indicated that traits characteristic of the narcissist are common features of terrorist personalities.

DSM-III (1980) noted that narcissists are likely to disregard "*the personal integrity and rights of others.*" Expanding further, Millon (1981) commented that "*. . . narcissists have learned to devalue others, not to trust their judgements, and to think of them as naive and simpleminded. Thus, rather than question the correctness of their own beliefs, they assume that it is the views of others that are at fault. Hence, the more disagreement they have with others, the more convinced they are of their own superiority and the more isolated and alienated they are likely to become.*"

This lack of regard for the welfare of others, fits very well with the nature of terrorist attacks, where innocent civilians, frequently totally uninvolved with the terrorists' real enemies and causes, are deliberately targeted. Women and children, normally shielded from conventional war, are placed in the front-line by terrorists. Such a profound lack of empathy is a hallmark of both the antisocial personality and the narcissistic personality. The fact that most terrorists belong to minority groups, and generally minorities within minorities, finds an echo in the narcissistic tendency to become increasingly alienated and isolated. The terrorist becomes segregated from mainstream society, first, by merging with that segment which condones the terrorist actions, then by moving into the faction which provides more tangible support for the terrorists, and finally by becoming an active member of the terrorist group itself. At each step, the individual becomes more secluded and alienated. One cannot help but believe that a narcissistic personality would slip from the majority to the final terrorist minority very easily due to their interpersonal attitudes.

Of further interest is the tendency for some commentators (e.g. Hassel, 1977; Johnson and Feldmann, 1992) to suggest that the narcissistic personality is particularly common among terrorist leaders. If true, this would not be especially surprising, for as Millon (1981) points out:

> . . . the sheer presumptuousness and confidence exuded by the narcissist often elicits admiration and obedience from others.

Continuing with the narcissistic personality, it is significant to note that one of the more common concurrent types involving the narcissist is found in combination with the antisocial personality type. This *narcissistic–antisocial mixed personality* (Millon, 1981) seems on surface overview ideally suited to a potential terrorist. Here we have an individual who takes from the narcissist a pronounced lack of regard and empathy for others, as well as a tendency to become marginalised and alienated from society, and melds these characteristics with the antisocial's willingness to use aggression and violence in order to maintain their own independence.

The Terrorist as Paranoid

The remaining personality of any significant interest to researchers is the paranoid personality disorder. DSM-III describes the paranoid as follows:

> The essential feature is a personality disorder in which there is a pervasive and unwarranted suspiciousness and mistrust of people, hypersensitivity, and restricted affectivity . . .

Individuals with this disorder are . . . viewed as hostile, stubborn and defensive. They tend to be rigid and unwilling to compromise. They often generate uneasiness and fear in others. Often there is an inordinate fear of losing independence or the power to shape events in accord with their own wishes. (DSM-III, 1980, p. 307–308)

Millon (1981) goes on to give a fuller picture of the typical paranoid:

> To assure their security, they go to great pains to avoid any weakening of their resolve and to develop new and superior powers to control others. One of their major steps in this quest is the desensitization of tender and affectionate feelings. They become hard, obdurate, immune, and insensitive to the sufferings of others . . .

> Fearful of domination, these personalities watch carefully to ensure that no one robs them of their will. Circumstances that prompt feelings of helplessness and incompetence, or decrease their freedom of movement, or place them in a vulnerable position subject to the powers of others, may precipitate a sudden and ferocious "counterattack." Feeling trapped by the dangers of dependency, struggling to regain their status and dreading deceit and betrayal, they may strike out aggressively and accuse others of seeking to persecute them.

Yet again the attraction for theorists is obvious. The paranoid's compulsion to strike at higher power seems to explain the terrorist's need to attack the incumbent state surrounding them. It certainly finds a comfortable home when considering nationalist/separatist terrorists who wish to become independent from a larger force, but paranoids are also associated with the ideologically motivated groups, take for example, Suellwold (1981) who claimed there was a high proportion of angry paranoids among the left-wing Red Army Faction.

The hostility and aggression of paranoids when they are in the weaker position, also seems to account for the violence of terrorists, who are a disempowered minority within a larger more powerful majority. Finally, the suggestion put forward by theorists such as Hassel (1977) and Turco (1987), that terrorist leaders tend to possess this personality type, finds support in the DSM-III (1980, p. 308) statement that paranoids *"avoid participation in group activities unless they are in a dominant position,"* and even stronger support from the DSM-III-R claim that *"people with this disorder may be over-represented among leaders of cults and fringe groups"* (1987, p. 338).

Hassel's (1977) suggestion that it is paranoid and/or narcissistic individuals who tend to become terrorist leaders is of interest, as the largest concurrent form of the paranoid disorder is the paranoid–narcissistic mixed personality. Millon (1981) notes that this personality type is much more prone to psychotic delusions than the more mildly dysfunctional narcissists. Millon goes on to say of the mixed variant, that "they may propose grandiose schemes for "saving the world," for solving insurmountable scientific problems, for creating new societies and so on. These schemes may be worked out in minute detail and are formulated often with sufficient logic to draw at least momentary attention and recognition from others" (Millon, 1981, p. 387).

Such a description seems to have utility in describing terrorist leaders whose stated aim is to bring about a better society (as they interpret it), and often have detailed manifestos as to how this "new order" will be achieved.

Another mixed personality of great relevance is the paranoid–antisocial mixed personality. Millon's (1981) comments on these individuals serves to highlight their significance to the discussion:

> These paranoids are characterised best by their power orientation, their mistrust and resentment of others, and by their belligerent and intimidating manner. There is a ruthless desire to triumph over others, to vindicate themselves for past wrongs by cunning revenge or callous force . . .

> Essential to these paranoids is their need to retain their independence from the malice and power of others . . . Paranoid persecutory themes are filled with dread of being forced to submit to authority, of being made soft and pliant, and to being tricked to surrender self-determination. (Millon, 1981, p. 387)

A revulsion of submitting to a higher authority, and a willingness to use "callous force" to maintain one's independence and "self-determination," seem to capture the heart of terrorist motivation and the ruthless nature of much terrorist violence.

For all of these personalities, we have seen time and again, their applied and implied connections to the terrorist. Every classification system of terrorists seems to have a place for the antisocial personality, most have roles for paranoids (especially among leaders), and roughly around half involve narcissistic personalities in some form. The reasons why theorists have returned again and again to these personalities has been described above—their relevance is self-apparent. That may be so, but does the theory correspond to the reality?

Evidence for the Cheshire-Cat Theory

It is surprising to discover, that despite the admittedly attractive theoretical reasons for linking terrorism and psychopathology, the evidence to support such coupling is neither plentiful nor of good quality.

Largely, the theorists who advocate the psychopathology model provide only anecdotal evidence to support their assertions. For example, Pearce (1977) stressed the importance of sociopathy in terrorism, but based his conclusions purely on secondary sources such as terrorist autobiographies, biographies and media interviews. In one case, Pearce made a diagnosis of psychopathy based mainly on an individual having tattoos on his torso.

Cooper (1978) adopts a similar approach to Pearce's, when he uses exposés of the career of German terrorist, Andreas Baader, to justify labelling Baader as a sociopathic personality. Another relevant case, is provided by Christopher Lasch (1979), who advocated a narcissistic personality explanation of terrorism. Again, the conclusions were based entirely on secondary sources, such as the public statements and autobiographical accounts provided by the terrorists. Lasch claimed there was sufficient evidence in these accounts to justify a diagnosis of narcissistic personality disorder.

Efforts such as Pearce (1977), Cooper (1978)

and Lasch (1979), are typical of the type of research used to support the notion of terrorist abnormality. Very few studies have attempted to provide stronger, more direct evidence, but one exception to this general trend, is work carried out by Hubbard (1978). Together with another psychiatrist, Hubbard examined 80 imprisoned terrorists in 11 countries. They found that nearly 90% of them had defective vestibular functions of the middle ear. In addition to causing poor balance and co-ordination, Hubbard claimed this impairment was linked with antisocial behaviour designed to gain attention and an inability to relate to other people. In essence, Hubbard seems to be suggesting that people had become terrorists because of an ear problem.

An unorthodox hypothesis to begin with, Hubbard's contention is weakened by concerns with the validity and reliability of his work. He never released detailed descriptions of the data he gathered or of his analysis procedures, and there have been no replications of his unusual finding.

Stronger evidence for abnormality is provided by Ferracuti and Bruno (1981). They analysed the few available case histories of individual left-wing Italian terrorists, and found that they rarely suffered from any serious personality defects. However, a similar analysis showed that among Italian "right-wing terrorists . . . disturbed, borderline, or even psychotic personalities have a much higher incidence." They went on to comment that, "*In right-wing terrorism; the individual terrorists are frequently psychopathological . . .*" and "*Even when they do not suffer from a psychopathological condition, their basic psychological traits reflect an authoritarian-extremist personality,*" which was composed of a mix of various unsavoury features (Ferracuti and Bruno, 1981, p. 209).

At first look, this result seems to be a godsend for the hard-pressed advocates of terrorist abnormality. However, the support is more ephemeral than it appears. Ferracuti and Bruno did not actually quote the figures or percentages behind their conclusions. Later, they would say that the incidence of abnormality among the right-wing terrorists was "limited" (Ferracuti and Bruno, 1983,

p. 307). Deeper examination revealed that the numbers involved were very small. True, the incidence of abnormality was higher among the right-wing terrorists than among the left-wing terrorists, (where abnormality was virtually unknown), but the numbers involved still composed just a tiny minority of the right-wing's overall membership.

Weakening the Italian's position further, was the conclusion of a similar, but more extensive West German study, which found that right-wing terrorists were no more unbalanced than their left-wing counterparts (Crenshaw, 1983, p. 386).

Terrorists in Wonderland: Evidence from Alice's Perspective

Overall then, the research supporting terrorist abnormality has been sparse and of questionable validity. In contrast, the research suggesting terrorist normality has been both more plentiful, and in general, of much greater scientific validity. On this latter point, take for example the case of Morf (1970), who failed to find any clinical evidence for the presence of narcissistic personality disorder among political terrorists, a finding in stark contrast to that of Lasch (1979). Significantly. Lasch based his conclusion solely on a study of secondary sources, whereas Morf's judgement was the result of personal interviews with the terrorists.

This is an important point—those who suggest abnormality are by and large making this inference from research on secondary sources. Rasch (1979) said this widespread habit was a scientific travesty, and that any explanation not backed by direct examination of terrorists, amounted to little more than "*idle speculation.*"

On the other hand, those who say terrorists are not abnormal tend to be those who have direct contact and experience with actual terrorists. The reality of close contact has displaced any comfortable notions of aberration that may have been harboured. They have learned that terrorism cannot be dismissed so easily. Yet, this seems to have been a remarkably slow lesson for others to learn.

Another early example of the value of direct-contact research is provided by Paine (1975), who reported that the psychiatrists who examined Koza Okamoto, the sole surviving Japanese terrorist of the Lydda airport massacre, found him to be absolutely sane and rational. In a similar vein, Wilfried Rasch has provided some excellent research dealing with German terrorists, and his 1979 paper is perhaps the most cited article in the debate on terrorist abnormality.

A psychiatry professor in Berlin, Rasch examined 11 captured terrorists, including the infamous Baader, Meinhof, Ensslin and Raspe. After extensive examination, Rasch wrote "nothing was found which could justify their classification as psychotics, neurotics, fanatics or psychopaths." Such a conclusion entirely contradicts Cooper's (1977) claim that Baader was a sociopath. Rasch also noted that the terrorists could not be diagnosed as "paranoid," and he mentions that this was particularly true in the case of Baader, and the other three already mentioned, which is notable as these individuals went on to commit suicide while in prison. Rasch's examination of 40 other suspected terrorists, also showed no sign of psychological disturbances.

Rasch's findings were supported by the work of Ferracuti and Bruno (1983) who in their study on captured terrorists could not find a "psychiatric explanation" for why these people were engaged in terrorism. Further work by Ken Heskin in Northern Ireland had similar results, concluding that IRA members could not be diagnosed as psychopathic or mentally abnormal (Heskin, 1980, 1984, 1994).

Continuing on this theme, Lyons and Harbinson (1986) provide even more compelling evidence. Taking their sample from the Northern Ireland prison population, they compared terrorist murderers with non-political murderers. They found that the politically motivated killers were generally more stable, showed a lower incidence of mental illness, and came from more stable family backgrounds than their non-political counterparts.

This work gains in significance when one realises the bias which existed in the sample. While representative of the non-political murderers, the sample was skewed for the political murderers. In Northern Ireland, murderers are routinely sent for psychiatric assessment, *unless* the killers are terrorists. Consequently, the vast majority of terrorists are never psychiatrically assessed. The only ones included in Lyons and Harbinson's study are those terrorists whose behaviour in custody was so abnormal that the authorities felt motivated to have them assessed. The majority of '*normal*' terrorists were thus never included. Even so, the '*abnormal*' terrorists still emerged as more normal and more mentally stable than the average non-political murderer.

The study found that 16% of the terrorists were mentally ill, but the researchers noted that this 16% was composed mainly of individuals "*who seemed to be operating on the fringe of a para-military organization and who were devoid of discipline. They killed in a most sadistic way while heavily intoxicated. This small group was by no means typical of the rest and raised the figures for those [political murderers] under the influence of alcohol. It included three who used a knife, which is a very rare method of political killing*" (Lyons and Harbinson, 1986, p. 197).

Even so, an incidence among this sub-group of only 16% is incredibly low, especially when compared with an incidence of 58% among the non-political offenders. The actual figure for terrorists on a whole is almost certainly far less than 16% but clarification of this point must wait until the authorities are prepared to allow random sampling of the terrorist population.

It is important to remember that the above research isn't saying that mentally unbalanced or pathological personalities are never present in terrorist organisations. On the contrary, both Rasch (1979) and Lyons and Harbinson (1986) did find such individuals in their samples. However, these individuals were a rarity, being the exception rather than the rule, a finding supported by Ferracuti and Bruno's (1981) survey. Further, the research also indicated that when they do appear, such personalities tend to be fringe members of the terrorist group, rather than central characters.

The Cheshire-Cat Returns: A New Interpretation of Terrorist Abnormality

Even with the best empirical studies rejecting the idea that terrorists are clinically abnormal, theorists are nevertheless still prone to the prevailing trend of believing terrorists possess many of the traits of pathological personalities (Bollinger, 1982; Ferracuti, 1983; Post, 1990). The current predilection seems to be one of placing terrorists in a twilight region bordering on pathology.

Take for example, Post (1987b) who seemed to accept the thrust of the empirical findings when he said "*most terrorists would be considered to fit within the spectrum of normality*," and even commented later that his own "*comparative research on the psychology of terrorists does not reveal major psychopathology*" (Post, 1990). So while on the one hand freely acknowledging the lack of "major" psychopathology, Post and many others have then been quick to switch the search towards finding some form of *minor* psychopathology. Note how Schmid and Jongman (1988) perceive this trend:

> Some authors see little prospect in the search for the terrorist personality and question whether a profile analogous to the "authoritarian personality" is possible at all. Walter Laqueur, for instance, holds that the search for a "terrorist personality" is a fruitless one, but a few pages earlier he notes that "Terrorists are fanatics and fanaticism frequently makes for cruelty and sadism." Paul Wilkinson is also ambiguous. On the one hand, he maintains that "We already know enough about terrorist behaviour to discount the crude hypothesis of a 'terrorist personality' or 'phenotype',," but at the same time he admits that "I do not believe we really understand much about the inner motivations of those who readily enunciated terrorist techniques."

Post (1987b) is more certain that some form of abnormality exists, and he confidently states his belief that "*individuals with particular personality dispositions are drawn to the path of terrorism*."

Such "dispositions" as described by Post, are largely variants of the three major personality types already discussed. For example, Shaw (1986) notes

that a narcissistic injury is commonly seen as a central feature of the terrorist's psychology, and he cites Kozo Okamoto as an example of such an individual. Yet, earlier we read how Okamoto had been found to be absolutely sane and rational by the team of psychiatrists who assessed him!

Terrorists are ascribed many pathological characteristics, yet in the new approach they somehow manage to avoid the actual diagnosis. Such fine distinctions are the hallmark of this entire trend. Consider the following from Post (1987b, p. 24):

> Without *being frankly paranoid*, there is an overreliance on the ego defence of projection. . . . Bollinger (1982) found psychological dynamics *resembling* those found in narcissistic borderlines . . . The terrorists he interviewed demonstrated a feature *characteristic* of individuals with narcissistic and borderline personalities—splitting, [italics mine]

In effect, Post is dancing around the psychopathology issue. Aware that terrorists cannot be clinically diagnosed, he has gone around this obstacle, and relentlessly ascribes to them many of the characteristics associated with such diagnoses. He does, however, appear aware of the weakness of such speculation. As he comments himself:

> It is not my intent to suggest that all terrorists suffer from borderline or narcissistic personality disorders or that the psychological mechanisms [related to such disorders] . . . are used by every terrorist. It is my distinct impression, however, that these mechanisms are found with extremely high frequency in the population of terrorists, and contribute significantly to the uniformity of terrorists' rhetorical style and their special psychologic. (Post, 1990, pp. 27–28)

However, Post is somewhat overstating the issue when he talks about an "extremely high frequency." In discussions of the personality flaws and life-style problems of terrorists, the figures involved rarely go higher than 33% of the populations considered. A large series of studies on 250 West German terrorists (Jager, Schmidtchen and Suellwold, 1981; von Baeyer-Kaette *et al.*, 1982), supplies much of the hard data behind this line of speculation. These studies revealed, among other things, that 25% of left-wing terrorists had lost one or both parents by age 14, that 33% reported severe conflict with parents, and that 33% had been convicted in juvenile court. Facts like this encouraged the German researchers to view terrorists as *"advancement orientated and failure prone."* Further, other researchers used this German work to form the basis of their contention that terrorists are *"marginal, isolated, and inadequate individuals from troubled families"* (Post, 1986, p. 211).

While of interest and suggestive, it is unwise to read too much into these figures. For a start, the statistics rarely composed a majority of the terrorist population. It would be one thing if 92% had lost a parent before 14, but 33% is of uncertain significance. It still leaves 67% with both parents, but who nevertheless went on to become terrorists. More important are the methodological flaws in this research, and in particular the lack of valid control groups in virtually all of the studies.

One exception is provided by Ferracuti (1983), who carried out a similar study to the above West German one, but used politically active youths as controls. Vitally, he found that the life patterns and backgrounds of the terrorists and the non-terrorists showed no significant differences. This finding is of considerable importance. If there is no meaningful difference with controls, it brings into question the whole validity of the line of reasoning adopted by Post and the others. Or at least it would, except that Ferracuti also reported that there existed some personality flaws in the terrorists which supported some of Post's earlier hypotheses.

Stronger evidence for those attempting to find some aberration in the psychology or upbringing of the terrorist, is provided by a suggestive piece of work looking at the membership of ETA. Clark (1983) found that although Basques with mixed parents (one Spanish–one Basque) form only 8% of the total Basque population, 40% of ETA is composed of such individuals. This intriguing finding has been a rich source of speculation for those looking for an aberration explanation of terrorists, but it is an isolated result. While it is possible to find some supporting anecdotal cases dealing with mixed parentage in other terrorist groups, there are no other large-scale studies with similar findings.

With Clark's study standing alone, and Ferracuti's controls having very similar backgrounds to the terrorists, all that's really left are the borderline characteristics which have received so much attention. However, such a focus must ultimately be unfair to the terrorists. Quite simply, the best of the empirical work does not suggest, and never has suggested, that such a borderline diagnoses is warranted. As Crenshaw (1981) notes, "what limited data we have on individual terrorists . . . suggest that the outstanding common characteristic of terrorists is their normality."

Speculation of the type offered by Post (1990) and others, including some like Ferracuti (1983) who supply mixed results, amounts to the second major attempt to set terrorists psychologically apart from the rest of the population. The first attempt in the 1970s was more direct, and because of its directness its tenets were easily tested, and the concept was refuted. This second wave, however, is more insidious. Its tenets are more subtle and less tangible, and it does not leave itself open to such direct testing. As such it is dangerously misleading. It encourages the notion that terrorists are in some respects psychologically abnormal, but it balks at going so far as to advocate clinical personalities. In the end, the trend has done little except taint terrorism with a pathology aura.

Conclusion

The issue of terrorist psychology is one of vital importance. Ultimately, the individuals involved in terrorism require a more complex response from society than simply a quest for their apprehension. Sooner or later, terrorists have to be dealt with in a different milieu, such as prisoners serving long sentences or as political opponents seated across a negotiating table. Believing distorted and deceptive characterisations must lead inevitably to flawed policies and bleak outcomes. Campaigns of violence are needlessly prolonged, property is wastefully destroyed and people are unnecessarily maimed and killed. This then, is why it so important to be concerned with any unfounded biases academic commentators and researchers may be harbouring in their considerations of terrorists.

Unfortunately, theorists have left the psychology of the individual corrupted in their wake. Blatant abnormality is rejected by most commentators, (though as we have seen, there is a steady stream of speculators who return to this notion). Instead, a pervasive perception exists that terrorists are abnormal *in more subtle ways.* We cannot believe normal people could commit terrorist acts, so we look for abnormality. As efforts to find gross abnormality fail again and again, attention has been turned to more subtle shades of aberration, in a seemingly never-ending effort to realise latent preconceptions.

The situation today is somewhat similar to that of the 1970s when the possibility that terrorists could be clinically abnormal was taken seriously. Eventually, empirical work, published in the late 70s and early 80s, largely—but not entirely—put paid to that extreme view. Now we must await the empirical research that can adequately assess the truth of the modern refined version of those original claims. However, with the research focus now firmly shifted to group psychology, a final rebuttal may be a long time in the coming.

The Cheshire-Cat theory of terrorists does not hold up to close scrutiny. While the attraction to view terrorists as being abnormal is understandable, for now, the evidence allows only one conclusion: terrorists are normal people. Without doubt, while the individual actors may be generally normal, the activity itself most certainly is not. This is the heart of the whole Alice in Wonderland argument, that normal people can do abnormal things.

Those who are content to adopt a Cheshire-Cat perception of terrorists, would do well to remember Alice's reaction to the grinning feline. To her credit, Alice was not convinced by the cat's reasoning and came up with her own theory to explain her predicament. Her answering logic was that she was *still* a normal, rational person, but that she was trapped in a very abnormal, bizarre place (i.e. Wonderland). As far as the Cat was concerned, simply being in Wonderland was enough to guarantee that an individual was mad, but Alice knew

better. It did not guarantee abnormality. It only guaranteed that others would prefer to see you as abnormal.

REFERENCES

American Psychiatric Association, (1980). *Diagnostic and statistical manual of mental disorders* (3rd edition), Washington, D.C.: American Psychiatric Association.

American Psychiatric Association, (1987). *Diagnostic and statistical manual of mental disorders* (3rd edition, revised), Washington, D.C.: American Psychiatric Association.

Bollinger, L. (1982). Analysen zum terrorismus 3: Gruppenprozesse. Cited in Post, J. M. (1987).

Carroll, L. (1865/1971). "Alice's Adventures in Wonderland." In D. J. Gray (Ed.), *Alice in Wonderland*, London: Norton.

Clark, R. P. (1983). Patterns in the lives of ETA members. *Terrorism*, **6**, 423–454.

Cooper, H. H. A. (1977). What is a terrorist: A psychological perspective. *Legal Medical Quarterly*, **1**, 16–32.

Cooper, H. H. A. (1978). Psychopath as terrorist. *Legal Medical Quarterly*, **2**, 253–262.

Corrado, R. R. (1981). A critique of the mental disorder perspective of political terrorism. *International Journal of Law and Psychiatry*, **4**, 293–309.

Crenshaw, M. (1981). The causes of terrorism. *Comparative Politics*, **13**, 379–399.

Crenshaw, M. (1983). The psychology of political terrorism. In M. G. Hermann (Ed.), *Political Psychology: Contemporary Problems and Issues*, London: Jossey-Bass.

Crenshaw, M. (1990). The logic of terrorism: terrorist behavior as a product of strategic choice. In W. Reich (Ed.), *Origins of Terrorism*, Cambridge: Woodrow Wilson Center.

Crenshaw, M. (1992). How terrorists think: what psychology can contribute to understanding terrorism. In L. Howard (Ed.), *Terrorism: Roots, Impact, Responses* (pp. 71–80), London: Praeger.

Dworetzky, J. P. (1988). *Psychology* (3rd Edition), St. Paul: West Publishing.

Eisen, S. V. (1979). Actor–observer differences in information inferences and causal attribution. *Journal of Personality and Social Psychology*, **37**, 261–272.

Ferracuti, F. (1983). Psychiatric aspects of Italian left wing and right wing terrorists. Paper presented to *VIIth World Congress of Psychiatry*, Vienna, Austria, July, 1983.

Ferracuti, F. and Bruno, F. (1981). Psychiatric aspects of terrorism in Italy. In I. L. Barak-Glantz and C. R. Huff (Eds.), *The Mad, the Bad and the Different: Essays in Honor of Simon Dinitz* (pp. 199–213), Lexington, Mass: Heath.

Ferracuti, F. and Bruno, F. (1983). Italy: a systems perspective. In A. P. Goldstein and M. H. Segall (Eds.), *Aggression in Global Perspective* (pp. 285–312), New York: Pergamon.

Friedland, N. (1992). Becoming a terrorist: social and individual antecedents. In L. Howard (Ed.), *Terrorism: Roots, Impact, Responses* (pp. 81–93), London: Praeger.

Hare, R. D. (1996). Psychopathy: theory, research, and implications for society. In D. J. Cooke, A. E. Forth, J. Newman, and R. D. Hare (Eds.), *International Perspectives on Psychopathy* (pp. 4–5), Leicester: The British Psychological Society.

Hassel, C. (1977). Terror: The crime of the privileged—an examination and prognosis. *Terrorism: An International Journal*, **1**, 1–16.

Heskin, K. (1980). *Northern Ireland: A Psychological Analysis*, Dublin: Gill and Macmillan.

Heskin, K. (1984). The psychology of terrorism in Northern Ireland. In Y. Alexander and A. O'Day (Eds.), *Terrorism in Ireland* (pp. 88–105), Beckenham, Kent: Croom Helm.

Heskin, K. (1994). Terrorism in Ireland: The past and the future. *The Irish Journal of Psychology*, **15**, 469–479.

Hodgins, S. (1995). Major mental disorder and crime: An overview. *Psychology, Crime and Law*, **2**, 5–18.

Hubbard, D. (1978). Terrorism and protest. *Legal Medical Quarterly*, **2**, 188–197.

Jager, H., Schmidtchen, G. and Suellwold, L. (Eds.) (1981). *Analysen Zum Terrorisms 2: Lebenslauf-Analysen*, Darmstadt: Deutscher Verlag.

Johnson, P. W. and Feldmann, T. B. (1992). Personality types and terrorism: Self-psychology perspectives. *Forensic Reports*, **5**, 293–303.

Laqueur, W. (1977). *Terrorism*, London: Weidefeld and Nicolson.

Lasch, C. (1979). *The Culture of Narcissism*, New York: W.W. Norton.

Lyons, H. A. and Harbinson, H. J. (1986). A comparison of political and non-political murderers in Northern Ireland, 1974–84. *Medicine. Science and the Law*, **26**, 193–198.

Millon, T. (1981). *Disorders of Personality: DSM-III: Axis II*, Chichester: John Wiley and Sons.

Morf, G. (1970). *Terror in Quebec—Case Studies of the F.L.Q.*, Toronto: Clark, Irwin.

Paine, L. (1975). *The Terrorists*, London: Robert Hale.

Pearce, K. I. (1977). Police negotiations. *Canadian Psychiatric Association Journal*, **22**, 171–174.

Pearlstein, R. M. (1991). *The Mind of the Political Terrorist*, Wilmington: Scholarly Resources.

Post, J. M. (1987a). Group and organisational dynamics of political terrorism: implications for counterterrorist policy. In P. Wilkinson and A. M. Stewart (Eds.), *Contemporary Research on Terrorism*, Aberdeen: Aberdeen University Press.

Post, J. M. (1987b). Rewarding fire with fire: effects of retaliation on terrorist group dynamics. *Terrorism*, **10**, 23–35.

Post, J. M. (1990). Terrorist psycho-logic: Terrorist behaviour as a product of psychological forces. In W. Reich (Ed.), *Origins of Terrorism: Psychologies, Ideologies, States of Mind*, New York: Cambridge University Press.

Quattrone, G. A. (1982). Overattribution and unit formation: When behaviour engulfs the person. *Journal of Personality and Social Psychology*, **36**, 247–256.

Raine, A. (1993). *The Psychopathology of Crime*, London: Academic Press.

Rasch, W. (1979). Psychological dimensions of political terrorism in the Federal Republic of Germany. *International Journal of Law and Psychiatry*, **2**, 79–85.

Rosenhan, D. L. (1973). On being sane in insane places. *Science*, **179**, 250–258.

Schmid, A. P. and Jongman, A. J. (1988). *Political Terrorism* (2nd Edition), Oxford: North-Holland Publishing Company.

Shafritz, J. M., Gibbons, E. F. Jr. and Scott, G. E. J. (1991). *Almanac of Modern Terrorism*, Oxford: Facts on File.

Shaw, E. D. (1986). Political terrorists: dangers of diagnosis and an alternative to the psychopathology model. *International Journal of Law and Psychiatry*, **8**, 359–368.

Silke, A. P. (1996). Terrorism and the blind men's elephant. *Terrorism and Political Violence*, **8**, 12–28.

Suellwold, L. (1981). Cited in J. M. Post (1987b). Rewarding fire with fire: effects of retaliation on terrorist group dynamics. *Terrorism*, **10**, p. 24.

Taylor, M. and Quayle, E. (1994). *Terrorist Lives*, London: Brassey's.

Turco, R. M. (1987). Psychiatric contributions to the understanding of international terrorism. *International Journal of Offender Therapy and Comparative Criminology*, **31**, 153–161.

von Baeyer-Kaette, W., Classens, D., Feger, H. and Neidhardt, F. (1982). Cited in J. M. Post (1990), Terrorist psycho-logic: Terrorist behaviour as a product of psychological forces. In W. Reich (Ed.), *Origins of Terrorism: Psychologies, Ideologies, States of Mind*, New York: Cambridge University Press, p. 28.

Wilkinson, P. (1977). *Terrorism and the Liberal State*, London: Macmillan.

READING 6

The Terrorists in Their Own Words: Interviews with 35 Incarcerated Middle Eastern Terrorists *

Jerrold M. Post, Ehud Sprinzak, and Laurita M. Denny

Using semi-structured interviews, 35 incarcerated Middle Eastern terrorists have been interviewed – 21 Islamic terrorists representing Hamas (and its armed wing Izz a-Din al Qassam), Islamic Jihad, and Hizballah, and 14 secular terrorists from Fatah and its military wing, PFLP and DFLP. The purpose of the research was to understand their psychology and decision-making in general, and with special reference to their propensity towards weapons of mass destruction.

This note is drawn from remarks presented at a memorial service for Ehud Sprinzak at Georgetown University on 2 November 2002:

I have been a close friend and collaborator with Ehud Sprinzak for more than 20 years. In our last luncheon together at Georgetown in August, we spoke together with excitement of future collaborations. What drew us together from the beginning was our common fascination with the mind of the extremist. Ehud had a remarkable capacity to engage with extremists from the far left – his doctoral dissertation was on the Weathermen – to the

extreme right – his award-winning study of the ascension of the radical right in Israel. There was a special vitality and solidity about Ehud that was compelling. One can't really pursue understanding the psychology of others without being quite comfortable with oneself, and Ehud was. In pursuing his fascination with what makes terrorists and extremists tick, he had this elegantly simple notion, that the best way to find out what leads people along the path of extremism, what leads people to be willing to kill in the name of their cause, is – to ask them!

Indeed, that was the central premise of our grant proposal to the Smith-Richardson Foundation which sponsored our project interviewing incarcerated Middle-East terrorists. The best way

* This research was conducted with the support of the Smith-Richardson Foundation.

to find out the interest of terrorists in using weapons of mass destruction was to ask them, and this we did, with the fascinating results reported below.

The findings are quite remarkable. Preliminary research suggested that the type posing greatest danger are religious fundamentalist terrorists, a population to which the Israeli team had ready access. The material elicited from the terrorists who were interviewed vastly exceeded our expectations. It provides rich contextual detail on their individual pathways into terrorism and the power of the group, the commitment to armed struggle, and the spectrum of rationalizations and justifications for their acts of terror. To provide a sense of the qualitative flavor of the interviews, excerpts have been included in this article.

Somewhat counter-intuitive, the backgrounds of the interview subjects varied widely and did not materially influence their decision as to whether to join the group. The boyhood heroes for the Islamist terrorists were religious figures, such as the Prophet, or the radical Wahabi Islamist, Abdullah Azzam; for the secular terrorists, revolutionary heroes such as Che Guevara or Fidel Castro were identified. Most had some high school, and some had education beyond high school. The majority of the subjects reported that their families were respected in the community. The families were experienced as being uniformly supportive of their commitment to the cause.

Clearly families that are politically active socialized their sons to the movement at an early age and were supportive of their involvement. However, families that were not politically active did not appear to dissuade active involvement by their children. The vast majority of both secular and Islamist group members reported that there were no other family members in the organization when they joined (70 per cent secular and 80 per cent Islamist) although several reported that younger brothers followed them. In most cases where a family member (father, older sibling) was already a member of an organization, the sons were more likely to join that same organization, and were more often members of the more

militant, or armed, wing. This was true of any group regardless of ideological affiliation. In a few cases, sons did not follow the path of an older sibling, however when this occurred, the younger sibling invariably joined a more radical group.

When looking at family activism, including support in the home for the struggle, we found that the vast majority of secular group members (almost 85 per cent) reported that their family was active at an average or below average level. Some 68 per cent of Islamist group members reported a similar experience. However, over 30 per cent of Islamist group members reported extensive or radical involvement by their family. Of those Islamist group members reporting a radical family background, all joined the militant armed wing of their respective organizations. In the secular groups, only 15 per cent report coming from radically active families and there is no correlation between radical family involvement and members joining the mainstream or militant wing of their organizations.

But it was clear that the major influence was the social environment of the youth. As one terrorist remarked, 'Everyone was joining'. Individuals from strictly religious Islamic backgrounds were more likely to join Islamist groups, while those who did not have a religious background might join either a secular or a religious group. The peer group was of much greater influence, and in many cases it was a friend or acquaintance in the group who recruited the subject. For the secular groups their social environment centered around school and social clubs, while for the Islamist group members, their social environment was dominated by the mosque, religious organizations and religious instruction.

Some 64 per cent of the secular group members, while only 43 per cent of the Islamist group members, report that the group they joined was the most active in their community. Over 50 per cent of the secular group members cite the involvement of their community or a youth club, such as Shabiba, as the primary influence in their recruitment. For the Islamist groups, almost 50 per cent cite the Mosque, Moslem Brotherhood or other religious influence as central, another 20 per cent cite their experience at the University or other professional school as of primary importance.

Only 30 per cent of the secular group members and not quite 20 per cent of Islamist group members report their families as a central influence in their decision to join an organization. Although introduction to 'the cause' varies among the interview subjects, almost all subjects report growing up in villages or refugee camps that were extremely active in the struggle. Over 80 per cent of the secular group members reported growing up in communities that were radically involved and slightly more than 75 per cent of the Islamist members report a similar experience. Less than 10 per cent of each group reports coming from communities that were not particularly active in the struggle.

The recruitment process is predominantly a casual or informal process among both secular and Islamist groups with only 15 per cent of secular group members reporting a formal recruitment process and 30 per cent of Islamist members reporting a similar experience. For the vast majority of those citing a formal recruitment process, the process involved either a formal swearing of allegiance or probationary period. Two Hizballah members reported the most formalized recruitment process of any of the interviewees involving multiple interviews with observers behind a mirrored window.

Over half the members of each group type knew their recruiter prior to recruitment. For some this was a family member, and for others someone from the community they knew casually. Another small percentage reported that their recruiter was introduced to them through a third party. 23 per cent of the secular and 16 per cent of the Islamist group members reported not knowing their recruiter before being approached about membership.

Two Islamist group members reported that they were confronted with information that they were collaborators and were given the option by their unknown recruiters to join the organization or be exposed. This however was the rare exception. A few members with active siblings or family members reported no recruitment process, their membership was a given within the family, the community and the organization.

At the time the interviews were conducted (before the collapse of the Camp David II talks and the resumption of the *intifada*), the secular terrorists, who sought a political solution, were turning away from violence as no longer necessary. This is almost certainly no longer the case. The secular terrorists did distinguish to some degree between legitimate military and government targets, and civilians, while the Islamists made no such distinction because Israelis all occupied Islamic territory.

Surprisingly, there was little attention to obtaining WMD weapons, but a desire to produce the largest number of casualties possible was evident, which they thought that conventional weapons could produce. If directed to use WMD weapons, they would not object, although several Islamist terrorists noted that the Koran proscribed the use of poisons. The two groups had different ultimate objectives. The secular terrorists sought an independent state, but the Islamists sought eradication of Israel in order to bring about the establishment of an Islamic state.

Both groups discussed the necessity of armed attacks. The Islamist terrorists believed that self-martyrdom ('suicide bombing') was the most valued technique of jihad, distinguishing this from suicide, which is proscribed in the Koran. Several Islamist terrorist commanders interviewed called the 'suicide bomber' holy warriors carrying out the highest level of jihad.

The prison experience was intense, especially for the Islamist terrorists. It further consolidated their identity and the group or organizational membership that provided the most valued element of personal identity. The impact of the prison experience showed more divergence between the secular and Islamist groups. While the incarcerated members felt that their prison experience brought them closer to the group they learned more about the group and were more committed to the cause following their incarceration. The percentage of Islamist group members describing this experience was much higher (77 per cent) than that of the secular groups (54 per cent).

Only a small percentage of either group stated

that they were less connected to the group after their incarceration. Of the interviewees 31 per cent of the secular group members and 29 per cent of the Islamist group members had served multiple prison sentences. While still loyal to the group, only 62 per cent of secular group members reported returning to activity with their organization, compared to 84 per cent of the Islamist group members who returned or plan to return upon their release. Some 75 per cent of the Islamist group members interviewed are still incarcerated, including three Izz a-Din al-Qassam members who are serving life (or multiple life) terms.

The prison experience also reinforced negative perceptions of Israelis and Israeli security forces. Most had never had any contact with Israelis before becoming terrorists. No regret was expressed by any of the terrorists for their actions; the majority expressed intense pride in their acts, and only regretted getting caught. For the secular terrorists, their acts were justified because they were at war. For the Islamist terrorists, their acts were in defense of their faith and commanded by their faith, and they received religious absolution for their acts.

Concerning the group dynamics of decision-making, both group types indicated that they were free to question operational details. It became clear they could question details, but not whether or not the authorized act should be carried out. The Islamic terrorists were less tolerant of dissent, but they were freer to act at a lower cell level, whereas the secular groups tended to be more hierarchical. Most striking in both cases was the fusion of the individual with the group.

The feelings of victimization, of being evicted from their family lands, and the sense of despair concerning their people's destiny referred to in the family background section contributed to the readiness to merge their individual identity with that of the organization in pursuit of their cause. Once recruited, there is a clear fusing of individual identity and group identity, particularly among the more radical elements of each organization.

There is a heightened sense of the heroic associated with fallen group members as the community supports and rallies around families of the dead or incarcerated members. Most interviewees reported not only enhanced social status for the families of fallen or incarcerated members, but financial and material support from the organization and community for these families as well. 'Success' within the community is defined as fighting for 'the cause' – liberation and religious freedom are the values that define success, not necessarily academic or economic accomplishment. As the young men adopt this view of success, their own self-image then becomes more intimately intertwined with the success of the organization. With no other means to achieve status and success, the organization's success become central to individual identity and provides a 'reason for living'.

As an individual succumbs to the organization, there is no room for individual ideas, individual identity and individual decision-making. As this occurs, individual measures of success become increasingly linked to the organization and stature and accomplishments within the organization. Individual self-worth is again intimately tied to the 'value' or prominence of the group – therefore each individual has a vested interest in ensuring not only the success of the organization, but to increase its prominence and exposure. The more prominent and more important (and often times the more violent) a group is, the greater the prestige that is then projected onto group members. This creates a cycle where group members have a direct need to increase the power and prestige of the group through increasingly dramatic and violent operations.

As the individual and group fuse, the more personal the struggle becomes for the group members. Regardless of group affiliation, interview subjects paint a similar picture of this personalization. Subjects were unable to distinguish between personal goals and those of the organization. In their discussion of group action, the success or failure of the group's action was personal – if the group succeeded, then as an individual they succeeded; if the group failed, they failed. Pride and shame as expressed by the individual were reflections of group actions, not individual actions, feelings or experiences.

An overarching sense of the collective consumes

the individual. This fusion with the group seems to provide the necessary justification for their actions with an attendant loss of felt responsibility for the individual member – if the group says it is required and justified, then it is required and justified. If the authority figure orders an action, then the action is justified. Guilt or remorse by the individual is not tolerated because the organization does not express it. Again this is intensified among Islamist groups who feel they have a religiously sanctioned justification – indeed obligation – for their actions.

The statements of individual members echoed, in some cases verbatim, the public rhetoric of the respective groups. As a member of a secular or Islamist group, individuals are able to establish their identity within a framework valued by their social community – the group provides others of a like mind with whom the individual has a common bond of belief. The need of individuals to control their own lives is paramount, but it is intensified in communities where segments are ostracized or persecuted. By belonging to a radical group, otherwise powerless individuals become powerful.

Socialization and Recruitment

Somewhat counter-intuitive, the backgrounds of the interview subjects varied widely and did not materially influence decisions as to whether to join the group. For both groups, joining the terrorist group seemed only natural. In effect, everyone was joining. Some from religious families joined a secular group, and vice versa, although a common pattern was the importance of those who recruited and sensitized the audience to the path of terrorism.

Islamist

I came from a religious family which used to observe all the Islamic traditions my initial political awareness came during the prayers at the mosque. That's where I was also asked to join religious classes. In the context of these studies, the sheik used to inject some historical background in which he would tell us how we were effectively evicted from Palestine.

The sheik also used to explain to us the significance of the fact that there was an IDF military outpost in the heart of the camp. He compared it to a cancer in the human body, which was threatening its very existence.

At the age of 16 I developed an interest in religion. I was exposed to the Moslem Brotherhood and I began to pray in a mosque and to study Islam. The Koran and my religious studies were the tools that shaped my political consciousness. The mosque and the religious clerics in my village provided the focal point of my social life.

Community support was important to the families of the fighters as well:

Families of terrorists who were wounded, killed or captured enjoyed a great deal of economic aid and attention. And that strengthened popular support for the attacks.

Perpetrators of armed attacks were seen as heroes, their families got a great deal of material assistance, including the construction of new homes to replace those destroyed by the Israeli authorities as punishment for terrorist acts.

The entire family did all it could for the Palestinian people, and won great respect for doing so. All my brothers are in jail, one is serving a life sentence for his activities in the Izz a-Din al-Qassam battalions. My brothers all went to school and most are university graduates.

The Emir blesses all actions.

Major actions become the subject of sermons in the mosque, glorifying the attack and the attackers.

Joining Hamas or Fatah increased social standing.

Recruits were treated with great respect a youngster who belonged to Hamas or Fatah was regarded more highly than one who didn't belong to a group, and got better treatment than unaffiliated kids.

Anyone who didn't enlist during that period (*intifada*) would have been ostracized.

The hatred towards Israelis was remarkable, especially given that few reported any contact with Israelis.

You Israelis are Nazis in your souls and in your

conduct. In your occupation you never distinguish between men and women, or between old people and children. You adopted methods of collective punishment, you uprooted people from their homeland and from their homes and chased them into exile. You fired live ammunition at women and children. You smashed the skulls of defenseless civilians. You set up detention camps for thousands of people in sub-human conditions. You destroyed homes and turned children into orphans. You prevented people from making a living, you stole their property, you trampled on their honor. Given that kind of conduct, there is no choice but to strike at you without mercy in every possible way.

Decision-Making and Military Hierarchy

There is a clear hierarchical structure, with orders passed on down to unquestioning members of the organization. The leaders made the key decisions:

And the rank and file were ready to follow through fire and water. I was subordinate to just one person. my relations with him were good, as long as I agreed to all that was asked of me. It was an organization with a very clear hierarchy, and it was clear to me that I was at the bottom of the ladder and that I had to do whatever I was told.

Commanders in the Hamas are commanders in every way. A commander's orders are absolutely binding and must not be questioned in substance.

View of Armed Attacks

Armed attacks are viewed as essential to the operation of the organization. There is no question about the necessity of these types of attacks to the success of the cause.

You have to understand that armed attacks are an integral part of the organization's struggle against the Zionist occupier. There is no other way to redeem the land of Palestine and expel the occupier. Our goals can only be achieved through force, but force is the means, not the end. history

shows that without force it will be impossible to achieve independence. Those who carry out the attacks are doing Allah's work . . .

The more an attack hurts the enemy, the more important it is. That is the measure. The mass killings, especially the martyrdom operations, were the biggest threat to the Israeli public and so most effort was devoted to these. The extent of the damage and the number of casualties are of primary importance.

The Justification of 'Suicide Bombings'

The Islamist terrorists articulated a religious basis for what the West has called 'suicide terrorism' as the most valued technique of jihad. One in fact became quite angry when the term was used in our question, angrily exclaiming:

This is not suicide. Suicide is selfish, it is weak, it is mentally disturbed. This is *istishad* (martyrdom or self sacrifice in the service of Allah.)

Several Islamist terrorist commanders interviewed called the 'suicide bomber' holy warriors carrying out the highest level of jihad:

A martyrdom operation is the highest level of jihad, and highlights the depth of our faith the bombers are holy fighters who carry out one of the more important articles of faith.[1]

It is attacks when a member gives his life that earn the most respect and elevate the bombers to the highest possible level of martyrdom.

I am not a murderer. A murderer is someone with a psychological problem; armed actions have a goal even if civilians are killed, it is not because we like it or are bloodthirsty. It is a fact of life in a people's struggle the group doesn't do it because it wants to kill civilians, but because the jihad must go on.

Quote from prisoner sentenced to 26 life terms for role in several suicide-bombing campaigns:

I asked Halil what it was all about and he told me that he had been on the wanted list for a long time and did not want to get caught without realizing his dream of being a martyrdom operation bomber. He was completely calm and explained to the other two bombers, Yusuf and Beshar, how to detonate the bombs, exactly the way he had explained things to the bombers in the Mahane Yehuda attack. I remember that besides the tremendous respect I had for Halil and the fact that I was jealous of him, I also felt slighted that he had not asked me to be the third martyrdom operation bomber. I understood that my role in the movement had not come to an end and the fact that I was not on the wanted list and could operate relatively freely could be very advantageous to the movement in the future.

Attitudes Toward Casualties and Weapons of Mass Destruction (WMD)

There was surprisingly little attention to obtaining WMD weapons. But it was asserted, there was no need, conventional weapons could cause such mass casualties. Many opined they were doing fine with conventional terrorism:

'Just give me a Kalishnikov'.

Another stated he did very well and will continue to do well with the weapons we had. Although they had not thought about them, they in general had few objections, indeed saw some advantages. One stated that he:

Personally I made do with a pistol. But I would like the organization to have arms that could wipe out a village or a neighborhood. Atomic and chemical weapons, and things like that, though, frighten me, and I would worry about their impact and consequences of using them.

Izz a-Din al-Qassam (the military wing of Hamas) members are overwhelmingly in favor of the use of weapons of mass destruction. One stated that they *would not hesitate to use them*.

The overwhelming view was that they would like the organization to have any kind of weaponry

That is necessary to defeat the enemy and to liberate our lands and can inflict damage to the enemy.

For Islamic Jihad members, not only was there no interest expressed in obtaining weapons of mass

destruction, but subject raised concerns regarding the use of such weapons being contravened by the Koran.

As for the question of weapons of mass destruction or nonconventional weapons, the question never arose. All I wanted was a pistol. But we did discuss the subject once. Islam wants to liberate, not kill. Under Islamic law, mass destruction is forbidden. For example, chemical, biological or atomic weapons damage the land and living things, including animals and plants, which are God's creations. Poisoning wells or rivers is forbidden under Islam.

Sense of Remorse/Moral Red Lines

When it came to moral considerations, we believed in the justice of our cause and in our leaders . . . I don't recall ever being troubled by moral questions.

The organization had no red lines or moral constraints in actions against Jews. Any killing of a Jew was considered a success, and the more the better.

The lack of remorse or moral considerations was particularly striking in the military wing of Hamas, Izz a-Din al Qassam. There is a deep sense of righteousness in their discussion of their actions and the legitimacy of action undertaken by the action in the fight for their cause. There is also a sense that the actions of the Israeli Security Forces provide justification for any action they might take. The language becomes more forceful in this section as the Israelis are referred to as 'the enemy' and 'foreign occupiers' – the Israelis are depicted as 'them', not as people living within the same community.

The organization has no moral red lines. We must do everything to force the enemy to retreat from out lands. Nothing is illegitimate in achieving this.

As for the organization's moral red lines, there were none. We considered every attack on the occupier legitimate. The more you hurt the enemy, the more he understands.

In a Jihad, there are no red lines.

Secular Groups

Family Background and Early Life

As with most other Palestinian terrorist organizations, there is a dichotomy between how families felt, in theory, about their sons joining organizations and how they felt in reality. Publicly, families supported the organization and were proud of their sons for joining. Privately, they feared for their sons and often for what the security forces might do to their families. Members were seen as heroes, but:

> On the other hand, families who had paid their dues to the war effort by allowing the recruitment of a son, tried to prevent other sons from enlisting too.

While most Fatah members reported their families had good social standing, their status and experience as refugees was paramount in their development of self-identity:

> I belong to the generation of occupation. My family are refugees from the 1967 war. The war and my refugee status were the seminal events that formed my political consciousness, and provided the incentive for doing all I could to help regain our legitimate rights in our occupied country.

For the secular terrorists too, enlistment was a natural step:

> Enlistment was for me the natural and done thing . . . in a way, it can be compared to a young Israeli from a nationalist Zionist family who wants to fulfill himself through army service.

> My motivation in joining Fatah was both ideological and personal. It was a question of self-fulfillment, of honor and a feeling of independence . . . the goal of every young Palestinian was to be a fighter.

> After recruitment, my social status was greatly enhanced. I got a lot of respect from my acquaintances, and from the young people in the village.

Decision-Making and Military Hierarchy

Like many of the other Palestinian terrorist organizations, there is a stark absence of critical thinking concerning following instructions and carrying out actions:

> There was no room for questioning. The commander got his orders from his superiors. You couldn't just take the initiative and carry out an armed attack without the commander's approval.

View of Armed Attacks

In addition to causing as many casualties as possible, armed action provided a sense of control or power for Palestinians in a society that had stripped them of it. Inflicting pain on the enemy was paramount in the early days of the Fatah movement:

> I regarded armed actions to be essential, it is the very basis of my organization and I am sure that was the case in the other Palestinian organizations. An armed action proclaims that I am here, I exist, I am strong, I am in control, I am in the field, I am on the map. An armed action against soldiers was the most admired. . . . The armed actions and their results were a major tool for penetrating the public consciousness.

> The various armed actions (stabbing, collaborators, martyrdom operations, attacks on Israeli soldiers) all had different ratings. An armed action that caused casualties was rated highly and seen to be of great importance. An armed action without casualties was not rated. No distinction was made between armed actions on soldiers or on civilians; the main thing was the amount of blood. The aim was to cause as much carnage as possible.

Attitudes Toward Casualties and Weapons of Mass Destruction

There was no discrimination between military and civilian targets. They were all occupiers of their land:

> The organization did not impose any limits with regard to damage or scope or nature of the armed

attacks. The aim was to kill as many Jews as possible and there was no moral distinction between potential victims, whether soldiers, civilians, women or children.

As for the kind of weaponry we would like to have, mass destruction or conventional weapons, we have never given it any thought.

Another ex-prisoner stated similarly that

As for non-conventional weapons and weapons of mass destruction, we never gave it any thought during the armed struggle, but morally I don't see any problem with using such weapons, and had I been able to get them, I would have used them gladly precisely because the casualties would have been that many times greater. I would not have had any problem with 200,000 casualties.

But another Fatah prisoner observed,

As for weapons of mass destruction and unconventional weapons, as an underground organization, we never needed anything more than light automatic weapons and grenades.

Before closing, we should distinguish the Palestinian 'suicide bombers' with the Al-Qaeda suicidal hijackers. The profile of a typical Palestinian is: age, 17–22, uneducated, unemployed, unmarried. Unformed youth. Once in the hands of Hamas and Islamic jihad, they are never let out of sight before an attack, lest they backslide.

This is in vivid contrast to the hijackers of Al-Qaeda. The latter were older; many had higher education. Atta, the alleged ringleader has an advanced degree from a technical university in Hamburg, Germany. The majority of the 11 September hijackers were from comfortable middle-class families in Saudi Arabia and Egypt. And, most importantly, on their own in the West for upwards of seven years, the 11 September hijackers experienced the opportunities of democratic society, yet maintained within them their mission to kill thousands while giving their own lives. These were fully formed adults, 'true believers', who have subordinated their individuality to the group, to the cause of radical Islam, as articulated by the destructive charismatic leader, Osama bin Laden.

These interviews have resulted in information not previously elicited from terrorists. We have gained invaluable insight that takes us further along the path of understanding the social context, mindset, motivations and recruitment of these individuals, a unique and invaluable insight into the tragedy unfolding before our eyes.

NOTE

1. Hassan Salame, responsible for the wave of suicide bombings in Israel in 1996, in which 46 were killed. He is now serving 46 consecutive life sentences.

Palestinian Suicide Terrorism in the Second Intifada: Motivations and Organizational Aspects

Assaf Moghadam*

Suicide terrorism has developed into a widely used tactic, and arguably one of the major strategic threats facing some countries. This article explores various issues related to Palestinian suicide terrorism by presenting a two-phase model to explain the processes and factors underlying the development of Palestinian suicide bombers, and the execution of suicide bombing attacks. The model is applied to the case of suicide attacks that have occurred in the course of the first 21 months of the Second Intifada, from September 2000 to June 2002. The assumptions of the model are tested by taking an in-depth look into the various motives leading individual Palestinians to volunteer for suicide missions, and by discussing the activities and major functions of the organizations that have employed this modus operandi in the specified time frame. It will be concluded that while a counter-terrorism strategy aimed at targeting terrorist organizations may offer short-term gains, in the long run Israel will need to identify ways of removing or reducing the incentives that lead some Palestinians to volunteer for suicide missions.

*The Fletcher School of Law and Diplomacy, Tufts University, Medford, MA, USA.
The author thanks Reuven Paz, Ariel Merari, and Jessica Stern for their invaluable comments, as well as John Parachini and Richard Shultz for encouraging this study from the outset. I am greatly indebted to my former colleagues at the Fletcher School of Law and Diplomacy, Chen Zak and Robert Kirsch, for helping me sharpen my arguments, and to Maria Mussler for her skillful editing.

Address correspondence to Assaf Moghadam, 15 Cutter Mill Road, Suite 252, Great Neck, NY 11021, USA. E-mail: assafm@hotmail.com

Since the 1980s, when Lebanon became the stage for several spectacular suicide terrorist attacks, suicide terrorism as a modus operandi has spread to a host of other countries, including Sri Lanka, Turkey, India, Pakistan, and other less publicized places, including Panama and Tanzania. However, few countries are more familiar with this tactic and its devastating consequences than the state of Israel.

Since the mid-1990s, suicide terrorism has developed into one of Israel's gravest strategic threats. Between 1993 and early August 2002, more than 135 Palestinian suicide bombers have detonated themselves in the vicinity of Israeli civilians or soldiers.[1] The majority of these suicide attacks have occurred during the current wave of Israeli–Palestinian hostilities, which erupted in late September 2000.[2] From the beginning of this latest round of violence until early August 2002, at least 260 Israelis have been killed, and over 2,200 wounded in suicide attacks (see Figure 7.1).[3] Although suicide attacks accounted for less than 1% of all Palestinian attacks since September 2000, almost 44% of all Israeli casualties that resulted from Palestinian attacks between September 2000 and August 2002 were killed in suicide terrorist attacks[4] (see Figures 7.2 and 7.3).

In academic literature, the phenomenon of suicide bombings has enjoyed little prominence to date.[5] Most studies on suicide terrorism concern themselves with particular aspects of suicide terrorism, such as religious, cultural, or psychological considerations of the phenomenon. Little, if any, effort has been made to devise an analytical framework for understanding the processes and factors that underlie the development of the suicide bomber and the execution of suicide bombing attacks. This article is an attempt to fill this gap.

The analytical framework offered here attempts to provide an overall model for a better understanding of the underlying motivations of Palestinian suicide bombers on the one hand, and the process in which suicide bombings are executed on the other. The model assumes that such an attack is the result of a two-phase process. Broadly speaking, this model first traces the underlying motives that drive organizations and individuals to perpetrate

acts of suicide terrorism. It then shows how, following the recruitment of the suicide candidate, organizations train and indoctrinate him or her into becoming a suicide bomber.

This study attempts to answer three central questions: (1) What instills individual Palestinians with a willingness to die, and which factors reinforce this mentality? (2) What motivates organizations such as Hamas, Palestinian Islamic Jihad (PIJ), Fatah, and PFLP to organize suicide attacks, and what are their goals? (3) What methods do these organizations use to mold motivated Palestinians who are willing to die into actual suicide bombers, and how do organizations plan and execute acts of suicide terrorism?

The two major aims of this article can therefore be summarized as follows: first, to offer a framework of analysis for understanding suicide terrorism as an individual and organizational phenomenon; second, to apply this model to the case of suicide bombings by Palestinians during the Second Intifada.

The study is structured as follows. Following this introduction, the first part of the article will present this new framework of analysis in greater detail. The next part will examine the set of motivations—religious, personal, nationalist, economic, and sociological—that play a role in generating and reinforcing individual Palestinians' willingness to die—the precondition for his or her selection as a "martyr." The argument will be made that it is a combination of motives among this "pool of personal motivations" that leads to and reinforces the readiness of some Palestinians to die.

The final part of the study focuses on organizational aspects of Palestinian suicide terrorism. It consists of two main sections: first, an overview over the four organizations that were responsible for suicide attacks in the first 21 months of the Second Intifada—a section that will also contain a summary of statistical data about suicide attacks between October 2000 and June 2002. The second section will discuss how these same organizations recruit, train, and indoctrinate the suicide bombers, and plan and execute suicide attacks. The findings of this study are summarized in a conclusion.

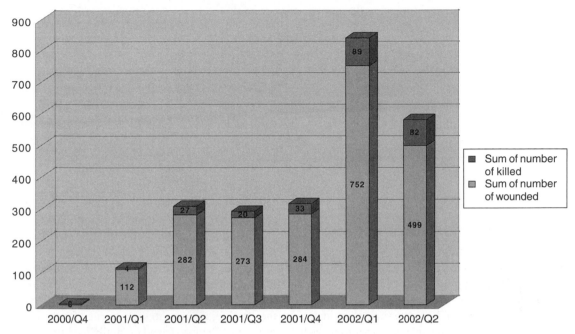

FIGURE 7.1 ■ Killed and wounded in Israel, Jerusalem, and West Bank and Gaza Strip (WBGS) by quarter.

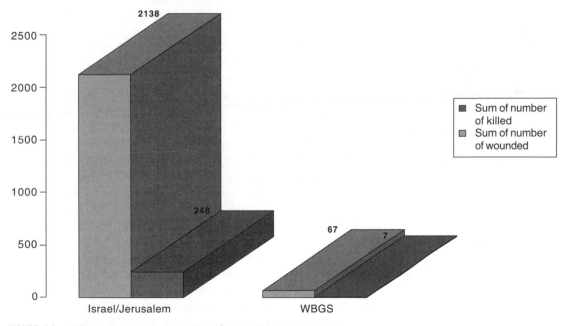

FIGURE 7.2 ■ Killed and wounded by region, October 2000–June 2002.

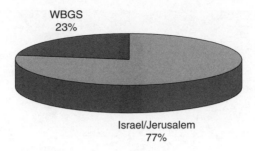

FIGURE 7.3 ■ Percentage of suicide attacks by region, October 2000–June 2002.

Framework of Analysis

Two-Phase Model of Suicide Bombings

In the academic literature to date, the phenomenon of suicide terrorism has not received the attention it deserves. Of the rare studies conducted on this modus operandi, few have emphasized the need to consider both individual aspects (i.e., what motivates the volunteer for the suicide mission) as well as organizational aspects (i.e., organizational goals and methods of training and indoctrination) of suicide terrorism.[6]

The framework of analysis offered here assumes that suicide terrorism is both an individual and an organizational phenomenon; in fact, it assumes that both aspects are integral and necessary parts of the process through which suicide attacks are organized and executed, and thus should be included in any discussion on suicide terrorism. The Israeli–Palestinian case shows that an individual Palestinian who is motivated to become a suicide bomber is likely to lack the resources, information, and organizational capacity needed to perpetrate such an act without the help of an organization. It is therefore not surprising that nearly all suicide bombings against Israeli targets are planned by one of several radical Palestinian organizations.[7] At the same time, it is clear that under normal circumstances, organizations themselves do not supply the pool of ripe suicide bombers from among their own ranks, but instead recruit individuals from outside the organization. It should also be kept in mind that the sheer fact that organizational leaders rarely put their own lives (or those of their relatives) at risk suggests that a clear distinction needs to be drawn

between individual motives on the one hand, and organizational goals and motives on the other.

With this key assumption in mind, the framework of analysis offered here focuses on two sets of motives: those of the individual Palestinian, and those relating to organizations.[8] Individual motives may include the desire to reap expected benefits in the afterlife, the urge to seek revenge for the death or injury of a close friend or family member, or the real or perceived humiliation brought about by Israeli occupation. The second set, which defines those goals and motives that lead organizations to plan suicide attacks, includes political aims of and tactical considerations for the use of suicide bombings (see Figure 7.4).

These two sets of motives converge at the recruitment stage, when organizations identify and mobilize individuals who have professed a willingness to die. At this stage, the two necessary conditions for suicide bombings merge: on the one hand, a willingness to kill that may stem from the individual or from the organization; and, on the other, a willingness to die on the part of the recruited individual. It is at the recruitment stage when the first phase, termed here the "Motivational Phase," ends, and where the second phase, the "Institutional Phase," sets in.

During the Institutional Phase, the "volunteer for martyrdom" comes entirely under the control of the organization. During this phase, the volunteer is indoctrinated and trained by the organization, which molds the individual who is ready to die into a highly committed "living martyr." The goal of the organization at this phase is to take all measures necessary to assure the individual's commit-

MOTIVATIONAL PHASE   INSTITUTIONAL PHASE

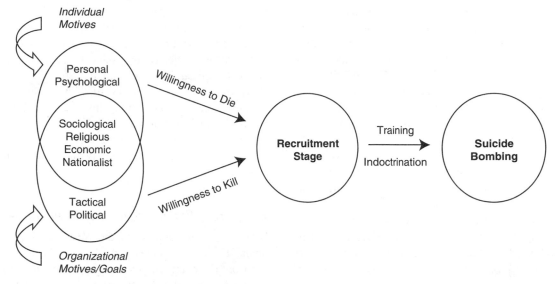

FIGURE 7.4 ■ Two-phase model of suicide bombings.

ment to perpetrate the act—in fact, to morally bind the volunteer to his commitment and to make sure that he will not change his mind. To achieve this goal, the organization, during this phase, will use several techniques, including peptalks, group pressure, and extrications of personal and public commitments from which the candidate will find it difficult, if not impossible, to turn back.[9] Toward the end of this phase, the volunteer for martyrdom reaches a "point of no return," to use Ariel Merari's term, and becomes a living martyr.[10] This Institutional Phase, which usually stretches over a number of days, culminates in the execution of the actual suicide terrorism attack.

The Motivations of the Suicide Bomber

Religious Motives

It is doubtful that a profound religious belief alone will generate a person's willingness to die. Similarly, it is doubtful whether other motivations taken alone—be they nationalist, economic, or personal—can shed light on the phenomenon without being considered in sum. If religious

fervor alone could explain the phenomenon of suicide terrorism, then acts of suicide terrorism should be expected to occur more frequently in countries where deep religious belief, let alone religious fundamentalism, is a powerful force. Similarly, if economic motives alone could explain the phenomenon, then more occurrences of suicide terrorism in much of the developing world would be expected. Because this is not the case, it will be argued here that a combination of some or all of the motives discussed in the following section are required to convince ordinary people that the benefits of martyrdom outweigh the costs.

Within this gamut of intentions, religious motives seem to play a comparatively important role.[11] Spokespeople for Hamas and PIJ, for example, confirmed to Nasra Hassan, a Pakistani journalist who interviewed nearly 250 "volunteers for martyrdom," that each of them was deeply religious. She was also told that all volunteers for a suicide mission have to be convinced of the religious legitimacy of the act.[12]

When assessing Hassan's reports, however, the statements about the deep piety of the candidates deserve some qualification. First, as Islamist groups, Hamas and PIJ only recruit deeply pious individuals in the first place, and thus exclude secular Palestinians who might be equally ready to become *shaheeds*, or martyrs. Second, after 2002, most suicide attacks were organized by Fatah, a secular Palestinian group, whose members need not necessarily be religious (see Figure 7.5).

To this day, Islamic scholars continue to debate whether suicide attacks against Israelis are legitimate. The religious among those who believe them to be a legitimate form of resistance, those who organize the attacks, and those who eventually carry them out, are usually associated with the radical Islamist branch of the Muslim tradition. Islamist groups and radical secular groups alike consistently use the terms *shaheed* and *istishhad* (martyrdom) when referring to suicide attackers and suicide attacks, respectively, since ordinary suicide (*intihar*), that is, suicide caused by personal distress, is expressly forbidden in Islam.

The Islamist interpretation of Jihad

Central to the religious motivation that plays a role in pushing some Palestinians to volunteer for suicide missions is the notion of Jihad, which carries two basic meanings that refer to the two fundamental struggles of the Muslim. *Jihad al nafs*, often described as "the struggle for one's soul against one's own base instinct," is an explanation that has been rejected by Islamists as heretical. *Jihad bi al saif* is the military struggle, the "holy war by means of the sword."[13] According to Islamists, the military fight against the nonbelievers is the real "Greater Jihad." To support their claims, they invoke only those Quranic sections that equate warfare with the duty of the faithful Muslim.

The perception of the enemy as an infidel

Islamists in general perceive the West, and in particular the United States and Israel, to be at the forefront of an anti-Islamic conspiracy that tries to undermine the religion, culture, and values of the Islamic world. The perceived threat to Islamic culture that emanates from the West and Israel leads the Islamist movement to claim that the Jihad is an act of self-defense against the "enemies of God." Thus suicide bombings and other violent acts are

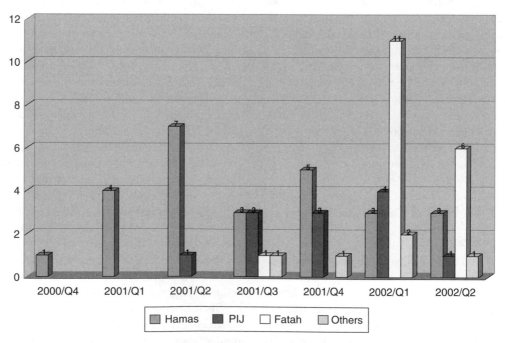

FIGURE 7.5 ■ Suicide attacks in Israel, Jerusalem, and WBGS by organizations—time series.

regarded as legitimate means of self-defense. In the words of the former spiritual leader of Hizballah, Sheikh Muhammad Hussein Fadlallah, those who commit such activities "are not preachers of violence . . . Jihad in Islam is a defensive movement against those who impose violence."[14]

Islam versus Judaism

More radical Islamists—many of whom can be found in territories under Palestinian control—consider the conspiracy against Islam to be spearheaded by Israel and by Judaism. The Israeli counterterrorism expert Reuven Paz argues that "after the establishment of Israel and the renaissance of the Islamist groups since the 1960s and 1970s," the perceived anti-Islamic conspiracy spearheaded by the West and Israel "came to be viewed as a constant and perhaps eternal struggle between Judaism and Islam."[15] Indeed, Palestinian rhetoric during the Second Intifada has been as anti-Jewish as it has been anti-Israeli in character.

The effect has been a drastic rhetorical escalation throughout the course of the Second Intifada, which has often resulted in calls to murder Jews. On 3 August 2001, for instance, Sheikh Ibrahim Madhi held a Friday sermon at the Sheikh Ijlin Mosque in Gaza, where he said that "[t]he Koran is very clear on this: The greatest enemies of the Islamic nation are the Jews, may Allah fight them. . . . The people who are the most hostile toward the believers are the Jews and the Polytheists. . . . Nothing will deter them except for us voluntarily detonating ourselves in their midst."[16]

Glorifying death and seeking martyrdom

Martyrdom has a long tradition in Islam, not only since the Ayatollah Khomeini declared no command "more binding to the Muslim than the command to sacrifice life and property to defend and bolster Islam."[17] Since the first suicide bombing by an Islamist Palestinian group in the West Bank on 16 April 1993, and especially since the beginning of the Second Intifada in late September 2000, more and more Palestinians have expressed their wish and willingness to become martyrs

by perpetrating martyrdom operations against Israelis.[18] Interviewed by Nasra Hassan, one leader of the Al-Qassam Brigades, the military arm of Hamas, said that "it is easy for us to sweep the streets for boys who want to do a martyrdom operation. Fending off the crowds who demand revenge and retaliation and insisting on a human bomb operation—that becomes our biggest problem."[19]

Juxtaposing Western cowardice with Muslim courage

During the Second Intifada, the mufti of Jerusalem, Ikrama Sabri, was quoted as saying "The Muslim embraces death. . . . Look at the society of the Israelis. It is a selfish society that loves life. These are not people who are eager to die for their country and their God. The Jews will leave this land rather than die, but the Muslim is happy to die."[20]

The mufti repeated a widely held belief that people in the West, including Israelis/Jews, fear death. Islamists juxtapose this perception of the death-fearing infidel with the readiness to die that is said to prevail among the true Muslim. Statements like the mufti's are highly prolific in Gaza and the West Bank, and are connected to the belief that the West, including the Israelis/Jews are—despite their military strength—morally corrupt, seeking the pleasures of the good life, "protect[ing] their lives like a miser protects his money,"[21] and thus are cowards.

Such a mode of thinking may prompt the shaheed to prove to the hedonist that, unlike the infidel, the shaheed is not afraid to lose his life. In the words of Reuven Paz, the members of the Islamist groups must show the enemy "that they are truly brave, because the ultimate bravery and heroism lie in seeking out death, thus showing the enemy as cowards and themselves as heroes."[22]

Personal Motives

Although religion seems to play an important role for many suicide bombers, there is no reason to assume that the shaheed's decision to embark on a martyrdom operation is entirely selfless. Although the literature describing the characteristics of an afterlife in paradise has flourished since the 1991 Gulf War, most original references to the benefits the martyr reaps in paradise can be found in *hadiths*—sayings attributed to the Prophet Muhammad that supplement the Quran as the source of Islamic law.[23] These benefits are said to include the forgiving of the martyr's sins; the redemption from the torments of the grave; security from the "fear of hell"; a crown of glory featuring a ruby "worth more than the world and all that is in it"; marriage to seventy-two huris, or black-eyed virgins; and the ability to extend these heavenly privileges to seventy relatives.[24]

Paradise seems to offer the martyr pleasures and benefits that he can only dream of in real life. If the shaheed, therefore, is convinced that he will enjoy these benefits in the afterlife, then candidates for martyrdom are confronted with a powerful incentive to swap the little they possess for the luxuries they are promised.

The suicide bomber's elevated status after death

An additional incentive to the suicide bomber is provided by the elevation of his status after the suicide mission is completed—an elevation that is given significant impetus by a virtual cult of the suicide bomber among many Palestinians.

This rise in social status after the suicide bomber's death seems all the more appealing when one considers that the Palestinian shaheeds are raised in a culture where honor and dignity are highly treasured, maybe even "in the nature of Islam," as one senior Hamas official put it,[25] and where becoming a martyr is among the highest, if not *the* highest, honor.

The elevated stature of the shaheed among Palestinians finds many expressions, beginning with the circulation of posters and leaflets carrying his name and picture. Perhaps most importantly, every attack is followed by a rally commemorating the suicide bomber, where the number of participants may reach into the thousands.

It is not difficult to imagine many a young Gazan looking at the glorification of this martyred Palestinian hero with a mixture of admiration and jealousy, and perhaps even hoping to reach the same kind of transcendent fame himself. In fact, he might rightfully regard martyrdom as the only way to attain a similar status, given his circumstances.

Benefits to the suicide bomber's family

A suicide bomber's mission will provide his family with both tangible and intangible rewards. After the suicide attack, both the material and the social status of the shaheed's family improve significantly. The family usually receives a cash payment of between $1,000 and several thousand dollars from Hamas, the PIJ, and sometimes from third parties, such as Iraqi leader Saddam Hussein.[26]

One journalist who visited the family of Ismail al-Masawabi, who killed himself and two Israeli sergeants on 22 June 2001 with a suicide device, described the material improvement of the family in an article in the *New York Times Magazine*. The Al-Masawabis, who used to live in a squalid refugee camp prior to the bombing, now live in an apartment that is "spacious by Gaza standards. . . . Everything in it looked new—the appliances, rugs and stuffed furniture, the gaudy wall clocks, even the bracelet and rings Ismail's mother was wearing."[27]

Revenge

An additional motivation to volunteer for a suicide mission may be for the shaheed to avenge the death or injury of a close friend or family member. Due to the tiny size of the area ravaged by decades of conflict, an extremely high population density, and high casualty and injury rates especially during the Second Intifada, scarcely any Palestinian has remained untouched by the violence, and many Palestinians—as well as Israelis—personally know someone who has been injured or killed during the conflict. As a result, calls for revenge have been extremely common on both sides of the conflict.

On the Palestinian side, revenge is often called for during funeral processions of Palestinians killed by Israeli forces.[28] Although a recent Israeli assessment found that revenge alone is seldom a motive,[29] and although those who train the shaheeds insist that revenge alone is not acceptable before Allah as a reason for seeking martyrdom,[30] it is not hard to fathom that many, if not most, suicide bombers share a desire to seek revenge. In addition, some suicide bombers have admitted that revenge was their primary motive. Nafez al-Nether, who detonated himself, killing several Israeli soldiers on 9 July 2001, said he wanted to avenge the blood of Palestinians killed by Israel. One of those Palestinians was Nafez's brother Fayez, who was killed during the First Intifada in clashes that took place in the Jabalya refugee camp.[31]

Dignity versus humiliation

There are numerous indications that a sense of humiliation, and the need to regain some pride through a dignified act, might also motivate a suicide bomber. There is no dearth of references to the humiliation felt by most Palestinians who continue to live under Israeli occupation, and to how this feeling motivates them to commit an act of terrorism. *Al Majallah*, a London-based, Saudi-owned Arabic weekly conducted an interview with a so-called living martyr—a volunteer for martyrdom who has been recruited and is currently undergoing training. The person, who identified himself as Ahmad, told the correspondent that "martyrdom is a duty and a right. There is no humiliation like that of living under the occupation."[32] In a similar statement, an Islamic Jihad operative told a reporter from the *Christian Science Monitor* that the Palestinians' "main objective is to satisfy God's will by undertaking Jihad." The other is to regain the Palestinians' "stolen land and dignity."[33] Hamas co-founder Abdul Aziz Rantisi agrees that dishonoring someone is the worst act that can be done, the only remedy being the regaining of one's dignity.[34]

The expectation of sexual benefits

Islamic scholars disagree over whether Islamic texts refer to sexual pleasures awaiting the martyrs, and an extensive discussion of the subject is beyond the scope of this article.[35] Ultimately, however, the question of whether Islamic texts promise

sexual pleasures to the martyr is less important than establishing whether religious leaders and operatives of Islamist and other radical groups attempt to and succeed in convincing young Palestinians that they will indeed attain such benefits in the afterlife. Statements collected by the Middle East Media Research Institute (MEMRI), as well as other sources, clearly indicate that not only do some operatives and religious scholars promote this belief, but a large number of youth are convinced they will attain future pleasures as a reward for martyrdom.[36]

Sixteen-year-old Bassam Khalifi, for instance, told Western journalists, "I know my life is poor compared to Europe and America, but I have something awaiting me that makes all my suffering worthwhile. . . . Most boys can't stop thinking about the virgins."[37]

In an even more compelling example, the Israeli daily *Ma'ariv* reported that one suicide bomber, Mahdi Abu Malek, whose attempt to commit an attack was foiled by the IDF, had wrapped toilet paper around his genitals. He evidently wanted to protect his genitals, given their importance in enjoying the pleasures of the Garden of Eden.[38]

In addition, the Palestinian press often prints death announcements of martyrs in the form of wedding announcements, corroborating the suspicion that martyrs expect to marry the "huris"—the "black-eyed virgins"—soon after their martyrdom. One representative "wedding announcement" read: "With great pride, the PIJ marries the member of its military wing . . . the martyr and hero Yasser Al-Adhami, to 'the black-eyed.' "[39]

Nationalist Motives

Many Palestinian suicide bombers appear to flock to Hamas, PIJ, and Fatah for nationalist reasons. Videotapes of suicide bombers, as well as statements of volunteers, living martyrs, or families of suicide bombers clearly suggest that many Palestinians perceive a deep injustice done to them by a "Zionist entity" that deprived Palestinians of their land and continues to deny them a worthy existence on what they regard to be Palestinian soil.

Most suicide bombers express a willingness to avoid the repetition of the 1948 *nakba*, that is, the "catastrophe" of the creation of the State of Israel, and clearly express their readiness to "die in defense of their land."[40] It should be kept in mind here that in the Middle Eastern tradition, the notion of territory, including the house, is extremely significant. The house is where the family is based—a social unit whose members are treated with utmost respect, and whose dignity and honor must be preserved at all costs. Considering that the house connects the victimized Palestinian resident to the territory of which he or she was deprived, it becomes an imperative to defend what little is left against any continued infringement on the part of the Israeli enemy.

Statements by Palestinian political leaders reflect the centrality of Palestinian nationalism as a motive. Reacting to the suicide bombing in front of Tel Aviv's Dolphinarium, top Hamas official Al-Rantisi told Al-Jazeera *TV* that Palestinians "will never approve of the occupation of [their] homeland."[41]

Without a doubt, these nationalist motives are intimately linked to and strengthened by the overwhelming sense of humiliation Palestinians have experienced over the five decades of Israeli occupation. Unlike in the First Intifada, which erupted in December 1987, Palestinians today live under Palestinian Authority rule. Nevertheless, the continued lack of territorial contiguity and the persistent division of clusters of autonomous Palestinian areas by Israeli roadblocks and army checkpoints generate frustrations similar to those Palestinians felt over a decade ago. In their seminal account of the First Intifada (1987–1993), Israeli journalists Ze'ev Schiff and Ehud Ya'ari described the expressed motives of some Palestinians detained by the IDF at the beginning of the First Intifada:

> All of them cited much the same motive: the feeling that they had suffered a grave personal injustice at the hands of their Jewish employers or colleagues. Each prisoner had his own story to tell, but the gist of their experiences was similar: at one time or another they had been subjected to verbal and even physical abuse, cheated out of their wages, set to work under inhuman conditions,

and exposed to the sweep of the dragnet that followed every act of terrorism. All complained of the insult and humiliation repeatedly suffered at army roadblocks and checkpoints: the nasty tone in which they were addressed, the body searches accompanied by shoves and shouts, the derision they were forced to endure in front of family and friends.[42]

Apart from feelings of humiliation, an additional catalyst for the Palestinian resistance against the Israeli occupation is what may be termed the "national Jihad"[43]—a struggle that serves to strengthen a Palestinian national entity and form a national heritage.

Fighting the national Jihad serves several purposes. It generates a sense of pride and belonging to a national group that fights a seemingly invincible enemy. This struggle can be fulfilling in the sense that the Zionist enemy's sense of invincibility is shattered, which in turn humiliates the enemy and provides the shaheed with a tremendous sense of achievement.

Suicide terrorism fulfills two tactical roles here. First, it is a highly effective tactic used in the asymmetric warfare against Israel. This is due in part to the fact that suicide bombings are a form of psychological warfare. As such, they fuel the belief that the enemy can be worn down over time, whereas the Palestinian nation is strengthened. In the process, Israeli society is instilled with fear. Following one suicide bombing, for example, one 19-year-old Palestinian laborer asked a journalist from the Associated Press, "Did you see how the Jews were crying on television? I want to become a martyr like that to scare the Jews, to send them to hell."[44]

Economic Motives

Living in economic distress can be an additional underlying motive in the formation of a willingness to die among many Palestinians in Gaza and the West Bank, though this motive is neither essential nor central. In the occupied territories, the most pressing economic and demographic problems are high population density and a high rate of unemployment, the result of which is a low standard of living,

The economic hardship that prevails in the Palestinian-controlled areas resulted from the post-1967 Israeli economic domination, which made any improvement in the Palestinian standard of living conditional on some direct connection to the economy in Israel proper. In addition, for most of the Israeli occupation, Palestinians have faced a stubborn and paralyzing Israeli bureaucracy. In the words of Schiff and Ya'ari, "the Palestinians found themselves completely at the mercy of the [Israeli] Civil Administration in every sphere of economic life. Each request for a permit, grant, or dispensation entailed an exhausting wrestle with a crabbed bureaucracy of mostly indifferent but sometimes hostile clerks and officials—a veritable juggernaut of 400 Jewish mandarins managing thousands of Arab minions bereft of all authority."[45]

Today, the Gaza Strip is home to roughly 1.2 million people—about half of whom are fourteen years old or younger—all sharing an area that is approximately twice the size of Washington, D.C.[46] In the early 1990s, unemployment in the West Bank and Gaza combined was under 5%, but it jumped to over 20% by the mid-1990s. From 1997 until September 2000, the economic situation in the Palestinian areas has generally improved, partly due to Israeli policies aimed at reducing the impact of closures and other measures. As a result, GDP in 1998 and 1999 grew by 5% and 6%, respectively, until the last quarter of 2000, when the outbreak of the Second Intifada led to renewed Israeli closures and the disruption of labor and trade movement in and out of the Palestinian self-rule areas.[47]

The Second Intifada has drastically worsened the economic plight of the over three million Palestinians living in the West Bank and Gaza. According to a report by the United Nations Special Commissioner on the Occupied Territories (UNSCO), unemployment rose to 25% one year after the beginning of the Second Intifada, while the underlying jobless rate in Gaza alone was as high as 50%.[48]

The UNSCO report said that the cost of the Second Intifada to the Palestinian economy after one year lay at between $2.4 and $3.2 billion. At the same time, revenues of the PA plummeted by 57% in the first nine months alone. Real incomes decreased by an average 37%, resulting in 46% of Palestinians living below the poverty line—twice as many as prior to the Second Intifada.[49]

Given these harsh economic realities prevalent in Gaza and the West Bank, some Palestinians may feel hopeless and desperate. Economic distress may also drive Palestinians to seek revenge against those they hold responsible for the conditions in which they find themselves. One elderly resident of the West Bank town of Jenin urged a journalist, "Look around and see how we live here. Then maybe you will understand why there are always volunteers for martyrdom. Every good Muslim understands that it's better to die fighting than live without hope."[50]

Economic deprivation in and of itself, however, is an insufficient explanation for the emergence of a widespread willingness to die among large parts of the Palestinian population. Not only have these harsh economic conditions existed before the emergence of suicide attacks in Israel, but some of the suicide bombers have come from relatively well-off families. Thus it seems that economic motives for the evolution of a willingness to die must interact with other motives in order to result in the use of suicide bombings by a particular group.

Sociological Aspects of Suicide Bombings

Sociological and psychological aspects of terrorism and violence may help shed further light on the phenomenon of suicide terrorism in general, and among Palestinians in particular.

Mark Juergensmeyer points out that, as is the case in many other societies, young Palestinians between the ages of 16 and 22 are in a "liminal state between two life stages," where they are neither children in their parents' families, nor have they created their own families. This stage can serve as a source of problems especially in societies that are built around family units. In such circumstances, religious movements may help fill the vacuum that the youth faces, and often provide a home and an extended kinship. This situation renders the youth "vulnerable to the voices of powerful leaders and images of glory."[51] Juergensmeyer's explanation seems particularly fitting for the West Bank and Gaza, where Palestinian youth are strongly influenced by religious authorities, and istishhad is glorified by many.

Another social phenomenon is the support that the volunteers for martyrdom receive among the Palestinian population. In the summer of 2001, popular support for suicide bombings among Palestinians reached an all-time high, with over 70% of Palestinians expressing their support for such attacks, according to a poll conducted by the Palestinian Center for Public Opinion.[52] When the same poll was conducted in the summer of 2002, support for suicide bombings had dropped slightly, but martyrdom operations were still supported by over two thirds of the respondents.[53]

Another sociological aspect relates to the harsh demographic realities of Gazan society described earlier. In one of the world's most densely populated regions plagued by economic difficulties, achieving any degree of economic or personal "success" may seem impossible. Becoming a martyr, on the other hand, may well present a remedy to this predicament by providing an opportunity to stand out of the crowd and become, literally, a celebrity. The shaheed is endowed with a sense of individuality that he is unlikely to achieve in any other way.

Organizational Aspects of Suicide Bombings

Organizations play a critical role in the recruitment stage, planning, and execution of a suicide attack. They provide the many resources and services necessary to sustain a prolonged and "effective" campaign of suicide terrorism, including fundraising; the procurement of weapons and the technical know-how for their assembly and use; the recruitment, training, and indoctrination of the shaheed; overall decision making and strategic planning; intelligence-gathering; target selection; and public relations.[54]

Organizational Goals and Motives

Apart from the motives of the Palestinian individual, the execution of a suicide attack also requires organizational motives—a concept that is closely linked to the goals of organizations in general. In the following section, several concepts relevant to organizational motives will be briefly discussed.[55]

Martha Crenshaw argues convincingly that terrorism can at times be understood as an expression of a political strategy. A group possesses collective preferences, or values, she writes, and "selects terrorism as a course of action from a range of perceived alternatives." Crenshaw is careful to add that strategic calculation is only one element "in the decision-making process leading to terrorism. But it is critical to include strategic reasoning as a possible motivation, at a minimum as an antidote to stereotypes of "terrorists" as irrational fanatics."[56]

Organizational theorists and terrorism analysts generally agree that the overarching goal of any organization is its own survival.[57] Apart from this overall goal, organizational theorists are distinguishing between "official" goals on the one hand, and "operative" goals on the other. Official goals tend to be more general because they provide a focus for the organization as a whole, whereas operative goals are more concrete goals that "focus attention on the issues that require effort on the part of specific units and particular employees."[58]

Applying these distinctions to Hamas, for example, one could distinguish between Hamas's official goal of destroying Israel,[59] and operative goals such as derailing the peace process, enhancing its prestige among Palestinians vis-à-vis the PA or other groups, increasing its appearance as a legitimate opposition, promoting ties with the Islamic world, and defying the Israeli enemy's real or perceived strength. It then becomes clear that Hamas may choose to employ a strategy of suicide bombings to fulfill either its official or its operative goals.

Intensifying the psychological warfare against the target audience, including through the media, is an additional operative goal of organizations.

Terrorist organizations are well aware of the fact that "terrorism and the media are bound together in an inherently symbiotic relationship," to use Bruce Hoffman's description.[60] At times, the sheer manipulation of their target audience may become an operative goal. Hamas, for example, often announces a series of ten or more suicide bombings in order to increase the psychological pressure on Israelis.[61]

Palestinian Organizations Employing Suicide Terrorism

Hamas—Izz-al-Din al-Qassam

Since the outset of the Second Intifada, no other Palestinian group has executed as many suicide attacks, or generated as many casualties among Israelis, as the radical Islamic organization Hamas, and in particular its military wing (see Figures 7.6 and 7.7).

Hamas asserts that its political and military wings are separate, with no direct links between the two[62]—a claim that appears to be justified.[63] The first squads of Hamas's military wing, Izz-al-Din al-Qassam,[64] were formed in early 1991, following a crackdown on Hamas' military infrastructure by Israeli security forces.

Izz-al-Din al-Qassam is responsible for most of the terrorist attacks executed in the name of Hamas since 1992. On 13 April 1994, the Brigades planned and executed the first major suicide bombing at the central bus station in the coastal Israeli town of Hadera, in which five people were killed.[65]

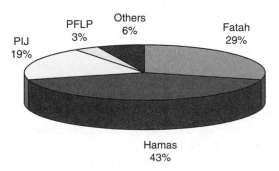

FIGURE 7.6 ■ Percentage of suicide attacks by organization, October 2000–June 2002.

The initial activities of Izz-al-Din al-Qassam had an internal focus, as the military wing kidnapped and executed Palestinians suspected of collaborating with Israel. In December 1991, Doron Shorshan became the first Israeli citizen to be killed by Izz-al-Din al-Qassam.[66]

The 5 January 1996 assassination of Yihye Ayyash, the mastermind behind several suicide bombings that killed and injured scores of Israelis, sparked a renewed wave of suicide bombings that persisted until late 1997. In early 1998, after a harsh crackdown on Hamas' military infrastructure by the Palestinian Authority, new insights into Izz-al-Din al-Qassam were gained. According to Shaul Mishal and Avraham Sela, interrogations of group members, many of whom were from Nablus, revealed:

> an extensive, compartmentalized, military apparatus, which maintained close contact with the Hamas headquarters in the Gaza Strip, Jordan, and Lebanon using advanced communications methods, including the internet. The activities of the *Izz-al-Din al-Qassam* squads were divided among several senior regional commanders, whose names were on Israel's "wanted" list. They were constantly on the move from one district to another, assisted by the clergy and personnel of the mosques. These senior activists organized new military cadres and supervised their training for military operations.[67]

At the time of this writing, Hamas has claimed responsibility for some 43% of all suicide attacks perpetrated against Israelis during the Second Intifada—more than any other Palestinian organization (see Figure 7.6). In the 26 successful attacks organized and executed by Hamas between September 2000 and the end of June 2002, some 161 Israelis have been killed, and over 1,100 injured (see Figures 7.5 and 7.8).

Hamas has demonstrated an extremely high degree of lethality in its attacks, a fact that hints at the effective organization and information-gathering capabilities that are at the group's disposal, in addition to its wealth of material and financial resources. As a result, Hamas has increased the number of Israeli casualties in almost every period under review, except for Quarter III in 2001, and Quarter II in 2002. In the first quarter of

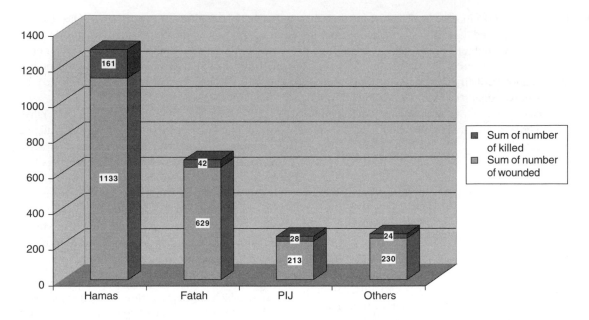

FIGURE 7.7 ■ Killed and wounded in Israel, Jerusalem, and WBGS by organization, October 2000–June 2002.

2002, for example, 55 Israelis were killed in three suicide attacks attributed to Hamas (Figure 7.8). Contrast this with Fatah's 11 attacks in the same quarter, in which 24 Israelis were killed—less than half as many as in attacks attributed to Hamas (see Figures 7.5 and 7.8). This trend repeated itself in the second quarter of 2002, when Hamas managed to inflict over twice as many Israeli casualties as did Fatah (43 and 18 Israelis killed, respectively) with only half the number of attacks (3 attacks compared to 6 by Fatah) (see Figures 7.5 and 7.8).

Hamas, unlike PIJ, has not focused its suicide attacks solely on civilian targets. At least six attacks since September 2000 have targeted the Israeli military (Figure 7.9). Figures 7.10 and 7.11 demonstrate Hamas's dominance in the Gaza Strip—all five suicide bombers who were from the Gaza Strip were members of Hamas.

Palestinian Islamic Jihad—the Jerusalem Brigades

Unlike Hamas, the radical Islamist organization Palestinian Islamic Jihad (*Harakat al-Jihad al-*

Islami al-Filastini) is dedicated exclusively to terrorist activities. Officially founded by Palestinian students in Egypt in 1980, PIJ, which is known for its secrecy and strict discipline, split from the Palestinian Muslim Brotherhood due to the latter's "lack of revolutionary spirit and style."[68] The group maintains offices in Beirut, Tehran, Damascus, and Khartoum, and wields more influence in the West Bank than in the Gaza Strip, where Hamas clearly dominates (see Figures 7.10 and 7.11).

According to Israeli and U.S. experts, PIJ's core consists of several cells numbering some several dozen members in the West Bank and Gaza Strip.[69] Like Hamas, PIJ is also divided into military and political wings. In an interview with Beirut's Al-Manar TV station in August 2001, PIJ leader Sheikh Ramadan Shallah said that it is PIJ's military wing, the so-called Jerusalem Brigades,[70] that determines the timing, venue, and type of suicide attacks. Shallah emphasized that "there is only one military wing and one fighting address under the banner of the Islamic Jihad Movement at this phase. It is the Al-Quds Squads [i.e., Jerusalem Brigades]. It is the party in charge of carrying out operations in the name of [the] Islamic Jihad Movement."[71]

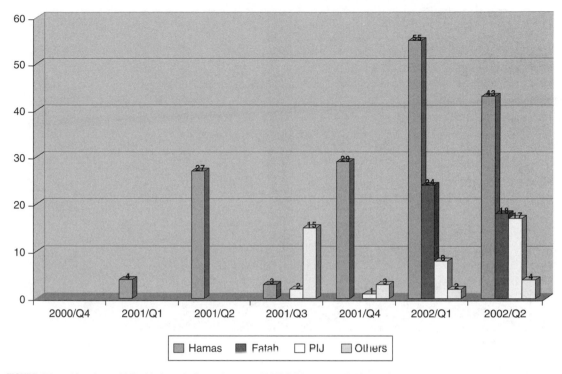

FIGURE 7.8 ■ Number of killed in Israel, Jerusalem, and WBGS by organization—time series.

PIJ began to carry out suicide attacks during the early wave of suicide bombings that hit Israel between 1994 and 1997. On 11 November 1994, a Palestinian recruited by PIJ detonated himself while he was riding a bicycle, killing three Israelis. PIJ is also responsible for one of the most deadly suicide attacks in Israeli history. On 22 January 1995 on the Israeli coastal plain, two bombs exploded at the Beit Lid junction, killing 18 Israeli soldiers and 1 civilian.[72]

Between the end of September 2000 and late June 2002—the initial 21 months of the Second Intifada—the PIJ has been responsible for roughly one fifth of all successful suicide attacks (see Figure 7.6), killing at least 28 Israelis, and injuring 213 (see Figure 7.7). Figure 7.5 shows that the number of attacks during the Second Intifada perpetrated by PIJ has been rising slowly, reaching four attacks in the first quarter of 2002 and leading to an increase in the number of Israelis killed by PIJ attacks to eight in the first quarter of 2002 (see Figure 7.8). Although PIJ executed only one attack

in the second quarter of 2002, the highly lethal attack on Bus Number 830 near the Megiddo Junction killed 17 Israelis—more than all of PIJ's four attacks in the preceding quarter combined. Moreover, Figures 7.9 and 7.11 show that PIJ's targets were predominantly civilians living in Israel proper, including Jerusalem.

Fatah, Tanzim, and the Al-Aqsa Martyrs

The third Palestinian organization to have employed suicide terrorism during the Second Intifada is Fatah, the dominant faction of the Palestine Liberation Organization (PLO), which in turn is headed by Yasser Arafat. As Figure 7.6 shows, Fatah has been responsible for almost a third of all suicide attacks since the beginning of the Second Intifada. More important, Figure 7.5 reveals that Fatah has become the most active organization in terms of numbers of attacks on Israelis. In 2002, it has perpetrated more suicide attacks than all the other groups combined (see Figure 7.5). As a result

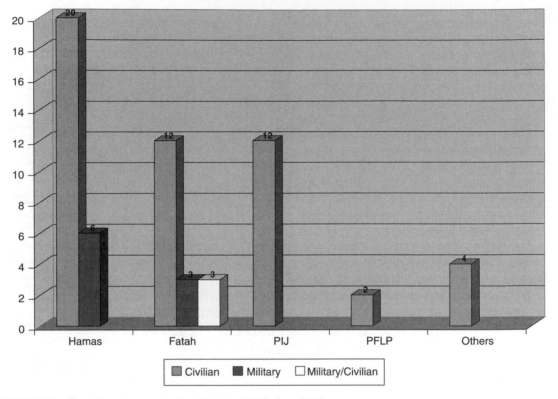

FIGURE 7.9 ■ Target type by organization, October 2000–June 2002.

of attacks by Fatah and affiliated organizations such as the Tanzim and Al-Aqsa Martyrs, 42 Israelis were killed, and 629 wounded between September 2000 and June 2002 (see Figure 7.7).

The armed wing of Fatah is known as the Tanzim, a group that has been responsible for much of the violence that erupted in the months following Ariel Sharon's visit to the Temple Mount. The first suicide attack in the course of the Second Intifada that has been attributed to Fatah's Tanzim took place on 17 January 2002 in Hadera, when 24-year-old Abdul Salaam Sadek Hassouneh, armed with a rifle and suicide belt, killed 6 Israelis.[73]

As the Second Intifada continues, a Fatah faction calling itself the Al-Aqsa Martyr Brigades has taken the lead in suicide attacks. In the first quarter of 2002, this group was responsible for over half of all suicide attacks against Israelis, rendering the group more active than any other, at least in the first half of 2002 (see Figure 7.5). It is partly due to the growing influence of Fatah's Al-Aqsa Martyr

Brigades that the State Department decided to put the group on its list of Foreign Terrorist Organizations (FTO) in March 2002.

The Al-Aqsa Martyr Brigades were formed after September 2000, and are said to consist of hundreds of members that are under the direct control of the Tanzim.[74] The links between Al-Aqsa and the PA leadership seem to be close. Maslama Thabet, a member of the Brigades, was quoted as saying, "we are Fatah itself, but we don't operate under the name Fatah. We are the armed wing of the organization. We receive our instructions from Fatah. Our commander is Yasser Arafat himself."[75] According to a former FBI terrorism analyst, "the infrastructure, funds, leadership, and operatives that comprise the Al-Aqsa Martyr Brigades and facilitate the group's activity all hail from Fatah. . . . Most of the Brigades' leadership are salaried members of the PA and its security forces. . . . Fatah is, by its own admission, Al-Aqsa's parent and controlling organization."[76]

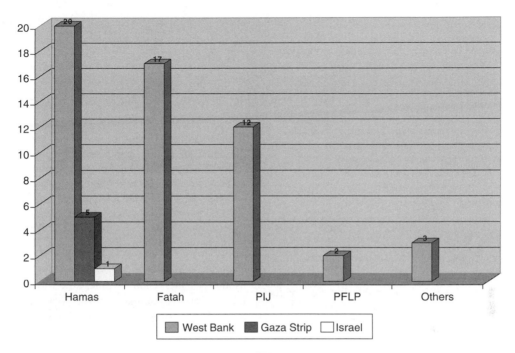

FIGURE 7.10 ▪ Origin of attacker by organization, October 2000–June 2002.

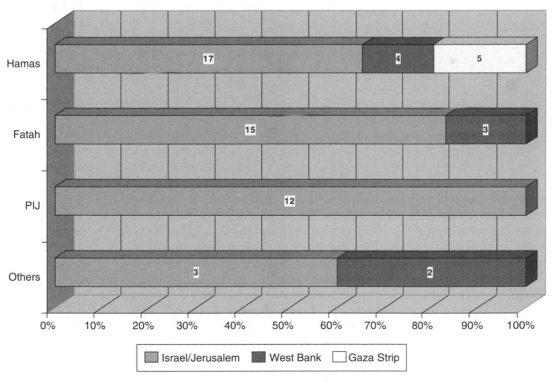

FIGURE 7.11 ▪ Target region by organization, October 2000–June 2002.

Fatah's formation of the Tanzim must be seen in the context of its attempt to channel and focus the passions of many Palestinians in the West Bank and Gaza away from Islamist groups. Fatah's success in doing this depends on Yasser Arafat's standing in the public, which oscillates with the political situation. Nevertheless, Fatah and the Tanzim are the most powerful secular force in the West Bank and Gaza, and offer a secular alternative to groups such as Hamas and PIJ.

The PFLP

The fourth organization that has executed a small number of suicide attacks during the Second Intifada is the Popular Front for the Liberation of Palestine (PFLP), a secular organization that originated from the PLO. Under the direction of its current leader, Ahmed Sadat, the PFLP carried out the assassination of right-wing Israeli Minister of Tourism Rehavam Ze'evi. On 16 February 2002, the PFLP took responsibility for a suicide bombing that killed 2 Israelis and injured 29 at the West Bank settlement of Karnei Shomron. Roughly 3 weeks later, the PFLP sent a suicide bomber to a hotel lobby in the settlement of Ariel, where 15 people were injured.

Recruitment, Training, and Indoctrination

Recruitment

To date, there is a relative dearth of open sources that reveal the methods employed by groups such as Hamas, PIJ, or Fatah to recruit, train, and indoctrinate Palestinians that have been selected for suicide missions. From the few open sources that are available, it appears that Hamas, PIJ, and Fatah have relatively similar processes of selection, recruitment, and training.

Typically, organizations will reject volunteers, and will select the candidates for suicide missions themselves. Because candidates are chosen on the basis of religious devotion, trust, and the ability to keep a secret, recruiters naturally prefer to pick candidates that they have known for a longer period of time. In addition, Hamas, PIJ, and other

groups expect Israelis to try to plant collaborators in their organizations, and are hesitant to accept volunteers.[77]

In an article that appeared in the journal *Studies in Conflict and Terrorism*, Harvey Kushner described the selection process as follows:

The selection process begins with members of the Izz-al-Din al-Qassam or even the Palestinian Islamic Jihad circulating among the organizations' schools and mosques during religious instruction. The recruiters broach the subject of dying for Allah with a group of students and watch the students' reactions. Students that seem particularly interested are immediately singled out for possible special merit.[78]

In a rare interview with Salah Shehadeh posted by the website "Islam Online," the former Izz-al-Din al-Qassam commander who was assassinated by the Israel Defense Forces on 22 July said that to Hamas, it is important that the recruit be a devout Muslim; that he comply "with his parents' wishes," not be an only child, or the head of a family; have the mental capacity to carry out the act; and that "his martyrdom should encourage others."[79] Hamas and other groups seem to place particular importance on a clean criminal record of the recruit, so as not to raise the suspicions of Israel's secret service;[80] the ability to withstand severe psychological pressure; and the ability of the recruit to keep a low profile.

Both Hamas and PIJ recruiters insist they do not select candidates who have a tendency to be suicidal. In an interview with the *New Yorker*, PIJ member Abdullah Shami told a reporter that PIJ does not recruit "depressed" people. "If there were a one-in-a-thousand chance that a person was suicidal, we would not allow him to martyr himself. In order to be a martyr bomber, you have to want to live."[81]

Shami and other PIJ members recruit their activists not only in mosques, but also on university campuses, through social activities, and even in Israeli jails. Ziad Abu-Amr, for example, writes that the PIJ leadership has been highly successful in recruiting new members in Israeli jails, and even suggests that this was one reason why the Israeli government began to deport PIJ leaders, rather than keeping them behind bars.[82]

Training and indoctrination

The training and indoctrination of the "candidate for martyrdom" are among the core tasks of organizations that use suicide bombings as a tactic. Here as well, little reliable unclassified information is available.

Most suicide bombers undergo between several weeks to several months of training,[83] with the length of the training differing, depending on the urgency of the timing of the operation. One high-ranking IDF official pointed out that the threat of assassination, for example, disrupts the smooth planning of suicide attacks, as the organizers are obliged to spend more time ensuring their personal safety, and thus have less time available to plan and organize suicide attacks.[84]

During the training period, the candidates are subjected to both religious indoctrination and anti-Israeli propaganda. Volunteers attend classes, usually between two and four hours a day, where emphasis is placed on those parts of the Quran and Hadith that glorify martyrdom, and that describe the benefits of the afterlife.[85] Harvey Kushner adds that "students are assigned various tasks to test their commitment: delivering weapons for use in clandestine activities is a popular way to judge the student's ability to follow orders and keep a secret."[86]

Besides indoctrination, the candidate will also undergo a process of cleansing and spiritual purification while he is being trained. He will go on lengthy fasts, will spend most of the nights praying, pay off all his debts, and ask for forgiveness for the sins and offenses he committed.[87]

When the candidate for the suicide mission has been indoctrinated, has proven his understanding and belief in the relevant parts of the Quran, and has manifested his courage as well as his ability to keep a secret, he will usually go through several final stages, shortly before he embarks on his mission.

In most cases, the candidate will "disappear," leaving his home and family without a trace.[88]

During this time, he will undergo intensive training for several days, and will acquaint himself with most operational aspects of his mission, including how to detonate the explosive device.[89]

In the last days before the bombing, the candidate will prepare his will in the form of a letter, audio tape, or video cassette, shot against the background of the sponsoring organization's banner. He will usually pose with the Quran in one hand, and a gun or a bomb in the other. In the video recording, the martyr will usually praise the holy war and call on his brethren to follow his example. He then will watch the tape over and over again in order to familiarize himself with his impending mission.[90] Just before the bomber sets out on his mission, Nasra Hassan writes,

> He performs a ritual ablution, puts on clean clothes, and tries to attend at least one communal prayer at a mosque. He says the traditional Islamic prayer that is customary before battle, and he asks Allah to forgive his sins and to bless his mission. He puts a Quran in his left breast pocket, above the heart, and he straps explosives around his waist or picks up a briefcase or a bag containing the bomb. The planner bids him farewell with the words "May Allah be with you, may Allah give you success so that you achieve Paradise." The would-be martyr responds, "Inshallah, we will meet in Paradise."

The purpose of the recruitment, training, and indoctrination process is for the organization to reach its goal of staging a terrorist attack, while minimizing the risks involved. These include the risk of failure, group exposure, and wasting resources. The organization attempts to achieve its objectives by recruiting the right candidates—those who remain terse and are committed to secrecy—and by training and indoctrinating these individuals. Both training and indoctrination involve the mental preparation to commit a highly violent act that will result in one's own death. To that end, the organization provides the candidate with religious and political indoctrination, in the course of which the terrorist act will be given a moral, political, and religious justification.

According to Ariel Merari, the organization and the individual form a kind of "social contract" that the candidate will find difficult, if not impossible, to break. The contract can be sealed at the end of a process consisting of three phases: first, long meetings between the trainee and trainers. During these "peptalks," several issues are discussed: the humiliation suffered as a result of the Israeli occupation; early Arab glory, juxtaposed with the current state of Arab and Islamic affairs; the glorification of martyrdom as a heroic act; and the benefits of being a martyr. Second, organizations use methods of group pressure. Third, the individual is compelled to commit himself personally and publicly by videotaping himself.[91]

Group leaders are well aware that group pressure, peptalks, and the recording of a videotape will all but seal the shaheed's fate. For organizations, preventing the candidate from changing his mind at the last moment is a top priority. By employing these forms of pressure, the organizations achieve their goal because the shaheed comes to understand that a sudden change of mind would be tantamount not only to betrayal, but also to tremendous shame. The shaheed reaches, as Merari says, a "point of no return." "From then on, he is the living martyr."[92]

Planning and execution

Suicide bombers are usually sent to perpetrate the attacks relatively soon after the training and indoctrination period for fear that they might change their minds. Organizations are also aware that the longer they remain living martyrs, the greater the chances they will let other people in on their secret, and the greater the risk that they will be intercepted by Israeli security forces.

The execution of any suicide bombing is an extremely secretive and carefully planned act, regardless of the sponsoring organization. Once the decision to perpetrate an attack has been made, the organization needs to gather intelligence, assemble the bomb material, and organize the departure for the attack target selected.[93] The following sections describe three key components of the logistical planning that takes place prior to the execution of the suicide bombing.

Weapon procurement

Most of the materials used in suicide bombings come from Egypt and are smuggled into the Gaza Strip either by sea or through underground tunnels. The seizure of the ship *Karine-A* in early 2002 suggested that Iran is another major supplier of weapons to the Palestinians. Among the weapons confiscated by an Israeli naval commando on the night of 3 January 2002 were about 1.5 tons of explosives believed by the Israeli military intelligence to have been destined for use in suicide bombings.[94]

Division of labor and compartmentalization

To guarantee the secrecy of the attack, the planning stage is highly compartmentalized. According to a report in the Israeli daily *Yediot Aharonot*, the following hierarchy prevails in the planning process: (1) The organizational leadership is the top decision-making body and determines the need to execute a suicide attack. (2) Next comes the "operator," who is responsible for the selection of the shaheed and his aides. (3) The aides, in turn, obtain the explosives, organize the means of transportation, and provide all other necessary items such as fake identity cards, Israeli army uniforms, wigs, or other types of camouflage. However, it is the operator who will eventually assemble the electronic apparatus for the explosive, which must be easy to operate.[95]

The so-called martyrdom cell (*Al khaliyya al istishhadiyya*) is the fundamental unit that organizes each suicide attack, and is tightly compartmentalized. The cell consists of the operator and two or three aides. The cell members, each of whom bears the title *al shaheed al hayy* (the living martyr), do not disclose their membership in the cell to their families and friends. Neither do they know the identity of the other cell members, except for that of the leader. At the end of each attack, the martyrdom cell is dissolved.[96]

The suicide bomber and the other cell members do not know the exact location of the attack, both for security reasons, as well as to prevent the suicide bomber from visiting the place in advance. The organization is concerned that the suicide bomber who visits the location in advance may change his mind about carrying out the operation due to a bad conscience.[97]

The suicide bomber will often be disguised as a religious Jew, an Israeli soldier, or a tourist. He will often have little difficulty crossing from the West Bank into Israel, given the highly porous nature of the Green Line.[98] It is generally more difficult to cross the border from the Gaza Strip to Israel, which explains why only five attacks (less than 10% of all attacks) in the first 21 months of the Second Intifada have been perpetrated in Gaza, by Gazans (see Figure 7.12).

Target selection

Israeli interrogations of suicide bombers have shed some light on some of the operational methods used by suicide bombers. According to a report in the Israeli daily *Ha'aretz*, Israeli interrogations of suicide bombers whose attacks have been foiled established that the shaheeds were instructed to target large public shopping or leisure venues, to attack crowds or civilians, to synchronize the detonation of an explosive with the gathering of a line at the entrance to a large public venue, and to avoid security check areas by finding an area at some distance from security personnel.[99]

Conclusion

The analytical framework introduced here is founded on the assumption that the phenomenon of suicide terrorism needs to be examined both at the individual and organizational levels. An organization without individuals that are willing to die will be unable to translate its goals into practice, whereas an individual who is willing to become a shaheed would normally lack the resources, information, and logistical capacity to turn his intentions into deeds.

Two major conclusions can be reached with regard to the motivations of those Palestinians that volunteer for suicide missions. First, most of the

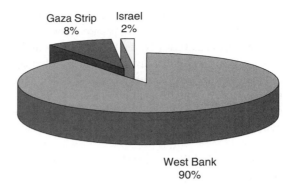

FIGURE 7.12 ■ Origin of attacker, October 2000–June 2002.

Palestinian individuals who volunteer for suicide missions seem to be influenced by several motivations at once, although the exact combination of these motivations varies from case to case. Therefore, although one volunteer for martyrdom may be most affected by, for example, religious and national motives, another may be more influenced by the promise of personal benefits, and may have been more susceptible to group pressure. It is impossible to delineate the exact combination of motives because many of them are difficult to distinguish from each other, and in fact often feed one another. It is difficult, for instance, to separate economic from personal motives when it is clear that economic distress has a bearing on the individual's dignity, or may create an urge to exact revenge against those held responsible for his misery.

It is unlikely—though it cannot entirely be ruled out—that a single motive among those identified would be sufficient cause for a Palestinian individual to be willing to sacrifice his life. Nationalist and economic motives alone, for example, are not sufficient explanations as to why groups employ suicide bombings as a tactic. Many other nations struggle for national self-determination without resorting to suicide terrorism, and the existence of economic hardship is a global phenomenon that does not necessarily lead to a "culture" of suicide bombings. The same can be said of religious motives, especially when it is considered that few Arab or Islamic countries—including those that host a relatively large number of radical Islamists—are plagued by this phenomenon.

More important may be the fact that the conflict bears a strong religious dimension, manifested by the fact that the terms Israeli, Jew, and Zionist are used virtually interchangeably. A deep-seated animosity toward Jews seems likely to serve as an additional incentive to commit acts of suicide terrorism.

It seems painfully obvious that many Palestinian suicide bombers believe that the benefits of becoming a martyr outweigh the costs. Becoming a martyr, many believe, is the fulfillment of a religious command. It provides an escape from the humiliation felt by most Palestinians. It provides the suicide bomber and his family with a multitude of tangible and intangible benefits, and offers an afterlife in paradise that is preferred to the reality of everyday life under Israeli occupation. Martyrdom bestows on the Palestinian youth a sense of achievement, and offers him an opportunity to stand out from the crowd. It lenables him to exact revenge on the despised Israeli/Jewish enemy while humiliating him and exposing his weaknesses. Last, but not least, the shaheed is fighting for the homeland he believes was illegally taken away from him and his family. A cost-benefit analysis undertaken by the volunteer for martyrdom, therefore, may result in his conviction that istishhad is a tempting, even attractive option, and that the rewards offered come at a relatively low price. That price may or may not include a mourning family. But, then again, the shaheed is likely convinced that he will rejoin his loved ones in heaven anyway.

Aware of what motivates the potential martyrs, organizations seek out candidates that demonstrate the highest promise to achieve the organization's goals while minimizing the risks of failure, exposure, and wasting of resources. The purpose of the training and indoctrination process, meanwhile, is to prepare the candidate mentally by inculcating religious and political propaganda that will justify his deed, while committing him psychologically to the eventual execution of the suicide attack.

Israel faces a particularly daunting task in addressing the phenomenon of suicide terrorism. The very multitude of motivations that provoke a person's decision to volunteer for a suicide mission makes it difficult to identify the root causes of the problem. Even if identified, it seems unlikely that any quick and easy solutions would be available to address those highly complex causes.

In the short run, therefore, the state confronted with this phenomenon would be hard pressed to find ways of removing the motivations that present themselves to young Palestinians. Given the pressure to act quickly, Israel will be more likely to target the more easily identifiable organizations that sponsor suicide missions. This may help explain Israel's attempt to "destroy the terrorist infrastructure"[100] by staging incursions into Palestinian cities during operations such as "Defensive Shield" of April 2002.

In the longer run, however, it is unlikely that targeting the organizations alone will prove to be the best strategy to fight this form of terrorism. A better long-term strategy would consist of a two-tiered approach targeting the organizations on one hand, and attempting to remove the incentives for individual Palestinians to volunteer for suicide missions on the other. Finding a way to address the individual motivations that play an integral role in suicide terrorism will certainly prove to be a major challenge for Israel in the years to come.

NOTES

1. See Israeli Ministry of Foreign Affairs website, 3 August 2002 (http://www.mfa.gov.il/). See also Ze'ev Schiff, "Strategic Dilemma," *Ha'aretz* (On-Line Edition), 9 August 2002.
2. See Ze'ev Schiff, "Strategic Dilemma," *Ha'aretz* (On-Line Edition), 9 August 2002.
3. See Israeli Ministry of Foreign Affairs website, 3 August 2002. See also Tracy Wilkinson, "Lives Forever Scarred after Suicide Bombings," *Los Angeles Times*, 21 July 2002, p. 1, which lists at least 270 Israelis killed and an estimated 2,500 wounded. Additional statistics on Israeli victims are available at the websites of the Israel Defense Forces (IDF) (http://www.idf.il/), and the website of B'Tselem, the Israeli Information Center for Human Rights in the Occupied Territories at (http://www.btselem.org/).
4. "Victims of Palestinian Violence and Terrorism," Israeli Ministry of Foreign Affairs, 3 August 2002, available at (http://www.mfa.gov.il/mfa/go.asp?MFAH0ia50/).

5. At the time of this writing, the only book that has dealt exclusively with the phenomenon of suicide terrorism is a collection of proceedings of an International Conference on Suicide Terrorism that was sponsored by the International Policy Institute for Counter-Terrorism (ICT) in Herzliya, Israel, on 20–21 February 2000. The book is titled *Countering Suicide Terrorism: An International Conference* (Herzliya, Israel: The International Policy Institute for Counter-Terrorism (ICT) at the Interdisciplinary Center, Herzliya, Israel, 2001).

6. Not all terrorism analysts agree on the importance of individual aspects of suicide terrorism. For example, Prof. Ariel Merari, a leading scholar on suicide bombings from Tel Aviv University, refers to suicide terrorism as an "organizational phenomenon." See lecture by Prof. Ariel Merari at the Fletcher School of Law and Diplomacy on 16 January 2002, summarized in Assaf Moghadam, "Fletcher Hosts Ariel Merari, Israeli Expert on Suicide Terrorism," *Fletcher Ledger*, 4 February 2002, available at (http://www.fletcherledger.com/archive/2002-02-04/020402-NfinalSuicideTerrorism.htm).

7. There are a few exceptions to this rule. In February 2001, for example, a 35-year-old Palestinian bus driver apparently acting on his own overran and killed eight Israelis.

8. It is assumed that some of these motives apply to both individuals and organizations.

9. Lecture by Ariel Merari at the Fletcher School of Law and Diplomacy, in Assaf Moghadam, "Fletcher Hosts Ariel Merari, Israeli Expert on Suicide Terrorism," *Fletcher Ledger*, 4 February 2002, available at (http://www.fletcherledger.com/archive/2002-02-04/020402-NfinalSuicideTerrorism.htm).

10. Ibid.

11. For in-depth discussions on religious aspects of suicide terrorism, see in particular the studies by Reuven Paz, including "Suicide and Jihad in Radical Palestinian Islam: The Ideological Realm," *Data and Analysis* (Netunim ve-Nituakh), Moshe Dayan Center for Middle Eastern and African Studies, Tel Aviv University, 1998 (in Hebrew); "The Islamic Legitimacy of Suicide Terrorism," in *Countering Suicide Terrorism: An International Conference* (Herzliya, Israel: The International Policy Institute for Counter-Terrorism (ICT) at the Interdisciplinary Center, Herzliya, Israel: 2001); and "Programmed Terrorists," ICT, 13 December 2001, available at (http://www.ict.org.il/articles/articledet.cfm?articleid=419); see also Abdul Hadi Palazzi, "Orthodox Islamic Perceptions of Jihad and Martyrdom," in ICT, *Countering Suicide Terrorism*.

12. Nasra Hassan, "An Arsenal of Believers: Talking to the 'Human Bombs,'" *The New Yorker*, 19 November 2001, p. 38.

13. Walter Laqueur (ed.), *The New Terrorism: Fanaticism and the Arms of Mass Destruction* (Oxford/New York: Oxford University Press, 1999), p. 130.

14. Quoted in Laura Marlowe, "A Fiery Cleric's Defense of Jihad," *Time*, 15 January 1996. See Bruce Hoffman, *Inside Terrorism* (New York: Columbia University Press, 1998), p. 97.

15. Reuven Paz, "The Islamic Legitimacy of Suicide Terrorism," p. 91.

16. "Friday Sermon on PA TV: Blessings to Whoever Saved a Bullet to Stick it in a Jew's Head," *Special Dispatch No. 252*, Middle East Media Research Institute (MEMRI), 7 August 2001, available at (http://www.memri.org/).

17. Quoted in Mark Juergensmeyer, *The New Cold War* (Berkeley: University of California Press, 1993), p. 153.

18. See, for example, "Hundreds of Men, Women, Volunteer for 'Martyrdom Operations,'" *Palestinian Information Center*, 19 May 2001, FBIS-NES, Document ID GMP20010519000045, "An Estimated 1,000 Martyrdom Bombers said Willing to Join Hamas' Military Wing," *Al-Majd*, 20 August 2001, FBIS-NES, GMP20010822000212.

19. Nasra Hassan, "An Arsenal of Believers," p. 39.

20. Quoted in Jeffrey Goldberg, "The Martyr Strategy: What Does the New Phase of Terrorism Signify?" *New Yorker*, 9 July 2001, p. 36.

21. "Egyptian Government Daily on the Muslims' Love of Death and Their Enemies' Love of Life," *Special Dispatch No. 289*, MEMRI, 19 October 2001, available at (http://www.memri.org/).

22. Reuven Paz, "The Islamic Legitimacy of Suicide Terrorism," p. 93.

23. Author's interview with Reuven Paz, 6 January 2002.

24. See, for example, David C. Rapoport, "Sacred Terror: A Contemporary Example from Islam," in Walter Reich (ed.), *Origins of Terrorism: Psychologies, Ideologies, Theologies, States of Mind* (Washington, DC: Woodrow Wilson Center Press, 1998), pp. 117–118.

25. See interview with Abdul Aziz al-Rantisi, in Mark Juergensmeyer, *Terror in the Mind of God: The Global Rise of Religious Violence* (Berkeley: University of California Press, 2000), pp. 187–188.

26. See, for example, Roni Shaked, "$10,000 per 'Shahid,'" *Yediot Ahronot*, 13 December 2000, available at (http://www.mfa.gov.il/). In March 2002, the *Sydney Morning Herald* reported that some 46 families of Tulkarm received checks of $25,000 for each martyr, and of $10,000 for each Palestinian shot by Israeli troops, from Saddam Hussein. See "Witwenrente von Saddam?" SPIEGEL Online, 26 March 2002, available at (http://www.spiegel.de/politik/ausland/0,1518,189096,00.html).

27. Joseph Lelyveld, All Suicide Bombers are Not Alike," *New York Times Magazine*, 28 October 2001, p. 50.

28. See, for example, "Hamas Military Wing Promises Suicide Operations to Avenge 11-Year-Old Boy," *London Quds Press*, FBIS-NES, GMP20010708000123.

29. "Profile of a Suicide Bomber: Single Male, Average Age 21," *Ha'aretz* (Online Edition), 24 August 2001.

30. Nasra Hassan, "An Arsenal of Believers," p. 41.

31. "Palestinian Suicide Bomber Dies in Gaza Blast," *Reuters*, 9 July 2001.

32. "Palestinian 'Suicide Bomber' Interviewed on Motives, Family Background," *Al Majallah*, 19 August 2001, in FBIS-NES, GMP20010822000152.

33. Cameron W. Barr, "A Suicide Bomber's World," *Christian Science Monitor*, 14 August 2001.

34. See Juergensmeyer, *Terror in the Mind of God*, p. 187.

35. For an extensive discussion on the subject, see Yotam Feldner, "72 Black-Eyed Virgins: A Muslim Debate on the Rewards of Martyrs," *Inquiry and Analysis No. 74, MEMRI*, 30 October 2001, available at (http://www.memri.org/).

36. Ibid.

37. Jack Kelley, "The Secret World of Suicide Bombers," *USA Today*, 26 June 2001, p. 1A.

38. Moshe Sunder, "The Lost Garden of Eden," *Ma'ariv* (Weekend Section), 17 August 2001, p. 28 (Hebrew).

39. Yotam Feldner, "72 Black-Eyed Virgins," *MEMRI*, 30 October 2001.

40. "Palestinian 'Suicide Bomber' Interviewed on Motives, Family Background," *Al Majallah*, 19 August 2001, in FBIS-NES, GMP20010822000152.

41. "Hamas Leader Al-Rantisi Reacts to Tel Aviv Explosion," *Doha Al-Jazeera Satellite Channel Television*, 1 June 2001, FBIS-NES GMP20010601000214.

42. Ze'ev Schiff and Ehud Ya'ari, *Intifada: The Palestinian Uprising—Israel's Third Front* (New York: Simon and Schuster, 1989), pp. 82–83.

43. Author's interview with Reuven Paz, Hertzliya, Israel, 6 January 2002.

44. Donna Abu Nasr, "Suicide Bombers United in Deadly Goal," *Ottawa Citizen*, 30 January 1995, p. A6.

45. Ze'ev Schiff and Ehud Ya'ari, *Intifada*, p. 91.

46. CIA World Factbook, 2001, 28 December 2001, available at (http://www.cia.gov/cia/publications/factbook/).

47. Ibid.

48. Harvey Morris, "Closures in West Bank and Gaza 'Hurting Israel,' UNSCO Report," *Financial Times*, 21 December 2001, p. 8. See also "Fifteen Months: Intifada, Closures, and Palestinian Economic Crisis—An Assessment," World Bank Report, 18 March 2002. The World Bank report data reflects that of the UNSCO report. The report is available at (http://lnweb18.worldbank.org/mna/mena.nsf/Attachments/complete/$File/complete.pdf/).

49. Ibid.

50. Philip Jacobson, "Home-grown Martyrs of the West Bank Reap Deadly Harvest," *Sunday Telegraph*, 19 August 2001, p. 20.

51. See Juergensmeyer, *Terror in the Mind of God*, p. 191.

52. Public Opinion Poll, June 2001, available at the website of the Jerusalem Media and Communication Centre (JMCC) (http://www.jmcc.org/publicpoll/pop/01/jun/pop4.htm/).

53. Jerusalem Media and Communication Centre Poll # 45, May–June 2002, available at (http://www.jmcc.org/publicpoll/results/2002/no45.htm/).

54. The author thanks Jessica Stern for her insightful comments on the role of organizations in terrorism.

55. The brevity of this section shall in no way indicate that organizational motives are less important than individual motives.

56. Martha Crenshaw, "The Logic of Terrorism: Terrorist Behavior as a Product of Strategic Choice," in Walter Reich (ed.), *Origins of Terrorism*, p. 8.

57. On organizational theorists, see Chester I. Barnard, *The Functions of the Executive* (Cambridge, MA: Harvard University Press, 1938), p. 216; and James Q. Wilson, *Political Organizations* (New York: Basic Books, 1973), pp. 30–36. On terrorism analysts, see for example Jerrold M. Post, who argues that "for any group or organization, the highest priority is survival. This is especially true for the terrorist group," in Jerrold M. Post, "Terrorist Psycho-Logic," in Walter Reich (ed.), *Origins of Terrorism*, p. 38.

58. See, for example, Mary Jo Hatch, *Organization Theory: Modern Symbolic and Postmodern Perspectives* (Oxford/New York: Oxford University Press, 1997) pp. 120–121.

59. See the Second Chapter of the Hamas Charter. The translation of the Hamas Charter used in this discussion can be found in the *Journal of Palestine Studies* XXII(4) (Summer 1993), pp. 122–134.

60. Bruce Hoffman, *Inside Terrorism*, p. 142.

61. See, for example, "Hamas Military Wing Promises 'Wave' of Suicide Operations," *Palestinian Information Center*, 17 July 2001, in FBIS-NES, Document ID GMP20010717000181.

62. See for example "Hamas Leader Al-Rantisi on Netanya Attacks, Suicide Operations," Doha Al Jazeera Satellite Channel Television, 8 January 2001, FBIS-NES, Document ID GMP20010108000280.

63. See for example, Khaled Abu Toameh, "From Cradle to Grave," *Jerusalem Report*, 4 September 1997, p. 34. At the time of this writing (April 2002), Israel conducts a self-declared "war on terrorism," during which it has occupied several cities under Palestinian control, including Ramallah, Bethlehem, and Nablus. In the course of Operation "Defensive Shield," as the operation has been labeled, Israel may find evidence that will lead to a reassessment of the nature of the relationship between Hamas's political and military wings.

64. The group's name is based on Izz-al-Din al-Qassam, considered a heroic figure by most Palestinian Islamic movements—a pioneer of the Palestinian armed resistance and the father of the armed Palestinian revolution. For information on Izz-al-Din al-Qassam the individual, see Ziad Abu-Amr, *Islamic Fundamentalism in the West Bank and Gaza: Muslim Brotherhood and Islamic Jihad* (Bloomington/Indianapolis: Indiana University Press, 1994), pp. 98–101.

65. See "Suicide and Car Bombings in Israel since the Declaration of Principles," Israeli Ministry of Foreign Affairs

website (http://www.mfa.gov.il/mfa/go.asp? MFAH0i5d0).

66. ICT, "Hamas (Islamic Resistance Movement)," available at (http://www.ict.org.il/).

67. Shaul Mishal and Avraham Sela, *The Palestinian Hamas: Vision, Violence, and Coexistence* (New York: Columbia University Press, 2000), p. 78.

68. See Ziad Abu-Amr, *Islamic Fundamentalism in the West Bank and Gaza*, p. xvii, p. 93.

69. See Jeffrey Goldberg, "The Martyr Strategy," p. 35.

70. Also known as Al-Quds [Jerusalem] Brigades, Al-Quds Squads, or Jerusalem Squads.

71. "Islamic Jihad Leader Interviewed on Jerusalem Operation, *Beirut Al-Manar Television*, 9 August 2001, in FBIS-NES, Document ID GMP20010809000114.

72. See, for example, the website of the Israeli Ministry of Foreign Affairs (http://www.mfa.gov.il/).

73. On the responsibility of Tanzim in the attack, see for example Ze'ev Schiff, "Israel Warns Hamas: Don't Use Rockets," *Ha'aretz* (On-Line Edition), 20 January 2002.

74. See Serge Schmemann, "In the Arabs' Struggle Against Israel, There are Many Players," *New York Times* (Internet Edition), 30 March 2002.

75. Matthew Levitt, "Designating the Al-Aqsa Martyr's Brigades," *PeaceWatch* # 371, The Washington Institute for Near East Policy, 25 March 2002, available at (http://www.washingtoninstitute.org).

76. Ibid.

77. See article by Ron Ben-Yishai, "Anatomy of a Suicide," *Yediot Aharonot*, 27 January 1995 (Hebrew).

78. Harvey Kushner, "Suicide Bombers: Business as Usual," *Studies in Conflict & Terrorism*, 19 (1996), pp. 329–337, on p. 332.

79. "A May 2002 Interview with the Hamas Commander of the Al-Qassam Brigades," translated by the Middle East Media Research Institute (*MEMRI*), Special Dispatch No. 403, 24 July 2002, available at (http://www.memri.org/).

80. See Jack Kelley, quoting "Hamas," in "The Secret World of Suicide Bombers," *USA Today*, 26 June 2001, p. 1A.

81. Jeffrey Goldberg, "The Martyr Strategy," p. 36; see also "A May 2002 Interview with the Hamas Commander of the Al-Qassam Brigades," *MEMRI*, Special Dispatch No. 403, 24 July 2002.

82. See Ziad Abu-Amr, *Islamic Fundamentalism in the West Bank and Gaza*, p. 95.

83. See Ariel Merari, quoted in Juergensmeyer, *Terror in the Mind of God*, p. 78.

84. Author's interview with a high-ranking IDF official.

85. The martyr is particularly encouraged to read six specific chapters of the Quran that feature such themes as jihad, the birth of the nation of Islam, war, Allah's favors, and the importance of faith. See Nasra Hassan, "An Arsenal of Believers," p. 41.

86. Harvey Kushner, "Suicide Bombers: Business as Usual," p. 333.

87. Nasra Hassan, "An Arsenal of Believers," p. 41.

88. In a recent article on the Al-Aqsa Martyrs Brigade, one candidate was said to have spoken to his mother while undergoing training. There is not enough information available at this point to establish whether this was an outlier case, or whether Fatah's training is less stringent than that of Hamas and PIJ, enabling the candidate to stay in touch with his family throughout the process. See Hala Jaber, "Inside the World of the Palestinian Suicide Bomber," *Sunday Times* (London), 24 March 2002.

89. Compare Boaz Ganor, "Suicide Attacks in Israel," in ICT, *Countering Suicide Terrorism*, p. 140. According to Ganor's excellent study, the bomber will understand *all* operational aspects during this stage. However, there are indications, which will be mentioned later, that the suicide bomber will be unaware of the location and type of attack until the very last moments before his mission.

90. Nasra Hassan, "An Arsenal of Believers," p. 41.

91. Lecture by Ariel Merari at the Fletcher School of Law and Diplomacy, in Assaf Moghadam, "Fletcher Hosts Ariel Merari, Israeli Expert on Suicide Terrorism," *Fletcher Ledger*, 4 February 2002, available at (http://www.fletcherledger.com/archive/2002-02-04/020402-NflualSuicideTerrorism.htm).

92. Ibid.

93. See Boaz Ganor, "Suicide Attacks in Israel," p. 141.

94. See, for example, Yossi Klein Halevi, "Stop Terror at its Source: Iran," *Los Angeles Times*, 8 January 2002, p. 11.

95. See Ron Ben-Yishai, "Anatomy of a Suicide," *Yediot Aharonot*, 27 January 1995. (Hebrew)

96. Nasra Hassan, "An Arsenal of Believers," p. 41.

97. See Ron Ben-Yishai, "Anatomy of a Suicide," *Yediot Aharonot*, 27 January 1995. (Hebrew)

98. A Palestinian man, Ibrahim Sarachne, who served as the driver for four aspiring suicide bombers between March and May 2002, and was subsequently arrested, described in a June 2002 interview the ease with which Palestinian attackers can cross Israeli roadblocks and closures. See "Guide for Bombers Maps His Methods," *Los Angeles Times*, 12 June 2002, p. 1.

99. Amos Harel, "Suicide Bombers Instructed to Aim for the Front of the Line," *Ha'aretz* (On-Line Edition), 16 July 2001.

100. According to former Israeli chief of staff, Lt.-Gen. Shaul Mofaz. Arieh O'Sullivan, "A War in Defense of Our Homes," *Jerusalem Post*, 16 April 2002, p. 7.

Received August 1, 2002
Accepted August 17, 2002 ■

Genesis of Suicide Terrorism

Scott Atran*

Contemporary suicide terrorists from the Middle East are publicly deemed crazed cowards bent on senseless destruction who thrive in poverty and ignorance. Recent research indicates they have no appreciable psychopathology and are as educated and economically well-off as surrounding populations. A first line of defense is to get the communities from which suicide attackers stem to stop the attacks by learning how to minimize the receptivity of mostly ordinary people to recruiting organizations.

According to the U.S. Department of State report *Patterns of Global Terrorism 2001* [1], no single definition of terrorism is universally accepted; however, for purposes of statistical analysis and policy-making: "The term 'terrorism' means premeditated, politically motivated violence perpetrated against noncombatant targets by subnational groups or clandestine agents, usually intended to influence an audience." Of course, one side's "terrorists" may well be another side's "freedom fighters" (Figure 8.1). For example, in this definition's sense, the Nazi occupiers of France rightly denounced the "subnational" and

FIGURE 8.1 ■ Chanting demonstrators in Pakistan-held Kashmir defending Osama bin Laden's actions and ambitions as freedom-fighting (November 2001). [PA Photos/Roshan Mugal]

"clandestine" French Resistance fighters as terrorists. During the 1980s, the International Court of Justice used the U.S. Administration's own

*CNRS–Institut Jean Nicod, 1 bis Avenue Lowendal, 75007 Paris, France, and Institute for Social Research, University of Michigan, Ann Arbor, MI 48106–1248, USA. E-mail: satran@umich.edu

Thanks to D. Medin, N. Chomsky, R. Gonzalez, M. Bazerman, R. Nisbett, and reviewers.

definition of terrorism to call for an end to U.S. support for "terrorism" on the part of Nicaraguan Contras opposing peace talks.

For the U.S. Congress, " 'act of terrorism' means an activity that—(A) involves a violent act or an act dangerous to human life that is a violation of the criminal laws of the United States or any State, or that would be a criminal violation if committed within the jurisdiction of the United States or of any State; and (B) appears to be intended (i) to intimidate or coerce a civilian population; (ii) to influence the policy of a government by intimidation or coercion; or (iii) to affect the conduct of a government by assassination or kidnapping."[2]. When suitable, the definition can be broadened to include states hostile to U.S. policy.

Apparently, two official definitions of terrorism have existed since the early 1980s: that used by the Department of State "for statistical and analytical purposes" and that used by Congress for criminal proceedings. Together, the definitions allow great flexibility in selective application of the concept of terrorism to fluctuating U.S. priorities. The special category of "State-sponsored terrorism" could be invoked to handle some issues[3], but the highly selective and politically tendentious use of the label terrorism would continue all the same. Indeed, there appears to be no principled distinction between "terror" as defined by the U.S. Congress and "counterinsurgency" as allowed in U.S. armed forces manuals[4].

Rather than attempt to produce a stipulative and all-encompassing definition of terrorism, this article restricts its focus to "suicide terrorism" characterized as follows: the targeted use of self-destructing humans against noncombatant— typically civilian—populations to effect political change. Although a suicide attack aims to physically destroy an initial target, its primary use is typically as a weapon of psychological warfare intended to affect a larger public audience. The primary target is not those actually killed or injured in the attack, but those made to witness it. The enemy's own information media amplify the attack's effects to the larger target population. Through indoctrination and training and under charismatic leaders, self-contained suicide cells canalize disparate religious or political sentiments of individuals into an emotionally bonded group of fictive kin who willfully commit to die spectacularly for one another and for what is perceived as the common good of alleviating the community's onerous political and social realities.

Recent History

Suicide attack is an ancient practice with a modern history (supporting online text). Its use by the Jewish sect of Zealots (*sicari*) in Roman-occupied Judea and by the Islamic Order of Assassins (*hashashin*) during the early Christian Crusades are legendary examples[5]. The concept of "terror" as systematic use of violence to attain political ends was first codified by Maximilien Robespierre during the French Revolution. He deemed it an "emanation of virtue" that delivers "prompt, severe, and inflexible" justice, as "a consequence of the general principle of democracy applied to our country's most pressing needs."[6]. The Reign of Terror, during which the ruling Jacobin faction exterminated thousands of potential enemies, of whatever sex, age, or condition, lasted until Robespierre's fall (July 1794). Similar justification for state-sponsored terror was common to 20th-century revolutions, as in Russia (Lenin), Cambodia (Pol Pot), and Iran (Khomeini).

Whether subnational (e.g., Russian anarchists) or state-supported (e.g., Japanese *kamikaze*), suicide attack as a weapon of terror is usually chosen by weaker parties against materially stronger foes when fighting methods of lesser cost seem unlikely to succeed. Choice is often voluntary, but typically under conditions of group pressure and charismatic leadership. Thus, the *kamikaze* ("divine wind") first used in the battle of the Philippines (November 1944) were young, fairly well educated pilots who understood that pursuing conventional warfare would likely end in defeat. When collectively asked by Adm. Takijiro Onishi to volunteer for "special attack" (*tokkotai*) "transcending life and death," all stepped forward, despite assurances that refusal would carry no shame or punishment. In the Battle of Okinawa (April 1945) some 2000 *kamikaze* rammed fully fueled fighter planes into more than 300 ships, killing 5000 Americans in the most costly naval battle in U.S. history. Because of such losses, there was support for using the atomic bomb to end World War II[7].

The first major contemporary suicide terrorist attack in the Middle East was the December 1981 destruction of the Iraqi embassy in Beirut (27 dead, over 100 wounded). Its precise authors are still unknown, although it is likely that Ayatollah Khomeini approved its use by parties sponsored by Iranian intelligence. With the assassination of pro-Israeli Lebanese President Bashir Gemayel in September 1982, suicide bombing became a strategic political weapon. Under the pro-Iranian Lebanese Party of God (Hezbollah), this strategy soon achieved geopolitical effect with the October 1983 truck-bomb killing of nearly 300 American and French servicemen. American and France abandoned the multinational force policing Lebanon. By 1985, these attacks arguably led Israel to cede most of the gains made during its 1982 invasion of Lebanon.

In Israel-Palestine, suicide terrorism began in 1993, with attacks by Hezbollah-trained members of the Islamic Resistance Movement (Hamas) and Palestine Islamic Jihad (PIJ) aimed at derailing the Oslo Peace Accords[8]. As early as 1988, however, PIJ founder Fathi Shiqaqi established guidelines for "exceptional" martyrdom operations involving human bombs. He followed Hezbollah in stressing that God extols martyrdom but abhors suicide: "Allah may cause to be known those who believe and may make some of you martyrs, and Allah may purify those who believe and may utterly destroy the disbelievers"; however, "no one can die except by Allah's leave"[9, 10] (Figure 8.2).

The recent radicalization and networking through Al-Qaida of militant Islamic groups from North Africa, Arabia, and Central and Southeast Asia stems from the Soviet-Afghan War (1979–1989). With financial backing from the United States, members of these various groups were provided opportunities to pool and to unify doctrine, aims, training, equipment, and methods,

FIGURE 8.2 ■ Wreckage in Gaza after an Israeli attack that killed Salah Shehadeh, Hamas military commander. It features the green Hamas flag, and Arabic graffiti reads: "We are resisters, death in the way of Allah is the life." [AP Photo/Adel Hana]

including suicide attack. Through its multifaceted association with regional groups (by way of finance, personnel, and logistics), Al-Qaida aims to realize flexibly its global ambition of destroying Western dominance through local initiatives to expel Western influences[11]. According to *Jane's Intelligence Review*: "All the suicide terrorist groups have support infrastructures in Europe and North America."[12].

Calling the current wave of radical Islam "fundamentalism" (in the sense of "traditionalism") is misleading, approaching an oxymoron (supporting online text). Present-day radicals, whether Shi'ite (Iran, Hezbollah) or Sunni (Taliban, Al-Qaida), are much closer in spirit and action to Europe's post-Renaissance Counter-Reformation than to any traditional aspect of Moslem history. The idea of a ruling ecclesiastical authority, a state or national council of clergy, and a religious police devoted to physically rooting out heretics and blasphemers has its clearest historical model in the Holy Inquisition. The idea that religion must struggle to assert control over politics is radically new to Islam[13].

Dubious Public Perceptions

Recent treatments of Homeland Security research concentrate on how to spend billions to protect sensitive installations from attack[14, 15]. But this last line of defense is probably easiest to breach because of the multitude of vulnerable and likely targets (including discotheques, restaurants, and malls), the abundance of would-be attackers (needing little supervision once embarked on a mission), the relatively low costs of attack (hardware store ingredients, no escape needs), the difficulty of detection (little use of electronics), and the unlikelihood that attackers would divulge sensitive information (being unaware of connections beyond their operational cells). Exhortations to put duct tape on windows may assuage (or incite) fear, but will not prevent massive loss of life, and public realization of such paltry defense can undermine trust. Security agencies also attend to prior lines of defense, such as penetrating agent-handling networks of terrorist groups, with only intermittent success.

A first line of defense is to prevent people from becoming terrorists. Here, success appears doubtful should current government and media opinions about why people become human bombs translate into policy (see also supporting online text on contrary academic explanations). Suicide terrorists often are labeled crazed cowards bent on senseless destruction who thrive in the midst of poverty and ignorance. The obvious course becomes to hunt down terrorists while simultaneously transforming their supporting cultural and economic environment from despair to hope. What research there is, however, indicates that suicide terrorists have no appreciable psychopathology and are at least as educated and economically well off as their surrounding populations.

Psychopathology: A Fundamental Attribution Error

U.S. President George W. Bush initially branded 9/11 hijackers "evil cowards." For U.S. Senator John Warner, preemptive assaults on terrorists and those supporting terrorism are justified because: "Those who would commit suicide in their assaults on the free world are not rational and are not deterred by rational concepts"[16]. In attempting to counter anti-Moslem sentiment, some groups advised their members to respond that "terrorists are extremist maniacs who don't represent Islam at all"[17].

Social psychologists have investigated the "fundamental attribution error," a tendency for people to explain behavior in terms of individual personality traits, even when significant situational factors in the larger society are at work. U.S. government and media characterizations of Middle East suicide bombers as craven homicidal lunatics may suffer from a fundamental attribution error: No instances of religious or political suicide terrorism stem from lone actions of cowering or unstable bombers.

Psychologist Stanley Milgram found that ordinary Americans also readily obey destructive orders under the right circumstances[18]. When told by a "teacher" to administer potentially life-threatening electric shocks to "learners" who fail to memorize word pairs, most comply. Even when subjects stressfully protest as victims plead and scream, use of extreme violence continues—not because of murderous tendencies but from a sense of obligation in situations of authority, no matter how trite. A legitimate hypothesis is that apparently extreme behaviors may be elicited and rendered commonplace by particular historical, political, social, and ideological contexts.

With suicide terrorism, the attributional problem is to understand why nonpathological individuals respond to novel situational factors in numbers sufficient for recruiting organizations to implement policies. In the Middle East, perceived contexts in which suicide bombers and supporters express themselves include a collective sense of historical injustice, political subservience, and social humiliation vis-à-vis global powers and allies, as well as countervailing religious hope (supporting online text on radical Islam's historical novelty). Addressing such perceptions does not entail accepting them as simple reality; however, ignoring the causes of these perceptions risks misidentifying causes and solutions for suicide bombing.

There is also evidence that people tend to believe that their behavior speaks for itself, that they see the world objectively, and that only other people are biased and misconstrue events[19]. Moreover, individuals tend to misperceive differences between group norms as more extreme than they really are. Resulting misunderstandings—encouraged by religious and ideological propaganda—lead antagonistic groups to interpret each other's views of events, such as terrorism/freedom-fighting, as wrong, radical, and/or irrational. Mutual demonization and warfare readily ensue. The problem is to stop this spiral from escalating in opposing camps (Figure 8.3).

Poverty and Lack of Education Are Not Reliable Factors

Across our society, there is wide consensus that ridding society of poverty rids it of crime[20]. According to President Bush, "We fight poverty because hope is the answer to terror. . . . We will challenge the poverty and hopelessness and lack of education and failed governments that too often allow conditions that terrorists can seize"[21]. At a gathering of Nobel Peace Prize laureates, South Africa's Desmond Tutu and South Korea's Kim Dae Jong opined, "at the bottom of terrorism is poverty"; Elie Wiesel and the Dalai Lama

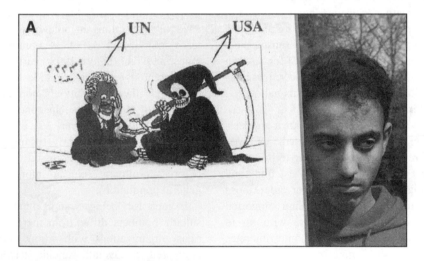

FIGURE 8.3 ■ Demonization works both ways. (A) Demonstrator's placard outside the Palestinian embassy in Beijing vilifying the United Nations and the United States (April 2002). [Reuters/Andrew Wong] (B) Anti-Moslem sign outside Jacksonville, Florida, church (January 2003).

concluded, "education is the way to eliminate terrorism"[22].

Support for this comes from research pioneered by economist Gary Becker showing that property crimes are predicted by poverty and lack of education[23]. In his incentive-based model, criminals are rational individuals acting on self-interest. Individuals choose illegal activity if rewards exceed probability of detection and incarceration together with expected loss of income from legal activity ("opportunity costs"). Insofar as criminals lack skill and education, as in much blue-collar crime, opportunity costs may be minimal; so crime pays.

Such rational-choice theories based on economic opportunities do not reliably account for some types of violent crimes (domestic homicide, hate killings). These calculations make even less sense for suicide terrorism. Suicide terrorists generally are not lacking in legitimate life opportunities relative to their general population. As the Arab press emphasizes, if martyrs had nothing to lose, sacrifice would be senseless[24]: "He who commits suicide kills himself for his own benefit, he who commits martyrdom sacrifices himself for the sake of his religion and his nation. . . . The Mujahed is full of hope"[25].

Research by Krueger and Maleckova suggests that education may be uncorrelated, or even positively correlated, with supporting terrorism[26]. In a December 2001 poll of 1357 West Bank and Gaza Palestinians 18 years of age or older, those having 12 or more years of schooling supported armed attacks by 68 points, those with up to 11 years of schooling by 63 points, and illiterates by 46 points. Only 40% of persons with advanced degrees supported dialogue with Israel versus 53% with college degrees and 60% with 9 years or less of schooling. In a comparison of Hezbollah militants who died in action with a random sample of Lebanese from the same age group and region, militants were less likely to come from poor homes and more likely to have had secondary-school education.

Nevertheless, relative loss of economic or social advantage by educated persons might encourage support for terrorism. In the period leading to the first Intifada (1982–1988), the number of Palestinian men with 12 years or more of schooling more than doubled; those with less schooling increased only 30%. This coincided with a sharp increase in unemployment for college graduates relative to high school graduates. Real daily wages of college graduates fell some 30%; wages for those with only secondary schooling held steady. Underemployment also seems to be a factor among those recruited to Al-Qaida and its allies from the Arabian peninsula[27].

The Institutional Factor: Organizing Fictive Kin

Although humiliation and despair may help account for susceptibility to martyrdom in some situations, this is neither a complete explanation nor one applicable to other circumstances. Studies by psychologist Ariel Merari point to the importance of institutions in suicide terrorism[28]. His team interviewed 32 of 34 bomber families in Palestine/Israel (before 1998), surviving attackers, and captured recruiters. Suicide terrorists apparently span their population's normal distribution in terms of education, socioeconomic status, and personality type (introvert vs. extrovert). Mean age for bombers was early twenties. Almost all were unmarried and expressed religious belief before recruitment (but no more than did the general population).

Except for being young, unattached males, suicide bombers differ from members of violent racist organizations with whom they are often compared[29]. Overall, suicide terrorists exhibit no socially dysfunctional attributes (fatherless, friendless, or jobless) or suicidal symptoms. They do not vent fear of enemies or express "hopelessness" or a sense of "nothing to lose" for lack of life alternatives that would be consistent with economic rationality. Merari attributes primary responsibility for attacks to recruiting organizations, which enlist prospective candidates from this youthful and relatively unattached population. Charismatic trainers then intensely cultivate mutual commitment to die within small cells of three to six members. The final step before a martyrdom operation is a formal social contract, usually in the form of a video testament.

From 1996 to 1999 Nasra Hassan, a Pakistani relief worker, interviewed nearly 250 Palestinian recruiters and trainers, failed suicide bombers, and relatives of deceased bombers. Bombers were men aged 18 to 38: "None were uneducated, desperately poor, simple-minded, or depressed. . . . They all seemed to be entirely normal members of their families"[30]. Yet "all were deeply religious," believing their actions "sanctioned by the divinely revealed religion of Islam." Leaders of sponsoring organizations complained, "Our biggest problem is the hordes of young men who beat on our doors."

Psychologist Brian Barber surveyed 900 Moslem adolescents during Gaza's first Intifada (1987–1993)[31]. Results show high levels of participation in and victimization from violence. For males, 81% reported throwing stones, 66% suffered physical assault, and 63% were shot at (versus 51, 38, and 20% for females). Involvement in violence was not strongly correlated with depression or antisocial behavior. Adolescents most involved displayed strong individual pride and social cohesion. This was reflected in activities: for males, 87% delivered supplies to activists, 83% visited martyred families, and 71% tended the wounded (57, 46, and 37% for females). A follow-up during the second Intifada (2000–2002) indicates that those still unmarried act in ways considered personally more dangerous but socially more meaningful. Increasingly, many view martyr acts as most meaningful. By summer 2002, 70 to 80% of Palestinians endorsed martyr operations[32].

Previously, recruiters scouted mosques, schools, and refugee camps for candidates deemed susceptible to intense religious indoctrination and logistical training. During the second Intifada, there has been a surfeit of volunteers and increasing involvement of secular organizations (allowing women). The frequency and violence of suicide attacks have escalated (more bombings since February 2002 than during 1993–2000); planning has been less painstaking. Despite these changes, there is little to indicate overall change in bomber profiles (mostly unmarried, average socio-economic status, moderately religious)[28, 30].

In contrast to Palestinians, surveys with a control group of Bosnian Moslem adolescents from the same time period reveal markedly weaker expressions of self-esteem, hope for the future, and prosocial behavior[30]. A key difference is that Palestinians routinely invoke religion to invest personal trauma with proactive social meaning that takes injury as a badge of honor. Bosnian Moslems typically report not considering religious affiliation a significant part of personal or collective identity until seemingly arbitrary violence forced awareness upon them.

Thus, a critical factor determining suicide terrorism behavior is arguably loyalty to intimate cohorts of peers, which recruiting organizations often promote through religious communion (supporting online text on religion's role)[33]. Consider data on 39 recruits to *Harkat al-Ansar*, a Pakistani-based ally of Al-Qaida. All were unmarried males, most had studied the *Quran*. All believed that by sacrificing themselves they would help secure the future of their "family" of fictive kin: "Each [martyr] has a special place—among them are brothers, just as there are sons and those even more dear"[34]. A Singapore Parliamentary report on 31 captured operatives from *Jemaah Islamiyah* and other Al-Qaida allies in Southeast Asia underscores the pattern: "These men were not ignorant, destitute or disenfranchised. All 31 had received secular education. . . . Like many of their counterparts in militant Islamic organizations in the region, they held normal, respectable jobs. . . . As a group, most of the detainees regarded religion as their most important personal value . . . secrecy over the true knowledge of *jihad*, helped create a sense of sharing and empowerment vis-à-vis others."[35].

Such sentiments characterize institutional manipulation of emotionally driven commitments that may have emerged under natural selection's influence to refine or override short-term rational calculations that would otherwise preclude achieving goals against long odds. Most typically, such emotionally driven commitments serve as survival mechanisms to inspire action in otherwise paralyzing circumstances, as when a weaker person convincingly menaces a stronger person into thinking twice before attempting to take advantage. In religiously inspired suicide terrorism, however, these emotions are purposely manipulated by organizational leaders, recruiters, and trainers to benefit the organization rather than the individual (supporting online text on religion)[36].

Rational Choice is the Sponsor's Prerogative, Not the Agent's

Little tangible benefit (in terms of rational-choice theories) accrues to the suicide bomber, certainly not enough to make the likely gain one of maximized "expected utility." Heightened social recognition occurs only after death, obviating personal material benefit. But for leaders who almost never consider killing themselves (despite declarations of readiness to die), material benefits more likely outweigh losses in martyrdom operations. Hassan cites one Palestinian official's prescription for a successful mission: "a willing young man . . . nails, gunpowder, a light switch and a short cable, mercury (readily obtainable from thermometers), acetone. . . . The most expensive item is transportation to an Israeli town"[30]. The total cost is about $150.

For the sponsoring organization, suicide bombers are expendable assets whose losses generate more assets by expanding public support and pools of potential recruits. Shortly after 9/11, an intelligence survey of educated Saudis (ages 25 to 41) concluded that 95% supported Al-Qaida[37]. In a December 2002 Pew Research Center survey on growing anti-Americanism, only 6% of Egyptians viewed America and its "War on Terror" favorably[38]. Money flows from those willing to let others die, easily offsetting operational costs (training, supporting personnel, safe houses, explosives and other arms, transportation, and communication). After a Jerusalem supermarket bombing by an 18-year-old Palestinian female, a Saudi telethon raised more than $100 million for "the Al-Quds Intifada."

Massive retaliation further increases people's sense of victimization and readiness to behave according to organizational doctrines and policies structured to take advantage of such feelings. In a poll of 1179 West Bank and Gaza Palestinians in spring 2002, 66% said army operations increased their backing for suicide bombings[39]. By year's end, 73% of Lebanese Moslems considered suicide bombings justifiable[38]. This radicalization of opinion increases both demand and supply for martyrdom operations. A December 2002 UN report credited volunteers with swelling a reviving Al-Qaida in 40 countries[40]. The organization's influence in the larger society—most significantly its directing elites—increases in turn.

Priorities for Homeland Security

The last line of defense against suicide terrorism—preventing bombers from reaching targets—may be the most expensive and least likely to succeed. Random bag or body searches cannot be very effective against people willing to die, although this may provide some semblance of security and hence psychological defense against suicide terrorism's psychological warfare. A middle line of defense, penetrating and destroying recruiting organizations and isolating their leaders, may be successful in the near term, but even more resistant organizations could emerge instead. The first line of defense is to drastically reduce receptivity of potential recruits to recruiting organizations. But how?

It is important to know what probably will not work. Raising literacy rates may have no effect and could be counterproductive should greater literacy translate into greater exposure to terrorist propaganda (in Pakistan, literacy and dislike for the United States increased as the number of religious *madrasa* schools increased from 3000 to 39,000 since 1978)[27, 38]. Lessening poverty may have no effect, and could be counterproductive if poverty reduction for the entire population amounted to a downward redistribution of wealth that left those initially better off with fewer opportunities than before. Ending occupation or reducing perceived humiliation may help, but not if the population believes this to be a victory inspired by terror (e.g.,

Israel's apparently forced withdrawal from Lebanon).

If suicide-bombing is crucially (though not exclusively) an institution-level phenomenon, it may require finding the right mix of pressure and inducements to get the communities themselves to abandon support for institutions that recruit suicide attackers. One way is to so damage the community's social and political fabric that any support by the local population or authorities for sponsors of suicide attacks collapses, as happened regarding the kamikaze as a by-product of the nuclear destruction of Hiroshima and Nagasaki. In the present world, however, such a strategy would neither be morally justifiable nor practical to implement, given the dispersed and distributed organization of terrorist institutions among distantly separated populations that collectively number in the hundreds of millions. Likewise, retaliation in kind ("tit-for-tat") is not morally acceptable if allies are sought[41]. Even in more localized settings, such as the Israeli-Palestinian conflict, coercive policies alone may not achieve lasting relief from attack and can exacerbate the problem over time. On the inducement side, social psychology research indicates that people who identify with antagonistic groups use conflicting information from the other group to reinforce antagonism[19]. Thus, simply trying to persuade others from without by bombarding them with more self-serving information may only increase hostility.

Other research suggests that most people have more moderate views than what they consider their group norm to be. Inciting and empowering moderates from within to confront inadequacies and inconsistencies in their own knowledge (of others as evil), values (respect for life), and behavior (support for killing), and other members of their group[42], can produce emotional dissatisfaction leading to lasting change and influence on the part of these individuals[43]. Funding for civic education and debate may help, also interfaith confidence-building through intercommunity interaction initiatives (as Singapore's government proposes)[35]. Ethnic profiling, isolation, and preemptive attack on potential (but not yet actual)

FIGURE 8.4 ■ Moslem youth with *Quran* dressed as a Palestinian suicide bomber demonstrating outside the United Nations office in Jakarta, Indonesia (April 2002). (Indonesia is the most populous Moslem nation.) [Reuters/Darren Whiteside]

supporters of terrorism probably will not help. Another strategy is for the United States and its allies to change behavior by directly addressing and lessening sentiments of grievance and humiliation, especially in Palestine (where images of daily violence have made it the global focus of Moslem attention)[44] (Figure 8.4). For no evidence (historical or otherwise) indicates that support for suicide terrorism will evaporate without complicity in achieving at least some fundamental goals that suicide bombers and supporting communities share.

Of course, this does not mean negotiating over all goals, such as Al-Qaida's quest to replace the Western-inspired system of nation-states with a global caliphate, first in Moslem lands and then everywhere (see supporting online text for history and agenda of suicide-sponsoring groups). Unlike other groups, Al-Qaida publicizes no specific demands after martyr actions. As with an avenging army, it seeks no compromise. But most people who currently sympathize with it might.

Perhaps to stop the bombing we need research to understand which configurations of psychological and cultural relationships are luring and binding thousands, possibly millions, of mostly ordinary people into the terrorist organization's martyr-making web. Study is needed on how terrorist

before implementation of "confidence building" measures, with an understanding by all parties of what to expect in the end, it is likely that doubts about ultimate intentions will undermine any interim accord—as in

every case since 1948. [S. Atran, *Politics and Society* **18**, 481 (1990)].

45. N. Chomsky, *9–11* (Seven Stories Press, New York, 2001).

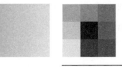

The Strategic Logic of Suicide Terrorism

Robert A. Pape*

Suicide terrorism is rising around the world, but the most common explanations do not help us understand why. Religious fanaticism does not explain why the world leader in suicide terrorism is the Tamil Tigers in Sri Lanka, a group that adheres to a Marxist/Leninist ideology, while existing psychological explanations have been contradicted by the widening range of socio-economic backgrounds of suicide terrorists. To advance our understanding of this growing phenomenon, this study collects the universe of suicide terrorist attacks worldwide from 1980 to 2001, 188 in all. In contrast to the existing explanations, this study shows that suicide terrorism follows a strategic logic, one specifically designed to coerce modern liberal democracies to make significant territorial concessions. Moreover, over the past two decades, suicide terrorism has been rising largely because terrorists have learned that it pays. Suicide terrorists sought to compel American and French military forces to abandon Lebanon in 1983, Israeli forces to leave Lebanon in 1985, Israeli forces to quit the Gaza Strip and the West Bank in 1994 and 1995, the Sri Lankan government to create an independent Tamil state from 1990 on, and the Turkish government to grant autonomy to the Kurds in the late 1990s. In all but the case of Turkey, the terrorist political cause made more gains after the resort to suicide operations than it had before. Thus, Western democracies should pursue policies that

* Robert A. Pape is Associate Professor, Department of Political Science, 5828 South University Avenue, The University of Chicago, Chicago, IL 60637 (r-pape@uchicago.edu).

I thank Robert Art, Mia Bloom, Steven Cícala, Alex Downs, Daniel Drezner, Adria Lawrence, Sean Lynn-Jones, John Mearsheimer, Michael O'Connor, Sebastian Rosato, Lisa Weeden, the anonymous reviewers, and the members of the program on International Security Policy at the University of Chicago for their superb comments. I especially thank James K. Feldman and Chaim D. Kaufmann for their excellent comments on multiple drafts. I would also like to acknowledge encouragement from the committee for the Combating Political Violence paper competition sponsored by the Institute for War and Peace Studies at Columbia University, which selected an earlier version as a winning paper.

teach terrorists that the lesson of the 1980s and 1990s no longer holds, policies which in practice may have more to do with improving homeland security than with offensive military action.

Terrorist organizations are increasingly relying on suicide attacks to achieve major political objectives. For example, spectacular suicide terrorist attacks have recently been employed by Palestinian groups in attempts to force Israel to abandon the West Bank and Gaza, by the Liberation Tigers of Tamil Eelam to compel the Sri Lankan government to accept an independent Tamil homeland, and by Al Qaeda to pressure the United States to withdraw from the Saudi Arabian Peninsula. Moreover, such attacks are increasing both in tempo and location. Before the early 1980s, suicide terrorism was rare but not unknown (Lewis 1968; O'Neill 1981; Rapoport 1984). However, since the attack on the U.S. embassy in Beirut in April 1983, there have been at least 188 separate suicide terrorist attacks worldwide, in Lebanon, Israel, Sri Lanka, India, Pakistan, Afghanistan, Yemen, Turkey, Russia and the United States. The rate has increased from 31 in the 1980s, to 104 in the 1990s, to 53 in 2000–2001 alone (Pape 2002). The rise of suicide terrorism is especially remarkable, given that the total number of terrorist incidents worldwide fell during the period, from a peak of 666 in 1987 to a low of 274 in 1998, with 348 in 2001 (Department of State 2001).

What accounts for the rise in suicide terrorism, especially, the sharp escalation from the 1990s onward? Although terrorism has long been part of international politics, we do not have good explanations for the growing phenomenon of suicide terrorism. Traditional studies of terrorism tend to treat suicide attack as one of many tactics that terrorists use and so do not shed much light on the recent rise of this type of attack (e.g., Hoffman 1998; Jenkins 1985; Laqueur 1987). The small number of studies addressed explicitly to suicide terrorism tend to focus on the irrationality of the act of suicide from the perspective of the individual attacker. As a result, they focus on individual motives—either

religious indoctrination (especially Islamic Fundamentalism) or psychological predispositions that might drive individual suicide bombers (Kramer 1990; Merari 1990; Post 1990).

The first-wave explanations of suicide terrorism were developed during the 1980s and were consistent with the data from that period. However, as suicide attacks mounted from the 1990s onward, it has become increasingly evident that these initial explanations are insufficient to account for which individuals become suicide terrorists and, more importantly, why terrorist organizations are increasingly relying on this form of attack (Institute for Counter-Terrorism 2001). First, although religious motives may matter, modern suicide terrorism is not limited to Islamic Fundamentalism. Islamic groups receive the most attention in Western media, but the world's leader in suicide terrorism is actually the Liberation Tigers of Tamil Eelam (LTTE), a group who recruits from the predominantly Hindu Tamil population in northern and eastern Sri Lanka and whose ideology has Marxist/ Leninist elements. The LTTE alone accounts for 75 of the 186 suicide terrorist attacks from 1980 to 2001. Even among Islamic suicide attacks, groups with secular orientations account for about a third of these attacks (Merari 1990; Sprinzak 2000).

Second, although study of the personal characteristics of suicide attackers may someday help identify individuals terrorist organizations are likely to recruit for this purpose, the vast spread of suicide terrorism over the last two decades suggests that there may not be a single profile. Until recently, the leading experts in psychological profiles of suicide terrorists characterized them as uneducated, unemployed, socially isolated, single men in their late teens and early 20s (Merari 1990; Post 1990). Now we know that suicide terrorists can be college educated or uneducated, married or single, men or women, socially isolated or integrated, from age 13 to age 47 (Sprinzak 2000). In other words, although only a tiny number of people become suicide terrorists, they come from a broad cross section of lifestyles, and it may be impossible to pick them out in advance.

In contrast to the first-wave explanations, this article shows that suicide terrorism follows a strategic logic. Even if many suicide attackers are irrational or fanatical, the leadership groups that recruit and direct them are not. Viewed from the perspective of the terrorist organization, suicide attacks are designed to achieve specific political purposes: to coerce a target government to change policy, to mobilize additional recruits and financial support, or both. Crenshaw (1981) has shown that terrorism is best understood in terms of its strategic function; the same is true for suicide terrorism. In essence, suicide terrorism is an extreme form of what Thomas Schelling (1966) calls "the rationality of irrationality," in which an act that is irrational for individual attackers is meant to demonstrate credibility to a democratic audience that still more and greater attacks are sure to come. As such, modern suicide terrorism is analogous to instances of international coercion. For states, air power and economic sanctions are often the preferred coercive tools (George et al. 1972; Pape 1996, 1997). For terrorist groups, suicide attacks are becoming the coercive instrument of choice.

To examine the strategic logic of suicide terrorism, this article collects the universe suicide terrorist attacks worldwide from 1980 to 2001, explains how terrorist organizations have assessed the effectiveness of these attacks, and evaluates the limits on their coercive utility.

Five principal findings follow. First, suicide terrorism is strategic. The vast majority of suicide terrorist attacks are not isolated or random acts by individual fanatics but, rather, occur in clusters as part of a larger campaign by an organized group to achieve a specific political goal. Groups using suicide terrorism consistently announce specific political goals and stop suicide attacks when those goals have been fully or partially achieved.

Second, the strategic logic of suicide terrorism is specifically designed to coerce modern democracies to make significant concessions to national self-determination. In general, suicide terrorist campaigns seek to achieve specific territorial goals, most often the withdrawal of the target state's military forces from what the terrorists see as national homeland. From Lebanon to Israel to Sri Lanka to Kashmir to Chechnya, every suicide terrorist campaign from 1980 to 2001 has been waged by terrorist groups whose main goal has been to establish or maintain self-determination for their community's homeland by compelling an enemy to withdraw. Further, every suicide terrorist campaign since 1980 has been targeted against a state that had a democratic form of government.

Third, during the past 20 years, suicide terrorism has been steadily rising because terrorists have learned that it pays. Suicide terrorists sought to compel American and French military forces to abandon Lebanon in 1983, Israeli forces to leave Lebanon in 1985, Israeli forces to quit the Gaza Strip and the West Bank in 1994 and 1995, the Sri Lankan government to create an independent Tamil state from 1990 on, and the Turkish government to grant autonomy to the Kurds in the late 1990s. Terrorist groups did not achieve their full objectives in all these cases. However, in all but the case of Turkey, the terrorist political cause made more gains after the resort to suicide operations than it had before. Leaders of terrorist groups have consistently credited suicide operations with contributing to these gains. These assessments are hardly unreasonable given the timing and circumstances of many of the concessions and given that other observers within the terrorists' national community, neutral analysts, and target government leaders themselves often agreed that suicide operations accelerated or caused the concession. This pattern of making concessions to suicide terrorist organizations over the past two decades has probably encouraged terrorist groups to pursue even more ambitious suicide campaigns.

Fourth, although moderate suicide terrorism led to moderate concessions, these more ambitious suicide terrorist campaigns are not likely to achieve still greater gains and may well fail completely. In general, suicide terrorism relies on the threat to inflict low to medium levels of punishment on civilians. In other circumstances, this level of circumstances as military coercion used by states, and these structural differences help to explain the logic of the strategy. In virtually all instances of international military coercion, the coercer is the stronger state and the target is the weaker state; otherwise, the coercer would likely be deterred or simply unable to execute the threatened military operations (Pape 1996). In these circumstances, coercers have a choice between two main coercive strategies, punishment and denial. Punishment seeks to coerce by raising the costs or risks to the target society to a level that overwhelms the value of the interests in dispute. Denial seeks to coerce by demonstrating to the target state that it simply cannot win the dispute regardless of its level of effort, and therefore fighting to a finish is pointless—for example, because the coercer has the ability to conquer the disputed territory. Hence, although coercers may initially rely on punishment, they often have the resources to create a formidable threat to deny the opponent victory in battle and, if necessary, to achieve a brute force military victory if the target government refuses to change its behavior. The Allied bombing of Germany in World War II, American bombing of North Vietnam in 1972, and Coalition attacks against Iraq in 1991 all fit this pattern.

Suicide terrorism (and terrorism in general) occurs under the reverse structural conditions. In suicide terrorism, the coercer is the weaker actor and the target is the stronger. Although some elements of the situation remain the same, flipping the stronger and weaker sides in a coercive dispute has a dramatic change on the relative feasibility of punishment and denial. In these circumstances, denial is impossible, because military conquest is ruled out by relative weakness. Even though some groups using suicide terrorism have received important support from states and some have been strong enough to wage guerrilla military campaigns as well as terrorism, none have been strong enough to have serious prospects of achieving their political goals by conquest. The suicide terrorist group with the most significant military capacity has been the LTTE, but it has not had a real prospect of controlling the whole of the homeland that

it claims, including Eastern and Northern Provinces of Sri Lanka.

As a result, the only coercive strategy available to suicide terrorists is punishment. Although the element of "suicide" is novel and the pain inflicted on civilians is often spectacular and gruesome, the heart of the strategy of suicide terrorism is the same as the coercive logic used by states when they employ air power or economic sanctions to punish an adversary: to cause mounting civilian costs to overwhelm the target state's interest in the issue in dispute and so to cause it to concede the terrorists' political demands. What creates the coercive leverage is not so much actual damage as the expectation of future damage. Targets may be economic or political, military or civilian, but in all cases the main task is less to destroy the specific targets than to convince the opposing society that they are vulnerable to more attacks in the future. These features also make suicide terrorism convenient for retaliation, a tit-for-tat interaction that generally occurs between terrorists and the defending government (Crenshaw 1981).

The rhetoric of major suicide terrorist groups reflects the logic of coercive punishment. Abdel Karim, a leader of Al Aksa Martyrs Brigades, a militant group linked to Yasir Arafat's Fatah movement, said the goal of his group was "to increase losses in Israel to a point at which the Israeli public would demand a withdrawal from the West Bank and Gaza Strip" (Greenberg 2002). The infamous fatwa signed by Osama Bin Laden and others against the United States reads, "The ruling to kill the Americans and their allies—civilians and military—is an individual duty for every Muslim who can do it in any country in which it is possible to do it, in order to liberate the al-Aqsa Mosque and the holy mosque [Mecca] from their grip, and in order for their armies to move out of all the lands of Islam, defeated and unable to threaten any Muslim" (World Islamic Front 1998).

Suicide terrorists' willingness to die magnifies the coercive effects of punishment in three ways. First, suicide attacks are generally more destructive than other terrorist attacks. An attacker who is willing to die is much more likely to accomplish the mission and to cause maximum damage to the target. Suicide attackers can conceal weapons on their own bodies and make last-minute adjustments more easily than ordinary terrorists. They are also better able to infiltrate heavily guarded targets because they do not need escape plans or rescue teams. Suicide attackers are also able to use certain especially destructive tactics such as wearing "suicide vests" and ramming vehicles into targets. The 188 suicide terrorist attacks from 1980 to 2001 killed an average of 13 people each, not counting the unusually large number of fatalities on September 11 and also not counting the attackers themselves. During the same period, there were about 4,155 total terrorist incidents worldwide, which killed 3,207 people (also excluding September 11), or less than one person per incident. Overall, from 1980 to 2001, suicide attacks amount to 3% of all terrorist attacks but account for 48% of total deaths due to terrorism, again excluding September 11 (Department of State 1983–2001).

Second, suicide attacks are an especially convincing way to signal the likelihood of more pain to come, because suicide itself is a costly signal, one that suggests that the attackers could not have been deterred by a threat of costly retaliation. Organizations that sponsor suicide attacks can also deliberately orchestrate the circumstances around the death of a suicide attacker to increase further expectations of future attacks. This can be called the "art of martyrdom" (Schalk 1997). The more suicide terrorists justify their actions on the basis of religious or ideological motives that match the beliefs of a broader national community, the more the status of terrorist martyrs is elevated, and the more plausible it becomes that others will follow in their footsteps. Suicide terrorist organizations commonly cultivate "sacrificial myths" that include elaborate sets of symbols and rituals to mark an individual attacker's death as a contribution to the nation. Suicide attackers' families also often receive material rewards both from the terrorist organizations and from other supporters. As a result, the art of martyrdom elicits popular support from the terrorists' community, reducing the moral backlash that suicide attacks might otherwise produce, and so establishes the foundation for credible signals of more attacks to come.

Third, suicide terrorist organizations are better positioned than other terrorists to increase expectations about escalating future costs by deliberately violating norms in the use of violence. They can do this by crossing thresholds of damage, by breaching taboos concerning legitimate targets, and by broadening recruitment to confound expectations about limits on the number of possible terrorists. The element of suicide itself helps increase the credibility of future attacks, because it suggests that attackers cannot be deterred. Although the capture and conviction of Timothy McVeigh gave reason for some confidence that others with similar political views might be deterred, the deaths of the September 11 hijackers did not, because Americans would have to expect that future Al Qaeda attackers would be equally willing to die.

The Record of Suicide Terrorism, 1980 to 2001

To characterize the nature of suicide terrorism, this study identified every suicide terrorist attack from 1980 to 2001 that could be found in Lexis Nexis's on-line database of world news media (Pape 2002).[3] Examination of the universe shows that

[3] This survey sought to include every instance of a suicide attack in which the attacker killed himself except those explicitly authorized by a state and carried out by the state government apparatus (e.g., Iranian human wave attacks in the Iran–Iraq war were not counted). The survey is probably quite reliable, because a majority of the incidents were openly claimed by the sponsoring terrorist organizations. Even those that were not were, in nearly all cases, reported multiple times in regional news media, even if not always in the U.S. media. To probe for additional cases, I interviewed experts and officials involved in what some might consider conflicts especially prone to suicide attacks, such as Afghanistan in the 1980s, but this did not yield more incidents. According to the CIA station chief for Pakistan from 1986 to 1988 (Bearden 2002), "I cannot recall a single incident where an Afghan launched himself against a Soviet target with the intention of dying in the process. I don't think these things ever happened, though some of their attacks were a little hare-brained and could have been considered suicidal. I think it's important that Afghans never even took their war outside their borders—for example they never tried to blow up the Soviet Embassy in Pakistan."

selves lowers the freedom rating of these states. Still, all these states elect their chief executives and legislatures in multiparty elections and have seen at least one peaceful transfer of power, making them solidly democratic by standard criteria (Boix and Rosato 2001; Huntington 1991; Przeworski et al. 2000).

The Kurds, which straddle Turkey and Iraq, illustrate the point that suicide terrorist campaigns are more likely to be targeted against democracies than authoritarian regimes. Although Iraq has been far more brutal toward its Kurdish population than has Turkey, violent Kurdish groups have used suicide attacks exclusively against democratic Turkey and not against the authoritarian regime in Iraq. There are plenty of national groups living under authoritarian regimes with grievances that could possibly inspire suicide terrorism, but none have. Thus, the fact that rebels have resorted to this strategy only when they face the more suitable type of target counts against arguments that suicide terrorism is a nonstrategic response, motivated mainly by fanaticism or irrational hatreds.

Terrorists' Assessments of Suicide Terrorism

The main reason that suicide terrorism is growing is that terrorists have learned that it works. Even more troubling, the encouraging lessons that terrorists have learned from the experience of 1980s and 1990s are not, for the most part, products of wild-eyed interpretations or wishful thinking. They are, rather, quite reasonable assessments of the outcomes of suicide terrorist campaigns during this period.

To understand how terrorists groups have assessed the effectiveness of suicide terrorism requires three tasks: (1) explanation of appropriate standards for evaluating the effectiveness of coercion from the standpoint of coercers; (2) analysis of the 11 suicide terrorist campaigns that have ended as of 2001 to determine how frequently target states made concessions that were, or at least could have been, interpreted as due to suicide attack; and (3) close analysis of terrorists' learning

from particular campaigns. Because some analysts see suicide terrorism as fundamentally irrational (Kramer 1990; Merari 1990; Post 1990), it is important to assess whether the lessons that the terrorists drew were reasonable conclusions from the record. The crucial cases are the Hamas and Islamic Jihad campaigns against Israel during the 1990s, because they are most frequently cited as aimed at unrealistic goals and therefore as basically irrational.

Standards of Assessment

Terrorists, like other people, learn from experience. Since the main purpose of suicide terrorism is coercion, the learning that is likely to have the greatest impact on terrorists' future behavior is the lessons that they have drawn from past campaigns about the coercive effectiveness of suicide attack.

Most analyses of coercion focus on the decision making of target states, largely to determine their vulnerability to various coercive pressures (George 1972; Pape 1996). The analysis here, however, seeks to determine why terrorist coercers are increasingly attracted to a specific coercive strategy. For this purpose, we must develop a new set of standards, because assessing the value of coercive pressure for the coercer is not the same problem as assessing its impact on the target.

From the perspective of a target state, the key question is whether the value of the concession that the coercer is demanding is greater than the costs imposed by the coercive pressure, regardless of whether that pressure is in the form of lives at risk, economic hardship, or other types of costs. However, from the perspective of the coercer, the key question is whether a particular coercive strategy promises to be more effective than alternative methods of influence and, so, warrants continued (or increased) effort. This is especially true for terrorists who are highly committed to a particular goal and so willing to exhaust virtually any alternative rather than abandoning it. In this search for an effective strategy, coercers' assessments are likely to be largely a function of estimates of the success of past efforts; for suicide terrorists, this means assessments of whether past suicide campaigns produced significant concessions.

A glance at the behavior of suicide terrorists reveals that such trade-offs between alternative methods are important in their calculations. All of the organizations that have resorted to suicide terrorism began their coercive efforts with more conventional guerrilla operations, nonsuicide terrorism, or both. Hezbollah, Hamas, Islamic Jihad, the PKK, the LTTE, and Al Qaeda all used demonstrative and destructive means of violence long before resorting to suicide attack. Indeed, looking at the trajectory of terrorist groups over time, there is a distinct element of experimentation in the techniques and strategies used by these groups and distinct movement toward those techniques and strategies that produce the most effect. Al Qaeda actually prides itself for a commitment to even tactical learning over time—the infamous "terrorist manual" stresses at numerous points the importance of writing "lessons learned" memoranda that can be shared with other members to improve the effectiveness of future attacks.

The most important analytical difficulty in assessing outcomes of coercive efforts is that successes are more ambiguous than failures. Whenever a suicide terrorist campaign, or any coercive effort, ends without obtaining significant concessions, presumably the coercers must judge the effort as a failure. If, however, the target state does make policy changes in the direction of the terrorists' political goals, this may or may not represent a coercive success for suicide attack in the calculations of the terrorists. The target government's decision could have been mainly or partly a response to the punishment inflicted by the suicide attacks, but it also could be a response to another type of pressure (such as an ongoing guerrilla campaign), or to pressure from a different actor (such as one of the target state's allies) or a different country, or the target's policy decision may not even have been intended as a concession but could have been made for other reasons that only coincidently moved in a direction desired by the terrorists. Different judgments among these alternatives yield different lessons for future usefulness of suicide attack.

Standard principles from social psychology suggest how terrorists are likely to resolve these ambiguities. Under normal conditions, most people tend to interpret ambiguous information in ways that are consistent with their prior beliefs, as well as in ways that justify their past actions (Jervis 1976; Lebow 1981). Suicide terrorists, of course, are likely to have at least some initial confidence in the efficacy of suicide attack or else they would not resort to it, and of course, the fact of having carried out such attacks gives them an interest in justifying that choice. Thus, whenever targets of suicide terrorism make a real or apparent concession and it is a plausible interpretation that it was due to the coercive pressure of the suicide campaign, we would expect terrorists to favor that interpretation even if other interpretations are also plausible.

This does not mean that we should simply expect terrorists to interpret virtually all outcomes, regardless of evidence, as encouraging further terrorism; that would not constitute learning and would make sense only if the terrorists were deeply irrational. To control for this possibility, it is crucial to consider the assessments of the same events by other well-informed people. If we find that when suicide terrorist leaders claim credit for coercing potential concessions, their claims are unique (or nearly so), then it would be appropriate to dismiss them as irrational. If, on the other hand, we find that their interpretations are shared by a significant portion of other observers, across a range of circumstances and interests—from target state leaders, to others in the terrorists' community, to neutral analysts—then we should assume that their assessments are as rational as anyone else's and should take the lessons they draw seriously. In making these judgments, the testimony of target state leaders is often especially telling; although states like the United States and Israel virtually never officially admit making concessions to terrorism, leaders such as Ronald Reagan and Yitzhak Rabin have at times been quite open about the impact of suicide terrorism on their own policy decisions, as we see below.

Finally, understanding how terrorists' assess the effectiveness of suicide terrorism should also be

Examination of these crucial cases demonstrates that the terrorist groups came to the conclusion that suicide attack accelerated Israeli's withdrawal in both cases. Although the Oslo Accords formally committed to withdrawing the IDF from Gaza and the West Bank, Israel routinely missed key deadlines, often by many months, and the terrorists came to believe that Israel would not have withdrawn when it did, and perhaps not at all, had it not been for the coercive leverage of suicide attack. Moreover, this interpretation of events was hardly unique. Numerous other observers and key Israeli government leaders themselves came to the same conclusion. To be clear, Hamas may well have had motives other than coercion for launching particular attacks, such as retaliation (De Figueredo and Weingast 1998), gaining local support (Bloom 2002), or disrupting negotiated outcomes it considered insufficient (Kydd and Walter 2002). However, the experience of observing how the target reacted to the suicide campaigns appears to have convinced terrorist leaders of the coercive effectiveness of this strategy.

To evaluate these cases, we need to know (1) the facts of each case, (2) how others interpreted the events, and (3) how the terrorists interpreted these events. Each campaign is discussed in turn.

Israel's withdrawal from Gaza, May 1994

The Facts. Israel and the Palestinian Liberation Organization signed the Oslo Accords on September 13, 1993. These obligated Israel to withdraw its military forces from the Gaza Strip and West Bank town of Jericho beginning on December 13 and ending on April 13, 1994. In fact, Israel missed both deadlines. The major sticking points during the implementation negotiations in Fall and Winter of 1993–94 were the size of the Palestinian police force (Israel proposed a limit of 1,800, while the Palestinians demanded 9,000) and jurisdiction for certain criminal prosecutions, especially whether Israel could retain a right of hot pursuit to prosecute Palestinian attackers who might flee into Palestinian ruled zones. As of April 5, 1994, these issues were unresolved. Hamas then launched two suicide attacks, one on April 6 and another on

April 13, killing 15 Israeli civilians. On April 18, the Israeli Knesset voted to withdraw, effectively accepting the Palestinian positions on both disputed issues. The suicide attacks then stopped and the withdrawal was actually conducted in a few weeks starting on May 4, 1994.[4]

These two suicide attacks may not originally have been intended as coercive, since Hamas leaders had announced them in March 1994 as part of a planned series of five attacks in retaliation for the February 24th Hebron massacre in which an Israeli settler killed 29 Palestinians and had strong reservations about negotiating a compromise settlement with Israel (Kydd and Walter 2002). However, when Israel agreed to withdraw more promptly than expected, Hamas decided to forgo the remaining three planned attacks. There is thus a circumstantial case that these attacks had the effect of coercing the Israelis into being more forthcoming in the withdrawal negotiations and both Israeli government leaders and Hamas leaders publically drew this conclusion.

Israeli and Other Assessments. There are two main reasons to doubt that terrorist pressure accelerated Israel's decision to withdraw. First, one might think that Israel would have withdrawn in any case, as it had promised to do in the Oslo Accords of September 1993. Second, one might argue that Hamas was opposed to a negotiated settlement with Israel. Taking both points together, therefore, Hamas' attacks could not have contributed to Israel's withdrawal.

The first of these arguments, however, ignores the facts that Israel had already missed the originally agreed deadline and, as of early April 1994, did not appear ready to withdraw at all if that meant surrendering on the size of the Palestinian police force and legal jurisdiction over terrorists. The second argument is simply illogical. Although Hamas objected to surrendering claims to all of historic Palestine, it did value the West Bank and Gaza as an intermediate goal, and certainly had no

---

[4] There were no suicide attacks from April to October 1994.

objection to obtaining this goal sooner rather than later.

Most important, other observers took explanations based on terrorist pressure far more seriously, including the person whose testimony must count most, Israeli Prime Minister Yitzhak Rabin. On April 13, 1994, Rabin said,

I can't recall in the past any suicidal terror acts by the PLO. We have seen by now at least six acts of this type by Hamas and Islamic Jihad. . . . The only response to them and to the enemies of peace on the part of Israel is to accelerate the negotiations. (Makovsky and Pinkas 1994)

On April 18, 1994, Rabin went further, giving a major speech in the Knesset explaining why the withdrawal was necessary:

Members of the Knessett: I want to tell the truth. For 27 years we have been dominating another people against its will. For 27 years Palestinians in the territories . . . get up in the morning harboring a fierce hatred for us, as Israelis and Jews. Each morning they get up to a hard life, for which we are also, but not solely responsible. We cannot deny that our continuing control over a foreign people who do not want us exacts a painful price. . . . For two or three years we have been facing a phenomenon of extremist Islamic terrorism, which recalls Hezbollah, which surfaced in Lebanon and perpetrated attacks, including suicide missions. . . . There is no end to the targets Hamas and other terrorist organizations have among us. Each Israeli, in the territories and inside sovereign Israel, including united Jerusalem, each bus, each home, is a target for their murderous plans. Since there is no separation between the two populations, the current situation creates endless possibilities for Hamas and the other organizations.

Independent Israeli observers also credited suicide terrorism with considerable coercive effectiveness. The most detailed assessment is by Efraim Inbar (1999, 141–42):

A significant change occurred in Rabin's assessment of the importance of terrorist activities. . . . Reacting to the April 1994 suicide attack in Afula, Rabin recognized that terrorists activities by Hamas and other Islamic radicals were "a form of

terrorism different from what we once knew from the PLO terrorist organizations. . . . "Rabin admitted that there was no "hermitic" solution available to protect Israeli citizens against such terrorist attacks. . . . He also understood that such incidents intensified the domestic pressure to freeze the Palestinian track of the peace process. Islamic terrorism thus initially contributed to the pressure for accelerating the negotiations on his part.

Arab writers also attributed Israeli accommodation to the suicide attacks. Mazin Hammad wrote in an editorial in a Jordanian newspaper:

It is unprecedented for an Israeli official like Y. Rabin to clearly state that there is no future for the settlements in the occupied territories. . . . He would not have said this [yesterday] if it was not for the collapse of the security Israel. . . . The martyrdom operation in Hadera shook the faith of the settlers in the possibility of staying in the West Bank and Gaza and increased their motivation to pack their belongings and dismantle their settlements. ("Hamas Operations" 1994)

Terrorists' Assessments. Even though the favorable result was apparently unexpected by Hamas leaders, given the circumstances and the assessments voiced by Rabin and others, it certainly would have been reasonable for them to conclude that suicide terrorism had helped accelerate Israeli withdrawal, and they did.

Hamas leader Ahmed Bakr (1995) said that "what forced the Israelis to withdraw from Gaza was the intifada and not the Oslo agreement," while Imad al-Faluji judged that

all that has been achieved so far is the consequence of our military actions. Without the so-called peace process, we would have gotten even more. . . . We would have got Gaza and the West Bank without this agreement. . . . Israel can beat all Arab Armies. However, it can do nothing against a youth with a knife or an explosive charge on his body. Since it was unable to guarantee security within its borders, Israel entered into negotiations with the PLO. . . . If the Israelis want security, they will have to abandon their settlements . . . in Gaza, the West Bank, and Jerusalem. ("Hamas Leader" 1995)

Further, these events appear to have persuaded terrorists that future suicide attacks could eventually produce still greater concessions. Fathi al-Shaqaqi (1995), leader of Islamic Jihad, said,

> Our jihad action has exposed the enemy weakness, confusion, and hysteria. It has become clear that the enemy can be defeated, for if a small faithful group was able to instill all this horror and panic in the enemy through confronting it in Palestine and southern Lebanon, what will happen when the nation confronts it with all its potential. . . . Martyrdom actions will escalate in the face of all pressures . . . [they] are a realistic option in confronting the unequal balance of power. If we are unable to effect a balance of power now, we can achieve a balance of horror.

Israel's withdrawal from West Bank towns, December 1995

The second Hamas case, in 1995, tells essentially the same story as the first. Again, a series of suicide attacks was associated with Israeli territorial concessions to the Palestinians, and again, a significant fraction of outside observers attributed the concessions to the coercive pressure of suicide terrorism, as did the terrorist leaders themselves.

The Facts.   The original Oslo Accords scheduled Israel to withdraw from the Palestinian populated areas of the West Bank by July 13, 1994, but after the delays over Gaza and Jericho all sides recognized that this could not be met. From October 1994 to April 1995, Hamas, along with Islamic Jihad, carried out a series of seven suicide terrorist attacks that were intended to compel Israel to make further withdrawals and suspended attacks temporarily at the request of the Palestinian Authority after Israel agreed on March 29, 1995 to begin withdrawals by July 1. Later, however, the Israelis announced that withdrawals could not begin before April 1996 because bypass roads needed for the security of Israeli settlements were not ready. Hamas and Islamic Jihad then mounted new suicide attacks on July 24 and August 21, 1995, killing 11 Israeli civilians. In September, Israel agreed to withdraw from the West Bank towns in December

(Oslo II) even though the roads were not finished. The suicide attacks then stopped and the withdrawal was actually carried out in a few weeks starting on December 12, 1995.[5]

Israeli and Other Assessments.   Although Israeli government spokesmen frequently claimed that suicide terrorism was delaying withdrawal, this claim was contradicted by, among others, Prime Minister Rabin. Rabin (1995) explained that the decision for the second withdrawal was, like the first in 1994, motivated in part by the goal of reducing suicide terrorism:

Interviewer: Mr Rabin, what is the logic of withdrawing from towns and villages when you know that terror might continue to strike at us from there?

Rabin: What is the alternative, to have double the amount of terror? As for the issue of terror, take the suicide bombings. Some 119 Israelis . . . have been killed or murdered since 1st January 1994, 77 of them in suicide bombings perpetrated by Islamic radical fanatics. . . . All the bombers were Palestinians who came from areas under our control.

Similarly, an editorial in the Israeli daily *Yediot Aharonot* ("Bus Attack" 1995) explained,

> If the planners of yesterday's attack intended to get Israel to back away from the Oslo accord, they apparently failed. In fact, Prime Minister Y. Rabin is leaning toward expediting the talks with the Palestinians. . . . The immediate conclusion from this line of thinking on Rabin's part—whose results we will witness in the coming days—will be to instruct the negotiators to expedite the talks with the Palestinians with the aim of completing them in the very near future.

Terrorists' Assessments.   As in 1994, Hamas and

---

[5] There were no suicide attacks from August 1995 to February 1996. There were four suicide attacks in response to an Israeli assassination from February 25 to March 4, 1996, and then none until March 1997.

Islamic Jihad came to the conclusion that suicide terrorism was working. Hamas's spokesman in Jordan explained that new attacks were necessary to change Israel's behavior:

> Hamas, leader Muhammad Nazzal said, needed military muscle in order to negotiate with Israel from a position of strength. Arafat started from a position of weakness, he said, which is how the Israelis managed to push on him the solution and get recognition of their state and settlements without getting anything in return. (Theodoulou 1995)

After the agreement was signed, Hamas leaders also argued that suicide operations contributed to the Israeli withdrawal. Mahmud al-Zahhar (1996), a spokesman for Hamas, said,

> The Authority told us that military action embarrasses the PA because it obstructs the redeployment of the Israeli's forces and implementation of the agreement. . . . We offered many martyrs to attain freedom. . . . Any fair person knows that the military action was useful for the Authority during negotiations.

Moreover, the terrorists also stressed that stopping the attacks only discouraged Israel from withdrawing. An early August Hamas communique (No. 125, 1995) read,

> They said that the strugglers' operations have been the cause of the delay in widening the autonomous rule in the West Bank, and that they have been the reason for the deterioration of the living and economic conditions of our people. Now the days have come to debunk their false claims . . . and to affirm that July 1 [a promised date for IDF withdrawal] was no more than yet another of the "unholy" Zionist dates. . . . Hamas has shown an utmost degree of self-restraint throughout the past period. . . . but matters have gone far enough and the criminals will reap what their hands have sown.

Recent Impact of Lessons Learned. In addition to the 1994 and 1995 campaigns, Palestinian terrorist leaders have also cited Hezbollah experience in Lebanon as a source of the lesson that suicide terrorism is an effective way of coercing Israel. Islamic Jihad leader Ramadan Shallah (2001) argued that:

> The shameful defeat that Israel suffered in southern Lebanon and which caused its army to flee it in terror was not made on the negotiations table but on the battlefield and through jihad and martyrdom, which achieved a great victory for the Islamic resistance and Lebanese People. . . . We would not exaggerate if we said that the chances of achieving victory in Palestine are greater than in Lebanon. . . . If the enemy could not bear the losses of the war on the border strip with Lebanon, will it be able to withstand a long war of attrition in the heart of its security dimension and major cities?

Palestinian terrorists are now applying the lessons they have learned. In November 2000, Khalid Mish'al explained Hamas's strategy for the second *intifada*, which was then in its early stages:

> Like the intifada in 1987, the current intifada has taught us that we should move forward normally from popular confrontation to the rifle to suicide operations. This is the normal development. . . . We always have the Lebanese experiment before our eyes. It was a great model of which we are proud.

Even before the second *intifada* began, other Hamas statements similarly expressed,

> The Zionist enemy . . . only understands the language of Jihad, resistance and martyrdom, that was the language that led to its blatant defeat in South Lebanon and it will be the language that will defeat it on the land of Palestine. (Hamas Statement 2000)

The bottom line is that the ferocious escalation of the pace of suicide terrorism that we have witnessed in the past several years cannot be considered irrational or even surprising. Rather, it is simply the result of the lesson that terrorists have quite reasonably learned from their experience of the previous two decades: Suicide terrorism pays.

The Limits of Suicide Terrorism

Despite suicide terrorists' reasons for confidence in the coercive effectiveness of this strategy, there are sharp limits to what suicide terrorism is likely to accomplish in the future. During the 1980s and 1990s, terrorist leaders learned that moderate punishment often leads to moderate concessions and so concluded that more ambitious suicide campaigns would lead to greater political gains. However, today's more ambitious suicide terrorist campaigns are likely to fail. Although suicide terrorism is somewhat more effective than ordinary coercive punishment using air power or economic sanctions, it is not drastically so.

Suicide Terrorism is Unlikely to Achieve Ambitious Goals

In international military coercion, threats to inflict military defeat often generate more coercive leverage than punishment. Punishment, using anything short of nuclear weapons, is a relatively weak coercive strategy because modern nation states generally will accept high costs rather than abandon important national goals, while modern administrative techniques and economic adjustments over time often allow states to minimize civilian costs. The most punishing air attacks with conventional munitions in history were the American B-29 raids against Japan's 62 largest cities from March to August 1945. Although these raids killed nearly 800,000 Japanese civilians—almost 10% died on the first day, the March 9, 1945, fire-bombing of Tokyo, which killed over 85,000—the conventional bombing did not compel the Japanese to surrender.

Suicide terrorism makes adjustment to reduce damage more difficult than for states faced with military coercion or economic sanctions. However, it does not affect the target state's interests in the issues at stake. As a result, suicide terrorism can coerce states to abandon limited or modest goals, such as withdrawal from territory of low strategic importance or, as in Israel's case in 1994 and 1995, a temporary and partial withdrawal from a more important area. However, suicide terrorism is unlikely to cause targets to abandon goals central to their wealth or security, such as a loss of territory that would weaken the economic prospects of the state or strengthen the rivals of the state.

Suicide terrorism makes punishment more effective than in international military coercion. Targets remain willing to countenance high costs for important goals, but administrative, economic, or military adjustments to prevent suicide attack are harder, while suicide attackers themselves are unlikely to be deterred by the threat of retaliation. Accordingly, suicide attack is likely to present a threat of continuing limited civilian punishment that the target government cannot completely eliminate, and the upper bound on what punishment can gain for coercers is recognizably higher in suicidal terrorism than in international military coercion.

The data on suicide terrorism from 1980 to 2001 support this conclusion. While suicide terrorism has achieved modest or very limited goals, it has so far failed to compel target democracies to abandon goals central to national wealth or security. When the United States withdrew from Lebanon in 1984, it had no important security, economic, or even ideological interests at stake. Lebanon was largely a humanitarian mission and not viewed as central to the national welfare of the United States. Israel withdrew from most of Lebanon in June 1985 but remained in a security buffer on the edge of southern Lebanon for more than a decade afterward, despite the fact that 17 of 22 suicide attacks occurred in 1985 and 1986. Israel's withdrawals from Gaza and the West Bank in 1994 and 1995 occurred at the same time that settlements increased and did little to hinder the IDF's return, and so these concessions were more modest than they may appear. Sri Lanka has suffered more casualties from suicide attack than Israel but has not acceded to demands that it surrender part of its national territory. Thus, the logic of punishment and the record of suicide terrorism suggests that, unless suicide terrorists acquire far more destructive technologies, suicide attacks for more ambitious goals are likely to fail and will continue to provoke more aggressive military responses.

Policy Implications for Containing Suicide Terrorism

While the rise in suicide terrorism and the reasons behind it seem daunting, there are important policy lessons to learn. The current policy debate is misguided. Offensive military action or concessions alone rarely work for long. For over 20 years, the governments of Israel and other states targeted by suicide terrorism have engaged in extensive military efforts to kill, isolate, and jail suicide terrorist leaders and operatives, sometimes with the help of quite good surveillance of the terrorists' communities. Thus far, they have met with meager success. Although decapitation of suicide terrorist organizations can disrupt their operations temporarily, it rarely yields long-term gains. Of the 11 major suicide terrorist campaigns that had ended as of 2001, only one—the PKK versus Turkey—did so as a result of leadership decapitation, when the leader, in Turkish custody, asked his followers to stop. So far, leadership decapitation has also not ended Al Qaeda's campaign. Although the United States successfully toppled the Taliban in Afghanistan in December 2001, Al Qaeda launched seven successful suicide terrorist attacks from April to December 2002, killing some 250 Western civilians, more than in the three years before September 11, 2001, combined.

Concessions are also not a simple answer. Concessions to nationalist grievances that are widely held in the terrorists' community can reduce popular support for further terrorism, making it more difficult to recruit new suicide attackers and improving the standing of more moderate nationalist elites who are in competition with the terrorists. Such benefits can be realized, however, only if the concessions really do substantially satisfy the nationalist or self-determination aspirations of a large fraction of the community.

Partial, incremental, or deliberately staggered concessions that are dragged out over a substantial period of time are likely to become the worst of both worlds. Incremental compromise may appear—or easily be portrayed—to the terrorists' community as simply delaying tactics and, thus, may fail to reduce, or actually increase, their distrust that their main concerns will ever be met. Further, incrementalism provides time and opportunity for the terrorists to intentionally provoke the target state in hopes of derailing the smooth progress of negotiated compromise in the short term, so that they can reradicalize their own community and

actually escalate their efforts toward even greater gains in the long term.[6] Thus, states that are willing to make concessions should do so in a single step if at all possible.

Advocates of concessions should also recognize that, even if they are successful in undermining the terrorist leaders' base of support, almost any concession at all will tend to encourage the terrorist leaders further about their own coercive effectiveness. Thus, even in the aftermath of a real settlement with the opposing community, some terrorists will remain motivated to continue attacks and, for the medium term, may be able to do so, which in term would put a premium on combining concessions with other solutions.

Given the limits of offense and of concessions, homeland security and defensive efforts generally must be a core part of any solution. Undermining the feasibility of suicide terrorism is a difficult task. After all, a major advantage of suicide attack is that it is more difficult to prevent than other types of attack. However, the difficulty of achieving perfect security should not keep us from taking serious measures to prevent would-be terrorists from easily entering their target society. As Chaim Kaufmann (1996) has shown, even intense ethnic civil wars can often be stopped by demographic separation because it greatly reduces both means and incentives for the sides to attack each other. This logic may apply with even more force to the related problem of suicide terrorism, since, for suicide attackers, gaining physical access to the general area of the target is the only genuinely demanding part of an operation, and as we have seen, resentment of foreign occupation of their national homeland is a key part of the motive for suicide terrorism.

---

[6] The Bush administration's decision in May 2003 to withdraw most U.S. troops from Saudi Arabia is the kind of partial concession likely to backfire. Al Qaeda may well view this as evidence that the United States is vulnerable to coercive pressure, but the concession does not satisfy Al Qaeda's core demand to reduce American military control over the holy areas on the Arab peninsula. With the conquest and long term military occupation of Iraq, American military capabilities to control Saudi Arabia have substantially increased even if there are no American troops on Saudi soil itself.

The requirements for demographic separation depend on geographic and other circumstances that may not be attainable in all cases. For example, much of Israel's difficulty in containing suicide terrorism derives from the deeply intermixed settlement patterns of the West Bank and Gaza, which make the effective length of the border between Palestinian and Jewish settled areas practically infinite and have rendered even very intensive Israeli border control efforts ineffective (Kaufmann 1998). As a result, territorial concessions could well encourage terrorists leaders to strive for still greater gains while greater repression may only exacerbate the conditions of occupation that cultivate more recruits for terrorist organizations. Instead, the best course to improve Israel's security may well be a combined strategy: abandoning territory on the West Bank along with an actual wall that physically separates the populations.

Similarly, if Al Qaeda proves able to continue suicide attacks against the American homeland, the United States should emphasize improving its domestic security. In the short term, the United States should adopt stronger border controls to make it more difficult for suicide attackers to enter the United States. In the long term, the United States should work toward energy independence and, thus, reduce the need for American troops in the Persian Gulf countries where their presence has helped recruit suicide terrorists to attack America. These measures will not provide a perfect solution, but they may make it far more difficult for Al Qaeda to continue attacks in the United States, especially spectacular attacks that require elaborate coordination.

Perhaps most important, the close association between foreign military occupations and the growth of suicide terrorist movements in the occupied regions should give pause to those who favor solutions that involve conquering countries in order to transform their political systems. Conquering countries may disrupt terrorist operations in the short term, but it is important to recognize that occupation of more countries may well increase the number of terrorists coming at us.

Appendix: Suicide Terrorist Campaigns, 1980–2001

TABLE 9.3.

Date	Group	Weapon	Target	Killed*
		Completed campaigns		
Campaign #1: Hezbollah vs. US, France				
1. April 18, 1983		Car bomb	US embassy, Beirut	63
2. Oct 23, 1983		Car bomb	US Marine barracks, Beirut	241
3. Oct 23, 1983		Car bomb	French barracks, Beirut	58
4. Dec 12, 1983		Grenades	US embassy, Kuwait	7
5. Dec 21, 1983		Car bomb	French HQ, Beirut	1
6. Sept 12, 1984		Truck bomb	US embassy, Beirut	14
Campaign #2: Hezbollah vs. Israel				
1. Nov 4, 1983		Car bomb	IDF post, Tyre, Lebanon	50
2. Jun 16, 1984		Car bomb	IDF post, south Lebanon	5
3. Mar 8, 1985		Truck bomb	IDF post	12
4. Apr 9, 1985		Car bomb	IDF post	4
5. May 9, 1985		Suitcase bomb	Southern Lebanese Army checkpoint	2
6. June 15, 1985		Car bomb	IDF post, Beirut	23
Campaign #3: Hezbollah vs. Israel and South Lebanon Army				
1. July 9, 1985		Car bombs	2 SLA outposts	22
2. July 15, 1985		Car bomb	SLA outpost	10

3. July 31, 1985	Car bomb	IDF patrol, south Lebanon	2
4. Aug 6, 1985	Mule bomb	SLA outpost	0
5. Aug 29, 1985	Car bomb	SLA outpost	15
6. Sept 3, 1985	Car bomb	SLA outpost	37
7. Sept 12, 1985	Car bomb	SLA outpost	21
8. Sept 17, 1985	Car bomb	SLA outpost	30
9. Sept 18, 1985	Car bomb	SLA outpost	0
10. Oct 17, 1985	Grenades	SLA radio station	6
11. Nov 4, 1985	Car bomb	SLA outpost	0
12. Nov 12, 1985	Car bomb	Christ. militia leaders, Beirut	5**
13. Nov 26, 1985	Car bomb	SLA outpost	20
14. April 7, 1986	Car bomb	SLA outpost	1
15. July 17, 1986	Car bomb	Jezzine, south Lebanon	7
16. Nov 20, 1986	Car bomb	SLA outpost	3

Campaign #4: Liberation Tigers of Tamil Eelam vs. Sri Lanka

1. Jul 12, 1990	Boat bomb	Naval vessel, Trincomalee	6
2. Nov 23, 1990	Mines	Army camp, Manakulam	0
3. Mar 2, 1991	Car bomb	Defense minister, Colombo	18**
4. Mar 19, 1991	Truck bomb	Army camp, Silavathurai	5
5. May 5, 1991	Boat bomb	Naval vessel	5
6. May 21, 1991	Belt bomb	Rajiv Gandhi, Madras, India	1**
7. June 22, 1991	Car bomb	Defense ministry, Colombo	27
8. Nov 16, 1992	Motorcycle bomb	Navy commander, Colombo	1**
9. May 1, 1993	Belt bomb	President of Sri Lanka, Colombo	23**
10. Nov 11, 1993	Boat bomb	Naval base, Jaffna Lagoon	0
11. Aug 2, 1994	Grenades	Air force helicopter, Palali	0
12. Sept 19, 1994	Mines	Naval vessel, Sagarawardene	25
13. Oct 24, 1994	Belt bomb	Presidential candidate, Colombo	53**
14. Nov 8, 1994	Mines	Naval vessel, Vettilaikerny	0

Campaign #5: LTTE vs. Sri Lanka

1. Apr 18, 1995	Scuba divers	Naval vessel, Trincomalee	11
2. Jul 16, 1995	Scuba divers	Naval vessel, Jaffna peninsula	0
3. Aug 7, 1995	Belt bomb	Government bldg, Colombo	22
4. Sep 3, 1995	Scuba divers	Naval vessel, Trincomalee	0
5. Sep 10, 1995	Scuba divers	Naval vessel, Kankesanthurai	0
6. Sep 20, 1995	Scuba divers	Naval vessel, Kankesanthurai	0
7. Oct 2, 1995	Scuba divers	Naval vessel, Kankesanthurai	0
8. Oct 17, 1995	Scuba divers	Naval vessel, Trincomalee	9
9. Oct 20, 1995	Mines	2 Oil depots, Colombo	23
10. Nov 11, 1995	Belt bombs	Army HQ, crowd, Colombo	23
11. Dec 5, 1995	Truck bomb	Police camp, Batticaloa	23
12. Jan 8, 1996	Belt bomb	Market, Batticaloa	0
13. Jan 31, 1996	Truck bomb	Bank, Colombo	91
14. Apr 1, 1996	Boat bomb	Navy vessel, Vettilaikerni	10
15. Apr 12, 1996	Scuba divers	Port building, Colombo	0
16. Jul 3, 1996	Belt bomb	Government motorcade, Jaffna	37
17. Jul 18, 1996	Mines	Naval gunboat, Mullaittivu	35
18. Aug 6, 1996	Boat bomb	Naval ship, north coast	0
19. Aug 14, 1996	Bicycle bomb	Public rally, Kalmunai	0
20. Oct 25, 1996	Boat bomb	Gunboat, Trincomalee	12
21. Nov 25, 1996	Belt bomb	Police chief vehicle, Trincomalee	0***
22. Dec 17, 1996	Motorcycle bomb	Police unit jeep, Ampara	1
23. Mar 6, 1997	Grenades	Air base, China Bay	0

(Continued overleaf)

TABLE 9.3. Continued

Date	Group	Weapon	Target	Killed*
24. Oct 15, 1997		Truck bomb	World Trade Centre, Colombo	18
25. Oct 19, 1997		Boat bomb	Naval gunboat, northeastern coast	7
26. Dec 28, 1997		Truck bomb	Political leader, south Sri Lanka	0***
27. Jan 25, 1998		Truck bomb	Buddhist shrine, Kandy	11
28. Feb 5, 1998		Belt bomb	Air Force headquarters, Colombo	8
29. Feb 23, 1998		Boat bombs	2 Landing ships off Point Pedru	47
30. Mar 5, 1998		Bus bomb	Train station, Colombo	38
31. May 15, 1998		Belt bomb	Army brigadier, Jaffna peninsula	1
32. Sep 11, 1998		Belt bomb	Mayor of Jaffna	20**
33. Mar 15, 1999		Belt bomb	Police station, Colombo	5
34. May 29, 1999		Belt bomb	Tamil rival leader, Batticaloa	2
35. Jul 25, 1999		Belt bomb	Passenger ferry, Trincomalee	1
36. Jul 29, 1999		Belt bomb	Tamil politician, Colombo	1**
37. Aug 4, 1999		Bicycle bomb	Police vehicle, Vavuniya	12
38. Aug 9, 1999		Belt bomb	Military commander, Vakarai	1
39. Sep 2, 1999		Belt bomb	Tamil rival, Vavuniya	3**
40. Dec 18, 1999		2 Belt bombs	President of Sri Lanka, Colombo	38***
41. Jan 5, 2000		Belt bomb	Prime minister of Sri Lanka, Colombo	11***
42. Feb 4, 2000		Sea diver	Naval vessel, Trincomalee	0
43. Mar 2, 2000		Belt bomb	Military commander, Trincomalee	1***
44. Mar 10, 2000		Belt bomb	Government motorcade Colombo	23
45. Jun 5, 2000		Scuba diver	Ammunition ship, northeast coast	5
46. Jun 7, 2000		Belt bomb	Industries Minister, Colombo	26**
47. Jun 14, 2000		Bicycle bomb	Air force bus, Wattala Town	2
48. Jun 26, 2000		Boat bomb	Merchant vessel, north coast	7
49. Aug 16, 2000		Belt bomb	Military vehicle, Vavuniya	1
50. Sep 15, 2000		Belt bomb	Hospital, Colombo	7
51. Oct 2, 2000		Belt bomb	Political leader, Trincomalee	22**
52. Oct 5, 2000		Belt bomb	Political rally, Medawachchiya	12
53. Oct 19, 2000		Belt bomb	Cabinet ceremony, Colombo	0
54. Oct 23, 2000		Boat bombs	Gunboat/troop carrier, Trincomalee	2
Campaign #6: Hamas vs. Israel				
1. Apr 6, 1994	Hamas	Car bomb	Afula	9
2. Apr 13, 1994	Hamas	Belt bomb	Hadera	6
Campaign #7: Hamas/Islamic Jihad vs. Israel				
1. Oct 19, 1994	Hamas	Belt bomb	Tel Aviv	22
2. Nov 11, 1994	Islamic Jihad	Bike bomb	Netzarim, Gaza	3
3. Dec 25, 1994	Hamas	Belt bomb	Jerusalem	0
4. Jan 22, 1995	Islamic Jihad	Belt bomb	Beit Lid Junction	21
5. Apr 9, 1995	IJ & H	2 Car bombs	Netzarim, Gaza	8
6. July 24, 1995	Hamas	Belt bomb	Tel Aviv	6
7. Aug 21, 1995	Hamas	Belt bomb	Jerusalem	5
Campaign #8: Hamas vs. Israel				
1. Feb 25, 1996	Hamas	Belt bomb	Jerusalem	25
2. Feb 25, 1996	Hamas	Belt bomb	Ashkelon	1
3. Mar 3, 1996	Hamas	Belt bomb	Jerusalem	19
4. Mar 4, 1996	Hamas	Belt bomb	Tel Aviv	13

Campaign #9: Hamas vs. Israel

1. Mar 21, 1997	Hamas	Belt bomb	Cafe, Tel Aviv	3
2. Jul 30, 1997	Hamas	Belt bomb	Jerusalem	14
3. Sept 4, 1997	Hamas	Belt bomb	Jerusalem	7

Campaign #10: Kurdistan Workers Party (PKK) vs. Turkey

1. Jun 30, 1996	Belt bomb	Tunceli	9
2. Oct 25, 1996	Belt bomb	Adana	4
3. Oct 29, 1996	Belt bombs	Sivas	4

Campaign #11: PKK vs. Turkey

1. Mar 4, 1999	Belt bomb	Batman	0
2. Mar 27, 1999	Grenade	Istanbul	0
3. Apr 5, 1999	Belt bomb	Governor, Bingol	0
4. Jul 5, 1999	Belt bomb	Adana	0
5. Jul 7, 1999	Grenades	Iluh	0
6. Aug 28, 1999	Bomb	Tunceli	0

Ongoing compaigns

Campaign #12: Al Qaeda vs. United States

1. Nov 13, 1995	Car bomb	US military base, Riyadh, SA	5
2. Jun 25, 1996	Truck bomb	US military base, Dhahran SA	19
3. Aug 7, 1998	Truck bombs	US embassies, Kenya/Tanzania	250
4. Oct 12, 2000	Boat bomb	USS Cole, Yemen	17
5. Sep 9, 2001	Camera bomb	Ahmed Shah Massoud, Afghanistan	1**
6. Sep 11, 2001	Hijacked airplanes	WTC/Pentagon	3037

Campaign #13: Chechen Separatists vs. Russia

1. Jun 7, 2000	Truck bomb	Russian police station, Chechnya	2
2. Jul 3, 2000	Truck bomb	Argun, Russia	30
3. Mar 24, 2001	Car bomb	Chechnya	20
4. Nov 29, 2001	Belt bomb	Military commander, Chechnya	1

Campaign #14: Kashmir Separatists vs. India

1. Dec 25, 2000	Car bomb	Srinagar, Kashmir	8
2. Oct 1, 2001	Car bomb	Legislative assembly, Kashmir	30
3. Dec 13, 2001	Gunmen	Parliament, New Delhi	7

Campaign #15: LTTE: vs. Sri Lanka

1. Jul 24, 2001	Belt bomb	International airport, Colombo	12
2. Sep 16, 2001	Boat bomb	Naval vessel, north	29
3. Oct 29, 2001	Belt bomb	PM of Sri Lanka, Colombo	3***
4. Oct 30, 2001	Boat bomb	Oil tanker, northern coast	4
5. Nov 9, 2001	Belt bomb	Police jeep, Batticaloa	0
6. Nov 15, 2001	Belt bomb	Crowd, Batticaloa	3

Campaign #16: Hamas/Islamic Jihad vs. Israel

1. Oct 26, 2000	Islamic Jihad	Bike bomb	Gaza	0
2. Oct 30, 2000	Hamas	Belt bomb	Jerusalem	15
3. Nov 2, 2000	Al Aqsa	Car bomb	Jerusalem	2
4. Nov 22, 2000	Islamic Jihad	Car bomb	Hadera	2
5. Dec 22, 2000	Al Aqsa	Belt bomb	Jordan valley	3
6. Jan 1, 2001	Hamas	Belt bomb	Netanya	10
7. Feb 14, 2001	Hamas	Bus driver	Tel Aviv	8
8. Mar 1, 2001	Hamas	Car bomb	Mei Ami	1
9. Mar 4, 2001	Hamas	Belt bomb	Netanya	3
10. Mar 27, 2001	Hamas	Belt bomb	Jerusalem	1

(Continued overleaf)

TABLE 9.3. Continued

Date	Group	Weapon	Target	Killed*
11. Mar 27, 2001	Hamas	Belt bomb	Jerusalem (2nd attack)	0
12. Mar 28, 2001	Hamas	Belt bomb	Kfar Saba	3
13. Apr 22, 2001	Hamas	Belt bomb	Kfar Saba	3
14. Apr 23, 2001	PFLP	Car bomb	Yehuda	8
15. Apr 29, 2001	Hamas	Belt bomb	West Bank	0
16. May 18, 2001	Hamas	Belt bomb	Netanya	5
17. May 25, 2001	Islamic Jihad	Truck bomb	Netzarim, Gaza	2
18. May 27, 2001	Hamas	Car bomb	Netanya	1
19. May 30, 2001	Islamic Jihad	Car bomb	Netanya	8
20. Jun 1, 2001	Hamas	Belt bomb	Nightclub, Tel Aviv	22
21. Jun 22, 2001	Hamas	Belt bomb	Gaza	2
22. Jul 2, 2001	Hamas	Car bomb	IDF checkpt, Gaza	0
23. Jul 9, 2001	Hamas	Car bomb	Gaza	0
24. Jul 16, 2001	Islamic Jihad	Belt bomb	Jerusalem	5
25. Aug 8, 2001	Al Aqsa	Car bomb	Jerusalem	8
26. Aug 9, 2001	Islamic Jihad	Belt bomb	Haifa	15
27. Aug 12, 2001	Islamic Jihad	Belt bomb	Haifa	0
28. Aug 21, 2001	Al Aqsa	Car bomb	Jerusalem	0
29. Sept 4, 2001	Hamas	Belt bomb	Jerusalem	0
30. Sept 9, 2001	Hamas	Belt bomb	Nahariya	3
31. Oct 1, 2001	Hamas	Car bomb	Afula	1
32. Oct 7, 2001	Islamic Jihad	Car bomb	North Israel	2
33. Nov 26, 2001	Hamas	Car bomb	Gaza	0
34. Nov 29, 2001	Islamic Jihad	Belt bomb	Gaza	3
35. Dec 1, 2001	Hamas	Belt bomb	Haifa	11
36. Dec 2, 2001	Hamas	Belt bomb	Jerusalem	15
37. Dec 5, 2001	Islamic Jihad	Belt bomb	Jerusalem	0
38. Dec 9, 2001	???	Belt bomb	Haifa	0
39. Dec 12, 2001	Hamas	Belt bomb	Gaza	4
		Isolated attacks		
1. Dec 15, 1981	???	Car bomb	Iraqi embassy, Beirut	30
2. May 25, 1985	Hezbollah	Car bomb	Emir, Kuwait	0***
3. Jul 5, 1987	LTTE	Truck bomb	Army camp, Jaffna Peninsula	18
4. Aug 15, 1993	???	Motorcycle bomb	Interior Minister, Egypt	3***
5. Jan 30, 1995	Armed Islamic Group	Truck bomb	Crowd, Algiers	42
6. Nov 19, 1995	Islamic Group	Truck bomb	Egyptian embassy, Pakistan	16
7. Oct 29, 1998	Hamas	Belt bomb	Gaza	1
8. Nov 17, 1998	???	Belt bomb	Yuksekova, Turkey	0
9. Dec 29, 1999	Hezbollah	Car bomb	South Lebanon	1

Note: Several reports of PKK suicide in May and June 1997 during fighting between PKK and Kurdish militias in Iraq, but coverage insufficient to distinguish suicide attack from suicide to avoid capture.
* Not including attacker(s).
** Assassination target killed.
*** Assassination target survived.
??? = unclaimed.

REFERENCES

al-Shaqaqi, Fathi. 1995. "Interview with Secretary General of Islamic Jihad." *Al-Quds*, 11 April. FBIS-NES-95-70, 12 April 1995.

al-Zahhar, Mahmud. 1996. "Interview." *Al-Dustur* (Amman), 19 February. FBIS-NES-96-034, 20 February 1996.

Art, Robert J., and Patrick M. Cronin. 2003. *The United States and Coercive Diplomacy*. Washington, DC: United States Institute of Peace.

Bakr, Ahmed. 1995. "Interview." *The Independent* (London), 14 March. FBIS-NES-95-086, 4 May 1995.

Bearden, Milton. 2002. Personal correspondence. University of Chicago, March 26.

Bloom, Mia. 2002. "Rational Interpretations of Palestinian Suicide Bombing." Paper presented at the Program on International Security Policy, University of Chicago.

Boix, Carlos, and Sebastian Rosato. 2001. "A Complete Dataset of Regimes, 1850–1999." University of Chicago. Typescript.

"Bus Attack Said to Spur Rabin to Speed Talks." 1995. *Yediot Aharonot*, July 25. FBIS-NES-94-142, 25 July 1995.

Clutterbuck, Richard. 1975. *Living with Terrorism*. London: Faber & Faber.

Crenshaw, Martha. 1981. "The Causes of Terrorism." *Comparative Politics* 13 (July): 397–99.

De Figueiredo, Rui, and Barry R. Weingast. 1998. "Vicious Cycles: Endogenous Political Extremism and Political Violence." Paper presented at the annual meeting of the American Political Science Association.

Department of State. 1983–2001. *Patterns of Global Terrorism*. Washington, DC: DOS.

Edler Baumann, Carol. 1973. *Diplomatic Kidnapings: A Revolutionary Tactic of Urban Terrorism*. The Hague: Nijhoff.

Elliott, Paul. 1998. *Brotherhoods of Fear*. London: Blandford.

George, Alexander, et al. 1972. *Limits of Coercive Diplomacy*. Boston: Little, Brown.

Greenberg, Joel. 2002. "Suicide Planner Expresses Joy Over His Missions," *New York Times*, 9 May.

Hamas Communique No. 125. 1995. *Filastin al-Muslimah* (London), August. FBIS-NES-95-152, 8 August 1995.

"Hamas Leader Discusses Goals." 1995. *Frankfurter Runschau*, 3 May. FBIS-NES-95-086, 4 May 1995.

"Hamas Operations Against Israel Said to Continue." 1994. *Al-Dustur* (Amman, Jordan), 14 April. FBIS-NES-94-072, 14 April 1994.

Hamas Statement. 2000. *BBC Summary of World Broadcasts*, 23 July.

Hoffman, Bruce. 1998. *Inside Terrorism*. New York: Columbia University Press.

Horowitz, Michael, and Dan Reiter. 2001. "When Does Aerial Bombing Work? Quantitative Empirical Tests, 1917–1999." *Journal of Conflict Resolution* 45 (April): 147–73.

Hroub, Khaled. 2000. *Hamas: Political Thought and Practice*. Washington, DC: Institute for Palestine Studies.

Huntington, Samuel P. 1991. *The Third Wave: Democratization in the Twentieth Century*. Norman: University of Oklahoma Press.

Inbar, Efraim. 1999. *Rabin and Israel's National Security*. Baltimore: John's Hopkins University Press.

Institute for Counter-Terrorism (ICT). 2001. *Countering Suicide Terrorism*. Herzliya, Israel: International Policy Institute for Counter-Terrorism.

Jenkins, Brian N. 1975. "Will Terrorists Go Nuclear?" Rand Report P-5541. Santa Monica, CA: Rand Corp.

Jenkins, Brian N. 1985. *International Terrorism*. Washington, DC: Rand Corp.

Jervis, Robert. 1976. *Perception and Misperception in International Politics*. Princeton, NJ: Princeton University Press.

Kaufmann, Chaim D. 1996. "Possible and Impossible Solutions to Ethnic Civil Wars." *International Security* 20 (Spring): 136–75.

Kaufmann, Chaim D. 1998. "When All Else Fails: Ethnic Population Transfers and Partitions in the Twentieth Century." *International Security* 23 (Fall): 120–56.

Kramer, Martin. 1990. "The Moral Logic of Hizballah." In *Origins of Terrorism*, ed. Walter Reich. New York: Cambridge University Press.

Kramer, Martin. 1996. "Fundamentalist Islam at Large: Drive for Power." *Middle East Quarterly* 3 (June): 37–49.

Kydd, Andrew, and Barbara F. Walter. 2002. "Sabotaging the Peace: The Politics of Extremist Violence." *International Organization* 56 (2): 263–96.

Laqueur, Walter. 1987. *The Age of Terrorism*. Boston: Little, Brown.

Lebow, Richard Ned. 1981. *Between Peace and War: The Nature of International Crisis*. Baltimore, MD: Johns Hopkins University Press.

Lewis, Bernard. 1968. *The Assassins*. New York: Basic Books.

Makovsky, David, and Alon Pinkas. 1994. "Rabin: Killing Civilians Won't Kill the Negotiations." *Jerusalem Post*, 13 April.

Merari, Ariel. 1990. "The Readiness to Kill and Die: Suicidal Terrorism in the Middle East." In *Origins of Terrorism*, ed. Walter Reich. New York: Cambridge University Press.

Mish'al, Khalid. 2000. "Interview." *BBC Summary of World Broadcasts*, 17 November.

Mishal, Shaul, and Avraham Sela. 2000. *The Palestinian Hamas*. New York: Columbia University Press.

Niebuhr, Reinhold. 1960. *Moral Man and Immoral Society*. New York: Scribner.

Nusse, Andrea. 1998. *Muslim Palestine: The Ideology of Hamas*. Amsterdam: Harwood Academic.

O'Neill, Richard. 1981. *Suicide Squads*. New York: Ballantine Books.

Pape, Robert A. 1996. *Bombing to Win: Air Power and Coercion in War*. Ithaca, NY: Cornell University Press.

Pape, Robert A. 1997. "Why Economic Sanctions Do Not Work." *International Security* 22 (Fall): 90–136.

Pape, Robert A. 2002. "The Universe of Suicide Terrorist

Attacks Worldwide, 1980–2001." University of Chicago. Typescript.

Post, Jerrold M. 1990. "Terrorist Psycho-Logic: Terrorist Behavior as a Product of Psychological Forces." In *Origins of Terrorism*, ed. Walter Reich. New York: Cambridge University Press.

Przeworski, Adam, Michael E. Alvarez, Jose Antonio Cheibub, and Fernando Limongi. 2000. *Democracy and Development: Political Institutions and Well-Being in the World, 1950–1990*. Cambridge, UK: Cambridge University Press.

Rabin, Yitzhaq. 1994. "Speech to Knessett." *BBC Summary of World Broadcasts*, 20 April.

Rabin, Yitzhaq. 1995. "Interview." *BBC Summary of World Broadcasts*, 8 September.

Rapoport, David C. 1971. *Assassination and Terrorism*. Toronto: CBC Merchandising.

Rapoport, David C. 1984. "Fear and Trembling: Terrorism in Three Religious Traditions." *American Political Science Review* 78 (September): 655–77.

Reagan, Ronald. 1990. *An American Life*. New York: Simon and Schuster.

Reich, Walter, ed. 1990. *Origins of Terrorism*. New York: Cambridge University Press.

Sauvagnargues, Philippe. 1994. "Opposition Candidate." *Agence France Presse*, 14 August.

Schalk, Peter. 1997. "Resistance and Martyrdom in the Process of State Formation of Tamililam." In *Martyrdom and Political Resistance*, ed. Joyed Pettigerw. Amsterdam: VU University Press, 61–83.

Schelling, Thomas. 1966. *Arms and Influence*. New Haven, CT: Yale University Press.

Schmid, Alex P., and Albert J. Jongman. 1988. *Political Terrorism*. New Brunswick, NJ: Transaction Books.

Sciolino, Elaine. 2002. "Saudi Warns Bush." *New York Times*, 27 January.

Shallah, Ramadan. 2001. "Interview." *BBC Summary of World Broadcasts*, 3 November.

Shiqaqi, Khalil, et al. 2002. *The Israeli-Palestinian Peace Process*. Portland, OR: Sussex Academic Press.

Sprinzak, Ehud. 2000. "Rational Fanatics." *Foreign Policy*, No. 120 (September/October): 66–73.

"Sri Lanka Opposition Leader Promises Talk with Rebels." 1994. *Japan Economic Newswire*, 11 August.

St. John, Peter. 1991. *Air Piracy, Airport Security, and International Terrrorism*. New York: Quorum Books.

Theodoulou, Michael. 1995. "New Attacks Feared." *The Times* (London), 21 August. FBIS-NES-95-165, 25 August 1995.

Tuchman, Barbara W. 1966. *The Proud Tower*. New York: Macmillan.

World Islamic Front. 1998. "Jihad Against Jews and Crusaders." Statement, 23 February.

Altruism and Fatalism: The Characteristics of Palestinian Suicide Terrorists

Ami Pedahzur,* Arie Perliger,* and Leonard Weinberg**

Over the last decade, the suicide method became one of the most prevalent tactics of Palestinian Terrorism in Israel. Who are those people, willing to sacrifice their lives in such in act, and what drives them to do such things? In our present analysis, we answer these questions, while relying on the concepts of altruistic and fatalistic suicide from Durkheim's typology of suicide behavior. Based on a newly established database compiled for this purpose—which includes information based on suicide, as well as non-suicide—Palestinian suicide terrorists from 1993 until the beginning of 2002, fit the "altruistic" type as well as some elements from the "fatalistic" and represent a combination of both types; thus they can be labeled under a new category of "fatalistic altruistic" suicide.

On the afternoon of Friday, April 16, 1993, Israeli radio reported a terrorist attack at a restaurant near Mechola in the Jordan Valley. In contrast to previous incidents, this time the terrorist, a member of the Hamas organization, parked a car loaded with explosives in between two buses next

to the restaurant and then, rather than leave the car behind, he chose to detonate the explosive device with himself inside. Despite the fact that, in terms of the number of casualties, the attack did not differ much from previous acts of terror perpetrated by Palestinian organizations, it was nevertheless unprecedented. This was the first time a Palestinian organization had initiated a suicide bombing against an Israeli target (Schweitzer 2001). The event in Mechola signaled the beginning of a long chain of suicide attacks executed by Palestinians against Israeli targets and, in effect, over the last

* University of Haifa, Mount Carmel, Haifa, Israel.
** University of Nevada, Reno, Reno, USA.
    Address correspondence to Arle Preliger, Department of Political Science, University of Haifa, Mount Carmel, 31905 Haifa, Israel. E-mail: aperliger@hotmail.com

territories and, on the other, the power of fundamentalist terrorist organizations has been on the rise. Furthermore, the increase in these trends witnessed a growth in suicide terrorism events.

Finally, we should note that the theoretical framework introduced above is closely related to socio-psychological approaches that deal in collective political violence, particularly, relative deprivation theories. In both cases, variables referring to the relation between stale and society (or individuals), and their impact on the individual subjective point of view, help determine the predisposition of the individual or group to act violently. In addition, both theories underscore the absence of alternatives to routes of violence. Hence, the next step would be to understand more fully the relations between theories dealing with individual political acts of violence and group violence.

REFERENCES

Andriolo, Karin. 2002. "Murder by Suicide: Episodes from Muslim History." *American Anthropologist.* 104(3): 736–42.

Brynen, Rex. 1995. "The Dynamic of Palestinian Elite Formation." *Journal of Palestinian Studies*, 24(3):31–43.

Dickey, Christopher, Mark Hosenball and Scott Johnson. 2001. "Training for Terror" *Newsweek*, 42.

Dublin, Leonard, 1963. *Suicide: A Sociological and Statistical Study.* New York: Ronald Free Press.

Durkheim, Emile. 1951. *Suicide.* Glenco: Free Press. (Originally published in 1897)

Ergil, Dogu. 2000. *Suicide Terrorism in Turkey: The Workers' Party of Kurdistan.* Countering Suicide Terrorism: An International Conference, Herzliya, Israel, International Policy Institute for Counter-Terrorism.

Flemming, Peter, Michael Stohl, and Alex Schmid. 1988. "The Theoretical Utility of Typologies of Terrorism: Lessons and Opportunities." Pp. 153–95 in *The Politics of Terrorism*, edited by Micheal Stohl. New York: Dekker.

Ganor, Bohaz. 2000. Suicide Terrorism: An Overview. Pp. 134–45 In *Countering Suicide Terrorism*, Erzlia: ICT

Gunaratna, Rohan. 2000. *Suicide Terrorism in Sri Lanka and India.* Countering Suicide Terrorism: An International Conference, Herzliya, Israel, International Policy Institute for Counter-Terrorism.

Hibbs, Jr. Douglas, A. 1973. *Mass Political Violence: A Cross-National Causal Analysis.* New York: John Wiley.

Israeli, Raphael. 1997. "Islamikaze and their Significance." *Terrorism and Political Violence* 9:96–121.

Johnson, Kathryn. 1979. "Durkheim Revisited: Why Do Women Kill Themselves?" *Suicide and Life-Threatening Behavior* 9: 145–53.

Joshi, M. I996. "On the Razor's Edge: The Liberation Tigers of Tamil Eelam." *Studies in Conflict and Terrorism.* 19:19–42.

Kushner, Harvey. W. 1996. "Suicide Bombers: Business, as Usual." *Studies in Conflict and Terrorism* 19:329–37.

Lehman-Wilzig, Sam N. 1990. *Still-Necked People, Bottle-Necked System: The Evolution and Roots of Israeli Public Protest*, 1949–1986. Bloomington, IN: Indiana University Press.

Merari, Ariel. 1990. "The Readiness to Kill and Die." Pp. 192–207, in *Origins of Terrorism*, edited By William Reich. Cambridge: Cambridge University Press.

Moghadam, Acliniu. 2002. "Fletcher Hosts Ariel Merari, Israeli Expert on Suicide Terrorism." *Fletcher Ledger* 3(8): Available online: http://www.fletcherledger.com/archive/

Peters, Guy B. 1998. *Comparative Politics: Theory and Methods*, New York: New York University Press.

Rex, Brynen. 1995. "The Dynamic of Palestinian Elite Formation" *Journal of Palestinian Studies* 24(3):31–43.

Riemer, W. Jeffrey. 1998. "Durkheim's 'Heroic Suicide' in Military Combat." *Armed Forces and Society* 25(1):103–20.

Rubin, Elizabeth. 2002. "The Most Wanted Palestinian." *The New York Times Magazine* (June 30, 2002):26–31, 42, 51–5.

Schbley, Ayla H. 2000. "Torn Between God, Family, and Money: The Changing Profile of Lebanon's Religious Terrorists" *Studies in Conflict and Terrorism* 23:175–96.

Schweitzer, Yoram. 2001. *Suicide Bombings—The Ultimate Weapon?* Available online: http://www.ict.org.il/articles

Shaul Shay and Yoram Schweitzer. 2002. The *Al-Aqsa Intifada: Palestinian-Israeli Confrontation.* Available online: http://www.ict.org.il

Sirriyeh, Hussein. 2000. "Democratization and the Palestinian National Authority: From State in the Making to Statehood." *Israel Affairs*, 7(1): 49–62.

Sprinzak, Ehud. 2000. "Rational Fanatics." *Foreign Policy* 120:66–73.

Stack, Steven. 1979. "Durkhiem's Theory of Fatalistic Suicide: A Cross-National Approach." *The Journal of Social Psychology* 107:161–68.

Taylor, Charles and David Jodice. 1983. *World Handbook of Political and social Indicators.* New Haven CT: Yale University Press.

Taylor, Steven. 1982. *Durkheim and the Study of Suicide.* London: Hutchinson.

Young, Lung-Chang. 1972. "Altruistic Suicide: A Subjective Approach." *Sociological Bulletin* 21(2):103–21.

Received October 2, 2002
Accepted January 16, 2003 ■

Why Would One Want to Become a Terrorist? Possible Economic or Political Origins of Terrorism

Articles in this section explore the role of larger socio-economic factors potentially related to the emergence of terrorist organizations and their appeal to aggrieved populations. Critiques of the psychopathological and individual difference explanations of terrorism—as well as the fact that wide swathes of various populations may feel sympathy toward terrorism and are apparently capable of radicalizing and evolving the readiness to engage in terrorism—directed the social science search light toward the social and economic situations potentially prompting terrorism. However, in this domain as well, the simplest explanations seem to command little empirical support. Thus, in a classical paper Krueger and Maleckova (Reading 11) report findings that cast serious doubt on the simplistic thesis that poverty or poor education explains terrorism. Neither the Palestinian terrorists nor their Jewish counterparts appeared to be particularly poor or uneducated. These authors further suggest that it is the content of the education (i.e., possible indoctrination into radical ideas) rather than the years of schooling that could be a contributing factor to terrorism. The paper by Li (Reading 12) reports an empirical investigation to address the thesis that the type of government (democratic versus totalitarian) may bear a significant relation to the risk of terrorism. This issue is of both theoretical and practical interest, since it bears on the question of whether promoting Western-style democracies in other parts of the world is likely to constitute an effective strategy to reduce terrorism. On the one hand, democracies are sensitive to individual grievances and offer individuals channels of recourse through which those grievances may be addressed. Thus, the *motivation* to engage in terrorism may be reduced in democracies. On the other hand, because of their sensitivity to individual rights of privacy, movement, and assembly, democracies may allow the formation of clandestine movements, hence contributing to the ability of terrorist organizations to form and function. Nonetheless, Li finds that democratic participation reduces the number of transnational incidents in a country, whereas government constraints increase the number of such incidents. In Reading 13, renowned Spanish terrorism authority Fernando Reinares provides insights into sociological evolution of the Euskadi Ta Askatasuna (ETA, "Basque Homeland and Freedom"), an organization that has terrorized Spain since 1959. The "permanent ceasefire" they announced in March of 2006 provided tantalizing hope that dialogue might resolve this bloody standoff—a possible model for collective disengagement from political violence. Those hopes were dashed by the announcement, in June of 2007, that "permanent ceasefire" was over.

Reading 11—Krueger and Maleckova (2002). Does Poverty Cause Terrorism?

Editors' Comments

The relation between poverty and terrorism is of considerable interest, among other reasons, because of the suggestion that if poverty is among the "root causes" of terrorism the problem of terrorism may be solved through monetary investment. As the authors note, establishment of a link between poverty and terrorism could also create perverse incentives for some groups to gain monetary rewards through engagement in terrorism. On cursory reflection, it would appear that the hypothesis of a link between poverty and terrorism is suspect from the outset. Osama bin Laden, Mohamed Atta, and many others in the history of terrorism do not appear to have been primarily poor or uneducated. From the psychological perspective, the hypothesized link between poverty and terrorism is suspect on conceptual grounds as well. Presumably, poverty breeds frustration and frustration produces aggression, and hence terrorism. But in psychological research the simplistic frustration–aggression hypothesis has been long abandoned. Rather than engaging in aggression, or joining a terrorist organization, frustrated individuals may become depressed, withdraw from the field, or engage in aggression against self rather than against others. It should not be surprising, therefore, that Krueger and Maleckova find no systematic relations between different indices of economic welfare and the frequency of terrorist acts in the Israel/Palestine arena.

Discussion Questions

1. According to what logic should poverty breed terrorism? Similarly, why should poor education breed terrorism? What is the connection between poverty and poor education as far as their alleged propensity to breed terrorism is concerned?
2. Why, in your opinion, was there a queue of willing participants in the suicide bombing enterprise in Palestine? What consequences did this apparently have on the selection of candidates? How does this bear on the presumed relation between poverty or low educational level and terrorism?
3. What is the current status of the evidence concerning the relation between poor economic conditions and violent crimes?

Suggested Readings

Bush, G. W. (2002). Remarks by the President at United Nations Financing for Development Conference, Cintermex Convention Center, Monterrey, Mexico. March 22 (http://www.whitehouse.gov/news/releases/2002/03/20020322-1.html).

Fearon, J., & Laitin, D. (2003). Ethnicity, insurgency, and civil war. *American Political Science Review, 97*, 75–90.

Hamermesh, D., & Soss, N. (1974). An economic theory of suicide. *Journal of Political Economy, 82*, 83–98.

Taylor, M. (1988). *The terrorist*. London: Brassey's Defence Publishers.

Reading 12—Li (2005). Does Democracy Promote or Reduce Transnational Terrorist Incidents?

Editors' Comments

The relation between systems of government and terrorism has been of considerable interest to researchers. It is also of interest to unpack different aspects of governance and examine their separate effects on individuals' motivation and ability to participate in terrorism. In this paper Li examines in these terms the relation between democracy and terrorism. Whereas prior studies looked at the relation between democracy and terrorism more globally, Li argues and finds that institutional constraints on democratic governments are positively related to the incidence of transnational terrorism, presumably by limiting the government's ability to fight terrorism. On the other hand, broad participation in the political process afforded in some democratic systems more than in others seems to be negatively related to the incidence of terrorism, presumably because of individuals' belief in their ability to address their grievances via the political process without the need to resort to an extra-systemic means such as terrorism. One implication of this important paper is that the concept of democracy is too broad and global to afford an unambiguous relation to terrorism. Democracies contain elements that promote the ability of terrorists to organize, and also elements that discourage terrorism, and these elements can be differentially emphasized in different democratic systems.

Discussion Questions

1. In what different ways, according to Li, might democracy encourage terrorism and in what ways might it discourage it?
2. Why should institutional constraints weaken governments' ability to deal with terrorism?
3. What are the differences between a proportional versus a majoritarian electoral system that are relevant to the incidence of terrorism?

Suggested Readings

Crenshaw, M. (1981). The causes of terrorism. *Comparative Politics*, *13*, 379–399.
Eubank, W., & Weinberg, L. (1994). Does democracy encourage terrorism? *Terrorism and Political Violence*, *6*, 417–443.
Eubank, W., & Weinberg, L. (2001). Terrorism and democracy: Perpetrators and victims. *Terrorism and Political Violence*, *13*, 155–164.

Reading 13—Reinares (2004). Who Are the Terrorists? Analyzing Changes in Sociological Profile among Members of ETA

Editors' Comments

In this paper, Fernando Reinares discusses intriguing sociological and demographic factors characterizing ETA. What is unique about this paper is that it combines statistical data (in terms of which the membership of ETA may be characterized) with illustrative interviews that explain the psychological and sociopsychological factors at work in prompting individuals to join a terrorist organization such as ETA, and how these may evolve over time. Note the issue of gender differences and the place of women in ETA, and also the interplay between age-related factors, ideology, and the tendency to join ETA.

Discussion Questions

1. What, in your opinion, may account for the fact that, over the three periods in the life of ETA that Reinares describes, the age of the recruits has gone down?
2. How does Reinares characterize the entry of women into ETA? In your opinion, do some of the same factors also apply to the men's entry?
3. How does having a family affect the tendency to join a terrorist organization? Can you think of a psychological explanation for why this may be so?

Suggested Readings

Benson, M., Evans, M., & Simon, R. (1992). Women as political terrorists. *Research in Law, Deviance and Social Control, 4*, 121–130.

Björgo, T., & Witte, R. (Eds.) (1993). *Racist violence in Europe.* Basingstoke, UK: Macmillan Press.

Morgan, R. (1989). *The demon lover: On the sexuality of terrorism.* New York: Norton and Company.

Reinares, F. (2003). Terrorism. In W. Heitmeier & J. Hagan (Eds.), *International handbook of violence research* (pp. 309–321). The Hague: Kluwer Academic.

READING 11

Does Poverty Cause Terrorism?

Alan B. Krueger and Jitka Maleckova

I

That investment in education is critical for economic growth, improved health, and social progress is beyond question. That poverty is a scourge that the international aid community and industrialized countries should work to eradicate is also beyond question. There is also no doubt that terrorism is a scourge of the contemporary world. What is less clear, however, is whether poverty and low education are root causes of terrorism.

In the aftermath of the tragic events of September 11, several prominent observers and policymakers have called for increased aid and educational assistance as a means for ending terrorism. "We fight against poverty," President George W. Bush has declared, "because hope is an answer to terror." But a careful review of the evidence provides little reason for optimism that a reduction in poverty or an increase in educational attainment would, by themselves, meaningfully reduce international terrorism. Any connection between poverty, education, and terrorism is indirect, complicated, and probably quite weak. Instead of viewing terrorism as a direct response to low market opportunities or lack of education, we suggest it is more accurately viewed as a response to political conditions and long-standing feelings of indignity and frustration (perceived or real) that have little to do with economics.

An understanding of the causes of terrorism is essential if an effective strategy is to be crafted to combat it. Drawing a false and unjustified connection between poverty and terrorism is potentially quite dangerous, as the international aid community may lose interest in providing support to developing nations when the imminent threat of terrorism recedes, much as support for development waned in the aftermath of the Cold War; and connecting foreign aid with terrorism risks the possibility of humiliating many people in less developed countries, who are implicitly told that they receive aid only to prevent them from committing acts of terror. Moreover, premising foreign aid on the threat of terrorism could create perverse incentives in which some groups are induced to engage in terrorism to increase their prospects of receiving aid. In our view, alleviating poverty is reason enough to pressure economically advanced countries to provide more aid than they are currently giving. Falsely connecting terrorism to poverty serves only to deflect attention from the real roots of terrorism.

To make any headway investigating the determinants of terrorism, one must have a working definition of terrorism. This is a notoriously

Alan B. Krueger is Bendheim Professor of Economics and Public Affairs at Princeton University. Jitka Maleckova is associate professor at the Institute for Middle Eastern and African Studies at Charles University in Prague.

difficult task. More than one hundred diplomatic and scholarly definitions of the term exist. The types of activities by various groups that are considered terrorist acts differ substantially across the definitions. The term "terrorism" has also evolved over time. It was first used in a political context during the French Revolution, when it was reserved for accusations against those who, like Robespierre, made use of violence in the name of the state. By the late nineteenth century, however, Russian and French anarchists proudly used the word "terrorism" to describe their violent endeavors against the state. A part of the difficulty in defining terrorism is that there are valid disputes as to which party is a legitimate government. During World War II, for example, the German occupation forces labeled members of the French Resistance terrorists.

A range of possible definitions exists. The State Department, which acknowledges that no single definition of terrorism has gained universal acceptance, seems to have captured what is considered terrorism by many governments and international organizations. Since 1983, it has employed this definition for statistical and analytical purposes: "The term 'terrorism' means premeditated, politically motivated violence perpetrated against noncombatant targets by subnational groups or clandestine agents, usually intended to influence an audience. The term 'international terrorism' means terrorism involving citizens or the territory of more than one country." The State Department also specifies that "the term noncombatant is interpreted to include, in addition to civilians, military personnel who at the time of the incident are unarmed and/or not on duty. . . . We also consider as acts of terrorism attacks on military installations or on armed military personnel when a state of military hostilities does not exist at the site, such as bombings against U.S. bases in the Persian Gulf, Europe, or elsewhere." The rub, of course, is that the definitions of "subnational" and "military hostilities" leaves much latitude for disagreement.

The definitions of terrorism used by scholars, by contrast, tend to place more emphasis on the intention of terrorists to cause fear and terror among a targeted population that is considerably larger than the actual victims of their attacks, and to influence the views of that larger audience. The actual victim of the violence is thus not the main target of the terrorist act. Scholarly definitions often also include nation-states as potential perpetrators of terrorism.

Rather than dogmatically adhere to one definition, we have analyzed involvement in or support for activities that, at least when judged by some parties, constitute terrorism. Still, in the incidents that we have analyzed, the line between terrorism and resistance is often blurred. At the least, all of the cases we examine could be thought of as involving politically motivated violence. Moreover, it is reassuring that our main conclusions appear to hold across a varying set of circumstances, cultures, and countries. (We do not examine state terrorism because we suspect that the process underlying participation in state terrorism is quite different from the process underlying sub-state terrorism, and would involve a different type of analysis. We do not dispute that state terrorism exists, and that it has at times generated sub-state terrorism as a response.)

In economics, it is natural to analyze participation in terrorism in the framework of occupational choice. As is conventional in economics, involvement in terrorism is viewed as a rational decision, depending on the benefits, costs, and risks involved in engagement in terrorism compared with other activities. Not surprisingly, the standard rational-choice framework does not yield an unambiguous answer to the question of whether higher income and more education would reduce participation in terrorism.

In this context, we have also reviewed evidence on "hate crimes," which can be viewed as a close cousin to terrorism in that the target of an offense is selected because of his or her group identity, not because of his or her individual behavior, and because the effect of both is to wreak terror in a greater number of people than those directly affected by the violence. A consensus is emerging in the social science literature that the incidence of hate crimes, such as lynchings of African Americans or violence against Turks in Germany, bears little relation to economic conditions.

Most significantly, we have considered data from a public-opinion poll conducted in the West Bank and Gaza Strip by the Palestinian Center for Policy and Survey Research (PCPSR). In December 2001, Palestinians were asked whether they supported attacks on Israeli civilian and military targets, and about whether they considered certain incidents acts of terrorism. Breaking down the data by education and occupation indicates that support for violence against Israeli targets is widespread in the Palestinian population, and at least as great among those with higher education and higher living standards as it is among the unemployed and the illiterate. Similarly, a review of the incidence of major terrorist acts over time in Israel, and an analysis that relates the number of terrorist acts each year to the rate of economic growth in that year or in the recent past, yields the same skepticism about the idea that poverty is a cause of terrorism.

The data on participation in and support for political violence, militancy, and terrorism that we have examined are meager, often indirect, and possibly nonrepresentative. In addition, participation in terrorist activities may be highly context-specific, and we have examined terrorism, militancy, and politically motivated violence in a small number of settings primarily in the Middle East. Consequently, our results must be considered tentative and exploratory. Yet we are not aware of compelling evidence that points in the opposite direction from what we have found. In light of our results, we would urge intellectuals and policymakers to exercise caution in presuming that poverty and education have a direct and causal impact on terrorism.

II

A simple view of terrorism is that participation in terrorism is akin to participation in crime in general. Economists have a well-developed and empirically successful theory of participation in criminal activities. As emphasized by Gary Becker, individuals should choose to allocate their time between working in the legal job market or working in criminal activities in such a way that maximizes their utility. After accounting for the risk of being caught and penalized, the size of the penalty, and any stigma or moral distress associated with involvement in crime, those who receive higher income from criminal activities would choose involvement in crime. According to this model, crime increases as one's market wage falls relative to the rewards associated with crime, and decreases if the risk of being apprehended after committing a crime, or the penalty for being convicted of a crime, rises. Available evidence suggests that individuals are more likely to commit property crimes if they have lower wages or less education; but the occurrence of violent crimes, including murders, is typically found to be unrelated to economic opportunities.

Some economists, notably William Landes, Todd Sandler, and Walter Enders, have applied the economic model of crime to transnational terrorism. They focus on how an increase in penalties and law enforcement influences the incentive to partake in terrorist activities. But the economic model yields few concrete predictions insofar as the relationship between market opportunities and participation in terrorism is concerned, because participation in terrorist acts by individuals with different characteristics depends on the probability that participation will bring about the desired political change, as well as the differential payoff for the various groups associated with achieving the terrorists' desired aims versus the penalties associated with failure. It is possible, for example, that well-educated individuals will disproportionately participate in terrorist groups if they think that they will assume leadership positions if they succeed, or if they identify more strongly with the goals of the terrorist organization than less-educated individuals.

Other important considerations include the relative pay of skilled and unskilled individuals for participation in terrorist organizations and how it compares to relative pay in the legal sector, and the selection of particular terrorists by terrorist organizations. Bill Keller recently reported in *The New York Times* that Iraq decided in March to increase the payment to families of suicide bombers in the West Bank and Gaza from $10,000 to $25,000. In the month after that decision, suicide bombings increased, though it is unclear whether the connection is causal.

Even before the increase in the payment to families of suicide bombers, there was a large supply of willing suicide bombers, as Nasra Hassan, a relief worker for the United Nations, reported last year in *The New Yorker*. Between 1996 and 1999, Hassan interviewed nearly two hundred fifty militants and associates of militants involved in the Palestinian cause, including failed suicide bombers, the families of deceased bombers, and those who trained and prepared suicide bombers for their missions. One Hamas leader whom Hassan interviewed remarked: "Our biggest problem is the hordes of young men who beat on our doors, clamoring to be sent [on suicide missions]. It is difficult to select only a few." A senior member of the al-Qassam Brigades said: "The selection process is complicated by the fact that so many wish to embark on this journey of honor. When one is selected, countless others are disappointed." Thus, the demand side is also part of the equation.

With a queue of willing participants, how do terrorist or militant groups choose their suicide bombers? A planner for Islamic Jihad explained to Hassan that his group scrutinizes the motives of a potential bomber to be sure that the individual is committed to carrying out the task. Now, a high level of educational attainment is probably a signal of one's commitment to a cause, as well as of one's ability to prepare for an assignment and carry it out. For this reason, the stereotype of suicide bombers being drawn from the ranks of those who are so impoverished that they have nothing to live for may be wildly incorrect. This interpretation is also consistent with another of Hassan's observations about suicide bombers: "None of them were uneducated, desperately poor, simple-minded, or depressed. Many were middle class and, unless they were fugitives, held paying jobs. More than half of them were refugees from what is now Israel. Two were the sons of millionaires."

Suicide bombers clearly are not motivated by the prospect of their own individual economic gain, although it is possible that the promise of larger payments to their families may increase the willingness of some to participate in these lethal missions. We suspect their primary motivation instead results from their passionate support for the ideas and the aims of their movement. "Over and over," Hassan reported, "I hear them say, 'The Israelis humiliate us. They occupy our land and deny our history.' " The eradication of poverty and the attainment of universal high school education are unlikely to change these feelings. Indeed, it is even possible that those who are well-off and welleducated experience such feelings more acutely.

Economic theory is unlikely to give a very convincing answer one way or the other as to whether poverty and education are important root causes of terrorism. One could construct plausible explanations for why a reduction in poverty and a rise in education might increase or decrease the incidence of terrorism. It might help to consider the evidence on hate crimes. Since the literature on participation in terrorism is less well developed than the literature on hate crimes, we begin by briefly reviewing evidence on the economic determinants of hate crimes, a phenomenon that many have considered closely related to terrorism.

Hate crimes are commonly defined as crimes against members of religious, racial, or ethnic groups because of their group membership, rather than because of their characteristics or actions as individuals. Hate crimes include acts of violence as well as destruction of property, harassment, and trespassing. Until recently, social scientists thought that economic deprivation was a crucial determinant of hate crimes, but new evidence strongly challenges the empirical basis for this conclusion. In fact, a new consensus is emerging that views hate crimes as independent of economic deprivation.

The original empirical support for the economic deprivation hypothesis stemmed mainly from historical evidence on anti-black lynchings in the southern United States. In his classic book *The Tragedy of Lynching*, which appeared in 1933, Arthur Raper documented a correlation of −0.532 between the number of lynchings in a year and the value of an acre of cotton (a measure of economic conditions) in that year, using data from 1882 to 1930. He concluded that "periods of relative prosperity bring reduction in lynching and periods of depression cause an increase." In 1940, the psychologists Carl Hovland and Robert Sears seized on this finding as support for the view that inter-group antagonism results from frustration accompanying economic contractions.

But a landmark study by Donald Green, Jack Glaser, and Andrew Rich overturned that conclusion in 1998. First, they showed that the correlation between lynchings and economic conditions vanished once secular trends in both variables were taken into account. That is, apart from the long-term tendency for the number of lynchings to decline and the economy to grow, lynchings were unrelated to year-to-year economic fluctuations. Second, when they applied Simon Kuznets's measure of real per capita GNP growth (which was unavailable to Raper) as a measure of economic conditions instead of the value of cotton, they found that lynchings and economic conditions were virtually unrelated.

Raper's sample ended just before the Great Depression. Lynchings did not rise during the Great Depression, despite the dramatic deterioration in economic conditions. When Green, Glaser, and Rich extended the original sample through 1938, they found an insignificant correlation between the number of anti-black lynchings and the value of an acre of cotton, and a positive correlation between anti-black lynchings and real GNP growth. It is almost certainly the case that the inverse correlation reported between economic conditions and anti-black lynchings that launched the "aggressionfrustration hypothesis" was spurious, a coincidence of two unrelated trends that happened to move in opposite directions at the turn of the twentieth century.

Moreover, evidence of a connection between economic conditions and other types of hate crimes in contemporary data is elusive as well. Green, Glaser, and Rich also report evidence on the incidence of hate crimes against blacks, Jews, Asians, and homosexuals using data from New York City each month from 1987 to 1995. They found that the incidence of these crimes was unrelated to the city's unemployment rate. And across regions in a given year, the occurrence of hate crimes and the prevalence of hate groups are also found to be unrelated to the economic circumstances of the area. In a study of the "geography of hate," Philip Jefferson and Frederic L. Pryor examined determinants of the existence of hate groups across counties in the United States in 1997. (About 10 percent of counties, they noted, are home to a hate group.) They found that the location of hate groups was unrelated to the unemployment rate, divorce rate, percentage of blacks, or gap in per capita income between whites and blacks in the county. The share of the adult population with a high school diploma or higher had a statistically significant positive association with the likelihood that a hate group was located in the area. They concluded that "economic or sociological explanations for the existence of hate groups in an area are far less important than adventitious circumstances due to history and particular conditions."

The findings for the United States do not appear to be unique. Germany experienced a rash of violence against foreigners in the early 1990s. Unemployment was high, particularly in the former East Germany. But economists who have studied the German case found no relationship between the unemployment rate and the incidence of ethnic violence across 543 counties in Germany, once they took account of whether the county was located in the former East or West Germany. Likewise, average education and the average manufacturing wage in the county was unrelated to the amount of violence against foreigners. Within the former East Germany, those counties located farthest from the West had the highest incidence of ethnic violence, a geographical pattern that may be explained by a failure of law enforcement farther east and a pent-up animosity that was suppressed during communism.

In sum: neither cyclical downturns nor longer-term regional disparities in living standards appear to be correlated with the incidence of a wide range of hate crimes. This is not proof of the absence of a causal relationship, of course; but if there were a direct causal effect one would expect hate crimes to rise during periods of economic hardship. Rather than to economic conditions, the hate crimes literature points to a breakdown in law enforcement, as well as official sanctioning and encouragement of civil disobedience, as significant causes of the occurrence of hate crimes.

III

The Palestinian Center for Policy and Survey Research (PCPSR) is an independent, nonprofit research organization in Ramallah that conducts policy analysis and academic research in the West Bank and Gaza. In December 2001, PCPSR conducted a public-opinion poll of 1,357 Palestinians eighteen years old or older in the West Bank and Gaza. The survey, which was conducted by in-person interviews, covered topics including the participants' views toward the September 11 attacks in the United States, the participants' support for an Israeli-Palestinian peace agreement, and their opinions about armed attacks against Israel. Under trying circumstances in the middle of one of the worst periods of the Israeli-Palestinian conflict, a researcher at the center kindly provided us with tabulations of key questions broken down by the educational level and the occupational status of the respondents.

Although public-opinion polls are subject to multiple interpretations, such data can provide indirect information about which segments of the population support terrorist or militant activities. The PCPSR poll reveals several things. First, the support for armed attacks against Israeli targets by the Palestinian population is widespread, though it is important to emphasize that there is a distinction between support for armed attacks expressed in a public-opinion poll at a particular point in time and participation in or active support for such attacks. Second, a majority of the Palestinian population believes that armed attacks against Israeli civilians have helped to achieve Palestinian rights in a way that negotiations could not have achieved. This finding raises obvious implications concerning the difficulty of ending the attacks, and may partially account for the Palestinian public's opposition to a United Nations initiative to fight terrorism, which was also found in the poll. If the Palestinian public believes the attacks are efficacious, they are unlikely to cease supporting additional attacks unless their demands are met. Another question asked was: "To what extent do you support or oppose the position taken by President Arafat and the [Palestinian Authority] regarding the U.S. campaign against terror?" Thirty-six percent supported or strongly supported the position of Arafat in this case, and 50.4 percent opposed it.

Moreover, a majority of the Palestinian population did not consider suicide bombings, such as the one that killed twenty-one Israeli youths at the Dolphinarium disco in Tel Aviv, terrorist events. Toward the end of the questionnaire, respondents were also asked whether they thought the international community considered the Dolphinarium bombing a terrorist event. Ninety-two percent responded yes. These results highlight important differences in interpreting the meaning of the word "terrorism."

Most important for our purposes, there is no evidence in these results that more highly educated individuals are less supportive of violent attacks against Israeli targets than are those who are illiterate or poorly educated. Consider the percentage of individuals who say they support or strongly support armed attacks against Israeli targets less those who say they oppose or strongly oppose such attacks. By a margin of 68 points, those with more than a secondary school education support armed attacks against Israeli targets, while the margin is 63 points for those with an elementary school education and 46 points for those who are illiterate.

A survey conducted by PCPSR in November 1994, before the current intifada, asked respondents whether they supported a dialogue between Hamas and Israel. Responses were reported by educational attainment. More highly educated respondents were less supportive of a dialogue with Israel: 53 percent of those with a B.A. and 40 percent of those with an M.A. or a Ph.D. supported a dialogue, compared with 60 percent of those with nine years of schooling or less. (Based on other questions, it is clear that supporters of dialogue generally favored a more peaceful coexistence with Israel.)

The PCPSR study in 2001 showed also that support for armed attacks against Israeli targets is widespread across all Palestinian occupations and groups, but particularly strong among students (recall that respondents are age eighteen or older) and merchants and professionals. Notably, the unemployed are somewhat less likely to support armed attacks against Israeli targets. If poverty was indeed the wellspring of support for terrorism or politically motivated violence, one would have expected the unemployed to be more supportive of armed attacks than merchants and professionals, but the public-opinion evidence points in the other direction.

The survey also found that the Palestinian population doubted Osama bin Laden's role in the September 11 attacks on New York and Washington. A subsequent poll of adults in nine Islamic countries by the Gallup Organization also found considerable skepticism toward the role of bin Laden's group in the attacks. Seventy-four percent of Muslim Lebanese, for example, did not believe news reports that groups of Arabs carried out the attacks, while 65 percent of Christian Lebanese accepted the veracity of the news reports. Respondents in the PCPSR survey were divided on whether they defined as a "terrorist event" the "destruction of the Twin Towers in New York City by people suspected to be members of Bin Laden's organization": 41.4 percent agreed and 53.1 percent disagreed.

It is possible to use public-opinion data to infer trends in economic expectations. On three occasions – in July/August 1998, in September 1999, and in February 2000 – PCPSR asked respondents in the West Bank and Gaza the following two questions: "How would you describe your economic situation over the last three years compared to the situation today? Better, Worse, Stayed the Same, or Don't Know?" and "Are you optimistic or pessimistic regarding your economic situation over the next three years? Optimistic, Pessi-

mistic, It will remain the same, No Opinion/Don't Know?"

The survey results indicate that between 1998 and 2000 the public perceived economic conditions to be improving. Optimism about the future was rising. The downward trend in the unemployment rate is also consistent with this interpretation of economic circumstances. There is little evidence here to suggest that a deteriorating economy or falling expectations for the economy precipitated the latest intifada, which began in September 2000, although it is possible that expectations could have changed between the PCPSR's last survey and the start of the intifada.

In 1995, Joshua Angrist closely examined Palestinian trends in school enrollment, earnings, and unemployment by level of education in a period encompassing the intifada in 1988. He found that college enrollment in the West Bank and Gaza increased rapidly in the early 1980s, doubling between 1981 and 1985. Between 1982 and 1988, the number of Palestinian men in the labor force with twelve or more years of schooling doubled, while the number with eleven or fewer years of schooling increased only by about 3 percent. This remarkable rise in the education of the workforce coincided with a sharp increase in the unemployment rate for college graduates relative to high school graduates in the 1980s. In addition, from 1985 to 1988 the real daily wage of college graduates fell by around 30 percent, while the real wage of those with twelve years of schooling held steady and the real wage of those with eleven or fewer years of schooling increased slightly. Angrist observes that the decline in Palestinian school enrollment in the early 1990s probably represents "a belated supply response to low returns to schooling."

Thus, the noteworthy increase in educational attainment of Palestinians in the 1980s coincided with a marked deterioration in the economic position of more highly educated Palestinians. Angrist and others speculate that the deterioration in economic opportunities for the highly educated contributed to the civil unrest that broke out in December 1987. Angrist notes, though, that the confluence of these developments could be unique to the Palestinian situation, and not a universal response to expanding educational opportunities. Importantly, the Israeli occupation of the territories and the lack of an effective capital market or banking system probably prevented the labor markets in the West Bank and Gaza from functioning smoothly, particularly in light of the fact that many Palestinians are dependent on Israel for jobs. Consequently, the link between an expansion in educational attainment, deteriorating economic conditions, and protest may not generalize. Indeed, the contrasting economic environments surrounding the intifadas in 1988 and 2000 suggest that protest, violence, and even terrorism can follow a rising economic tide or a declining one.

We also performed a detailed analysis of participation in Hezbollah in Lebanon, which has reportedly instructed Palestinian extremist groups on the use of suicide bomb attacks. We compared the background characteristics of 129 members of Hezbollah's militant wing who died in action mostly in the late 1980s to those of a random sample of 121,000 young people in the Lebanese population. Many of these militants died fighting Israeli occupation, while others died in suicide bomb attacks or while planting booby traps. The Hezbollah militants in this sample are likely to be representative of those who engaged in terrorist acts, and some were carrying out terrorist acts when they died. Compared to the general Lebanese population from the same age group and region, the Hezbollah militants were actually slightly less likely to come from impoverished households, and were more likely to have attended secondary school or higher. These results suggest that the militants were not particularly drawn from those with the least opportunities in society.

And this conclusion is ratified by political violence on the other side as well. In the late 1970s and early 1980s, numerous violent attacks against Palestinians were conducted by Israeli Jews in the West Bank and Gaza. These attacks included attempts to kill three Palestinian mayors of West Bank cities and attempts to blow up the Dome of the Rock mosque in Jerusalem. From 1980 to 1984, a total of twenty-three Palestinians were killed in attacks by what became known among Israelis as the Jewish Underground, and 191 Palestinians were injured. The *International Encyclopedia of Terrorism* (1997) refers to these attacks as acts of terrorism. In a ruling in 1985, an Israeli court convicted three Israeli settlers of murder and found others guilty of violent crimes in cases involving attacks in the West Bank.

What were the biographical backgrounds of those involved in these violent attacks by Israeli Jewish extremists? A list may be compiled of the name, the age, the occupation, and the nature of underground activity for twenty-seven individuals involved in the Jewish Underground in the early 1980s, based mainly on a memoir of the Jewish Underground by Haggai Segal, one of its members. It is clear from such a chart that these Israeli extremists were overwhelmingly well-educated and in high-paying occupations. The list includes teachers, writers, university students, geographers, an engineer, a combat pilot, a chemist, and a computer programmer. As Donald Neff observed in 1999 about the three men convicted of murder, "all were highly regarded, well-educated, very religious." Although we have not statistically compared the backgrounds of these extremists to the wider Israeli population, these twenty-seven individuals certainly do not appear to be particularly underprivileged or undereducated.

IV

The evidence that we have assembled and reviewed suggests that there is little direct connection between poverty, education, and participation in or support for terrorism. Indeed, the available evidence indicates that compared with the relevant population, participants in Hezbollah's militant wing in the late 1980s and early 1990s in Lebanon were at least as likely to come from economically advantaged families and to have a relatively high level of education as they were to come from impoverished families without educational opportunities. We should caution, however, that the evidence we have considered is tentative due to data limitations. In addition, our focus has been primarily on the Middle East, so our conclusions may not generalize to other regions or circumstances.

Still, less quantitative studies of participants in a variety of forms of terrorism in several different settings have reached a conclusion similar to ours. We are particularly struck by Charles Russell and Bowman Miller's work in this regard. In 1983, to derive a profile of terrorists, they assembled demographic information on more than three hundred fifty individuals engaged in terrorist activities in Latin America, Europe, Asia, and the Middle East from 1966 to 1976 based on newspaper reports. Their sample consisted of individuals from eighteen revolutionary groups known to engage in urban terrorism, including the Red Army in Japan, the Baader-Meinhof Gang in Germany, the Irish Republican Army in Northern Ireland, the Red Brigades in Italy, and the People's Liberation Army in Turkey. Russell and Miller found that "the vast majority of those individuals involved in terrorist activities as cadres or leaders is quite well educated. Infact, approximately two-thirds of those identified terrorists are persons with some university training, university graduates or postgraduate students." They also report that more than two-thirds of arrested terrorists "came from the middle or upper classes in their respective nations or areas."

Maxwell Taylor likewise concluded from his survey of the literature, in his book *The Terrorist* in 1988, that "neither social background, educational opportunity or attainment seem to be particularly associated with terrorism." And this conclusion also accords with the conclusion of the Library of Congress's report "The Sociology and Psychology of Terrorism: Who Becomes a Terrorist and Why?" This report was prepared for the CIA in September 1999 and foresaw the possibility of Al Qaeda crashing explosive-laden airplanes into the Pentagon, the CIA, or the White House. After reviewing profiles of terrorists, the report observed that "terrorists in general have more than average education," and questioned whether there is a typical terrorist profile.

While economic deprivation may not be associated with participation in terrorism and political violence at the individual level, it may nonetheless matter at the national level. If a country is impoverished, a minority of the relatively well off in that country may turn to terrorism to seek to improve the conditions of their countrymen. One might question, though, whether the goal of many terrorist organizations is to install a political regime that is likely to reduce poverty. In addition, there are well-documented cases of homegrown terrorism in economically advanced countries (remember Timothy McVeigh?), so it is far from clear that poverty at a national level is associated with support for terrorism. Of course, this question can only be addressed by cross-country analyses.

In addition, poverty may indirectly affect terrorism through the apparent connection between economic conditions and the proclivity for countries to undergo civil wars. James Fearon and David Laitin have found that GDP per capita is inversely related to the onset of civil war, and Paul Collier and Anne Hoeffler have found that the growth rate of GDP per capita and the male secondary-school enrollment rate are inversely related to the incidence of civil war. Lebanon, Afghanistan, and Sudan are high-profile examples of countries where civil war provided a hospitable environment for international terrorists to operate. But there are other situations in which countries undergoing a civil war did not provide a breeding ground for international terrorism, so it is unclear how much one should extrapolate from the relationship between economic development and civil war. And terrorism has arisen in many countries that were not undergoing a civil war.

Enough evidence is accumulating that it is fruitful to begin to conjecture why participation in terrorism and political violence is apparently unrelated – or positively related – to individuals' income and education. The standard economic model of crime suggests that those with the lowest value of time should engage in criminal activity. But we would hypothesize that in most cases terrorism is less like property crime and more like a violent form of political engagement. More-educated people from privileged backgrounds are more likely to participate in politics, probably in part because political involvement requires some minimum level of interest, expertise, commitment to issues, and effort, all of which are more likely if people are educated enough and prosperous enough to concern themselves with more than economic subsistence. These factors could outweigh the effect of opportunity cost on individuals' decisions to become involved in terrorism.

The demand side for terrorists must be considered as well as the supply side. Terrorist organizations may prefer highly educated individuals over less-educated ones, even for suicide bomb attacks. In addition, educated middle-class or upper-class individuals are better suited to carry out acts of international terrorism than are impoverished illiterates, because the terrorists must fit into a foreign environment to be successful. This consideration suggests that terrorists who threaten economically developed countries will disproportionately be drawn from the ranks of the relatively well off and highly educated.

On the whole, we must conclude that there is little reason to be optimistic that a reduction in poverty or an increase in educational attainment will lead to a meaningful reduction in the amount of international terrorism without other changes. Jessica Stern has observed that many madrasahs, or religious schools, in Pakistan are funded by wealthy industrialists, and that those schools deliberately educate students to become foot soldiers and elite operatives in various extremist movements around the world. She further reported that "most madrasahs offer only religious instruction, ignoring math, science, and other secular subjects important for functioning in modern society." These observations suggest that, in order to use education as part of a strategy to reduce terrorism, the international community should not limit itself to increasing years of schooling, but should consider very carefully the content of education.

Alan B. Krueger and Jitka Malecková are writing a history of hate crimes and terrorism.

Post date June 20, 2002
Issue date June 24, 2002 ■

Does Democracy Promote or Reduce Transnational Terrorist Incidents?

Quan Li*

This article studies the various mechanisms by which democracy affects transnational terrorism. New theoretical mechanisms are identified that either complement or encompass existing arguments. Different effects of democracy on transnational terrorism are assessed for a sample of about 119 countries from 1975 to 1997. Results show that democratic participation reduces transnational terrorist incidents in a country, while government constraints increase the number of those incidents, subsuming the effect of press freedom. The proportional representation system experiences fewer transnational terrorist incidents than either the majoritarian or the mixed system.

How does democracy affect transnational terrorist activities? Two theoretical arguments in the literature posit opposite expectations (see, e.g.,

*Department of Political Science, The Pennsylvania State University.

Author's note: The author wishes to thank Todd Sandler, Bruce Russett, Navin Bapat, Alex Braithwaite, Pat James, Leonard Weinberg, and the anonymous referees for their helpful comments and suggestions. Young Hun Kim and Tatiana Vashchilko provided valuable research assistance. An earlier version of this article was presented at the annual meeting of International Studies Association, Montreal, Canada, March 2004. The replication data set is available at http://www.yale.edu/unsy/jcr/jcrdata.html.

Schmid 1992; Eubank and Weinberg 1994, 1998, 2001; Eyerman 1998; Ross 1993). The first argument expects that democracy reduces transnational terrorism. Democratic societies offer access for citizens to seek recourse to their grievances, while democratic rules ensure the nonviolent resolution of conflicts of interest. Hence, groups in democratic societies are more likely to pursue nonviolent alternatives rather than costly terrorist activities to further their interest. The second argument, however, suggests that democracy encourages terrorism. Democratic countries provide relatively more freedom of speech, movement, and association, permitting parochial interests to get organized and reducing the costs of conducting terrorist activities. Open democratic societies therefore facilitate terrorism.

Most but not all of the empirical evidence to date supports the notion that democracy encourages transnational terrorism. In a pioneering paper, Eubank and Weinberg (1994) examine whether democratic or authoritarian regimes host more terrorist groups. They find that terrorist groups are more often found in democratic societies than in authoritarian ones. They conclude that political and civil liberties are positively associated with political terrorism. Sandler (1995) challenges the finding by Eubank and Weinberg on methodological grounds. He argues that events data, rather than the number of terrorist groups, are more appropriate for assessing the relationship between democracy and terrorism. In response, Eubank and Weinberg (1998) reanalyze the relationship between democracy and terrorism by employing the international terrorist events data from the RAND–St. Andrews Chronology of International Terrorism and the U.S. State Department. They investigate whether political regime type is linked to the frequency of international terrorist events within countries in 1994 and 1995. They find that terrorist events are substantially more likely to occur in free and democratic countries. Moreover, countries undergoing regime change are more likely to experience transnational terrorism. Meanwhile, however, Eyerman (1998) finds somewhat contradictory evidence based on a multivariate negative binomial regression using the ITERATE (International Terrorism: Attributes of Terrorist Events) database. He finds that established democracies experience fewer terrorist events than nondemocracies, while new democracies tend to have more terrorist incidents than other types of states. In a follow-up analysis, Eubank and Weinberg (2001) also employ the ITERATE database to classify terrorist events according to their location, the perpetrator nationality, and the victim nationality. They find that terrorist attacks occur most often in stable democracies and that both the perpetrators and victims of those attacks are from the same democratic states. Recently, Li and Schaub (2004) have used the ITERATE data to analyze how economic globalization affects terror-

ist incidents. From their multivariate negative binomial regression, they find that democracy as a control variable has a statistically significant positive effect on the number of transnational terrorist incidents in countries.

While most empirical evidence shows that democracy encourages transnational terrorism, extant theoretical and empirical work suffers several important weaknesses. First, at the theoretical level, the positive effect of civil liberties on transnational terrorism is epiphenomenal of some other fundamental regime attribute. I argue that it is the institutional constraints on the government that drive the positive effect of democracy on terrorism. In addition, previous arguments in the literature have ignored the heterogeneity of democratic systems across countries. I argue that such institutional differences account for cross-country variations in transnational terrorist activities.

Second, there exists a disconnection between theoretical arguments and empirical analyses in the literature. Competing theoretical expectations are derived from consideration of different attributes of democracy. Existing empirical analyses, however, all employ some aggregate indicator of political regime type. This approach is problematic because an aggregate indicator cannot offer an empirical separation of the positive and negative effects of democracy if competing effects are at work at the same time. Hence, aggregate indicators of regime type are not useful for evaluating arguments on disparate effects of different attributes of democratic institutions.

Finally, the widely cited analyses by Eubank and Weinberg (1994, 1998, 2001) do not control for additional factors such as economic development and income inequality that may confound their findings. The multivariate analysis by Eyerman (1998) fails to address important statistical problems such as heteroskedasticity and serial correlation in the error term that may affect statistical inferences. These empirical issues need to be addressed.

In this article, I focus on the various mechanisms by which democracy affects transnational terrorism. I identify new theoretical mechanisms that either complement or encompass existing arguments. Different effects of democracy are assessed using a multivariate analysis in a sample of about 119 countries from 1975 to 1997 using the ITERATE database. The findings have important policy implications for the war on terrorism and for promoting democracy around the world.

Theoretical Argument

In this analysis, terrorism is defined as the premeditated or threatened use of extranormal violence or force to obtain a political, religious, or ideological objective through the intimidation of a large audience (e.g., Enders and Sandler 1999, 2002). Because extant empirical evidence in the democracy-terrorism literature is exclusively based on transnational terrorism data, I choose to focus on transnational terrorist incidents in this article. A transnational terrorist incident in a country involves victims, perpetrators, targets, or institutions of another country. Based on the incident venue, transnational terrorist incidents can involve (1) terrorist attacks initiated by foreign terrorists against some domestic target in a country, (2) attacks by domestic terrorists against some foreign target in a country, or (3) attacks by foreign terrorists against some other foreign target in a country.

Democracy in this article refers to the notion of representative democracy that typically implies free and fair elections of the executive and legislative offices, the right of citizens to vote and compete for public office, and institutional guarantees for the freedom of association and expression such as an independent judiciary and the absence of censorship (Dahl 1971, 1998). Distinct institutional characteristics of democratic polity produce different effects on transnational terrorism.

Negative Effect of Democratic Participation

One argument in the democracy-terrorism literature posits that aspects of democracy reduce terrorism. In nondemocratic societies, the lack of opportun-

ities for political participation induces political grievances and dissatisfaction among dissenters, motivating terrorism (Crenshaw 1981, 383). In contrast, in democratic societies, free and fair elections ensure that rulers can be removed and that desirable social changes can be brought about by voters, reducing the need to resort to violence (Schmid 1992). Democratic rules enable nonviolent resolution of political conflict. Democracies permit dissenters to express their policy preferences and seek redress (Ross 1993). Different social groups are able to participate in the political process to further their interest through peaceful means, such as voting and forming political parties (Eubank and Weinberg 1994, 2001). Since democracy lowers the cost of achieving political goals through legal means, groups find costly illegal terrorist activities less attractive (Ross 1993; Eyerman 1998).

Wide democratic participation also has beneficial consequences that remain largely unnoticed in the literature. To the extent that democratic participation increases political efficacy of citizens, terrorist groups will be less successful recruiting new members in democracy than in autocracy. This may reduce the number of terrorist attacks in democracy. Within the context of transnational terrorism, wide democratic participation helps to reduce incentives of domestic groups to engage in terrorist activities against foreign targets in a country. When citizens have grievances against foreign targets, greater political participation under a democratic system allows them to exert more influence on their own government so that they can seek favorable policy changes or compensation more successfully. Joining a terrorist group and attacking the foreign target become less appealing options. To the extent that democratic participation leads to public tolerance of counterterrorist efforts, a democratic government will be more effective stopping a variety of terrorist attacks, including those by domestic terrorists against foreign targets as well as those committed by foreign terrorists in the country.

Hypothesis 1: Greater democratic participation reduces the number of transnational terrorist incidents in a country.

Civil Liberties, Reporting Bias, and Positive Effect of Government Constraints

A second argument in the literature claims that democracy encourages terrorism. This is based on the premise that democracies provide greater civil liberties (e.g., Schmid 1992). By guaranteeing civil liberties, democracies allow terrorists to become organized and maneuver easily, reducing the costs of conducting terrorist activities (Ross 1993; Eyerman 1998). Expansive and secure civil liberties also make it harder for the legal systems in democracies to convict terrorists and for democratic governments to prevent or retaliate against terrorism (Schmid 1992; Eubank and Weinberg 1994, 2001). As Crenshaw (1981, 383) notes, "The desire to protect civil liberties constrains security measures."

The hypothesized effect of civil liberties, however, involves two confounding issues. First, civil liberties may also generate a mitigating effect on terrorism. Citizens enjoying more civil liberties are more likely to influence the political process successfully. To the extent that civil liberties reduce political grievances, they may also reduce terrorist activities. Therefore, civil liberties alone do not help us separate the positive and negative effects of democracy, either theoretically or empirically.

Second, press freedom, as part and parcel of civil liberties, may induce possible terrorist incident reporting bias and create an additional incentive for terrorism. The bias in the reporting of terrorist incidents between different regime types has been widely recognized (see, e.g., Schmid 1992; Eubank and Weinberg 1994; Sandler 1995; Li and Schaub 2004). Terrorist incidents are more likely to be reported in democratic countries but less so in nondemocratic ones. This is so because democratic countries place fewer restrictions on the media, the less restrained news-seeking media in democracies tend to provide more extensive coverage of terrorist events, or both. In contrast, reporting of such incidents in nondemocratic countries is heavily controlled and censored. Since data on terrorist incidents are collected from open sources, one is likely to conclude that democracies have more terrorist incidents. Even if nondemocratic countries experience the same number of incidents, observers may never find out, using data collected from open sources. The reporting bias may falsely cause one to observe a positive correlation between the level of civil liberties and the number of terrorist events.

The reporting bias, however, may be more real than it seems. A terrorist group succeeds because of its ability to terrorize. To terrorize a wide audience, terrorists pursue recognition and attention by seeking to expand publicity and media coverage of their activities (see, e.g., Crenshaw 1981; Atkinson, Sandler, and Tschirhart 1987). Press freedom increases the opportunities for terrorists to be heard and watched by a large audience and hence their ability to create widespread fear. All else equal, that press freedom can satisfy the desire of terrorists for publicity creates greater incentives for terrorist activities. In addition, because of the newsworthiness of terrorist events, free press often reports terrorist incidents with excessive details, helping to recruit, teach, and train new terrorists (Schmid 1992). Press freedom and its alleged reporting bias thus generate a real positive effect on transnational terrorist incidents.

I argue that the positive effect of civil liberties, particularly press freedom, on terrorism is epiphenomenal of a crucial attribute of democratic governance—the institutional constraints on the decision-making power of government. The enormous freedom of speech, movement, and association in democracy terrorists take advantage of is contingent in nature. Regardless of regime type, a country that experiences terrorist attacks often attempts to prevent future attacks by adopting policies that circumscribe the freedom of terrorists. These counterterrorist strategies, however, often restrict civil liberties for society as a whole. Counterterrorist intelligence gathering, for example, infringes on personal privacy for all citizens. Because the state monopolizes the legitimate use of force, the degree of civil liberties depends on the strength of institutional constraints on the freedom of action of the government.

The freedom of action of an autocratic government is largely defined by the support of the elite. The democratic government, in contrast, is held accountable to the legislature and the electorate through checks and balances and elections. Relative to the autocratic ruler, the democratic government faces a wider range of institutionalized constraints over its exercise of power. This institutional difference between regime types means that there are more veto players over government policy in democracy than in autocracy. Such political constraints prevent the democratic government from encroaching on civil liberties. Democracies with inadequate executive constraints are less likely to respect civil rights. Therefore, the effect of civil liberties on terrorism is epiphenomenal of the institutional constraints on government because the extent of civil liberties, particularly press freedom, is fundamentally determined by the strength of those constraints.

Institutional constraints on the democratic government are likely uncorrelated with the negative effect of democracy on terrorism. Policy inaction and political deadlock often occur in democratic polities as a result of the constraints on the policy-making power of government. To the extent that policy inaction and political deadlock fail to reduce grievances but heighten public frustration, government constraints do not reduce but rather encourage terrorism. If one considers the implication of Fearon and Laitin's (2003) argument on civil war, terrorist groups are typically extremely marginal groups whose political grievances are too narrow to be resolved through a democratic system. Policy inaction and political deadlock, induced by institutional checks and balances, will increase the grievances of marginalized groups, pushing them toward violence.

More important, I argue that institutional constraints significantly weaken the ability of the democratic government to fight terrorism. Because the winning coalition in democracy tends to be larger, institutional checks and balances hold the democratic government accountable to a broader range of societal interests. It is, therefore, difficult for democracies to enact antiterrorist strategies that are as strict as those commonly adopted by nondemocratic regimes (Wilkinson 2001). Enacting repression and effective deterrence is more costly to the government in a competitive political system because it may harm political support and cause the government to lose power. In contrast, the largely unconstrained, repressive military regime, for example, can disregard civil liberties, effectively crush terrorist organizations, and reduce terrorist incidents (Crenshaw 1981).

Finally, I also argue that institutional constraints perversely strengthen the strategic position of terrorists in their interactions with the government. Institutional checks and balances allow a broad range of interests to influence government policy making and involve careful and regular oversight and scrutiny of government performance and policy failures. As a result, the security of a vast number of citizens becomes the concern of the democratic government. Creating a general terrorist threat that affects most citizens is likely to be effective in democratic countries. Also, the cost of generating such a threat is low because of the abundance of targets valuable to the democratic government. In nondemocratic countries, the government is constrained only by the ruling elite, so an effective terrorist threat need only target those in the small ruling coalition. Because the ruling elite are easier to protect than the general population, an effective terrorist threat is much more costly and difficult to mount in nondemocratic regimes.

Within the context of transnational terrorism, the effect of government constraints applies to both domestic terrorists and foreign terrorists in a country, thus influencing all three types of transnational terrorist attacks.

Hypothesis 2: Countries with more institutional constraints on their governments experience more transnational terrorist incidents.

Different Effects of Alternative Democratic Systems

Democracies are not homogeneous but have different electoral systems. As these systems aggregate preferences differently, they influence citizen satisfaction and political grievances differently, producing disparate effects on the incentives to engage in terrorism. Huber and Powell (1994) explore how two different democratic systems affect the congruence between citizen preferences and public policies. The majoritarian system creates single-party majority governments, while the proportional representation system produces legislatures that often represent the preferences of all citizens. In the majoritarian system, the government winning the election is committed to policies corresponding to the preferences of the median voter. In the proportional system, bargaining in the legislature that reflects the preferences of all citizens results in policies that are linked to the position of the median voter. With regression analysis of the proportional, mixed, and majoritarian systems in twelve nations in the late 1970s and early 1980s, Huber and Powell show that, on average, the proportional system leads to closer congruence between citizen self-placements and the estimated positions of governments than the other two systems.

Analyzing the effects of different democratic systems on civil wars, Marta Reynal-Querol (2002) argues that the proportional system has a lower probability of group rebellion than the majoritarian system. This is so because the opportunity cost of rebellion is higher under the more participatory proportional system than under the majoritarian system. She finds that countries of the proportional system have a lower probability of experiencing civil wars than those of the majoritarian system.

Based on the analyses by Huber and Powell (1994) and Reynal-Querol (2002), I argue that variations in democratic electoral systems also systematically influence transnational terrorism. Because the proportional system is most inclusive and has the closest congruence between citizen preferences and public policies, the proportional system is more likely to resolve political grievances than either the majoritarian or the mixed system, reducing incentives to resort to terrorism. Alternative nonviolent solutions to grievances also are more accessible under the proportional system

than under the majoritarian system. Within the context of transnational terrorism, citizens under the proportional system will have less incentive to turn violent against some foreign target within their countries than those under the majoritarian or the mixed system. Different democratic systems will experience different frequencies of terrorist attacks.

Hypothesis 3: Democratic countries with the proportional system have fewer transnational terrorist incidents than those with the majoritarian or the mixed system.

Research Design: Measures, Data, and Methods

An empirical analysis is designed to test the above hypotheses. The unit of analysis is country year. The main estimation sample covers about 119 countries from 1975 to 1997. The dependent variable is the annual number of transnational terrorist events that occur in a country. Data are from the ITERATE database (Mickolus et al. 2003). The ITERATE database includes 12,104 incidents from 1968 to 2001. The estimation sample is smaller due to data availability of the independent variables.

A measure of *democratic participation* for testing hypothesis 1 combines the electoral participation variable in Vanhanen's (2000a, 2000b) Polyarchy data set with a dichotomous indicator of democracy.[1] A country is defined as a democracy if the widely used composite indicator of regime type from POLITY IV (Marshall and Jaggers 2000), computed as the difference between the 10-point democracy index (DEMOC) and the 10-point autocracy index (AUTOC), is greater

---

[1] For robustness check, I also use the index from Freedom House instead of the POLITY scale. The overall freedom index codes each country's overall status as being free, partly free, or not free, based on the combined average of each country's political rights and civil liberties ratings. Using the Freedom House index as the democracy cutoff does not change the results of variables.

than or equal to 6.[2] Vanhanen's electoral participation variable is the percentage of the population that actually voted in general elections. *Democratic participation* is coded as equal to Vanhanen's electoral participation variable only if a country is a democracy and coded zero for nondemocracies.[3]

Two issues related to the variable are worthy of clarification. First, voter turnout may be high in nondemocratic countries because of the repressive nature of the regime (e.g., Iran, Libya). While these countries have high voter turnout records based on Vanhanen's (2000a, 2000b) electoral participation data, turnout is not voluntary since absence may lead to political persecution. Hence, the statistics for this type of countries should not be used to measure the extent to which their citizenry are participatory and satisfied with their political regime. This justifies coding *democratic participation* as equal to the voter turnout only if a country is democratic. Second, voter turnout in some highly advanced countries such as the United States is often low, not because the citizens are unhappy but arguably because they are generally satisfied and rarely have serious grievances against the political system. To control for this confounding effect, real gross domestic product (GDP) per capita is included in the model.[4] In addition, these cases only make it harder for the effect of *democratic participation* to be statistically significant, posing a tougher test of hypothesis 1. *Democratic participation* is expected to have a negative effect.

Govt constraint measures the extent of institutionalized constraints on the decision-making power of chief executives, reflecting the checks and balances in the policy-making process. This variable is based on the executive constraints variable from the POLITY IV database (Marshall and Jaggers 2000). It is on a 7-point scale, with 1 indicating *unlimited authority* and 7 denoting *executive parity or subordination.*[5] *Govt constraint* should have a positive effect.

To test hypothesis 3, I construct three dummy variables following Huber and Powell (1994). *Proportional* (or *majority* or *mixed*) is coded 1 if a country is democratic, based on the POLITY IV data and the same coding rule discussed above, and if it also has a proportional representation (or majoritarian or mixed) system and zero otherwise. The excluded reference category is the nondemocratic system. Testing hypothesis 3 requires the equality tests between *proportional*, on one hand, and *majority* and *mixed*, respectively, on the other hand. Data are from Golder (forthcoming), which record the years of all institutional changes for 199 countries from 1946 to 2000.[6]

The control variables include economic development, income inequality, regime durability, country size, government capability, history of terrorist incidents, post-cold war change, military conflict involvement, and regional differences. Details of these control variables are in the appendix. While most of the control variables follow those in Li and Schaub (2004), the history of terrorist incidents is measured differently, and regime durability is a new variable, both requiring clarification.

Regime durability is the number of years since the most recent regime change.[7] The variable is too important to exclude. Several previous studies (e.g., Eubank and Weinberg 1998; Eyerman 1998)

---

[2] The cutoff value of 6 follows the conventional practice of many other international relations scholars (see, e.g., Dixon 1994).

[3] The behavior-based electoral participation variable may correlate with other regime variables in the model. To reduce collinearity, the electoral participation variable is centered before being used to construct *democratic participation*. This procedure follows the suggestion of Aiken and West (1991).

[4] Because such countries typically belong to the Organization for Economic Cooperation and Development (OECD) group, I assess whether the results are sensitive to the OECD membership. Including the OECD dummy does not change the results.

[5] Following the suggestion of Aiken and West (1991), the variable is centered to reduce collinearity.

[6] Reynal-Querol (2002) uses data from Colomer (2001) to create these variables. I use data from Golder (forthcoming) instead because Colomer (2001) covers only eighty-four countries.

[7] This is defined as a 3-point change in the POLITY score over a period of three years or less, with the end of the transition period defined by the lack of stable political institutions, or the year 1900, whichever came last. The variable is log transformed to address skewed distribution.

find that countries undergoing regime changes are more likely to experience terrorist incidents and that new democracies experience more terrorist incidents than other countries. The confounding effect of regime change thus must be controlled for in analyzing the effect of democracy. The variable should have a negative effect.

Past incident measures the history of a country as a venue of terrorist incidents. Many countries experience persistence of terrorism (e.g., Israel). Li and Schaub (2004) control for this path dependence effect by including the lagged dependent variable. The use of the lagged dependent variable, however, has two weaknesses. First, it takes up too much variation in the dependent variable that should be explained by other substantive variables (see, e.g., Achen 2000). Second, the lagged dependent variable reflects the immediate past. A country's historical involvement with terrorism runs much longer than that. *Past incident* is the logged average annual number of terrorist incidents within each country since 1968 or since independence if after 1968.

Because the dependent variable is event count, ordinary least squares (OLS) estimates can be inefficient, inconsistent, and biased (Long 1997). The negative binomial regression (Negbin I) is thus applied (Cameron and Trivedi 1986). Robust standard errors clustered by country are estimated, producing standard errors robust to both heteroskedasticity and a general type of serial correlation within the cross-sectional unit (Rogers 1993; Williams 2000). *Past incident* and *post-cold war* dummy also help to control for temporal dependence. One-tailed tests are applied because the hypotheses are directional. Because terrorist incidents may affect many of the right-hand variables (e.g., GDP per capita), all independent variables are lagged one year behind the dependent variable to control for possible simultaneity bias.

Findings

Table 12.1 presents the statistical results. Model 1 provides the benchmark test of hypotheses 1 and 2 based on central arguments of the study. The effect

of *democratic participation* is statistically significant and negative, consistent with hypothesis 1. Voter turnout in democratic societies reduces the number of transnational terrorist attacks in these countries. This finding stands in contrast with previous research, which has failed to find any systematic evidence that can substantiate the mitigating effect of democracy on transnational terrorism.

The effect of *govt constraint* is positive and statistically significant, consistent with hypothesis 2. Institutional constraints on government increase the number of transnational terrorist attacks within a country. This finding supports my argument on the role of government constraints.

For a one-point increase in the government constraint variable, the expected number of transnational terrorist incidents increases by 6.3 percent in the country; for a one–standard deviation (2.4) increase, the expected number of incidents rises by about 16 percent. In contrast, with a one-unit increase in the voter turnout in a democracy, the expected number of terrorist incidents in the country declines by about 1 percent; with a one–standard deviation (13 percent) increase, the expected number of incidents drops by 11 percent.

The results of many of the control variables are consistent with the findings of Li and Schaub (2004). The level of economic development of a country, measured by real GDP per capita, reduces the number of transnational terrorist incidents in a country. Income inequality is positive but insignificant, possibly due to its high correlation with GDP per capita. The two variables are negatively correlated at 0.76 in the sample. The variance inflation factor (VIF) scores for income inequality and GDP per capita are the highest among all variables, 6.72 and 6.03, respectively.

Countries going through regime changes are vulnerable to more transnational terrorist attacks, while countries with stable regimes tend to experience fewer incidents. Larger countries are exposed to more transnational terrorist attacks than are smaller ones.

Countries with more capable governments tend to experience more terrorist incidents. While they may have more resources to crack down on terrorists, they are more attractive and salient targets for publicity-seeking terrorists. Terrorist activities against more capable governments receive more media coverage, wider influence, and better recruits. While terrorists may have to pay high costs for acting against these governments, the expected returns also are likely to be high.

Military conflict involvement reduces the number of terrorist incidents in the country. While external military conflict creates grievances and opportunities for terrorists, it often leads to tightened domestic security measures, raising the costs of terrorist activities.

Countries with a history of terrorist activities continue to have more terrorist events. Terrorist groups, once operational organizationally, tend to continue their activities. Consistent with the finding of Enders and Sandler (1999), transnational terrorist incidents declined in the post-cold war era. The Middle East and Europe are most susceptible to terrorist attacks, while Asia, America, and Africa experience fewer incidents relative to the Middle East.[8]

Effect of Press Freedom

Models 2 to 3 evaluate the effect of press freedom on transnational terrorism and the results in model 1. *Press freedom* is based on the measure developed by Van Belle (1997, 2000). Using the descriptive summaries of the International Press Institute's annual reports, country reports by area experts, and other country-specific historical documents, Van Belle codes a country's level of press freedom into five categories: nonexistent press, free press, imperfectly free press (due to corruption or unofficial influence), restricted press, and government-controlled press. Consistent with Van Belle, press freedom is coded 1 if a country's press is clearly free and zero otherwise. As an initial analysis, model 2 includes press freedom but excludes democratic participation, government constraints, and past incident that confound the impact of the temporally stable press freedom variable. Model 3 includes model 1 plus press freedom.

Model 2 shows that in the absence of confounding variables, press freedom has a statistically significant positive effect on the number of transnational terrorist incidents in a country. Once we add press freedom to the full model as in model 3, the effect of press freedom turns statistically insignificant, while the effects of key independent variables remain consistent with those in model 1. Democratic participation reduces terrorist incidents, while government constraints increase them. The impact sizes of these two variables also remain unchanged.

While press freedom and government constraints are highly correlated (0.69) in the estimation sample, their VIF scores are 2.86 and 2.66, respectively, and do not exceed the threshold of 10 for serious multicollinearity. More important, the significance of government constraints and the lack of significance of press freedom indicate that the former explains more variations in terrorist incidents than the latter.

In an additional analysis not reported for the sake of space, model 3 is reestimated, with *govt constraint* replaced by the unexplained residual from a Tobit regression of *govt constraint* on press freedom, for the purpose of obtaining a measure of the former independent of the latter.[9] This operationalization attributes to press freedom their shared covariance, which favors press freedom but biases against finding a significant effect of

---

[8]I assess the influence of multicollinearity on the results in model 1 by estimating the variance inflation factor (VIF) diagnostics. With multicollinearity, regression coefficients remain unbiased, but their standard errors are large, causing insignificant coefficients. Multicollinearity is a concern when model average VIF is above 1 and the VIF for any variable is above 10 (Chatterjee, Hadi, and Price 2000). For model 1, individual VIF scores range from 1.07 to 6.72. The average VIF is 3.2, which is largely a function of the regional variables (almost all above 4), as well as the real gross domestic product (GDP) per capita and income inequality (both above 6). The VIF scores for the democracy variables are all below 2.55.

---

[9]Because the government constraint variable is bounded between 1 and 7, I apply Tobit regression to restrict the predicted value to the range. Results using ordinary least squares (OLS) remain largely unchanged.

TABLE 12.1. Effects of Democracy on Transnational Terrorist Incidents within Countries, 1975–1997

	Model 1	Model 2	Model 3	Model 4	Model 5	Model 6	Model 7	Model 8	Model 9	Model 10
Democratic participation	-0.009** (2.26)		-0.009** (1.99)		-0.008** (1.80)	-0.010** (2.14)	0.003 (0.64)	-0.013*** (2.75)	-0.010*** (2.45)	-0.009** (2.19)
Govt constraint	0.061*** (2.62)		0.062*** (2.43)		0.066* (1.57)	0.060*** (2.44)	0.110*** (5.47)	0.059** (2.26)	0.062*** (2.66)	0.062*** (2.65)
Press freedom		0.550** (2.18)	0.066 (0.33)							
Proportional				0.072 (0.51)	-0.086 (0.34)					
Majority				0.269* (1.57)	0.078 (0.29)					
Mixed				0.383** (1.82)	0.217 (0.79)					
Income inequality	0.001 (0.04)	-0.009 (0.56)	-0.003 (0.21)	0.004 (0.27)	0.005 (0.34)	0.001 (0.03)	0.020** (1.98)	0.014 (1.19)	0.001 (0.07)	-0.0002 (0.01)
GDP per capita	-0.177* (1.63)	-0.087 (0.68)	-0.183* (1.58)	-0.202** (1.88)	-0.191** (1.82)	-0.163* (1.48)	-0.125 (1.18)	-0.153* (1.47)	-0.171* (1.59)	-0.189* (1.71)
Regime durability	-0.076* (1.63)	-0.215*** (3.33)	-0.093** (1.65)	-0.100** (2.18)	-0.080* (1.64)	-0.077* (1.64)	-0.047* (1.38)	-0.102*** (2.52)	-0.068* (1.42)	-0.075* (1.59)
Size	0.118*** (2.66)	0.345*** (6.14)	0.121*** (2.68)	0.094** (1.99)	0.103** (2.21)	0.119* (2.67)	-0.015 (0.30)	0.219* (6.01)	0.102* (1.93)	0.122*** (2.75)
Govt capability	0.275** (2.01)	0.627*** (3.39)	0.290* (2.00)	0.295** (2.18)	0.297* (2.13)	0.263** (1.80)	0.242** (2.08)	0.136 (1.10)	0.268** (1.98)	0.293** (2.20)
Past incident	0.547*** (12.17)		0.545*** (11.91)	0.543*** (12.13)	0.545*** (11.83)	0.551*** (12.19)	0.219*** (4.59)	0.570*** (13.45)	0.545*** (12.04)	0.547*** (12.25)
Post-cold war	-0.578*** (5.95)	-0.252*** (2.46)	-0.373*** (3.88)	-0.544*** (5.54)	-0.589*** (6.09)	-0.180 (0.82)	-0.668*** (9.12)	-0.418*** (4.19)	-0.571*** (5.79)	-0.587*** (6.01)
Conflict	-0.170* (1.51)	-0.025 (0.18)	-0.199* (1.68)	-0.150* (1.38)	-0.164* (1.45)	-0.082 (0.73)	-0.151 (1.22)	-0.225* (1.36)	-0.179* (1.59)	-0.171* (1.52)
Europe	0.221 (1.10)	-0.133 (0.44)	0.168 (0.88)	0.234 (1.19)	0.281* (1.41)	0.229 (1.09)	-0.047 (0.20)	0.509*** (2.60)	0.232 (1.15)	0.219 (1.10)
Asia	-0.494** (1.99)	-0.949*** (3.24)	-0.521** (2.11)	-0.398* (1.73)	-0.492** (2.00)	-0.502* (1.93)	-0.217 (0.89)	-0.690*** (3.24)	-0.479** (1.95)	-0.500** (2.01)
America	-0.349*** (2.37)	-0.214 (0.80)	-0.324** (2.22)	-0.286** (1.78)	-0.328** (2.17)	-0.364** (2.40)	-0.272* (1.43)	-0.451** (2.92)	-0.380*** (2.55)	-0.341** (2.30)
Africa	-0.423*** (2.38)	-0.757*** (2.78)	-0.410** (2.26)	-0.357** (1.78)	-0.448** (2.22)	-0.443** (2.42)	-0.672*** (2.40)	-0.851*** (3.67)	-0.443** (2.47)	-0.405** (2.28)

	(1)	(2)	(3)	(4)	(5)	(6)	(7)	(8)	(9)	(10)
Trade									-0.001 (0.71)	
Contraction										0.026 (0.40)
Constant	-0.443 (0.29)	-5.307*** (2.63)	-0.318 (0.21)	-0.120 (0.08)	-0.391 (0.25)	-0.698 (0.44)	-0.360 (0.27)	-2.372** (1.75)	-0.146 (0.09)	-0.468 (0.30)
Observations	2,232	2,039	1,974	2,293	2,232	2,232	2,218	1,685	2,218	2,219
Dispersion = 1	4.59	6.72	4.57	4.72	4.53	4.36			4.60	4.57
Wald test (χ^2)	1,151	158	1,043	1,114	1,418	1,753	212	706	1,196	1,153
Equality tests (χ^2)										
Proportional = majority				1.74*	0.95					
Proportional = mixed				2.24*	2.76**					

Note: Robust z-statistics, adjusted over countries, in parentheses, except for in models 7 (country fixed effects) and 8 (population averaged). GDP = gross domestic product.
* Significant at 10 percent. **Significant at 5 percent. ***Significant at 1 percent.

government constraints, presenting a tougher test of hypothesis 2. In this analysis, press freedom has a statistically significant positive effect on terrorist incidents. The effect of government constraints unexplained by press freedom remains statistically significant, positive, and the same in magnitude, as in model 1. The effect of democratic participation also remains the same.

These results confirm that the influence of press freedom on transnational terrorist incidents is encompassed and driven by the impact of government constraints. The effect of government constraints is demonstrably stronger.

Effect of Alternative Democratic Systems

Model 4 includes the three electoral system variables but excludes democratic participation and government constraints to avoid the confounding effect of their high correlation with the former. Model 5 puts participation and government constraints back in to assess the robustness of model 1. The coefficients for *proportional*, *majority*, and *mixed* represent their respective effects relative to the nondemocratic system. To test hypothesis 3, equality tests between *proportional* and *majority* and between *proportional* and *mixed* are presented at the bottom of Table 12.1.

Model 4 shows that in terms of the number of terrorist incidents in countries, the proportional system is not statistically different from the nondemocratic system, while the majoritarian and mixed systems tend to experience more incidents. Turning to testing hypothesis 3, the coefficient of the proportional system is statistically smaller than those of the majoritarian and mixed systems. As expected, the proportional system experiences fewer terrorist incidents than either the majoritarian or the mixed system. In terms of the effect size, the majoritarian and mixed systems can expect to have about 22 percent and 37 percent more transnational terrorist incidents, respectively, than the proportional system. Relative to the nondemocratic system, the majoritarian and mixed systems can expect to have 31 percent and 47 percent more terrorist incidents, respectively.

In model 5, the inclusion of democratic participation and government constraints makes all the electoral system variables statistically insignificant, except for the difference between the proportional system and the mixed system. The effects of democratic participation and government constraints, however, remain statistically significant and in the expected directions, as in model 1. These two dimensions of the democratic polity are more powerful predictors of transnational terrorist incidents than variations in the electoral system.

Further Robustness Tests

Models 6 to 8 evaluate the robustness of the results in model 1 under three different statistical estimators. Model 6 controls for time-specific unit effects by including year dummies because some years witness large numbers of terrorist incidents while others are relatively tranquil. Results show that government constraints and democratic participation both have statistically significant effects in the expected directions, as in model 1.

Model 7 presents results from the country fixed-effects negative binomial regression. The effect of government constraints remains positive and significant. But the effect of democratic participation becomes statistically insignificant, which is not surprising. It is well known that the cross-sectional dummies in the fixed-effects estimator absorb excessively between-country variations attributable to substantive variables, especially those that are temporally stable (see, e.g., Beck and Katz 2001). In addition, unless the number of time periods approaches infinity, the estimated effects are inconsistent for the country fixed-effects estimator (Greene 1997, 632). As the voter turnout figure remains the same between elections and we have only twenty-seven years in the sample, the large number of country dummies makes it difficult for the participation variable to remain significant.

Model 8 employs the population-averaged negative binomial estimator that allows for an AR(1) correlation structure. Estimation of the AR(1) correlation structure leads to a smaller sample. As in model 1, the effect of democratic participation is negative and significant, while the effect of government constraints is positive and significant.

Models 9 to 10 assess whether the results of model 1 are sensitive to the inclusion of additional control variables. The effect of trade openness on transnational terrorism is debated in the literature on how globalization affects terrorism, which is studied in detail by Li and Schaub (2004). Model 9 adds trade openness to examine whether the effect of democracy on terrorism is confounded by globalization. Model 9 shows that the effect of trade openness is statistically insignificant, consistent with the finding of Li and Schaub. The results for democratic participation and government constraints remain the same as those in model 1.

Blomberg, Hess, and Weerapana (2004) model the interactions between terrorism and national economic conditions as a bivariate Markov process, estimating the transitional probabilities among four regimes that are defined by the combinations of terrorism or peace and contraction or expansion in a country. They find that periods of economic weakness increase the likelihood of terrorist activities. To assess whether my results in model 1 are sensitive to economic contraction or expansion, I construct the same contraction variable as they do. *Contraction* is coded 1, referring to recession if a country has negative growth of real GDP per capita in a year, and zero otherwise. Model 10 shows that the effects of government constraints and democratic participation remain robust as those in model 1. The effect of economic contraction, however, is not statistically significant. In an additional analysis not reported, I use annual GDP growth rate to measure short-run economic conditions instead of the contraction dummy. Results for participation and government constraints remain robust as in model 1. Growth is statistically significant and negative, consistent with the finding of Blomberg, Hess, and Weerapana.

In addition to the above analyses, I also conduct several more tests that are not reported due to space. One may plausibly argue that the dependent variable, the number of terrorist incidents, has measurement error in event count. To assess whether the results in model 1 are sensitive to this possibility, the dependent variable is recoded as dichotomous, equal to 1 if a country experiences any incident in a year and zero otherwise. Within the estimation sample, the recoding produces a dependent variable with 1,085 country years of zero incidents and 1,147 country years of at least one incident. Probit with robust standard errors clustered over country is applied. Government constraints remain positive and significant. Democratic participation becomes statistically insignificant. This is not surprising because the advantage of the democratic participation variable is its ability to explain the count of terrorist attacks, not whether a country has any incident.

In another test, I evaluate whether the results of model 1 are sensitive to the inclusion of a measure of civil liberties. The measure is from Freedom House (2000), ranging from 1 to 7 and inverted so that higher values indicate the lack of civil rights. It is argued, however, that the Freedom House data are not appropriate for temporal analysis because the scale for the Freedom House data changes over time, and some cases rose and fell in scale even though they had no institutional change (see, e.g., Neumayer, Gates, and Gleditsch 2003). Despite the measurement error, democratic participation and government constraints remain highly robust in terms of the directions and statistical significance of their effects. The effect of civil liberties is positive but statistically insignificant, consistent with my expectation that the effect of civil liberties is epiphenomenal of the institutional constraints on government.

Finally, I also assess the effect of applying the zero-inflated negative binomial model. In the ITERATE database, a few countries never experience any terrorist incident. It is plausible that the complete absence of any terrorist attack in a country over time is explained by causal mechanisms that are different from those that account for the number of incidents in countries with at least some incident. In this study, I deal with the heterogeneity in the data generation process by excluding those states that never experience any terrorist incident in the sample period. An alternative is to apply the zero-inflated negative binomial estimator, modeling the complete absence of terrorist attack in a country over time with probit and the count of terrorist attacks with negative binomial. But this estimator requires the modeler to have two separate, a priori theories for the two different processes. Applying the same set of variables implies that the data generation process is one and the same, apparently inconsistent with the rationale for using the zero-inflated estimator. Lacking strong theoretical priors, I choose not to use this estimator for the main analysis in the article. Nonetheless, I estimate the zero-inflated negative binomial for robustness check, with the same set of independent variables for both stages. Among the democracy-related variables, only democratic participation is significant in the negative binomial model and has a negative sign as expected. Government constraints fail to explain the number of terrorist incidents.[10] Neither variable explains the complete absence of transnational terrorist incidents in some countries.

Conclusion

Two main arguments in the democracy-terrorism literature expect contradictory effects of democracy on transnational terrorism. Previous empirical work, however, has relied on using some aggregate indicator of regime type, failing to separate the positive and negative effects of democracy.

In this article, I investigate the various mechanisms by which democracy affects transnational terrorism. New theoretical mechanisms are advanced that either complement or encompass existing arguments. First, democratic participation reduces transnational terrorism in ways in addition to those conceived in the literature. It increases satisfaction and political efficacy of citizens,

reduces their grievances, thwarts terrorist recruitment, and raises public tolerance of counterterrorist policies. Second, the institutional constraints over government play a fundamental role in shaping the positive relationship between democracy and transnational terrorism. Institutional checks and balances create political deadlock, increase the frustration of marginal groups, impose on the democratic government the tough task of protecting the general citizenry against terrorist attacks, and weaken the government's ability to fight terrorism. The effect of civil liberties on terrorism popularized in the literature is more complex than commonly recognized. Finally, heterogeneous democratic systems have different implications for transnational terrorist activities.

Effects of different aspects of democracy on transnational terrorism are assessed in a multivariate analysis for a sample of about 119 countries from 1975 to 1997. Results show that democratic participation reduces transnational terrorist incidents in a country. Government constraints, subsuming the effect of press freedom, increase the number of terrorist incidents in a country. The proportional representation system experiences fewer transnational terrorist incidents than either the majoritarian or the mixed system. Overall, democracy is demonstrated to encourage and reduce transnational terrorist incidents, albeit via different causal mechanisms.

The findings suggest several important policy implications for the war on terrorism. Democracy does not have a singularly positive effect on terrorism as is often claimed and found. By improving citizen satisfaction, electoral participation, and political efficacy, democratic governments can reduce the number of terrorist incidents within their borders.

Limiting civil liberties does not lead to the expected decline in terrorist attacks, as is sometimes argued. Restricting the freedom of press, movement, and association does not decrease the number of transnational terrorist incidents. Strategic terrorists simply select alternative modes to engage in violence, as argued by Enders and Sandler (2002).

[10] Applying the zero-inflated estimator without appropriate substantive theories is problematic. Since the errors of the two equations (probit and negative binomial) are correlated, correct model specification is critical. In this case, the zero-inflated model is not necessarily superior.

We may just have to acknowledge and accept the fact that aspects of democratic polity are associated with more terrorist incidents. Institutional constraints over the government and the majoritarian system tend to bring with them more terrorist incidents, but these institutional features are undesirable, difficult to change, or both. Citizens under these institutional configurations need to be aware of those inherent risks, particularly in a world of growing uncertainty.

Appendix

List of Control Variables

Control variable	Sign	Definition	Source
GDP per capita	−	Real gross domestic product (GDP) per capita, adjusted for purchasing power parity (PPP), logged	Heston, Summers, and Aten (2002)
Income inequality	+	Gini ranging from 0 to 100 (missing values are filled following Feng and Zak 1999; Li and Reuveny 2003)	Deininger and Squire (1996)
Regime durability	−	The number of years since the most recent regime change, logged	Marshall and Jaggers (2000)
Size		Total population, logged	World Bank (2002)
Govt capability	−	Logged annual composite percentage index of a state's share of the world's total population, GDP per capita, GDP per unit of energy, military manpower, and military expenditures	Li and Schaub (2004)
Past incident	+	Average annual number of terrorist incidents that have occurred in a country since 1968	Computed using ITERATE (International Terrorism: Attributes of Terrorist Events)
Conflict	+	Coded 1 if a state is engaged in interstate military conflict or war and zero otherwise	Gleditsch et al (2002)
Region dummies		Europe, Africa, Asia, and America (relative to the Middle East)	
Post-cold war	−	Coded 1 since 1991 and zero otherwise	Enders and Sandler (1999)

REFERENCES

Achen, Christopher H. 2000. Why lagged dependent variables can suppress the explanatory power of other independent variables. Working paper, Society for Political Methodology, St. Louis, WA. Accessed from http://www.polmeth.ufl.edu/working00.alpha.html/.

Aiken, L. S., and S. G. West. 1991. *Multiple regression: Testing and interpreting interactions*. Newbury Park, CA: Sage.

Atkinson, Scott, Todd Sandler, and John Tschirhart. 1987. Terrorism in a bargaining framework. *Journal of Law and Economics* 30 (1): 1–21.

Beck, Nathaniel, and Jonathan Katz. 2001. Throwing out the baby with the bathwater: A comment on Greene, Yoon and Kim. *International Organization* 55 (2): 487–95.

Blomberg, S. Brock, Gregory D. Hess, and Akila Weerapana. 2004. Economic conditions and terrorism. *European Journal of Political Economy* 20 (2): 463–78.

Cameron, A. Colin, and Pravin K. Trivedi. 1986. Economic models based on count data: Comparisons and applications of some estimators & tests. *Journal of Applied Econometrics* 1 (1): 29–53.

Chatterjee, S., A. S. Hadi, and B. Price. 2000. *Regression analysis by example*. New York: John Wiley.

Colomer, Josep M. 2001. *Political institutions: Democracy and social choice*. New York: Oxford University Press.

Crenshaw, Martha. 1981. The causes of terrorism. *Comparative Politics* 13 (4): 379–99.

Dahl, Robert A. 1971. *Polyarchy: Participation and opposition*. New Haven, CT: Yale University Press.

——. 1998. *On democracy*. New Haven, CT: Yale University Press.

Deininger, Klaus, and Lyn Squire. 1996. A new dataset measuring income inequality. *World Bank Economic Review* 10:565–91.

Dixon, William J. 1994. Democracy and the peaceful settlement of international conflict. *American Political Science Review* 88:14–32.

Enders, Walter, and Todd Sandler. 1999. Transnational terrorism in the post–cold war era. *International Studies Quarterly* 43 (1): 145–67.

——. 2002. Patterns of transnational terrorism 1970–99: Alternative time series estimates. *International Studies Quarterly* 46 (2): 145–65.

Eubank, William, and Leonard Weinberg. 1994. Does democracy encourage terrorism? *Terrorism and Political Violence* 6 (4): 417–43.

——. 1998. Terrorism and democracy: What recent events disclose. *Terrorism and Political Violence* 10 (1): 108–18.

——. 2001. Terrorism and democracy: Perpetrators and victims. *Terrorism and Political Violence* 13 (1): 155–64.

Eyerman, Joe. 1998. Terrorism and democratic states: Soft targets or accessible systems. *International Interactions* 24 (2): 151–70.

Fearon, James, and David Laitin. 2003. Ethnicity, insurgency, and civil war. *American Political Science Review* 97 (1): 75–90.

Feng, Yi, and Paul J. Zak. 1999. The determinants of democratic transitions. *Journal of Conflict Resolution* 43 (2): 162–77.

Freedom House. 2000. *Annual surveys of freedom country ratings 1972–73 to 1999–00*. New York: Freedom House. Available: www.freedomhouse.org.

Gleditsch, Nils Petter, Peter Wallensteen, Mikael Eriksson, Margareta Sollenberg, and Håvard Strand. 2002. Armed conflict 1946–2001: A new dataset. *Journal of Peace Research* 39 (5): 615–37.

Golder, Matt. Forthcoming. Democratic electoral systems around the world, 1946–2000. *Electoral Studies*.

Greene, William H. 1997. *Econometric analysis*. Englewood Cliffs, NJ: Prentice Hall.

Heston, Alan, Robert Summers, and Bettina Aten. 2002. *Penn world table version 6.1*. Philadelphia: Center for International Comparisons at the University of Pennsylvania (CICUP).

Huber, John D., and G. Bingham Powell Jr. 1994. Congruence between citizens and policymakers in two visions of liberal democracy. *World Politics* 46 (3): 291–326.

Li, Quan, and Rafael Reuveny. 2003. Economic globalization and democracy: An empirical analysis. *British Journal of Political Science* 33 (1): 29–54.

Li, Quan, and Drew Schaub. 2004. Economic globalization and transnational terrorist incidents: A pooled time series analysis. *Journal of Conflict Resolution* 48 (2): 230–58.

Long, J. Scott. 1997. *Regression models for categorical and limited dependent variables*. Thousand Oaks, CA: Sage.

Marshall, Monty G., and Keith Jaggers. 2000. Polity IV project: Political regime characteristics and transitions, 1800–2000 dataset users manual. Retrieved February 5, 2003, from http://www.bsos.umd.edu/cidcm/inscr/polity/index.htm#data/.

Mickolus, Edward F., Todd Sandler, Jean M. Murdock, and Peter Flemming. 2003. *International terrorism: Attributes of terrorist events, 1968–2001*. Dunn Loring, VA: Vinyard Software.

Neumayer, Eric, Scott Gates, and Nils Petter Gleditsch. 2003. Environmental commitment, democracy and inequality. Background paper to World Development Report 2003, World Bank, Washington, D.C.

Reynal-Querol, Marta. 2002. Political systems, stability and civil wars. *Defence and Peace Economics* 13 (6): 465–83.

Rogers, William H. 1993. Regression standard errors in clustered samples. *Stata Technical Bulletin* 13:19–23.

Ross, Jeffrey Ian. 1993. Structural causes of oppositional political terrorism: Towards a causal model. *Journal of Peace Research* 30 (3): 317–29.

Sandler, Todd. 1995. On the relationship between democracy and terrorism. *Terrorism and Political Violence* 12 (2): 97–122.

Schmid, Alex P. 1992. Terrorism and democracy. *Terrorism and Political Violence* 4 (4): 14–25.

Van Belle, Douglas. 1997. Press freedom and the democratic peace. *Journal of Peace Research* 34 (4): 405–14.

——. 2000. *Press freedom and global politics*. Westport, CT: Praeger.

Vanhanen, Tatu. 2000a. A new dataset for measuring democracy, 1810–1998. *Journal of Peace Research* 37 (2): 251–65.

——. 2000b. The Polyarchy dataset: Vanhanen's index of democracy. Accessed from http://www.svt.ntnu.no/iss/data/vanhanen/.

Wilkinson, Paul. 2001. *Terrorism versus democracy: The liberal state response*. Portland, OR: Frank Cass.

Williams, Rick L. 2000. A note on robust variance estimation for cluster-correlated data. *Biometrics* 56 (2): 645–46.

World Bank. 2002. *The 2002 world development indicators CD-ROM*. Washington, D.C.: World Bank.

Who Are the Terrorists? Analyzing Changes in Sociological Profile among Members of ETA

Fernando Reinares*

Based on quantitative data extracted from a wide sample of ETA militants, this article offers an empirical assessment about their evolving social and demographic characteristics. Oral testimonies coming from individual interviews with former terrorists help to interpret statistics. Findings related to sex, age, and marital status when joining, also type of habitat they shared, are consistent with existing knowledge on the members of other contemporary terrorist organizations. By contrast, facts about occupation and social class are rather uncommon. Information gathered on more specific and situational variables reveals how these ethno-nationalist terrorists were not homogeneously recruited across its population of reference. Moreover, an inversion in the sociological profile of ETA activists took place over time, suggesting the extent to which membership traits may vary during the life cycle of a terrorist organization.

Studying terrorism at an individual level of analysis requires collecting and interpreting

* King Juan Carlos University, Madrid, Spain.

Research on which this article is based was made possible thanks to a grant from the Harry Frank Guggenheim Foundation.

Address correspondence to Fernando Reinares, Facultad de Ciencias Jurídicas y Sociales, Universidad Rey Juan Carlos, Campus de Vicálvaro, 28032 Madrid, Spain. E-mail: freinares@fcjs.urjc.es

data about those who actually engage in such type of violence. For instance, they may exhibit common social and demographic traits, although variations could be expected between terrorists pertaining to different political sectors within the same country or coming from a basically similar ideological frame but across cultures and even civilizations. Their sociological profile may significantly coincide or differ with the prevailing one among the surrounding population, a topic also to be investigated. Moreover, the characterization of terrorists according to a series of relevant structural variables may evolve over time, changes perhaps reflecting external socioeconomic transformations, internal organizational dynamics, or both. However, all these and other related issues remain largely unexplored in the specialized literature on terrorism.[1] This article is therefore intended as a contribution to this field of research by quantitatively and qualitatively analyzing changes in sociological profile among members of ETA.

ETA (*Euskadi ta Askatasuna* or Basque Homeland and Freedom) is a terrorist organization formed during the late sixties, in the context of a dictatorial regime, namely Francoism. It evolved as a radicalized expression of Basque ethnic nationalism, an ideology and a movement dating back to the end of the nineteenth century. However, its violent campaign escalated dramatically along the second half of the seventies, as Spain underwent a process of democratic transition from authoritarian rule. Nevertheless, terrorism arising from separatist nationalism declined in frequency during the eighties, as the new democracy consolidated and an autonomous Basque government institutionalised, and much more so through the nineties. This was due to the combined effect of sound governmental antiterrorist policies, massive popular reaction against ETA within Basque society and, last but certainly not least, international cooperation.[2]

Who joined ETA? What are the underlying social and demographic traits they have in common, if at all? What type of geographical and cultural background do they share, if any? How has the sociological profile of these ethno-nationalist terrorists evolved over time? From a social science perspective, empirically addressing these questions is of both substantive and theoretical interest in the study of terrorism and the terrorists. Accordingly, this article offers an analysis of data corresponding to over 600 individuals who became militants of ETA between the early seventies and the late nineties. Data was collected directly by the author using judicial summaries and proceedings carried out from 1977 to 1998 in the Juzgado Central de Instrucción number two of the Audiencia Nacional in Spain, a national court endowed with exclusive jurisdiction over terrorist crimes. Then, data was treated statistically. The sample of militants, thus avoiding the category of collaborators, corresponds to nearly half of all those who were recruited by ETA since the early seventies.

In order to better describe changes in sociological profile among members of the terrorist organization, the tables included in this article segregate the different variables under consideration along three consecutive periods of time. The first of these periods extends from 1970 to 1977. By the former year, still under Francoist dictatorship, ETA had already adopted the internal structure and contentious repertoire of a terrorist organization. 1977 was the year when, amid the democratic transition, a general amnesty was granted and the first free general elections were held. The second period, extending from 1978 to 1982, starts with the drafting and approval of a new democratic Constitution in Spain, ending with the self dissolution of one of the two factions into which ETA previously split, an event that took place shortly after the establishment in 1980 of a widely legitimized Basque autonomous community having political institutions embodied with extensive powers, and also following a failed coup d'etat in 1981. The third and last period covers between 1983 and 1995. That is the period when the progressive and sustained decay of the terrorist organization became even more notorious. Numerical data has been complemented with illustrative extracts from semi structured and taped individual interviews with former ETA militants conducted personally by the author between 1994 and 1999.

Men, Women, and Terrorism

The overwhelming majority of those who joined ETA have been men. Nine out of every ten, according to data from the wide sample on which this article is elaborated, although the percentage of women recruited increased slightly over the years (Table 13.1). This distribution of membership by sex is common to the terrorist organizations known during the past three decades both in industrial advanced societies and elsewhere. Even when

TABLE 13.1. ETA Militants According to their Sex, by Periods of Time (in Percentages)

Sex	1970–1977	1978–1982	1983–1995	Total
Male	95.8	93.6	88.8	93.6
Female	4.2	6.4	11.2	6.4
Total	(190)	(202)	(90)	(482)
Missing data: 132				

actual figures may denote some significant variations from one case to the other, it can be asserted that contemporary terrorism is predominantly a male phenomenon. This empirical fact has been subject to two different interpretations.[3] On the one hand, as evidence that men, as opposed to women, are especially prone to aggressive behavior in general and terrorism in particular. On the other, as empirical proof that violent forms of political action are strongly influenced by cultures or subcultures within which markedly patriarchal values and behavior patterns tend to prevail.

As to the first of these explanations, it is no doubt striking that women who accepted recruitment into ETA frequently did so because of personal bonds with men already belonging to the terrorist organization. More concretely, because of their relationship with male members whom those females eventually becoming militants had previously been maintaining close affective ties. More often than not, at least until the early nineties, this would occur after a boyfriend had been forced to seek refuge in France because police identified him as a member of ETA in Spain. Terse but nonetheless revealing accounts of how these sentimental liaisons led to a number of women becoming involved with ETA are reproduced here. First, by a Navarrese woman who ended up in the terrorist organization during the period of democratic transition, when she was 23 years old. The second testimony was provided by another woman, born in the province of Alava, who joined ETA around the middle eighties, aged just 19:

> They just suggested it to me. There was this guy I was going out with. He joined and I did, too.

> I had this boyfriend and there were these police round ups in our village. He was afraid, so I went with him. I was afraid they'd arrest me because I

was his girlfriend. Then he went to Iparralde, you know, the northern Basque Country. And I went with him.

All this is not to mean that young women so recruited lacked ideological affinity with the subculture of radical Basque nationalism. It would also be a mistake to assume that they were not at all involved in mobilizations pertaining to that same political sector until the moment of their recruitment. Evidence suggests, however, that an emotional relation such as the one just described was ultimately critical for these women to accept membership in the terrorist organization, a commitment many of them would otherwise be likely to avoid due to reservations concerning the practice of violence. An additional account from the first of the two former female militants quoted, who joined at the end of the seventies, appears to corroborate this hypothesis. She joined ETA at the request of her boyfriend and, although insisting that she would never have done so on her own initiative, nevertheless acknowledges her sympathy and even support for the terrorist organization before recruitment actually took place. Something similar is to be found in the subsequent remarks made by another woman recruited in the early eighties. In those days, she was 21 years old, had completed primary education, and was performing unskilled jobs. She also followed her boyfriend to the then-called French sanctuary but had previously been involved in collaborative activities with the terrorist organization:

> I think it never once entered my mind that I might actually become part of ETA, you know? But there were other things that definitely did occur to me ... they might ask me to do something for them, by way of infrastructure or whatever. I mean they might ask you ... look, there's this person

coming, and he's with ETA, and you've got to take him into your home and hide him, for example. Well, anyway, I didn't have too much of a problem with that. Because if you are defending their struggle, you are defending them and shouting *Gora ETA*! or *Gora ETA militarra*! or *Gora ETA politico militarra!* and someone comes up to you, you're not just going to tell him no. So it seemed perfectly logical, perfectly congruent and well, there you are. But going all the way never crossed my mind.

I went to the other side, well, because he went over. And I was out of work just then. And anyway, I wasn't feeling too good about myself in a lot of ways and I sort of said to myself: right now I haven't got too much going for me here so I might as well see what happens there, do you see? So I went to live with him.... Although to some extent you could say I had already been implicated. Helping them out from the sidelines with a couple of things that were a fairly big deal, but never actually becoming a militant. And I don't think I ever would have if this situation hadn't come up. Even though later on, well, I always say it was a mistake, you know, one of these awful, huge mistakes everyone makes. Getting involved with something when you're not totally convinced of the methods being used.

Some additional evidence presented along these same lines now follows, but this time in the words of a former male militant from Vizcaya who was recruited by ETA during the late seventies, at the age of 22. As in the case of many other male militants, once inside the terrorist organization he managed to convince his girlfriend to also accept clandestine membership. It is particularly interesting to note how this man comments on the fact that, before his girlfriend actually joined ETA, she was no more than simply a regular voter for the political party established and sponsored by the terrorist organization at the end of that decade:

> She was a sympathizer of *Herri Batasuna*.... She was, well, this kid who would never have got into any political move, other than voting, like a lot of people did, for the *abertzale* candidates and all, but without too much an idea of what it was about.

However, the predominance of men among members of ETA could also be related to structural conditions and cultural patterns associated with the division of roles in public life according to sex or gender. Moreover, it is plausible to affirm that terrorist organizations formed in a context where women have traditionally been relegated to the private sphere of family and household, where patriarchal norms and values are particularly salient, would tend to show a proportion of female militants notably lower than those arising from more egalitarian societies. Past militants of ETA often precisely explain in these terms the large majority of male militants found inside their former terrorist organization. Examples are provided in the words of two men who joined ETA during the years of post-Francoism. One of them, recruited by the terrorist organization at the age of 19, was born in Alava and comes from an urban working class and Castilian speaking family. The other one, 20 years old at the time of his recruitment, is a Guipuzcoan, also from a working class background, grown up in a home where the vernacular Basque language was usually spoken:

> I guess maybe it is more cultural than . . . I don't really know if you could call it a macho thing. An always existing culture about men and women. And it goes without saying that in the Basque Country it's a very rooted thing, the idea that the mother, the *etxekoandre*, is the boss, but strictly in the home. And out there, well, that's what you get.

> Let's see, I knew this woman who was an assistant to Txomin. Well, let's see, other than that, I never came across any women occupying positions of importance. And forget about them being part of armed units. Back in those days there simply weren't any. No question that was on account of the fact that we Basques have always had this extremely macho hang-up. That's for sure. Woman's place is in the home, if you ask me.

In this same respect it is worth giving careful consideration to the following statement provided by a Guipuzcoan woman, Basque vernacular speaker since childhood, originally from a middle-class family with nationalist antecedents and settled in a mid-sized town. She was finishing her vocational studies in the late seventies when she decided to join ETA at the age of 18. As she saw it at the time of interviewing her, men are more likely to join a terrorist organization because of their different upbringing. Interestingly enough, she emphasizes how family reactions in general and more concretely those of her own mother were to a political commitment, like her decision to join ETA, understood by close relatives as something rather more appropriate for men:

> I suppose it's easier for men to take a step like this, because of the way they've been brought up, right? In any case, it was a really big deal at home. For everybody concerned, no matter how much you may be in favor. It's all fine and dandy if it's your neighbor's son who's taking the step, but if it's your own, maybe not so fine and dandy. This is perfectly normal. It's just human. But the thing is, what if it's your daughter? What I mean is that to go off and leave home when you're 18 years old, and especially when you're a woman, well, it sure cost my mother a lot, you know? Because if it were a man, she would still suffer, logically, it being her son, but being a woman it's like this tare you carry around inside.

The same cultural patterns determining the extent to which it is considered adequate for women to take part in public life regardless of means may also appear as outright rejection by male militants of a terrorist organization who eventually had to consider allowing women to get involved in their activities. For instance, when men members argue that the presence of female members was sure to cause them trouble, especially as it may well give rise to sentimental ties considered inappropriate for their clandestine lifestyle. As the argument goes, since men would then feel themselves obliged to go to dangerous lengths in looking after their women partners, something male members perceived as likely to cause serious security problems in a tight spot. Actually, this is how a former ETA male member seems to reflect on this kind of situation. The following is from a Guipuzcoan native who was raised in a lower middle-class urban environment, and who took some college courses but left without a degree prior to joining ETA in late eighties, at the age of 24:

> We didn't want any of it. There was one of the guys in the unit with us who was dead set on getting a girl in for cover and so on and so forth. Well, we weren't having any of that because it would only create problems. When you're young and normally you haven't been in any real relationship, one thing leads to another and you've got this close thing going. And what was really out of the question for a girl to get involved in the organization or in the unit. Then we'd have problems trying to find this girl. If it had ever happened that there was this girl, I suppose we would have . . . we could have worked with her just as if she had been a man. I guess so. Then, later on, when push comes down to shove, if you're into something dangerous well, everyone of us knew what to do and where to aim, and if there's this girl with you, then you're in a sort of ashamed, what I mean is, should I help her out? or . . . I just don't know. Anyway, later on we did get these women who have done a really outstanding job in the units. But if you want my opinion, well, like I'm telling you, it's thanks but no thanks.

Accordingly, it would hardly be surprising to observe inside ETA similar attitudes and behavioral patterns concerning the role of women, to the extent that these were noted in the society considered by the terrorists as their population of reference. In this sense, attention should be paid to the following statements of three women, all of them natives of Guipúzcoa, who joined ETA during the second half of the seventies. The first, a vernacular speaker since childhood and coming from a middle-class family, had taken some vocational training courses by the time of recruitment, aged 18. Her remarks underscore the conventional nature of the role assigned to those women inducted into the terrorist organization because of their already engaged husbands or, as is mostly the case, boyfriends. The second is a Castilian speaker who grew up in a working-class family and joined at the age of 21, while finishing up a secondary education. Her statement refers to a number of disagreeable aspects of what she and other female members experienced as refugees or fugitives in the French Basque Country. The final excerpt recounts what can be recognizable as a case of sexual harassment. Testimony comes this time from a woman of *baserritarra* or rural origins, born in a family where Basque language was spoken and nationalist ideology shared, employed as an unskilled worker when recruited into ETA at the age of 20:

> What usually happens is that women, unfortunately, get in because of their husbands or because of their boyfriends, and once they are inside they functioned as women. All I mean by that is that ETA was a true reflection of the surrounding society as far as machismo is concerned. Just as I suppose would be the case in the other kinds of organizations, right?
>
> In the other side, my experience as a woman was just horrible. I mean really horrible. . . . They were all these disgusting macho types. And with a few exceptions, the majority were real jerks. There were so few women around, you can just imagine what it was like. These characters would try to climb into bed with me just like . . . and you told them to get lost. I mean . . . well, and then you had these famous games. I managed to stay out of them but there might have been two or three girls at one of these dinners they used to have. Fifteen or twenty people in a little flat. And late at night they'd play these cute little games where you'd take off all your clothes. And the goal of the game was to get to see these girls in the nude, of course. Well, they never got to see me. Not by a long shot, you understand? And as far as everything else was concerned, it came down to taking care of, well, the domestic chores, you know? Just everyday housework, cleaning up and all. . . .
>
> There was one of these clowns who, well, who wanted to have sex with me. And I didn't want. So he said, watch out, or I'll send in bad report about you. Yeah, there was blackmail of that sort, for sure. Sometimes this happened and it would just totally screw me up.

From all accounts, women who joined ETA have been much less directly involved in acts of violence than men militants. Similarly, their access to command positions inside the terrorist organization has been rather exceptional when compared with the experience of male members. In this sense, it is highly illustrative to consider what happened when ETA leaders decided in the mid-

dle eighties to make credible their threats against any member or former activist who may dissociate from the terrorist organization by accepting reinsertion measures or individual pardons offered by the Spanish authorities since the early eighties in exchange for renouncing violence. Of all possible candidates for punishment, among well over a hundred former militants who had openly renounced violence and already returned to a normalized civilian existence, ETA leaders targeted precisely one of the very few women who had ever risen to the directorate of this terrorist organization. She was María D. González Catarain, better known as *Yoyes*, shot dead on September 1985 by two ETA gunmen while she was out for a walk in the native hometown of Ordizia with her small child, who witnessed the assassination. Paradoxically, one of these two terrorists who perpetrated the crime formally asked for reinsertion benefits some years later, following his arrest and imprisonment.

Even though there are some exceptions to the rule, generally speaking women who have joined ETA tend to admit not only that they were typically relegated to functions of merely supporting male militants, as we can see in the next testimony. They also acknowledge the difficulties placed in their way so as to prevent them from rising to command or leadership positions within the terrorist organization. These grievances are reiterated by the Guipuzcoan woman quoted next, another one coming from a rural, *baserritarra* background and a vernacular Basque-speaking home with strong nationalist leanings. She was recruited into ETA at the age of 21, in the early eighties:

> Women have really got a lousy deal out of this whole thing, you know? Women have been used. And what's more, back then they made no bones about us being, you know, the warrior's consolation. And a lot of women have got such a raw deal because they were part of the infrastructure or whatever but as soon as the unit is broken up or one of its members gets caught, they've had to make a run for it and they have been really and truly blown. These women really got the short end of the stick. There were always fewer women than

men. There's been all this theorizing, but when it comes right down to having a woman take over some command position, something important, you have to . . . how shall I put it? You have to show them that you're twice as deserving as the next guy in line.

Her view of things is confirmed by another significant testimony, but this time from a Vizcayan men who joined ETA when he was 27, in the early eighties. He was born in a middle-class family with no antecedents of ideological attachment to Basque nationalism. His comments refer to two women, among the most notorious recent female militants of the terrorist organization, whom he knew personally and with which he had extensive dealings. The relevant observation he makes is that, according to his perception, women of ETA invariably felt under constant pressure to prove themselves, not solely in order to advance their position inside the terrorist organization but just to be fully respected and acknowledged as militants by their fellow male companions:

> Women have always come into ETA under a disadvantage, with this slight handicap. They've always got to prove something. They themselves were the first ones to tell me so. Take Idoia López Riaño, for instance, the one they call The Tigress. She used to say that a woman in ETA has to show twice as many balls as a man just to be accepted as a militant. And I'd say to her, don't worry, you just do your job and you'll be recognized for it. And in the case of Belén González Peñalva, you heard the same thing from her, that they have got to show everyone they were twice as good as the next guy. So what happens is that they want to show more than the rest and they really can't manage it, well, what you've got is a nice little conflict of interests, that leads to a lot of screw ups. And . . . I don't know . . . that's where you get real personality conflicts, right?

With the foregoing testimony in mind, the next one offered by that same former ETA militant seems somewhat curious and even paradoxical. During the first half of the eighties, ETA sent a good number of its members to military training facilities in Algeria, at the invitation of its authorities. Each member of the terrorist organization

would usually stay there for two months at a time. However, with the knowledge and consent of ETA leaders, the hosting country would openly discriminate against the women who were part of the group sent for training, as can be deduced from this account:

> The only problem we had is that these two women went with us. So what happened is that being these Arab countries, women weren't accepted any too well. What happened was that they made us go running. Well, maybe that's putting it too strongly, we were the ones who asked to work out a little. They didn't want to do any running, they were pretty laid back about the whole thing. They just wanted to shoot and run away, you know? Well, we wanted to get in shape and work out and do some running. So we started running on this dirt track through the desert and the women, the two of them, weren't allowed to run with us. Because they said, no way, women were inferior to men and then. . . . So, anyway, the truth is that as far as being in good physical shape goes, they were a lot worse off than we were. But they made those two women run by themselves. That whole business was just unbelievable. But since we didn't want to have any problems or hassles with them, we just went along with it.

Fact is that women recruited into ETA were usually assigned by their predominantly male colleagues tasks of organizational maintenance or information gathering. This is due not only to probable sexist prejudices but also because they considered that female militants would be more effective in such functions. This is clearly stated in the words of a woman who joined the terrorist organization when she was 20 years old. A Guipuzcoan of rural or *baserritarra* origin, born in a Basque-speaking family where nationalist sympathies prevailed, her testimony calls attention to the small number of women who were involved with ETA in the immediate post-Francoist period, even though figures did not show strong variations later on. Immediately afterwards, a male member of ETA makes it rather clear why terrorist leaders assigned a woman to accompany him when carrying out their killing commands from city to city throughout Spain. The more they appeared as ordinary couple, as he explains, the less notice would be taken of them:

> We went to Madrid, back in the days when Fraga was around. Now I can talk about it because it all came to nothing, we couldn't do a thing about it, but we were supposed to execute Fraga, how about that? That was in 1975, I'm pretty sure or maybe it was '76. In Vitoria, Gasteiz, five workers were killed that year taking part in a demonstration on the third of March or whenever it was, and the next year we wanted to do something to get back at Fraga. So I went around with my eyes open, trying to figure out how to locate him, going to all the masses that he went to. And in the end I tracked him down to this church where he was attending mass with his daughter. . . . Well, sure, we were girls and nobody paid that much attention to us. So to verify, to take a look around, to track someone down, to find out where he was, they would send us girls. But there were scarcely more than a handful of us.

> We were living just like any other perfectly normal, perfectly ordinary couple in Madrid, where I would go out pounding the pavement and looking for information, looking for data and files and she, well, she stayed at home. Sometimes she'd go out with me.

Young, Single, and Violent

A large majority of those who have joined ETA did so during their late teens or early twenties (Table 13.2), more often than not, after having participated in informal groups or formal associations active within the ideological sector of radical Basque nationalism. Often enough, they join after having been initiated in violent activities such as vandalism against institutions considered as pertaining to the enemy or the harassment of people labeled as political adversaries. Recruitment into the terrorist organization tends to occur, however, not only because an individual becomes ideologically predisposed and has been socialized in the use of violence but mainly when he or she is available in terms of time and personal responsibilities. Seven out of every ten ETA militants were actually

recruited between the ages of 18 and 23. As concerned anthropologists have argued, the willingness to terrorize other human beings usually stems from a lack of measure associated to juvenile hybris, those years along the lifecycle that follow immediately on childhood and precede adulthood.[4] Three extracts from interviews held with former militants of ETA who reflect on their past experiences precisely evoke this linkage between age, political ideas, and membership in a terrorist organization. The first testimony comes from a Guipuzcoan woman who joined ETA in the middle seventies, the second is provided by a man from Álava who was recruited once the transition from authoritarian rule was initiated, and the third corresponds to a Vizcayan male who entered the terrorist organization around the end of the eighties:

> Well, sure. I'm looking back on it when I'm 37 years old. What I mean is that if I were going through that same sort of thing now, at the age of 37, as I was back then, well, maybe it would be a whole other story. You know what I mean. The thing was the . . . atmosphere, and the age, too. I think that age had a whole lot to do with my being where I was at that particular moment.

> It's a time of your life. . . . I think that age had got lots to do with it, right? You feel all this vitality inside you that, I don't know, it means you want to pull out all the stops. And at the same time you're totally identified with the problem. So there you are and everything's fine.

> You want me to help out? Sure thing, anything you say. You're nineteen years old and ready to go take on the world. I know it's not the usual thing, but . . . they came to me and I told them, yes. And I did it as wholeheartedly as I've ever done anything, because I was convinced that it had to be done.

The fact that ETA militants were typically recruited between the last years of their teens and the beginning twenties may indeed reflect certain mental characteristics predicated with respect to the adolescent mind. As a distinctive stage in the psychological development of individuals, which tends to be extended and prolonged in modern

TABLE 13.2. ETA Militants According to their Age at the Moment of Recruitment, by Periods of Time (in Percentages)

Age at the moment of recruitment	1970–1977	1978–1982	1983–1995	Total
Under 18	1.8	1.5	10.6	3.6
18 to 20	7.2	49.2	45.5	33.2
21 to 23	29.7	37.7	28.8	32.9
24 to 26	33.3	7.7	13.6	18.2
27 to 29	14.4	0.8	1.5	5.9
30 and over	13.5	3.1	—	6.2
Total	(111)	(130)	(67)	(308)

Missing data: 306

societies, adolescence is particularly vulnerable to the attractiveness of lifestyles and political practices that combine the allure of adventure and expectations for radical social change. Militancy in terrorist organizations could thus be appealing enough to some youngsters in both of these senses.[5] The following account by a former member of ETA is noteworthy for the frankness and clarity with which he actually makes this point. Guipuzcoan and a Basque vernacular speaker since childhood, born in a low-class family devoid of nationalist political traditions whatsoever, he was recruited around the mid-seventies, aged 16, just at the time he began employment as a skilled industrial worker:

Man, we all had this conspiratorial mindset, you know? This way of thinking that if we really hit them right where it hurts, or if we got a lucky break, well, we could change history. You know, this thing about believing that we could help bring a whole new world into existence overnight. It's one of those exciting things . . . apart from the fact that you might call it romanticism, there was a real over the top romanticism. But it's also this . . . really exciting thing, a really awesome feeling, that's for sure. And I couldn't help but being attracted to it. I mean it was like that for me, personally. All the other stuff . . . whatever you think of it. There's also this sense of adventurous spirit, something of that sort is absolutely fundamental. It might be different for somebody else, somebody who thinks the whole thing is fine, who might want to do it, but when it comes to the crunch says no, sorry, I just can't do it.

Interestingly enough, even those who eventually

did end up joining ETA tended to relate alternative, nonviolent possibilities of political engagement existing across the broad Basque nationalist sector with different age cohorts or generations. Militancy in the terrorist organization, for instance, was perceived by them as a much more exciting option than any other form of political involvement. Indeed, the mainstream moderate and conservative *Partido Nacionalista Vasco* (PNV or Basque Nationalist Party) was likely to be identified as something more the sort of choice for committed but far from innovative adults, a political organization that had not yet managed to shake off the passivity it acquired during its long period underground during the Franco years or simply became autonomist instead of separatist. This critical view affected also its youth wing, *Eusko Gaztedi* (EGI or Basque Youth). On the contrary, ETA was envisaged as the leading actor of a collective mobilization process much more appropriate for demanding and contentious young people. In their own words, first from a Basque speaking Vizcayan *baserritarra*, employed as mechanical worker and aged 19 when he joined ETA near the mid-seventies, and then from another native vernacular speaker born in a low-class family who was performing an unskilled job at the time of his recruitment around the same period, aged 17:

Why ETA and not EGI, say, since that could be considered one of the options? Because I felt you had to do something more, if know what I mean. To do something more than all that folklore, what simply wasn't getting done in those days. The way I saw it, the PNV, EGI were doing absolutely nothing. That is, they were well organized and all, but there wasn't any . . . any task they were carrying out. And those other guys, well, at least they were pretty dynamic, you know? When you're young it's easier to get hooked by something dynamic, something along those lines, right?

Well, actually, back in those days the only alternative you had was the PNV, I guess. Anyway, as far as we were concerned, the PNV was the party for . . . I don't know how to put it . . . for grownups, I guess.

As data at hand suggest, the frequency of people recruited yearly by ETA has fallen notoriously and consistently since at least the mid-eighties, perhaps even earlier. At the same time, however, the average age at the moment of recruitment became considerably lower than had previously been the case. During the first half of the seventies, that is still under the dictatorship, and throughout the early years of transition from authoritarian rule, only 9 percent of new militants were aged 20 or less when recruited by the terrorist organization. According to the sample used as basis for this study, by the mid-eighties and throughout the nineties that figure had soared to nearly 60 percent of the total. Across the seventies and early eighties, ETA leadership could count on a broad mobilization potential and was able to maintain several operative armed units. Those were the days when it was unusual to see someone other than a male aged between 21 and 26 enlisting the organization. It was also a virtual requisite for those joining the group to have already completed the then compulsory military service. ETA leaders were rather reluctant to include teenagers among their militants, among other things because they considered this would have a negative impact on the image still enjoyed by the terrorist organization within Basque society.

Here is a woman born in Guipúzcoa who precisely joined ETA during the democratic transition period and recalls how their clandestine leadership used to turn down adolescents wanting to volunteer themselves. A man from the same province, who became a member of the terrorist organization in the immediate post-Francoism, relates that he had a hard time being recruited because of his then just 20 years of age and the fact that he had not been conscripted into the Spanish army. A stint as a draftee was considered by ETA leaders as a good way of getting the enemy to provide your own militants with costless basic training in the use of arms and even explosives. Moreover, the experience of conscripts during military service would often leave them with an edge of additional hostility toward the Spanish armed forces, traditionally depicted by ETA as an occupation army keeping the Basque people, at least on the southern side of the Pyrenees, in submission:

> Well, I remember that whenever we'd ask to do something serious as far as the organization was concerned, they would tell us no way. This was in the beginning, when we were 17, and they would say no . . . because we were just a bunch of kids, we were simply too young. I suppose they figured that if some 17 year old got arrested with a pistol on him, it would make the organization look pretty bad, right? But let me also tell you, being 17 years old politically back in those days was nothing like being 17 years old politically is now. But of course, in personal terms, you were just a kid.

> Let's see, the thing was that I hadn't been drafted. In those days, they made a point of not having that hanging over you, and stuff like that, they wanted people who had come of age. Then, afterwards, they started taking on these other kind of people, younger, you know? But at that time they had more militants than they knew what to do with. And I even remember [hearing them say] look, we've got plenty of people, we just want the qualified ones. As in more mature. And I was still young.

Apart from the demographical evolution and population dynamics inherent to Basque society, it has been quite some time since ETA leaders were in a position to pick and choose new members for the terrorist organization. From at least the mid-eighties and much more so during the nineties, they tended to accept whoever is available, regardless of their age, in order to sustain not several but simply one or two, perhaps three operational units the terrorist themselves call *comando* or *talde* in the vernacular, usually composed of between three and five militants who may be helped by some ten to twelve collaborators. A no doubt eloquent testimony in this sense is the following one, provided by a Guipuzcoan male raised inside an urban and middle-class family, who joined ETA in the early eighties, when he was 24 years old:

> In those days there was nothing like it is now. Before you could get into an armed unit, you would have to pass through a long series of activities. So it came as sort of the culmination. It's not like that any more. Nowadays, the people in one of the units get handed a gun and go out shooting, you know? Of course, it was a whole other story in those days. There was lots of raw material, lots of possibilities.

Consistent with the usual age of their recruitment in ETA, those who have joined the terrorist organization are typically single and most of them tend to remain so as long as they sustain their militant commitment (Table 13.3). Indeed, only one out of every ten of the individuals included in the sample was married at the time of becoming a member of ETA. However, this can also be seen as indicative of the obvious difficulties entailed in conciliating a high-risk, clandestine activity with the daily routines and responsibilities of a family life, particularly if there are children to care for. The next two excerpts transcribe the taped words of a like number of former ETA militants who do not mind admitting as much. The first is a *baserritarra* from Guipúzcoa recruited by ETA in the early seventies, still under the dictatorship, whereas the second, quoted previously in this article, is an Álava native having an urban and working class family background, who joined the terrorist organization in the immediate aftermath of Francoism:

> My love life in ETA before I got sent to jail was nonexistent. I suffered a lot emotionally because . . . well, I couldn't even think about. . . . I

couldn't make any plans for having a family or a girlfriend, because they might get me from one day to the next. . . . It didn't look good to me having some of the comrades living a family life. I saw the family as an obstacle to ETA's struggle . . . well, within ETA, at least.

> By the time I got a girlfriend, and later on I even got married, I was already on my way out of the organization. I mean, we were already sort of sitting it out on the sidelines. The way I've always seen it is that you should never let one thing mix with another, for your own sake as well as everyone else's. What I mean is that if I had had a family, I would have . . . I would have participated with my ideas, in some whole other way. Politically, most probably.

Certainly, there has always been few notorious exceptions to the single marital status as a rule among those who ended up joining ETA. Such as in the case of this former member of the terrorist organization, once again a Guipuzcoan man with both urban and working class origins, Basque-speaking background, and a limited degree of nationalist tradition in his family. He was married and had children already at the time of being recruited by the terrorist organization, around the mid-seventies. Nevertheless, this individual was rather surprisingly capable of compaginating, during nearly thirteen years, his ordinary public life as a sales agent and family father with underground violent activities that frequently resulted in bloodshed. All this went on for well over a decade, without evoking more than bewilderment and suspicions at home. At least, that is the way he personally saw it:

> Yeah, my wife . . . well, it's pretty much impossible to keep your wife in the dark over a long

TABLE 13.3. ETA Militants According to their Marital Status at the Moment of Recruitment, by Periods of Time (in Percentages)

Marital status	1970–1977	1978–1982	1983–1995	Total
Single	78.5	92.9	100	88.1
Married	20.7	7.1	—	11.6
Other	0.8	—	—	0.3
Total	(121)	(140)	(42)	(303)
Missing data: 311				

period of time, right? So my wife, shit, she knew something was going on, you know? But she had no idea the whole business was so . . . that I was so involved up to my ears, right?

Guipuzcoans, Above All

ETA is more a Guipuzcoan than an encompassing Basque phenomenon. What does this mean? It means that practically half of all past and present members of the terrorists organization originated from Guipúzcoa (Table 13.4). That is to say, one of the four provinces in Spain where Basque collective identity is geographically predicated upon and one out of seven territories if those across the border in France are to be included. Interestingly, Basque nationalism in general and radical nationalism in particular are most strongly implanted in that province than anywhere else across the Basque Country. Guipuzcoan population accounts, however, for some 25 percent of the Basques in Spain, including Navarre. Moreover, a majority of those ETA militants who came from Guipúzcoa were actually born in the provincial capital town, San Sebastián or Donostia, as well as in its surrounding municipalities. It is often taken for granted in the mass media that *Goiherri*, that is Ordizia and the surrounding villages located in the inner and mountainous area of Guipúzcoa, has supplied the greater percentage of militants in ETA, but this is actually not the case. The misunderstanding probably arises from the fact that members born in such mountainous and highly industrialized areas have typically been over-represented among leaders of ETA.

Over the three consecutive periods considered in this study, the percentage of ETA members coming from Vizcaya has held consistently at around 34 percent of the total. Two out of every three of them were born in or long-time residents at the metropolitan area of Bilbao, also known as the Gran Bilbao, before being recruited by the terrorist organization. Since the mid-eighties, as the yearly number of young people joining ETA continues to fall, those born in the autonomous community of Navarra have proportionally increased, although they never amounted to more than half the percentage of Vizcayans and not even a third of those coming from Guipúzcoa. According to the data herewith collected, it can be suggested that a significant amount of these Guipuzcoans and Vizcayan who have joined the terrorist organization were in fact residing in Álava and Navarra at the time of their recruitment (Table 13.5). They probably induced further ETA recruitment in these two territories. In turn, those members of the terrorist organization born in Álava have always constituted a very small percentage of the total, one invariably surpassed even by militants who were born outside the Basque Country.

That is why it is worth paying particular attention to the oral testimony coming from a former militant quoted next. He was born and raised in a Castilian-speaking family with no nationalist leanings whatsoever, and became a member of ETA in the late seventies. Before joining the terrorist organization, this individual embraced some usual prejudices of Basque nationalism in its original and mainstream version by repudiating Álava, his own province of birth, on the account of

TABLE 13.4. ETA Militants According to their Territory or Province of Birth, by Periods of Time (in Percentages)

Territories or provinces	1970–1977	1978–1982	1983–1995	Total
Álava	4.3	4.9	3.5	4.4
Guipúzcoa	49.1	45.6	43.0	46.4
Navarra	4.3	7.7	14.0	7.7
Vizcaya	34.4	36.3	32.6	34.8
Other	8.0	5.5	7.0	6.7
Total	(163)	(182)	(87)	(432)
Missing data: 182				

TABLE 13.5. ETA Militants According to their Territory or Province of Residence at the Moment of Recruitment, by Periods of Time (in Percentages)

Territories or provinces	1970–1977	1978–1982	1983–1995	Total
Álava	2.3	2.9	9.1	3.5
Guipúzcoa	51.1	50.0	34.1	48.2
Navarra	7.0	5.7	22.7	8.6
Vizcaya	38.8	40.0	34.1	38.7
Other	0.8	1.4	—	1.0
Total	(129)	(140)	(44)	(313)

Missing data: 301

its predominantly Castilian-speaking interface, cultural mixture, and even frontier situation. While still a teenager and before being recruited by ETA, he actually made the decision to move and live in Guipúzcoa, mainly if not exclusively because such territory was considered to be more genuinely Basque than the other ones:

> I've always felt much more identified with Guipúzcoa than with Álava, for example. Well, I guess, I don't know . . . there was this feeling that over there everything was so much more . . . so much more radical, so much more Euskadi, you know, more so than Álava. Because in Álava, you see, everything has been more influenced by La Rioja and Castile, you know? the nearest areas. So . . . I don't know if it was on account of that. I believe maybe you could say that yes. I always could feel myself drawn to Guipúzcoa that much more strongly.

Guipúzcoa and the Guipuzcoans are thus a fundamental reference for many of those relatively few members of ETA who come from southern Basque provinces. The landscape of Guipúzcoa corresponds much better to the mythical image of a wilder, evergreen, and inaccessible Euskal Herria, which literally means the land where the Basque language is spoken. Guipúzcoa is by far the territory with a largest number of people who can claim the Basque vernacular as their primary tongue. For many of those militants born in Álava or Navarre, Guipúzcoa was usually regarded as something like the quintessential Euskal Herria, the cradle of Basque idiosincracy and distinctiveness. The following is a testimony precisely offered by a Navarrese woman who explains the meaning

Guipúzcoa and the Guipuzcoans had for her, the daughter of an urban middle-class family where Castilian was the sole language spoken and nationalism did not form part of her upbringing. She decided to join ETA during the democratic transition period, at the age of 23:

> Guipúzcoa was always the . . . sort of the . . . it more or less was a case of the Guipuzcoans being the best there is going. Guipúzcoa was like, well, the Guipuzcoans! Going to Guipúzcoa was a little like going back to the cradle, you know?

All throughout the seventies, young people recruited by ETA came predominantly from rural or semirural inland areas, more concretely from winding mountain valleys where primordial elements of the autochthonous Basque culture clashed head on with an accelerated process of industrialization that began in the fifties and reached a feverish pitch during the following decade. Data gathered indicates that, from the early seventies until the post-Francoist period, seven out of every ten militants of ETA shared a common rural or semirural background (Table 13.6). In the years from the democratic transition through approximately the mid-eighties, over half of those who joined the terrorist organization were still born in small and medium-sized towns where the density of social networks is significantly higher when compared to that of urban or metropolitan areas.[6] Since the mid-eighties, however, an inversion has occurred in this sociological profile, also as far as habitat of origin is concerned. From then on, almost 70 percent of all those who have joined ETA were born in urban or metropolitan areas.

TABLE 13.6. ETA Militants According to the Size of their Town of Birth, by Periods of Time (in Percentages)

Size of birth town (population)	1970–1977	1978–1982	1983–1995	Total
Under 2,000	15.5	7.7	2.5	9.6
2.000 to 10,000	15.5	11.8	8.9	12.6
10.001 to 50,000	40.6	34.9	21.5	34.3
50.001 to 100,000	2.7	4.2	6.3	4.1
Over 100,000	25.7	41.4	60.8	39.4
Total	(148)	(169)	(80)	(397)

Missing data: 217

TABLE 13.7. ETA Militants According to the Size of their Town of Residence at the Moment of Recruitment, by Periods of Time (in Percentages)

Size of residence town (population)	1970–1977	1978–1982	1983–1995	Total
Under 2,000	8.6	4.3	4.5	6.1
2.000 to 10,000	16.4	13.0	6.8	13.5
10.001 to 50,000	46.1	46.5	34.1	44.5
50.001 to 100,000	5.5	8.7	9.1	7.4
Over 100,000	23.4	27.5	45.5	28.4
Total	(128)	(138)	(44)	(310)

Missing data: 304

This fact is highly significant, even if the percentage lowers when taking into consideration the size of those municipalities where incoming militants were residing at the time of their recruitment into the terrorist organization (Table 13.7).

Interestingly, this means as well that ETA militants have been extracted, since the mid-eighties, mainly in those areas where the primordial attributes most closely related with traditional Basque culture are less vigorous. According to the sample used as the basis for this analysis, four in every ten members recruited by the terrorist organization from the early eighties to the end of the century came from a linguistic environment where less than 10 percent of the people as an average knew how to express themselves correctly in the autochthonous vernacular. Overall, 75 percent of them were born in places where no more than 40 percent of the inhabitants were fluent *euskera* speakers (Table 13.8). No doubt a most significant change from the first of the three periods accounted for in this study, spanning the end of the Franco dictatorship and early transition years, throughout which the majority of those who joined the terrorist

organization came from areas where the rate of vernacular speakers amounted to over 60 percent of the population (Table 13.9). Indeed, more than half of these new militants came during that first period from small towns or medium-sized localities where Basque vernacular was the language in which 40 percent or more of the inhabitants expressed themselves in everyday life.

All this evidence may possibly help to better understand why it is that six out of every ten ETA militants who joined the terrorist organization during the seventies had both paternal and maternal autochthonous family names, a proportion exactly inverted during the third period under consideration, until the late nineties (Table 13.10). Nowadays, 60 percent of those recruited by the terrorist organization have only one autochthonous surname or none at all. A great many of these are probably the sons and daughters of immigrant families that moved to the north during the fifties and sixties from the less developed regions of Spain. Actually, many of those former ETA militants who do share the vernacular as mother tongue, have autochthonous last names and are truly adhered to

TABLE 13.8. ETA Militants According to the Number of *Euskera* Speakers in their Town of Birth, by Periods of Time (in Percentages)

Percentage of *euskera* speakers in birth town	1970–1977	1978–1982	1983–1995	Total
Less than 10%	17.6	36.1	40.5	30.1
11% to 20%	2.7	2.9	2.5	2.8
21% to 40%	25.7	16.0	31.7	22.7
41% to 60%	24.3	28.4	15.2	24.2
More than 60%	29.7	16.6	10.1	20.2
Total	(148)	(169)	(80)	(397)

Missing data: 217

TABLE 13.9. ETA Militants According to the Number of *Euskera* Speakers in their Town of Residence when Recruited, by Periods of Time (in Percentages)

Percentage of Basque vernacular speakers in residence town	1970–1977	1978–1982	1983–1995	Total
Less than 10%	22.6	28.3	43.2	28.1
11% to 20%	3.9	5.1	4.5	4.5
21% to 40%	25.0	18.8	27.3	22.6
41% to 60%	21.9	29.0	15.9	24.2
More than 60%	26.6	18.8	9.1	20.6
Total	(128)	(138)	(44)	(310)

Missing data: 304

TABLE 13.10. ETA Militants According to the Origin of their Surnames, by Periods of Time (in Percentages)

Origin of surnames	1970–1977	1978–1982	1983–1995	Total
Both surnames autochthonous	60.6	51.5	41.6	53.2
Only one surname autochthonous	17.8	28.3	25.8	23.7
Neither surname autochthonous	21.6	20.2	32.6	23.1
Total	(185)	(198)	(90)	(473)

Missing data: 141

the ideas of an ethnic separatism find it increasingly disturbing to perceive how the terrorist organization ended up recruiting people with little or no primordial traits as part of their individual profile. This point of view comes clearly across in the following statement from a Vizcayan man who grew up in a middle-class home where Basque language was indeed spoken and nationalist leanings were palpable. He joined ETA in the late seventies, at the age of 18:

> The precise base of those who are keeping with us . . . generally from the other side, the side of San-

turce and that, much less nationalist, far more concerned about the social question, more with the social outcasts issues, the whole situation, unemployment. Affected by this sort of facts. And a pretty high proportion, maybe 85 percent. . . . well, I shouldn't be spouting off numbers. . . . I really don't know for sure. But if you look at the people who are being arrested and pay attention to their surnames, you'll see that they've got little or nothing to do with the autochthonous people, who have been living here always. And are people coming from the immigration. A marginal substratum, that is to say.

As to the occupation held by ETA militants at the time of their recruitment, it is likewise interesting to observe how this variable evolved over the years. According to the data under review, no less than half of those who joined ETA during the first period considered in the present study, that is to say from the early seventies through the first post-Francoist years, were skilled industrial workers (Table 13.11). Throughout the third period, between the mid-eighties and the late nineties, this same category has shrunk dramatically to only 16 percent of all those recruited by the terrorist organization. This evolution may be related to changes in the Basque social structure but also to the declining mobilization potential of ETA, insofar as the predominance of militants coming from the working class has been empirically associated to the persistence of separatist terrorist organizations in the context of Western industrialized societies.[7]

On the other hand, students accounted for only 5 percent of all those recruited by ETA during the first period under consideration, yet this subgroup had multiplied by six in the third period and now accounts for 33 percent of the total, making students the largest single category among all those who have joined since the mid-eighties. They are mainly secondary school students. Taken as a whole, therefore, the proportion of ETA militants from a working-class background has been steadily declining among members of the terrorist organization over the last three decades. Their place has been taken by members who can be broadly categorized, considering the occupational status they enjoyed immediately before recruitment, as belonging to the new middle classes (Table 13.12).

Apparently, the sociological profile of those who have joined ETA evolved in such a way that is has come to closely resemble that which characterizes

TABLE 13.11. ETA Militants According to their Occupation at the Moment of Recruitment, by Periods of Time (in Percentages)

Occupational categories	1970–1977	1978–1982	1983–1995	Total
Industrial or tertiary sector self-employed	0.8	0.7	—	0.6
Agricultural small holders	1.6	—	—	0.6
Managers and executives	—	0.7	—	0.3
Admistrative, sales & technical personnel	20.6	20.6	24.3	21.0
Services sector personnel	5.6	8.2	8.1	7.1
Specialized industrial and services workers	50.0	35.6	16.2	39.3
Industrial & services nonspecialized workers	11.1	11.6	13.5	11.7
Agricultural workers	1.6	0.7	—	1.0
Unemployed	—	0.7	2.7	0.6
Students	5.5	21.2	32.5	16.2
Other categories	3.2	—	2.7	1.6
Total	(126)	(146)	(38)	(310)
Missing data: 304				

TABLE 13.12. ETA Militants Distributed According to their Social Class Sector, by Periods of Time (in Percentages)

Social class sector	1970–1977	1978–1982	1983–1995	Total
Upper classes	—	—	—	—
Old middle class	1.7	—	—	0.8
New middle class	30.2	38.6	52.2	36.0
Working classes	68.1	61.4	47.8	63.2
Total	(116)	(114)	(24)	(254)
Missing data: 360				

juvenile, urban, and anomic radicalism as it is manifested in a number of European countries.[8] Nowadays, this radicalism tends to express its discontent and disaffection by way of xenophobic, racist, or totalitarian movements endorsing a neonazi orientation. In the Basque Country, this wave of urban juvenile radicalism expresses its disruptive aggressiveness through the existing offer of collective violence managed by the leaders of a terrorist organization, namely ETA and practiced by both underground militants and above the ground supporters. Next quote is extracted from the testimony of a native Vizcayan, born in a working-class, urban family. Having joined ETA at the end of the eighties, when he was just 19 years old, he recalls the alternatives that were available to him and his peers, who were not prepared to enter the workforce at that point in their respective lives but neither had the desire to go on with their formal education. As is often the case with individuals immersed in the anomic, discontented, and even marginalized segments of contemporary youth in large cities, the two basic options presented upon them were to either go on drugs or get involved in disruptive activities:

> Young people ... I mean those who went to school with me or who looked like they'd be going on to university. . . . I guess they would have had their political ideas, just like anybody else. But in any rate, they pretty much kept them to themselves, they didn't go out of their way to get involved in things. Then you had the ones like me who had been working since they were 16. And then there were those who didn't want to finish their studies, only they didn't want to go out and get a job, either. So then, it was like this automatic thing. If you didn't get involved in something political, you turned into a druggie. It was as simple as that.

That *something political*, literally alluded in this testimony as an alternative to the world of drugs, no doubt refers in situational terms to get drawn into violent mobilizations within the radical Basque nationalist sector, one that became increasingly self-enclosed, sectarian, and cut off from external reality. More concretely, to get drawn into the thematic associations and sectorialized move-

ments where a constant to decreasing estimate of perhaps between 200 and 400 adolescents and youngsters underwent political socialization and learned the use of violence during the nineties. A number of them may later on become members of ETA, particularly the more obstacles this organization eventually found in developing open recruitment practices, although the violence they engage in is not necessarily expressive nor goal oriented, but essentially antisystem. This fact seems to be reflected in the following comments by the same former militant of ETA whose testimony was extracted in the previous quote:

> Smash, smash, smash. . . . Smash for the sake of smashing. Take anything you can get and just smash it to pieces. Nothing happened, nothing was going on, there was no pressure from the cops. I don't know. But . . . all you need is a couple of drinks to go out and tear apart a phone booth.

Actually, many former members of ETA have been scathingly critical of the teenagers being recruiting by the terrorist organization, particularly since the mid-eighties and throughout the nineties. Three such illustrative comments follow. The first one comes from a Guipuzcoan already quoted, who joined the terrorist organization at the end of the Franco period. The second is provided by an old gunman born in the same province who was recruited by ETA during the post-Francoist years, at the age of 20. The third and last is offered by a Vizcayan who joined the terrorist organization in the democratic transition period, at the age of 18. In one way or another, all these former militants of the terrorist organization underscore their disapproval of an antisystem violence that they perceive as unrelated with grievances and demands voiced by Basque nationalists:

> Man, there's the difference between the people that were in before, and the ones they've got in today. Because nowadays for example, if someone is out of a job and can't find a girlfriend, he ends up getting caught up in a place or an entity to raise hell. Because he has to raise hell. You get involved in the *Gestoras*, you get involved anywhere else, solely for the sake of . . . well, letting all that

adrenaline flow a little. Because they're absolutely right, they're pissed off, and any way they want to protest is just fine, right?

They never had to live under repression, they never had to go through repression. It's these characters who have swallowed what they read in three or four books and heard in three or four speeches, and the ideas they've had poured into their heads through a funnel and that's it, as far as they're concerned. It's always that bunch. They have this whole idea of what life is about and it is totally impossible to put into practice in Euskadi and what's worse, it would turn other people totally against. What I mean is they are supposed to be idealists, but I swear I don't know what kind of world they're living in. What I mean is they're full of Marx and Lenin. They haven't got the slightest idea of . . . how shall I put it? What the Basque roots are and what this struggle is all about. They haven't got the slightest idea, none. They weren't living under Franco and they haven't lived through anything. . . . About all they know is that this is Euskadi and that's as far as it goes. And as much as I can make out, they have no other . . . in other words, they just aren't nationalists.

In those days, the underpinning of our movement was above all nationalistic. However, this has changed. Changed as far as the movement's feeding sources are concerned, not to mention its procedures and goals. These have changed, too. So, what does it all mean? Well, it's like this, it used to be that a militant was a militant because he knew why he was a militant and knew what he was fighting for. Now this has trailed off into something that is borderline criminal, borderline social misfit. Things are moving further in that direction so that nowadays if what you want is a militant who raises the red revolutionary banner, the first thing you've got to do is reeducate him, you have sit him down and tell him that even though the Iron Curtain has come down, the values it represents are still standing because they are the values that praise men, and so on and so forth, and you have to completely reeducate him this way. But for a militant like us, above all nationalist, well, you know. . . . Nobody has to tell me which one is and where is my homeland. I already know it, and that I should love my homeland. I already know that.

And either I love it or I don't love it, but at least I know all that.

Conclusions

As data retrieved in this study shows, the overwhelming majority of those who joined ETA have been single men. Most of them were recruited between their late teens and early twenties, born in and residents of urban settings. This basic distribution of membership by sex, age, and marital status at the time of recruitment, as well as habitat of origin these violent ethno-nationalists tended to share, is consistent with existing information on members of other secular insurgent terrorist organizations known since the late sixties in Western developed societies. The prevalence of male militants is determined by a cultural context impregnating attitudes and behavior inside the terrorist organization. Adolescents and young people are the majority due to their much greater availability in terms of time and personal responsibilities, as well as perceptions associated to these age cohorts. However, in contrast with evidence about contemporary terrorists elsewhere, the largest proportion of ETA members were skilled industrial workers at the time of their recruitment, an occupational category followed by low middle-class, white-collar employees, not unlike a few other lasting terrorist organizations active during the past three decades in a similar socioeconomic and cultural context.

Interestingly enough, information gathered on more casuistic and situational variables reveals how ETA members were not homogeneously extracted across its population of reference. As to more specific traits such as geographical origins, it is worth mentioning how nearly half the militants of the terrorist organization originated from Guipúzcoa, although this province, one of the four in Spain where Basque collective identity is affirmed, accounts for just a quarter of the Basque population, a proportion decreasing if the French Basque Country would have to be considered. However, it is precisely in that territory where a series of primordial elements more closely associated with the autochthonous Basque culture are most prevailing and ethnic nationalism has been better rooted. Nevertheless, it is also true that a third of all those who have joined the terrorist organization came from localities where only a small proportion of its inhabitants were actually able to speak the vernacular language or *euskera*. Moreover, ETA militants having only autochthonous surnames equate in numbers those with just one local surname or no local family names at all. A great many of these latter are probably the sons of mixed families or immigrant families altogether, which moved to the north of Spain, particularly to the industrialized and comparatively wealthier Basque provinces during the fifties and sixties from less developed regions.

Moreover, an astonishing inversion in the sociological profile of ETA activists has taken place over time, thus suggesting the extent to which membership traits may vary during the lifecycle of a terrorist organization. As ETA evolved between the early seventies and the mid-nineties, intensifying its lethal activities and growing in size at the end of the first of these decades, to decline afterward both in terms of mobilization potential and frequency of violent operations, significant if not dramatic changes became evident in the social and demographic characterization of its militants. For instance, the percentage of women recruited increased slightly over the years. But a true inversion in the sociological profile of ETA terrorists can also be observed in a number of other variables. Initially, that is during the seventies, a majority of members joined in their early twenties, shared a common rural or semirural background, came from areas with a medium or high rate of vernacular speakers, most had two autochthonous surnames and, more often than not, were skilled industrial workers at the time of their recruitment.

As from the mid-eighties, the majority of those who decided to join ETA were in their late teens as an average, usually born in urban and metropolitan environments, extracted mainly from cities with a medium or low proportion of actual *euskera* speakers, had typically only one autochthonous surname or none at all. As from the mid-eighties,

secondary high school or vocational students below the college level became the largest occupational category among those adolescents and youngsters recruited by ETA, somewhat replacing the progressive defection of skilled industrial workers. Therefore a profile, in terms of age, habitat of origin, and occupation, apparently close if not identical to the ones exhibited by neo-nazi, xenophobic, and antisystem violent militants active in a number of both established and new European democracies during well over the past twenty years. Is it because current totalitarian movements adopting the form and structures of terrorist organizations tend to converge in this sense, despite differences of political discourse or ideological orientation?

NOTES

1. Fernando Reinares, "Terrorism," in *International Handbook of Violence Research*, eds. Wilhelm Heitmeyer and John Hagan (The Hague: Kluwer Academic Publishers, 2003), pp. 309–321.
2. Fernando Reinares, "Sociogénesis y Evolución del Terrorismo en España," in *España: Sociedad y Política*, ed. Salvador Giner (Madrid: Espasa Calpe, 1990), pp. 353–396; Fernando Reinares and Oscar Jaime, "Countering Terrorism in a New Democracy: The Case of Spain," in *European Democracies Against Terrorism: Governmental Policies and Intergovernmental Cooperation*, ed. Fernando Reinares (Aldershot, Hampshire: Ashgate, 2000), pp. 119–145; Fernando Reinares, "Democratization and State Responses to Protracted Terrorism in Spain," in *Confronting Terrorism. European Experiences, Threat Perceptions and Policies*, ed. Marianne van Leeuwen (The Hague: Kluwer Law International, 2003), pp. 57–71.
3. Mike Benson, Mariah Evans and Rita Simon, "Women as Political Terrorists," *Research in Law, Deviance and Social Control* 4 (1992), pp. 121–130; Robin Morgan, *The Demon Lover. On the Sexuality of Terrorism* (New York and London: Norton and Company, 1989).
4. Julio Caro, *Terror y Terrorismo* (Barcelona: Plaza y Janés, 1989).
5. Richard G. Braungart and Margaret M. Braungart, "From Protest to Terrorism: the Case of SDS and the Weathermen," *International Social Movement Research* 4 (1992), pp. 45–78.
6. Robert Clark, *The Basque Insurgents. ETA, 1952–1980* (Madison: University of Wisconsin Press, 1984), pp. 141–165; Ernest Lluch, "Els Orígens Econòmics de la Violència Basca," *L'Avenç* 191 (1995), pp. 30–55; David Laitin, "Nationalist Revivals and Violence," *Archives Européennes de Sociologie* 36 (1) (1995), pp. 3–43.

7. Peter Waldmann, *Radicalismo Etnico. Análisis Comparado de las Causas y Efectos en Conflictos Etnicos Violentos* (Madrid: Akal, 1997).

8. Tore Björgo and Rob Witte, eeds., *Racist Violence in Europe* (Basingstoke, Hampshire: Macmillan Press, 1993) and Tore Björgo, ed., *Terror from the Extreme Right* (London: Frank Cass, 1995).

Received August 10, 2004
Accepted August 10, 2004 ■

Why Would Terrorists Enjoy Wide Popular Support?

One of the observations that has most baffled and distressed societies that are targets of terrorism is the apparent support, sympathy, and even enthusiasm for terrorist behaviors expressed by substantial proportions of the populations from which terrorists arise. Of course, this varies greatly according to the particular terrorist campaign. There was little evidence of broad popular support for the German Red Army Faction (also known as the Baader-Meinhof Group) or for the Italian Red Brigades in the 1970s. There was virtually no community support for the lone wolf terrorist, Theodore Kaczynski. Yet survey research suggests that many groups that claim to fight for independence, oppression, or freedom from occupation—such as Hamas, Hizbullah, ETA, or the IRA—have enjoyed considerable support from broad segments of their respective societies. Perhaps even more worrisome from the point of view of long-term global security, the Pew Global Attitude Surveys suggest that roughly one quarter of Europe's 15–20 million Muslims support terrorism.

This observation may be explained, in part, by a maxim as simple as the "one man's freedom fighter is another man's terrorist" formulation, yet psychology seeks a more robust and nuanced understanding. When a group of people feel affiliative bonds and common identity, and when that group perceives itself as literally at risk of annihilation, one can well imagine a collective setting aside of restraints on intergroup aggression. When a high proportion of a group has suffered humiliation, perceived injustice, or explicit and unequivocal violence to person or property (as, by one survey, 60% of Palestinians have suffered at the hands of Israeli soldiers), the urge for communal self-defense by any means, for revenge, for demonstrating group efficacy in the face of insurmountable odds, or even for the stress relief of externalizing behaviors as an alternative to despair may help to explain the occurrence of terrorism as well as the acquiescence or support of significant segments of society.

While a great deal of empirical research has measured the fact of support for terrorism, less is known about the "why" of it. Moreover, one suspects that different people in the same circumstances may support terrorism for different reasons. The Basque, Tamil, or Palestinian teen may be more excited by mental images of glorious action, whereas their adult counterparts may be more hopeful and passionate for political change. The "why" may be the key to meaningful changes in policy. If, for example, we knew that the primary driver of community support for terrorism was perceived injustice, it might lead to de-emphasizing notions of a definitive military counterterrorism solution, since cutting the head off the snake cannot suppress a social urge—as the French learned in Algiers. If, on the other hand, research determined that social support was primarily driven by allegiance to a charismatic figure, the security policy implications might be quite different.

In this section we will consider two of modern social psychology's most important contributions to answering the "why" question: social dominance orientation (SDO) and terror management theory (TMT). Each of these theories helps to illuminate why individuals and groups might be provoked by certain circumstances to hate, to fear, or to conceive violent ideas and intentions against another group—potent psychological mechanisms that apply not just to terrorism but to war.

Reading 14—Levin et al. (2003). Social Dominance and Social Identity in Lebanon: Implications for Support of Violence Against the West

Editors' Comments

Social dominance theory is based on the observation that groups of people tend to sort into social hierarchies, with one group hierarchically dominant over another. So, for example, Whites (Euro-Americans) in the USA tend to enjoy a higher status than do Blacks or Latinos. What is more, people in each group exhibit individual differences in the degree to which they accept the hierarchy. Whites who identify strongly with their ingroup—and who favor the existing hierarchy—are said to have *high* social dominance orientation (SDO). In contrast, Blacks in the USA who identify with their own lower status group and reject the status quo are said to have *low* SDO (also known as "counterdominance" orientation). This paper empirically examines SDO among Lebanese civilians. There appear to be strong links between Arab identification and counterdominance orientation. There are also clear links between Arab or Muslim identification and support for anti-Western violence—including the attacks of 9/11. An interesting finding, however, was that the support for terrorism was not necessarily mediated by counterdominance orientation. Blood (historical ethnicity) and religion may be thicker than SDO.

Discussion Questions

1. Social dominance theory posits that people vary in the degree to which they embrace an established hierarchy of power or status. According to this theory, if a person is a member of the subordinate group and if they reject the status quo, are they more likely to identify with their own group or with the group in the dominant position?
2. A higher level of ingroup identification is sometimes associated with hostility and aggression against the outgroup, and sometimes not. What determines the difference?
3. In this study, Arab identification was negatively correlated with SDO, while Lebanese identification was positively correlated with SDO. Why?
4. In this study, some Lebanese college students supported the terrorist organization and thought that the World Trade Center attacks of 9/11 were justified. Which factor seems to have explained such support: Arab/Muslim group identification or counterdominance orientation?

Suggested Readings

Pratto, F., Sidanius, J., Stallworth, L. M., & Malle, B. F. (1994). Social dominance orientation: A personality variable predicting social and political attitudes. *Journal of Personality and Social Psychology*, *667*, 741–763.

Sidanius, J., & Pratto, F. (1999). *Social dominance*. Cambridge, UK: Cambridge University Press.

Van Hieel, A., & Mervielde, I. (2002). Explaining conservative beliefs and political preferences: A comparison of social dominance orientation and authoritarianism. *Journal of Applied Social Psychology*, *32*, 965–976.

Reading 15—Sidanius et al. (2004). Arab Attributions for the Attack on America

Editors' Comments

This paper compares the explanatory power of two alternative explanations for hostility of Arab young people toward the USA: a "clash of civilizations" versus the social dominance perspective. Since Huntington published his very influential and rather provocative 1996 book, *The clash of civilizations and the remaking of world order*, a debate has raged regarding the premise that a massive conflict is on the way, pitting Muslims against non-Muslims across the globe. This paper reports a research project that investigates the validity of the Huntington premise. Rather than a supposed anti-non-Muslim mindset, Sidanius and colleagues find that the anti-Western orientation of Arab youth is associated with rejection of a domineering group over a struggling subordinate group. This discovery, if replicated, is extremely helpful for making sense out of the challenge faced by both sides. Religion *qua* religion may be much overestimated as the wellspring of the conflict and of anti-Western terrorism. Instead, Arab and Persian rage and sympathy for attacks on US civilians may be based more on the straightforward and understandable distress and ambitions expected of *any* subordinate group.

Discussion Questions

1. Sidanius et al. begin with the poignant question, "Why do they hate us so?" What answers to that question seem to fall out of this research project?
2. This article examines the interpretative framework popularized by Samuel P. Huntington in his 1996 book, *The clash of civilizations and the remaking of world order.* According to this framework, one might see support for anti-Western terrorism as part of a grand conflict between the Muslim and non-Muslim worlds. Does this research support that view?
3. Which factors seem to drive Lebanese students' support for anti-Western terrorism more strongly: American support for Israel or the conflict between Islamic and Western values?
4. Based on the results of this research, what foreign policy changes would you predict might reduce Arab support for terrorism against the USA?

Suggested Readings

Echebarria-Echabe, A., & Emilia Fernández-Guede, E. (2006). Effects of terrorism on attitudes and ideological orientation. *European Journal of Social Psychology*, *36*, 259–265.

Henry, P. J., Sidanius, J., Levin, S., & Pratto, F. (2005). Social dominance orientation, authoritarianism, and support for intergroup violence between the Middle East and America. *Political Psychology*, *26*, 569–583.

Huntington, S. P. (1996). *The clash of civilizations and the remaking of world order.* New York: Simon and Schuster.

Hussein, A. D. (2001). On the end of history and the clash of civilization: A dissenter's view. *Journal of Muslim Minority Affairs*, *21*, 25–38.

Reading 16—Pyszczynski et al. (2006). Mortality Salience, Martyrdom, and Military Might: The Great Satan versus the Axis of Evil

Editors' Comments

This paper introduces the powerful role of *mortality salience* in political attitudes. We will all die eventually, but culturally bound worldviews such as the orderly nature of society and the universe help to defend us against the terror of that fact. Psychologists have observed for two decades that when people are reminded of the terrifying fact that they will die someday—when our mortality becomes *salient* in our conscious minds—it is not only upsetting but also shifts one's attitudes about one's group. Mortality salience seems to elevate the us-versus-them feelings and cognitions that drive intergroup conflict. Pyszczynski et al. apply this theory in fascinating parallel studies of Iranian and American college students. When Iranians are reminded of death, they support martyrdom operations against the West. When Westerners are reminded of death, they support extreme, preemptive, and indiscriminate military campaigns against countries they perceive as threatening. The lesson of this superb paper is human universality, and the results may help to explain the view, held for several years by a plurality of US voters and their elected representatives, that war was the best answer to Iraq's equivocal threat.

Discussion Questions

1. Terror management theory observes that we usually set aside thoughts of death, but that reminders that we are bound to die have a powerful influence on our attitudes and behaviors. In the course of the "war on terrorism" since 9/11, what have been some of the main death reminders for Western citizens and for Middle Eastern Muslims?
2. When people are confronted with frequent reminders of death, who are they more likely to vote for: a candidate who provides a grand vision of ingroup superiority or a candidate who emphasizes that we all share a common humanity? Why?
3. For a young Muslim in Iran, to what degree do reminders of death affect his or her willingness to join pro-martyrdom causes?
4. According to this research, when young US citizens are provoked by death reminders (mortality salience), some express more support for extreme military actions against groups perceived to be threatening, including preemptive attacks and the use of chemical weapons. Did mortality salience have equally strong affects among conservative and liberal students?

Suggested Readings

Dunkel, C. S. (2002). Terror management theory and identity: The effect of the 9/11 terrorist attacks on anxiety and identity change. *Identity*, 2, 287–301.

Greenberg, J., Pysczcynski, T., & Solomon, S. (1986). The causes and consequences of a need for self-esteem: A terror management theory. In R. F. Baumeister (Ed.), *Public self and private self* (pp. 189–192). New York: Springer-Verlag.

Jost, J. T., Glaser, J., Kruglanski, A. W., & Sulloway, F. J. (2003). Political conservatism as motivated social cognition. *Psychological Bulletin*, *129*, 339–375.

Pyszczynski, T., Solomon, S., & Greenberg, J. (2002). *In the wake of 9/11: The psychology of terror*. Washington, DC: American Psychological Association.

Social Dominance and Social Identity in Lebanon: Implications for Support of Violence Against the West

Shana Levin, P. J. Henry, Felicia Pratto, and Jim Sidanius

We examined various group identifications among Lebanese Muslims and Christians after the events of September 11 2001 and how these identifications related to social dominance orientation (SDO) and support for violence against the West. We expected stronger identification with less powerful groups to be associated with lower SDO (i.e. greater desires for group equality), and stronger support for terrorist organizations and violent acts against powerful nations. Consistent with these expectations, we found that SDO related negatively to identification with Arabs, and this group identification related positively to support for terrorist organizations and feelings that the September 11 attack was justified. Furthermore, we found that the direct negative effect of SDO on support for terrorism was mediated by Arab identification. Efforts to reduce conflict are discussed in terms of recognizing the anti-dominance elements of Arab identification in Lebanon, and the powerful implications that this subordinate group identification has for continued support of terrorist organizations and violence against the West.

Shana Levin, Claremont McKenna College; P. J. Henry, Yale University; Felicia Pratto, University of Connecticut; and Jim Sidanius, University of California, Los Angeles.

Author's note. Address correspondence to: Shana Levin, Department of Psychology, Claremont McKenna College, 850 Columbia Avenue, Claremont, CA 91711, USA [email: shana_levin@mckenna.edu].

This research was supported by a grant from the American University of Beirut Office of Grants and Contracts. Special thanks are due to Diala Nammour for her help in data collection, and to the American University of Beirut post office for their help in distribution of the questionnaires.

The attacks of September 11 2001 very likely made national, religious, and ethnic identities salient, not just for Americans, but for people in all regions implicated in the ensuing conflict (Pyszczynski, Solomon, & Greenberg, 2003). In situations of uncertainty and threat, people are motivated to repair the psychological difficulties such situations bring by identifying with people they define as having a common group membership, such as their co-nationals, or those who share their religion or cultural worldview (e.g. Hogg & Abrams, 1990). A major social danger of this solution is that when intergroup competition and threat are heightened, identifying with an ingroup often leads people to demean and discriminate against outgroups (e.g. Brewer, 2001). As violent conflicts are erupting and threatening to erupt in many regions of the world, it is important to understand the psychological factors related to identification with various social groups, and how these social identifications are related to support for violence directed at particular groups.

Although a great deal of empirical research has examined the role of social identity in driving intergroup conflict, considerably less attention has been devoted to the factors that influence the strength of ingroup identification (Huddy, 2001). Social dominance theory offers one possibility. Broadly speaking, social dominance theory assumes that conflicts develop among groups of people as a result of basic human tendencies to form systems of group-based dominance, in which certain groups are at the top of the social hierarchy and other groups are at the bottom (Sidanius & Pratto, 1999). Although systems of group-based dominance are created and maintained by interacting forces at several levels of analysis (see Sidanius & Pratto, 1999), one contributor to this phenomenon at the level of individual differences is people's desires for group-based dominance, or social dominance orientation (SDO). According to social dominance theory, ingroup identification contributes to intergroup strife but is itself associated with one's level of SDO. Specifically, higher SDO should be associated with stronger ingroup identification among members of high-status groups and weaker ingroup identification among members of low-status groups. According to social dominance theory, members of high-status groups with greater desires for group inequality should have higher levels of ingroup identification because connections with the dominant ingroup facilitate access to social and economic resources that can be used to reinforce group-based status differences (Sidanius & Pratto, 1999). For members of low-status groups, on the other hand, ingroup identification implies a counter-dominance orientation, or a rejection of the social system in which one's group is relegated to a subordinate position. As predicted, previous research has shown that in both the USA and Israel, members of higher status ethnic groups (i.e. White Americans and Israeli Jews, respectively) identify more strongly with their groups to the extent they are high in SDO, whereas members of lower status ethnic groups (i.e. Latino Americans and Israeli Arabs, respectively) identify more strongly with their groups to the extent they are low in SDO (Levin & Sidanius, 1999; Pratto, 1999; Sidanius, Pratto, & Rabinowitz, 1994).

However, because this research is correlational in nature, it does not allow us to determine whether higher SDO leads to greater ingroup identification among members of high-status groups, or whether greater ingroup identification leads to higher SDO among these group members. The same is true for the causal direction of the negative relationship between SDO and ingroup identification among members of low-status groups: higher SDO may lead to weaker ingroup identification, or weaker ingroup identification may lead to higher SDO among these group members. Social identity theory is most likely to expect SDO to be a function of social identity (see e.g. Schmitt, Branscombe, & Kappen, in press). According to social identity theory, one way members of low-status groups may react to the negative social identity conferred by their low status is by adopting a social change belief structure (Tajfel & Turner, 1986). Because a negative social identity is more threatening to those who identify strongly with their low-status ingroup, these group members may be especially likely to adopt such an identity-protecting belief structure. One manifestation of such a belief structure may be stronger desires for group equality and beliefs that 'inferior' groups should *not* stay in their place.

While most of the empirical research inspired by social dominance theory thus far has modeled the strength of one's social identity as a function of one's level of SDO (e.g. Levin & Sidanius, 1999; Pratto, 1999; Sidanius et al., 1994), it is also consistent with social dominance theory to suspect that social identity has prior causal status. That is, people adopt levels of SDO that are perceived to be in the interests of the social groups with which they are identified. Because a positive social identity is more self-enhancing for those who identify strongly with their high-status ingroup, these group members may be especially likely to display greater desires for group inequality and beliefs that 'superior' groups should dominate 'inferior' groups. This is the primary reason why social dominance theorists have argued that members of high-status groups should have higher SDO scores than members of low-status groups, everything else being equal (see Sidanius & Pratto, 1999, p. 40). At the same time, those people who are predisposed to favor hierarchical and dominant/ subordinate relationships among social groups are also more likely to identify with strong and dominant groups and to disidentify with weak and subordinate groups. Thus, social dominance theorists would argue that the true causal relationship between SDO and social identity is probably reciprocal and bidirectional (see Sidanius & Pratto, in press).

In the current study, we explore the role of both group identification and SDO in mediating the effect of the other on support for intergroup violence. We focus particularly on subordinate group members' support for violence against the dominant group in a conflict. First we explore the role of subordinate group identification in mediating the effect of SDO on support for intergroup violence. Among subordinate group members, low SDO may lead to greater ingroup identification and stronger support for intergroup violence. People with low SDO are expected to show stronger support for violence against dominant groups because such violence serves to attenuate the

hierarchical social arrangements that they oppose (see Henry, Sidanius, Levin, & Pratto, 2003). Furthermore, low SDO may be associated with stronger support for intergroup violence precisely because it leads to greater identification with the subordinate ingroup. That is, opposition to the domination of 'inferior' groups by 'superior' groups may mobilize identification with the subordinate group in a conflict, which may then become a key factor in driving support for violence against the dominant group. We also explore the role of SDO in mediating the effect of subordinate group identification on support for intergroup violence. Among subordinate group members, high ingroup identification may lead to lower SDO and more support for intergroup violence. Furthermore, strong identification with the subordinate ingroup may be associated with greater support for intergroup violence precisely because it leads to lower SDO. That is, identification with the subordinate ingroup may stimulate opposition to hierarchical social arrangements, which may then become a critical factor in driving support for violence against the dominant outgroup. The intergroup context we examine is the conflict between Arabs and Americans after the events of September 11, 2001. Arabs have less power than Americans do in this conflict, not only by objective standards (see, e.g. United Nations Development Program, 2003), but also according to subjective Lebanese perceptions of power differences (Alexander, Levin, & Henry, in press). We examine social identification among Lebanese university students, who have several salient social identities they could draw upon—social identities that, if they were to become politically mobilized, could draw them deeper into the 'war on terrorism'.

Intergroup Relations in Lebanon

The intergroup landscape in Lebanon makes it an ideal place to study the dynamics of social identification and their possible relation to support for intergroup violence. Lebanon is an Arab country, but is atypical of Arab countries in having a sizable Christian population (roughly 23%), and in that Christians enjoy more power and social status than the Muslim majority, including, according to constitutional decree, the presidency. Although Lebanon does not command as much American attention as other Arab states, Lebanon might be considered one of the Arab nations most embroiled in the Palestinian/Israeli conflict. Lebanon is currently home to approximately 350,000 Palestinians. Israel invaded Lebanon in 1982 and the radical anti-West, anti-Israel organization Hizbullah was formed there in 1983. Given the majority Arab population in Lebanon, one group identity that could potentially be mobilized for political ends in the current 'war on terrorism' is Arab identification.

In the current study, we examine whether higher levels of Arab identification are associated with greater support for anti-US violence among this Lebanese population. Although empirical research has demonstrated that ingroup identification is often coupled with ingroup favoritism (Brewer, 1979), ingroup identification does not always lead to outgroup derogation and aggression (e.g. Hinkle & Brown, 1990; Levin & Sidanius, 1999; Struch & Schwartz, 1989). Rather, ingroup identification seems to lead to outgroup hostility mainly when groups are competing for social regard or material resources (Brewer, 2001; Hinkle & Brown, 1990). Given Lebanon's proximity to the sites of Palestinian–Israeli violence and involvement in the current 'war on terrorism', we expect that our participants will perceive the material and symbolic interests of Arabs to be in conflict with those of the West. We therefore expect Arab identification to relate positively to support for anti-West violence. Previous research has found that Lebanese who are lower in SDO also tend to support greater violence against the West (Henry et al., 2003). If identification with Arabs (i.e. the subordinate group in the conflict) is driven at least in part by an anti-dominance orientation, then the effect of SDO on support for terrorism against the West may be mediated by Arab identification.

On the other hand, it is also possible that Arab identification has a positive effect on anti-West violence because identification with such a subordinate group reduces one's level of SDO, which then increases support for anti-West violence.

Consistent with this direction of causality, desires for social change may be adopted in order to enhance the negative social identity conferred by identification with a subordinate group. If this is the case, then one should expect that a desire for social change, or a low SDO, is driven at least in part by identification with Arabs, and that the effect of Arab identification on support for terrorism may be mediated by SDO.

We also examine whether national identification with the Lebanese relates to SDO on the one hand and support for anti-West violence on the other. In other work using the Lebanese sample, we examined whether religious identities were related to several political beliefs and attitudes concerning the events of September 11. We found that Lebanese Muslims were more opposed to US activities in the 'war on terrorism', showed more support for organizations that the US State Department has classified as terrorist organizations (i.e. Popular Front for the Liberation of Palestine, Hamas, Islamic Jihad, and Hizbullah), and were less opposed to the September 11 attack on the World Trade Center compared with Lebanese Christians (Henry, Sidanius, Levin, & Pratto, 2002). Our analyses also revealed that opposition to US 'counterterrorism' activities and support for terrorist organizations increased with increasing religious identification among Lebanese Muslims and decreased with increasing religious identification among Lebanese Christians. Another study showed that Lebanese Christians and Muslims differed in their attributions for the attack on the World Trade Center and in their level of opposition to the attack: Muslims felt more that the attack was an act of anti-dominance (i.e. that the attack was caused by American support of Israel, anger at American imperialism and arrogance, the Israeli–Palestinian conflict, American mistreatment of Iraq, and the presence of American soldiers in Saudi Arabia), whereas Christians attributed the attack more to a 'clash of civilizations' (i.e. the conflict between Christianity and Islam, the clash between Islamic and Western values, and dislike of democracy; Sidanius, Henry, Pratto, & Levin, in press). These findings indicate the importance of religious-group membership and religious identification in driving attitudes and attributions relevant to contemporary geo-political conflicts. The present work goes beyond religious identification to examine how broader social identifications—including Arab and Leba-nese identification—relate to social dominance orientation and support for anti-West violence.

Method

Procedure

A questionnaire assessing reactions to the September 11 attacks on the Pentagon and the World Trade Center and attitudes toward various organizations classified as terrorist by the US State Department was distributed to a random sample of 596 out of 5808 possible graduate and undergraduate student mailboxes at the American University of Beirut in the late fall of 2001. The name 'American University of Beirut' is somewhat deceiving, and might lead one to assume that any sample drawn from it is not truly Arab but instead is composed of Americans or American sympa-thizers. This is a reasonable assumption to make: courses at the American University of Beirut are taught in English and the university is administered out of New York City. Nevertheless, there are a number of reasons to believe that, in fact, this sample from the American University of Beirut is truly not 'American'. First, most of the students at the University have citizenship in at least one Arab or Muslim country, and as an additional precaution, we selected for our sample only those participants who had Lebanese citizenship. Second, the university serves as an important rallying center for the Palestinian cause and the broader Arab/Muslim cause as well, and may be as highly politicized today as American campuses were during the 1960s (Faour, 1998). Third, com-parative data between an American student sample and our sample from the American University of Beirut have shown significant and powerful differences in support for American anti-Arab policy (Henry et al., 2003), suggesting that this sample is not particularly sympathetic with Ameri-can policy. These reasons made us confident that our sample represented, as Edward Said once said of the students at the American University of Beirut, 'the vanguard for the new citizens of the Middle East' (Said, 2000).

The cover letter to the questionnaire indicated that the study was part of an international assess-ment of student reactions to the events of September 11, and that participation was voluntary and anonymous. The questionnaire was written in English, which is the language used in teaching classes at the American University of Beirut (students are required to pass basic English fluency tests as part of admission to the university). A total of 145 questionnaires were completed, yielding a response rate of 24%. Response rates for mail-in questionnaires typically range from 10% to 50% (Weisberg, Krosnick, & Bowen, 1996).

Participants

Lebanese, Arab, and religious group member-ship were assessed by asking participants to identify, through checklists, the groups of which they consider themselves to be members. Only Lebanese citizens who were either Muslim (Sunni or Shiite) or Christian (Maronite, Catholic, or Orthodox) were selected for analysis in the current study. Of the 108 Lebanese respondents, 51 classi-fied themselves as Muslim and 57 classified themselves as Christian. At the national level the religious breakdown is roughly 70% Muslim and 23% Christian, but the ratio is much more balanced at the American University of Beirut (United Nations Development Program, 1998). Our sample reflects the more balanced religious demographic trend of the university. Of the Muslim respondents, 88% classified themselves as Arab, and of the Christian respondents, 25% clas-sified themselves as Arab. There were 54 males and 54 females in the study, with a range in age from 18 to 34 years ($M = 20.56$, $SD = 2.56$).

Measures

We measured various social identifications, SDO, support for organizations classified as terrorist, and support for the World Trade Center attack on September 11, 2001.

Social identifications

Arab and Lebanese identification were assessed with two-item scales: 'How strongly do you identify with Arabs/the Lebanese?' (1 = not at all, 7 = very strongly) and 'How close do you feel to Arabs/ the Lebanese?' (1 = not at all, 7 = very close). Both scales exhibited high reliability (Arab identification: $a = .87$; Lebanese identification: $a = .88$).

SDO

SDO was measured with the full 16-item SDO$_6$ scale (Pratto, Sidanius, Stallworth, & Malle, 1994). Participants were asked to rate the degree to which they agreed or disagreed with the following 16 statements on a scale of '1–strongly disagree' to '7–strongly agree': (1) Some groups of people are just more worthy than others. (2) In getting what your group wants, it is sometimes necessary to use force against other groups. (3) Superior groups should dominate inferior groups. (4) To get ahead in life, it is sometimes necessary to step on other groups. (5) If certain groups of people stayed in their place, we would have fewer problems. (6) It's probably a good thing that certain groups are at the top and other groups are at the bottom. (7) Inferior groups should stay in their place. (8) Sometimes other groups must be kept in their place. (9) It would be good if all groups could be equal (reverse-coded). (10) Group equality should be our ideal (reverse-coded). (11) All groups should be given an equal chance in life (reverse-coded). (12) We should do what we can to equalize conditions for different groups (reverse-coded). (13) Increased social equality (reverse-coded). (14) We would have fewer problems if we treated different groups more equally (reverse-coded). (15) We should strive to make incomes more equal (reverse-coded). (16) No one group should dominate in society (reverse-coded). The scale was highly reliable ($a = .89$). As shown in these statements, the SDO items themselves do not refer to any particular groups, but rather to groups in general. This ambiguity allows different meanings to be assigned to the groups mentioned in the SDO scale by making different intergroup contexts (e.g. Arab–West) salient before the scale is completed. As emphasized by Levin (in press), it is important to measure SDO after a series of questions that highlight the intergroup context of particular relevance to the research question examined in a study. In the current study, we measured SDO at the very end of the questionnaire, after participants had been asked a series of questions about their reactions to the events of September 11, 2001. Because we were interested in examining the relationships among SDO, Arab and Lebanese identification, and support for terrorism, these questions about the events of September 11, 2001 highlight the intergroup context of particular relevance to our research questions.

Support for terrorist organizations

This scale was computed as the average degree of support for the following four organizations categorized as terrorist by the US State Department as of February, 2002: Popular Front for the Liberation of Palestine (PFLP), Hamas (Islamic Resistance Movement), Islamic Jihad, and Hizbullah (Party of God). Ratings ranged from '1–Strongly oppose' to '7–Strongly support' ($a = .93$).

Support for the World Trade Center attack

This variable was assessed by asking respondents, 'How much, if at all, do you feel that the attack on the World Trade Center in New York City was justified?' (1 = not at all justified, 7 = very much justified).

Results

Preliminary Analyses

To first understand which group identities were most important to participants, and whether

Christians and Muslims differed in their identification with different groups, we compared Christians and Muslims on degree of identification with Arabs and Lebanese. Paired samples t tests revealed significant differences in mean levels of Arab and Lebanese identification among both Christians ($t(56) = -12.42$, $p < .001$), and Muslims ($t(50) = -2.06$, $p = .04$). Among Christians, Lebanese identification ($M = 6.02$, $SD = 1.12$) was the highest and Arab identification ($M = 3.23$, $SD = 1.60$) was considerably lower. Among Muslims, Lebanese identification was also the highest ($M = 5.88$, $SD = 1.39$), but Arab identification was quite high as well ($M = 5.40$, $SD = 1.41$). Independent samples t tests also indicated that compared to Christians, Muslims had higher levels of Arab identification ($t(106) = 7.47$, $p < .001$), but there was no difference between the two religious groups in how much they identified as Lebanese ($t(106) = -.56$, $p = .58$). These findings reveal that both Christians and Muslims identify strongly as Lebanese, but Muslims feel closer to Arabs than Christians do.

Associations Among SDO and Social Identifications

The correlations among SDO and the social identification variables are shown in Table 14.1. As expected, SDO was significantly negatively correlated with Arab identification ($r = -.28$, $p = .01$), but not with Lebanese identification ($r = -.05$, $p = .65$). In order to examine the unique effects of SDO on Arab and Lebanese identification, over and above the effects of Arab and religious group memberships, we conducted a series of multiple regression analyses. Separate analyses were run for Arab and Lebanese identification as the dependent variables. In these analyses, the terms for Arab (dummy-coded with Arabs = 1 and non-Arabs = 0) and religious group membership (dummy-coded with Muslims = 1 and Christians = 0) were entered simultaneously with SDO. As can be seen in Table 14.1, results indicated that, not surprisingly, Arabs were higher in Arab identification than non-Arabs ($\beta = .52$, $p < .001$), and Muslims were higher in Arab identifica-

tion than Christians ($\beta = .22$, $p = .02$). More interesting for our purposes here, findings showed that, above and beyond the effects of these group memberships, SDO had a significant negative effect on Arab identification ($\beta = -.16$, $p = .03$). These results suggest that Arab identification implies a *counter*-dominance orientation. Unlike the case for Arab identification, however, the analysis for Lebanese identification indicated that SDO did not have a significant unique effect ($\beta = -.06$, $p = .59$). Given these results, it is not surprising that when the effects of both Arab and Lebanese identification on SDO were examined after the effects of Arab and religious group membership were taken into account, this analysis indicated a significant effect for Arab identification ($\beta = -.32$, $p = .03$), but not for Lebanese identification ($\beta = .02$, $p = .88$; overall model: $F(4, 95) = 2.09$, $p = .09$; $R^2_{adj} = .04$).

Associations Among Social Identifications and Support for Terrorism

Correlations

The correlations among the social identification variables and the support for terrorism variables can be found in Table 14.2. These analyses revealed strong and consistent positive relationships between Arab identification on the one hand and support for terrorist groups and activities on the other hand. The positive correlation between Arab identification and support for the World Trade Center attack was statistically significant and moderate in magnitude ($r = .31$, $p = .001$). What really stands out in these analyses is the very large, positive correlation between Arab identification and support for terrorist organizations ($r = .74$, $p < .001$), indicating that Arab identification alone is able to explain 55% of the variance in support for PFLP, Hamas, Islamic Jihad, and Hizbullah. These organizations are evidently successful in mobilizing Arab identification.

TABLE 14.1. Social Identification Variables Regressed on Group Memberships and SDO

	Outcome variable			
	Arab identification		Lebanese identification	
Predictor variable	r	β	r	β
Group membership				
Muslim	.59***	.22*	−.05	−.04
Arab	.68***	.52***	−.05	−.03
Group orientation				
SDO	−.28**	−.16*	−.05	−.06
R^2_{adj}		.51***		−.03

$* p < .05; ** p < .01; *** p < .001.$

Notes: Table entries are Pearson correlation coefficients and standardized multiple regression coefficients. 'Muslim group membership' is dummy-coded such that Muslim = 1, Christian = 0; 'Arab group membership' is dummy-coded such that Arab = 1, non-Arab = 0. SDO and the identification variables are coded such that higher numbers indicate greater levels of the construct.

Regressions of support for terrorist organizations

In Table 14.2, we also see the results of regression analyses examining the effects of the group memberships, social identifications, and SDO on support for terrorism. Results of the analyses for support for terrorist organizations can be found on the left side of Table 14.2. These analyses revealed several noteworthy results. First, when entered at the first step in a hierarchical regression analysis, both Muslim group membership ($\beta = .42, p < .001$) and Arab group membership ($\beta = .28, p = .01$) contributed to support for terrorist organizations (overall regression equation: $F(2, 94) = 30.83, p < .001; R^2_{adj} = .38$). Second, quite impressively, adding the identification variables to the regression equation significantly increased the percentage of explained variance in support for terrorist organizations from 38% to 57% (overall regression equation: $F(4, 92) = 32.46, p < .001; R^2_{adj} = .57; F_{change} (2, 92) = 20.98, p < .001$). This means that by themselves, these psychological variables (mainly Arab identification) were able to explain a substantively and statistically significant amount of variance in a variable that has caught the world's attention since September 11: support for terrorist organizations that have claimed responsibility for devastating missile attacks and suicide bombings among civilian populations. Third, once the identification and group membership variables were

entered together at Step 2, Arab identification ($\beta = .63, p < .001$) had an even stronger effect than Arab group membership per se ($\beta = −.06, p = .59$). Findings that the significant direct effect of Arab group membership on support for terrorist organizations became nonsignificant when the effects of the identification variables were taken into account suggest that group identification fully mediates the effect of Arab group membership on support for terrorist organizations. Figure 14.1 shows the fully mediated effect of Arab group membership on support for terrorist organizations through Arab identification alone. Fourth, adding SDO to the regression equation already containing the group membership and identification variables neither increased the percentage of explained variance in support for terrorist organizations, nor reduced the effects of the identification variables (overall regression equation: $F(5, 91) = 26.57, p < .001; R^2_{adj} = .57; F_{change}(1, 91) = 1.83, p = .18$). This final analysis indicates that the effects of the identification variables on support for terrorist organizations were not mediated by SDO. If SDO had served as a mediator, we would have seen a decline in the direct effect of group identification on support for terrorist organizations when SDO was added to the equation, as well as a significant effect of SDO when the effects of group identification were taken into account.[1]

We also explored the possibility that Arab

TABLE 14.2. Terrorism Variables Regressed on Group Memberships, Social Identification Variables and SDO

Predictor variable	Outcome variable							
	Support for terrorist organizations				Support for the World Trade Center attack			
	r	β (Step 1)	β (Step 2)	β (Step 3)	r	β (Step 1)	β (Step 2)	β (Step 3)
Group membership								
Muslim	.60***	.42***	.26**	.26**	.22*	.17	.07	.06
Arab	.55***	.28**	−.06	−.05	.18+	.04	−.19	−.18
Group orientation								
Arab ID	.74***		.63***	.59***	.31***		.42**	.38*
Lebanese ID	.08		−.02	−.02	−.09		−.18+	−.19+
SDO	−.31**			−.10	−.22*			−.15
R^2_{adj}		.38***	.57***	.57***		.02	.09**	.11**

+ p < .10; * p < .05; ** p < .01; *** p < .001.
Notes: Table entries are Pearson correlation coefficients and standardized multiple regression coefficients. 'Muslim' is dummy-coded such that Muslim = 1, Christian = 0; 'Arab' is dummy-coded such that Arab = 1, non-Arab = 0. SDO, the identification (ID) variables, and the terrorism variables are coded such that higher numbers indicate greater levels of the construct.

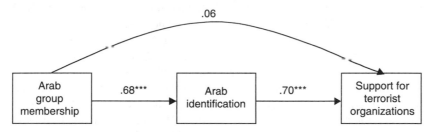

FIGURE 14.1 ■ Role of Arab identification in mediating the effect of Arab group membership on support for terrorist organizations. *Note*: Path entries are standardized regression coefficients. The direct effect of Arab group membership on support for terrorist organizations was r = .55, p < .001. *** p < .001.

identification mediated the effect of SDO on support for terrorist organizations. Specifically, we ran three separate analyses to determine whether the conditions for mediation outlined by Baron and Kenny (1986) were met: (1) SDO (the independent variable) must be directly related to Arab identification (the mediator) and support for terrorist organizations (the dependent variable), (2) Arab identification must be related to support for terrorist organizations, and (3) the direct effect of SDO on support for terrorist organizations must decline in magnitude once the effect of Arab identification is taken into account. Correlation analyses indicated that SDO had a direct effect on both Arab identification (r = −.28, p = .01) and support for terrorist organizations (r = −.31, p = .002). An additional regression analysis indicated that the

effect of SDO on support for terrorist organizations was nonsignificant when the effect of Arab identification was taken into account (β = −.10, p = .18), but the effect of Arab identification on support for terrorist organizations remained strong when the effect of SDO was taken into account (β = .71, p < .001). Figure 14.2 shows the mediated effect of SDO on support for terrorist organizations through Arab identification. These findings therefore indicate that desires for group *equality* are manifested in greater identification with Arabs, and it is this greater group identification that relates to stronger support for terrorist organizations. Desires for group equality are not associated with stronger support for terrorist organizations once the mediating effect of Arab identification is taken into account.

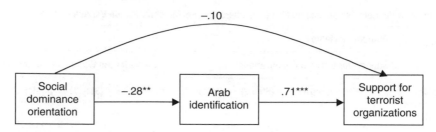

FIGURE 14.2 ■ Role of Arab identification in mediating the effect of SDO on support for terrorist organizations. *Note*: Path entries are standardized regression coefficients. The direct effect of SDO on support for terrorist organizations was $r = -.31, p = .002.$ **$p < .01$; ***$p < .001$.

Regressions of support for the World Trade Center attack

In Table 14.2, we also see the effects of the group memberships, social identifications, and SDO on feelings that the World Trade Center attack was justified. Overall, results indicated that, when entered at the first step in the hierarchical regression analysis, none of the effects of the group memberships were statistically significant, and together they accounted for far less variance in support for the World Trade Center attack than they did in support for terrorist organizations (overall regression equation: $F(2, 95) = 2.00, p = .14; R^2_{adj} = .02$). This may be because overall this sample strongly opposed the attack. However, when added at the second step in the regression equation, the identification variables together substantially increased the amount of explained variance in support for the attack (overall regression equation: $F(4, 93) = 3.51, p = .01; R^2_{adj} = .09; F_{change}(2, 93) = 4.85, p = .01$). Particularly noteworthy in this analysis is the effect of Arab identification, which was stronger than any other variable ($\beta = .42, p = .004$). Arab identification clearly plays an important role in driving support for the attack. Interestingly, the effect of Lebanese identification was negative, although only marginally significant ($\beta = -.18, p = .08$). Lastly, as was the case for support for terrorist organizations, adding SDO at the next step in the regression equation neither increased the percentage of explained variance in support for the World Trade Center attack nor reduced the effects of the identi-

fication variables (overall regression equation: $F(5, 92) = 3.26, p = .01; R^2_{adj} = .11; F_{change}(1, 92) = 2.12, p = .15$). Again, this analysis indicates that the effects of the identification variables on support for terrorism were not mediated by SDO.[2]

We ran additional analyses in order to determine whether Arab identification mediated the effect of SDO on support for the World Trade Center attack as it did for support for terrorist organizations. Correlation analyses indicated that SDO had a direct effect on both Arab identification ($r = -.28, p = .01$) and support for the World Trade Center attack ($r = -.22, p = .03$). An additional regression analysis indicated that the effect of SDO on support for the attack was no longer significant when the effect of Arab identification was taken into account ($\beta = -.15, p = .13$), although in absolute terms there was only a modest decline in the magnitude of the effect. The effect of Arab identification on support for the attack, however, remained significant when the effect of SDO was taken into account ($\beta = .26, p = .01$). Figure 14.3 shows the mediated effect of SDO on support for the World Trade Center attack through Arab identification. Again, these findings indicate that desires for group *equality* are manifested in greater identification with Arabs, and it is this greater group identification that relates to stronger support for the World Trade Center attack. Desires for group equality are not significantly associated with stronger support for terrorism once the mediating effect of Arab identification is taken into account.

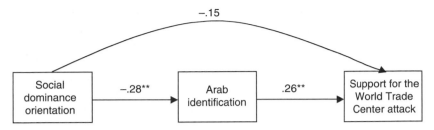

FIGURE 14.3 ■ Role of Arab identification in mediating the effect of SDO on support for the World Trade Center attack. *Note*: Path entries are standardized regression coefficients. The direct effect of SDO on support for the World Trade Center attack was $r = -.22$, $p = .03$. **$p < .01$.

The case of Lebanese identification

The correlations between Lebanese identification and the support for terrorism variables can be found in Table 14.2. Unlike the case for Arab identification, Lebanese identification was not related to support for terrorist organizations ($r = .08$, $p = .45$) or support for the World Trade Center attack ($r = -.09$, $p = .34$), although Lebanese identification was moderately correlated with Arab identification ($r = .19$, $p = .05$). Hierarchical regression analyses also indicated that none of the effects of Lebanese identification were statistically significant. Of the kinds of group identification studied, then, Lebanese identification appears to be the most politically neutral.

Discussion

In the aftermath of the September 11 attacks on the United States, international public opinion polls indicated widespread anger at the US among Muslim populations ('Poll Says Muslims Angry at US', 2002). Lebanon is a particularly interesting place to study support for violence against the US because the Lebanese Christians, although fewer in number in Lebanon compared to Muslims, are higher in status (see Seaver, 2000) and more pro-Western in their orientation (Henry et al., 2002). Although Muslim group membership certainly plays a large role in explaining support for violence against the US, there is considerable variability within the religious groups that contributes to these attitudes as well. The current study examined

differences in two types of social identifications in Lebanon: identification with Arabs and the Lebanese.

Our first step was to identify the factors that are associated with social identification. Social dominance theory suggests one possibility: desires to express one's values concerning group-based dominance. According to the theory, people high in SDO will identify more strongly with dominant groups as a way of positioning themselves within group-based dominance systems that they endorse. People who desire group equality, on the other hand, will identify more strongly with subordinate groups, with whom they have empathy. Because Arabs are a subordinate group in the conflict with the Western superpower, we expected that greater desires for group-based dominance would be associated with lower levels of identification with this less powerful group. An implication of our analysis is that Arab identification can be mobilized for political ends because it implies a *counter-dominance* orientation.

Rather than viewing group conflict as stemming from attempts to assert identity per se, social dominance theory views group conflict as stemming from attempts to support or resist group-based domination. In his analysis of the wars in the former Yugoslavia, political anthropologist Thomas Eriksen describes a similar view of group conflict in the Balkans: 'The conflicts involving Serbs, Croats, Bosnian Muslims, Slovenes, and Albanians were never conflicts over the right to assert one's ethnic or cultural identity, but were based on competing claims to rights such as employment, welfare, and political influence' (2001, p. 49). In other words, the conflicts over these resources were framed in ethnic terms but were more fundamentally about competition over material and symbolic resources.

The present results indicated strong support for this interpretation in the current Middle East conflict. Lower levels of social dominance orientation were associated with higher levels of Arab identification, even when the effects of important group memberships (i.e. Muslim and Arab) were taken into account. As expected, the more *egalitarian* participants were in their general orientations toward social groups, the more strongly they identified with the subordinate group in the conflict with the West: Arabs. However, it is important to note that because the data are correlational, we cannot isolate the direction of causality. While the logic of social dominance theory argues for a reciprocal and bidirectional relationship between social identity and SDO, it must be left to future research, using qualitatively different methodologies, to uncover the strength and precise circumstances under which this reciprocal causal structure actually holds.

One additional caveat that must be kept in mind is that because SDO was measured after a series of questions about the events of September 11, the SDO–identification link we have found may depend on whether this intergroup context is in mind when the SDO questions are answered. The salience of the intergroup context, however, cannot account for findings that Arab identification is more likely to mediate the effect of SDO on support for terrorism than SDO is to mediate the effect of Arab identification. Specifically, these mediational analyses indicated that not only are desires for group equality manifested in greater identification with Arabs, this anti-dominance sentiment is also indirectly related to support for terrorist organizations through its effect on Arab identification. That is, it is precisely because this anti-dominance orientation leads to higher Arab identification that it has its effect on increasing support for terrorist organizations: although SDO was directly related to support for terrorist organizations (see Henry et al., 2003), the negative effect

of SDO was no longer significant when we controlled for the powerful effects of social identification. On the other hand, the direct effect of Arab identification on support for terrorist organizations remained strong even when we controlled for SDO. These results suggest that anti-dominance motives drive support for terrorist organizations in the Arab world only to the extent that they elevate identification with the subordinate group in the conflict with the West.

Arab identification also contributed substantially to support for the World Trade Center attack, and when its contribution was accounted for, no other variable could explain a significant amount of additional variance. Furthermore, although SDO was directly related to support for the World Trade Center attack (see Henry et al., 2003), the negative effect of SDO was no longer significant (although it was only slightly smaller in magnitude) when we controlled for the effects of social identification. It is clear from these results that we cannot fully understand support for terrorist organizations in general and the attack on the World Trade Center in particular without considering the powerful influence of group identification—not just being an Arab or a Muslim.

Interestingly, Arab identification was even more important than Arab group membership per se in explaining support for terrorism, especially support for terrorist organizations. By itself, Arab identification explained 55% of the variance in support for terrorist organizations, and together with Lebanese identification, it added 19% of explained variance in support for these organizations once the effects of important group memberships (i.e. Muslim and Arab) were taken into account. Furthermore, Arab identification fully mediated the effect of Arab group membership on support for terrorist organizations. From a psychological perspective, these findings are astounding. They indicate that Arab group membership drives support for organizations that have claimed responsibility for hundreds of civilian casualties only to the extent that such group membership entails a *psychological identification* with the subordinate group.

However, it is important to point out that not all

social identifications in Lebanon have anti-dominance elements. Specifically, unlike Arab identification, Lebanese identification was neither negatively associated with SDO nor positively associated with support for terrorism. In fact, when the effects of SDO and Arab identification were controlled in the regression analysis, Lebanese identification was marginally *negatively* associated with support for the World Trade Center attack. Lebanese identification may be less politically volatile because its current function may be more to unify Muslims and Christians following years of devastating civil war than to mobilize outgroup aggression. As such, Lebanese identity may be tied more to common history and culture than to religious and dominance battles. If this is the case, researchers of intergroup relations should theorize more explicitly about when national identities may serve as unifying, common ingroups that could potentially reduce conflict between subnational groups, rather than as identities that foment aggression against outgroup nations. For example, Gaertner and Dovidio (2000) have proposed a common ingroup identity model, in which they advocate the creation of a superordinate group identity in order to reduce conflict between members of different subnational groups. From this perspective, encouraging members of different religious groups in Lebanon to embrace a common Lebanese identity could reduce inter-religious conflict familiar to the Lebanese by extending the ingroup favoritism formerly lavished solely on fellow religious group members to all fellow Lebanese. This process of recategorization (i.e. extending the boundaries of the ingroup to include former outgroup members) elevates the evaluation of previous outgroup members to the level of ingroup members, thus reducing intergroup bias and discrimination. Complementing this model, social dominance theory specifies the conditions facilitating the development of a viable common ingroup identity. In order to be viable, social dominance theory argues that a superordinate group identity must be endorsed to approximately the same extent by members of all subgroups and must complement rather than contradict subgroup identification (Levin, Sinclair, Sidanius, & van Laar,

2003; Sidanius & Petrocik, 2001). The results of this study offer preliminary good news regarding the viability of Lebanese identity as a common ingroup identity: mean levels of Lebanese identification were higher than those of Arab identification among both Christians and Muslims, and both religious groups exhibited similarly high levels of Lebanese identification.

In conclusion, social identity theory suggests that when comparisons with outgroups threaten important bases of ingroup evaluation, group members who identify strongly with their ingroup become motivated to derogate outgroups in order to restore positive ingroup evaluation. Realistic competition with outgroups over scarce material resources can also threaten the ingroup and result in outgroup hostility when ingroup identification is high (see Brewer, 2001). Given that the clash between the Arab and Western worlds has been characterized as a conflict over both competing collective identities and material resources (e.g. Kelman, 2001), we expected and found identification with the subordinate group in the conflict to be associated with support for terrorist organizations and support for the World Trade Center attack. This very powerful overlap between Arab identification and support for terrorist organizations and activities speaks not only to the depth of the present conflict between the Western and Arab worlds, but also to social psychological factors associated with it. As we have seen in other conflicts around the world, such as those in the former Yugoslavia, intergroup tensions are heightened when social identities become mobilized for political ends. The findings here that Arab identification is closely associated with support for terrorist organizations and activities suggest that such a mobilization of social identity has occurred in Lebanon as well. Moreover, findings that this powerful social identity is associated with a counter-dominance orientation imply that subordinate group identity in the Middle East is being mobilized toward political ends not only because it reflects religious and moral values that clash with those of the West, but also because it reflects desires to change the existing system of group-based dominance in which Arabs are subordinated.

Efforts to reduce conflict between the Arab and Western worlds must therefore address both the anti-dominance elements of social identity in the Middle East after the events of September 11, and the powerful implications that subordinate group identity has for continued support of terrorist organizations and violence against the West.

NOTES

1. We also checked for interactive effects of SDO and Arab identification on support for terrorist organizations by entering the interaction term into our hierarchical regression analysis. We did not find a significant interaction between the variables ($\beta = -.25, p = .27$).

2. We also checked for interactive effects of SDO and Arab identification on support for the World Trade Center attack by entering the interaction term into our hierarchical regression analysis. We did not find a significant interaction between the variables ($\beta = -.48, p = .16$).

REFERENCES

Alexander, M. G., Levin, S., & Henry, P. J. (in press). Image theory, social identity, and social dominance: Structural characteristics and individual motives underlying international images. *Political Psychology*.

Baron, R. M., & Kenny, D. A. (1986). The moderator–mediator variable distinction in social psychological research: Conceptual, strategic, and statistical considerations. *Journal of Personality and Social Psychology, 51*, 1173–1182.

Brewer, M. B. (1979). In-group bias in the minimal intergroup situation: A cognitive-motivational analysis. *Psychological Bulletin, 86*, 307–324.

Brewer, M. B. (2001). Ingroup identification and intergroup conflict: When does ingroup love become outgroup hate? In R. D. Ashmore, L. Jussim, & D. Wilder (Eds.), *Social identity, intergroup conflict, and conflict resolution* (pp. 17–41). New York: Oxford University Press.

Eriksen, T. H. (2001). Ethnic identity, national identity, and intergroup conflict: The significance of personal experiences. In R. D. Ashmore, L. Jussim, & D. Wilder (Eds.), *Social identity, intergroup conflict, and conflict resolution* (pp. 42–68). New York: Oxford University Press.

Faour, M. (1998). *The silent revolution in Lebanon: Changing values of the youth*. Beirut: American University of Beirut.

Gaertner, S. L., & Dovidio, J. F. (2000). *Reducing intergroup bias: The common ingroup identity model*. Philadelphia: Psychology Press.

Henry, P. J., Sidanius, J., Levin, S., & Pratto, F. (2002). *Social dominance orientation, authoritarianism, religious identification, and support for terrorism in the Middle East*. Working Paper # 186. New York: Russell Sage Foundation.

Henry, P. J., Sidanius, J., Levin, S., & Pratto, F. (2003). *Social dominance orientation, authoritarianism, and support for intergroup violence between the Middle East and America*. Manuscript submitted for publication.

Hinkle, S., & Brown, R. (1990). Intergroup comparisons and social identity: Some links and lacunae. In D. Abrams & M. Hogg (Eds.), *Advances in social identity theory* (pp. 48–70). New York: Harvester Wheatsheaf.

Hogg, M. A., & Abrams, D. (1990). *Social identifications: A social psychology of intergroup relations and group processes*. London: Routledge.

Huddy, L. (2001). From social to political identity: A critical examination of social identity theory. *Political Psychology, 22*, 127–156.

Kelman, H. C. (2001). The role of national identity in conflict resolution: Experiences from Israeli–Palestinian problem-solving workshops. In R. D. Ashmore, L. Jussim, & D. Wilder (Eds.), *Social identity, intergroup conflict, and conflict resolution* (pp. 187–212). New York: Oxford University Press.

Levin, S. (in press). Perceived group status differences and the effects of gender, ethnicity, and religion on social dominance orientation. *Political Psychology*.

Levin, S., & Sidanius, J. (1999). Social dominance and social identity in the United States and Israel: Ingroup favoritism or outgroup derogation? *Political Psychology, 20*, 99–126.

Levin, S., Sinclair, S., Sidanius, J., & van Laar, C. (2003). *In search of a viable common ingroup identity: A social dominance perspective*. Manuscript submitted for publication.

Poll says Muslims angry at US. (2002, February 27). BBC News.

Pratto, F. (1999). The puzzle of continuing group inequality: Piecing together psychological, social, and cultural forces in social dominance theory. In M. P. Zanna (Ed.), *Advances in experimental social psychology* (Vol. 31, pp. 191–263). San Diego, CA: Academic Press.

Pratto, F., Sidanius, J., Stallworth, L.M., & Malle, B.F. (1994). Social dominance orientation: A personality variable predicting social and political attitudes. *Journal of Personality and Social Psychology, 67*, 741–763.

Pyszczynski, T., Solomon, S., & Greenberg, J. (2003). *In the wake of 9/11: The psychology of terror*. Washington, DC: American Psychological Association.

Said, E. (2000). American University of Beirut, commencement speech. Retrieved from http://www.aub.edu.lb/activities/public/graduation/ed-said.html.

Schmitt, M. T., Branscombe, N. R., & Kappen, D. (in press). Attitudes toward group-based inequality: Social dominance or social identity? *British Journal of Social Psychology*.

Seaver, B. (2000). The regional sources of power-sharing failure: The case of Lebanon. *Political Science Quarterly, 115*. Retrieved from http://web.macam.ac.il/~arnon/Int-ME/extra/THE%20CASE%20OF%20LEBANON.htm

Sidanius, J., Henry, P. J., Pratto, F., & Levin, S. (in press). Arab attributions for the attack on America: The case of Lebanese sub-elites. *Journal of Cross-Cultural Psychology*.

Sidanius, J., & Petrocik, J. R. (2001). Communal and national identity in a multiethnic state: A comparison of three perspectives. In R. D. Ashmore, L. Jussim, & D. Wilder (Eds.), *Social identity, intergroup conflict, and conflict reduction* (pp. 101–129). New York: Oxford University Press.

Sidanius, J., & Pratto, F. (1999). *Social dominance: An intergroup theory of social hierarchy and oppression*. New York: Cambridge University Press.

Sidanius, J., & Pratto, F. (in press). Social dominance theory and the dynamics of inequality: A reply to Schmitt, Branscombe, & Kappen and Wilson & Liu. *British Journal of Social Psychology*.

Sidanius, J., Pratto, F., & Rabinowitz, J. (1994). Gender, ethnic status, ingroup attachment and social dominance orientation. *Journal of Cross-Cultural Psychology, 25,* 194–216.

Struch, N., & Schwartz, S.H. (1989). Intergroup aggression: Its predictors and distinctiveness from ingroup bias. *Journal of Personality and Social Psychology, 56,* 364–373.

Tajfel, H., & Turner, J. (1986). The social identity theory of intergroup behavior. In S. Worchel & W. G. Austin (Eds.), *Psychology of intergroup relations* (pp. 7–24). Chicago: Nelson-Hall.

United Nations Development Program (1998). *The national human development report, Lebanon 1998: Youth and development*. New York: United Nations Publications.

United Nations Development Program. (2003). *The Arab human development report 2002: Creating opportunities for future generations*. New York: United Nations Publications.

Weisberg, H. F., Krosnick, J. A., & Bowen, B. D. (1996). *An introduction to survey research, polling, and data analysis (3rd ed.)*. Thousand Oaks, CA: Sage.

Received October 22, 2002
Revised version accepted March 30, 2003 ■

Arab Attributions for the Attack on America: The Case of Lebanese Subelites

Jim Sidanius, P. J. Henry, Felicia Pratto, and Shana Levin

There are at least two major ways of understanding the attributions that Arab young people used to explain the September 11th attack on the World Trade Center: (a) in terms of a so-called clash of civilizations or an inherent conflict between Muslim and Western values or (b) in terms of an antidominance reaction to perceived American and Israeli oppression of Arabs in general and Palestinians in particular. The authors compare the relative validities of these two framings using a sample of Lebanese students from the American University of Beirut. The results from analysis of variance, regression, and structural equation modeling showed strong, clear, and consistent support for the antidominance attributions and essentially no support for the clash-of-civilizations attributions.

"**W**hy do they hate us so?" is the question that has been reverberating off the walls of American minds ever since the day that changed the world: September 11, 2001. At least in the United States, one of the most popular and widespread answers to this question has been the thesis

Jim Sidanius, University of California, Los Angeles; P. J. Henry, American University of Beirut; Felicia Pratto, University of Connecticut; and Shana Levin, Claremont McKenna College.

on the clash of civilizations first proposed by Bernard Lewis (1990) and later popularized and expanded on by Samuel Huntington (1993).[1] In his original formulation of this hypothesis, Lewis (1990) suggested that Islamic hatred of the United States and the West

> goes beyond hostility to specific interests or actions or policies or even countries and becomes a rejection of Western civilization as such, not only what it does but what it is, and the principles and values that it practices and professes. These are indeed

seen as innately evil, and those who promote or accept them as the "enemies of God."

Seen from this perspective, the attack of September 11th, 2001, is simply the latest and most dramatic manifestation of the very deep and fundamental conflict between rival social and spiritual systems that has lasted since the advent of Islam 14 centuries ago.

Another, but by no means the only, alternative to this clash-of-civilizations paradigm could be labeled the *antidominance perspective*. This perspective begins with the assumption that the relationships between states, just as with the relationships between social groups within states (see Sidanius & Pratto, 2001), can be thought of as hierarchically structured such that dominant states have disproportionate influence over the terms and conditions of international relations compared to subordinate states. As Seifudein Adem Hussien (2001) remarks,

> International hierarchy is in part an extension of an innate human predisposition. Human beings naturally tend to rank and order events, peoples, states, collectivities, however more or less systematic the process may be. . . . There is ample empirical evidence that human perception operates in a context of hierarchy—imagined or real. It could thus make sense for Dumont [1980] to argue that we should refer to ourselves as "Homo-Hierarchicus." (pp. 33–34)

In contemporary international politics, there is little question that the United States is the dominant power and stands without peer at the top of the hierarchically structured state system. The military and economic dominance of the United States is now so extreme that this nation is often referred to as a "hyperpower."

Although human social groups, including states in the international state system, will have a tendency to organize themselves into hierarchically ordered, dominant-subordinate structures, it is also true that these hierarchical structures will not go completely unchallenged by the subordinate members of these systems (see e.g., Scott, 1990). From this perspective, the conflict in the Middle East can be seen as one of several areas around the world

where the policies of near hegemonic American power are now under challenge. Consistent with the results from a recent Gallup poll of public opinion across nine Muslim countries (BBC News, 2002), there is good reason to believe that Arabs perceive the American support of Israel, the apparent lack of concern for the loss of Palestinian life in the West Bank and Gaza Strip, American hostility toward Iraq, and the stationing of American troops in Saudi Arabia as expressions of American desire for continued dominance and hegemony. Thus, from this generalized dominance perspective (see Sidanius & Pratto, 2001), Arab popular support for "terrorist"[2] organizations in general and the recent attack on the Word Trade Center in particular could be seen as reactions to and psychological resistance against this perceived domination. In other words, "terrorism" can be seen as an antidominance project by the weak against the strong (see also Chomsky, 2001; Henry, Sidanius, Levin, & Pratto, 2002).

Despite the popularity of these two interpretative frameworks, there has been very little, if any, empirical work exploring the attributions used by Arabs for the September 11 attacks or the manner in which people in the Arab world frame the present conflict between East and West. This article is a modest attempt to help fill this lacuna. Using data collected in Lebanon, we explore the degree to which Arab reactions to the events of September 11 are consistent with the clash-of-civilizations perspective or the antidominance perspective.

Specifically, we explored the relative plausibilities of the clash-of-civilizations and antidominance framings in four ways. First, and most directly, we simply asked a sample of Lebanese university students to indicate whether they thought clash-of-civilizations or antidominance attributions were the most plausible causes of the attacks of September 11th. Second, we examined differences between Lebanese Muslims and Christians in their attributions for the World Trade Center (WTC) attack. If people in the Arab and Muslim world are tempted to understand the WTC attack in clash-of-civilizations terms, then there is strong reason to expect that this framing should be more attractive to Lebanese Muslims than to Lebanese Christians.

Third, and following up on the second analysis, if the clash-of-civilizations attribution is a salient and accessible framing for members of the Muslim community in particular, then there is also reason to expect that the greater the importance and salience of their social identities as Muslims, the greater should be the tendency to frame the events of September 11 in clash-of-civilizations terms. Fourth, and finally, to explore more general reasons for support of the WTC attack, we used structural equation modeling to examine whether reactions to the WTC attack are, at least in part, determined by general support for "terrorist" organizations (e.g., Islamic Jihad) and opposition to antiterrorist efforts and whether these sentiments are, in turn, partly determined by membership in the Muslim versus the Christian community. In this final analysis, we explored the relative power of clash-of-civilizations versus antidominance attributions to explain reactions to the WTC attack while considering the manner in which generalized terrorism attitudes are affected by and affect other factors.

Method

Respondents

The respondents consisted of 145 graduate and undergraduate students from the American University of Beirut, Lebanon. Because the study participants were students who volunteered to be part of the study, this should be considered a convenience sample. The analyses were restricted to members of the two largest religious communities: Christians ($N = 61$; 27 females and 34 males) and Muslims ($N = 63$; 39 females and 24 males). The average age was 20.51 years. The American University of Beirut is an elite, private university founded in 1866, where English is the language of instruction. As a result, this population is particularly interesting because it consists of the subelite and the pool from which the future leaders of Lebanese society will be disproportionately recruited (Said, 2000).

Although the university is called "American," the largest proportion of students comes from Lebanon and other parts of the Middle East. Our sample was composed completely of citizens of Middle East countries, including Lebanon, Syria, and Jordan (with one exception: a citizen of Cyprus).

In the late fall of 2001, each respondent was given a questionnaire assessing reactions to the September 11 attacks on the Pentagon and the WTC and attitudes toward "terrorist" organizations and "antiterrorism" efforts.

Measures

WTC attack attributions

All respondents were asked to indicate why they thought the hijackers attacked the WTC on September 11, 2001. The stem question read as follows:

> There are many possible reasons why the hijackers attacked the World Trade Center in New York. Using the scale from 1 *(not at all a cause)* to 7 *(very important cause)*, please rate how important each possible cause of the attack was.

The respondents were given eight possible attributions to choose from. All attributions were assumed to fall within one of two attributional categories: (a) clash-of-civilizations attributions and (b) antidominance attributions. The clash-of-civilizations attributions were (a) "clash between Islamic and Western values (e.g., role of women in society)," (b) "the conflict between Christianity and Islam," and (c) "the attackers' dislike of democracy." The antidominance attributions were (a) "American support of Israel," (b) "the Israeli-Palestinian conflict," (c) "American mistreatment of Iraq," (d) "the presence of American soldiers in Saudi Arabia," and (e) "anger at American imperialism and arrogance."[3]

WTC attack justified

All respondents were asked to indicate the degree to which they felt that the September 11 attack on the WTC was justified. The response scale ranged from 1 *(not at all justified)* to 7 *(very much justified)*.

Support for "terrorist" organizations

Respondents were asked to indicate their support for four organizations listed as "terrorist" by the United States Department of State as of February, 2002.[4] The organizations were (a) the Popular Front for the Liberation of Palestine, (b) Hamas (Islamic Resistance Movement), (c) Islamic Jihad (al-Jihad), (d) Fatah, and (e) Hezbollah (Party of God). Ratings ranged from 1 (*strongly oppose*) to 7 (*strongly support*) (Cronbach's $a = .93$).

Support for "antiterrorism" policies

Support for "antiterrorism" policies consisted of support for military action carried out by the United States and Israel and targeted against "terrorists" and their organizations. There were eight items comprising this "antiterrorism" scale: (a) "Osama bin Laden should be found by the U.S. military, arrested and tried in the U.S."; (b) "Afghanistan should be invaded or bombed until they surrender bin Laden"; (c) "The U.S. has no right to bomb Afghanistan" (reverse coded); (d) "Israel should stop targeted assassinations of Palestinians" (reverse coded); (e) "Military action in response to the events of September 11th should be led by the U.S."; (f) "The U.S. should not engage in any military action that will kill civilians, no matter how few" (reverse coded); (g) "The U.S. should cease bombing Afghanistan and offer to negotiate" (reverse coded); and (h) "Osama bin Laden must be stopped by any means necessary" ($a = .83$).

Religious identification

All respondents were asked to specify to which religious community they belonged (e.g., Muslim, Christian). Following this question, they were immediately asked a series of four questions indicating the degree to which they identified with this religious community. The questions read as follows: (a) "How strongly do you identify with other members of your religious community?" (1 = *not at all*, 7 = *very strongly*); (b) "How important is your religion to your identity?" (1 = *not at all*, 7 = *very important*); (c) "How often do you think of

yourself in terms of your religious beliefs?" (1 = *not at all*, 7 = *very often*); and (d) "How close do you feel toward other members of your religious community?" (1 = *not at all*, 7 = *very close*). These four identity questions were averaged to form an overall religious identity scale with a substantial level of reliability (i.e., Cronbach's $a = .88$).[5]

Results

WTC Attack Attributions

To establish whether the eight WTC attack attributions actually defined the two distinct attributional dimensions of *clash of civilizations* and *antidominance*, we performed a confirmatory, two-dimensional factor analysis using LISREL 8.03 (see Jöreskog & Sörbom, 1993). The results of these analyses confirmed expectations and showed that a two-dimensional antidominance and clash-of-civilizations structure gave a very good fit to the data (i.e., $\chi^2[19] = 25.60$, $p = .14$; NNFI = .96, RMSEA = .056, SRMR = .054). All five antidominance indicators were significantly related to the latent dimension of antidominance. In order of importance, this dimension was most strongly defined by the following: American support of Israel ($\lambda = .86$, $p < .001$); the Israeli-Palestinian conflict ($\lambda = .73$, $p < .001$); American mistreatment of Iraq ($\lambda = .66$, $p < .001$); American soldiers in Saudi Arabia ($\lambda = .40$, $p < .001$); and anger at American imperialism and arrogance ($\lambda = .38$, $p < .001$). Similarly, all three items hypothesized to define the clash-of-civilizations dimension were strongly and significantly related to this latent continuum. In order of magnitude, this dimension was defined by the following: the conflict between Christianity and Islam ($\lambda = .84$, $p < .001$); the clash between Islamic and Christian values ($\lambda = .81$, $p < .001$); and dislike of democracy ($\lambda = .55$, $p < .001$).

It is also quite noteworthy that these two factors were essentially orthogonal to one another (i.e., $\varphi = -.05$, ns). This is important because it suggests that respondents' endorsement of a clash-of-civilizations framing does not generally preclude their endorsement of an antidominance framing.

We took the unweighted averages of the items defining each dimension to operationalize measures of antidominance and clash of civilizations ($a = .74$ and $.75$, respectively).

Having established that we have theoretically congruent measures of two distinct dimensions, our first approach to the relative validities of the clash-of-civilizations versus the antidominance interpretation of respondent opinion was simply to inspect the degree to which respondents attributed the attack on the WTC to each of the eight possible causes (see Table 15.1). The attributions in Table 15.1 are arranged in the order that the respondents endorsed them as attributions for the WTC attack.

The first thing of note in Table 15.1 is the fact that respondents assigned greater importance to antidominance rather than clash-of-civilizations attributions for the attack on the WTC. Secondly, even though Christians and Muslims assigned slightly different relative importance to clash-of-civilizations versus antidominance attributions for the attack on the WTC, both Christians and Muslims were in strong agreement that the WTC attack was more attributable to antidominance explanations (e.g., "American support of Israel," "anger at American imperialism") than to clash-of-civilization explanations. The degree of attributional profile similarity in the means of the attributions for the two religious groups was quite high ($r = .92$, $p < .01$).

To formally test the significance of the differential importance assigned to antidominance versus clash-of-civilizations attributions for the attack on the WTC, we used the composite clash-of-civilizations and antidominance scores and performed a 2×2 ANOVA with repeated measures over the two attributions and the groups factor consisting of the contrast between Muslims and Christians. Consistent with the impression given in Table 15.1, there was a very powerful and statistically significant difference in the amount of importance assigned to antidominance versus clash-of-civilizations explanations for the attack on the WTC (i.e., $M = 4.76$ vs. $M = 2.32$; $F[1, 117] = 194.53$, $p < 10^{-12}$, $\eta = .79$). Furthermore, the interaction between religious group membership (i.e., Muslim vs. Christian) and attributional importance was also statistically significant. Thus, although both Christians and Muslims felt that antidominance motives were more important than clash-of-civilization motives, Muslims gave more importance to antidominance motives than did Christians ($M = 5.05$ vs. $M = 4.47$), whereas Christians gave more explanatory power to clash-of-civilizations motives than did Muslims ($M = 2.81$ vs. $M = 1.84$; interaction effect: $F[1, 117] = 19.81$, $p < .001$, $\eta = .38$).

This last finding is theoretically important because if the clash-of-civilizations interpretation of reactions to the WTC attack is correct, we should expect to find Muslims endorsing this attack

TABLE 15.1. Means and Standard Deviations for Lebanese Muslims and Christians on Eight Attributions for the Attack on the World Trade Center

Variable	Muslims		Christians	
	M	SD	M	SD
Antidominance attributions				
American support of Israel	5.97	1.27	5.53	1.59
Anger at American imperialism	5.42	1.77	5.03	1.90
Israeli-Palestinian conflict	5.31	1.81	4.61	2.11
American mistreatment of Iraq	4.77	2.02	4.32	1.97
American soldiers in Saudi Arabia	3.64	2.07	2.74	1.79
Clash-of-civilizations attributions				
Conflict between Christianity and Islam	2.03	1.47	3.17	2.34
Dislike of democracy	1.97	1.49	2.44	1.69
Clash between Islamic and anti-Islamic values	1.47	0.98	2.64	2.04

attribution to a greater extent than Christians, and not the reverse. However, not only did Muslims show very low mean endorsement of this clash-of-civilizations attribution in absolute terms, the degree to which Muslims endorsed this attribution was significantly lower than that found among Christians, and the effect size of this group difference was far from trivial ($F[1, 117] = 13.23$, $p < .001, \eta = .32$).

As a way of further exploring the attributional differences between the Christian and Muslim communities, we also regressed the endorsement of clash-of-civilization attributions on the degree of religious identification separately among both Christians and Muslims. We reasoned that if the clash-of-civilizations interpretation of reactions to the WTC attack is correct, then the greater the level of religious identification among Muslims, the greater the degree to which they would attribute the WTC attack to clash-of-civilizations attributions. Furthermore, this should happen to a greater extent among Muslims than among Christians. However, examination of these regression coefficients within each religious community directly contradicted these expectations. Among Muslims, clash-of-civilizations attributions did not increase with increasing levels of religious identification ($b = -.02$, ns). However, this relationship was found among Christians: The greater the degree to which Christians identified with their religious community, the more they attributed the attack on the WTC to clash-of-civilization attributions ($b = .38$, $p < .05$). Furthermore, use of hierarchical regression analysis showed that this slope difference between the Muslims and Christian students was statistically significant ($t = -2.53$, $p < .01$).[6] Thus, not only did Christians give more importance to clash-of-civilizations motives than did Muslims, but these attributions were also significantly more strongly related to sense of religious community.

Causal Models of WTC Attack Justification

Finally, we used structural equation modeling to explore the degree to which the respondents thought the WTC attack was justified as a function of their WTC attack attributions, their general support of "terrorist" and "antiterrorist" activities and their religious affiliations (i.e., Muslim vs. Christian).[7] We included the respondents' attitudes about terrorist organizations and antiterrorist policies to see if the WTC attack attributions could explain the degree to which the respondents felt the WTC attack to be justified over and above these generalized attitudes toward terrorism. Among other things, this structural equation approach will allow us to test the degree to which both the clash-of-civilizations and antidominance models provide statistically adequate fits to the empirical data, as well as to explore the direct and indirect effects of all variables on beliefs that the WTC attacks were justified.

The correlation matrix used to produce both the clash-of-civilizations and antidominance models is found in Table 15.2. In both models, one's religious community was assumed to be related to support of "terrorist" organizations and antiterrorist activities, which, in turn, were assumed to be related to WTC attack attributions and ultimately to feelings that the WTC attack was justified.

Clash-of-civilizations model

The major idea behind this model is that clash-of-civilization attributions are assumed to affect WTC attack justification, whereas the effects of antidominance attributions on WTC attack justification are constrained to zero (see Figure 15.1).

This model showed that Muslims were indeed more supportive of "terrorist" organizations than Christians ($\gamma = .62$, $p < .05$) while being less supportive of American antiterrorist activities than Christians ($\gamma = -.48$, $p < .05$). Support for "terrorist" groups was positively related to both endorsement of antidominance attributions ($\beta = .30$, $p < .05$) and thinking that the WTC attack was justified ($\beta = .34$, $p < .05$). Support for "antiterrorism" was positively related to clash-of-civilizations attributions ($\beta = .22$, $p < .05$) and negatively related to thinking that the WTC attack was justified ($\beta = -.18$, $p < .05$). However, support for "antiterrorism" was not significantly related to antidominance attributions ($\beta = -.11$, ns).

TABLE 15.2. Means, Standard Deviations, and Intercorrelations Used for Structural Equation Modeling

M	SD	WTC attack justified	Anti-dominance	Clash of civilizations	Terrorism support	Antiterrorism	Muslim
2.77	1.98	WTC attack justified					
4.79	1.33	Antidominance	.39				
2.24	1.51	Clash of civilizations	−.22	−.04			
3.15	1.80	Terrorism support	.45	.30	−.26		
2.70	1.28	Antiterrorism	−.36	−.21	.27	−.45	
0.31	0.50	Muslim (Muslim = 1,					
		Christian = 0)	.23	.23	−.29	.62	−.48

Note: WTC = World Trade Center.

Despite a number of significant and expected relationships among these variables, there are several aspects of these findings that cast doubt on the validity of the clash-of-civilizations model. First, the clash-of-civilizations attribution was not found to make a statistically significant contribution to feeling that the WTC attack was justified, and to the extent that these variables were related at all; the nature of this relationship contradicts what a clash-of-civilizations interpretation would expect. This is to say that, net of the other factors in the model and to the extent that the variables were related at all, the more the WTC attack was perceived to be motivated by clash-of-civilizations motives, the less justified it was felt to be ($\beta = -.10$, *ns*). Second, using the clash-of-civilizations framework, we would also expect that those supporting "terrorist" organizations should also be those most likely to endorse clash-of-civilizations attributions. However, the exact opposite trend was found. Although not statistically significant, the data indicated that those who supported "terrorist" organizations were less—not more—likely to endorse clash-of-civilizations attributions ($\beta = .20$, *ns*). Third, and finally, this clash-of-civilizations model was found to give a rather poor fit to the data as a whole ($\chi^2[5] = 15.25$, $p = .009$; NNFI = .78, RMSEA = .14, SRMR = .06).

Antidominance model

The only way that this antidominance model differs from the clash-of-civilizations model above is that the antidominance attributions are assumed to affect WTC justification, whereas clash-of-civilizations attributions are constrained to zero. Although most of the coefficients remained stable in the two models, the results also show that the antidominance model gives a much better fit to the data (see Figure 15.2). First, we see that antidominance attributions for the WTC attack were significantly related to feeling that the WTC was justified ($\beta = .32$, $p < .05$), even after simultaneously considering the effect of generalized support of terrorist organizations ($\beta = .27$, $p < .05$). Net of the other factors in the model, the more respondents felt that the WTC attack was motivated by reactions to antidominance, the more justified the attack was seen to be.

Second, as was the case with the model above, those supporting terrorist organizations were still less—not more—likely to endorse clash-of-civilizations attributions ($\beta = -.20$, *ns*). Interestingly enough, endorsement of clash-of-civilization attributions was most likely among those supporting antiterrorism ($\beta = -.22$, $p < .05$). Finally, and in contrast to the clash-of-civilizations model, the antidominance model provided a strong fit to the empirical data as a whole ($\chi^2[5] = 6.68$, $p = .25$; NNFI = .96, RMSEA = .056, SRMR = .03).

Both models together

To see if the addition of clash-of-civilizations effects could still increase the fit of the model over and above antidominance attributions, a third model was run in which the path from clash-of-civilizations attributions to WTC justification was added. The results showed that this additional path did not significantly improve model fit (i.e., change

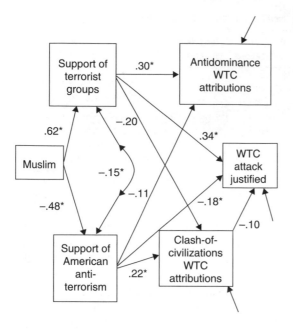

Chi-square = 15.25, df = 5; p <.009; NNFI = .78
RMSEA = .14; SRMR = .06

FIGURE 15.1 ■ Clash-of-civilizations attribution model for the World Trade Center attack. *Note*: WTC = World Trade Center.

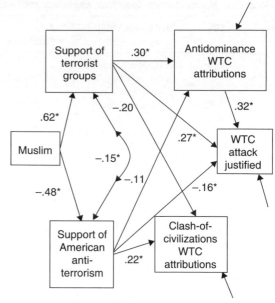

Chi-square = 6.68, df = 5; p <.25; NNFI = .96
RMSEA = .06; SRMR = .03

FIGURE 15.2 ■ Antidominance attribution model for the World Trade Center attack. *Note*: WTC = World Trade Center.

in $\chi^2[1] = 1.29$, $p > .26$). Therefore, the clash-of-civilizations model is rejected.

Discussion

This article has examined the comparative validities of two attributional framings of the bloody events of September 11, 2001, among young subelites in the Middle East. These attributional framings have been labeled the *clash-of-civilizations* and the *antidominance* perspectives. Regardless of whether one directly asks the respondents why the terrorists attacked the WTC or whether one examines the relationships between these attributions and the respondents' sense that the attacks were justified, all analyses support the same general conclusions. Young people from the Arab subelite framed and understood the events of September 11 as being more attributable to antidominance motives than to any perceived clash of civiliza-

tions. Not only did our participants think that antidominance was the more likely cause of the attacks, but the extent to which they saw it as a likely cause influenced the extent to which they saw it as a good cause, enough to shift their level of perceived justification of the WTC attacks. Such a relationship did not hold for the clash-of-cultures attributions.

Thus, in the minds of these Arab students, the ferocious and deadly attack on the United States was primarily driven by reaction to American support of Israel and the Israeli-Palestinian conflict and anger at perceived American imperialism, arrogance, and disregard for the lives and welfare of people in the Arab world. Not only were both Lebanese Christians and Muslims unlikely to attribute the events of September 11 to clash-of-civilizations motives, but Muslim respondents put even less weight on these motives than did Christians.

Thus, whereas the clash-of-civilization attributional perspective does appear to comprise a meaningful and coherent dimension of public opinion among these subelites, not only does this dimension of public opinion appear unrelated to these young people's reaction to the September 11 events, but this clash-of-civilization framing also has relatively little to do with the degree of support for terrorist organizations (e.g., Islamic Jihad, Hamas) in general. Thus, whereas those supporting terrorist organizations were more likely to understand these events as a reaction against American Middle East policy, support for these organizations was clearly not associated with the tendency to view Islam as locked in some millennial conflict with the West. Even more tellingly, to the degree that clash-of-civilizations attributions and terrorism support were related at all, they tended to be negatively rather than positively correlated. This is to say that the more respondents framed the conflict in terms of the clash-of-civilization attributions, the less they supported terrorist organizations.

Clearly, then, in the minds of these young Arab subelites, the events of September 11 are not framed or understood as a rejection of Western values, a rejection of democracy, some vague desire to return to the 14th century, or as a desire to exert dominance over the West. These results are quite consistent with evidence from recent polls in the Middle East that have shown that discontent with the United States is not due to a dislike of American values (DeYoung, 2002). Rather, these subelites in our sample seem to frame the events of September 11 as a project of antidomination. This antidominance interpretation is given further support by the results of Henry et al. (2002), using the same data set. In this work, Henry and his colleagues explored the relationship between social dominance orientation (i.e., the desire to establish hierarchical and dominant-subordinate relationships among social groups; see Pratto, Sidanius, Stallworth, & Malle, 1994; Sidanius & Pratto, 2001) and support for terrorist organizations and the attack on the WTC. In line with this antidominance interpretation of the data, the researchers found that support of terrorism and the attack on the WTC were associated with low, rather than high, levels of social dominance orientation. In

other words, these forms of terrorism were most strongly supported by those who rejected hierarchical and dominant-subordinate relationships among social groups.

However, we must also underline a number of important caveats and clearly emphasize what we are not saying. First, and most importantly, although we feel we are in the position to make statements about the manner in which these young people from a Lebanese Arab subelite understand and frame the events of September 11 and the ongoing terrorism wars, we do not mean to imply that clash-of-civilizations dynamics play no role at all in the present conflict, even within the population in which these respondents can be considered representative. This implies that we are not in the position to make statements about what motives might or might not actually be driving the present terrorism conflict. The ability to make statements about the actual motives behind support for the September 11 attacks would entail methodologies well beyond that of which this and almost all other public opinion surveys are capable. Rather, this study was devoted to the exploration of the manner in which young subelite Arabs frame and understand the present conflict. Rather than being of minor importance, we submit that understanding how young Arab subelites frame and understand this conflict is of major import if one is to successfully attempt a resolution of the conflict.

Second, and more obviously, we must also keep in mind that we have only sampled opinion from one university and one nation within the Middle East. The degree to which our conclusions generalize to other subelite populations across a broader section of the Arab world is yet to be determined. On the other hand, one could also argue that if the clash-of-civilizations framing is a powerful lens through which Middle Easterners are tempted to frame the present conflict, then Lebanon is one of the most likely countries in the Middle East where this framing should be used. This argument is based on the fact that Lebanon has had a large and politically mobilized Christian population since before the time of the crusades and the fact that Lebanese Christians and Muslims, among others, have been recently engaged in very bitter

the World Trade Center (WTC) and Pentagon and the U.S. military actions in Afghanistan and Iraq, rhetoric from all sides of this conflict continues to escalate. From the perspective of terror management theory (TMT; Greenberg, Pyszczynski, & Solomon, 1986), people who would not normally condone violent attacks on others can be motivated to support acts of aggression and sometimes even take up arms themselves when their need for protection from existential fear is heightened and they are confronted with an outgroup that explicitly or implicitly challenges core aspects of their cultural worldview. Although Pyszczynski, Solomon, and Greenberg (2003) recently applied this analysis to the ongoing strife in the Middle East, to date there are no data documenting the role of terror management processes in fueling hostile attitudes on either side of this conflict. If the TMT analysis of the motivational underpinnings of this conflict is sound, then reminders of death should increase the willingness of people in both the United States and parts of the Islamic world to support violent action against each other. The two experiments reported here investigated the effect of mortality salience on support for martyrdom attacks against Americans among young Iranians and on support for extreme military interventions in the Middle East among young Americans.

Terror Management Theory

TMT posits that the uniquely human awareness of the inevitability and potential finality of death creates the potential for existential terror, which is controlled by (a) maintaining faith in an internalized cultural worldview and (b) obtaining self-esteem by living up to the standards of value prescribed by that worldview. Because one's cultural worldview is a symbolic psychological construction and because people are aware that there are many different worldviews that provide alternative ways of construing reality, confidence in one's own worldview, and thus the protection from existential anxiety that it provides, depends on consensual validation from others. When others share one's worldview, faith in it increases, making it more effective as a buffer against existential

anxiety. However, the mere existence of people with different worldviews undermines this much-needed consensus, thereby threatening faith in the absolute validity of one's own worldview and reducing its anxiety-buffering effectiveness. People attempt to defuse the threat posed by alternative worldviews by disparaging them and those who subscribe to them, attempting to convert their adherents to one's own worldview, or simply killing them, thus eliminating the threat to consensus and asserting the superiority of one's own worldview.

To date, more 250 experiments conducted in 14 different countries have provided support for TMT hypotheses (for reviews, see Greenberg, Solomon, & Pyszczynski, 1997; Pyszczynski et al., 2003). Of particular relevance to present concerns, research has shown that reminders of death (*mortality salience*, MS) lead people to conform more closely to the norms of their culture, punish violators of those norms more severely, and react more negatively toward those whose worldviews conflict with one's own. The most common finding has been that MS increases *worldview defense*. For example, studies of American college students have shown that MS engenders more negative evaluations of those who criticize the United States and greater aggression toward those with divergent political orientations (Greenberg et al., 1997). Similarly, following MS, German college students exhibit more negative evaluations of and physical distancing from foreigners (Ochsmann & Mathey, 1994), Israeli children have more negative impressions of Russian Jewish immigrants (Florian & Mikulincer, 1998), and Japanese participants are more derogatory toward those who criticize Japan (Heine, Harihara, & Niiya, 2002).

Findings supporting TMT hypotheses have been obtained using a variety of operationalizations of MS, including the typical open-ended questions employed in the present research, death anxiety questionnaires, requests to write a single sentence about death, gory accident footage, proximity to funeral homes and cemeteries, and subliminal presentations of the words *death* and *dead* (Greenberg et al., 1997). Parallel comparison conditions in which participants are induced to think about failure, embarrassment, physical pain, uncertainty, social exclusion, paralysis, or meaninglessness do not produce these results, suggesting that MS effects are specific to thoughts of death (e.g., Baldwin & Wesley, 1996; Greenberg et al., 1995; Landau, Johns, et al., 2004). Other research has provided a detailed account of the conscious and nonconscious cognitive processes through which thoughts of death exert their effects on judgments and other behavior (Pyszczynski, Greenberg, & Solomon, 1999). This work shows that stimuli that lead to heightened death thought accessibility reliably produce worldview defense and that worldview defense effectively reduces death thought accessibility to baseline levels. Although MS inductions typically do not arouse negative affect (e.g., Rosenblatt, Greenberg, Solomon, Pyszczynski, & Lyon, 1989), recent research indicates that they increase the potential to experience anxiety and that it is this increased potential that motivates worldview defense (Greenberg et al., 2003). These studies provide converging support for the TMT proposition that cultural worldviews and self-esteem provide protection against the problem of death by reducing the potential for anxiety engendered by the heightened accessibility of death-related thoughts.

Do Some Worldviews Provide Better Protection Than Others?

What is it about cultural worldviews that provide protection from existential fear? This is a complex question in that beliefs and values probably provide protection in a variety of ways. The original presentation of TMT argued that worldviews provide protection by "providing a view of the world as orderly, predictable, meaningful, and permanent" (Greenberg et al., 1986, p. 198). Consistent with this view, Landau, Johns, et al. (2004) demonstrated that MS increases people's preference for well-structured information and encourages closure upon simple solutions to inferential problems, particularly for people high in personal need for structure. More recently, a complementary set of studies (Landau, Greenberg, Solomon, Pyszczynski, & Martens, 2005) showed that MS reduces

liking for art that seems to lack clear structure or meaning. This work suggests that all else being equal, worldviews that offer a clear vision of an orderly meaningful world are likely to be particularly appealing when thoughts of mortality are activated.

In addition, in accord with TMT, research has shown that ideologies depicting one's group as special and uniquely valuable are especially effective for terror management purposes. One recent study showed that MS increased preference for a hypothetical charismatic gubernatorial candidate who promoted a grand vision emphasizing the superiority of the ingroup but not for candidates who emphasized accomplishing tasks or egalitarian relationships (Cohen, Solomon, Maxfield, Pyszczynski, & Greenberg, 2004). These findings suggest that worldviews that enhance the perceived value of one's group are likely to be especially appealing as buffers against existential anxiety.

Ernest Becker (1975), Eric Fromm (1969), Otto Rank (1958), and Robert J. Lifton (1999) argued that worldviews that depict one's group as engaged in a heroic struggle against evil may be particularly effective for enhancing the meaningfulness of one's worldview and the value of one's group and therefore especially useful for warding off death-related fear. Thus, when death thought accessibility is heightened, leaders who help people feel good about themselves by portraying their groups as undertaking a righteous mission to obliterate evil might be particularly alluring. In support of this proposition, four recent studies demonstrated that MS increased American college students' support for George W. Bush, a leader who has portrayed the United States as engaged in a mission to vanquish evil around the globe (Landau, Solomon, et al., 2004). Study 1 showed that relative to a neutral control condition, MS increased agreement with an essay praising Bush and his policies in Iraq. Study 2 established that subliminal presentation of the number *911* or the letters *WTC*, both closely associated with the terrorist attacks, increased the accessibility of death-related thoughts relative to a neutral control condition. Study 3 demonstrated that relative to thinking about an upcoming exam, both MS and reminders of the September 11 terrorist attacks increased agreement with the pro-Bush essay. Finally, Study 4 showed that although American college students in a control condition focused on thoughts of intense pain preferred Democratic presidential nominee John Kerry over President Bush, this preference was completely reversed after exposure to MS. Indeed, Cohen, Ogilvie, Solomon, Greenberg, and Pyszczynski (in press) found that although registered voters in a control condition preferred Kerry by a 4 to 1 margin, in an MS condition, Bush was preferred by a 2.5 to 1 ratio.

This reversal of preference in the MS condition reflects a departure from most previous TMT research in that it suggests that heightened death concerns can lead people to shift from the worldviews with which they affiliate under less threatening conditions, or at least shift toward emphasizing different elements of their overall worldview.

These findings are consistent with the notion that MS increases the appeal of worldviews in which one's own group is portrayed as pursuing a heroic fight against evil. However, President Bush differs from Kerry in a variety of ways, so the Bush findings could have resulted from factors other than his emphasis on the heroic triumph over evil. The present research was designed to provide additional evidence regarding the appeal of ideologies that focus on a clash between one's own people and evil forces, particularly with regard to the role that terror management processes might be playing in the current "clash of civilizations" (Huntington, 1996) occurring between parts of the Middle East and Western world.

Specifically, we examined the effect of death-related concerns on support for extremist solutions to the ongoing conflict between the United States and some segments of the Islamic world. Whereas George W. Bush has designated some nations in this region as spokes in an "axis of evil" and supporters of martyrdom attacks as "evil-doers," in some parts of the Middle East, the United States is referred to as the "Great Satan" and an "enemy of Allah." Some Islamic fundamentalist groups, such as Al Qaeda, take this view to the extreme, advocating martyrdom in the form of suicide bombings

against the United States and its allies as the highest form of heroism and service to Allah and their culture. In a parallel manner, some Americans support preemptive war against countries that might threaten our security in the future and the use of "shock and awe-inspiring" military force that could kill thousands of innocent civilians as part of the "war on terror." If such attitudes serve a terror management function, then reminders of death should increase support for martyrdom attacks against Americans among persons in Middle Eastern cultures and increase Americans' support for extreme military action against those who oppose the United States in the Middle East.

Study 1: TMT and Support for Martyrdom Attacks Against Americans

Study 1 examined the effect of MS on support for martyrdom attacks against the United States among young adults in a Middle Eastern country. To this end, we conducted one of the first TMT studies with an Islamic population in Iran, a country with a long and ongoing history of conflict with the United States. Whereas the majority of TMT research has been conducted in North America, Europe, and Israel, and some studies have been conducted in Eastern Asia and Australia, only a very few as yet unpublished studies have been conducted in the predominantly Islamic countries of the Middle East. Given that Muslims make up approximately 18% of the world's population and that Islam is the world's fastest growing religion (Esposito, 2000), this is a serious gap in the TMT literature. In addition to the primary goal of addressing the important global issue of understanding psychological factors that increase support for martyrdom attacks, Study 1 was designed to provide information about the role of TMT processes in this understudied segment of the world's population.

Although there has been a tremendous amount of scholarly discussion and informed speculation about what leads people to support terrorist violence, very little empirical research on this topic has been conducted. Indeed, to our knowledge this is the first experimental investigation of a psychological variable posited to have a causal impact on such tendencies. Available evidence from demographic and case studies shows that contrary to common stereotypes, suicide bombers tend to be psychologically well adjusted, well educated, and financially well off compared to their countrymen. Based on interviews with members of Japan's Aum Shinrikyo cult, which was responsible for the 1995 nerve gas attack on a Tokyo subway, Lifton (1999) noted that the members' "familiar ordinariness" was one of their most disturbing characteristics. Interviews with suicide bombers and other terrorists suggest some similarity between the recruitment, commitment, and solidarity-producing strategies used by their organizations and those used by other cults (e.g., Ignatieff, 1993).

In *Terror in the Name of God*, Jessica Stern (2003) concluded from a series of in-depth interviews with a variety of religious terrorists from diverse groups (Christian, Muslim, Jewish, Hindu) that alienation from the mainstream, feelings of humiliation for both oneself and one's people, a desire to avenge past and present grievances, and most important, a desire to restore order and morality to a world viewed as bereft of these qualities play major roles in inspiring terrorist violence and support for it among those who do not directly participate in it. Similarly, Bruce Hoffman (1993) proposed that for religious terrorists, "Violence [is] first and foremost a sacramental act or divine duty executed in direct response to some theological demand or imperative" (p. 2). Stern's and Hoffman's ideas are thoroughly compatible with TMT in that these terrorists seem to be strongly focused on heroically contributing to a triumph over what they perceive to be a great evil. Thus, we believe that TMT provides an overarching theoretical framework for delineating at least one basic motive underlying efforts to use extreme violence against those viewed as evil. Study 1 provided an initial test of the TMT analysis by examining the effect of reminders of death on support for martyrdom missions against Americans. We hypothesized that MS would lead to more favorable evaluations of a "fellow student" who supported martyrdom attacks relative to a student who

opposed them and would also increase interest in joining the martyrdom cause.

Method

Participants and experimental design

In Study 1, 40 undergraduates (14 women and 26 men; mean age = 22.46) at two universities in Iran were randomly assigned to MS or aversive thought control conditions and then read and evaluated questionnaires supposedly completed by two fellow students at their universities, one supporting and one opposing martyrdom attacks; thus, the design was a 2 × 2 mixed factorial.

Materials and procedure

Participants were tested individually; all verbal instructions and materials were presented in Farsi. After obtaining informed consent, participants were told that the study was an investigation of the effects of personality on impression formation. They then completed a questionnaire containing filler items to sustain the cover story, followed by the MS manipulation (Rosenblatt et al., 1989) presented as a new personality measure. The MS induction consisted of two open-ended questions: "Please, briefly describe the emotions that the thought of your own death arouses in you" and "Jot down, as specifically as you can, what you think will happen to you as you physically die." The dental pain control condition, used in many previous MS studies, consisted of parallel questions about experiencing dental pain. Participants then completed the Positive and Negative Affect Scale (PANAS; Watson, Clark, & Tellegen, 1988) followed by a word search task to provide a delay and distraction before obtaining the dependent measures.

Participants were then told that the next part of the study involved reading some questionnaires completed by other students at their university and rating their impressions of them. They were then given two questionnaires supposedly filled out by other students that started with background information, followed by the critical items used to vary that person's attitudes about martyrdom attacks. These materials were designed to be representative of commonly expressed views among this population. A pilot study with a separate sample showed that the materials were understandable and did not arouse suspicion.

In the promartyrdom condition the "other student's" responses to the critical items were as follows:

- What do you feel to be the most pressing world issue? Showing the world that deaths in the name of Allah will bring an end to the imperialism practiced in the West.
- Do you have a life motto? One should treat all other true believers as brothers; everyone else should be considered enemies of Allah.
- How do you perceive the role of the United States in the Middle East? I believe the United States' presence is wrong. They are invading our holy land and threatening our way of life.
- Are martyrdom attacks on the United States justified? Yes. The United States represents the world power which Allah wants us to destroy.

In the antimartyrdom condition, the "other student" replied,

- What do you feel to be the most pressing world issue? Convincing others in the world that Islam is a peaceful religion and that Allah loves all men. The world must know that not all Muslims are motivated by the hatred and misguided beliefs that have led to many needless deaths in the name of Allah.
- Do you have a life motto? One should treat other humans with respect and care, no matter what racial, ethnic, or religious background.
- How do you perceive the role of the United States in the Middle East? Although I believe the United States' presences is somewhat intrusive, they did remove a tyrannical leader from power in hope of establishing a more democratic system of government.
- Are martyrdom attacks on the United States justified? No. Universally speaking, human life is too valuable to be used as a means of producing change.

After reading each questionnaire (presented in counterbalanced order), participants indicated their impressions of the student by responding to the following questions on 9-point scales (1 = *most negative response*, 9 = *most positive response*): How much do you think you would like this person? How much do you agree with this person's opinion? How intelligent do you believe this person to be? and To what degree do you respect this person? To get a more direct assessment of participants' support for martyrdom attacks, the final item asked them to "Rate the degree to which you would consider joining their cause."

After each session, participants were debriefed; none showed any suspicions.

Results and Discussion

Reliability analyses of the four items evaluating the "other student" indicated high internal consistency, with Cronbach's alpha of .95 and .90 for the pro- and antimartyrdom conditions, respectively. Therefore, composite measures of participants' evaluations of the two "other students" were computed by taking the mean of the four questions. A 2 (MS vs. control) × 2 (pro- vs. antimartyrdom) ANOVA yielded a significant main effect for MS, $F(1, 38) = 19.86$, $p < 0001$, and more important, a significant MS × Martyrdom Attitude interaction, $F(1, 38) = 66.04$, $p < .0001$.[1] Relevant means are in Figure 16.1. Pairwise comparisons revealed that although participants preferred the student who opposed martyrdom attacks over the one who supported martyrdom attacks in the dental pain control condition, $t(38) = 5.47$, $p < .0001$, MS led to a dramatic reversal of this pattern such that after being reminded of their mortality participants preferred the student who supported martyrdom attacks over the one who opposed them, $t(38) = 6.02$, $p < .0001$. Looked at differently, MS led to significantly more favorable evaluations of the promartyrdom student, $t(38) = 10.45$, $p < .0001$, and a trend toward less favorable evaluations of the antimartyrdom student, $t(38) = 1.86$, $p = .071$.

To get a more direct assessment of the effect of MS on participants' willingness to personally get

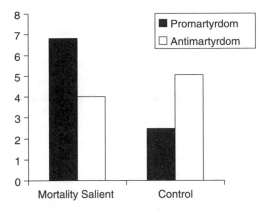

FIGURE 16.1 ■ Evaluation of persons supporting and opposing martyrdom attacks as a function of mortality salience. Higher scores indicate more positive evaluation of that person.

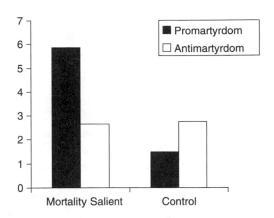

FIGURE 16.2 ■ Willingness to consider joining pro- and antimartyrdom causes as a function of mortality salience. Higher scores indicate greater willingness to consider joining the cause.

involved in martyrdom attacks, we conducted a parallel ANOVA on their responses to the item that assessed their willingness to consider joining their cause. This analysis revealed significant main effects of MS, $F(1, 38) = 33.85$, $p < .0001$; martyrdom attitude, $F(1, 38) = 6.31$, $p < .02$; and the predicted MS × Martyrdom Attitude interaction, $F(1, 38) = 32.87$, $p < .0001$. Relevant means are displayed in Figure 16.2. Although dental pain control participants indicated greater interest in joining the antimartyrdom than the promartyrdom cause, $t(38) = 2.28$, $p < .05$, MS participants indicated greater interest in joining the promartyrdom cause than the antimartyrdom cause, $F(1, 38) = 5.83$, $p < .0001$. Whereas MS increased interest in joining the promartyrdom cause, $t(38) = 9.40$, $p < .0001$, it had no effect on interest in joining the antimartyrdom cause, $t(38) < 1$.

To determine whether MS affected mood, we ran separate ANOVAs on the subscales of the PANAS. As in previous studies (Goldenberg, Pyszczynski, McCoy, Greenberg, & Solomon, 1999; Rosenblatt et al., 1989), MS did not affect mood on any subscales (all $Fs < 1$), thus ruling out the possibility that subjective mood produced by MS is responsible for the change in attitudes toward martyrdom.

The results of Study 1 support TMT predictions. MS produced a significant increase in both the favorability ratings of the promartyrdom target person and willingness to consider joining his or her cause. Thus, thoughts of death led young people in the Middle East who ordinarily preferred a person who took a pacifist stance to switch their allegiance to a person who advocated suicide bombings. These data support the proposition that worldviews that construe one's people as part of a sacred campaign to triumph over evil are especially appealing when terror management needs are heightened, even to the point of pulling people from the values that guide their attitudes and evaluations under conditions of lower threat. This shift in allegiance will be considered in greater detail in the general discussion. These findings provide the first experimental evidence documenting psychological determinants of the appeal of martyrdom and suggest that TMT may provide useful insights into the psychological forces that encourage such behavior.

Because we wished to make the target persons in this study as realistic as possible, the pacifist and radical target persons differed in several ways, including their feelings regarding nonbelievers, their statements about the United States, and their support of martyrdom per se. Thus, it is unclear exactly which aspects of the target persons' attitudes were most influential in determining evaluations of the targets. However, the views expressed by the target persons reflect attitudes that tend to go together in contemporary Islamic culture. People who support martyrdom are unlikely to hold more positive attitudes toward the United States than those opposed to it.

It is worth noting that reminders of death influenced attitudes and evaluations even in a country where death is dealt with in a much more open manner than in the West. For example, many older Muslim men and women buy themselves a burial shroud and visit it once in a while, and for some it is a common practice to crawl down into their future graves to pray. Indeed, many Muslims in the Middle East report that they look forward to their death so they can join Allah in paradise. The present findings show that reminders of death increase cultural allegiances even in cultures where death is openly celebrated; this adds to other recent findings indicating that TMT applies to non-Western cultures with very different ideologies regarding death (e.g., Halloran & Kashima, 2004; Heine et al., 2002).

Whereas Study 1 demonstrated the effect of MS on support for martyrdom attacks among Iranian college students, from the perspective of TMT, this tendency for existential fear to increase support for extreme and violent solutions to international conflicts is a general characteristic of the human condition. This suggests that similar forces are likely involved in fueling some Americans' support for extreme military interventions in the Middle East. Study 2 investigated American college students' support for the use of extreme military force as appropriate tactics for use in the war against terrorism.

Study 2: TMT and Support for Extreme Military Solutions among Americans

Study 2 examined Americans' support for preemptive wars, the use of nuclear and chemical weapons, and the killing of thousands of innocent people as collateral damage in the quest to destroy Osama bin Laden. The theoretical rationale was identical to that leading to Study 1: If viewing one's nation as pursuing a valiant battle against evil serves a terror management function, then reminders of one's mortality should increase support for extreme lethal measures as a means of vanquishing that evil. One particularly common reminder of mortality that is often raised in discussions of contemporary American foreign policy centers around the September 11, 2001, terrorist attacks on the World Trade Center and Pentagon. Landau, Solomon, et al. (2004, Study 2) showed that even subliminal presentation of the letters *WTC* or the numbers *911* increase the accessibility of death-related thoughts. Thus, it was predicted that reminders of both one's own death and the 9/11 attacks would increase support for a variety of extreme military solutions to the current conflict in the Middle East among American college students.

We also addressed an additional question in Study 2: Does MS affect support for extreme military force among all people, or does it primarily affect those with political orientations or personality characteristics that are associated with support for such measures? This gets back to the complex issue of how cultural worldviews serve their terror management function. Wicklund (1997) raised the question of whether MS leads people to gravitate toward their existing worldview or toward worldviews that reduce ambiguity. More recently, Jost, Glaser, Kruglanski, and Sulloway (2003) proposed that MS pushes people toward supporting more conservative ideologies. According to TMT, when the need for protection from existential fears is heightened, people will gravitate toward whatever is most likely to provide effective protection from this potential terror. Because the individual's cultural worldview functions to provide this fortification, MS will generally lead to greater commitment to and perhaps more extreme ways of affirming that worldview. However, cultural worldviews are complex structures that contain many elements, some of which may be in conflict with others. There may thus be situations in which less dominant thoughts and values may be more effective in providing protection than those that make up the person's central attitudes and values. In these instances, MS may lead people to gravitate toward positions associated with enhanced security that they might otherwise eschew when their need for existential protection is less.

Supporting extreme military solutions in a war against evil may be a particularly potent way of protecting oneself from existential anxiety. Vanquishing an enemy that is construed as evil is likely to boost one's self-esteem by asserting one's greater strength and moral superiority while at the same time affirming the values that differentiate one's own group from the outgroup. On the other hand, some worldviews may view lethal violence as unacceptable or as a form of evil itself and thus steer those who subscribe to such views away from supporting solutions to conflicts that entail the killing of others. Clearly in the United States, political conservatives are more prone to negative attitudes toward out-groups (Jost et al., 2003) and are more supportive of taking military action against Iraq (Gallup, 2005). Thus, MS seems most likely to increase support for extreme military actions among conservatives. Therefore, in Study 2, we examined whether participants' political orientation moderates the hypothesized effect of MS on support for American use of extreme military tactics in the Middle East. However, prior TMT research is somewhat equivocal on this issue. On one hand, Greenberg, Simon, Pyszczynski, Solomon, and Chatel (1992) found that conservatives became more negative toward a different other after MS, but liberals did not. On the other hand, Landau, Solomon, et al. (2004) found that MS increased liberals' as well as conservatives' support for President Bush. Therefore, there was no strong basis for an a priori prediction as to whether political orientation would or would not moderate the predicted effect of MS on Americans' support for extreme military actions.

Method

Participants

In this study, 127 Rutgers university undergraduate students (95 women and 32 men) were recruited to participate.

Procedure

The experimenter introduced the study as concerning the relationship between personality attributes and opinions about matters of public interest. Participants were given a booklet, told to work through it in order, to respond to the questions with their "gut reactions," and informed that they could withdraw from the study at any time.

This questionnaire packet began with two filler questionnaires to sustain the cover story followed by the MS induction, parallel questions focused on intense physical pain (used in Landau, Johns, et al., 2004, Study 4), or a terrorism prime condition. Terrorism salience participants were asked to "Please describe the emotions that the thought of the terrorist attacks on September 11, 2001, arouses in you" and "Write down as specifically as you can, what happened during the terrorist attacks on September 11, 2001." All participants then completed the PANAS and a short passage to serve as a distraction.

Participants then completed the dependent measure consisting of the following five statements:

1. It is entirely appropriate to engage in preemptive attacks on countries (e.g., Iran, Syria, North Korea) that may pose a threat to the United States in the future, even if there is no evidence they are planning to attack us right now.
2. If necessary, the United States should use nuclear weapons to defend our interests at home and abroad.
3. If necessary, the United States should use chemical weapons to defend our interests at home and abroad.
4. If we could capture or kill Osama bin Laden we should do it, even if thousands of civilians are injured or killed in the process.
5. The Patriot Act should be strengthened, even if we have to relinquish personal freedoms to make our country more secure.

Participants indicated their agreement with each statement on 5-point scales (1 = *strongly disagree*; 5 = *strongly agree*).

Participants then completed a final page of the booklet soliciting demographic information;

specifically, gender, ethnicity, religion, and political orientation ("How would you describe your political orientation?" on a 9-point scale; 1 = *very conservative*; 5 = *moderate*; 9 = *very liberal*). Participants were subsequently debriefed and thanked.

Results and Discussion

Support for extreme force

The four items measuring support for extreme force revealed acceptable internal consistency, Cronbach's alpha of .83. Consequently, a composite index was formed by calculating the mean score on these four items. An ANOVA revealed no effect of the priming manipulation on political orientation, $F(2, 125) = 1.23$, $p = .30$; consequently, political orientation was used as a predictor in the primary analyses.

The composite index served as the dependent variable in a regression analysis with priming condition (MS vs. pain control vs. 9/11), political orientation, and the product of the two as predictors. Priming condition was dummy coded, yielding separate vectors for the MS versus pain control and 9/11 salience versus pain control contrasts and for the interaction of each of these contrasts with political orientation (Aiken & West, 1991). The only significant main effect to emerge was for the MS versus control contrast, $\beta = .21$, $SE = .21$, $t = 2.04$, $p = .04$. This MS main effect was qualified by two significant interactions: Political Orientation × MS versus control, $\beta = -.25$, $SE = .12$, $t = 2.27$, $p = .03$, and Political Orientation × 9/11 versus control, $\beta = -.28$, $SE = .10$, $t = 2.26$, $p = .03$ (see Figure 16.3).

Analyses of simple slopes suggest that political orientation predicts variation in support for extreme military interventions within the MS ($\beta = -.44$, $SE = .09$, $t = -2.59$, $p = .01$) and 9/11 ($\beta = -.38$, $SE = .07$, $t = -2.83$, $p = .005$) conditions but not within the control condition ($\beta = .07$, $SE = .08$, $t = .47$, $p = .64$); higher levels of political conservatism were associated with greater support for extreme military measures in these two conditions. To provide tests of the differential effects of the two primes for people on the liberal and conserva-

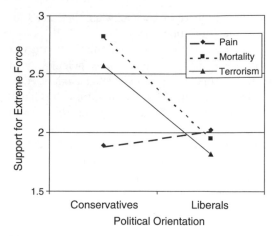

FIGURE 16.3 ■ Support for the use of extreme military force as a function of mortality salience, 9/11 salience, and political orientation. Higher scores indicate greater support for use of military force.

tive ends of the political spectrum, we compared the projected means in the MS and 9/11 salience conditions with that of the control condition at one standard deviation above and below the mean on the political orientation scale (Aiken & West, 1991). These analyses revealed that the contrasts MS versus pain, $\beta = .45$, $SE = .33$, $t = 2.80$, $p = .006$, and 9/11 versus pain, $\beta = .36$, $SE = .28$, $t = 2.44$, $p = .01$, reached significance among conservatives but not among liberals. None of the other contrasts were significant ($ps \geq .36$). As Figure 16.3 shows, liberals' support for extreme force remained relatively low across the different priming conditions, whereas conservatives' support for extreme force significantly increased in both the MS and 9/11 salience conditions relative to the control condition, with MS and 9/11 salience moving them across the midpoint of the scale.

Support for the Patriot Act

The item assessing support for the Patriot Act was subjected to the same regression analysis. A main effect was found for both MS, $\beta = .22$, $SE = .25$, $t = 2.30$, $p = .02$, and 9/11 salience, $\beta = .21$, $SE = .25$, $t = 2.16$, $p = .03$. These main effects were moderated by political orientation; Political Orientation × MS versus control: $\beta = -.32$, $SE = .14$, $t = 3.01$, $p =$

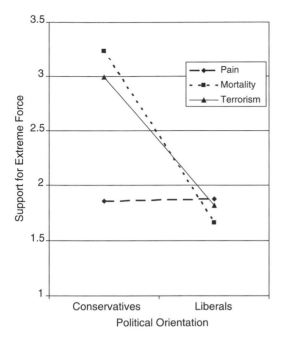

FIGURE 16.4 ■ Support for the Patriot Act as a function of mortality salience, 9/11 salience, and political orientation. Higher scores indicate greater support for use of military force.

.003; Political Orientation × 9/11 versus control: $\beta = -.30$, $SE = .12$, $t = 2.54$, $p = .01$. As Figure 16.4 shows, the simple slopes for political orientation predicting support of the Patriot Act were significant in the MS and 9/11 salience conditions, $\beta = -.63$, $SE = .11$, $t = -3.93$, $p < .001$ and $\beta = -.47$, $SE = .08$, $t = -3.71$, $p < .001$, but not in the control condition, $\beta = .01$, $SE = .09$, $t = .05$, $p = .96$. We followed the same procedure as described earlier to further explore the significant interactions. These analyses revealed that MS and 9/11 salience led to increased support for the Patriot Act among conservatives, $\beta = .57$, $SE = .37$, $t = 3.75$, $p < .001$, $\beta = .45$, $SE = .36$, $t = 3.13$, $p = .002$, but not among liberals, $ps \geq .46$.

Study 2 conceptually replicated and extended Study 1 by demonstrating that reminders of both one's own mortality and the 9/11 attacks on the Pentagon and World Trade Center increased support for both extreme military interventions in the Middle East and the Patriot Act among politically conservative Americans. However, these inductions had no effect on either measure among politically liberal Americans. Similar to the present findings, Greenberg et al. (1992, Study 1) found that political conservatives responded to MS with more negative evaluations of political liberals but that political liberals' evaluations of political conservatives were not affected by MS. Greenberg et al. argued that the value of tolerance that is central to liberal ideology is inconsistent with hostile reactions toward those who are different, making negative reactions to MS a potential threat to self-esteem and thereby preventing liberals from responding to MS in this way. Consistent with this reasoning, a follow-up study by Greenberg et al. (1992, Study 2) demonstrated that when the value of tolerance is primed, neither liberals nor conservatives derogated attitudinally dissimilar others in response to MS. Thus, it seems likely that liberals did not become more supportive of extreme military interventions or the Patriot Act in response to reminders of death or 9/11 in the present study because the values of their worldviews typically oppose such measures.

Perhaps somewhat surprisingly, political orientation was not associated with scores on either measure in the control condition. This might reflect the extreme nature of the attitudes assessed (e.g., using nuclear and chemical weapons); indeed, our conservative participants tended to oppose both extreme military force and the Patriot Act in the control condition, just as our Iranian participants preferred the antimartyrdom target in Study 1. However, when reminded of either death or 9/11, politically conservative participants' support for these issues rose just past the midpoint of the scales. These findings show that MS can lead to an expression of attitudinal tendencies that are not exhibited under less threatening conditions.

General Discussion

The present findings demonstrate that thoughts of death increases people's readiness to support extreme violent solutions to global conflicts. The same induction that increased Iranians' support for martyrdom attacks against Americans

uncertainty salience replicates MS effects on responses to perceived unfair treatment and inequity. Based on this work, one could plausibly argue in the present context that the uncertainty produced by thoughts of death motivated the preference for decisive measures directed toward eradicating evil. This view cannot be ruled out for the present studies; however, both conceptual and empirical issues cast some doubt on this interpretation.

First, it is not clear why the MS induction would produce more uncertainty than the controls used in these studies, dental pain and intense pain, or in other studies (e.g., worries after college, social exclusion, giving a speech in public). In one important sense, death is the only certain future event. What is uncertain about it is when and how it will happen and what happens afterward. Interestingly, Iranians generally seem far more certain about what happens afterward than Americans, so that aspect may be less uncertain for them, yet the MS induction clearly affects them. People are likely to be uncertain about worries after college, about when and how intense pain or dental pain will occur and what that and its aftermath will be like, and matters like how they will do on upcoming exams. Thus, when MS has different effects than such aversive future events, it seems unlikely that uncertainty is the operative factor. More damaging to an uncertainty interpretation, a substantial set of recent studies has found quite different effects for the MS induction used here and uncertainty salience (e.g., Friedman & Arndt, in press; Landau, Johns, et al., 2004; Routledge, Arndt, & Goldenberg, 2004). Despite this evidence supporting the discriminant validity of the MS induction, the relationships among death, uncertainty, and other existential threats is surely a worthy topic for further investigation.

The Axis of Evil Versus the Great Satan

From a TMT perspective, people protect themselves from the fear of death inherent in the human condition by aligning themselves with aspects of cultural worldviews that enable them to view themselves as significant contributors to a meaningful and enduring reality. Because some Islamic groups and leaders advocate martyrdom against the United States as a heroic means of vanquishing evil, alignment with martyrdom causes has become a means of attaining this sense of death-transcending significance. Some Islamic sects preach that martyrdom attacks are the duty of all good Muslims and that those who do so will be rewarded by a blissful afterlife, the ultimate victory over death. Similarly, President Bush has repeatedly construed U.S. military campaigns in the Middle East as part of a "war on terror" in which "lovers of freedom" pursue a valiant mission to root out "evil-doers" who "hate freedom."

Our findings are consistent with the view that MS increased attraction to martyrdom and extreme military measures because these positions are specifically directed toward eradicating evil. It may be that for most people, inhibitions against killing other people can be overcome only when the target is viewed as inherently evil. However, these positions are associated with a variety of other attitudes and beliefs, so at this point, we cannot be sure that this specific aspect of the worldview was responsible for these effects. More precisely controlled studies are clearly needed to determine the specific role the desire to vanquish evil, isolated from associated attitudes and beliefs, plays in these findings and terror management in general.

Of course, our primary goal with these studies was to enhance our understanding of the psychological forces that encourage support for violent solutions to the ongoing conflicts in the Middle East. This research indicates that the increased awareness of death can lead people to desire to inflict harm on those who are construed as enemies. This suggests that the frequent reminders of death that inevitably result from armed conflicts may be fanning the passions that sustain these conflicts. Although TMT theorists have argued that terror management processes play an important role in the problems in the Middle East (Pyszczynski et al., 2003), these studies provide much needed evidence that this is indeed likely to be true.

Polarization of Worldviews or Shift Toward Security-Providing Worldview Elements?

The question of whether thoughts of death push people to confirm their preexisting worldviews or to move toward belief systems that are especially likely to provide security (cf. Jost et al., 2003; Wicklund, 1997) is a complex one. Although a large research program will be necessary to fully address this question, the present findings do bear on it. In both studies, the MS inductions led participants to move toward supporting positions that were generally not supported in the control conditions. This shift toward positions not favored under neutral conditions has emerged in several other TMT studies. For example, Cohen et al. (2004) showed that MS greatly increased support for a charismatic leader who garnered little support under control conditions; Landau, Solomon, et al., (2004) demonstrated that MS led to a dramatic reversal of preferences for George Bush over John Kerry among college students who were registered and intended to vote in the 2004 American presidential election; and Schimel et al. (1999) found that MS led participants who preferred a stereotype disconfirming African American under control conditions to prefer an African American who confirmed widely shared racial stereotypes. It seems clear that reminders of mortality do not simply lead to an amplification of tendencies that exist under more neutral conditions. Rather, MS leads people to gravitate toward conceptions of reality that provide security in one way or other. Often this entails affirming the dominant aspects of one's worldview, but as the present and other results demonstrate, sometimes this entails moving toward less dominant aspects of the worldview that are heavily associated with feelings of superiority, structure, and security.

Study 2 provides additional insight into this issue by demonstrating that preexisting differences in political orientation predicted which participants responded to MS by increasing their support for extreme military policies. When reminded of their mortality, conservative but not liberal participants increased their support for the use of such tactics.

Perhaps the inhibitions against such tactics were simply stronger for liberal participants, or the threat posed by Middle Eastern radicals was perceived as stronger for conservative participants. Although these findings suggest that preexisting attitudes play an important role in determining how people will protect themselves from existential concerns, we suspect that other factors are involved as well. The logic of TMT suggests that reminders of death should lead people to gravitate toward whatever aspect of one's worldview is expected to provide the best protection at the time the protection is needed. Providing a clearer explication of the factors that determine which aspects will provide superior protection is an important challenge for future work.

Conclusion

In our view, the most important contribution of this research is to show that common psychological forces contribute to support for extreme solutions to the current conflict in the Middle East in both the United States and Iran. The same variable that increases support for martyrdom attacks in the Middle East increases support for use of extremely lethal military force in the United States. To our knowledge, these are the first studies to examine common psychological determinants of attitudes on both sides of this volatile international conflict. These studies show that scientifically rigorous research can yield insights into the forces that encourage allegiance to good versus evil ideologies that are currently threatening the peace in much of the world. Given what is at stake, a scientifically informed understanding of the forces responsible for escalating the conflict between the United States and the Islamic world is sorely needed. Although frightening in their implications, the convergence in findings across the two nations raises the hope that recognizing the role of a common psychological force in fueling hostilities in both nations might create at least some empathy within each country for people in the other and perhaps even provide some impetus for finding additional common ground that could be used as a basis for seeking more peaceful resolutions to the issues that divide us.

Cultural worldviews have been characterized as fitting one of two types (Pyszczynski et al., 2003). The first type, "the rock," is a relatively secure, rigid conception that emphasizes absolutes of good and evil; proponents of such worldviews hold them with great certainty, and the primary negative emotion they experience when their worldview is threatened is anger directed toward that which is designated as evil. The second type, "the hard place," is a more flexible and hence less secure worldview that emphasizes the relativity and complexity of assessments of right and wrong; proponents of such worldviews live with uncertainty, and the primary negative emotion they experience is anxiety. The present research suggests that when thoughts of death are highly accessible, people, especially those with prior leanings in this direction, gravitate toward the former rock type of worldview, an inclination that can contribute to a cycle of violence as groups lash out at the "evil" they perceive in those whose worldview is different from their own.

NOTE

1. In both studies, there were no significant effects of gender and no significant effects on the mood measures.

REFERENCES

Abdollahi, A. (2004, July). *Effects of mortality salience on judgment, choice, self-esteem and behavior.* Poster session presented at the 18th International Society for the Study of Behavioural Development Meeting, Ghent, Belgium.

Aiken, L. S., & West, S. G. (1991). *Multiple regression: Testing and interpreting interactions.* Newbury Park, CA: Sage.

Arndt, J., Cook, A., & Routledge, C. (2004). The blueprint of terror management: Understanding the cognitive architecture of psychological defense against the awareness of death. In J. Greenberg, S. Koole, & T. Pyszczynski (Eds.), *The handbook of experimental existential psychology* (pp. 35–53). New York: Guildford.

Arndt, J., Greenberg, J., Pyszczynski, T., & Solomon, S. (1997). Subliminal exposure to death-related stimuli increases defense of the cultural worldview. *Psychological Science, 8,* 379–385.

Baldwin, M. W., & Wesley, R. (1996). Effects of existential anxiety and self-esteem on the perception of others. *Basic and Applied Social Psychology, 18,* 75–95.

Becker, E. (1975). *Escape from evil.* New York: Free Press.

Cohen, F., Ogilvie, D. M., Solomon, S., Greenberg, J., & Pyszczynski, T. (in press). American roulette: The effect of reminders of death on support for George W. Bush in the 2004 presidential election. *Analyses of Social Issues and Public Policy.*

Cohen, F., Solomon, S., Maxfield, M., Pyszczynski, T., & Greenberg J. (2004). Fatal attraction: The effects of mortality salience on evaluations of charismatic, task-oriented, and relationship-oriented leaders. *Psychological Science, 15,* 846–851.

Esposito, J. (2000). *The Oxford history of Islam.* Oxford, UK: Oxford University Press.

Florian, V., & Mikulincer, M. (1998). Terror management in childhood: Does death conceptualization moderate the effects of mortality salience on acceptance of similar and different others? *Personality and Social Psychology Bulletin, 24,* 1104–1112.

Friedman, R. S., & Arndt, J. (in press). Reconsidering the connection between terror management theory and dissonance theory. *Personality and Social Psychology Bulletin.*

Fromm, E. (1969). *Escape from freedom.* New York: Henry Holt.

Gallup. (2005, March 15). *Would public back military action in "trouble spots"?* Retrieved March 15, 2005, from http://www.gallup.com/poll/anaylses/goverPolit/

Goldenberg, J. L., Pyszczynski, T., McCoy, S. K., Greenberg, J., & Solomon, S. (1999). Death, sex, love, and neuroticism: Why is sex such a problem? *Journal of Personality and Social Psychology, 77,* 1173–1187.

Greenberg, J., Martens, A., Jonas, E., Eisenstadt, D., Pyszczynski, T., & Solomon, S. (2003). Detoxifying thoughts of death: Eliminating the potential for anxiety eliminates the effects of mortality salience on worldview defense. *Psychological Science, 14,* 516–519.

Greenberg, J., Pyszczynski, T., & Solomon, S. (1986). The causes and consequences of a need for self-esteem: A terror management theory. In R. F. Baumeister (Ed.), *Public self and private self* (pp. 189–192). New York/Berlin: Springer-Verlag.

Greenberg, J., Pyszczynski, T., Solomon, S., Simon, L., & Breus, M. (1994). Role of consciousness and accessibility of death-related thoughts in mortality salience effects. *Journal of Personality and Social Psychology, 67,* 627–637.

Greenberg, J., Simon, L., Harmon-Jones, E., Solomon, S., Pyszczynski, T., & Lyon, D. (1995). Testing alternative explanations for mortality salience effects: Terror management, value accessibility, or worrisome thoughts? *European Journal of Social Psychology, 25,* 417–433.

Greenberg, J., Simon, L., Pyszczynski, T., Solomon, S., & Chatel, D. (1992). Terror management and tolerance: Does mortality salience always intensify negative reactions to others who threaten one's worldview? *Journal of Personality and Social Psychology, 63,* 212–220.

Greenberg, J., Solomon, S., & Pyszczynski, T. (1997). Terror management theory of self-esteem and cultural worldviews:

Empirical assessments and conceptual refinements. In M. P. Zanna (Ed.), *Advances in experimental social psychology* (Vol. 29, pp. 61–139). San Diego, CA: Academic Press.

Halloran, M. J., & Kashima, E. S. (2004). Social identity and worldview validation: The effect of ingroup identity primes and mortality salience on value endorsement. *Personality and Social Psychology Bulletin, 30,* 915–925.

Heine, S. J., Harihara, M., & Niiya, Y. (2002). Terror management in Japan. *Asian Journal of Social Psychology, 5,* 169–185.

Hoffman, B. (1993). *"Holy terror": The implications of terrorism motivated by a religious imperative.* Santa Monica, CA: RAND.

Huntington, S. (1996). *The clash of civilizations and the remaking of the world order.* New York: Simon & Schuster.

Ignatieff, M. (1993). *Blood and belonging: Journeys into the new nationalism.* New York: Farrar, Straus & Giroux

Jost, J. T., Glaser, J., Kruglanski, A. W., & Sulloway, F. J. (2003). Political conservatism as motivated social cognition. *Psychological Bulletin, 129,* 339–375.

Landau, M. J., Greenberg, J., Solomon, S., Pyszczynski, T., & Martens, A. (2005). *Windows into nothingness: Terror management, meaninglessness, and negative reactions to modern art.* Unpublished manuscript, Tucson, AZ.

Landau, M. J., Johns, M., Greenberg, J., Pyszczynski, T., Martens, A., Goldenberg, J. L., et al. (2004). A function of form: Terror management and structuring the social world. *Journal of Personality and Social Psychology, 87,* 190–210.

Landau, M. J., Solomon, S., Greenberg, J., Cohen, F., Pyszczynski, T., Arndt, J., et al. (2004). Deliver us from evil: The effects of mortality salience and reminders of 9/11 on support for President George W. Bush. *Personality and Social Psychology Bulletin, 30,* 1136–1150.

Lifton, R. J. (1999). *Destroying the world to save it: Aum Shinrikyo, apocalyptic, violence, and the new global terrorism.* New York: Metropolitan Books.

McGregor, I., Zanna, M. P., Holmes, J. G., & Spencer, S. J. (2001). Compensatory conviction in the face of personal uncertainty: Going to extremes and being oneself. *Journal of Personality and Social Psychology, 80,* 472–488.

Ochsmann, R., & Mathey, M. (1994). *Depreciating of and distancing from foreigners: Effects of mortality salience.* Unpublished manuscript, Universitat Mainz, Germany.

Pyszczynski, T., Greenberg, J., & Solomon, S. (1999). A dual process model of defense against conscious and unconscious death-related thoughts: An extension of terror management theory. *Psychological Review, 106,* 835–845.

Pyszczynski, T., Solomon, S., & Greenberg, J. (2003). *In the wake of 9/11: The psychology of terror.* New York: American Psychological Association.

Rank, O. (1958). *Beyond psychology.* New York: Dover.

Rosenblatt, A., Greenberg, J., Solomon, S., Pyszczynski, T., & Lyon, D. (1989). Evidence for terror management theory I: The effects of mortality salience on reactions to those who violate or uphold cultural values. *Journal of Personality and Social Psychology, 57,* 681–690.

Routledge, C., Arndt, J., & Goldenberg, J. L. (2004). A time to tan: Proximal and distal effects of mortality salience on sun exposure intentions. *Personality and Social Psychology Bulletin, 30,* 1347–1358.

Schimel, J., Simon, L., Greenberg, J., Pyszczynski, T., Solomon, S., Waxmonski, J., et al. (1999). Support for a functional perspective on stereotypes: Evidence that mortality salience enhances stereotypic thinking and preferences. *Journal of Personality and Social Psychology, 77,* 905–926.

Stern, J. (2003). *Terror in the name of God: Why religious militants kill.* New York: HarperCollins.

van den Bos, K. (2001). Uncertainty management: The influence of uncertainty salience on reactions to perceived procedural fairness. *Journal of Personality and Social Psychology, 80,* 931–941.

Watson, D., Clark, L. A., & Tellegen, A. (1988). Development and validation of brief measures of positive and negative affect: The PANAS scales. *Journal of Personality and Social Psychology, 53,* 1063–1070.

Wicklund, R. A. (1997). Terror management accounts of other theories: Questions for the cultural worldview concept. *Psychological Inquiry, 8,* 54–58.

Received March 18, 2005
Revision accepted July 16, 2005 ■

SECTION V

How Does One Become a Terrorist?
Social and Psychological Factors in Terrorism

"Terrorism" is often discussed as if it were a unitary phenomenon: a plague of ghastly, immoral behavior committed by "them" against "us." While it is impossible to deny the horrors of attacks on innocent civilians, psychology seeks to understand the origins of this terrible form of human aggression, at least in part hoping to identify modifiable risk factors. We know that humans often engage in violent conflicts, be they individual or collective. We know that some of these conflicts involve a good deal of terrorism, and some do not. Two questions come to mind. First, given the fact that violent conflict between individuals or groups has probably been a feature of human behavior since the dawn of our species, why does the behavior we call terrorism (attacks on innocent non-combatants to advance a political agenda) become a notable characteristic of some conflicts and not others? Why, for example, were there relatively few deliberate attacks on innocent White South Africans during the apartheid era, compared with relatively more attacks on White Rhodesians and thousands of attacks on innocent Israelis during the intifadas? Second, why do some people who share a grievance commit acts of terrorism, while most do not? Clearly, even in the most distressing conditions, only a relative handful of individuals turn to terrorism. Why, for example, might large population groups such as the Tamils in Sri Lanka, the Chechens in Russia, or the Kurds in Turkey suffer discriminatory or oppressive experiences, while only a very small subgroup of these people join terrorist groups? What makes joiners different from everyone else?

To say that psychology has the answer would be a hollow boast. The study of terrorism as an important behavioral phenomenon is in its infancy. Moreover, a tension exists between those who focus on "the mind of the terrorist" at the individual level and those who focus on terrorism as a group activity. That having been said, superb scholars have put their minds to work trying to answer these questions for several decades. Some examine the question from the sociological perspective; authorities such as Donna della Porta (Reading 17) and Marc Sageman (Reading 21) apply this top-down perspective, seeking to identify the broad social conditions and structural factors that tend to inspire violent extremist movements and the networks of human affiliation that supply members. Others scholars, such as McCauley and Segal (Reading 19), focus on the process of radicalization from the point of view of classic experiments in social psychology. Sprinzak (Reading 18) also explores the radicalization process, emphasizing the psychological differences between the many who may feel disenfranchised and the few who take up arms. And Merari and Friedland (Reading 20) attend to yet another aspect of the social psychology of terrorism: Since the success of a terrorist campaign relates to the public's perception that they are terrorized, one wants to know what factors increase or decrease that dreadful feeling.

After reading this section, one comes to the inescapable conclusion that terrorism cannot be understood from any single disciplinary outlook. Indeed, allegiance to one or another perspective—such as individual psychology, group behavior, or structural sociology—will blind us to the extraordinary heterogeneity and complexity of this dangerous problem. The generation of terrorism scholars that will make a difference will be the one that eschews disciplinary blinders and plunges, eyes wide open, into the data.

Reading 17—della Porta (1988). Recruitment Processes in Clandestine Political Organizations: Italian Left-Wing Terrorism

Editors' Comments

Donatella della Porta has made major contributions to our understanding of European terrorism of the 1970s and 1980s. By combining careful reviews of criminal trial records with personal interviews, she has developed new insights into both the role of social networks and the role of past political activities in the building of extremist groups.

In this paper, she applies a theory of "consensus mobilization," or the process by which groups of people come to form networks predisposed to political action. Based on data regarding more than 1200 individual militants, she concludes that both personal associations, such as friendship or kinship, and shared ideology are important factors in the decision to join politically violent groups. Yet even the combination of these two factors is not sufficient to explain who joins and who does not. Given the risks involved, she suggests that deep personal loyalties, long-time acquaintanceship, past experience of using violence to address problems, and "symbolic incentives" all add to the mix and far outweigh practical or economic motives. Yet she concludes: "Analyzing recruitment is not sufficient to give a full account of individual motivations in joining underground groups." Political realities also figure in the recipe. The harsh, repressive behavior of police seems to have been a key factor in provoking a cycle of violence in Italy in the 1970s. It appears that special combinations of personal connection, political milieu, and bilateral physical aggressiveness may be recipes for radical extremism.

Discussion Questions

1. This study reports that multiple factors seem to contribute to recruitment. How might one sort out the relative contribution of each? For example, is there any practical way for us to determine whether friendship is more or less important than ideology?
2. Some people seem more likely than others to join groups, and some are more likely than others to get politically involved. Do the data in this study suggest that the urge to join groups, in and of itself, may be a factor in becoming a terrorist?
3. della Porta states that previous experience of violence is a predisposing factor to involvement in terrorist groups, yet only 67 of the 1214 militants in her sample had prior convictions for violent crimes. Do the data in this study support the conclusion that prior experience of violent behavior plays a significant role in joining terrorist organizations?

Suggested Readings

della Porta, D. D. (1995). *Social movements, political violence, and the state: A comparative analysis of Italy and Germany*. Cambridge, UK: Cambridge University Press.

Hoffer, E. (1951). *The true believer: Thoughts on the nature of mass movements*. New York: HarperPerennial.

Jenkins, J. C. (1983). Resource mobilization theory and the study of social movements. *Annual Review of Sociology*, 9, 527–553.

Ruggiero, V. (2005). Brigate Rosse: Political violence, criminology, and social movement theory. *Crime, Law, and Social Change*, 43, 289–307.

Tarrow, S. (1998). *Power in movement: Social movements and contentious politics*. Cambridge, UK: Cambridge University Press.

Reading 18—Sprinzak (1990). The Psychopolitical Formation of Extreme Left Terrorism in a Democracy: The Case of the Weathermen

Editors' Comments

The late Ehud Sprinzak was a towering figure in the early studies of the psychology of terrorism. In this paper (a chapter from Walter Reich's now classic 1990 book, *Origins of terrorism: Psychologies, ideologies, states of mind*), Sprinzak addresses the rather bizarre case of the Weathermen. This small, fractious group arose when the USA was in the throes of a crisis of legitimacy, as national leaders prosecuted the increasingly unpopular Vietnam War and as police violently attacked the protestors against that war. Hijacking a more liberal and non-violent group—the Students for a Democratic Society—the small self-selected Weatherman cohort preached rejection of virtually all Western values, from democracy to maternal love. Barbarism in the name of Communist revolution was their catchword and modus operandi. Sprinzak explores the psychology of this violent but ineffectual little group, tracking its evolution through three stages: (1) a crisis of confidence, in which large segments of the US population began doubting the wisdom and intentions of the government, (2) a conflict of legitimacy in which a smaller group becomes enraged at the failures of moderate methods to move the intransigent, repressive authorities and feels a need to channel their frustration into more militant behaviors, and (3) a crisis of legitimacy in which an even smaller group delegitimizes the authorities and everything connected with them. Having rejected the entire value system of their culture, the Weathermen were obliged by their own rhetoric to adopt an entirely antisocial (and ultimately self-destructive) way of living, replete with orgies, drug abuse, and largely indiscriminate violence.

Discussion Questions

1. Sprinzak theorizes that extraparliamentary politics is an expected part of modern society, while ideological terrorism only occurs when several conditions are met. What are those conditions?
2. In this paper, the author concludes that ideological terrorism represents a "fantasy war," or a "simulated revolution of the isolated few." Yet real and successful large-scale revolutions such as those in France and Russia perhaps also began with the radicalization of the "isolated few." Would one expect a psychological difference between those who commit terrorist violence in small-scale abortive movements and those who do so in history-making revolutions?
3. The conditions that Sprinzak describes as precipitating the rise of the Weathermen—an unpopular war, a crisis of confidence, and ready models of urban guerilla behavior—seemed virtually identical in the USA to 1969–1970 and 2004–2008. Why did we not see a mass anti-Iraq war protest movement and a smaller White-led anti-war terrorist movement?

Suggested Readings

Ferracuti, F. (1982). A sociopsychiatric interpretation of terrorism. *Annals of the American Academy of Political and Social Science, 463*, 129–149.

Gurr, T. (1970). *Why men rebel*. Princeton, NJ: Princeton University Press.

Tajfel, H., & Turner, J. C. (1979). An integrative theory of intergroup conflict. In W. G. Austin & S. Worchel (Eds.), *The social psychology of intergroup relations* (pp. 33–48). Monterey, CA: Brooks/Cole.

Tilly, C. (1978). *From mobilization to revolution*. Reading, MA: Addison-Wesley.

Reading 19—McCauley and Segal (1987). Social Psychology of Terrorist Groups

Editors' Comments

In this incisive, ambitious paper, the authors undertake a very large task. They examine terrorists as individuals but set aside that approach quickly, arguing that little is known about definitive or deterministic personality traits that distinguish terrorists from non-terrorists. They focus instead on terrorism as a group phenomenon. Like Sprinzak, they observe radicalization as an incremental process and outline the rewards and challenges of group membership. The special value of this paper is the authors' effort to explore how key discoveries in social psychology may help us to better understand terrorism. First, cult recruitment has been studied among the membership of the Unification Church; the combination of deprivation with exposure to a social network of members seems to be a powerful factor in recruitment. Second, social psychology explains the shift of groups from moderate toward extreme as a quest for consensus and an urge to be "above average" in expressing favored opinions. Third, Milgram's famous studies of obedience (in which subjects were willing to shock others at progressively higher voltages) may help to explain why a person joining a terrorist group might be willing to abandon familiar moral guidelines and acquiesce to escalated violence.

Discussion Questions

1. McCauley and Segal review several important social psychological domains, including cult recruitment, group extremity shift, and obedience. What social conditions might increase or decrease a person's vulnerability to these group dynamics?
2. This paper identifies many parallels between cult group recruitment and terrorist group recruitment. What are the differences?
3. This paper concludes that terrorism is "not understandable in terms of individual psychopathology" but is the product of group dynamics, yet it is obvious that some people approached for recruitment join and others do not. Given equal political grievances and hopes, what factors might distinguish joiners from non-joiners?

Suggested Readings

Lofland, J., & Stark, R. (1965). Becoming a world-saver: A theory of conversion to a deviant perspective. *American Sociological Review, 30*, 862–875.

Milgram, S. (1974). *Obedience to authority*. New York: Harper.

Smelser, N. J. (1963). *Theory of collective behavior*. New York: Free Press.

Traub, S. H., & Little, C. B. (1980). *Theories of deviance* (2nd ed.). Itasca, NY: Peacock.

4. Like della Porta, Sageman found that networks of friendship or kinship seem to play a very important role in recruitment to terrorist groups. One counterterrorism approach would be to target the people who are the "hubs" of such networks, yet the virtual communities of the Internet may be playing an increasingly important role. Has modern technology leap-frogged some counterterrorism initiatives by facilitating new avenues to human affiliation?

Suggested Readings

Burt, R. S. (1982). *Toward a structural theory of action: Network models of social structure, perception, and action.* New York: Academic Press.

Freeman, L. C., White, D. R., & Romney, A. K. (1992). *Research methods in social network analysis.* New Brunswick, NJ: Transaction Publishers.

Passy, F., & Giugni, M. (2001). Social networks and individual perceptions: Explaining differential participation in social movements. *Sociological Forum, 16,* 123–153.

Sageman, M. (2004). *Understanding terror networks.* Philadelphia: University of Pennsylvania Press.

Recruitment Processes in Clandestine Political Organizations: Italian Left-Wing Terrorism

Donatella della Porta

Recruitment in Terrorist Organizations: An Introduction

Of all the phenomena that characterized the history of Italy in the 1970s, terrorism has had the most dramatic impact on the collective memory. At that time many questions arose about the causes of such a widespread and lasting wave of political violence. The peculiarity of the political culture and the gravity of some social problems were singled out as the environmental preconditions for its emergence. Some legal organizations were accused of offering structures and legitimation to terrorist groups. The fact that a large number of people were believed to be involved increased the need to understand the motivations that led to the violent behavior of individuals who had been politically socialized in a consolidated democratic regime.

Many of these questions remained unanswered at the time. It is only recently, with the change in the political climate and the availability of new sources of information, that it has become possible to analyze this phenomenon with a greater degree of historical precision. As part of a wider research project on Italian left-wing terrorism (della Porta in preparation), this essay deals with one aspect of individual motivations for engaging in noninstitutional forms of political behavior; recruitment into clandestine organizations.

In the sociological literature the most radical forms of protest have often been explained by the assumed pathology of the militants. In the case of clandestine political groups, participation has been related to personality dependence, low intelligence, egocentrism (Livingstone 1982), and frustrated attempts to build positive identities (Billing 1984; Ivianski 1983; Russell and Miller 1983; Knutson 1981; Steinoff 1976). These interpretations, however, have never been proven true by empirical research. In the few cases in which former terrorists were given personality tests, the tests were administered after their arrest, that is after the individuals involved had passed through at least two total institutions, the clandestine organization and the prison system.

Considering terrorist groups as forms of political organizations, albeit with particular characteristics, may suggest alternative hypotheses about individual participation. As I have

The information used in this paper has been gathered by the author as part of a wider research program on "Political Violence and Terrorism" coordinated by the Carlo Cattaneo Institute of Bologna, Italy.

Continua (Continuous Struggle) is quite high. These organizations have often been accused of having provided the structures for the emerging terrorist groups, in particular by forming semi-legal bodies that have been defined as "strategic articulations of an organic terrorist project" (Ventura 1984). My data show that the breakdown of *Potere Operaio*, as well as the almost contemporaneous crisis of *Lotta Continua*, had important effects on the fortunes of the Italian radical left. But the careers of individual militants show that very few people shifted to terrorism directly from these two groups. Rather, the breakdown of these groups gave rise to a process of "autonomization" of *Comitati di Base* (Rank and File Committees) and *Collettivi Operai* (Workers Collectives) from under the guardianship of the more structured groups of the New Left (Palombarini 1982). It was in these small political nuclei, characterized by radical ideologies and violent repertoires, that many future terrorists continued their political involvement.

But the number of late 1960s militants who chose a radicalization of the conflict was quite small. The sharp increase in recruitment came about only when the entrepreneurial efforts of these people found a large potential base in another group of violence-prone political militants. While the breakdown of *Lotta Continua* and *Potere Operaio* occurred in 1973, only after 1976 did a large number of people, as many as 78% of all the recruits, join terrorist groups. Too young to have been involved in the first phases of the late 1960s protest cycle, the members of the "second generation" of terrorists began their political socialization in those groups which had their origins in the crisis of the New Left. As many as 84% of the terrorists had been active in the nuclei that formed around 2 magazines called *Rosso* (Red) or *Senza Tregua* (Without Truce), in the *Circoli del Proletariato Giovanile* (Circles of Youth Proletariat), or in the small *Comitati di Quartiere* active in the working-class neighborhoods of the largest cities.

One characteristic of these groups was their very small size. In Table 17.3, the category "Autonomous Collectives" combines 93 sub-categories. In at least 89 of these sub-categories, the size of the organization was small enough to suggest that strong personal bonds developed among all the members. In 65 of these sub-categories the frequency is more than 1; in other words, within these groups, at least 2 future terrorists were sharing the same legal political experience. Very often the decision to join a clandestine organization involved an even larger network of "political" companions: 47 of these groups produced at least three future terrorists; 35 at least 4; and 112 more than 5. Decisions to join the "armed struggle" were, in all these cases, collective ones.

In-depth interviews and examinations allow for a better interpretation of these quantitative data. As the testimony of former members reveals, membership in the small legal political group was of great importance in their daily lives. Even where friendship ties external to the political milieu did exist their importance tended to diminish as political socialization developed. In a spiraling series of interrelationships, as the amount of time a member spent in political activities increased, so did his contacts with political companions. At the same time, the strengthening of friendship ties inside the political environment increased the value attached to political involvement and encouraged people to dedicate more and more time to political activities. In this way, other ties lost their power to exert countervailing effects on the formation of the personality. As Keniston (1968) has suggested is typical of other kinds of political socialization, commitment among the militants involved a process of isolation from the outside world, and this isolation reinforced loyalty to the new group. Political friends became the most important peer group, capable of influencing any individual choice.

Terrorist Militancy and Political Identities

To summarize what has been said so far, Italian clandestine organizations recruited their militants from tight-knit networks of social relations in which political ties were strengthened by primary solidarity based on friendship and kinship relations. These networks offered loyalty channels of communication to the underground groups. Individual motivations can be traced, to a large extent, to solidarity with groups of people with whom an individual shared a political identity. But the understanding of personal motivation requires a deeper analysis of the process of political socialization that helps to build a collective identity.

Examinations and interviews with former terrorists support the hypothesis, that the formation of collective political identities is influenced by the political climate in which sectors of the population have their first political experiences. Specific political sub-cultures influence both the degree of importance political identity has in a person's life and the specific meaning that political activities have for an individual.

Life stories of Italian terrorists confirm that a characteristic of people recruited to clandestine organizations is previous experience of using violence as a political means. Many of the members of armed groups had previously belonged to the semimilitary structures of nonclandestine organizations. They had been involved, for example, in the *servizio d'ordine* (marshall body) of *Lotta Continua*, in the semilegal structures of *Potere Operaio* and of the groups organized around the review *Linea di Condotta* (Line of Conduct), and in the military body of *Rosso*, the so-called *Brigate Comuniste* (Communist Brigades), appointed for the armed defense of public demonstrations and illegal activities. Some of the militants of *Nuclei Armati Proletari* and of *Proletari Armati per il Comunismo* were experienced in illegal activities, though, in the case of ordinary delinquents who became involved in politics during their stay in prison, for nonpolitical aims. Many of the small clandestine groups that arose after 1979 were founded by terrorists from the major armed organizations. And, conversely, many people recruited into the larger terrorist organizations had previously been involved with illegal groups active in some working class neighborhoods.

The relevance of the previous use of violent repertoires in the political socialization of Italian terrorists is indicated by other data as well. Previous legal convictions for violent crime were traced in 67 cases. Moreover, many of the younger terrorists of the late seventies had been charged with the "proletarian expropriations" and "armed demonstrations" carried out by semilegal groups. A number of others had been prosecuted as members of the most violent groups of *Autonomia Operaia* (Workers Autonomy), the *Collettivo di Via dei Volsci* in Rome, for instance.

The importance of previous experiences with violence is often stated in former militants' accounts of their lives. The political episodes most frequently mentioned are squattings, confrontations with police, fascist assaults, and use of "Molotov cocktails" to "defend" marches and arrests. The use of violence by right-wing activists and police is cited as a justification for personal involvement in illegal and violent activities. The militants' emphasis on their participation in violent events is, therefore, often a device to justify choices that were seen as a necessary response.

To conclude, previous experience in violent political activities predisposes individuals to involvement in terrorist groups. My analysis suggests that participation in violent practices produces a kind of militant for whom political commitment is identified with physical violence rather than with negotiation. The lack of possibilities for concrete gains through bargaining activities increases the need for symbolic substitutes, which are often found in radical ideologies that maintain that social changes can be obtained only through a long war against the enemy.

The spread of terrorist organizations in Italy was, therefore, connected to the presence of political militants whose political socialization took place in the long protest cycle of the late sixties–early seventies. In this period, political activities were characterized by strategies aimed at the formation of new collective identities, rather than at the use of already existing solidarity bonds for bargaining (Pizzorno 1978b). When the protest cycle was over, networks of militants—more accustomed to physical violence than to mediation—constituted a potential base for violent political groups. This group of people interacted, then, with other militants who were politically socialized during periods of identity building and high violence rates. This interaction produced the base from which the second generation of terrorists would emerge. For these people, the use of physical violence preceded rather than followed the joining of terrorist organizations. The threshold of clandestinity was often passed involuntarily and sometimes even unconsciously.

A fair conclusion would be, therefore, that an individual has a greater propensity to become involved in terrorist activities when she or he belongs to tight-knit political networks and has been socialized to accept violent forms of action.

The Recruitment to Clandestine Organizations as a Case of Political Participation: A Conclusion

Analyzing recruitment is not sufficient to give a full account of individual motivations in joining underground groups. We must examine other processes in order to understand the way in which the militants were integrated in the organizations and the evolution of their activities in them. In concluding, I will simply summarize my main findings, arranging them around three foci of attention: mobilization potential, consensus mobilization, and action mobilization (Klandermans 1984 and 1985; Tarrow 1985).

Consensus mobilization, that is, "the creation of network arenas and mentalities in which predispositions favorable to action mobilization are formed" (Tarrow 1985. p. 15) has been the main focus of my analysis. Our findings show that terrorist groups are able to recruit in homogeneous political networks. The reservoir for terrorist organizations is composed of people who share (1) strong political identities, that is, people whose personality-building process relies heavily upon a political commitment; and (2) a political socialization to violence, that is, people, whose political ideology and, in particular, whose practice, admits the use of physical violence.

The high risks involved in terrorist recruitment may require a greater emphasis on personal networks in terrorist organizations than in other political groups. Moreover, the total commitment that a terrorist organization requires may dramatically increase the degree of personality investment in political participation.

Even allowing for important peculiarities, some general statements can be made here. First, the categories of social network and political ideology are only partially useful in defining consensus mobilization. Neither participation in a social network nor adoption of a certain ideological framework is indeed sufficient to foster political loyalties. They can, in fact, be important constraints on the formation of collective political identities. Second, solidarities that develop during the formation of these collective identities tend to persist and often to direct the groups of people they bind together toward political problem solving attitudes. Faced with crises in social movements, groups of friends keep their solidarity with each other by looking together for other political involvements. Third, collective identities are formed during periods of regular contact, a fact that in turn helps explain why some individuals consider their political role so important to the structure of their personality.

Although this research concentrated on consensus mobilization, it also offers insights into the other two levels of analysis of political participation. As far as the mobilization of people into action is concerned, the main findings refer to the importance of symbolic incentives. Such incentives are somewhat specific to terrorist organizations, because the high risks involved in participation, diminish the importance of economic incentives. Actually, this situation seems to hold true for other kinds of social movement organizations as well. Indeed, social movements in general are rarely able to offer more than very low-paying and temporary jobs and rely heavily upon volunteer work.

The third subject for analysis, the structural factors that produce groups and individuals with a predisposition to left-wing clandestine organization has not been systematically reviewed. Nevertheless, my data suggest that left-wing groups emerged in Italy as the unforeseen consequences of harsh social conflicts (on this point, see Caselli et al. 1984; della Porta et al. 1986). The lack of a timely policy response to the late 1960s protest cycle, together with the relatively high level of police intervention, favored a gradual deterioration of the repertoires. In the second half of the seventies a very intense outburst of youth protest quickly gave rise to violence. One of the reasons for this outburst may be found in the repressive way through which the new demands were dealt with. In both cases, the environmental conditions encouraging the emergence of terrorism were characterized by the spread of violent patterns of political behavior. The presence of violent repertoires, indeed, creates the preconditions for political entrepreneurs to orient their efforts to a specific constituency formed by those who use radical forms of action.

While these structural preconditions may seem very specific to terrorist groups, nonetheless some general conclusions can be drawn on this point. First, political variables have to be taken into account in analyzing mobilization potential. This potential is defined not only by class position or economic variables but also by the structure of political opportunities (Tarrow 1983). Second, political variables are particularly necessary when the research addresses the potential constituency, not of a social movement in general, but of a specific social movement organization. The two problems have to be differentiated analytically. Third, the mobilization potential is not a naturally existing reservoir; rather, it is in some way shaped by the political organization. The organization's strategic choices define the boundaries of a certain constituency and in this way contribute, if not to the creation, at least to the exploitation of some structural preconditions.

REFERENCES

Aveni, Adrian F. 1977. "The not-so-lonely crowd: Friendship groups in collective behavior." *Sociometry* 40:96–99.

Aveni, Adrian F. 1978. "Organizational linkages and resource mobilization: The significance of linkage strength and breath." *Sociological Quarterly* 19:185–202.

Barnes, J.A. 1969. "Network and political process." Pages 51–76 in J. Mitchell (ed.), *Social Networks in Urban Situations*. Manchester: Manchester University Press.

Billing, Otto. 1984. "The case history of a German terrorist." *Terrorism: An International Journal* 7:1–10.

Burt, Ronald S. 1980. "Models of network structure." *Annual Review of Sociology* 6:79–141.

Caselli, Giancarlo and Donatella della Porta, 1984. "La storia delle Brigate Rosse: Strutture organizzative e strategie d'azione." In Donatella della Porta (ed.), *Terrorismi in Italia*. Bologna: Il Mulino.

Coombs, G. 1979. "Network and exchange: The role of social relations in a small voluntary association." *Journal of Anthropological Research* 29:96–112.

Court of Turin. 1980. "Left-wing terrorism in Italy during the seventies: The formation of terrorist organizations." Paper presented at the 13th International Conference of the IPSA, Paris, July.

della Porta, Donatella and Sidney Tarrow. 1986. "Unwanted children: Political violence and the cycle of protest in Italy, 1966–1973." *European Journal of Political Research* 14: 607–32.

della Porta, Donatella. In preparation. *Il Terrorismo di Sinistra in Italia*.

Elder, Glen. 1981. "History and the life course." In D. Bertaux (ed.), *Biography and Society*. Beverly Hills: Sage.

Erickson, Bert H. 1981. "Secret societies and social structures." *Social Forces* 60:188–210.

Garner, Roberta and Mayer N. Zald. 1983. "Social movement sectors and systemic constraints: Towards a structural analysis of social movements." University of Michigan, CRSO Working Paper No. 238.

Gerlach, Luther P. 1970. "Corporate groups and movement networks in America." *Anthropological Quarterly* 43:123–45.

Gerlach, Luther P. and Virginia H. Hine 1970. *People, Power, Change: Movements of Social Transformation*. New York; Bobbs-Merrill.

Hirschman, Albert O. 1982. *Shifting Involvements: Private Interest and Public Action*. Princeton: Princeton University Press.

Homans, George C. 1958. "Social behavior as exchange." *American Journal of Sociology* 63:596–606.

Ivianski, Zeev. 1983. "A chapter in the story of individual terror: Andrey Zhelyabol." In L. Z. Freedman and Y. Alexander (eds.), *Perspectives on Terrorism*. Wilmington, Del.: Scholarly Resource.

Keniston, Kenneth. 1968. *Young Radicals: Notes on Committed Youth*. New York: Harcourt, Brace and World.

Klandermans, Bert C. 1984. "Mobilization and participation: Social-psychological expansions of resource mobilization theory." *American Sociological Review* 49:583–600.

Klandermans, Bert. 1986. "New social movements and resource mobilization: The European and the American approach." *International Journal of Mass Emergencies and Disasters*. Special issue, *Comparative Perspectives and Research on Collective Behavior and Social Movements* 4:13–37.

Knutson, Jeanne N. 1981. "Social and psychological pressures toward a negative identity: The case of an American revolutionary terrorist." In Y. Alexander and J. M. Gleamson (eds.), *Behavioral and Quantitative Perspectives on Terrorism*. New York: Pergamon.

time there's going to be people hitting pigs. . . . The focal point is here in Chicago. We've got to show people that white kids are willing to fight on the side of black people and on the side of revolution around the world. If you're not going to right, then you're not part of us. It's as simple as that.[3]

Violence occurred as soon as the march began. Weathermen first attacked the North Federal Savings and Loan Building, breaking its large plate-glass windows with rocks. As they moved down Clark Street they started to run, systematically smashing windows of buildings and parked cars on both sides of the street. People trying to protect their cars were beaten and left bleeding on the streets. The police, caught by surprise, did not interfere. Later, when a police line formed, the demonstrators charged into it and the line was broken.

Assessing the first evening of what became known in the history of the American protest movement as the "Days of Rage," Stephen Zicher, a Chicago assistant corporation counsel, said, "We never expected this kind of violent demonstration. There always has been a big difference between what they say and what they do."[4] And Tom Hayden, a central figure in the protest movement of the 1960s, later said of the Weatherman action:

We never did what the government accused us of in 1968 [at the Democratic National Convention in Chicago], but the Weathermen did it in 1969. What we did in 1968 prefigured Weathermen; a few karate and snake dance exercises, some disruption, a lot of running in the streets, and at the end of Convention Week, a prediction that a fighting force would be created which would bring the war in Vietnam home. It remained for the government to develop this seed into a paranoid image of crazy, unruly, drug-ruined, club-carrying, Communist-inspired mobs rampaging in the Loop, and for Weathermen to fulfill the image one year later. Many Weathermen leaders were shaped by the events of Chicago '68. When our legal protest was clubbed down they became outlaws. When our pitiful attempts at peaceful

confrontation were overwhelmed, they adopted the tactic of offensive guerrilla violence.[5]

As on other occasions, Tom Hayden was not attempting to make a detached and theoretical observation about the behavior of radicals in a time of national crisis, but in his acute and peculiar way he managed to do so. What he observed and described was the development of a crisis of legitimacy in a democracy.[6] Like Zicher, Hayden noticed that rhetoric and symbols expressing an attitude of delegitimation vis-à-vis the regime were now being matched by overt and intentional illegal behavior, and that this second generation of radicals was ready to challenge not only the elected authorities but also their agencies of physical coercion. American observers of the student protest movement had witnessed worse scenes of student violence. But the violence in those previous scenes had not been planned; it was shaped primarily by the unintended interaction of committed activists, uncommitted observers, and the appearance of the police. The violence in Chicago, in 1969, was planned.

Soon after the "Days of Rage," the Weathermen leaders, at that time in command of the national headquarters of the Students for a Democratic Society (SDS) in Chicago, closed the offices of that organization and entrusted its massive archives to the State Historical Society of Wisconsin in Madison. Their new mood was reflected well in a headline in the Weatherman's journal, *Fire:* "DURING THE 1960S THE AMERICAN GOVERNMENT WAS ON TRIAL FOR CRIMES AGAINST THE PEOPLE OF THE WORLD. WE NOW FIND THE GOVERNMENT GUILTY AND SENTENCE IT TO DEATH ON THE STREETS."[7]

---

[3] Ibid., 199.
[4] Ibid., 204.

[5] Tom Hayden, *Trial* (New York: Holt, Rinehart and Winston, 1970), 91–2.
[6] For an earlier analysis of this phenomenon see Ehud Sprinzak, "The Revolt Against the Open Society and the Phenomenon of Delegitimation: The Case of the American New Left," in *The Open Society in Theory and Practice*, Dante Geimino and Klaus von Beime, eds. (The Hague: Martinus Neijhof, 1974). See also Jurgen Habermas, *Legitimation Crisis* (Portsmouth, N.H.: Heinemann, 1976).
[7] See Larry Grathwohl, *Bringing Down America* (New Rochelle, N.Y.: Arlington House Publishers, 1976), 84.

In a three-day "war council" in Flint, Michigan, the Weathermen came to the conclusion that they now had to become real revolutionaries. Bernardine Dohrn, the most determined leader of the organization, made it clear that "white kids," unlike their black counterparts, were not risking themselves sufficiently. Real revolution meant violence and terrorism, and this had to be the Weatherman's course. Suzan Stern, a participant at the "war council," reported on the themes that dominated the discussion:

> There was a history for us to follow. The Algerian guerrilla terrorists did play a big role in freeing Algeria from the French tyranny; [Viet Cong] terrorists, the Huks in the Philippines, the Tupamaros in Uruguay . . . the Palestinian Liberation Front. The topic was not approached lightly; it was a deadly serious meeting. Everyone knew the implications of even *talking* about terrorism. And we were discussing what would be necessary to actually do it.[8]

By the end of 1969 the course was set. The Weatherman, whose members already lived in very closed "collectives," went underground; it declared war on the government of the United States and announced its intention to build a Leninist vanguard and a "red army."[9] Splitting itself into small, secret, action-oriented "affinity groups" that were subject to the hierarchical command of the "Weather Bureau," it armed itself heavily and enforced strict rules of secrecy upon its members.[10] Through anonymous telephone calls and letters to the underground press, it claimed responsibility for otherwise unsolved cases of bombing and subversive operations.[11]

The New "Barbarism"

The political transformation of the large SDS into the small and self-selected Weather organization, and of the "Weather People" into self-conscious terrorists, was not the only transformation these young people went through. Shreds of information surfacing from the American underground have suggested a remarkable story of personal-psychological transformation. Based on memoirs of former Weathermen, it is possible to reconstruct some of these transformations. The Weathermen appear to have developed antinomian norms of behavior. Out of their outrage and desperation they came to reject every rule and value they had known and had been socialized to respect. The whole symbolic framework within which they now operated was elaborated in Flint, Michigan, by the concept of "barbarism": "A new Weatherman catchword was 'barbarism.' The Weathermen see themselves as playing a role familiar to that of the barbaric tribes such as the Vandals and the Visigoths, who invaded and destroyed the decadent, corrupt Rome. (Some Weathermen even suggested changing their name to the Vandals.)"[12]

This "barbaric" dehumanization of the existing social structure was not only ideological, it pertained to culture and morality as well. In addition to their previous involvement with the counterculture of drugs and free love, the members of the Weatherman assumed, as a group, a "negative identity," and challenged the normative order of the bourgeois society.[13] They created a new and all-inclusive *Weltanschauung* of their own. Young

[8] Suzan Stern, *With the Weatherman* (Garden City, N.Y.: Doubleday, 1975), 204.

[9] Karin Ashley, Bill Ayers, Bernardine Dohrn, John Jacobs, Jeff Jones, Gerry Long, Howie Machtinger, Jim Mellen, Terry Robbins, Mark Rudd, and Steve Tappis, "You Don't Need a Weatherman to Know Which Way the Wind Blows," in Jacobs, *Weatherman*, 87–90.

[10] See Harold Jacobs, "Inside the Weather Machine: Introduction," in Jacobs, *Weatherman*, 302–3.

[11] Ibid., 345.

[12] Stern, *With the Weatherman*, 114–15.

[13] I find Knutson's concept of "negative identity," which she uses to denote the psychology of the would-be terrorist, extremely useful for the portrayal of the group psychology of the would-be terrorists. See Jeanne N. Knutson, "Social and Psychodynamic Pressures Towards a Negative Identity: The Case of An American Revolutionary Terrorist" in *Behavioral and Quantitative Perspectives on Terrorism*, edited by Yona Alexander and John M. Gleason (New York: Pergamon Press, 1981), chapter 7. See also Martha Crenshaw, "The Psychology of Political Terrorism" in *Political Psychology*, edited by Margaret G. Hermann (San Francisco: Jossey-Bass, 1986), 393.

couples living in "Weather collectives" were required to "smash monogamy" and to reject natural parenthood. The "Weather Bureau" ordered that all female revolutionaries sleep with all male revolutionaries, and vice versa.[14] Women were also to make love to each other. Private relations of love and affection were declared counterrevolutionary, because they represented bourgeois habits.

"Weather" mothers who were suspected of devoting too much time to their babies (born in the course of the "revolution") were told to give the revolution first priority.[15] There were cases in which they were even ordered to give their babies to other, less committed, members of the organization, so that they could devote all of their energies to the cause. Public sessions of self-criticism and collective criticism were frequently held. Persons who could not conform fully to the rigid authoritarian line dictated by the "Bureau" were scolded by the whole group; they were forced to confess and to admit to their mistakes, and were frequently tested for their sincerity. The ordeals of these "deviants" were not stopped even in cases of nervous breakdown.[16] If a terror campaign against the outside world was to start soon, there could be no room for human compassion or exaggerated sensitivity. Everyone had to conform to the "group-think" and to be ready for the revolution.[17]

Perhaps the most bizarre and antinomian act of the Weathermen was the applause they gave to the murder of movie actress Sharon Tate and her friends by Charles Manson and his "family," who tortured their victims and desecrated their bodies. Their slogan, "Helter-Skelter," and their "fork" sign, which were left behind, terrified and haunted

the country. But the Weathermen celebrated the event as an act of liberation of utmost significance. The brutal murder fit their new *Weltanschauung* perfectly. "Almost everybody in the Bureau," wrote Suzan Stern, "ran around saluting people with the fork sign. . . . There was a picture of Sharon Tate on the wall."[18] And in Flint, Michigan, the final assessment of the murder, and the crowning of the new morality of dehumanization, was voiced by Bernardine Dohrn: "Dig it, first they killed those pigs then they ate dinner in the same room with them, then they even shoved a fork in the victim's stomach! Wild!"[19]

The Radicalization of the SDS

What is so intriguing about the activities of the Weatherman, from a historical and theoretical perspective, is not so much the group's antinomian delegitimation of the entire American value system in 1969 but the fact that it was the direct offspring of a student organization, the Students for a Democratic Society (SDS), which in 1962 had constituted itself as a liberal and democratic movement in order to promote the value of a "democracy of individual participation."[20]

It is true that, in its founding manifesto, the Port Huron Statement, the SDS severely criticized the Democratic and Republican parties for being equally insensitive to the cold war, the third world, and racial discrimination at home.[21] But the conclusion of this critique was neither a call for antidemocratic revolution nor a quest for a political system guided by a Leninist party representing the proletariat. Rather, it projected a system of "Two genuine parties, centered around issues and essential values . . . with sufficient party

[14] Larry Grathwol, *Bringing Down America*, 149–50.

[15] Stern, *With the Weatherman*, 187–90.

[16] Ibid., 204.

[17] See Jerrold M. Post (following Janis), "Group and Organizational Dynamics of Political Terrorism: Implications for Counter Terrorist Policy," paper prepared for the International Conference on Terrorism Research, University of Aberdeen, Scotland, 21–23 April 1986, p. 12; and Jeanne N. Knutson, "The Terrorists' Dilemmas: Some Implicit Rules of the Game," *Terrorism: An International Journal* 4 (1980): 211–12.

[18] Stern, *With the Weatherman*, 191.

[19] Jacobs, ed., *Weatherman*, 347.

[20] "SDS: Port Huron Statement," in *The New Left: A Documentary History*, edited by Massimo Teodori (New York: Bobbs-Merrill, 1969), 167. (References to the complete text of the Port Huron Statement are made only when the texts referred to are omitted by Teodori.)

[21] Ibid., 170.

disagreement to dramatize major issues, yet sufficient party overlap to guarantee stable transition from administration to administration."[22] Indeed, the SDS saw itself as a spearhead of a "New Left" concentrated on the American campus. Yet this New Left was very peaceful and nonviolent. It did not try to "outrevolutionize" the Old Left, but to "underrevolutionize" it. Commenting on Marx, Tom Hayden, the cofounder of the SDS, maintained that although "Marx, the humanist, has much to tell us . . . his conceptual tools are outmoded and his final vision implausible."[23] He was equally unhappy with the "non-ideological" thinking of revolutionary leaders of the rising nations such as Che Guevara.[24] Not only did the SDS of the early 1960s reject the traditional solutions of the extreme left of the pre–World War II era, it also refused to grant membership to members of Communist and, in general, "totalitarian" organizations. The SDS constitution declared: "SDS is an organization of democrats. It is civil libertarian in its treatment of those with whom it disagrees, but clear in its opposition to any totalitarian principle as a basis for government or social organization. Advocates or apologists for such a principle are not eligible for membership."[25]

Reflecting the impact of another student organization—the black Student Nonviolent Coordinating Committee (SNCC), an organization that fought for civil rights in the South and thereby became to the SDS a subject of great admiration and respect—the Port Huron Statement insisted on a basic commitment to a philosophy of nonviolence:

> We find violence to be abhorrent because it requires generally the transformation of the target, be it a human being or a community of people, into a depersonalized object of hate. It is imperative that the means of violence be abolished and

the institutions—local, national, international—that encourage nonviolence as a condition of conflict be developed.[26]

The SDS conceived commitment to nonviolence not as a useful tactical means to be applied temporarily against a resourceful and powerful rival but as a normative ethical principle. Violence as a political means was to be abolished because it was basically a dehumanizing pattern of behavior. Politics could do well without violence, and institutions encouraging nonviolence had to be devised. The SDS's commitment to nonviolence was thus fully Congruent with its idealistic vision of the desired performance of liberal democracy as well as with its criticism of the actual performance of this system in the United States.

What happened in the seven years between the creation of the SDS and the rise of the Weatherman was the development of a process of group radicalization in which the SDS first grew into a radical mass movement and then split and shrank. The young, liberal critics of 1962 were swept up by the events of their stormy decade to an extent that neither they nor others thought possible. And in 1969 they themselves were left behind by a second generation of radicals that they had helped socialize into the politics of protest. A retrospective examination of two dimensions of this process of radicalization, the acts and practices of the radicals, on the one hand, and their symbolic behavior and rhetoric, on the other, is highly revealing.[27] It illustrates the collective psychopolitical process that turns some young, educated, sensitive human beings into tough revolutionaries and brutal killers.

As early as 1963, the young theoreticians of the New Left started to refer to their activities as "insurgent politics" and to refer to themselves as

[22] *The Port Huron Statement* (New York: SDS Pamphlet, 1964), 46–7.
[23] Thomas Hayden, "A Letter to the New (Young) Left," in *The New Student Left*, edited by M. Cohen and D. Hale (Boston: Beacon Press, 1968), 3.
[24] Ibid.
[25] "SDS Constitution" (mimeographed pamphlet, 1963).
[26] "SDS: Port Huron Statement," in Teodori, *The New Left*, 168.
[27] The methodological justification for the emphasis on these two behavioral dimensions as indexes of delegitimation cannot be developed here in greater detail. It can be found in E. Sprinzak, "Democracy and Illegitimacy: A Study of the American and the French Student Protest Movements and Some Theoretical Implications" (Ph.D. dissertation, Yale University, 1972).

"new insurgents."[28] Recalling methods used by the civil rights and peace movements—sit-ins, protests, and demonstrations—they tried to identify types of political action that would defy the rules of the prevailing American game without being illegal. At the same time, these New Left theoreticians started to refer to the system against which they were protesting as "corporate liberalism."[29] They frequently repeated the phrase introduced by President Eisenhower and used in the Port Huron Statement, "the military-industrial complex."[30] In addition, as a result of their bitter experiences with the most brutal representatives of American authority—particularly the sheriffs of the South— the activists of the New Left started to see "participatory democracy" as an alternative type of democracy, thereby rejecting party and interest group politics.[31] This tendency greatly deepened in the summer of 1964, when young radicals failed to unseat the official Mississippi delegation to the Democratic National Convention held in Atlantic City. Having demonstrated the discriminatory practices of the official Democratic party of Mississippi, they came to the convention with the duly elected Mississippi Freedom and Democratic party (MFDP) as an alternative delegation; but the new party was rejected by the convention.[32]

Soon after, in February 1965, the United States began bombing North Vietnam. The SDS, already a radical organization, was discovered by many disenchanted students. It quickly tripled its membership and became the most vocal opponent of the war and the spearhead of the emerging antiwar movement. It was at this time of intense protest that the language and mentality of delegitimation first entered the vocabulary of the New Left, making its appearance in a discussion of the meaning of revolution in an article by Staughton Lynd, a historian and self-styled ideologue of the New Left:

> So long as a revolution is pictured as a violent insurrection, it seems to me both distasteful and unreal. The traditional alternative, the social Democratic vision of electing more and more radical legislators until power passes peacefully to the left, seems equally illusory. However, the events of the past year—the creation of the MFDP and the protest against the war in Vietnam— suggest a third strategy. One can now begin to envision a series of nonviolent protests which would, from the beginning, question the legitimacy of the Administration's authority where it has gone beyond constitutional and moral limits and might, if this insane foreign policy continues, culminate in the decisions of hundreds of thousands of people to recognize the authority of alternative institutions of their own making.[33]

Although Lynd cautiously avoided a comprehensive presentation of the system as illegitimate and did not attack democracy in principle, he went beyond the charge that the government was acting unconstitutionally. He argued that it was immoral and insane and suggested that the charges of unconstitutionality and immorality could be first steps in questioning the legitimacy of the administration's authority. These first steps could then lead to the recognition of alternative (legitimate) institutions. What Lynd did, apart from his explicit argument, was to introduce the terminology and imagery of delegitimation into the "groupthink" of the New Left.

Tom Hayden, former president of the SDS, presented the case for alternative institutions in even stronger terms:

> The Movement is a community of insurgents sharing the same radical values and identity, seeking

---

[28] "SDS: America and New Era," in Teodori, ed., *The New Left*, 180–2.

[29] This image was coined by the editorial board of *Studies On the Left*, a New Left journal. See James P. O'Brien, "The Development of a New Left in the United States 1960–1965" (Ph.D. dissertation, University of Wisconsin, 1971), 237.

[30] *The Port Huron Statement*, 17.

[31] See Staughton Lynd, "The New Radicals and Participatory Democracy," *Dissent* (Summer 1965).

[32] The MFDP was offered by the Credentials Committee of the Democratic Party two "delegates-at-large," an offer that was bluntly rejected. The story of the conflict regarding the MFDP can be found in *Black Power: the Politics of Liberation in America*, edited by Stokely Carmichael and Charles V. Hamilton (New York: Random House, 1967), 86–97.

[33] Staughton Lynd, "Coalition Politics or Nonviolent Revolution," in Teodori, ed., *The New Left*, 199.

an independent base of power wherever they are. It aims at a transformation of society led by the most excluded and unqualified people. Primarily, this means building institutions outside the established order which seek to become the genuine institutions of the total society: community unions, freedom schools, experimental universities, community-formed policy review boards, people's own antipoverty organizations fighting the federal money.... Ultimately, this movement might lead to a continental congress called by all the people who feel excluded from the higher circles of decision making in the country.[34]

The New Left was a movement motivated and directed by students, and these students' growing sense that the prevailing political authorities lacked legitimacy inevitably affected their attitude toward academic authorities, whom they came to view as part of the same system against which they were protesting.[35] In the fall of 1964, student activists of the Free Speech Movement (FSM) at Berkeley, many of whom had participated in earlier civil rights actions in the South, sent shock waves through the American academic world when they took over the administration building at their university. Mario Savio, one of the leaders of the FSM, stated clearly that what was happening in Mississippi was closely connected with what was going on at Berkeley:

> In Mississippi an autocratic and powerful minority rules, through organized violence, to suppress the vast, virtually powerless, majority. In California, the privileged minority manipulates the university bureaucracy to suppress the students' political expression. That "respectable" bureaucracy masks the financial plutocrats; that impersonal bureaucracy is the efficient enemy in a "Brave New World."[36]

The SDS soon issued a demand for "student power."[37] This demand signaled a growing split with the academic authorities in the universities and reflected another process of radicalization taking place in the United States, a process experienced by the black liberation movement. The SNCC had also become radicalized. In 1966 it had dropped its previous liberal identity and its commitment to nonviolence in order to become a militant antigovernment organization. It now adopted "black power" as its slogan and developed an ideology of national liberation.[38] The government of the United States was presented as an illegitimate "colonial" ruler, necessitating an "anticolonial struggle" of the "black colonies."

At its 1965 national convention, the SDS dropped from its constitution the "exclusionist" clause that had denied eligibility for membership to "advocates or apologists" of "totalitarian principle." It did so because of its growing conflict with the political system responsible for the intervention in Vietnam and because of its need to join forces with those who shared with it the psychology of resistance.[39] Members of the Maoist Progressive Labor party (PLP) were now eligible for SDS membership. They streamed in, formally accepting the idea of "participatory democracy" but intending to take control of the SDS and bend it in their direction. The Maoists soon started a "Marxization" of the organization. Many SDS veterans were aware of the PLP's takeover intentions and were highly resentful of the whole process. They could not, however, resist the growing pressure from the local branches of their loose organization to implement these changes.[40] They

---

[34] Tom Hayden, "The Politics of the Movement," *Dissent* (January–February 1960): 87.

[35] For a good analysis of the emergence of the student movement, see Michael Miles, *The Radical Probe* (New York: Atheneum, 1971), 88–108.

[36] Mario Savio, "An End to History," in *The Berkeley Student Revolt*, edited by S. M. Lipset and S. S. Wolin (New York: Doubleday, 1965), 216.

[37] Karl Davidson, "Toward Student Syndicalism," *New Left Notes*, 9 September 1966.

[38] *Black Power, SNCC Speaks for Itself: A Collection of Statements and Interviews* (Boston: New England Free Press, 1966).

[39] On the issue of nonexclusionism, see Alan Haber, "Nonexclusionism: The New Left and the Democratic Left," in Teodori, ed., *The New Left*, 218–28.

[40] For an analysis of the struggles within SDS, see Andrew Kopkind, "The Real SDS Stands Up," in Jacobs, ed., *Weatherman*, 15–28.

were especially helpless against the delegitimating magic of the Marxist ideological categories, which were now so appealing. Convinced that the system was structurally corrupt, these veterans themselves searched independently for a new, symbolic frame of reference that would express their sense of delegitimation toward the regime without succumbing to the growing pressures of the PLP.

Early in 1967, an influential group within the SDS published a paper titled "Towards a Theory of Social Change in America," in which a theory of the "new working class" was formulated.[41] Gregory Calvert, the president of SDS, elaborated this new theory in a speech at Princeton University. He suggested that students were themselves part of a "new working class," created and exploited by "this super-technological capitalism."[42] The former image of "corporate liberalism" was replaced by "corporate capitalism." ("American corporate capitalism is an incredibly brutal and dehumanizing system whether at home or abroad.") The system was challenged not by "new insurgents" and "alternative institutions" but by the working class heading toward revolution. At the core of the new theory was the idea that modern society had created a new proletariat composed of middle-class and professional workers. This "new working class" was presented as a class not because of its relation to the means of production but because of conditions of "unfreedom" in society, conditions affecting deprived minorities, high-salaried, middle-class professionals, and students living in "factory-like multiversities."[43]

The new theory, and especially its conceptualization of a "new working class," had little relation to classical Marxism and no empirical support. How could one seriously create a class out of such diverse groups and believe that such a class could carry out a revolution? To be sure, Marxist concepts were, as Tom Hayden had noted in 1962,

"outmoded" for diagnosing the American social, economic, and political realities. But in 1967 and 1968, the New Left did not need an analytically valid and reliable social theory. It needed, instead, a cultural system of symbols expressing its deep psychopolitical rejection of the established order. It was in the right mental state to adopt a new ideological master-key that would sanction a moral disengagement from the entire American way of life. In the late 1960s, Marxism had become such a master-key. It provided a framework for a rebellious "groupthink."[44] When, in the summer of 1969, the SDS split into three factions—each adhering to a different tactical and strategic perspective—they all had one thing in common: they presented their case in militant Marxist language directed at a discredited and illegitimate political system.[45]

The Marxization of many segments within the New Left betokened a principled delegitimation of liberal democracy. But this symbolic transformation was not used to justify illegal behavior and violence. Draft card burning, for example, was presented in the courts as a constitutional act falling within the First Amendment.[46] The practices of confrontation with public authorities and the police, extolled by the SDS and other radical groups after 1967, also were not clear cases of illegal action. They were an extreme application of earlier tactics of direct action.[47] If intensive violence occurred—and it did occur increasingly after 1967—it was usually not planned in advance but was a result of the interaction between impatient police and passionate demonstrators.

---

[41] David Gilbert, Robert Gottlieb, and Gerry Tenny, "Toward a Theory of Social Change," *New Left Notes*, 23 January 1967.
[42] Gregory Calvert, "In White America: Radical Consciousness and Social Change," in Teodori, ed., *The New Left*, 417.
[43] Ibid., 415.

[44] See Ehud Sprinzak, "Marxism As a Symbolic Action," in *Varieties of Marxism*, edited by Shlomo Avineri (The Hague: Martinus Neijhof, 1977). See also Edward E. Ericson, Jr., *Radicals in the University* (Stanford: Hoover Institution Press, 1975), 28–34.
[45] See *Debate Within SDS* (Detroit: Radical Education Project pamphlet, Summer 1969).
[46] Lawrence R. Velvel, "Freedom of Speech and the Draft Card Burning Cases," *Kansas Law Review* 16 (1968).
[47] See J. H. Skolnick, *The Politics of Protest* (New York: Ballantine Books, 1969), 106–9.

But the experience of low-grade violence, and the intensive use of symbols of delegitimation, have their own logic of incremental development.[48] The tactics of confrontation were soon supplemented by the bombings of induction centers. The radical Black Panthers, who armed themselves heavily and fought the police fiercely, provided an attractive model to follow. They also produced an immense sense of guilt in the hearts of the young radicals, who believed in the same cause but did not get the same brutal treatment from the authorities. Also important was the "urban guerrilla" model provided by then Tupamaros in Uruguay.[49] It remained for the Weatherman leaders, the second generation of the SDS who were politically socialized by the violent confrontations of the previous three years, to bring the process to its peak. This process—a psycho-political crisis of legitimacy—was marked by a syndrome consisting of four components: (1) a political language of delegitimation of the regime, (2) rhetoric and symbols of depersonalization and dehumanization of individuals belonging to the system, (3) intended and planned violence, and (4) terrorism.

As a terror underground the Weatherman was a failure. It did not succeed, as the Red Army Faction did in West Germany, to shock an entire country. It was unable, as the Italian Red Brigades were able, to hold up a modern society at gun point. In fact, it never recruited more than four hundred members and followers, and most of the time its inexperienced leaders and recruits worried not about the revolution but about their hideouts, survival logistics, and internal group relations. Although the organization was responsible for dozens of bombings in 1970—and scored some spectacular successes, such as the explosions that took place in the Capitol, the Pentagon, and New York police headquarters—its greatest damage

was self-inflicted: three leaders of the organization blew themselves up in a New York townhouse while manufacturing a bomb.[50] Despite the Weatherman's high-revolutionary rhetoric, its young leaders never recovered from this loss; the accident greatly diminished their enthusiasm for terrorism.[51] In their last public document, *Prairie Fire*, published in 1974, Weatherman leaders restated their revolutionary commitment to armed struggle and took credit for twenty explosions and other operations initiated over the previous years.[52] But they admitted, at the same time, that very little had been achieved in the United States and that a long and protracted world struggle was still ahead. Nothing of significance has been heard from them since.

The Formation of Ideological Terrorism: Some General Conclusions

What is the theoretical lesson to be drawn from this developmental analysis of the Weatherman? What can be learned from a comparative observation of similar New Left terror organizations in Europe and Japan that emerged in the 1960s and operated mainly in the 1970s? Is it possible to identify some universal behavior patterns that govern the rich historical context of ideological terrorism in a democracy? Can we make some general sense of the political psychology of ideological terrorism?

All these questions can be answered constructively if the two most significant observations emerging from fifteen years of terrorism research are taken into consideration:

1. Terrorism is neither a sui generis plague that comes from nowhere, nor an inexplicable, random strike against humanity.

---

[48] See Albert Bandura, "Social Learning Theory of Aggression," in *The Control of Aggression: Implications from Basic Research*, edited by John F. Knutson (New York: Hawthorn, 1973).

[49] Stuart Daniels, "The Weatherman," *Government and Opposition* 9 (1974): 449–51.

[50] See *The Weather Underground: Report of the Subcommittee to Investigate the Administration of the Internal Security Act and Other Internal Security Laws of the Committee on the judiciary, United States Senate*, January 1975, 133.

[51] Daniels, "The Weatherman," 445.

[52] *Prairie Fire*, an underground document, 1974.

2. Terrorism is not the product of mentally deranged persons.

Terrorism, and ideological terrorism in particular, is a political phenomenon par excellence and is therefore explicable in political terms. It is an extension of opposition politics in democracy, a special case of an ideological conflict of authority. It is, furthermore, the behavioral product of a prolonged process of delegitimation of the established society or the regime—a process whose beginning is, almost always, nonviolent and nonterroristic. In the main, the process does *not* involve isolated individuals who become terrorists on their own because their psyche is split or they suffer from low esteem and need extravagant compensation.[53] Rather, it involves a group of true believers who challenge authority long before they become terrorists, recruit followers, clash with the public agencies of law enforcement from a position of weakness, obtain a distinct collective world view, and, in time, radicalize within the organization to the point of becoming terroristic. The terrorist collectivity is almost always an elite group that is headed by well-educated middle-class or upper-middle-class young people, usually college students or dropouts.[54]

Although neither supernatural nor rationally inexplicable, the process that leads to ideological terrorism is nevertheless extraordinary, because for the people concerned it involves a remarkable personal and political transformation. An understanding of this group process and its painful developmental stages seems to be much more

important than an understanding of the individual terrorists' personal psychology.[55] This understanding of the evolutionary group psychology to terrorists seems crucial for the explanation of the ease with which young, educated, middle-class, normal people with no previous experience with violence are able to desecrate all of the norms of organized society, commit the worst atrocities, and feel good about it all.

The experience of the Weatherman organization shows that the process of delegitimation, through which ideological terrorism is formed, can be divided into three stages: (1) crisis of confidence, (2) conflict of legitimacy, and (3) crisis of legitimacy. Each of these stages identifies a particular collective psychopolitical identity reached by an ideologically motivated group. This group identity, which changes rapidly as radicalization proceeds, contains a combination of political-behavioral components, ideological and symbolic tenets, and psychological traits. It appears that, as radicalization deepens, the collective group identity takes over much of the individual identity of the members; and, at the terrorist stage, the group identity reaches it peak.[56] The individual terrorists may not lose their former identity, but their actual behavior can best be explained by the psychology of the larger group.

If this analysis is correct, then the study of ideological terrorism, including its psychological dimension, can proceed fruitfully without clinical interviews (which are, in any case, very hard to obtain). If much of the terrorist's activity is determined by group identity, an empirical examination of the following two variables may help a great deal:

1. The changing symbolic behavior of the activists involved—the ways in which they talk, categor-

[53] This statement should not be mistaken for the claim that individuals are drawn to the terrorist organization at random. Studies in the psychology of terrorism have shown certain peculiar commonalities among terrorists; see Jerrold M. Post, "Notes on a Psychodynamic Theory of Terrorist Behavior," *Terrorism: An International Journal 7.* no. 3 (1984): 244–6. The argument is that these peculiarities *do not explain* the phenomenon of terrorism.

[54] For a comprehensive summary of the sociopsychology of radical students and young intellectuals, see Christopher A. Roots, "Student Radicalism: Politics of Moral Protest and Legitimation Problems of the Modern Capitalist State," *Theory and Society 9* (1980).

[55] According to Jerrold M. Post. "The predominant determinant of terrorist action is the internal dynamic of the terrorist group"; see Post, "Group and Organizational Dynamics," p. 16. See also Crenshaw, "The Psychology of Political Terrorism," pp. 395–400; and Abraham Kaplan, "The Psychodynamics of Terrorism," *Terrorism: An International Journal* 1, no. 3/4 (1978): 248.

[56] See Knutson, "The Terrorists' Dilemmas," 212–15.

ize, theorize, and stigmatize the world, both their own and that of the enemy[57]

2. The changing political and legal behavior of the activists involved—the ways in which they interact with the prevailing political and legal system.

An examination of the interplay of these two dimensions helps to identify the general features of the three stages of the process of delegitimation.

Crisis of confidence is the psychopolitical stage reached by a movement, or a challenge group, whose confidence in the existing political government is greatly eroded. Crisis of confidence implies a conflict with specific rulers or policies. It does not presume a structural delegitimation because, at this stage, the foundations of the established political system are not yet questioned or challenged. In many cases, crisis of confidence involves an angry critique of the established authorities or rulers from the very ideological assumptions on which the regime itself is founded. The existing "masters" are projected as wrong not because of some fundamental faults in the system itself but because of their own misleading behavior or misguided policies.

Although a crisis of confidence does not indicate a complete ideological break with the powers that be, it nevertheless represents a profound conflict with what is seen as "the establishment" and goes far beyond ordinary political opposition.

From an empirical perspective, the crisis of confidence is marked by the appearance of an enraged ideological challenge group (or movement, or counterculture) that refuses to play according to the established political rules of the game. The group will usually articulate its critique of the establishment in ideological terms, will dissent from mainstream politics, and will engage in protests, demonstrations, symbolic resistance, and other forms of "direct action."[58] Although not illegal, its behavior, group mentality, and language are likely to be countersystemic. Early confrontations with the authorities and the police, including small-scale and unplanned violence, are very likely.

Conflict of legitimacy is the radicalized continuation of the crisis of confidence. It is the behavioral stage that evolves when a challenge group previously engaged in antigovernment criticism is ready to question the very legitimacy of the whole system. Conflict of legitimacy emerges when the challenge group discovers that the erroneous rulers are able to "mislead the people" not because they shrewdly manipulate the otherwise benign system but because the system itself is manipulative and repressive. The way to do away with the oppressive rulers is to transform the system altogether. Conflict of legitimacy implies the emergence of an alternative ideological and cultural system, one that delegitimates the prevailing regime and its code of social norms in the name of a better one.

The conflict of legitimacy is usually precipitated by a great disappointment on the part of the challenge group with its previous stage of radicalization. The formerly "moderate" radicals are frustrated either by the government's hostile (and sometimes excessively violent) response to their passionate critique or by their own failure to score successes. They develop a need to channel their frustration into a more extreme form of protest. What follows is the development of an ideology of delegitimation, which articulates a break with the

[57] For a general theoretical elaboration on the meaning of symbolic behavior in politics see Murray Edelman, *Politics as Symbolic Action* (Chicago: Markham Publishing Co., 1971). For attempts to read the terrorists' minds through their own words and expressions, see Konrad Kellen, "Terrorists: What Are They Like? How Some Terrorists Describe Their World and Actions," in *Terrorism and Beyond: An International Conference on Terrorism and Low-Level Conflict*, edited by Brian Jenkins (Santa Monica: Rand Corporation, 1982); Bonnie Cordes, "Euroterrorists Talk About Themselves: A Look at the Literature," paper delivered at the International Conference on Terrorism Research, University of Aberdeen, Scotland, 15–17 April 1986; David C. Rapoport, "The World as Terrorist Leaders See It: A Look at the Memoirs," paper delivered at the American Political Science Association convention, 28–31 August 1986, Hilton Hotel, Washington, D.C.

[58] See April Carter, *Direct Action and Liberal Democracy* (New York: Harper and Row, 1973), 26–7; Donald Light, Jr., John Spiegel, et al., *The Dynamics of University Protest* (Chicago: Nelson-Hall Publishers, 1977), chapter 4.

prevailing political order.[59] The new frame of reference is, in most cases, an already-existing ideology. Very few radicals are capable, during their intense process of delegitimation, of developing a new system of critical thought that fits the new situation analytically and empirically. It is much easier to take over an existing ideology of delegitimation (such as Marxism, Maoism, or third-world Trotskyism) and to believe that it is relevant to the situation at hand. It is of some interest that the ideology adopted need not be foreign. If the national culture of the country involved contains historical images of successful revolutions (such as the French or the American), these images may be rediscovered and reused with great effectiveness.

The evolution of the conflict of legitimacy is marked not only by ideological, symbolic, and psychological changes, but also by intense political action that ranges from angry protest (demonstrations, confrontations, and vandalism) to the application of small-scale violence against the regime.[60] The challenge group or the movement, which is the concrete collective carrier of the conflict of legitimacy, lives now in a stage of intense radicalization. It solidifies itself and closes ranks. The individuals involved are totally consumed by the great moments and emotionally change a great deal. Their language and rhetoric—which is the expression of their inner collective identity—is revolutionary, and their jargon is full of slanders and desecrations.

Crisis of legitimacy is the behavioral and symbolic culmination of the two preceding psychopolitical stages. Its essence lies in the extension of the previous delegitimation of the system to every person associated with it. Individuals who are identified with the rotten, and soon-to-be-destroyed, social and political order are depersonalized and dehumanized. They are derogated to the ranks of subhuman species. Dehumanization makes it possible for the radicals to be disengaged morally and to commit atrocities without a second thought. It bifurcates the world into the sons of light and the sons of darkness, and makes the "fantasy war" of the former versus the latter fully legitimate.[61] It makes the few radicals who have made it to the third stage of the process of delegitimation, usually a second generation of radicals, accomplished terrorists. Each person who belongs to the establishment, or who is perceived as belonging to it, becomes a potential target for assassination or indiscriminate murder.

The first external indication of the evolution of the crisis of legitimacy is linguistic and symbolic. Expressions of political delegitimation are no longer limited to political terms or social concepts but are extended to a language of objects, animals, or "human" animals. The regime and its accomplices are now portrayed as "things," "dogs," "pigs," "Nazis," or "terrorists." The portrayal is not accidental and occasional but repeated and systematic. It is part of a new lexicon. The "pigs," "Nazis," or "terrorist lackeys" can be killed or eliminated because they are, by definition, not human and do not belong to the legitimate community of "the people."

The crisis of legitimacy—which brings together all of the earlier clusters of the process of radicalization—presupposes an acute stage of psychological transformation. The group that undergoes this profound mental change often displays antinomian behavior.[62] Its members free themselves from the yoke of conventional morality and engage in sexual perversity, excessive drug orgies, and criminality of many forms. The boundaries between political and personal illegality are totally removed, and certain forms of deviant behavior are hailed as

---

[59] See Sprinzak, "Marxism as a Symbolic Action."

[60] See Carter, *Direct Action*, 74–7; and Rob Kroes, "Violence in America: Spontaneity and Strategy," in *Urban Guerilla*, edited by Joane Niezing (Rotterdam: Rotterdam University Press, 1974), 82–7.

[61] Franco Ferracuti, "A Sociopsychiatric Interpretation of Terrorism," *Annals of the American Academy of Sciences* 463 (September 1982): 136–7.

[62] For the relationships between terrorism and antinomian ethos in messianic and millenarian movements, see David C. Rapoport, "Why Does Messianism Produce Terror?" paper presented at the American Political Science Association meeting, New Orleans, 27 August—1 September 1985, 12–13.

right and even sacred. A new revolutionary morality emerges, and an antinomian *Weltanschauung* is articulated.

The political manifestation of the crisis of legitimacy is strategic terrorism. It consists of the formation of a small terror underground that engages in unconventional attacks on the regime and its affiliates and that is capable of committing a wide range of atrocities. As a social unit, the terrorist underground is isolated from the outside world. It constructs a reality of its own and a whole new set of behavioral and moral standards that are strictly enforced. The members of the group are so involved with each other that every individual act has a collective meaning of utmost importance. The psychodynamics of the whole unit, including its acts of terrorism against the outside society, assume an internally consistent logic that may be unrelated to external factors.[63] Very few of the terrorists who reach the crisis of legitimacy, and are fully consumed by it, are capable of reversing their radicalization to the point of returning to normal life. Their immense personal transformation—which, in many cases, leads them to nihilism, despair, and extreme fear of the group's punishment—may drive them to suicide.

Although all three stages of the process of delegitimation can be seen in most modern ideological terrorist organizations, they need not be. First, groups may not develop beyond the first or second stage. And even if a group does move through all these stages, individual members of that group may not.

It is important to recognize that the conditions that promote the evolution of ideological terrorism are very different from the conditions that promote the evolution of protest and extraparliamentary politics. Most modern societies experience, at some time, some form of a crisis of confidence.

The accepted repertoire of political action of modern democracy includes extraparliamentary politics of different types. The growing literature on collective and political action is full of cases and useful examples of such politics.[64] Even groups that delegitimate each other often coexist. Communists, third-world Marxists, extreme neofascists, and religious fanatics coexist in the margins of most modern societies. Many of them are engaged in one or another form of antigovernment action or are waiting for the opportunity to do so. For ideological terrorism to develop, another set of conditions is required. It is one that entails a perception of harsh governmental repression, and a profound disillusionment (as well as a sense of guilt) among idealistic and young middle-class intelligentsia regarding society and their role in it.[65] External models of revolt and terrorism also must be available.[66] The New Left terrorism that emerged in the late 1960s doubtless could not have come to existence without two critical historical conditions: the disillusionment with the war in Vietnam and the attractive models of terrorism and the urban guerrilla that developed after 1950 in the third world.

Despite the image of a widespread New Left terrorism that prevailed in the 1970s, it is important to remember that even at that time ideological terrorism was the exception rather than the rule. Most processes of delegitimation never reach the full maturation necessary for the formation of terrorism.

---

[63] See Jerrold M. Post, "Notes on a Psychodynamic: Theory," 250–3; Knutson, "The Terrorists' Dilemmas," 211–5; Crenshaw, "The Psychology of Political Terrorism," 395–400; Fred and Phyllis Wright, "Violent Groups," *Group 6*, no. 2 (Summer 1982): 31–4.

[64] See Carter, *Direction Action*; E. N. Muller, *Aggressive Political Participation* (Princeton, N.J.: Princeton University Press, 1979); Neil Smelser, *Theory of Collective Behavior* (New York; Free Press, 1962); Charles Tilly, *From Mobilization to Revolution* (Reading. Pa.: Addison-Wesley, 1978).

[65] For an excellent discussion of the conditions for terrorism, see Martha Crenshaw, "The Causes of Terrorism," *Comparative Politics* 13 (July 1981).

[66] Students of terrorism discuss this issue in relation to the "contagion" of terrorism; see Manu I. Midlarsky, Martha Crenshaw, and Fumihico Yoshida, "Why Violence Spreads," *International Studies Quarterly* 24 (June 1980); Kent Layne Oots and Thomas C. Weigele, "Terrorist and Victim: Psychiatric and Physiological Approaches From a Social Science Perspective," *Terrorism: An International Journal 8*, no. 1 (1985): 8–13.

It is also important to recognize that radicalization is a demanding and dangerous process. The radicals are always outnumbered. The more violent they become, the harsher the official reaction is likely to be. In addition to the forceful response of the police and the military—which in most cases outbrutalizes the brutality of the inexperienced activists—the society around them is likely to remain unmoved and hostile. Very few radicals, who usually come from the second generation that was socialized directly to the "conflict of legitimacy," are capable of becoming terrorists and of adhering to terrorism over a long period of time.[67] Those who do display either reckless optimism or profound pessimism and helplessness. Terrorism is violent, cruel, antinomian, and, most of all, deadly. People get killed or mutilated. For the radicals involved, just as for their victims, this is by far the most dangerous form of political action or warfare.

Most of the radicals who do not achieve the stage of terrorism stay at the psychopolitical level of the crisis of confidence or at the level of the conflict of legitimacy. It is thus possible to distinguish between the avant garde of the process of delegitimation—the terrorists—and the rear-guard, the great number of the other radicals who remain behind.[68] The terrorists are usually scornful and critical of the rearguard. They see themselves as the *crème de la crème* of the revolution and perceive the others as fakes or failures. But politically and operationally they need the rearguard a great deal. No terror underground is capable of sustaining itself without a nonterrorist support system—friends and accomplices who provide information, hideouts, escape routes, and supplies. To the degree that the New Left terrorists were able to survive, they did it with the support of the less-committed rearguardists.

Ideological terrorism does not emerge from a vacuum or from an inexplicable urge on the part of a few unstable radicals to go berserk. Rather, it is the psychopolitical product of a profound process of delegitimation that a large number of people undergo in relation to the established social and political order. Although most of the participants in this process are capable of preserving their sense of reality, a few are not. Totally consumed by their radicalism, they imagine a nonexistent "fantasy war" with the authorities and expend themselves in the struggle to win it. Idological terrorism, in the final analysis, is the simulated revolution of the isolated few.

---

[67] See Crenshaw, "The Psychology of Political Terrorism," 398–9.

[68] For the development of the distinction between the avant garde of the process of delegitimation and its rearguard, see Sprinzak, *Democracy and Illegitimacy*, chapter 7.

Social Psychology of Terrorist Groups

Clark R. McCauley and Mary E. Segal

Every year, hundreds of terrorist incidents occur around the world. Some, like the 1985 Palestinian hijacking of a TWA jet airliner, create international crises as the television cameras roll. Others, the work of obscure groups with causes we perceive dimly or not at all, receive barely a squib in the morning newspaper. The tactics are now familiar: bombings, hijackings, seizure of embassies, kidnappings, and assassinations. Terrorist activity appears to be increasing steadily (Cordes et al., 1984, p. 46), and although governments have scored some important gains, terrorism has proved remarkably resistant to efforts to control it.

It is often said that one man's terrorist is another man's freedom fighter. For instance, do their gasoline "necklaces" make the African National Congress a terrorist organization? Schmid (1983, p. 6–158) has reviewed the complexities of distinguishing terrorism from violence, anarchism, guerrilla warfare, and crime; here we (somewhat arbitrarily) adopt the following definition: The use or threat of violence, by small groups against non-combatants of large groups, for avowed political goals (see Kellen, 1979, p. 9). We restrict our analysis to what Laqueur (1977, p. 7) has called terrorism "from below," that is, concerned with grievances or ideologies opposed to the existing state, as distinct from state-directed terrorism imposed on citizens from above. Although state-directed terrorism is certainly the larger contributor to human misery, its understanding calls for a psychology of bureaucracy substantially different from the social psychology of terrorism from below.

Our survey of the literature suggests that a central aspect of terrorist activity is often largely ignored: Terrorism is a *group* phenomenon. Terrorist organizations are not just collections of separate individuals: they are functioning units that exert strong pressures on their members and hold out powerful rewards. In this chapter, we examine data and theory from three areas of research relevant to the social psychology of terrorist groups: religious conversion to cults, extremity shift of group opinions, and individual extremity shift in obedience studies. First, we present an overview of what is known about terrorist groups and their members, and then demonstrate how a social psychological framework can be useful in the analysis of terrorist behavior.

Not surprisingly, most of the literature on terrorist groups and their members is recent, and Laqueur's (1977) already-classic work is one of the oldest in the field. This is because terrorism has emerged only during the last several years as a pressing issue among industrialized nations; a quantitative escalation of terrorist violence has been accompanied by increasingly more lethal and less discriminant choices of targets (Cordes et al., 1984, p. vi). In addition to its immaturity, the literature suffers from methodological constraints: Obvious hazards preclude original field studies; content analyses of terrorists' public declarations are more revealing of what terrorists wish us to think than of the reality of their experiences; and post hoc interviews with ex-terrorists are problematic in terms of subjects' selective and reconstructive recall. Nevertheless, the beginnings of a consensus appear to be emerging in the description of terrorist groups and their members.

Terrorists as Individuals

A few demographic generalizations can be made with confidence, among them the fact that terrorists are predominantely male (Laqueur, 1977. p. 121; Russell & Miller, 1983). Exceptions include the nineteenth-century Russian terrorists, in which one-quarter of the membership was composed of women, and the Baader-Meinhof group, in which one-third of the operational personnel were women. Although a few other groups have included a woman in a position of leadership, these are isolated cases; in general, women have tended to occupy secondary support roles at the periphery of the organizations (for an interesting discussion of women as terrorists, see Georges-Abeyie, 1983).

Terrorists are also young, usually in their (often early) twenties, although leaders may be in their thirties and older (Russell & Miller, 1983; Laqueur, 1977, p. 120). Most terrorists come from middle-class or professional families. Many have at least some university education; indeed, nineteenth-century Russian, as well as contemporary West German, Italian, United States, Japanese, and Uruguayan terrorist movements have been direct outgrowths of student unrest (Crenshaw, 1981). Sixty-five percent of the Baader-Meinhof group has been estimated to be middle class; 80% had at least some university training (Russell & Miller, 1983). Similar profiles are characteristic of Japanese and U.S. terrorist groups, which have included a large number of university dropouts (Laqueur, 1977, p. 123). In Turkish, Iranian, and Palestinian terrorist groups, the great majority are middle- and upper-class students and professionals. South American terrorist groups follow a similar pattern: The Argentinian ERP and Monton-

eros were both middle class (with some working class in the latter); the urban terrorists active in Venezuela in the early 1960s were predominately students; and 90% of the Tupamaros in Uruguay were middle and upper-class students and young professionals. (Sec Table 19.1 for explication of ERP and later abbreviations of the names of terrorist groups.) Crenshaw (1985) notes that the leader of the Shining Path organization in Peru is a former philosophy professor, and that the entire movement was first a product of the university, and only later enlisted peasant support. The Italian Red Brigade appears to be an exception to the general rule, as it was at least initially composed mainly of working class members (Laqueur, 1977, p. 211).

Post (1985) has made an interesting distinction between two types of terrorists: the "anarchic-ideologues" and the "nationalist-separatists." The former are committed to the overthrow of the government and social order that are supported by their parents (examples are the German Red Army Faction and the Italian Red Brigade), while the latter attempt to redress grievances held against the prevailing order by their parents (e.g., the Basque ETA and the Armenian ASALA). In general, nationalist-separatist groups appear to draw more heavily on the working class for membership than do anarchic-ideologue groups. The FLN in Algeria were mostly of modest means from small towns and villages; many had been in the French army (Hutchinson, 1978, p. 7). Forty percent of the

TABLE 19.1. Abbreviations of Names of Terrorist Groups

Armenian ASALA	Armenian Secret Army for the Liberation of Armenia
Argentinian ERP	People's Revolutionary Army
Basque ETA	Euzkadi Ta Askatasuna
Algerian FLN	National Liberation Front (Front de Liberation Nationale)
Canadian FLQ	Quebec Liberation Front (Front de Liberation du Quebec)
Irish IRA	Irish Republican Army
Palestinian PFLP	Popular Front for the Liberation of Palestine
German RAF	Red Army Faction

Basque ETA have some university training (Russell & Miller, 1983), but this figure is considerably lower than those reported for anarchic-ideologue groups such as the Baader-Meinhof (80%) or the Tupamaros (75%). The IRA are predominantly members of the working and lower-middle classes (Laqueur, 1977, p. 119). As noted above, the Palestinians provide at least one exception to this generalization.

Thus, terrorists can be demographically characterized as male, young, and middle or professional class (with more working-class members represented in nationalist-separatist groups). Psychological generalizations are more elusive. Perhaps the best-documented generalization is negative; Terrorists do not show any striking psychopathology (Post, 1985). According to Crenshaw (1981, p. 390), "the outstanding common characteristic of terrorists is their normality." Potential recruits into terrorist organizations who seem to be merely seeking danger and excitement are not encouraged. Laqueur (1977, p. 121) notes that the nineteenth-century Russian terrorists were in general balanced, normal people. Hutchinson (1978, p. 142) points out that in the FLN in Algeria during the 1950s, "terrorism was basically a reasonable and considered political choice," and terrorists were, on the whole, normal people. Members of the IRA in Northern Ireland do not appear to be clinically disturbed by any measure (Heskin, 1984).

Further evidence of terrorists' lack of overt psychopathology is found in reports of their ambivalence toward the human suffering caused by their violent actions (Knutson, 1981). Burton (1978; quoted in Heskin, 1984) suggests that depression, self-doubt, and guilt are not uncommon among IRA activists. The Red Army Faction leader Ulrike Meinhof was terrified of guns (Demaris, 1977, p. 220). Crenshaw (1986) notes the PFLP terrorist Leila Khaled was able to deal with the presence of children on a plane she hijacked only by closing her mind to the possible consequences of the hijacking for them. These feelings are hardly consistent with our general notions of pathologically disturbed individuals.

Beyond suggesting an absence of pathology, attempts to delineate a "terrorist personality" have

not been very fruitful. A suggestion worth further investigation has been made by Heskin (1984), who has noted that the single most likely characteristic of IRA members is authoritarianism. A generalization that has received some support across various terrorist groups was made by Laqueur (1977, p. 147), who suggested that terrorists possess a kind of "free-floating activism." Becker (1977) frequently refers to the Baader-Meinhof group's impatience with words and desire for action. Crenshaw (1986) notes that the Basque ETA came to place a premium on armed conflict as an end, rather than as a means toward obtaining other objectives, and mentions the South American terrorist theoretician Marighella's focus on revolutionary action as opposed to discussion.

If terrorists are in general rather normal individuals who are inclined toward direct action regarding some perceived grievance or ideological position, we still have not come very far in describing characteristics that might predispose them toward terrorist activity. Hoffman (1985a) reports on studies of terrorist prisoners in countries, including Italy, Germany, and Turkey, that suggest that an individual's decision to join a left-wing, as opposed to a right-wing, organization is often a matter of little more than chance. Something more powerful than ideology is at work. Bollinger (1981; quoted in Billig, 1985) has suggested that social deficits in West German terrorists' personal lives may have been key factors in their attraction to group membership in the RAF; Post (1985) believes that joining an extremist group represents above all an attempt to belong. As Crenshaw (1985, p. 471) explains, "The group, as selector and interpreter of ideology, is central." We focus next on the group context of terrorist activities.

Terrorist Groups

The Increasingly Extreme Behavior of Members of Terrorist Groups

In understanding how normal and even idealistic people can become terrorists, it is important to recognize that their radical behavior is acquired gradually, progressing from the less to the more extreme. Often, an individual will join a succession of groups and causes, beginning with ones that advocate relatively pacifist goals (Crenshaw, 1985); in some cases, the commitment to terrorism may be made only when it appears to the individual that terrorist action is the only possible alternative in effecting social or political change. The German RAF leader Meinhof headed community efforts in the city of Munster opposing nuclear weapons during the 1950s; her increasing disillusionment with society occurred gradually throughout the following decade until she became a leader of the Baader-Meinhof group (Demaris, 1977, p. 218). Horst Mahler, another RAF leader, was a member of the moderate Social Democratic Party of Germany and the Socialist German Student Society, but left these organizations before helping to found the RAF (Billig, 1985). In a case study of a second-generation RAF terrorist referred to as "Rolfe," Billig (1984) notes that his subject joined radical groups and student Vietnam protests in late adolescence, and then went on to start a venture that printed literature for some radical organizations before actually being recruited into the RAF.

It is also possible that an individual member becomes more extreme as the whole group undergoes radical change. For example, the nineteenth-century Russian terrorist group known as "The People's Will" (Narodnaya Volya) broke off from a larger revolutionary movement because its leaders advocated terrorism. "The person who has become extremely dependent on the group will move with it to the new activity, without necessarily having made an independent choice" (Crenshaw, 1985, p. 477). Salvioni and Stepbanson (1985; quoted in Crenshaw, 1986) note that early Red Brigade activity in Italy centered on issues such as the campaign in Milan for free mass transit, and later escalated to violence justified by the terrorists as retribution for working class injustice. The German RAF's declarations suggest that the group's mission changed from (an albeit) limited commitment to working inside the social structure toward purely illegal activities (see "The concept of the urban guerrilla," published in 1971; reprinted in Laqueur, 1978, p. 179). Bollinger (1982, p. 118) discusses a

process of "double marginalization" among the members of the RAF, first in the leftist student movement, and then beyond the limits of that movement into a distinct subculture in which a separate system of norms gradually developed.

Furthermore, it should be recognized that there is specialization and hierarchy of violent behavior in terrorist groups; thus, depending upon their roles and status within the organization, terrorists vary in the extremity of their actual behavior. Division of labor has been documented in the Argentinian Montoneros, which included divisions for logistics, documents, planning, and psychological action (Crenshaw, 1985), and in the Algerian ALN, the military arm of the FLN, which included separate sections for bombings, attacks on police, logistics, and so forth. These divisions themselves were compartmentalized: The bomb section, for example, included laboratory work, transportation, storage, distribution, and placement (Hutchinson, 1978, p. 10). Thus, all terrorists are not required to hijack planes or plant bombs.

Once connected with an extreme group, a new recruit may gradually move from peripheral activities designed to support the group's terrorist tactics to the acts of violence that are central to the group's purpose. Thus the RAF member "Rolfe" mentioned above, who was eventually arrested in the kidnap-murder of the German industrialist Hans-Martin Schleyer in 1977, began his career with the RAF as a courier (Billig, 1984). Clark (1983) mentions a similar gradation in the recruitment phases of the Basque ETA membership.

Conflict in Terrorist Groups

In understanding the social psychological factors in terrorist organizations, it is important to recognize that all extreme groups, including anarchic-ideologues as well as nationalist-separatists, are at the apex of a much larger number of sympathizers and supporters. As Laqueur (1977, p. 110) points out, a measure of popular support is crucial for a terrorist organization. After RAF leader Meinhof's suicide in 1976, 4,000 mourners attended her funeral (Becker, 1977, p. 282). Crenshaw (1985, p. 467) notes that the IRA and the ETA are "components of broader organizational structures and possess a reservoir of support in society because the grievances of (their) communities . . . remain unsolved."

An important factor in the psychosocial reality of terrorist groups is constant and pervasive conflict. Obviously, terrorists are in conflict with the prevailing social and political order. A factor less often recognized is that extremist groups, particularly nationalist-separatist groups, must deal with their supporters—people in basic sympathy with their goals who nevertheless do not condone violent tactics beyond a certain limit—as another potential source of conflict. Thus the French Canadian community that supported the separatist goals of the FLQ was deeply disturbed by the group's 1970 kidnap-murder of Laporte (Laqueur, 1977, p. 196). The IRA is concerned about the organization's public image, and recognizes the importance of avoiding any backlash in the general population (Crenshaw, 1984). Thompson (1985) provides a vivid example: In 1977 the Provisional IRA murdered a woman, a part-time member of the Ulster Defence Regiment, while she slept in her home, and shot at her three-year-old daughter. The action was widely denounced by IRA supporters. Thompson notes that shared extra-political values operate in such situations as constraints against further escalation.

Intergroup conflict is also not unusual. Rivalry between the Provisional IRA and the official IRA (from which the provos had split) resulted in outright assassination plots during the 1970s (Laqueur, 1977, p. 189). Often, rivalry between competing terrorist groups causes an escalation of violence against the commonly perceived enemy. Thus the IRA assassination of Lord Mountbatten in 1979 may have been in response to escalated attacks on the British by the Irish National Liberation Army (Crenshaw, 1984). Palestinian terrorist attacks are frequently aimed not only at the intimidation of Israel, but also at influence among competing Palestinian factions (Crenshaw, 1981). Hoffman (1985b) interprets both the 1985 TWA hijacking and the seizure of the luxury liner *Achille Lauro* as attempts by Palestinian terrorists to gain advantage over rival groups. Other nations with feuding

terrorist groups include Italy, Armenia, and Argentina (Crenshaw, 1985).

Finally, and perhaps most important, intragroup conflict leads to constant and powerful tensions among group members (Post, 1985). Bollinger (1982, p. 118) suggests that in the RAF, there was a great deal of infighting and rivalry, "even rivalry about the topic who is the most leftist or the most determined." Demaris (1977, p. 232) mentions the frequent conflicts among the RAF leaders, notably between Baader and Meinhof; Billig (1985) maintains that relations were equally strained between Mahler and Meinhof. Laqueur (1977, p. 125) describes a grisly 1972 incident in which some 14 members of the Japanese United Red Army were slain by fellow terrorists. As Zawodny (1983) notes, an important function of external violence is to restore cohesion within the terrorist group. Without action and external threat, the group may destroy itself.

The conflict among group members may be especially threatening because individual survival depends on group solidarity. A member's defection is extremely upsetting to those who remain (Post, 1985). Thus strong group norms develop against any form of rebellion; indeed, any questioning of authority amounted to risking one's place in the Baader-Meinhof group (Post, 1985). Such sanctions can be powerful pressures toward conformity, particularly because members need the group as protection against an unfriendly outside world. Although it is possible for a member of an extreme group to leave the organization, it is generally difficult and dangerous to do so (Crenshaw, 1985). Ex-terrorists are pursued by both government forces and their former comrades.

However, members do in fact leave: Post (1985, p. 11) cites findings that as many as 23% of the RAF dropped out. In general, the dropouts were "ambivalent on joining, never fully resolved their doubts, and increasingly questioned the espoused goals of the group and whether the group's actions actually served those goals." On the average, they dropped out after only one year of active membership; 36% of the dropouts had lasted only six months in the organization. The numerous Italian Red Brigade defections in response to government

titled "Becoming a World Saver" chronicled the beginnings of the UC in America, and its surprise value was its emphasis on the importance of social networks in religious conversion. The first missionary began her work in Eugene, Oregon, in 1961 and her first convert contributed a social network that was exploited for additional recruits. Indeed, "the great majority of converts in Eugene were linked by long-standing relationships prior to any contact with Moon's movement" (Stark & Bainbridge, 1980, p. 1379). The importance of this social network was made plain to Lofland and Stark when the group left Eugene for San Francisco— and stopped growing for lack of social ties to potential recruits in the Bay Area. Recruiting efforts during the early sixties in San Francisco were not the sophisticated and successful techniques for which the group is known today. Rather, they were "weak, haphazard, and bumbling" (Lofland, 1977). Improved techniques were evidently more the product of trial and error than of theory, but did finally succeed by providing a means of reaching out to develop personal relationships with newcomers to the Bay Area. Stark and Bainbridge (1980) point out that this solution was satisficing rather than maximizing, since recruiting was slower than if new converts had provided local acquaintance networks within which to attract additional converts. Compared with geometric progression in Eugene, recruiting in the Bay Area was reduced to arithmetic progression.

The emphasis given by Lofland and Stark (1965) to social networks was a watershed in the study of cults. The established view (Clark, 1937; Linton, 1943; Smelser, 1963) pointed to the match between the needs of the individual and the ideology of the group to explain why some people and not others join a cult or sect. This view assumes that any deviant group will tend to attract individuals with a grievance or deprivation for which the group offers some interpretation and remedy. In retrospect, the deprivation explanation was always too broad, because most individuals who suffer a particular deprivation do not ever join a deviant group. Thus Lofland and Stark did not so much contradict the established view as complement it. Perceived deprivation establishes the pool of potential converts to a particular cult, but social networks determine who among the many in the pool are likely to be among the few actually recruited.

The interaction of deprivation and social networks in predicting cult recruitment is nowhere better represented than in some remarkable studies of the UC carried out by an investigator with the cooperation of church leaders. Galanter, Rabkin, Rabkin, and Deutsch (1979) obtained 237 completed questionnaires from a representative sample of UC members living in the church's residences in a large metropolitan area. Most were unmarried (91%), white (89%), and young (mean age 25 years). Consistent with the deprivation hypothesis, most (67%) had been at least moderately committed to their family's religion before the age of 15, but had lost this commitment: 90% reported at least some commitment to an Eastern or fundamentalist Christian sect before joining the UC. Half reported some previous commitment to a political party or movement. More than half had attended college, although only a quarter held degrees. Thirty percent had experienced emotional problems leading them to seek professional help and 6% had been hospitalized for such problems. This is a picture of individuals dissatisfied and seeking support, and indeed 91% seem to have found some help in the UC, as evidenced by recollection of more psychological distress before joining than after. The same study also shows the importance of interpersonal bonds during the conversion period. Sixty-seven percent reported having felt during this period much more than usual "a great deal of respect for another person," 48% felt more than usual "close or intimate with another person," and 43% felt more than usual "cheered up."

Another study by Galanter (1980) provides questionnaire and outcome data for 104 individuals who began the 21-day sequence of lectures and group activities that ends with a decision whether or not to join the UC. Most of these individuals had been invited by a UC member whom they had met in some public place. Demographic and background data indicated that the 104 who attended the first weekend at a rustic center outside a metropolitan area in Southern California were very similar to

UC membership as surveyed in the questionnaire study described above. Despite this similarity, 74 guests left at the end of the first weekend. Those who left differed from those who stayed in reported feelings toward "the ten or so people from the workshop (from outside the workshop) you know best," with dropouts reporting both less feeling for insiders and more feelings for outsiders. Dropouts also reported less acceptance of UC religious beliefs. Of the 30 guests who stayed at the center past the first weekend, 21 dropped out between days 3 and 22, and 9 ultimately joined the Church on day 22. The late dropouts did not differ from joiners in positive feelings toward workshop members or in acceptance of UC beliefs, but did report more positive feelings toward those outside the church. Galanter concludes that an important factor in joining the UC is lack of interpersonal attachments outside the church, and pays special attention to the power of the relationship with the UC host who, after inviting a guest, stays with that guest through the weeks of the recruiting sequence.

And what keeps the recruits in the cult? As indicated above (Galanter et al. 1979), cult members feel themselves less stressed than they were before joining. In this sense the cult experience is not a fraud and does fulfill the promise held out to recruits. The importance of social bonds to cult members has already been emphasized. But here we want to underscore what Stark and Bainbridge (1980, p. 1393) called the "missing factor" in understanding cults: the very concrete and material rewards of membership. Groups that live communally, such as the UC and the Hare Krishnas, combine the security of a family with the opportunities of a corporation. Stark and Bainbridge point out that such groups clothe, feed, and shelter their members, and provide opportunities within the movement to achieve positions of status and power. In this connection it must be recognized that the cult members encountered in public fund-raising or proselytizing are the cream of the movement. A look in the lobby of the old New Yorker hotel in New York City, now owned by the UC, will reveal a considerable number of crippled, ugly, nonyoung members going about their chores. These, the unwanted of our society, find in the UC a home that

gives them meaning, work, and affection as well as material security.

The importance of personal ties in UC recruitment appears to fit what is known about other cults as well. For instance, Bainbridge (1978) found that interpersonal bonds were critical in both the formation and expansion of a Satanic cult he studied from 1970 to 1976. A doomsday cult studied by Hardyck and Braden (1962) offers similar evidence. Though the original report is familiar to social psychologists as a test of dissonance theory predictions, Hardyck recently reviewed her field notes (see Stark & Bainbridge, 1980) and reported that 75% of adult members of the cult formed a single kinship network. These and other explanations are reviewed by Stark and Bainbridge to argue that developing interpersonal bonds, in combination with ideology responsive to perceived deprivation, are at the bottom of recruitment to both cults and more traditional religious groups.

Another aspect of the experience of cult groups worth noting is the constant flux in the members' identities and levels of commitment. At any given time, some individuals are beginning to find out about a particular group, others are becoming committed, others are firmly committed, others becoming less committed, and still others are in the process of leaving entirely. Bird and Reimer (1982) examine survey data from Montreal and from the Bay Area of California and conclude that about 20% of the adult population has participated to some extent in a nontraditional religious or quasi-religious movement (including Charismatics, Buddhists, Scientologists, EST, and other groups of Western, Eastern, and "scientific" disciples). The typical participant establishes a not-very-strong relationship with one of these groups and then drops out. Three-quarters of the Montreal respondents who had ever participated in one of these groups had dropped out, and fewer than 10% of all respondents were current members of any group. This larger picture from survey data is entirely consistent with our description earlier of UC recruitment, during which the great majority of guests at the UC center dropped out, leaving only a few converts at the end of 21 days. Perhaps part of the success of the UC technique is the compression into only

21 days of the winnowing of potential converts that occurs in any religion.

Even this brief review indicates a number of obvious parallels with what is known about recruitment into terrorist groups: Both pull mostly from the ranks of middle-class, twenty-year-olds with some college. Both depend for recruits on a pool of seekers or sympathizers much larger than the numbers actually recruited. Both require a socialization period during which recruits are brought to full commitment, with a constant flux of dropouts from the path that leads to full commitment and from among those already committed. It does seem that commitment is faster and dropping out likewise faster for cults than for terrorist groups. But this quantitative difference is easily attributable to the greater barriers to both entrance and exit from terrorist groups—barriers that stem from their greater deviance from the norms of the larger society. In terms of group dynamics, both cults and terrorist groups offer a full array of reinforcements to members: affective, social, cognitive, and material. These rewards depend in both kinds of groups on powerful interpersonal bonds among group members, bonds that appear to be very important in explaining how only a few of the many seekers or sympathizers are actually recruited.

A big difference between cults and terrorist groups appears to be the relative lack of intragroup conflict in the cults in comparison with the high levels of conflict reported within terrorist groups. One possible explanation of the difference is the norm of interpersonal warmth and sharing that is part of cult ideology. In contrast, terrorist groups have in common only their enemy and their action. What Marxist ideology is to be found among members of terrorist groups does not include norms of interpersonal intimacy. Another way of putting this possibility is to say that cults are closer to experiential groups (Back, 1972) than terrorist groups are. A prediction from this view is that movement from one group or cell to another should be easier and more frequent within a cult than within a terrorist organization.

Another possibility is that the high level of conflict within terrorist groups is attributable to their cellular organization, where contact with other cells and terrorist leadership must be minimized for reasons of security. The kind of continuous and hierarchical communication required for one person to control many is difficult when the followers are underground, particularly for a charismatic leader who depends on personal contacts for his impact. Strong and centralized leadership is common in cults and relatively rare in terrorist groups, especially radical terrorist groups where the RAF appears to be a rare example of centralization. But the leadership difference is understandable in terms of situational differences that do not get in the way of the substantial parallels in recruitment and group dynamics.

Studies of cult formation and recruitment have been primarily sociological in emphasis, and Stark and Bainbridge (1979, p. 130) argue that cults can be valuable as models of the evolution of culture and institutions. Similarly, cults have potential as natural laboratories for the study of personality and social psychology. Issues of leadership, affiliation, compliance and internalization, affect and cognition, attitudes and behavior, in-group and out-group perceptions—these familiar issues are raised, and we believe likely to be illuminated, by research on cults. Similarly, a comparison of cult dropouts with terrorist dropouts, especially as their perceptions and evaluations of their groups change with time since dropping out, could provide data of interest for issues of self-justification and in-group/out-group perceptions. Social psychologists could profit by taking up an interest in cults that has languished since prophecy failed (Festinger, Riecken, & Schachter, 1956) and failed again (Hardyck & Braden, 1962) for dissonance theorists.

Group Extremity Shift

An observation about terrorist groups is that they become more extreme only gradually over a period of time. This can be understood in terms of several different kinds of social psychological theory and research. First, the shift to extremity occurs as a function of change in the membership of the group. Festinger's (1950) theory of informal social communication specifies that strong differences of opinion on important issues in a group will lead to communication aimed at reducing opinion discrepancy. If this communication does not succeed in reducing difference of opinion to tolerable levels, the theory predicts rejection of the group members holding the most deviant opinions (Schachter, 1951). Thus activist groups do not turn one day to full blown terrorist activity, but develop slowly as an ever more like-minded nucleus is condensed from a cloud of less committed and less extreme opinions. The Baader-Meinhof gang condensed out of German antiwar activists, the Weatherman out of American student activists, and the IRA out of the long history of anti-English sentiment in Ireland.

Groups become more extreme in another and perhaps more impressive way: The same membership may become more extreme over time. In other words, the average of group members' opinions and behaviors becomes more extreme. Put in this fashion, the transition to terrorism is a case of what has been studied in social psychology as group extremity shift. The beginning of this literature was the observation that the average opinion of group members became more risky after group discussion of a series of decisions involving risk (Stoner, 1961). Then it was noted that group opinions sometimes became more risky and sometimes more cautious, depending on the issue discussed (Stoner, 1968). Moscovici and Zavalloni (1969) broadened the scope of the phenomenon when they showed analogous group shifts after discussion of issues of opinion and judgment having nothing to do with risk. The consistent pattern of group shifts, whether or not involving risk, was that average opinion became more extreme after discussion in the direction of the side of issue favored by average opinion before discussion (Myers, 1978). Beyond the laboratory, natural examples of group polarization—for example, in group conflict and group counseling—have been cited (Myers, 1982) as supporting the significance and generalizability of group extremity shifts.

After a few false starts in the direction of leadership, diffusion of responsibility, and familiarization, research on group extremity shifts settled down to two competing explanations. The first,

relevant arguments, asserts that the shift is caused by exposure to a biased set of arguments in the course of discussion, arguments reflecting the relative strength of the values invested in the sides of an issue (Burnstein & Vinokur, 1977). These values bias the initial group opinions in one direction or another and bias the production of arguments in discussion so as to push group members still further toward the favored side as they hear arguments that had not previously considered. This is a rationalist explanation of the group shift—a picture of members swayed by argument.

The competing explanation of the group shift is less rationalist. Called social comparison theory, this explanation holds that the group shift is caused by the desire of group members not to fall behind in their apparent recognition of and devotion to the side of an issue favored by the majority (Sanders & Baron, 1977). According to social comparison theory, group members tend to admire persons with positions more extreme than their own on the favored side and want to be at least as extreme as the average of their group. In other words, everyone wants to be above average in exemplifying group anchored values. Discussion reveals the distribution of others' opinions and those who are less-than-average extreme are moved to become more extreme.

It is now generally accepted that both relevant arguments and social comparison contribute to the group shift effect (Myers, 1983; Brown, 1986). Furthermore, these two explanations have been linked to familiar processes of group dynamics, in particular to the distinction between normative and informational social influence (Deutsch & Gerard, 1955). Sanders and Baron (1977) and Myers (1983) identify relevant arguments with informational social influence and social comparison with normative social influence.

There is some evidence to support this identification of group shift mechanisms with the familiar processes of group dynamics. Group shift experiments consistently found decreased variance of opinions after group discussion, and there has never been any doubt (Brown, 1965) that this effect of group discussion is to be explained in terms of group dynamics. But there is evidence (McCauley,

1972) that, for both risk and attitude issues, the decrease in variance is larger for groups showing the larger group extremity shift. If the variance decrease is clearly an effect of the usual group dynamics processes, then the group extremity shift associated with the variance decrease is plausibly an effect of these same processes.

The implication of the group shift research for terrorist extremity shifts, then, is that shifts can be understood as the product of normal group dynamics such as have been studied in thousands of groups of college student subjects. As groups shed less extreme opinions about how to solve political problems, the opinions of group members become more homogeneous. These more homogeneous opinions interact in group discussion to become even more homogeneous (variance decrease) and more extreme (group shift). At the bottom of the group shift to more extreme political action are processes of relevant arguments and social comparison that are expressions of normative and informational social influence.

A problem remains in this analysis. Terrorist groups move toward extremity not only in the sense that the average opinion of the group becomes more extreme, but in the sense that the average individual becomes more extreme. The latter sense was implied by Moscovici and Zavalloni (1969) in describing group shift as a phenomenon of polarization. But McCauley (1972) found that, for both risk and nonrisk issues, extremity shift can occur for the group average opinion but not for the average individual opinion. That is, the group average moves farther from neutrality on an opinion scale after discussion, but the average individual is not farther from neutrality. This can happen because some individuals start off on the opposite side of the scale neutral point from the group average and, after group discussion, move only to neutrality or to mildly favoring the side of the issue favored by the majority. Thus individual extremity shifts in terrorist groups should occur after the group has shed the deviate opinions that favored inaction or only legitimate action—that is, after all the members of the group are on the same side of neutrality on issues of political action (see Myers & Bishop, 1970). A testable prediction from this analysis is

that laboratory group shifts should continue over multiple discussions of the same issue, if the issue is of sufficient interest that multiple and continuing discussions do not lead merely to boredom. After group members are all on the same side of the opinion scale, further discussion should produce both group and individual extremity shift. As far as we are aware, group shift research has been limited to studying the impact of a single group interaction involving only one discussion of a particular issue.

Individual Extremity Shift and Milgram's Studies of Obedience

Individual extremity shift in terrorist groups can also be understood by reference to Milgram's (1974) studies of obedience. The results of this paradigm are well known: Normal subjects given the role of teacher in a psychology experiment will give high levels of shock to a protesting "victim" in the role of learner. The strength of the situation is apparent in the high percentage of subjects who are completely obedient (over 60% in the strongest version of the situation), and the subtlety of this strength is apparent in the failure of psychiatrists, college students, and middle-class adults to predict that even one subject would be completely obedient. Complete obedience requires the subject to raise the level of shock administered from 15 to 450 volts, with an increase of 15 volts every time the learner makes a mistake. This escalation is a shift to increased extremity of behavior in the sense that the higher levels of shock are increasing violations of the norm against hurting an innocent other, and we are not the first (see Heskin, 1984) to see Milgram's obediently paradigm as a model relevant to understanding terrorists' escalation of violence.

Milgram theorized about the power of his situation in terms of the structure of authority and an "agentic shift" in which subjects moved from seeing themselves as responsible for their behavior to seeing themselves as responsible to the experimenter. Without detracting from the value of this analysis, we follow Gilbert (1981) in emphasizing an aspect of the paradigm that receives only one paragraph of attention in Milgram's book (p. 149): the gradual and sequential nature of the shock escalation. All subjects were given a "demonstration" 45-volt shock that most people perceive as little more than a tickle. Thus subjects have no reason not to give the first low level shocks, especially as they cannot know ahead of time how many mistakes the learner will make and the level of shocks they will be required to administer. Once started administering the shocks, a subject is on slippery slope. To refuse to give the next shock is inconsistent with having given the previous shock and requires the subject to question what he has done to this point. A psychology of self-justification is set in motion that Milgram (1974, p. 149) recognized as consistent with the predictions of dissonance theory. Whether dissonance is understood, as in Festinger (1957), as pure cognitive inconsistency, or whether it is understood, as Aronson (1969) later suggested, as inconsistency between behavior and a positive self-image, there is clearly dissonance created for a subject who breaks off at the nth shock after having already administered n–1 shocks.

An extension of social comparison theory (Festinger, 1954) provides another way of thinking about the difficulty subjects experience in breaking off the escalation of shocks in Milgram's paradigm. In the same way that we need to compare ourselves with others, we need to compare ourselves with our previous selves. Albert (1977) has argued that the predictions of social comparison can be directly translated into predictions concerning when and about what we most need to compare our present selves with the series of past selves that stretches back in time. Thus a subject looking back at n–1 shocks administered is looking back at n–1 interpretations of the situation from a self who, on the basis of attractiveness, is a powerful influence toward a similar interpretation and a similar choice for the nth shock. We might say that the most credible and trustworthy source of persuasion on the nth trial is not the experimenter, but the subject himself or herself (see Bem, 1967).

Both the dissonance and the social comparison understandings of the power of Milgram's situation point to the importance of the small gradations in the escalation of shock. As Milgram (1974, p. 149) points out, the subject "is implicated into the destructive behavior in piecemeal fashion." Although theologians have long been concerned about the slippery slope from small sin to great evil, social psychologists have not much inclined to see the devil emerging piecemeal from behavior. There has been little research that builds on Milgram's paradigm, although, as Gilbert (1981) points out, the "foot in the door" effect (Freedman & Fraser, 1966) can be considered an example of the power of a graded behavior sequence with the gradations reduced to only two.

An example of more gradual escalation to extreme behavior—in this case self-destructive behavior—is provided by the form of funny business called a "jam joint" (McCauley & Handelsman, 1976). A jam joint is a store, usually working off the sidewalks or boardwalks of a resort area, where a special sales technique is used to sell poor quality merchandise for inflated prices. The technique is complex, but depends notably on harnessing group pressure, greed, and small gifts to shape a slow escalation of two behaviors: saying "yes" and passing forward increasing sums of money to the jammers. The pressure for self-justification is so strong that victims seldom come back to the jam joint to complain.

This analysis of Milgram's situation leads to a testable prediction (Gilbert, 1981): Less gradual steps of escalation should lead to reduced obedience. As far as we know, neither Milgram nor any later investigator has examined the effect of manipulating the number and gradualness of steps in the escalation of extreme behavior. Harrison and Pepitone (1972) came close to the kind of study needed in their examination of contrast effects in the use of punishment. They showed that adding a high but "forbidden" shock level to the control panel increased the amount of moderate shock subjects would administer to a "learner" rat. Though a manipulation of the range of alternatives, this study does not provide evidence concerning the effect of manipulating the gradations within a given range. Even in the absence of direct evidence, however, we feel confident that the extreme form of an ungraduated shock series—15 volts to 450 volts as

Post, J. M. (1985). Hostilite, conformite, fraternite: The group dynamics terrorist behavior. *International Journal of Group Psychotherapy, 36*, 211–224.

Rubin, J. Z., & Friedland, N. (1986, March). Theater of terror. *Psychology Today, 20*, 18–28.

Russell, C. V., & Miller, B. H. (1983). Profile of a terrorist. In L. Z. Freedman & Y. Alexander (Eds.), *Perspectives on terrorism* (pp. 45–60). Wilmington, DE: Scholarly Resources.

Salvioni, D., & Stephanson, A. (1985). Reflections on the Red Brigades. *Orbis, 29*, 489–506.

Sanders, G. S., & Baron, R. S. (1977). Is social comparison irrelevant for producing choice shifts? *Journal of Experimental Social Psychology, 13*, 303–314.

Schachter, S. (1951). Deviation, rejection and communication. *Journal of Abnormal and Social Psychology, 46*, 190–207.

Schmid, A. P. (1983). *Political terrorism: A research guide to concepts, theories, data bases and literature.* Amsterdam: North-Holland.

Schmid, A. P., & de Graaf, J. (1982). *Violence as communication.* Newbury Park, CA: Sage Publications.

Smelser, N. J. (1963). *Theory of collective behavior.* New York: Free Press.

Stark, R., & Bainbridge, W. S. (1979). Of churches, sects, and cults: Preliminary concepts for a theory of religious movements. *Journal for the Scientific Study of Religion, 18*, 117–133.

Stark, R., & Bainbridge, W. S. (1980). Networks of faith: Interpersonal bonds and recruitment to cults and sects. *American Journal of Sociology, 85*, 1376–1395.

Stoner, J.A.F. (1961). *A comparison of individual and group decision including risk.* Unpublished master's thesis, School of Industrial Management, Massachusetts Institute of Technology.

Stoner, J.A.F. (1968). Risky and cautious shifts in group decisions: The influence of widely help values. *Journal of Experimental Social Psychology, 4*, 442–459.

Sutherland, E. H. (1955). *Principles of criminology* (rev. by D. R. Cressey). Chicago: Lippencott.

Thompson, J.L.P. (1985). *Crime, social control, and political killing.* Paper presented at the Annual Conference of the Sociological Association of Ireland, Belfast, Northern, Ireland.

Traub, S. H. & Little, C. B. (1980). *Theories of deviance* (2nd ed.). Itasca, IL: Peacock.

Wardlaw, G. (1982). *Political terrorism: Theory, tactics and counter-measures.* New York: Cambridge University Press.

Zawodny, J. K. (1983). Infrastructures of terrorist organizations. In L.Z. Freedman & Y. Alexander (Eds.), *Perspectives on terrorism* (pp. 61–70). Wilmington, DE: Scholarly Resources.

READING 20

Social Psychological Aspects of Political Terrorism

Ariel Merari and Nehemia Friedland

As a social and political phenomenon, terrorism is undoubtedly older than recorded history. The use of assassinations, bombings, and other forms of violence to achieve political ends did not start in this century. Yet, since 1968, terrorism has increasingly attracted public attention worldwide. (Among the many definitions of political terrorism that have been suggested (see Schmid, 1984), the one employed in this chapter is the systematic utilization of actual or threatened violence by nonstate groups, aimed to achieve political objectives.)

Several reasons may explain this sudden interest. Among them is the fact that, although it is doubtful that domestic (intrastate) terrorism has grown much recently, there has been a marked rise since 1968 in international terrorism, defined as an incident of terrorism involving more than one country in any possible way. Official U.S. statistics tally 142 international terrorist incidents in 1968 and 760 in 1980 (U.S. Central Intelligence Agency, 1981); 794 such incidents reportedly occurred in 1982 (U.S. Department of State, 1983). Another explanation is the growing lethality of terrorism. In the words of a Rand Corporation report: "1983 was the bloodiest year yet for terrorist activity, with 720 fatalities and 963 injuries. . . . Since 1977, the number of international terrorist incidents resulting in fatalities has increased each year. . . . Terrorists

seem to be less and less reluctant to inflict casualties, demonstrating an increased willingness to kill" (Cordes et al., 1984, pp. 6–7). According to the same source, among incidents with fatalities, the share of those with multiple fatalities increased from 33 percent in 1982 to 59 percent in 1983. Last, terrorism is increasingly being used by states as a tool of foreign policy. Whatever the reason, it seems that political terrorism as a phenomenon is currently at the center of political, media, and, increasingly, academic interest.

References to terrorism can be found in the writings of psychiatrists, sociologists, criminologists, political scientists, and historians. Social psychologists, on the other hand, have shown little interest in the topic. This chapter examines social psychology's potential contribution to the study of terrorism and to the development of means to cope with it.

The student of terrorism has to overcome three major obstacles: a scarcity of data, the heterogeneity of the phenomenon, and the ambiguity surrounding its causes. These are discussed in the first section of this chapter. The second and third sections define a role for social psychology by portraying terrorism as a sophisticated form of psychological warfare. As such, terrorism employs fear induction to maximize its attitudinal impact on target publics. A social psychological analysis of determinants of this impact is presented in the fourth section. The fifth section evaluates the potential contribution of social psychology to designing procedures whereby target publics' ability to withstand this impact can be bolstered.

Terrorism: Heterogeneity and Ambiguity

The subject of terrorism does not lend itself easily to research. In the first place, although several academic, government, and commercially run data bases routinely document international terrorist events, data on the larger group of domestic terrorist incidents are lacking. Second, contrary to the loose common usage of the term "terrorism," the phenomenon it denotes is not uniform. Terrorist groups vary greatly in size, from less than a score of members to thousands, as well as in national composition and cultural background. Responsibility for international terrorist incidents that took place in 1982 was claimed by 125 different organizations (as compared to 61 in 1970), of 75 different nationalities (U.S. Department of State, 1983). The number and diversity of terrorist groups involved in domestic terrorism is considerably greater. Data on 500-odd groups, active during the last decade, have been compiled by the Jaffee Center for Strategic Studies at Tel Aviv University.

The declared motivations of terrorist groups are rather diverse. Some are nationalistic, others are separatist. Social ideologies from the extreme right to the extreme left are well represented among present-day terrorist groups: A variety of neo-Nazis and neo-Fascists can be found on one side and a plethora of Leninist, Maoist, Trotskyist, and anarchist groups on the other.

Among religious terrorist groups are ones formed by Catholics, Protestants, Jews, Shi'ite Moslems, and Sunnite Moslems. Other terrorist groups have a racial motivation: white, black, or red. To further complicate the picture, quite often a terrorist group's credo is a composite one (though most present-day separatist groups espouse a leftist ideology), and some groups have changed ideology in midcourse (e.g., the Colombian M-19, that started

as a right-wing-oriented, populist movement and turned to Marxism). In sum, as a social, political, and psychological phenomenon, terrorism is very heterogenous, and there is no sound, a priori reason to assume much in common between different terrorist groups (e.g., the anarchist German Revolutionary Cells and the Argentinian populist Montoneros).

The heterogeneity of terrorism might be responsible for the current failure to formulate a coherent, well-grounded theory of its causes. Explanations of the phenomenon range from in-depth psychological analyses of individual terrorists to general sociopolitical interpretations. The former, which have been primarily undertaken by psychiatrists, psychologists, and criminologists, sought to chart the "terroristic personality" and to determine the dynamics that turn an individual into a terrorist (e.g., Hacker, 1976, 1980; Kellen, 1979). Such clinically oriented analyses have typically been carried out on a small number of cases, and their conclusions are frequently overgeneralized. Moreover, even if it were possible to identify some common attributes of the terrorist personality, transformation of such information into an explanation would be hindered by its predictive irreversibility. That is, the fact that terrorists share certain characteristics or traits by no means implies that any person who has these traits is bound to become a terrorist. This kind of irreversibility also limits the usefulness of statistical profiles of the "typical" terrorist, such as Jenkins's (1982) conclusion that the typical terrorist is male, in his early twenties, single, from middle- to upper-class urban family, well educated, and has some university training.

An alternative approach depicts terrorism as a group phenomenon (e.g., Turk, 1982). It primarily derives from theories and studies of social destabilization (e.g., Lipset, 1960; Davies, 1962, 1973; Johnson, 1966; Huntington, 1968; Gurr, 1970, 1973; Muller, 1979; Monti, 1980). Yet, identification of correlates of destabilization goes only part way toward the explanation of terrorism: The process whereby destabilization generates terrorism remains undetermined. Moreover, destabilization theories rely quite heavily on "blockade" or frustration-aggression hypotheses, or on assumed gaps between expectations and their fulfillment. It is therefore somewhat difficult to reconcile such theories with the recent proliferation of terrorism in democracies or with the fact that terrorists are not necessarily underprivileged. (For a more extensive criticism of frustration-aggression theories of terrorism see, for instance, Schmid, 1984, pp. 161–166.)

Terrorism as Psychological Warfare

The great diversity of terrorism and the ambiguity surrounding its cause notwithstanding, terrorists of all nationalities, races, religions, and ideological or political leanings employ the same tactics and strategy. All of them wage a sophisticated form of psychological warfare. That is, by bearing on target publics' emotions and attitudes, terrorists create an impact that disproportionately exceeds the physical consequences of their action. Clearly, on a national scale, such consequences are negligible. According to the U.S. Department of State (1983), in the 10-year period from 1973–1982, international terrorism around the globe resulted in the death of 3509 persons. As a manifestation of a severe international or national problem, this figure is quite small, considering that in the United States alone, the annual death toll in road accidents is approximately 45,000. To illustrate this point further, one of the deadliest terrorist incidents in history was the October 23, 1983 suicidal car-bomb attack on the U.S. Marine headquarters in Beirut, in which 241 American soldiers were killed. This event instigated vocal criticism of the U.S. administration by politicians and the media, and was arguably a precipitating factor in the ultimate decision to evacuate United States troups from Lebanon. Thus, the death of several hundred men, in a single incident, had a profound effect on a superpower policy in a critical region and, quite possibly, on the fate of Lebanon as a state.

The preceding example points to the essence of terrorist tactics, which is to draw authorities into public, widely exposed confrontations, and let the public judge their course and pass the verdict on their outcome. A successful terrorist incident is one that maneuvers authorities into "no win" situations. Consider the contrast, for instance, with a criminal kidnap case, where the kidnapper will often strive to maximize the amount of ransom extorted. The sophisticated political terrorist, on the other hand, might minimize the ransom demands, such that authorities' refusal to concede would be perceived as unduly intransigent, whereas a concession, albeit trivial, could nevertheless be construed as capitulation. From this line of reasoning, terrorism can be seen as "the indirect strategy that wins or loses only in terms of how you respond to it. . . . Terrorism wins only if you respond to it in the way the terrorists want you to; which means that its fate is in your hands and not in theirs" (Fromkin, 1975, p. 697).

What can Social Psychology Contribute?

Our portrayal of terrorism gives rise to some doubts about the feasibility of eradicating it. The multiplicity of causes espoused by terrorists and uncertainty about the dynamics that turn individuals into terrorists make it difficult, if not impossible, to follow the advice that lasting solutions to problems require the uprooting of their antecedents. As regards terrorism, a root treatment would necessitate removal of the terrorists' political motivation —a solution to their grievances. Such a treatment, however, is impossible in many cases where terrorism, as argued by Ferracuti, "is a fantasy war, real only in the mind of the terrorist" (1982, p. 137). Moreover, accepting the claims of one group might infuriate another segment of the population. For instance, a negotiated settlement between the British government and the Catholic IRA would almost certainly unleash Protestant terrorism in Ulster. In retrospect, it can be shown that terrorism ceased when its perpetrators gained full power (the FLN in Algeria or Mau-Mau in Kenya) or when they were forcefully crushed (the SLA in California or the Second of June movement in West Germany). We do not recall any instance in which a violent subversive group halted its activity in the context of a mutually agreed-upon compromise with authorities.

The difficulty of addressing the root causes of terrorism does not preclude a potentially more promising attempt to cope with its consequences. In terms of the analogy drawn by Brian Jenkins (1975) between terrorism and a theater, one may say that what really counts is not the activity on stage but the audience responses. Thus, the main battle against terrorism has to be fought in the arena of public opinion. Much in the same way as terrorism is an indirect strategy—a sophisticated form of psychological warfare—we hold that the response and counterstrategy ought to be largely indirect and to use psychological tactics. More specifically, we propose that the core of an effective containment strategy consists of denying terrorists the most essential condition for their success: namely, a responsive and excitable public.

This proposition highlights the potential contribution of social psychologists to the struggle against terrorism. The challenge is twofold. First, social psychological methods should be harnessed to investigate factors that determine the potency of terrorism's effect on public opinion. Identification and understanding of such factors is an indispensible prerequisite for assessment and prediction of the impacts of terrorism. Second, social psychologists should formulate principles and devise means for bolstering public resistance to the attitudinal effects of terrorism. In the following sections we offer some preliminary observations that are based on our own research studies and firsthand practical experience with certain aspects of the response to political terrorism. We hope that these observations will stimulate other social psychologists to join the effort.

Factors Influencing Public Attitudes toward Terrorism

Though definitions of terrorism vary, all stress the induction of fear and intimidation as the means used by terrorists to effect political change: for example, "coercive intimidation" (Wilkinson, 1977, p. 48); "putting the public in fear" (Mickolus, 1980, p. 295); "Terrorism is aimed at the people

watching. Fear is the intended effect, not the byproduct of terrorism" (Jenkins, 1975, p. 1).

These definitions pose two key, fundamental questions to the student of terrorism. One, is terrorism an effective means of political influence? Two, is the extent of attitude and behavior change induced by terrorists linearly related to the intensity of fear elicited by their actions? That is, should we accept the intuitively compelling assumption that the more severe and threatening the terrorists' assault, the greater the target's willingness to give in?

Historical precedents show that the above questions cannot be answered in the affirmative. The number of cases in which political change can be unequivocally attributed to terroristic activity is rather small. Furthermore, most of those cases were in the category of anticolonial struggle (e.g., the Jewish groups in Palestine, EOKA in Cyprus, and Mau-Mau in Kenya against the British, the FLN in Algeria against the French, and FRELIMO in Mozambique against the Portuguese). That is, in all these cases, terrorists fought against a foreign rule and occupying forces. On the other hand, domestic terrorism, in which the insurgents rose against people in their own country, has been largely unsuccessful. Although most terroristic activity in the last half of the century may be categorized as domestic, in only six instances did terrorists carry out successful campaigns that overturned existing regimes in their native countries (Cuba, Nicaragua, Cambodia, Laos, Iran, and Rhodesia). In Europe, where scores of terrorist groups have been active, there has not been a single case of an insurgent group gaining power since the end of World War II.

This historical pattern is intriguing, for domestic terrorism appears to be more threatening both in its modus operandi and in its potential lethality than anticolonial terrorism. In the colonial situation, the typical targets are soldiers, policemen, and officials of the occupying country who are stationed in the colony, and the ruling nation's homeland is usually immune to danger. Domestic terrorism, on the other hand, is characteristically less discriminating. Ideologically motivated terrorists usually target whole classes of people associated with the regime, with ethnic or religious groups, or even just the population at large. Such randomly targeted, seemingly senseless attacks (e.g., the bombing of a railway station in Bologna, Italy, which resulted in 83 dead, or of a crowd celebrating the Munich Oktoberfest, which killed 13) turn every member of the population into a potential victim and thereby induce much fear and anxiety. Moreover, no terrorist campaign against a foreign rule compared to the lethality of domestic terrorism in El Salvador, where 8,000 to 10,000 are estimated to have died in recent years; or in Turkey, where approximately 2,000 persons were killed annually in the period preceding the 1980 coup; or in northern Ireland, where thousands have died as a result of terrorist activity since 1969. It is quite surprising, therefore, that on the whole, domestic terrorist groups have been considerably less successful than anticolonial groups in achieving their political objectives.

Empirical Evidence

Historical analyses such as this are obviously tentative. However, the possibility that—contrary to a commonly held belief—terrorism's ability to effect social or political change is not a simple, direct function of the amount of fear it induces has also been supported by empirical research. In 1979, during a period of relatively intense terroristic activity in Israel, we conducted a nationwide survey that was designed to assess Israelis' emotional and attitudinal reactions to terrorism (Friedland & Merari, 1985). The results confirmed the notion that terrorism induces fear beyond its physical significance. Although only 23 Israelis were killed and 344 were wounded in 1979 as a result of Palestinian terrorism, 93 percent of our respondents expressed "worry" or "extreme worry" about terrorism in the country. Close to three-quarters stated that they were "worried" or "extremely worried" about the possibility that they or members of their families might get hurt by terrorism.

Despite these high levels of expressed anxiety, the respondents maintained an uncompromising position vis-à-vis the terrorists' political objectives. More than 90 percent regarded terrorism as a

reason to deny the PLO a representative status and to avoid political change in the areas occupied by Israel (i.e., either the establishment of an independent Palestinian state or the granting of autonomy to the Palestinian population). Furthermore, very large majorities favored the use of radical counter-terrorist measures, including the demolition of houses whose owners harbored terrorists (79.5 percent support), deportation of individuals who held contacts with terrorist organizations (90 percent), imposition of curfews (87 percent), shelling of terrorist bases, even if it jeopardized civilians (75.5 percent), and assassination of terrorist leaders (92 percent).

Effects of the Intensity of Threat

Taken together, historical evidence and our survey data suggest the need to reconsider the pattern of relationship between the determinedness of a target population to adhere to its political positions and the intensity of an actual or potential terrorist assault. The already mentioned assumption that the two are linearly related might have been valid if the cost of adhering to their positions were the sole determinant of the public's resolve to resist terrorist pressure. There is reason to believe, however, that two conflicting processes shape individuals' willingness to change their attitudes and behavior as a function of the intensity of attempts to effect such change. On one hand, utilitarian considerations and the cost of resistance to change tend to produce a positive relationship between individuals' readiness to change and the intensity of raw power that is brought to bear on them. On the other hand, the perception of threats as illegitimate means of influence might promote reactance and resentment (Brehm, 1966; Friedland, 1976). As a result, reluctance to change might grow stronger as the attempts to induce such change become more persistent. (This effect is likely to be particularly potent when terrorism is employed to compel political change.)

Combined, the conflicting effects just described yield a curvilinear relationship between public steadfastness in the face of terrorism and the intensity of threat. Below a certain level of intensity, the lethal effects of terrorists' actions are too weak to compel the public to reconsider the costs and benefits of adhering to its political positions, but sufficient to arouse animosity toward terrorists and their causes. Hence, in the range of low to moderate threat intensities, terrorism might result in a radicalization of public attitudes in a direction *opposed* to the terrorists' interests. Within this range, the more severe the threat, the stronger the public's opposition. Beyond a certain threshold of suffering, however, public steadfastness is likely to erode, and then the greater the severity of terrorists' assaults, the more inclined toward concessions the public is likely to be. Cohen (in press) described this curvilinear or biphasic effect, based on interviews with officials who held high ranking positions in the British government before 1948, during the British rule in Palestine:

> To the extent that public opinion influenced British policy, it was mainly affected by the actions of the IZL and LHI [Jewish terrorist organizations in Palestine]. Terrorism influenced public opinion in two opposing directions. Initially it aroused and stimulated the public against the Zionist struggle and created disgust and weakened the support of Zionism. In a later phase, this disgust had a cumulative effect that brought about public opinion pressure to evacuate [Palestine]. The public became tired of the loss of soldiers' lives.

Importance of the Issues

The effect of the intensity of terrorism on public steadfastness interacts with two additional factors: the importance of the issues at stake, and public hopefulness. As regards the former, it is hardly necessary to assert that individuals' resistance to relinquishing their attitudes and political positions, even in the face of threats to their physical safety, is related to the importance that they assign to the contested issues. Although fear is a potent motivation, under certain circumstances individuals and collectives adhere to opinions, attitudes, and behaviors despite extreme danger. Such has been true of POWs who stood up to their captors and nations that fought "lost wars" for the sake of honor or other intangible rewards. Hence, the curvilinear

function described above is, in effect, a family of functions, as shown in Figure 20.1.

Two parameters of the proposed functions are noteworthy. One, the greater the perceived importance of the issues at stake, the higher the threshold that must be reached before the cost and intensity of terrorism will start eroding public resistance. Two, the greater the perceived importance of the issues at stake, the steeper the negative part of the function and the more moderate its positive part. That is, antiterrorist attitudes are likely to crystallize faster and the erosion of public resistance to terrorism is likely to be slower when the issue of conflict is vitally important to the target public than when it is less important. These functions, then, can explain the seemingly, self-contradictory findings that intense terrorism of the domestic kind is usually less effective than the typically less intense anticolonial terrorism, and that terrorism's success in inducing fear does not necessarily enhance the target public's willingness to concede. The hardening of Israelis' attitudes, for instance, or the finding that 94 percent of the Protestants and even 55 percent of the Catholics in Ulster advocated harsher British action against the IRA (Moxon-Browne, 1981), can be attributed to the fact that in both Israel and Ulster terrorism concerns issues of a truly existential nature for the target populations. By contrast, most modern anticolonial struggles were carried out to obtain concessions that had no

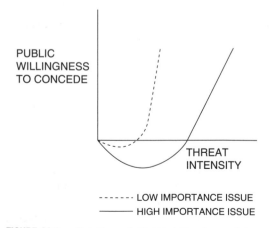

FIGURE 20.1 ■ Relation of threat intensity and issue importance to public willingness to concede to terrorism.

immediate or direct effect on the beleaguered public. Consequently, in these cases, concessions were more readily granted, even though the intensity of terrorism was considerably lower than in most instances of domestic terrorism.

Taken to its extreme, our analysis would appear to suggest that when terrorism threatens the very existence of a nation or strives to alter the character of a society in a manner wholly, unacceptable to the majority of its members, it is unlikely to prevail. After all, nations have withstood wars that claimed more lives and caused more material damage than any known or conceivable terrorist campaign. This suggestion is not entirely valid, however, as there exist two fundamental differences between conventional wars and terrorism. First, attacks on civilian populations during conventional wars are usually patterned (e.g., German air raids on Britain took place at night, against major cities) and have a specific nature (e.g., bombings). Hence, early warning is feasible and the population can be trained to take evasive action. Terrorist attacks, on the other hand, are usually more random in their timing, location, and targeting, and are considerably more varied with respect to method. In war, then, the targets of violence have a greater degree of predictability and control over their fate than in terrorist campaigns. Second, the course and dynamics of conventional wars usually enable the involved parties to form at least tentative expectations about their ending. Terrorism, on the other hand, often lacks a clear and determinable point of extinction (see Devine & Rafalko, 1982). As one Israeli official recently commented, "The public ought to become reconciled to bearing a hundred years of terrorism." Thus, a second factor that distinguishes between individuals' ability to withstand the hardships of war and their resilience in the face of terrorism may be termed "hopefulness."

Public Hopefulness

The possibility that hopefulness has a decisive effect on a public's ability to withstand terrorism was recently illustrated by the collapse of the white regime in Rhodesia. After several years of contained, albeit continuous, terrorist attacks by the ZAPU and ZANU black insurgents, the white regime decided to yield. Thus, despite the fact that by all indications the whites had enough strength to continue their struggle indefinitely, and that the very existence of a dominant white society in Rhodesia was at stake, opposition to terrorism suddenly collapse. We would speculate that this sudden surrender resulted from the loss of hope, caused by the white regime's growing isolation in the international community and failure to see an end to its predicament.

Turning back to the functions described in Figure 20.1, we propose that the position of the threshold beyond which public steadfastness will start to erode, and the rate and intensity of such erosion, are affected by the degree of hopefulness. Taking the hopefulness factor into consideration, we can enlarge our family of curves, as shown in Figure 20.2.

Our analysis of factors that determine the attitudinal impact of terrorism is clearly preliminary. A systematic investigation of these factors is sorely needed in order to arrive at a valid and comprehensive model that explains the processes whereby public opinion regarding terrorism is shaped. Such a model is an indispensable foundation for the measuring, monitoring, and prediction of public reactions to terrorism.

Prediction of Responses to Terrorism

The practical importance of this investigation can hardly be exaggerated. If public opinion is the

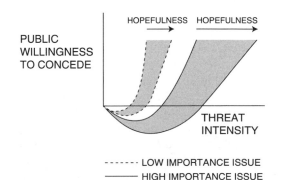

FIGURE 20.2 ■ Addition of the factor of public hopefulness in explaining reactions to terrorism.

key to terrorists' success or failure, then its constant monitoring can provide authorities with "intelligence" needed to combat terrorism. For example, it often appears that although the returns from investments in the prevention of road accidents, crime, and diseases would be considerably greater than from investments in counterterrorist action, governments are more willing to make the latter investment (Alon, 1980). Such a disproportionate investment is usually justified by "public morale" considerations, yet governments rarely bother actually to measure public morale. Thus, the monitoring of public opinion could provide valuable information for the allocation of national resources.

The intelligence that is essential for authorities' effective response to terrorism consists not only of actual public reactions but also of projections to the future. Since terrorism might plague a society for an extended period of time, authorities could benefit immensely from predictions about the long-term, cumulative effects of a drawn-out exposure to terrorism. Furthermore, decision making and policymaking could be aided by predictions of public reactions to contingencies that are currently hypothetical but have a high probability of materializing in the future. For instance, a government that seeks to implement a credible "no ransom" policy in order to stem hostage-taking tactics might be compelled to sacrifice individuals who have been taken hostage. Advance knowledge of public reaction to such an event could help the government decide whether or not to adopt the policy.

Projections into the future are of course risky, yet their importance is so great that even approximations are valuable. Several methods may be employed. The routine measurement of public attitudes can eventually provide a data base for detecting regularities of change in public opinion. These may then be extrapolated to forecast future trends. Such extraplations are at best tentative, as it is impossible to foresee all future events that might affect public reaction. On the other hand, some confidence regarding their reliability may be drawn from the fact that the characteristics of the relevant target population are unlikely to undergo rapid changes.

Surveys can also be used to present respondents with scenarios to which they are asked to respond. Our use of this procedure, as part of the nationwide survey we conducted in 1979, yielded data that attest to its usefulness. Respondents were given three barricade-and-hostage scenarios, two of which had actually occurred—the Ma'alot incident in 1974 and the Savoy Hotel incident in 1975. In both, heavy casualties were sustained in the course of rescue operations. The third was a hypothetical scenario that ruled out a military rescue operation, due to technical constraints. The respondents were asked to indicate the policies that in their view should have been implemented in the three cases, as well as their general preferences for the handling of various kinds of barricade-and-hostage situations differing in the number and type of hostages, the magnitude of terrorist demands, and the feasibility of military rescue operations. The results showed that about one-third of the public opposed any concession to terrorists' demands, the cost of hostages' lives notwithstanding. Less than 10 percent preferred always to concede so as not to jeopardize hostages. The position of the remaining 60 percent of the public depended on the specifics of the situation, with the feasibility of forceful rescue appearing to be the decisive factor. Whereas only 33 percent of the sample advocated no concessions to terrorists in the hypothetical scenario, where no military rescue was possible, 65 percent recommended this policy in the Savoy scenario and 58 percent in the Ma'alot case. It should be noted that in the latter, opting for forceful action actually led to the death of 22 high school students who were held hostage. These findings on specific scenarios were consistent with policy preferences that were expressed in response to general questions. Combined, they suggest that public steadfastness in situations where military options were available did not stem from an expectation that such options would necessarily increase the chance of saving the hostages. A majority of the public appeared willing to sustain losses in the process of an active attack on the terrorists, but would yield to some demands if military action were impossible. The number and kind of hostages appeared to have less importance as a determinant of public policy preferences. Although responses to the general questions revealed a greater importance of these factors than responses to the scenarios, we believe the latter provide a better reflection of public attitude.

The validity of public-reaction assessments can be further enhanced by increasing individuals' perceived involvement in relevant situations. We refer here to the use of experimental simulations in which individuals are asked to assume the roles of decision makers or policymakers. Such an application of the experimental method might prove fruitful in providing information on the effects of a wide variety of factors. Although simulations have sometimes been criticized on the grounds that they lack realism, our own experience and that of others (e.g., Zimbardo, 1971) suggests that a faithful reproduction of the key characteristics of a real-life situation is entirely possible.

Each of the research avenues suggested above has its shortcomings. Hence the generation of predictions about a target public's behavior must be methodologically eclectic. We believe that, despite any shortcomings, the data that such methods might yield would provide a sounder basis for decision making than the guesswork on which many decisions concerning the response to terrorism are based. From a practical point of view, such data might constitute the single most important contribution of social psychologists to combating terrorism.

Enhancing Public Resistance to the Impacts of Terrorism

Social psychologists' second potential contribution to the struggle against terrorism involves planning interventions designed to bolster public resistance to the effects of terrorism. After extensive thought on this topic, we have concluded that existing social psychological knowledge offers little help here. Although social psychologists have made some headway on procedures for enhancing resistance to influence (e.g., Freedman & Sears, 1965; Haas & Grady, 1975; McGuire, 1964; McGuire & Papageorgis, 1962; Petty, Brock, & Brock, 1978;

Petty & Cacioppo, 1977), their contribution is mostly limited to the inducement of cognitive resistance to persuasive arguments. Little is known, on the other hand, about ways to hinder influence attempts that are aimed at arousal of primitive motivations such as fear.

Having failed to find ready-made solutions, we attempted to design interventions that we could suggest if asked to help in enhancing the public's resistance to the impacts of terrorism. This attempt was rather frustrating, for the outcome was quite meager, and the uniqueness of our inputs as psychologists was not apparent. The following pages of discussion illustrate this predicament and indicate that the needed breakthroughs have yet to be made.

Although our analysis of factors that determine the impact of terrorism indicated that fear is just one determinant, nevertheless fear is a critical factor, and its attenuation could weaken the power wielded by terrorists.

The fear of terrorism is largely a fear of the unknown. Anxiety and apprehension stem not only from what terrorists have already done but from unrealistic projections as to what they might be capable of doing. Faced with an ambiguous threat, such as a force that strikes at random, individuals tend to expect the worst (see Kupperman, 1977). Fear and worry are further fueled by the magnifying effect of the news media and by their depiction of terrorists as desperate, ideology-driven persons who are willing to sacrifice everything for a cause (see Netanyahu, 1979). Authors of fiction have contributed their share by weaving intricate plots suggesting that terrorists are sophisticated planners and faultless strategists (e.g., Harris, 1976; Collins & Lapierre, 1980; Mills, 1977). And governments and politicians, in an effort to justify counterterrorist acts and policies, tend at times to present terrorism in more dramatic colors than it actually warrants.

The above arguments suggest that the fear of terrorism can be considerably alleviated by making terrorism known, that is, by disseminating valid and accurate information about terrorism, terrorists, and their capabilities. This is not to suggest that terrorism should be trivialized or that its targets should be lulled into a false sense of security, for terrorism is dangerous. Yet the danger might be exacerbated if its dimensions are exaggerated. The dissemination of accurate information about terrorism might lead the public to realize that terrorism, in Jenkins's (1982, p. 13) words, "is a pain, not a mortal danger."

The main culprits in magnifying the perceived might of terrorism are doubtlessly the news media. Their role in the "theater of terrorism" has been extensively discussed elsewhere (e.g., Netanyahu, 1979; Alexander, 1979). Here it is sufficient to point out the ways in which the media serve terrorism. First, the printed space and broadcast time devoted to terrorism and terrorist incidents turn terrorism into an ever present threat in individuals' consciousness. Second, the media's technical capabilities, which allow them to convey information in real time, by word, sound, and image, force millions to experience vicariously the horrors of terrorism. Third, modern journalists provide not only news but also background and "in depth" analyses; and journalistic explanations of terrorism—which are almost invariably of a social nature—have sometimes combined with a tendency to forgive whatever is "socially explainable" to exculpate terrorism (Podhoretz, 1979). Fourth, Western journalism often adopts an adversarial position vis-à-vis authorities, and as a result, some reports of terrorist incidents have been more critical of the authorities than of the terrorists. To the extent that one of the major aims of terrorism is to discredit authorities, journalists sometimes act as valuable allies of terrorists (Netanyahu, 1979).

In principle, the damage caused by the news media could be prevented if the operating philosophy and practices of the news media were changed. It would not seem to be a gross violation of the "public's right to know" if, for instance, a terrorist incident were not reported while it was unfolding, or if the occurrence were made known without being shown. Difficulty would arise, however, in implementation of such changes, which might entail a serious infringement on the freedom of the press. As social psychologists we can only stress that a fundamental change in journalists'

modus operandi might be the single most important antiterrorist remedy.

Terrorism derives much of its power from the randomness of its attacks. Terrorism, in other words, is potentially powerful because it may come to be perceived as unpredictable and uncontrollable, and thereby induce a feeling of helplessness. The power of terrorism can therefore be weakened by preventing the public from adopting a passive stance vis-à-vis terrorism; that is, by teaching the public that terrorism can be coped with actively.

Active coping with terrorism can take a variety of forms. On a most elementary level, individuals can be taught and encouraged to take certain precautionary and defensive actions that, aside from their practical utility, could also ward off feelings of helplessness. In Israel, for instance, where bombing attacks are commonplace, authorities routinely encourage the public to keep on the alert for suspicious objects and parcels found in public places, and they provide information on the various methods that terrorists can employ to plant bombs. The frequent early discovery of bombs, by civilians, has reinforced public alertness and, we believe, instilled confidence that the threat can be coped with. There is no evidence whatsoever that the planting of bombs has deterred Israelis from frequenting public places or from using public transportation, which is a popular target of bombing attacks. It should be immediately stressed, however, that in encouraging the public to become actively involved in its own protection, one should be careful to avoid excesses. Unnecessarily exaggerated safety measures might become a burden and interfere with daily routines to a degree that could by itself be considered a small victory for terrorism. Additionally, the human tendency to rationalize action could turn such measures into fear stimulants.

Individuals' perceived control over the threats posed by terrorism derives not only from coping behaviors that they themselves are capable of undertaking. In times of stress, individuals' dependence on authorities is enhanced, and authorities' performance in dealing with terrorism becomes a yardstick by which the public assesses the likelihood that there will be an end to its ordeal.

During the last two decades, most Western governments have been notably hesitant in their response to terrorism. Many have favored the so called "flexible response" policy (see Friedland, 1983), which advocates the adoption of ad hoc responses, in accordance with conditions prevailing in each terrorist incident. The inevitable resultant inconsistency is detrimental in two important respects. Authorities might come to be regarded as inept and noncredible. The Israeli government has many times stated its opposition to dealing with terrorists; yet it traded 3500 jailed terrorists for the release of 6 Israelis held captive by the PLO and may thus have impaired its ability to inspire public trust. Second, authorities' indecisiveness might be interpreted as evidence that the problem is insurmountable. We therefore submit that the public's confidence that "something can be done" and its hope that "there is light at the end of the tunnel" have to be nurtured by authorities' adoption of clear and consistent policies regarding terrorism and by their visibly undertaking decisive counterterrorist action. Our 1979 public opinion survey, referred to above, revealed that the Israeli public strongly supported the implementation of extreme counterterrorist measures.

Underneath the desire for action, revealed by our research and that of others (see Jenkins, 1982), there lurks an elementary psychological phenomenon: namely, the helplessness-reducing or stress-reducing quality that activity, whether instrumental or not, can have in threatening situations. In our view, authorities should be better attuned to this psychological need of their constituents. Our own experience has taught us that officials and politicians entrusted with the response to terrorism often act on the basis of misconceptions of public attitudes. Thus, for instance, the worry and concern of the close relatives of kidnap victims and their understandable desire to assure the victims' release at any cost has sometimes been interpreted as the attitude of the public at large and thus led to unwise decisions. Such seems to have been the case in the Israeli government's agreement to release 76 convicted terrorists, some of them sentenced to life terms for multiple murders, in exchange for a single Israeli soldier who was held captive by a terrorist group. Our 1979 survey, conducted shortly after the exchange, showed that 81.5 percent of the public thought that the government had conceded too much in this case.

To reiterate, authorities should pay closer attention to psychological processes that could enhance the public's ability to withstand terrorism. In so doing, they might discover that their indecisiveness, which they often rationalize as "public concern," is ill-founded. Governments are frequently paralyzed by the fear that they would be damned if they energetically responded to terrorism—and in so doing impinged on the rights, freedoms, and welfare of their constituents—and would be equally damned if they tried to weather the threat passively. The dilemma is genuine, and the importance of carefully weighing the intensity and scope of counterterrorist action can hardly be exaggerated. Nevertheless, the guiding question for authorities should not be whether the public will tolerate action, but rather, how will it fare without action?

The Relevance of Social Psychology

Although the present wave of political terrorism is by now 16 years old and seems to be growing, it has not yet attracted the attention and interest of mainstream social psychology or other branches of psychology. The *Psychological Abstracts* listed no reference to terrorism or to related terms such as "hostages" or "hijacking" until the end of 1981. By this criterion, official psychology only recognized the problem of terrorism in 1982, when 10 publications were listed under that heading. Meanwhile, from 1967 through October 1981, there were 19,450 listings for the subject "rats," 243 for goldfish, and 52 for seagulls. By contrast, during the aforementioned period, only 42 items were listed under "nationalism" and 32 under "political revolution."

A detailed analysis of the reasons for this apparent indifference to problems of immense social importance is beyond the scope of the present chapter. Some of the more salient reasons can nevertheless be pointed out. The traditional emphasis on individuals and small groups rather than on mass

Understanding Terror Networks

Marc Sageman*

After leaving the CIA, I was happy in my naive belief that I had left all that behind me. But after 9-11, like everyone, I wanted to do something. What people were saying about the perpetrators shortly after the attacks was simply not consistent with my own experience. I began to apply the principles of evidence-based medicine to terrorism research, because there really was no data on the perpetrators. There were theories, opinions, and anecdotal evidence, but there was no systematic gathering of data.

I started gathering terrorist biographies from various sources, mostly from the records of trials. The trial that took place in New York in 2001 in connection with the 1998 embassy bombing, for instance, was 72 days long and had a wealth of information, 9,000 pages of it. I wanted to collect this information to test the conventional wisdom about terrorism. With some 400 biographies, all in a matrix, I began social-network analysis of this group.

*University of Pennsylvania and The Foreign Policy Research Institute.

Marc Sageman, M.D., Ph.D. Correspondence concerning this article should be sent to email: sageman@post.harvard.cdu

Background

We all know that Al Qaeda is a violent, Islamist, revivalist social movement, held together by a common vision of a Salafi state. Al Qaeda proper is just a small organization within this larger social movement. We often mistake the social movement for Al Qaeda and vice versa because for about five years, Al Qaeda had more or less control of the social movement.

The segment that poses a threat to the United States came out of Egypt. Most of the leadership and the whole ideology of Al Qaeda derives from Egyptian writer Sayyid Qutb (1906–66) and his progeny, who killed Anwar Sadat and were arrested in October 1981. President Mubarak generously allowed them to be released in 1984.

Many of the released men, harassed by the Egyptian police, migrated to Afghanistan. With the end of the Soviet-Afghan War, they continued on to jihad. These Arab outsiders actually did not fight in the Soviet-Afghan War except for one small battle at Jaji/Ali Kheyl, which was really defensive: the Arabs had put their camp on the main logistic supply line, and in the spring of 1987 the Soviets tried to destroy it. So they were really more the recipient of a Soviet offensive, but they really did not fight in that war and thus the U.S. had absolutely no contact with them. I heard about the battle of Jaji at the time, and it never dawned on me to ask the Afghans I debriefed who the Arabs were. They turned out to be bin Laden and his men at the Al-Masada (Lion's Den) camp.

After the war, a lot of these foreigners returned to their countries. Those who could not return because they were terrorists remained in Afghanistan. In 1991, Algeria and Egypt complained to Pakistan that it was harboring terrorists, so Pakistan expelled them. Thus the most militant of these terrorists made their way to Khartoum, where they were invited by Hassan al-Turabi of the National Islamic Front in Khartoum.

The Khartoum period is critical, because what these violent Salafists basically want to do is to create a Salafi state in a core Arab country. Salafi (from Salaf, "ancient ones" or "predecessors" in Arabic) is an emulation, an imitation of the mythical Muslim community that existed at the time of Mohammed and his companion, which Salafists believe was the only fair and just society that ever existed. A very small subset of Salafis, the disciples of Qutb, believe they cannot create this state peacefully through the ballot-box but have to use violence. The Utopia they strive for is similar to most Utopias in European thought of the nineteenth to the twentieth centuries, such as the communist classless society.

In Khartoum, the Salafists theorized that the reason they had been unable to overthrow their own government (the "near enemy") was because it was propped up by the "far enemy"—the United States. So they decided to redirect their efforts and, instead of going after their own government, to attack the "far-enemy." In 1996, for many reasons, Hassan al-Bashir, the President of Sudan, had to expel Al Qaeda after the imposition of international sanctions, because the Sudanese Government was implicated in the attempt to assassinate Egyptian President Mubarak in Addis Ababa in 1995. In August 1996, within two months of returning to Afghanistan, bin Laden issued a fatwa declaring war on the United States.

The fatwa clearly articulated the new goals of this movement, which were to get the U.S. out of the Middle East so they would be free to overthrow the Saudi monarchy or the Egyptian regime and establish a Salafi state. This remains their goal and is why 9-11 happened. This is why the embassy bombing happened. It's really not so much to destroy the United States, something they know they cannot do right now. This is all why I put the start of the threat against us at 1996.

The Data

The 400 terrorists on whom I've collected data were the ones who actually targeted the "far enemy," the U.S., as opposed to their own governments. I wanted to limit myself for analytical purity to that group, to see if I could identify anything different from other terrorist movements, which were far more nationalistic.

Most people think that terrorism comes from poverty, broken families, ignorance, immaturity, lack of family or occupational responsibilities, weak minds susceptible to brainwashing—the sociopath, the criminals, the religious fanatic, or, in this country, some believe they're just plain evil.

Taking these perceived root causes in turn, three quarters of my sample came from the upper or middle class. The vast majority—90 percent—came from caring, intact families. Sixty-three percent had gone to college, as compared with the 5–6 percent that's usual for the third world. These are the best and brightest of their societies in many ways.

Al Qaeda's members are not the Palestinian fourteen-year-olds we see on the news but join the jihad at the average age of 26. Three-quarters were professionals or semi-professionals. They are engineers, architects, and civil engineers, mostly scientists. Very few humanities are represented, and quite surprisingly very few had any background in religion. The natural sciences predominate. Bin Laden himself is a civil engineer, Zawahiri is a physician, Mohammed Atta was, of course, an architect; and a few members are military, such as Mohammed Ibrahim Makawi, who is supposedly the head of the military committee.

Far from having no family or job responsibilities, 73 percent were married and the vast majority had children. Those who were not married were usually too young to be married. Only 13 percent were madrassa-trained and most of them come from what I call the Southeast Asian sample, the Jemaah Islamiyya (JI). They had gone to schools headed by Sungkar and Bashir. Sungkar was the head of JI; he died in 1999. His successor, Bashir, is the cleric who is being tried for the Jakarta Marriott bombing of August 2003; he is also suspected of planning the October 2002 Bali bombing.

As a psychiatrist, originally I was looking for any characteristic common to these men. But only four of the 400 men had any hint of a disorder. This is below the worldwide base rate for thought disorders. So they are as healthy as the general population. I didn't find many personality disorders, which makes sense in that people who are antisocial usually don't cooperate well enough with others to join groups. This is a well-organized type of terrorism: these men are not like Unabomber Ted Kaczynski, loners off planning in the woods. Loners are weeded out early on. Of the nineteen 9-11 terrorists, none had a criminal record. You could almost say that those least likely to cause harm individually are most likely to do so collectively.

At the time they joined jihad, the terrorists were not very religious. They only became religious once they joined the jihad. Seventy percent of my sample joined the jihad while they were living in another country from where they grew up. So someone from country A is living in country B and going after country C—the United States. This is very different from the usual terrorist of the past, someone from country A, living in country A, going after country A's government. I want to remind that I'm addressing my sample of those who attacked the U.S., not Palestinians, Chechens, Kashmiris, etc.

France happened to generate a lot of my sample, fourth behind Saudi Arabia, Egypt, and Morocco. Eighty percent were, in some way, totally excluded from the society they lived in. Sixty-eight percent either had preexisting friendships with people already in the jihad or were part of a group of friends who collectively joined the jihad together: this is typical of the Hamburg group that did 9-11, the Montreal group that included Ahmed Ressam, the millennial bomber. Another 20 percent had

close family bonds to the jihad. The Khadr family from Toronto is typical: the father, Ahmed Saeed Khadr, who had a computer engineering degree from Ottawa and was killed in Pakistan in October 2003, got his five sons involved: all of them trained in Al Qaeda camps and one has been held for killing a U.S. medic. Their mother is involved in financing the group.

So between the two, you have 88 percent with friendship/family bonds to the jihad; the rest are usually disciples of Bashir and Sungkar. But that's not the whole story. They also seem to have clustered around ten mosques worldwide that generated about 50 percent of my sample. If you add the two institutions in Indonesia, twelve institutions generated 60 percent of my sample. So, you're talking about a very select, small group of people. This is not as widespread as people think.

So what's in common? There's really no profile, just similar trajectories to joining the jihad and that most of these men were upwardly and geographically mobile. Because they were the best and brightest, they were sent abroad to study. They came from moderately religious, caring, middle-class families. They're skilled in computer technology. They spoke three, four, five, six languages. Most Americans don't know Arabic; these men know two or three Western languages: German, French, English.

When they became homesick, they did what anyone would and tried to congregate with people like themselves, whom they would find at mosques. So they drifted towards the mosque, not because they were religious, but because they were seeking friends. They moved in together in apartments, in order to share the rent and also to eat together—they were mostly halal, those who observed the Muslim dietary laws, similar in some respects to the kosher laws of Judaism. Some argue that such laws help to bind a group together since observing them is something very difficult and more easily done in a group. A micro-culture develops that strengthens and absorbs the participants as a unit. This is a halal theory of terrorism, if you like.

These cliques, often in the vicinity of mosques that had a militant script advocating violence to

conflict—for instance, terrorists and governments— arrive at surprisingly counterintuitive but nonetheless predictable behavioral choices. In this realm of decision theory, "rational" means "instrumental." In other words, if an action makes sense as an instrumental means to an end, however grisly the means and however abhorrent the end may be to us, a person who takes that action is a rational actor.

Several terrorism experts have explicitly addressed the question of the rationality of terrorist behaviors. The two papers we have included represent the tip of the iceberg and reflect two somewhat different approaches. Political scientist and eloquent terrorism authority Martha Crenshaw (Reading 22) provides a concise summary of terrorism as a logical means to a political end. Sandler et al. (Reading 23) come from a more quantitative tradition—the economic analysis of terrorist behaviors. Together, these papers serve as an introduction to an entirely different facet of the psychology of terrorism.

context (1995), remains a landmark in the field. Technically, she is a political scientist rather than a psychologist, but this technicality is irrelevant, given her penetrating and compelling insights into the social psychology of political violence. In this paper, she has acquiesced to Walter Reich's request that she summarize the instrumental or rational choice position in terrorism research. It is by no means her sole perspective; she acknowledges the contribution of personality and psychological pressures. Yet her essay and her explication of the framework of rational choice—cost–benefit analysis, "public goods," and "free-riders"—offers a clear and intelligible starting point for examining the history of terrorism as a story of strategic decisions.

[Note to readers: Jerrold Post's 1998 essay "Terrorist psycho-logic" was prepared as a companion piece to Crenshaw's essay. The reader may wish to refer to the Post paper for a contrasting, psychiatrically informed perspective.]

Reading 22—Crenshaw (1998). The Logic of Terrorism: Terrorist Behavior as a Product of Strategic Choice

Editors' Comments

Martha Crenshaw is one of the towering figures of terrorism scholarship. Her edited text, *Terrorism in*

Discussion Questions

1. Crenshaw emphasizes that terrorism is a "weapon of the weak." She offers three explanations for the relationship between weakness and the decision to commit terrorist acts. What are they? Are they equally compelling?

2. Crenshaw proposes that terrorism has an "excitational function," acting as a catalyst for broader social mobilization. How much might the efficacy of this strategy depend on the population's average level of grievance?
3. Government repression and limitation of civil liberties is an understandable response to terrorism. Crenshaw points out that this response might exacerbate the very problem it is intended to suppress. How so?

Suggested Readings

Crenshaw, M. (1995). The effectiveness of terrorism in the Algerian war. In M. Crenshaw (Ed.), *Terrorism in context* (pp. 473–513). University Park, PA: Pennsylvania State University Press.

Midlarsky, M. I., Crenshaw, M., & Yoshida, F. (1980). Why violence spreads: The contagion of international terrorism. *International Studies Quarterly*, *24*, 262–298.

O'Brien, C. C. (1983). Terrorism under democratic conditions: The case of the IRA. In M. Crenshaw (Ed.), *Terrorism, legitimacy, and power: The consequences of political violence*. Middletown, CN: Wesleyan University Press.

Post, J. M. (1998). Terrorist psycho-logic: Terrorist behavior as a product of psychological forces. In W. Reich (Ed.), *Origins of terrorism: Psychologies, ideologies, theologies, states of mind* (pp. 25–40). Washington, DC: Woodrow Wilson Center Press.

Reading 23—Sandler et al. (1983). A Theoretical Analysis of Transnational Terrorism

Editors' Comments

Todd Sandler is an innovator. An expert in the international relations implications of quantitative economics and game theory, he was definitely among the first to recognize how this framework can help to explain terrorism. This paper by Sandler and colleagues is one of the earliest and most accessible discussions of that perspective. The paper considers terrorists as rational actors engaged in an effort to obtain certain outcomes, communicating via behaviors such as hostage taking and negotiating with governments. The problem for both sides is uncertainty. One can never be altogether sure if the opponent has the resources they claim or is negotiating in good faith. So how does a government decide the most advantageous way to resolve a crisis? (Do not be deterred by the jargon of decision making or by the mathematical formulae! You will find that the authors provide abundant narrative explanation and that the take-away messages are quite vivid.)

Discussion Questions

1. Sandler et al. begin with the premise that terrorists are rational actors who optimize their chances of achieving a goal (or "utility"), subject to constraints. What are some of the constraints faced by terrorists and by governments?

2. This article develops two models. The first depicts the dilemma of terrorists trying to decide whether to follow legal means or resort to illegal activity. According to this model, what will limit the demands that terrorists make?

3. This article proposes a "linked model" describing the terrorist–government negotiation process. How might terrorist attitudes about level of demands and likelihood of concessions become clear to the government?

4. At the core of the quantitative modeling approach to terrorism is the assumption that terrorists truly want the things they publicly demand. Is that a reasonable assumption?

Suggested Readings

Arce, D. G., & Sandler, T. (2005). Counterterrorism: A game theoretic analysis. *Journal of Conflict Resolution*, *49*, 183–200.

Camerer, C. F. (2003). *Behavioral game theory: Experiments in strategic interaction*. New York: Russell Sage Foundation.

Enders, W., & Sandler, T. (2006). *The political economy of terrorism*. Cambridge, UK: Cambridge University Press.

Neumann, J. V., & Morgenstern, O. (1944). *The theory of games and economic behavior*. Princeton, NJ: Princeton University Press.

Sandler, T. (2005). Collective versus unilateral responses to terrorism. *Public Choice*, *124*, 75–93.

READING 22

The Logic of Terrorism: Terrorist Behavior as a Product of Strategic Choice

Martha Crenshaw

This chapter examines the ways in which terrorism can be understood as an expression of political strategy. It attempts to show that terrorism may follow logical processes that can be discovered and explained. For the purpose of presenting this source of terrorist behavior, rather than the psychological one, it interprets the resort to violence as a willful choice made by an organization for political and strategic reasons, rather than as the unintended outcome of psychological or social factors.[1]

In the terms of this analytical approach, terrorism is assumed to display a collective rationality. A radical political organization is seen as the central actor in the terrorist drama. The group possesses collective preferences or values and selects terrorism as a course of action from a range of perceived alternatives. Efficacy is the primary standard by which terrorism is compared with other methods of achieving political goals. Reasonably regularized decision-making procedures are employed to make an intentional choice, in conscious anticipation of the consequences of various courses of action or inaction. Organizations arrive at collective judgments about the relative effectiveness of different

---

[Original] Editor's Note: The purpose of this chapter is, in a way, contrapuntal. The main theme of this volume is a psychological one: In chapter after chapter, it explores the psychological underpinnings of terrorist motivations and behaviors. In focusing on this theme, it could well leave the impression that psychology more than any other factor—or, indeed, *instead of* any other factor—determines terrorist behavior. The author of this chapter agrees that psychology is indeed important in determining such behavior, but she has been asked by the editor, in order to balance the perspective of the book and to place its main theme within a realistic context, to identify the main nonpsychological—that is, the instrumental—bases of terrorist actions.

This chapter, then, and the succeeding one, by Jerrold Post, which lays out the main arguments for the psychological approach to terrorism, together identify the poles of the explanatory debate about terrorist motivations and actions—the strategic pole, at one end, and the psychological pole, at the other. In the opinion of the editor, as well as the authors of both this chapter and the next, both poles must be recognized as delimiting the boundaries of an explanatory landscape. This chapter focuses on one; the next, and much of the rest of the book, focuses on the other.

---

[1] For a similar perspective (based on a different methodology) see James DeNardo, *Power in Numbers: The Political Strategy of Protest and Rebellion* (Princeton, N.J.: Princeton University Press, 1985). See also Harvey Waterman, "Insecure 'Ins' and Opportune 'Outs': Sources of Collective Political Activity," *Journal of Political and Military Sociology* 8 (1980): 107–12, and "Reasons and Reason: Collective Political Activity in Comparative and Historical Perspective," *World Politics* 33 (1981): 554–89. A useful review of rational choice theories is found in James G. March, "Theories of Choice and Making Decisions," *Society* 20 (1982): 29–39.

strategies of opposition on the basis of observation and experience, as much as on the basis of abstract strategic conceptions derived from ideological assumptions. This approach thus allows for the incorporation of theories of social learning.

Conventional rational-choice theories of individual participation in rebellion, extended to include terrorist activities, have usually been considered inappropriate because of the "free rider" problem. That is, the benefits of a successful terrorist campaign would presumably be shared by all individual supporters of the group's goals, regardless of the extent of their active participation. In this case, why should a rational person become a terrorist, given the high costs associated with violent resistance and the expectation that everyone who supports the cause will benefit, whether he or she participates or not? One answer is that the benefits of participation are psychological. Other chapters in this volume explore this possibility.

A different answer, however, supports a strategic analysis. On the basis of surveys conducted in New York and West Germany, political scientists suggest that individuals can be *collectively* rational.[2] People realize that their participation is important because group size and cohesion matter. They are sensitive to the implications of free-riding and perceive their personal influence on the provision of public goods to be high. The authors argue that "average citizens may adopt a collectivist conception of rationality because they recognize that what is individually rational is collectively irrational."[3] Selective incentives are deemed largely irrelevant.

One of the advantages of approaching terrorism as a collectively rational strategic choice is that it permits the construction of a standard from which deviations can be measured. For example, the central question about the rationality of some terrorist organizations, such as the West German groups of the 1970s or the Weather Underground in the United States, is whether or not they had a sufficient grasp of reality—some approximation, to whatever degree imperfect—to calculate the likely consequences of the courses of action they chose. Perfect knowledge of available alternatives and the consequences of each is not possible, and miscalculations are inevitable. The Popular Front for the Liberation of Palestine (PFLP), for example, planned the hijacking of a TWA flight from Rome in August 1969 to coincide with a scheduled address by President Nixon to a meeting of the Zionist Organization of America, but he sent a letter instead.[4]

Yet not all errors of decision are miscalculations. There are varied degrees of limited rationality. Are some organizations so low on the scale of rationality as to be in a different category from more strategically minded groups? To what degree is strategic reasoning modified by psychological and other constraints? The strategic choice framework provides criteria on which to base these distinctions. It also leads one to ask what conditions promote or discourage rationality in violent underground organizations.

The use of this theoretical approach is also advantageous in that it suggests important questions about the preferences or goals of terrorist organizations. For example, is the decision to seize hostages in order to bargain with governments dictated by strategic considerations or by other, less instrumental motives?

The strategic choice approach is also a useful interpretation of reality. Since the French Revolution, a strategy of terrorism has gradually evolved as a means of bringing about political change opposed by established governments. Analysis of the historical development of terrorism reveals

[2] Edward N. Muller and Karl-Dieter Opp, "Rational Choice and Rebellious Collective Action," *American Political Science Review* 80 (1986): 471–87.

[3] Ibid., 484. The authors also present another puzzling question that may be answered in terms of either psychology or collective rationality. People who expected their rebellious behavior to be punished were more likely to be potential rebels. This propensity could be explained either by a martyr syndrome (or an expectation of hostility from authority figures) or intensity of preference—the calculation that the regime was highly repressive and thus deserved all the more to be destroyed. See pp. 482 and 485.

[4] Leila Khaled, *My People Shall Live: The Autobiography of a Revolutionary* (London: Hodder and Stoughton, 1973), 128–31.

similarities in calculation of ends and means. The strategy has changed over time to adapt to new circumstances that offer different possibilities for dissident action—for example, hostage taking. Yet terrorist activity considered in its entirety shows a fundamental unity of purpose and conception. Although this analysis remains largely on an abstract level, the historical evolution of the strategy of terrorism can be sketched in its terms.[5]

A last argument in support of this approach takes the form of a warning. The wide range of terrorist activity cannot be dismissed as "irrational" and thus pathological, unreasonable, or inexplicable. The resort to terrorism need not be an aberration. It may be a reasonable and calculated response to circumstances. To say that the reasoning that leads to the choice of terrorism may be logical is not an argument about moral justifiability. It does suggest, however, that the belief that terrorism is expedient is one means by which moral inhibitions are overcome, as Albert Bandura argues in Chapter 9 of this volume.

The Conditions for Terrorism

The central problem is to determine when extremist organizations find terrorism useful. Extremists seek either a radical change in the status quo, which would confer a new advantage, or the defense of privileges they perceive to be threatened. Their dissatisfaction with the policies of the government is extreme, and their demands usually involve the displacement of existing political elites.[6] Terrorism is not the only method of working toward radical goals, and thus it must be compared to the alternative strategies available to dissidents. Why is terrorism attractive to some opponents of the state, but unattractive to others?

The practitioners of terrorism often claim that they had no choice but terrorism, and it is indeed true that terrorism often follows the failure of other methods. In nineteenth-century Russia, for example, the failure of nonviolent movements contributed to the rise of terrorism. In Ireland, terrorism followed the failure of Parnell's constitutionalism. In the Palestinian-Israeli struggle, terrorism followed the failure of Arab efforts at conventional warfare against Israel. In general, the "nonstate" or "substate" users of terrorism—that is, groups in opposition to the government, as opposed to government itself—are constrained in their options by the lack of active mass support and by the superior power arrayed against them (an imbalance that has grown with the development of the modern centralized and bureaucratic nation-state). But these constraints have not prevented oppositions from considering and rejecting methods other than terrorism. Perhaps because groups are slow to recognize the extent of the limits to action, terrorism is often the last in a sequence of choices. It represents the outcome of a learning process. Experience in opposition provides radicals with information about the potential consequences of their choices. Terrorism is likely to be a reasonably informed choice among available alternatives, some tried unsuccessfully. Terrorists also learn from the experiences of others, usually communicated to them via the news media. Hence the existence of patterns of contagion in terrorist incidents.[7]

Thus the existence of extremism or rebellious potentials necessary to the resort to terrorism but does not in itself explain it, because many revolutionary and nationalist organizations have explicitly disavowed terrorism. The Russian Marxists argued for years against the use of terrorism.[8] Generally, small organizations resort to violence to compensate for what they lack in numbers.[9] The

---

[5] See Martha Crenshaw, "The Strategic Development of Terrorism," paper presented at the 1985 Annual Meeting of the American Political Science Association, New Orleans.

[6] William A. Gamson, *The Strategy of Social Protest* (Homewood, Illinois: Dorsey Press, 1975).

[7] Manus I. Midlarsky Martha Crenshaw and Fumihiko Yoshida "Why Violence Spreads: The Contagion of International Terrorism," *International Studies Quarterly* 24 (1980): 262–98.

[8] See the study by David A. Newell, *The Russian Marxist Response to Terrorism: 1878–1917* (Ph.D. dissertation, Stanford University, University Microfilms, 1981).

[9] The tension between violence and numbers is a fundamental proposition in DeNardo's analysis; see *Power in Numbers*, chapters 9–11.

374 ■ Psychology of Terrorism: Key Readings

imbalance between the resources terrorists are able to mobilize and the power of the incumbent regime is a decisive consideration in their decision making.

More important than the observation that terrorism is the weapon of the weak, who lack numbers or conventional military power, is the explanation for weakness. Particularly, why does an organization lack the potential to attract enough followers to change government policy or overthrow it?

One possibility is that the majority of the population does not share the ideological views of the resisters, who occupy a political position so extreme that their appeal is inherently limited. This incompatibility of preferences may be purely political, concerning, for example, whether or not one prefers socialism to capitalism. The majority of West Germans found the Red Army Faction's promises for the future not only excessively vague but distasteful. Nor did most Italians support aims of the neofascist groups that initiated the "strategy of tension" in 1969. Other extremist groups, such as the *Euzkadi ta Akatasuna* (ETA) in Spain or the Provisional Irish Republican Army (PIRA) in Northern Ireland, may appeal exclusively to ethnic, religious, or other minorities. In such cases, a potential constituency of like-minded and dedicated individuals exists, but its boundaries are fixed and limited. Despite the intensity of the preferences of a minority, its numbers will never be sufficient for success.

A second explanation for the weakness of the type of organization likely to turn to terrorism lies in a failure to mobilize support. Its members may be unwilling or unable to expend the time and effort required for mass organizational work. Activists may not possess the requisite skills or patience, or may not expect returns commensurate with their endeavors. No matter how acute or widespread popular dissatisfaction may be, the masses do not rise spontaneously; mobilization is required.[10] The

organization's leaders, recognizing the advantages of numbers, may combine mass organization with conspiratorial activities. But resources are limited and organizational work is difficult and slow even under favorable circumstances. Moreover, rewards are not immediate. These difficulties are compounded in an authoritarian state, where the organization of independent opposition is sure to incur high costs. Combining violent provocation with nonviolent organizing efforts may only work to the detriment of the latter.

For example, the debate over whether to use an exclusively violent underground strategy that is isolated from the masses (as terrorism inevitably is) or to work with the people in propaganda and organizational efforts divided the Italian left-wing groups, with the Red Brigades choosing the clandestine path and Prima Linea preferring to maintain contact with the wider protest movement. In prerevolutionary Russia the Socialist-Revolutionary party combined the activities of a legal political party with the terrorist campaign of the secret Combat Organization. The IRA has a legal counterpart in Sinn Fein.

A third reason for the weakness of dissident organizations is specific to repressive states. It is important to remember that terrorism is by no means restricted to liberal democracies, although some authors refuse to define resistance to authoritarianism as terrorism.[11] People may not support a resistance organization because they are afraid of negative sanctions from the regime or because censorship of the press prevents them from learning of the possibility of rebellion. In this situation a radical organization may believe that supporters exist but cannot reveal themselves. The depth of this latent support cannot be measured or activists mobilized until the state is overthrown.

Such conditions are frustrating, because the likelihood of popular dissatisfaction grows as the likelihood of its active expression is diminished.

[10] The work of Charles Tilly emphasizes the political basis of collective violence. See Charles Tilly, Louise Tilly, and Richard Tilly, *The Rebellious Century 1830–1930* (Cambridge: Harvard University Press, 1975), and Charles Tilly, *From Mobilization to Revolution* (Reading, Mass.: Addison-Wesley, 1978).

[11] See Conor Cruise O'Brien, "Terrorism under Democratic Conditions: The Case of the IRA," in *Terrorism, Legitimacy, and Power: The Consequences of Political Violence*, edited by Martha Crenshaw (Middletown, Conn.: Wesleyan University Press, 1983).

Frustration may also encourage unrealistic expectations among the regime's challengers, who are not able to test their popularity. Rational expectations may be undermined by fantastic assumptions about the role of the masses. Yet such fantasies can also prevail among radical undergrounds in Western democracies. The misperception of conditions can lead to unrealistic expectations.

In addition to small numbers, time constraints contribute to the decision to use terrorism. Terrorists are impatient for action. This impatience may, of course, be due to external factors, such as psychological or organizational pressures. The personalities of leaders, demands from followers, or competition from rivals often constitute impediments to strategic thinking. But it is not necessary to explain the felt urgency of some radical organizations by citing reasons external to an instrumental framework. Impatience and eagerness for action can be rooted in calculations of ends and means. For example, the organization may perceive an immediate opportunity to compensate for its inferiority vis-à-vis the government. A change in the structure of the situation may temporarily alter the balance of resources available to the two sides, thus changing the ratio of strength between government and challenger.

Such a change in the radical organization's outlook—the combination of optimism and urgency—may occur when the regime suddenly appears vulnerable to challenge. This vulnerability may be of two sorts. First, the regime's ability to respond effectively, its capacity for efficient repression of dissent, or its ability to protect its citizens and property may weaken. Its armed forces may be committed elsewhere, for example, as British forces were during World War I when the IRA first rose to challenge British rule, or its coercive resources may be otherwise overextended. Inadequate security at embassies, airports, or military installations may become obvious. The poorly protected U.S. Marine barracks in Beirut were, for example, a tempting target. Government strategy may be ill-adapted to responding to terrorism.

Second, the regime may make itself morally or politically vulnerable by increasing the likelihood that the terrorists will attract popular support.

Government repressiveness is thought to have contradictory effects: it both deters dissent and provokes a moral backlash.[12] Perceptions of the regime as unjust motivate opposition. If government actions make average citizens willing to suffer punishment for supporting antigovernment causes, or lend credence to the claims of radical opponents, the extremist organization may be tempted to exploit this temporary upsurge of popular indignation. A groundswell of popular disapproval may make liberal governments less willing (as opposed to less able) to use coercion against violent dissent.

Political discomfort may also be internationally generated. If the climate of international opinion changes so as to reduce the legitimacy of a targeted regime, rebels may feel encouraged to risk a repression that they hope will be limited by outside disapproval. In such circumstances the regime's brutality may be expected to win supporters to the cause of its challengers. The current situation in South Africa furnishes an example. Thus a heightened sensitivity to injustice may be produced either by government actions or by changing public attitudes.

The other fundamental way in which the situation changes to the advantage of challengers is through acquiring new resources. New means of financial support are an obvious asset, which may accrue through a foreign alliance with a sympathetic government or another, richer revolutionary group, or through criminal means such as bank robberies or kidnapping for ransom. Although terrorism is an extremely economical method of violence, funds are essential for the support of full-time activists, weapons purchases, transportation, and logistics.

Technological advances in weapons, explosives, transportation, and communications also may enhance the disruptive potential of terrorism. The invention of dynamite was thought by nineteenth-century revolutionaries and anarchists to equalize the relationship between government and

---

[12] For example, DeNardo, in *Power in Numbers*, argues that "the movement derives moral sympathy from the government's excesses" (p. 207).

challenger, for example. In 1885, Johann Most published a pamphlet titled *Revolutionary War Science*, which explicitly advocated terrorism. According to Paul Avrich, the anarchists saw dynamite "as a great equalizing force, enabling ordinary workmen to stand up against armies, militias, and police, to say nothing of the hired gunmen of the employers."[13] In providing such a powerful but easily concealed weapon, science was thought to have given a decisive advantage to revolutionary forces.

Strategic innovation is another important way in which a challenging organization acquires new resources. The organization may borrow or adapt a technique in order to exploit a vulnerability ignored by the government. In August 1972, for example, the Provisional IRA introduced the effective tactic of the one-shot sniper. IRA Chief of Staff Sean Mac-Stiofain claims to have originated the idea: "It seemed to me that prolonged sniping from a static position had no more in common with guerrilla theory than mass confrontations."[14] The best marksmen were trained to fire a single shot and escape before their position could be located. The creation of surprise is naturally one of the key advantages of an offensive strategy. So, too, is the willingness to violate social norms pertaining to restraints on violence. The history of terrorism reveals a series of innovations, as terrorists deliberately selected targets considered taboo and locales where violence was unexpected. These innovations were then rapidly diffused, especially in the modern era of instantaneous and global communications.

It is especially interesting that, in 1968 two of the most important terrorist tactics of the modern era appeared—diplomatic kidnappings in Latin America and hijackings in the Middle East. Both were significant innovations because they involved the use of extortion or blackmail. Although the nineteenth-century Fenians had talked about kidnapping the prince of Wales, the People's Will (Narodnaya Volya) in nineteenth-century Russia had offered to halt its terrorist campaign if a constitution were granted, and American marines were kidnapped by Castro forces in 1959, hostage taking as a systematic and lethal form of coercive bargaining was essentially new. This chapter later takes up the issue in more detail as an illustration of strategic analysis.

Terrorism has so far been presented as the response by an opposition movement to an opportunity. This approach is compatible with the findings of Harvey Waterman, who sees collective political action as determined by the calculations of resources and opportunities.[15] Yet other theorists—James Q. Wilson for example—argue that political organizations originate in response to a threat to a group's values.[16] Terrorism can certainly be defensive as well as opportunistic. It may be a response to a sudden downturn in a dissident organization's fortunes. The fear of appearing weak may provoke an underground organization into acting in order to show its strength. The PIRA used terrorism to offset an impression of weakness, even at the cost of alienating public opinion: in the 1970s periods of negotiations with the British were punctuated by outbursts of terrorism because the PIRA did want people to think that they were negotiating from strength.[17] Right-wing organizations frequently resort to violence in response to what they see as a threat to the status quo from the left. Beginning in 1969, for example, the right in Italy promoted a "strategy of tension," which involved urban bombings with high numbers of civilian casualties, in order to keep the Italian government and electorate from moving to the left.

---

[13] Paul Avrich, *The Haymarket Tragedy* (Princeton: Princeton University Press, 1984), 166.

[14] Sean MacStiofain, *Memoirs of a Revolutionary* (N.p.: Gordon Cremonisi, 1975), 301.

[15] Waterman, "Insecure 'Ins' and Opportune 'Outs' " and "Reasons and Reason."

[16] *Political Organizations* (New York: Basic Books, 1973).

[17] Maria McGuire, *To Take Arms; My Year with the IRA Provisionals* (New York: Viking, 1973), 110–11, 115, 118, 129–31, and 161–62.

Calculation of Cost and Benefit

An organization or a faction of an organization may choose terrorism because other methods are not expected to work or are considered too time-consuming, given the urgency of the situation and the government's superior resources. Why would an extremist organization expect that terrorism will be effective? What are the costs and benefits of such a choice, compared with other alternatives? What is the nature of the debate over terrorism? Whether or not to use terrorism is one of the most divisive issues resistance groups confront, and numerous revolutionary movements have split on the question of means even after agreeing on common political ends.[18]

The Costs of Terrorism

The costs of terrorism are high. As a domestic strategy, it invariably invites a punitive government reaction, although the organization may believe that the government reaction will not be efficient enough to pose a serious threat. This cost can be offset by the advance preparation of building a secure underground. *Sendero Luminoso* (Shining Path) in Peru, for example, spent ten years creating a clandestine organizational structure before launching a campaign of violence in 1980. Furthermore, radicals may look to the future and calculate that present sacrifice will not be in vain if it inspires future resistance. Conceptions of interest are thus long term.

Another potential cost of terrorism is loss of popular support. Unless terrorism is carefully controlled and discriminate, it claims innocent victims. In a liberal state, indiscriminate violence may appear excessive and unjustified and alienate a citizenry predisposed to loyalty to the government. If it provokes generalized government repression, fear may diminish enthusiasm for resistance. This potential cost of popular alienation is probably least in ethnically divided societies, where victims can be clearly identified as the enemy and where the government of the majority appears illegal to

the minority. Terrorists try to compensate by justifying their actions as the result of the absence of choice or the need to respond to government violence. In addition, they may make their strategy highly discriminate, attacking only unpopular targets.

Terrorism may be unattractive because it is elitist. Although relying only on terrorism may spare the general population from costly involvement in the struggle for freedom, such isolation may violate the ideological beliefs of revolutionaries who insist that the people must participate in their liberation. The few who choose terrorism are willing to forgo or postpone the participation of the many, but revolutionaries who oppose terrorism insist that it prevents the people from taking responsibility for their own destiny. The possibility of vicarious popular identification with symbolic acts of terrorism may satisfy some revolutionaries, but others will find terrorism a harmful substitute for mass participation.

The Advantages of Terrorism

Terrorism has an extremely useful agenda-setting function. If the reasons behind violence are skillfully articulated, terrorism can put the issue of political change on the public agenda. By attracting attention it makes the claims of the resistance a salient issue in the public mind. The government can reject but not ignore an opposition's demands. In 1974 the Palestinian Black September organization, for example, was willing to sacrifice a base in Khartoum, alienate the Sudanese government, and create ambivalence in the Arab world by seizing the Saudi Arabian embassy and killing American and Belgian diplomats. These costs were apparently weighed against the message to the world "to take us seriously." Mainstream Fatah leader Salah Khalef (Abu Iyad) explained: "We are planting the seed. Others will harvest it. . . . It is enough for us now to learn, for example, in reading the Jerusalem Post, that Mrs. Meir had to make her will before visiting Paris, or that Mr. Abba Eban had to travel with a false passport."[19] George Habash of the

---

[18] DeNardo concurs; see *Power in Numbers*, chapter 11.

[19] See Jim Hoagland, "A Community of Terror," *Washington*

PFLP noted in 1970 that "we force people to ask what is going on."[20] In these statements, contemporary extremists echo the nineteenth-century anarchists, who coined the idea of propaganda of the deed, a term used as early as 1877 to refer to an act of insurrection as "a powerful means of arousing popular conscience" and the materialization of an idea through actions.[21]

Terrorism may be intended to create revolutionary conditions. It can prepare the ground for active mass revolt by undermining the government's authority and demoralizing its administrative cadres—its courts, police, and military. By spreading insecurity—at the extreme, making the country ungovernable—the organization hopes to pressure the regime into concessions or relaxation of coercive controls. With the rule of law disrupted, the people will be free to join the opposition. Spectacular humiliation of the government demonstrates strength and will and maintains the morale and enthusiasm of adherents and sympathizers. The first wave of Russian revolutionaries claimed that the aims of terrorism were to exhaust the enemy, render the government's position untenable, and wound the government's prestige by delivering a moral, not a physical, blow. Terrorists hoped to paralyze the government by their presence merely by showing signs of life from time to time. The hesitation, irresolution, and tension they would produce would undermine the processes of government and make the Czar a prisoner in his own palace.[22] As Brazilian revolutionary Carlos Marighela explained: "Revolutionary terrorism's great weapon is initiative, which guarantees its survival and continued activity. The more committed terrorists and revolutionaries devoted to anti-dictatorship terrorism and sabotage there are, the more military power will be worn down, the more time it will lose following false trails, and the more fear and tension it will suffer through not knowing where the next attack will be launched and what the next target will be."[23]

These statements illustrate a corollary advantage to terrorism in what might be called its excitational function: it inspires resistance by example. As propaganda of the deed, terrorism demonstrates that the regime can be challenged and that illegal opposition is possible. It acts as a catalyst, not a substitute, for mass revolt. All the tedious and time-consuming organizational work of mobilizing the people can be avoided. Terrorism is a shortcut to revolution. As the Russian revolutionary Vera Figner described its purpose, terrorism was "a means of agitation to draw people from their torpor," not a sign of loss of belief in the people.[24]

A more problematic benefit lies in provoking government repression. Terrorists often think that by provoking indiscriminate repression against the population, terrorism will heighten popular disaffection, demonstrate the justice of terrorist claims, and enhance the attractiveness of the political alternative the terrorists represent. Thus, the West German Red Army Faction sought (in vain) to make fascism "visible" in West Germany.[25] In Brazil, Marighela unsuccessfully aimed to "transform the country's political situation into a military one. Then discontent will spread to all social groups and the military will be held exclusively responsible for failures."[26]

But profiting from government repression depends on the lengths to which the government is

---

Post, 15 March 1973, pp. 1 and 13; also *New York Times*, 4 March 1973, p. 28. Black September is widely regarded as a subsidiary of Fatah, the major Palestinian organization headed by Yasir Arafat.

[20] John Amos, *Palestinian Resistance: Organization of a Nationalist Movement* (New York: Pergamon, 1980), 193; quoting George Habash, interviewed in *Lift Magazine*, 12 June 1970, 33.

[21] Jean Maitron, *Histoire du mouvement anarchiste en France (1880–1914)*, 2d ed, (Paris: Société universitaire d'éditions et de librairie, 1955), 74–5.

[22] "Stepniak" (pseud. for Sergei Kravshinsky), *Underground Russia: Revolutionary Profiles and Sketches from Life* (London: Smith, Elder, 1883), 278–80.

[23] Carlos Marighela, *For the Liberation of Brazil* (Harmondsworth: Penguin, 1971), 113.

[24] Vera Figner, *Mémoires d'une révolutionaire* (Paris: Gallimard, 1930), 206.

[25] *Textes des prisonniers de la "fraction armée rouge" et dernières lettres d'Ulrike Meinhof* (Paris: Maspéro, 1977), 64.

[26] Marighela, *For the Liberation of Brazil*, 46.

willing to go in order to contain disorder, and on the population's tolerance for both insecurity and repression. A liberal state may be limited in its capacity for quelling violence, but at the same time it may be difficult to provoke to excess. However, the government's reaction to terrorism may reinforce the symbolic value of violence even if it avoids repression. Extensive security precautions, for example, may only make the terrorists appear powerful.

Summary

To summarize, the choice of terrorism involves considerations of timing and of the popular contribution to revolt, as well as of the relationship between government and opponents. Radicals choose terrorism when they want immediate action, think that only violence can build organizations and mobilize supporters, and accept the risks of challenging the government in a particularly provocative way. Challengers who think that organizational infrastructure must precede action, that rebellion without the masses is misguided, and that premature conflict with the regime can only lead to disaster favor gradualist strategies. They prefer methods such as rural guerrilla warfare, because terrorism can jeopardize painfully achieved gains or preclude eventual compromise with the government.

The resistance organization has before it a set of alternatives defined by the situation and by the objectives and resources of the group. The reasoning behind terrorism takes into account the balance of power between challengers and authorities, a balance that depends on the amount of popular support the resistance can mobilize. The proponents of terrorism understand this constraint and possess reasonable expectations about the likely results of action or inaction. They may be wrong about the alternatives that are open to them, or miscalculate the consequences of their actions, but their decisions are based on logical processes. Furthermore, organizations learn from their mistakes and from those of others, resulting in strategic continuity and progress toward the development of more efficient and sophisticated tactics. Future choices are modified by the consequences of present actions.

Hostage Taking as Bargaining

Hostage taking can be analyzed as a form of coercive bargaining. More than twenty years ago, Thomas Schelling wrote that "hostages represent the power to hurt in its purest form."[27] From this perspective, terrorists choose to take hostages because in bargaining situations the government's greater strength and resources are not an advantage. The extensive resort to this form of terrorism after 1968, a year that marks the major advent of diplomatic kidnappings and airline hijackings, was a predictable response to the growth of state power. Kidnappings, hijackings, and barricade-type seizures of embassies or public buildings are attempts to manipulate a government's political decisions.

Strategic analysis of bargaining terrorism is based on the assumption that hostage takers genuinely seek the concessions they demand. It assumes that they prefer government compliance to resistance. This analysis does not allow for deception or for the possibility that seizing hostages may be an end in itself because it yields the benefit of publicity. Because these limiting assumptions may reduce the utility of the theory, it is important to recognize them.

Terrorist bargaining is essentially a form of blackmail or extortion.[28] Terrorists seize hostages in order to affect a government's choices, which are controlled both by expectations of outcome (what the terrorists are likely to do, given the government reaction) and preferences (such as humanitarian values). The outcome threatened by the terrorist—the death of the hostages—must be worse for the government than compliance with terrorist demands. The terrorist has two options, neither of which necessarily excludes the other: to

---

[27] Schelling, *Arms and Influence* (New Haven, Conn.: Yale University Press, 1966), 6.

[28] Daniel Ellsburg, *The Theory and Practice of Blackmail* (Santa Monica: Rand Corporation, 1968).

make the threat both more horrible and more credible or to reward compliance, a factor that strategic theorists often ignore.[29] That is, the cost to the government of complying with the terrorists' demands may be lowered or the cost of resisting raised.

The threat to kill the hostages must be believable and painful to the government. Here hostage takers are faced with a paradox. How can the credibility of this threat be assured when hostage takers recognize that governments know that the terrorists' control over the situation depends on live hostages? One way of establishing credibility is to divide the threat, making it sequential by killing one hostage at a time. Such tactics also aid terrorists in the process of incurring and demonstrating a commitment to carrying out their threat. Once the terrorists have murdered, though, their incentive to surrender voluntarily is substantially reduced. The terrorists have increased their own costs of yielding in order to persuade the government that their intention to kill all the hostages is real.

Another important way of binding oneself in a terrorist strategy is to undertake a barricade rather than a kidnapping operation. Terrorists who are trapped with the hostages find it more difficult to back down (because the government controls the escape routes) and, by virtue of this commitment, influence the government's choices. When terrorists join the hostages in a barricade situation, they create the visible and irrevocable commitment that Schelling sees as a necessary bond in bargaining. The government must expect desperate behavior, because the terrorists have increased their potential loss in order to demonstrate the firmness of their intentions. Furthermore, barricades are technically easier than kidnappings.

The terrorists also attempt to force the "last clear chance" of avoiding disaster onto the government, which must accept the responsibility for noncompliance that leads to the deaths of hostages. The

seizure of hostages is the first move in the game, leaving the next move—which determines the fate of the hostages—completely up to the government. Uncertain communications may facilitate this strategy.[30] The terrorists can pretend not to receive government messages that might affect their demonstrated commitment. Hostage takers can also bind themselves by insisting that they are merely agents, empowered to ask only for the most extreme demands. Terrorists may deliberately appear irrational, either through inconsistent and erratic behavior or unrealistic expectations and preferences, in order to convince the government that they will carry out a threat that entails self-destruction.

Hostage seizures are a type of iterated game, which explains some aspects of terrorist behavior that otherwise seem to violate strategic principles. In terms of a single episode, terrorists can be expected to find killing hostages painful, because they will not achieve their demands and the government's desire to punish will be intensified. However, from a long-range perspective, killing hostages reinforces the credibility of the threat in the next terrorist incident, even if the killers then cannot escape. Each terrorist episode is actually a round in a series of games between government and terrorists.

Hostage takers may influence the government's decision by promising rewards for compliance. Recalling that terrorism represents an iterative game, the release of hostages unharmed when ransom is paid underwrites a promise in the future. Sequential release of selected hostages makes promises credible. Maintaining secrecy about a government's concessions is an additional reward for compliance. France, for example, can if necessary deny making concessions to Lebanese kidnappers because the details of arrangements have not been publicized.

Terrorists may try to make their demands appear legitimate so that governments may seem to satisfy

[29] David A. Baldwin, "Bargaining with Airline Hijackers," in *The 50% Solution*, edited by William I. Zartman, 404–29 (Garden City, N.Y.: Doubleday, 1976), argues that promises have not been sufficiently stressed. Analysts tend to emphasize threats instead, surely because of the latent violence implicit in hostage taking regardless of outcome.

[30] See Roberta Wohlstetter's case study of Castro's seizure of American marines in Cuba: "Kidnapping to Win Friends and Influence People," *Survey* 20 (1974): 1–40.

popular grievances rather than the whims of terrorists. Thus, terrorists may ask that food be distributed to the poor. Such demands were a favored tactic of the *Ejercito Revolucionario del Pueblo* (ERP) in Argentina in the 1970s.

A problem for hostage takers is that rewarding compliance is not easy to reconcile with making threats credible. For example, if terrorists use publicity to emphasize their threat to kill hostages (which they frequently do), they may also increase the costs of compliance for the government because of the attention drawn to the incident.

In any calculation of the payoffs for each side, the costs associated with the bargaining process must be taken into account.[31] Prolonging the hostage crisis increases the costs to both sides. The question is who loses most and thus is more likely to concede. Each party presumably wishes to make the delay more costly to the other. Seizing multiple hostages appears to be advantageous to terrorists, who are thus in a position to make threats credible by killing hostages individually. Conversely, the greater the number of hostages, the greater the cost of holding them. In hijacking or barricade situations, stress and fatigue for the captors increase waiting costs for them as well. Kidnapping poses fewer such costs. Yet the terrorists can reasonably expect that the costs to governments in terms of public or international pressures may be higher when developments are visible. Furthermore, kidnappers can maintain suspense and interest by publishing communications from their victims.

Identifying the obstacles to effective bargaining in hostage seizures is critical. Most important, bargaining depends on the existence of a common interest between two parties. It is unclear whether the lives of hostages are a sufficient common interest to ensure a compromise outcome that is preferable to no agreement for both sides. Furthermore, most theories of bargaining assume that the preferences of each side remain stable during negotiations. In reality, the nature and intensity of preferences may change during a hostage-taking episode. For example, embarrassment over the Iran-*contra* scandal may have reduced the American interest in securing the release of hostages in Lebanon.

Bargaining theory is also predicated on the assumption that the game is two-party. When terrorists seize the nationals of one government in order to influence the choices of a third, the situation is seriously complicated. The hostages themselves may sometimes become intermediaries and participants. In Lebanon, Terry Waite, formerly an intermediary and negotiator, became a hostage. Such developments are not anticipated by bargaining theories based on normal political relationships. Furthermore, bargaining is not possible if a government is willing to accept the maximum cost the terrorists can bring to bear rather than concede. And the government's options are not restricted to resistance or compliance; armed rescue attempts represent an attempt to break the bargaining stalemate. In attempting to make their threats credible—for example, by sequential killing of hostages—terrorists may provoke military intervention. There may be limits, then, to the pain terrorists can inflict and still remain in the game.

Conclusions

This essay has attempted to demonstrate that even the most extreme and unusual forms of political behavior can follow an internal, strategic logic. If there are consistent patterns in terrorist behavior, rather than random idiosyncrasies, a strategic analysis may reveal them. Prediction of future terrorism can only be based on theories that explain past patterns.

Terrorism can be considered a reasonable way of pursuing extreme interests in the political arena. It is one among the many alternatives that radical organizations can choose. Strategic conceptions, based on ideas of how best to take advantage of the possibilities of a given situation, are an important determinant of oppositional terrorism, as they are of the government response. However, no single explanation for terrorist behavior is satisfactory.

---

[31] Scott E. Atkinson, Todd Sandler, and John Tschirhart, "Terrorism in a Bargaining Framework," *Journal of Law and Economics* 30 (1987): 1–21.

Strategic calculation is only one factor in the decision-making process leading to terrorism. But it is critical to include strategic reasoning as a possible motivation, at a minimum as an antidote to stereotypes of "terrorists" as irrational fanatics. Such stereotypes are a dangerous underestimation of the capabilities of extremist groups. Nor does stereotyping serve to educate the public—or, indeed, specialists—about the complexities of terrorist motivations and behaviors.

A Theoretical Analysis of Transnational Terrorism

Todd Sandler,* John T. Tschirhart,** and Jon Cauley***

This article presents some "rational-actor" models that depict the negotiation process between terrorists and government policymakers for those incidents where hostages or property are seized and demands are issued. The models account for the objectives and constraints faced by both the terrorists and the policymakers. Uncertainty is introduced through probability constraints (i.e., chance constraints) requiring a specific likelihood of some event occurring. Implications are subsequently extracted from the comparative static analysis as the models' parameters are changed. The last part of the article presents a club theory analysis concerning the sharing of transnational commando forces.

. . . what should be the response of a government when faced with a hostage situation? The choice has been somewhere on a continuum ranging from never negotiating, which is the stated policy of the United States and Israel, to giving in to the terrorist's demands. Each approach is based on implicit theories regarding the driving mechanisms of terrorist behavior, but such theories have never been adequately spelled out (Mickolus 1976, p. 1314).

Terrorism is an activity that has probably characterized modern civilization from its inception.[1] In the past decade, however, terrorist activity has increased in frequency and has taken on important, novel dimensions.[2] For example, incidents are

---

* University of Wyoming and Australian National University.
** University of Wyoming.
*** University of Hawaii-Hilo.

While assuming sole responsibility for the article's contents, the authors gratefully appreciate helpful comments provided by Donna Lake, Ronald Cummings, Dina Zinnes, and the anonymous referees. Helpful assistance was provided by Paul Kalsbeek.

[1] One of the earliest recorded examples is the *sicarii*, a highly organized religious sect consisting of "men of lower orders" in the Zealot struggle in Palestine (A.D. 66–73). See Laqueur (1978, p. 7).

[2] The following sources provide an overview of transnational terrorism and its trends: Pierre 1976; Jenkins, Johnson, and Ronfeldt 1977; Gurr 1979; Mickolus 1980; Corsi 1981; Russell et al. 1979; and Stohl 1979. Also see Zartman (1977) on negotiation models.

being employed more as a means of political expression and are becoming characterized by a transnational element (Mickolus 1980, p. xv). As a consequence of these developments, scholars have begun to focus their research on this critical problem. Nevertheless, there is a paucity of rigorous modelling of terrorism. Some interesting inductive models have examined the spread of terrorism as a contagion phenomenon by analyzing the goodness of fit between some statistical distributions and the actual distribution of terrorist incidents (Midlarsky 1970, 1978; Midlarsky, Crenshaw, and Yoshida 1980; Hamilton and Hamilton 1981). Although these models have had success in documenting the transmission process of terrorism within and across national boundaries, they have not provided an a priori explanation for the spread of terrorism, the choice of terrorist tactics, or the process of negotiation.

The purpose of this article is to present some "rational-actor" models that analyze important terrorist phenomena. In particular, models are presented which depict the negotiation process that takes place between terrorists and government negotiators. Such an analysis attempts to supply the theory that Mickolus has indicated is missing. The models developed are sufficiently general to analyze the planning stage and the negotiation process surrounding an incident. The implications of the models offer negotiation strategies that may someday be effective in reducing terrorist demands. However, these strategies *must not* be followed until the assumptions of the models are thoroughly tested, since different assumptions imply different conclusions.

The analysis demonstrates that the stability of negotiations and the terrorists' response to government actions depend on risk attitudes of both the terrorists and the policymakers. A no-negotiation policy is shown not to be best in all situations, but appears effective when confronting groups who prefer risky ventures, as demonstrated by the group's past behavior. Moreover, the models predict that government actions that raise the price or costs of engaging in terrorist incidents may not work unless the flow of resources to the terrorists is stemmed as well. The analysis also indicates how stalemated negotiations may be circumvented.

No model of terrorism could possibly apply to all incidents, since assumptions must be made for tractability. The negotiation models here only deal with those situations where a terrorist group seizes hostages or property and holds them at known or unknown locations for the purpose of making demands in terms of money, released prisoners, or the airing of propaganda statements (Mickolus 1976; Corsi 1981).[3] The models analyze a democratic government's response to these terrorist incidents.

The last portion of the article presents a rational-actor model, which examines the feasibility of sharing commando forces among nations. This analysis investigates the interactions among sovereign governments, in contrast to the negotiation models that study the interactions between the terrorists and a single government.

In the analysis below, a number of important conclusions are derived. Some of these conclusions have been previously offered in the literature; however, they are now derived from rigorous models whose assumptions and predictions can be tested. The models demonstrate that ambiguous and aberrant cases, those against conventional wisdom, are possible when special conditions exist.

The body of the article contains five major sections. The following section presents preliminaries, including a justification of the assumptions and methodology of the negotiation model, the differences between the approach taken here and elsewhere, and the usefulness of our approach in studying economic and political science problems. The negotiation models are presented in the second section, and implications are derived in the third. Commando forces and other terrorist-thwarting activities are analyzed in the fourth section, and conclusions follow in the last section.

---

[3] In a recent article, Corsi (1981, p. 51) denoted these types of operations as Type 1 and Type 2. He also listed characteristics of each type (p. 53); the assumptions made in this article agree with those characteristics.

Preliminaries

Terrorism has been defined as the premeditated, "threatened or actual use of force or violence to attain a political goal through fear, coercion, or intimidation" (Russell, Banker, and Miller 1979, p. 4). Political goals can be served through the publication of propaganda, the acquisition of money, and the release of prisoners.[4] The negotiation models here apply to those incidents where bargaining occurs between the terrorists and the government negotiators. Corsi (1981) and Mickolus (1980, p. xxiii) documented that such incidents include kidnappings ($61.2 million in ransoms have been paid from 1968 to 1979), barricade and hostage taking, and hijackings. Mickolus's (1976, Table VI, p. 1322) data indicated that money or release of prisoners or both were demanded in 62 percent of kidnappings, 50 percent of the barricade and hostage situations, and 72.5 percent of the aerial hijackings. Hence, by analyzing those incidents where money or prisoners are demanded, our models relate to a large percentage of incidents. However, the negotiation models do not apply to bombings and assassinations, where in over 93 percent of the incidents examined by Corsi (1981, Table 4, p. 60) no demands were issued.

The negotiation models primarily concern transnational terrorism, in which terrorists or government participants from two or more countries are involved. Incidents originating in one country and terminating in another are transnational in character, as are incidents involving demands made of a nation other than the one where the incident occurs.

The negotiation models assume that the terrorists are bargaining with a democratic government. Since terrorist acts occur in democracies, autocracies, and mixed political systems, this assumption further limits the models' applicability. Fortunately, a large proportion of the types of terrorist acts analyzed by the negotiation models has taken place in industrialized democracies. For example,

Gurr (1979, p. 43) indicated that 52 of 84 more durable terrorist campaigns occurred in democracies because democracies attempt to accommodate diverse political views. The freedom of the media, characteristic of most democracies, allows for the coverage many terrorist groups seek. A recent U.S. Central Intelligence Agency (CIA) report (1981) on terrorism stated that 2,949 out of 6,714 incidents involved the United States. The report indicated that 30 percent of all transnational terrorist attacks occurred in Western Europe, and 10 percent took place in North America. Mickolus (1980, p. xix) noted that nearly half of all transnational terrorism was recorded in culturally "western" democracies. In particular, his data (1976, Tables III and IV, pp. 1312–13; 1980, pp. xiii–xxx) showed that democracies, especially those with high per-capita gross national products, were frequently chosen as hostage contributors.

This article utilizes rational-actor models to examine various aspects of terrorism. A rational-actor model depicts an individual or collective as optimizing some goal, usually that of utility, subject to a set of constraints, restricting the actions that can be taken. These constraints indicate the limits imposed by resources (e.g., time and money), legal rules, and institutional rules. In some cases, restrictions imposed by uncertainty can be introduced in the form of probability constraints, as is done in the negotiation models through the use of "chance constraints."

Once a solution is characterized to a rational-actor model, parameters (or restrictions) can be altered and new solutions can be found. Such an exercise is called *comparative statics,* because different optimal equilibriums at various points in time can be compared as parameters are altered. For example, one can determine how individuals would spend their incomes among alternative products to maximize their utility. In comparative statics, the price of a product is allowed to change and the resulting effects on the person's expenditure on that and other goods are determined.

Rational-actor models and comparative statics have had a rich and fruitful history in economics. The theory of markets and the analysis of economic policy have relied on both modelling

---

[4] Political goals can also be furthered with assassinations and anarchistic activities that seek to embarrass a government.

techniques. Recently, rational-actor models and comparative statics have been used by Becker (1968), Ehrlich (1973), and Heineke (1975) to investigate criminal behavior. These investigators depicted the criminal as maximizing expected utility from legal and criminal activities, which have different expected payoffs owing to different rewards and success probabilities. The deterrent effect of punishment was analyzed by examining the influence that harsher sentences (a comparative static change) have had on a criminal's choice of activities. Such an analysis is fruitful because it leads to implications and policy conclusions that subsequently can be tested.

In political science, rational-actor models and comparative statics have been utilized by Downs (1957) to study a candidate's or party's best election strategy when faced with resource constraints in terms of staff, contributions, and time. A whole field of research known as *public choice* has employed these techniques to examine voting behavior, lobbying strategies, and bureaucratic behavior (see, especially, Mueller 1979). These techniques can also be used to study revolutions, coups, and terrorism.

Some people would object to the use of a rational-actor model to study terrorism: they would argue that terrorists are irrational or mad, a view often fostered by the news media. However, a number of political scientists have disputed this characterization. Stohl (1979) has argued that the madman depiction is a myth, because many terrorist groups have particular goals that are sought as part of an ongoing political struggle. Stohl cited (pp. 6–7) numerous instances where careful negotiations regarding the terrorist demands led to peaceful solutions to hostage incidents. Obviously, one cannot negotiate with madmen.

Gurr (1979, p. 38), Mickolus (1980, pp. xix, xxv) and the U.S. Central Intelligence Agency (1981, p. 11) have shown that political terrorists rank the tactics that they adopt with respect to such factors as risk, time, and the probability of confrontation with authorities. High-risk activities like hijacking and barricade and hostage taking have the smallest incidence; low-risk tactics like bombings and assassinations have the highest (Mickolus

1980, pp. xii–xxx). For example, explosives and incendiary devices were utilized in 69 percent of terrorist incidents. This pattern of behavior suggests a rational response to risk. Mickolus (1980, p. xxv) noted, as did the U.S. CIA (1981) report, that measures taken to raise the costs of certain types of terrorist activities (e.g., metal detectors at airports, more guards at embassies) have immediately induced terrorists to choose other types of tactics whose costs have not risen. Such a response again implies terrorist rationality.

Furthermore, Jenkins, Johnson, and Ronfeldt (1977, p. 1) reported that hostage-taking terrorists are successful almost 80 percent of the time. Such a high percentage of success would presumably attract rational individuals with strongly held political beliefs.

Based upon this type of evidence, we assume that the terrorists are rational actors. One must remember that an actor's goals do not determine rationality; rather, an actor's pursuit of these goals in the face of constraints indicates rationality—i.e., terrorists and law-abiding citizens have different goals, but both are said to be rational when they *efficiently* utilize scarce resources to achieve their respective goals and effectively respond to changes in their constraints.

A final preliminary concerns a comparison between our approach and those of Midlarsky (1970, 1978), Corsi (1981), and Midlarsky, Crenshaw, and Yoshida (1980). Corsi provided a useful typology of terrorist incidents, a typology that we use above and elsewhere in the article. Corsi (1980, pp. 73–76) also suggested an extensive-game approach to modelling terrorist-government negotiations. In the negotiation model, we present a nonextensive-game approach that can capture many of the illustrative scenarios indicated by Corsi. Our approach goes beyond his by depicting the form of the utility functions and the constraints of the terrorists and the government policymakers. Moreover, the stability of negotiations and the comparative static results are examined here.

The deductive models here differ from Midlarsky's contagion models since those models are inductive. Both approaches are concerned with the uncertainty surrounding terrorist incidents and with analyzing what terrorist tactics are used. But our models attempt to explain why certain tactics are utilized more frequently, whereas the contagion approach simply documents which tactics are most contagious. The contagion model is concerned with the overall terrorist pattern; the negotiation model offers better crisis management strategies.

The Negotiation Models

Two models are developed: the first depicts the problem confronted by the terrorists; the second explores the dilemma faced by the government. Both models contain random elements to capture the idea that neither the terrorist nor the government can be certain about the actions the other might pursue. The models are later linked in order to investigate possible negotiation outcomes when terrorists present the government with demands, and the government responds with concessions. Demands and concessions are assumed to be continuous variables, amenable to quantification.[5]

The models employ a chance-constrained programming paradigm rather than a state-preference approach. In the former, an agent maximizes an objective (e.g., utility) subject to constraints, at least one of which is a probability requirement that some event will occur. Thus, uncertainty is introduced through the probability constraint(s). When, however, a state-preference approach is used, an agent maximizes the expected value of an objective where uncertainty is reflected by the probabilities concerning the likelihood of different states (or events) of the world. This latter approach can examine the choice between legal and illegal activities prior to an incident (Becker 1968; Ehrlich 1973); however, the state-preference approach does not lend itself to an examination of the negotiation process once an incident happens.

To the best of our knowledge, this is the first time that chance-constrained programming has been used to generate reaction paths describing the negotiation process. In a non-negotiation setting, chance-constrained models have been used to examine capacity planning for both electric public utilities and home solar-heating systems. In the former, the public utility faces a stochastic demand for its service, where randomness is largely the result of weather. If the public utility installs too little productive capacity, some demand may go unsatisfied. Alternatively, too much capacity means wasted resources. Thus, the utility must choose a capacity level that will fully meet demand with a particular probability (Meyer 1975). In the United States, typical values of this probability exceed 99.9 percent. For solar heating, the availability of solar energy is a random variable associated with cloud cover. A solar-heating system will therefore satisfy heating needs with a particular probability. The owner must plan to minimize the cost of the heating system subject to a chance constraint, ensuring that adequate heat will be available with an acceptable probability (Hamlen and Tschirhart 1980).

The Terrorist Model

The terrorists are characterized as having a choice between engaging in legal activities to further their cause, or planning and executing an illegal activity. Let L be a measure of the gain from a legal activity, and D be the demands against the government as a result of an illegal activity. Since both legal and illegal activities are costly to pursue, there are prices that the terrorists must pay to engage in them. Let p_L and p_D be the unit prices of pursuing legal gains and demands, and let R represent the total amount of resources available to the terrorists. Given these definitions, the terrorists face the following budget constraint:

$$p_L L + p_D D = R, \qquad (1)$$

requiring the expenditure of resources in legal and illegal pursuits to equal available resources.

The greater the terrorist demands, the greater the resources needed to achieve them. Although

---

[5] Although quantification may be difficult in specific cases, demands such as amounts of money or number of political prisoners to be freed can certainly be quantified. Even some forms of propaganda demands, such as the length of a broadcast, can be quantified.

virtually anyone could carry out a terrorist activity and make demands of the government, some minimum level of resources is necessary to make the threat appear viable. The price, p_D, gives the minimum resource expenditure required to make a unit of D credible. For specificity, R can be measured in dollars. L may, for example, be the number of propaganda leaflets distributed, and p_L the dollars needed to make and distribute a leaflet; or L may be a measure of lobbying efforts, and p_L the dollars spent per unit of that effort. Similarly, if D is the number of political prisoners demanded to be freed, then p_D is the dollars expended per political prisoner to make the terrorist threat viable; or if D is a ransom amount, then p_D is the money spent per dollar requested to make the threat believable.

The use of per-unit prices in equation (1) may not reflect accurately expenditures on all types of activities, since there may be nonlinear relationships between costs and activity levels. For instance, the total costs of making and distributing a thousand leaflets can be far less than ten times the costs for one hundred. In this case, $p_L L$ could be replaced by a function, say $T = T(L)$, giving the total costs for L leaflets. This alteration would not significantly change the analysis. The crucial point is that both legal and illegal activities require resources; the terrorists are thus constrained by an expression similar to equation (1). As shown later, the allocation of resources among activities crucially depends on their relative costs, which for the linear case is represented by the price ratio.

Only one legal gain and one demand are depicted in equation (1). This is solely for ease of exposition. Both L and D could be vectors of legal gains and demands, whereas p_L and p_D could be vectors of prices.

The terrorists' preferences are represented by a twice-differentiable utility function with arguments L, D, Π, and parameter C^*, where Π is the probability that demands are met and C^* is the most recent concession made by the government in response to terrorist demands. A twice-differentiable utility function is assumed so that both changes (i.e., first derivatives) and rates of change (i.e., second derivatives) of utility with respect to its arguments can be analyzed. The twice-differentiable assumption simply ensures the existence of these rates of change, which determine the shape (or convexity) of the function. Second derivatives also indicate the sufficient conditions for an optimal solution to exist (i.e., minimums can then be distinguished from maximums). The terrorists' utility function is written as:

$$U = U(L, D, \Pi; C^*). \tag{2}$$

A general utility function is depicted in equation (2), so that the model can apply to a wide range of different types of terrorist groups. Each terrorist group will have its own specific utility function, indicating the satisfaction it receives from different goals. If, for example, a specific group was being analyzed, then empirical evidence would have to be used to test the exact form for its utility function. The marginal utility for each of the three arguments in equation (2) is assumed positive; thus, greater levels of legal activity, greater demands, and greater probabilities of success all increase terrorist satisfaction. Although terrorists are not usually associated with legal activities, an increase in these activities is assumed to add utility since legal acts can further a terrorist group's goals. If terrorists did not receive positive utility from legal acts, they would not engage in them; e.g., the PLO and the IRA would not circulate pamphlets.[6] In the planning stage preceding an illegal act, C^* can be set at zero in equation (2), since the government has not yet received a demand to which it must respond. Since $U = U(L, D, \Pi; C^*)$, from equation (1) it follows that

$$U = U (R/p_L - p_D D/p_L, D, \Pi), \tag{3}$$

where C^* is zero initially.

The chance constraint,

$$Pr\,\{\hat{C} \geq D\} \geq \Pi, \tag{4}$$

---

[6] Some nihilistic groups may receive negative marginal utility from legal activities owing to their interest in bringing down all established order. For these groups, the marginal utility would be negative, and the model would predict that no legal acts would be performed.

ensures that the probability of receiving a government concession of at least D dollars is greater than or equal to Π. Pr denotes probability, and $\hat{C}$ is a *random variable* serving as a proxy for the government concessions policy. Figure 23.1 illustrates this concept. In the right-hand graph, the terrorist demands are measured along the horizontal axis, and government concessions are depicted on the vertical. From the terrorists' vantage point, the government concession is random; past government behavior provides information about what policy might be forthcoming. This is shown in the left-hand graph, where concessions are on the vertical axis and the associated probabilities are on the horizontal. This graph is essentially a probability density function for concessions from the terrorists' perspective. Since the terrorists have knowledge of the density function from past government behavior, the historic mean and variance of concessions are known.

To illustrate how Figure 23.1 is interpreted, suppose the terrorists take an action and the government responds according to the seriousness of the threat. One response might be to adopt a policy such as $\hat{C} = C'$ associated with curve Oab, in which any demand accompanying a threat less than D' is met, while any demand greater than D' is not. If, for example, D' is requested, the government would only concede C'. Segment Oa of Oab lies on the 45° line and not above, since the government would not make concessions greater than demands. Thus, demands of $D°$ are met with concessions of $C°$ under policy C'.

To see how probability enters, suppose the terrorists take action and demand D^*. If the government uses the policy associated with Oab and C', the demand would not be fully met—only C' would be conceded. If, however, the government adopts a concession policy associated with $\hat{C} = C''$ and curve Ocd, the demand D^* would be exactly met. In fact, a concession policy associated with any $\hat{C}$ at or above C^* would ensure satisfaction of demands of D^*. From the terrorists' viewpoint, the probability that the government responds with C^* is given by the shaded area between C^* and C_{max}, an area based on past concessions granted.

Concessions range from zero to some maximum value. Lower values of demands mean a larger shaded area or a higher success probability for the terrorists. The diagram shows that outrageously large demands have little likelihood of being met, whereas the reverse is true for modest demands. In maximizing utility, the terrorists must therefore balance demands with the probability of receiving them.

Constraint (4) can be written more conveniently as

$$\sigma N(1 - \Pi) + \mu - D \geq 0, \tag{5}$$

where μ and σ are the mean and standard deviation of $\hat{C}$, and the function $N(1 - \Pi)$ defines the number of standard deviations that D must be from the mean so as to satisfy the constraint.[7]

Maximizing equation (3) subject to equation (5) yields the following first-order or necessary conditions:[8]

$$D: U_D - U_L p_D/p_L - \lambda = 0 \tag{6}$$

$$\Pi: U_\Pi - \lambda \sigma N' = 0 \tag{7}$$

$$\lambda: \sigma N + \mu - D = 0, \tag{8}$$

where $D > 0$, $\Pi > 0$, and $\lambda > 0$. λ is a Lagrangian multiplier associated with the constraint. Such a multiplier represents the implied cost, in terms of the objective (i.e., utility), associated with the constraint. Subscripts on U denote partial derivatives, and N' is the derivative of N. For example, U_D is the utility gained from additional demands (i.e., $U_D = \partial U/\partial D$). Conditions (6) and (7) can be used to obtain

[7] Constraint (4) can be rewritten as $Pr\{(\hat{C} - \mu)/\sigma \geq (D - \mu)/\sigma\} \geq \Pi$ where $(\hat{C} - \mu)/\sigma$ is a normalized random variable with distribution function $F[(C - \mu)/\sigma]$. Letting $N = F^{-1}$, we have $1 - F[(D - \mu)/\sigma] \geq \Pi$, which implies $(D - \mu)/\sigma \leq N(1 - \Pi)$. The latter can be rewritten as equation (5).
[8] For notational convenience, the arguments have been dropped from the functions. The Lagrangian multiplier technique of constrained optimization is explained in Chiang (1974, Chapter 12).

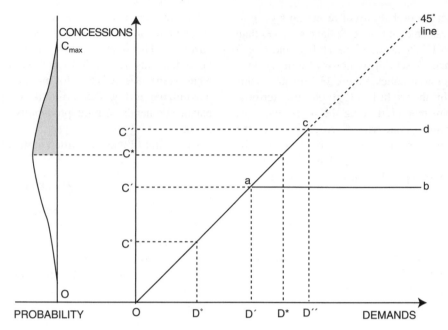

FIGURE 23.1 ■ Government's historic response.

$$\frac{U_D}{p_D} = \frac{U_L}{p_L} + \frac{U_\Pi}{p_D \, \sigma N'} . \qquad (9)$$

The terrorists choose optimum values, D^*, L^*, and Π^* such that condition (9) is satisfied. Thus, demands are increased to the point where the marginal utility from the last unit of resources spent on demands (i.e., the additional benefits from increasing demands) is equated with the marginal utility from the last unit of resources spent on legal activities, plus the marginal utility from the last unit of resources spent on improving the probability of success. But the only way to improve the success probability is to decrease demands; hence, the third term of equation (9) represents a marginal cost associated with increased demands—namely, the resulting marginal disutility of a lower success probability. Both terms on the right-hand side therefore express the marginal opportunity costs of increasing demands in terms of foregone legal activities and a reduced likelihood of success. Hence, equation (9) equates the marginal benefits and the marginal costs associated with increased terrorist demands.

After solving this problem and executing the illegal activity, the terrorists present D^* to the government in the hopes of gaining a concession. The existence of a solution does not guarantee success; rather, the terrorists attempt to succeed with probability Π^*. If $C^* = D^*$ (recall $C^* > D^*$ is ruled out) when the government responds, the terrorists are successful and the illegal activity is completed. But if $C^* < D^*$, negotiations begin and a stalemate may occur. The terrorists must then solve a second problem where utility is again given by equation (2), except that C^*, the actual concession offered, is updated. The government concession enters parametrically in the utility function and acts as a shift parameter. The second round of terrorist demands will be a function of C^*.

The Government Model

The government must decide whether to grant concessions, to wait it out, or to end an incident with force. The government policymaker's utility function, G, is represented by

$$G = G(C, \Omega, a_2; D^*), \qquad (10)$$

which is a twice-differentiable function. C is the concession policy chosen by the government, Ω is the probability of reelection, a_2 denotes the amenities of office, and D^* represents the actual demands of the terrorists. The latter serves as a shift parameter. The policymaker is interested in the reelection probability because either he holds an elective office or is responsive to an elected official, since a democratic government is assumed. Amenities of office may consist of the monetary value of time spent in vacation retreats (e.g., Camp David), or the value of personal services provided by one's staff.[9]

The policymaker confronts two constraints: a resource constraint and a chance constraint. The former is given by

$$a_1 + a_2 + pC = \hat{a}. \qquad (11)$$

where a_1 is the value of resources used to gain reelection, a_2 is the value of the amenities of office, $\hat{a}$ is the value of the policymaker's resource endowment, and p is the price, in terms of resources, required per unit of concession made to the terrorists. However, the pC term does not represent the actual ransom or payment made to the terrorist; rather, it measures the allocation of policymaker's staff and resources to negotiate an agreement. Since the staff could be used to help win reelection or to increase amenities, a real cost is paid by the official when these resources are spent on negotiations with terrorists. President Carter's efforts to end the Iranian hostage crisis clearly took away resources from campaigning and the pursuit of amenities.

The probability of reelection constraint is given by

$$Pr\{v(C, a_1, u) \geq \hat{v}\} \geq \Omega, \qquad (12)$$

where $v(C, a_1, u)$ is a function giving the number of votes the policymaker, or his elected superior, receives in the next election. The vote total depends on the concession policy of the government, the resources used in the reelection campaign, and a random variable, u, serving as a proxy for the competition from other political parties. For simplicity, u is assumed to be an additive disturbance term so that $v(C, a_1, u) = v(C, a_1) + u$. The more resources devoted to the campaign, the greater is the number of votes expected (i.e., $v_{a1} = \partial v/\partial a_1 > 0$). The effect of concessions on votes is ambiguous, however. A negative effect (i.e., $v_C < 0$) implies that voters blame the government for making concessions, because they feel either that no concessions should be considered or that government was at fault for allowing an environment where an incident could occur. A positive effect implies that voters may feel concessions are necessary on humanitarian grounds and at the same time do not fault the officeholder for situations beyond the government's sphere of influence. The possibility that v_C has both a positive and negative range is explored below.

For reelection in democracies, some minimum number of votes is required, usually 50 percent of the votes plus one; this number is $\hat{v}$ in equation (12). The government therefore commits resources and sets concession policy to ensure that the perceived number of votes equals or exceeds $\hat{v}$ with probability Ω. The more risk-averse the officeholder, the higher Ω will be set, and this in turn requires more campaign resources for each concession level.

By using equation (11) to eliminate a_2 from equation (10) and rewriting equation (12) in a more convenient form (see footnote 7), the government problem becomes

$$\max G(C, \Omega, \hat{a} - a_1 - p\hat{C}; D^*) \qquad (13)$$

subject to

$$\sigma_u M(1 - \Omega) + \mu_u - \hat{v} + v(C, a_1) \geq 0,$$

where σ_u and μ_u are the standard deviation and the mean of u, and $M(1 - \Omega)$ is the number of standard deviations from the mean required to attain an Ω probability of reelection. Maximizing with respect to C, Ω, a_1, and a Lagrangian multiplier, γ, yields the following necessary conditions for an optimum:

---

[9] Each of these amenities can be valued by finding the costs of an equivalent vacation or service in the private sector. The model does not, however, imply that political officials remain in office to receive amenities. Instead, the model simply indicates that office amenities provide satisfaction.

$$C: \quad G_C - pG_{a_2} + \gamma v_C = 0 \qquad (14)$$

$$\Omega: \quad G_\Omega - \gamma \sigma_u M' = 0 \qquad (15)$$

$$a_1: \quad -G_{a_2} + \gamma v_{a_1} = 0 \qquad (16)$$

$$\gamma: \quad \sigma_u M + \mu_u - \hat{v} + v(C, a_1) = 0, \qquad (17)$$

where C, Ω, a_1, and γ are positive; subscripts on G and v denote partial derivatives; and the prime on M indicates a total derivative.

From equation (14), either G_C, γv_C, or both are positive because pG_{a_2} is unambiguously positive. Thus, there must be some benefits associated with concessions, either to the policymaker directly or to the voters and then to the policymaker indirectly through the election process. If there are no benefits, the left-hand side of equation (14) is negative and $C^* = 0$. Conditions (14) through (16) can be arranged to obtain

$$\frac{G_C}{p} + \frac{G_\Omega}{\sigma_u M'} \frac{v_C}{p} = G_{a_2}. \qquad (18)$$

The policymaker chooses the optimum values, C^*, Ω^*, a_1^*, and a_2^* to satisfy equation (18). Concessions are thus increased until the policymaker's marginal utility associated with concessions *plus* the marginal utility (or disutility) of the resulting change in the election probability [i.e., the second term on left-hand side of equation (18)] *equal* the marginal utility of the policymaker's foregone amenities. Both expressions on the left-hand side are evaluated in terms of the resources required of the policymaker to make the concession (i.e., p is in the denominator). Equation (18) indicates that policymakers must sacrifice some amenities when negotiating with terrorists. Unless offsetting benefits arise in terms of political stability or direct utility gains, the policymaker will not negotiate.

The Negotiated Equilibrium

Since the actual demand (i.e., D^*) faced by the government comes from the terrorists' optimal choice of D (given the concession offered), and the actual concession (i.e., C^*) offered to the terrorists

derives from the policymaker's optimal choice of C (given the demands made), the two models can be simultaneously solved for the Nash, or independent adjustment, equilibrium.[10] This equilibrium gives the values for D^*, Π^*, λ^*, C^*, Ω^*, a_1^*, and γ^* as the simultaneous solution to equations (6), (7), (8), (14), (15), (16), and (17), and such that $D^* = C^*$. A graphical interpretation of this solution is given at the end of the next section.

Comparative Statics: The Models' Implications

By analyzing the effects that changes in the parameters (e.g., σ, p_D, R) have on the terrorists' optimal choice of demands, the comparative statics suggest important implications concerning the influence of changing the variance in granting concessions or the effect of increasing the price of terrorist activities. The analysis shows that the outcome of these actions as well as others depends on the terrorist group's attitudes to risk, as defined below.[11] These implications crucially depend on our assumptions and may not hold in general.

The comparative static derivation and assumptions are discussed in the mathematical Appendix. As with most comparative static investigations, some of the results are ambiguous. Part of this ambiguity is eliminated by assuming diminishing marginal utilities (e.g., $\partial^2 U/\partial L^2 = U_{LL} < 0$) and separability of the utility function. Diminishing marginal utility or returns implies that the additional satisfaction derived from increases in an activity declines after some point. This is a standard assumption in economics. The separability assumption eliminates some income influences and highlights substitution effects resulting from relative price changes (i.e., changes in p_D/p_L). If price

---

[10] A Nash equilibrium gives the optimal values of the choice variables of one agent (say the terrorist) under the assumption that the other agent (say the policymaker) maintains his choice variables' values.

[11] Chance-constrained models do not yield the usual definition of risk aversion owing to different arguments in the utility function (Pyle and Turnovsky 1971).

changes are small, income effects are then tiny, and their elimination causes little distortion. For large price changes, however, income effects can be important and should not be eliminated unless they reinforce the substitution influence and only the direction of change is of interest.

Other ambiguities disappear by signing some cross partials (e.g., $U_{D\Pi}$) based on a definition of terrorists' risk attitudes. Some ambiguity cannot be removed until more empirical information concerning the functional specifications is available. Nevertheless, many comparative static partials are signed and are consistent with intuition and available data, thus suggesting the appropriateness of our assumptions. The discussion focuses on the terrorist side, since the comparative static results of the government model are more ambiguous owing to a greater number of endogenous variables (four instead of three).

The Terrorist Model's Comparative Statics

If government action raises the price of terrorist activities, then equation (19) indicates that terrorist demands will decrease.

$$\partial D^*/\partial p_D = -(\sigma N')^2 [U_L p_L^{-1} - U_{LL}D(p_D/p_L^2)]/|H_T| < 0, \quad (19)$$

where $|H_T|$ is the determinant of the Hessian matrix of second-order partials (see Appendix). This determinant must be positive if the necessary conditions [i.e., equations (6) – (8)] are also sufficient for optimality. Equation (19) indicates that any government action that increases the severity of sentencing, the likelihood of apprehension, or the difficulty of reaching an intended target would raise p_D and thwart terrorist activities, regardless of terrorists' risk attitudes. Thus, an increase in the effectiveness of a commando force would decrease terrorist activities (see the next section). This comparative static result is in keeping with the evidence. For example, Mickolus (1979, p. 152) showed that air hijackings dropped severely after tighter controls were instituted in 1973. He further noted in 1976–1977 a decline in attempted takeovers of embassies after security improvements

(1980, Introduction). The U.S. CIA (1981) also documented a reduction in hostage taking after the government improved its ability to deal with these episodes.

If p_D is a vector of the prices of activities, an increase in one terrorist activity's price with others held constant would decrease the demands associated with that activity, but would raise those associated with activities whose prices have remained constant. Thus, the government must carefully consider this substitution phenomenon when allocating its resources among different thwarting programs (see the next section). The current increase in assassinations (see U.S. CIA 1981) may have come as a result of terrorist substitution from those activities where government crackdowns have occurred.

An increase in the amount of resources available to the terrorist group is seen in Equation (20) to increase demands unambiguously:

$$\partial D^*/\partial R = -[(\sigma N')^2(p_D/p_L^2) U_{LL}]/|H_T| > 0. \quad (20)$$

This result has significant implications for transnational terrorism owing to transnational cooperation among terrorist groups (Mickolus 1980, pp. xxv–xxvii). Such cooperation serves to increase a group's resource endowment and, from equation (20), to increase terrorist demands. Thus, government activities inhibiting this resource flow will curb terrorism. The strength of the resource effect depends, among other things, on p_D: a large p_D indicates a greater augmentation in terrorist demands resulting from increased resources. If the government succeeds in raising p_D but does not stem the transnational resource flow to the terrorist, demands may still increase, owing to the adverse resource influence. Hence, the model indicates that a government must attempt to *raise p_D and to reduce resource inflows; neither action by itself may be very effective.*

Other comparative static results of interest concern the concession-making policy of the government. Some governments have adopted a no-negotiation policy with terrorists as a means to deter terrorism. The analysis below shows that whether such a negotiation strategy will succeed depends on the risk attitudes of the terrorists. A government's concession-making behavior is characterized by the mean concession granted (μ) and the standard deviation about this mean (σ). By examining the effects that changes in μ and σ have on terrorist demands, we can analyze the influence that changing the government's concession-making policy is expected to have on terrorism.

The effect of a change in the mean concession is depicted as:

$$\partial D^*/\partial\mu =$$
$$[\sigma N' U_{D\Pi} - U_{\Pi\Pi} - \lambda\sigma N''] \, |H_T|. \quad (21)$$

In equation (21), σ and N' are always positive, while $U_{\Pi\Pi}$ is negative by the diminishing marginal utility assumption. N'' is zero for a uniform distribution and is approximately zero for a normal distribution; hence, the last term in the square brackets will be ignored. If U_D is positive, $\partial D^*/\partial\mu$ will be positive, indicating that a rise in the mean concession will increase terrorist demands. A terrorist group whose $U_{D\Pi}$ is positive may be characterized as risk averse, since a decline in the probability of success decreases the marginal utility of demands. In contrast, a negative $U_{D\Pi}$ indicates that as success likelihood *declines* (i.e., more risky acts are chosen), the marginal utility of demands increases. A group displaying a negative $U_{D\Pi}$ appears to enjoy risk, since the marginal benefits derived from demands are higher when risks are greater. Thus, we associate negative values of $U_{D\Pi}$ with risk-preferring or risk-loving tastes. Returning to equation (21), a risk-averse group will increase its demands when the government's mean concession is raised—this result agrees with intuition. The sign of equation (21) is equivocal when a risk-preferring group is considered. If the risk-loving influence is especially strong, large enough to outweigh the diminishing returns influence (i.e., $U_{\Pi\Pi}$), then demands and activities of the group may fall with a rise in μ.

Terrorists' attitudes toward risk, as indicated by $U_{D\Pi}$, are also an important determinant of the effect of changing the standard deviation associated with concession granting. As this measure of variation increases, the uncertainty surrounding

negotiations increases. Equation (22) depicts the effect of σ on terrorist demands:

$$\partial D^*/\partial\sigma = [\sigma N' N U_{D\Pi} + \sigma N'^2\lambda - N U_{\Pi\Pi}$$
$$- N\lambda\sigma N''] \, / \, |H_T|. \quad (22)$$

Once again, we ignore the term involving N'' and consider two cases: negative and positive $U_{D\Pi}$. For the former, the first two terms in the square brackets are positive, because $N < 0$ and $\lambda = U_\mu > 0$.[12] The third term is negative. Thus, if the risk-preferring influence and the direct marginal utility associated with the mean outweigh the diminishing-returns influence, a greater variation in concession granting would increase rather than decrease terrorist demands. Intuitively, this result means that governments should choose little variance in their concessions when dealing with a risk-preferring group, since these groups enjoy uncertainty.

The opposite tendency is associated with risk-averse groups. In this case, the second term in the square brackets is positive, but the first and third terms are negative, indicating that risk avoidance and diminishing returns influences reinforce one another. If these latter influences outweigh the second term, then maintaining a high variation in granting concessions would probably curb terrorism for risk-averse groups.

A no-negotiation strategy would presumably have both a low μ and σ. To determine the efficacy of such an action, the relative strengths of the $\partial D^*/\partial\mu$ and $\partial D^*/\partial\sigma$ terms must be compared, since they are opposing influences. By substituting equation (21) into equation (22), the resulting equation provides the comparison:

$$\partial D^*/\partial\sigma = N(\partial D^*/\partial\mu) + (\sigma N'^2\lambda) \, / \, |H_T|. \quad (23)$$

The last term is positive, and hence equation (23) indicates that $\partial D^*/\partial\sigma$ is a stronger influence than $\partial D^*/\partial\mu$ when the latter is negative (since $N < 0$), as

[12] $N < 0$ follows when $\Pi > 50$ percent. Jenkins, Johnson and Ronfeldt (1977, p. 1) and Mickolus (1980) indicated that on the average, transnational terrorism succeeds in approximately 80 percent of the cases. $\lambda = U_\mu > 0$ follows from the envelope theorem.

expected for some risk-preferring groups. This analysis suggests that a no-negotiation strategy is usually best when dealing with risk-preferring groups. Similarly, a concession policy displaying high variance appears most efficacious when confronting risk-averse groups, which include the majority of terrorist groups (see Jenkins, Johnson, and Ronfeldt 1977 and Mickolus 1980 who showed that easier targets are most often chosen).

The Israelis' no-negotiation policy appears proper for them because the Palestinian terrorist groups (e.g., Black September, PFLP) whom the Israelis confront tend to engage in the relatively riskier activities, such as aerial hijackings and barricade and hostage taking. In fact, Mickolus's data (1980, p. 937) showed that 31 percent of all transnational acts of barricade and hostage taking was excuted by Palestinian terrorists. Moreover, 22.5 percent of aerial hijackings in Mickolus's sample (p. 935) was performed by Palestinian terrorists. No other group accounted for more than 3 or 4 percent of these risky operations! Thus, the Palestinian terrorist groups apparently prefer risky operations, and thus the model implies that the Israelis' policy is best for dealing with them. However, countries confronting risk-averse groups should choose a concession-granting policy with a low μ and high σ. Once again, we caution the reader that these implications only hold for these models and their assumptions.

Since the best concession-granting policy usually differs when dealing with risk-preferring and risk-avoiding groups, policy-makers facing both types must determine which kind is most prevalent and destructive. Once determined, the concession policy must be designed to thwart that type of group. This is a novel and important conclusion.

Another comparative static result involves the change in demands that follows from a change in the concessions offered to the terrorists during the

negotiation process (i.e., $\partial D^*/\partial C^*$). This partial derivative is the slope of the negotiation reaction path for the terrorists. This reaction path is presented below and is used to determine the stability of negotiations by showing the response of one group to offers or demands from the other. The comparative static influence is

$$(\partial D^*/\partial C^*) = \sigma N'[\sigma N' U_{DC^*} - U_{\Pi C^*}]/|H_T|. \quad (24)$$

In equation (24), the expected sign of U_{DC^*} is positive, since concessions are probably complementary or supportive of demands; the sign of $U_{\Pi C^*}$ is equivocal and will probably agree with the sign of $U_{D\Pi}$. Thus, a risk-loving group will probably exhibit a positive $\partial D^*/\partial C^*$. The sign of $\partial D^*/\partial C^*$ is equivocal for risk-averse groups and will be positive when the complementarity of D and C^* dominates.

Space does not permit a discussion of the effects that the parameters have on the terrorists' optimum choice of the success probability associated with the chance constraint. In Table 23.1, the signs of the comparative static partials are indicated for the risk-averse and risk-preferring groups in rows 1 and 2.

The Government Model's Comparative Statics

Unfortunately, the additional endogenous variable in the government model causes great difficulty when the signs of the comparative static influences are analyzed. Consequently, only one comparative static result will be presented. We have chosen to present $\partial C^*/\partial D^*$ [see equation (25)] because it represents the slope of the government's negotiation reaction path and therefore is crucial in determining the stability of the negotiation process as discussed in the next subsection.

$$\partial C^*/\partial D^* = \{- G_{CD^*} [-(\sigma_u M')^2 F - v_{a_1}^2 E]$$

TABLE 23.1.

Group type/partials	$\partial\Pi^*/\partial\mu$	$\partial\Pi^*/\partial p_D$	$\partial\Pi^*/\partial R$	$\partial\Pi^*/\partial\sigma$	$\partial\Pi^*/\partial p_L$	$\partial\Pi^*/\partial C^*$
Risk averse	+	+	−	−	?	?
Risk preferring	?	+	−	?	?	−

$$+ G\Omega_{D*}[-v_{a_1} B\sigma_u M' + \sigma_u M' Fv_C$$

$$- v_{a_1}^2 G_{C\Omega}]\}/|H| \qquad (25)$$

$$\text{where} \quad \begin{cases} F = G_{a_2 a_2} + \lambda v_{a_1 a_1} \\ E = G_{\Omega\Omega} + \gamma\sigma_u M'' \\ B = pG_{a_2 a_2} + \gamma v_{Ca_1}. \end{cases}$$

To insure that $\partial C^*/\partial D^*$ is positive, $G_{C\Omega}$ and G_{CD*} must be positive, and $G_{\Omega D*}$ and v_{Ca_1} must be negative, provided that the sufficiency condition is satisfied (i.e., $|H| < 0$). These requirements imply a risk-averse attitude for the policymaker and a complementarity between demands and concessions. The remaining two partials are difficult to interpret. Risk-averse policymakers would seek a high re-election probability and consequently would allocate large amounts of resources to campaigning. Furthermore, they would be especially responsive to the effects of concessions on reelection.

A Diagrammatic Presentation of the Linked Model

The terrorist-government negotiation process embodied in the chance-constrained models can be depicted in terms of reaction paths. In Figure 23.2, the horizontal axis measures the terrorist demands; the vertical depicts the government concessions. The terrorist reaction path, *OA* (ignoring *OA'* for the moment), indicates the terrorists optimal demands for each level of government concessions offered. This path represents the solutions (for each *C**) to the terrorist model. Its slope is $\partial D^*/\partial C^*$ and is shown as positive in Figure 23.2. The convexity of the path implies that the terrorist demands will increase at a *decreasing* rate as concessions are raised. The actual convexity depends on the terrorists' attitudes and can be inferred from a few rounds of negotiations by determining whether the terrorists increase their demands at an increasing *or* decreasing rate in response to concessions. Similarly, the government's reaction path, *OB*, shows the government's optimal concessions for each level of demands requested. This path depicts graphically the solution to the government model. Its slope is $\partial C^*/\partial D^*$. The government reaction path must lie on or below the 45° line to rule out the possibility that a government will offer a concession greater than the demands requested. In Figure 23.2, the government is willing to match terrorist demands until level *g*; thereafter, the

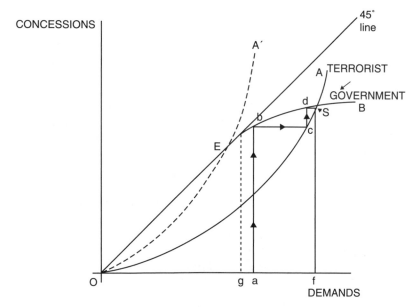

FIGURE 23.2 ■ Terrorist negotiations.

government offers a concession smaller than the demands requested.

The 45° line indicates those positions in which concessions equal demands. The adjustment path *abcd* . . . shows that a stable equilibrium[13] at *S* will be reached if the terrorists make an initial demand of *a*. The arrow above *S* indicates that initial demands greater than *f* will also lead to *S* via an adjustment path in which demands are reduced over time with concessions. Cases where demands increase during negotiations and where demands decrease during negotiations have been observed in recent terrorist incidents (see Corsi 1981, p. 69).

The stable equilibrium, *S*, is a *stalemate equilibrium*, since concessions are not equal to demands. Thus, the incident will continue until the government sends in the troops or else the reaction paths shift in order to produce an equilibrium on the 45° line (e.g., point *E*). Shifts will occur in response to changes in the parameters of the model. For example, if the government succeeds in reducing the terrorists' resources, then the comparative static result, $\partial D^*/\partial R < 0$, means that the terrorist reaction path will shift leftward indicating a reduced demand for each concession level. If the shift is to *OA'* in Figure 23.2, a nonstalemate equilibrium, *E*, is attained. Situations of stalemate have been observed in 35.5 percent of transnational terrorist incidents from 1970 to 1974 (Corsi 1981, Table 7, p. 69). Incidents lasting for a long time that were finally settled peacefully (e.g., the Iranian take-over of the U.S. embassy in Tehran; the March 1981 hijacking of a Pakistanian airplane on route to Kabul, Afghanistan) were cases where the stalemate was eventually overcome by an apparent shift in one or more of the reaction paths.

The reaction paths in Figure 23.2 apply both to the planning stage and to the actual incident, since once the incident occurs, the terrorists and the government must constantly reevaluate their options in light of the negotiations and constraints. Consequently, shifts in the reaction paths may occur during the incident's planning stage and during the incident itself. Government actions affecting the mean and variance of concessions granted will cause shifts in the terrorist curve at the planning stage and *may* keep an incident from occurring if the terrorists expect less than a minimally acceptable equilibrium concession. An improvement in the government's commando force may also cause a leftward shift of the terrorist curve during the planning stage.

During the negotiation stage, the government can shift the terrorist curve leftward by either raising p_D or reducing terrorists' resources. By allowing the negotiations to drag on for a long time, the government will be doing both. Thus, the model supports drawn-out negotiation. When terrorists are interested in media coverage of their escapade, the passage of time may automatically shift terrorist reaction curves leftward, because a greater fulfillment of a publicity goal may mean a willingness to reduce other demands.[14]

The stability of the negotiation process depends on the slopes of the reaction paths and their convexity. In Figure 23.3, an unstable situation is depicted. Unlike Figure 23.2, terrorists now increase their demands at an increasing rate as concessions are offered. Since stability depends on the slopes and convexity of the reaction paths and these, in turn, are determined by risk attitudes, political constraints, resource constraints, and tastes, these same factors determine the stability of the negotiation process. Thus, the dynamics of negotiations depend on the mix of risk attitudes and the constraints of both the policymakers and the terrorists. Multiple equilibriums are also possible when the convexity of the reaction paths varies over the quadrant.

When the negotiation process is unstable, an increasing divergence between demands and concessions will occur over time as negotiations continue. For stable negotiations, demands and concessions will converge with time.

---

[13] This position is the simultaneous solution to equations (6), (7), (8), (14), (15), (16), and (17). The actual solution is in a higher dimensional space of D, C, Π, Ω, a_1, γ, and λ.

[14] Media effects could be modelled by making D a vector of demands, one component of which is media coverage. A third participant, the media, could be introduced, and reaction equilibriums between the three types of participants analyzed.

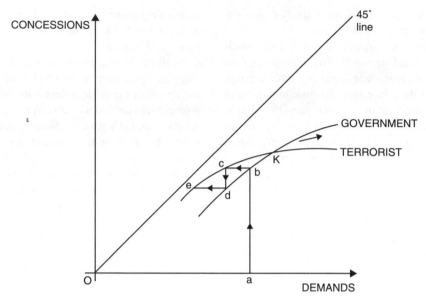

FIGURE 23.3 ■ Unstable negotiations.

Other Rational-Actor Models of Government Behavior

In this section, two additional models are applied to the study of terrorist-inhibiting activities. In particular, a "club theory" analysis is presented to examine the provision of a transnational commando force. Club theory studies the voluntary sharing by two or more individuals (or nations) of a good having benefits that can be withheld from noncontributors or free riders.[15] In a club, tolls are collected as the good is utilized and serve to finance the good's provision.

Although club theory is applied here to the commando force issue only, it could be used to study many aspects of terrorism. For example, other types of terrorist-thwarting linkages between countries (e.g., the sharing of information networks and the joint utilization of police) could be examined. It could also analyze cooperation among and

within terrorist groups, since groups share arsenals, information networks, personnel, and training programs (Russell, Banker, and Miller 1979).[16]

Transnational Commando Forces

Nations experiencing significant terrorist activity have formed their own commando units to deal with terrorist incidents, rather than developing a transnational unit that could be shared internationally. Thus, the United States, Egypt, Israel, United Kingdom, West Germany, France, Switzerland, Belgium, Denmark, Italy, the Netherlands, Norway, Austria, and Indonesia all have commando

---

[15] For a detailed analysis of clubs, see Sandler and Tschirhart (1980).

[16] A few examples of jointly executed transnational terrorist operations include: the Japanese Red Army (JRA), and Popular Front for the Liberation of Palestine (PFLP), and German terrorist collaboration in the May 1972 attack on the Lod Airport in Israel; the PFLP and JRA cooperation in an incident involving a Shell Oil facility in Singapore during January 1974; and German and Palestinian terrorists involvement in the December 1975 assault on the OPEC ministerial conference held in Vienna (Russell, Banker, and Miller 1979, pp. 9–10).

forces (Mickolus 1980, pp. 734–35). This duplication of effort raises the question whether resource allocative efficiency, in terms of cost savings, could be promoted by forming one or more transnational commando forces. The released resources could be reassigned to other ways of curbing terrorism. In so doing, the net inhibition of terrorism resulting from a given resource expenditure might be enhanced.

A commando unit produces multiple benefits or outputs; i.e., joint products exist. Some outputs are purely public to the sharing nations (e.g., deterrence of transnational terrorist activities); others are impurely public (e.g., crisis management of an incident); and still others represent private benefits to a nation (e.g., maintenance of domestic order).[17]

To examine the efficiency of a transnational commando unit, the character of these joint products must be examined. The troublesome one concerns the deterrence owing to its publicness. That is, the unit's deterrence of terrorism yields nonrival *and* nonexcludable benefits to all nations sharing it. Feasibility problems concern the nonexcludability characteristic since some nations will contribute little in the hopes of receiving a free ride from those who give more. Nations with risk-averse policymakers and high levels of terrorist activities are more apt to contribute to the maintenance of the commando unit, whereas those with less risk-averse policymakers and fewer terrorist activities will try to free ride on nations with more incidents. Overall, contributions will be suboptimal.

Olson and Zeckhauser (1966, pp. 268–71) noted a different type of free riding for allied nations sharing an arsenal consisting of strategic weapons, whose primary purpose is deterrence; they showed that a disproportionate burden of the alliance expenditures would be shouldered by the large,

rich allies, since these allies would have the most to gain from effective deterrence. This correlation between country size and free-riding behavior *is not* expected to characterize the sharing of a commando force, because many large nations have little or no terrorist activities and thus would not be highly motivated to contribute to a unit's maintenance and provision. During the period from 1968 to 1977, large nations such as Canada, Australia, and China had relatively few transnational terrorist incidents, whereas small nations such as Israel, Lebanon, and Greece had many (see Mickolus 1980, pp. xvi–xvii).

Even with deterrence as a benefit, Sandler and Forbes (1980) have shown that Pareto optimality can be approached by a club, provided that the bulk of the benefits from a shared arsenal are impurely public or private to the allies.[18] The analysis clearly applies to commando units, because such units primarily provide impurely public benefits in the form of crisis management and damage-limiting capabilities once an incident occurs. Both of these benefits are excludable since the commandos can be withheld unless the requesting nation pays a user charge for the unit's deployment. The country or group of countries providing the commando force, therefore, has leverage over free riders.

Unlike deterrence, damage-limiting activities are subject to consumption rivalry, as one or more nations simultaneously try to use the same commando force to cope with multiple incidents. This rivalry takes the form of a *thinning of forces*, as a smaller proportion of the force can be assigned to each incident occurring simultaneously.

Thinning is related to both the total quantity of defense (X) provided by the commando group *and* the total utilization of the group ($\sum_{i=1}^{n} x^i$, where n is the number of sharing nations) within a given time period. When the total usage of the commando unit

---

[17] A pure public good is totally nonrival in consumption, since its consumption by one individual (nation) does not detract in the slightest from the consumption opportunities available to other persons (nations). Moreover, the benefits of a pure public good are nonexcludable; once it is provided, the good is available to all. In contrast, a private good (e.g., food) is totally rival and its benefits are excludable. Impure public goods exhibit varying degrees of rivalry and excludability.

[18] Pareto optimality refers to a position where no one can be made better off without hurting someone else. A Pareto-optimal move helps at least one individual without harming anyone.

is increased by extending its services to another incident while holding the unit's size constant, thinning becomes more pronounced. In contrast, an increase in the force size, given total usage, reduces thinning and thereby enhances the well-being of the sharing nations. By making thinning (t) depend on the average utilization rate (k) of the commando force, both aforementioned influences on thinning are present in the ensuing club model. Equation (26) indicates the form of the thinning function:

$$t = t(k) \text{ where } k = \sum_{i=1}^{n} x^i/X \qquad (26)$$

with $t/\partial k = t_k > 0$, $\partial t/\partial x^i = t_k/X > 0$, and $\partial t/\partial X = -kt_k/X < 0$. The sign of t_k indicates that an increase in average utilization creates more thinning. The $\partial t/\partial X$ term depicts the thickening effect that occurs via a reduction in the average utilization rate, resulting from increased provision of the commando unit. Finally, the $\partial t/\partial x^i$ term represents the thinning that follows from increased utilization of the force.

The utility function for the ith nation depends on its consumption of the unit (x^i), a private numeraire good (y^i), and thinning, i.e.,

$$G^i = G^i [x^i, y^i, t(k)],$$

where $\partial G^i/\partial t < 0$ and $i = 1, \ldots, n$. (27)

To find the Pareto-optimal toll and provision conditions, any user's utility function must be maximized subject to the following constraints: the constancy of the other users' utilities (required for Pareto optimality), a private good consumption-distribution constraint, a production possibility frontier (depicting production capabilities), and the requirement that no nation utilizes the entire commando unit throughout the time period (i.e., $x^i < X$ for all i). Equations (28) and (29) are simplified representations for the provision and the toll conditions.[19]

$$\text{(Provision)} \sum_{i=1}^{n} MBT^i = MC_x \qquad (28)$$

$$\text{(Toll)} \sum_{i=1}^{n} MTC^i = MB^p \text{ (for all } p) \qquad (29)$$

As the capacity of the commando unit is increased, a nonrival benefit in the form of troop thickening is conferred on the sharing nations. Troop thickening occurs when the size of the force is increased or their weaponry is improved. In the former case, more forces are available for any incident; in the latter, the same sized troop can be more effective in confronting an incident. For optimal provision, the sum of the marginal benefits associated with troop thickening (ΣMBT^i) is equated to the marginal costs of increased provision (MC_x). Since each sharing nation benefits from a larger or better-equipped commando force, the resulting marginal benefits must be summed over the sharing nations.

In equation (29), tolls are set equal to the sum of the marginal thinning costs (ΣMTC^i) imposed upon the users as utilization increases, and the pth nation uses the commando unit until its marginal benefits from utilization equals the sum of marginal thinning costs. The toll condition charges the same user fee for each terrorist incident that the force is dispatched to handle, since the same marginal thinning costs are expected to result from each incident.[20] Nevertheless, the total tolls paid for the commando unit vary among nations according to their revealed intensity of utilization. This intensity depends on the number of incidents involving their territory, persons, property, the risk aversion of their policymakers, and their proclivity to concede to the terrorist demands.

Such a toll scheme will finance the marginal cost associated with the optimal provision amount, but

---

[19] See Sandler (1977, p. 451) and Sandler and Tschirhart (1980, pp. 1488–89) for more detailed expressions.

[20] If some incidents require a longer dispatchment of troops than others, a per-day toll can then be charged instead of a per-incident charge. For this scheme, the per-day toll would be identical to all users, but those nations utilizing the commando force for more days would pay more in total tolls. Hence, the marginal unit of utilization is a day's use of the force rather than an incident's use.

it will not finance total cost unless nonincreasing returns to scale characterize provision (Sandler and Tschirhart 1980, p. 1496). Increasing returns mean that per-unit cost falls with increased provision; per-unit cost will then be less than marginal cost. Consequently, covering marginal cost will not cover per-unit or total costs. To make up the deficit, an additional charge must be collected from the sharing nations to supplement the tolls.

In summary, a club arrangement can be used by nations to share a commando force whenever the force's principal function is to limit damage once an incident occurs. By avoiding needless duplication of forces and by exploiting scale economies (i.e., per-unit cost reductions), this arrangement can foster economic efficiency. Repeated use of the same force will increase their effectiveness. Under existing circumstances where many countries maintain their own forces, these forces are often idle and do not gain experience. Moreover, the associated communication and information linkages formed by the club can be used to coordinate other efforts in deterring terrorism. Another major advantage of the proposed scheme concerns its administrative simplicity; nations need contribute only on a per-utilization basis. Frequent meetings of ministers are not required once the force is established. In fact, an individual nation can set up the unit and charge interested nations for its dispatchment; no permanent transnational organization is even required.

There are a few problems that limit the efficiency of this arrangement. The first problem concerns measurement of the marginal thinning costs experienced by each sharing nation when utilization of the unit increases. Such measurement would be far from perfect with existing technologies, but could be approximated by the increased expenditures on manpower and equipment required to offset the thinning costs associated with a given dispatchment. Furthermore, measurement entails administration costs which, in turn, can inhibit optimality. Another measurement problem concerns the provision condition and its implementation. Each country must base its estimate of the marginal benefits of troop thickening on the expected number of terrorist incidents, since these

benefits increase as the number of incidents increases. If the average annual number of incidents is stable, then this estimation can be made easily. Mickolus's (1980, p. xviii) data showed that during the 1970s, the number of transnational incidents ranged from 301 to 480 per year. On a per-country basis, the variation was also large. Hence, estimating the benefits from thickening will be difficult.

The major potential difficulty with the club approach concerns the existence of the jointly produced, pure public output of deterrence, since the club cannot force payment for this output. In contrast, the jointly produced, private outputs pose no problem since they can be priced and sold separately. Private benefits are conferred to those nations where the commando units are permanently based. These nations receive an added deterrence and foreign exchange benefit not experienced by the other nations, and presumably can be charged for them. Since both the damage-limitation output and the private output(s) can be allocated by a toll or a price, the extent of suboptimality of the club arrangement depends upon the ratio of the pure public outputs to the sum of the excludable outputs. As this ratio goes to zero, suboptimality disappears, since the excludable outputs serve a privatizing function, which reduces free riders (Sandler and Culyer 1982).

Allocating Resources among Terrorist-Thwarting Activities

The comparative static analysis above shows that a government's effort to reduce one type of activity causes the terrorist to shift into another. Thus, how best to assign the government's resources among terrorist-reducing activities where each involves different risks and expected returns is an important question. Space does not permit a full analysis, but a chance-constrained portfolio model can be suggested and sketched. In essence, the government must assign its resources among the various terrorist-inhibiting actions to maximize the resources' mean return, subject to a chance constraint. The latter requires the probability that the return falls below a minimally acceptable level to be less than some percentage. The resulting allocation can then be shown to depend on the policymaker's attitude toward risk. If the policymaker is risk averse, an increase in available resources would induce that person to assign relatively more to a set of actions having a smaller coefficient of variation (i.e., σ/μ.). Other conclusions could also be derived.

Conclusions

An entire series of terrorist negotiation situations could be modelled by modifying the models presented above. For example, by changing the government's utility function and constraints, terrorist negotiations with an autocratic (or mixed) government could be analyzed in a comparative static framework similar to the one here. The terrorist objective function and constraints could be altered to study groups and operations not represented by the models above. Time could also be introduced into the models, and a terrorist group's *time preference*, as reflected by its desired trade-off between current and future rewards, could then be related to negotiation strategies, much like risk attitudes have been related here. Furthermore, non-Nash type behavior could be examined.[21] Thus, an essential contribution of this article has been to present a theoretical methodology that could be modified and applied to a wide-range of terrorist situations.

By subjecting the models to testing, their usefulness can be ascertained and improved models can be developed to rectify shortcomings. The following conclusions were derived from the models and only hold for their assumptions:

1. A no-negotiation strategy is *not best in all situations*. The efficacy of this strategy depends on the risk attitudes of the terrorists and appears best for risk-preferring groups.
2. If a government confronts risk-preferring *and* risk-averse terrorist groups, then the govern-

ment's long-term concession-granting policy must be geared to thwart the type of group that imposes the greatest threat, since the best policy differs between the two groups.
3. Raising the price to terrorists may not work unless the transnational flow of resources is also curbed. Piecemeal policies may exacerbate the problem!
4. The stability of the negotiation process depends on the risk attitudes and constraints of both the terrorists and the policymakers.
5. Government long-term actions to lower the mean concession and its variance or to increase the commando force's effectiveness can decrease incidents by making contemplated actions unattractive to terrorists at the planning stage.
6. Crisis management actions that reduce terrorist resources or raise the costs to the terrorist can remove a stalemate by shifting the negotiation reaction paths. Media payoffs may do the same.
7. Commando units can be shared by nations based on a toll or utilization fee. Such an arrangement can increase the commando force's effectiveness and release resources to be used elsewhere.

Appendix

Second-order sufficiency conditions for both the terrorist and government problems are now presented. It is assumed that the solution to both problems is such that the optimum values of all variables are positive. The second-order conditions can then be used to obtain the comparative static properties in the text owing to the implicit function theorem (see Chiang 1974, pp. 222–38).

In the terrorist problem, the utility function is assumed to be separable so that $U(L, D, \Pi; C^*) = U(L) + U(D, \Pi; C^*)$. The bordered Hessian matrix of second-ordered partials associated with the partial derivatives of equations (14) through (17) is

$$
H_T = \begin{bmatrix} U_{DD} + (p_D/p_L)^2\, U_{LL} & U_{D\Pi} & -1 \\ U_{D\Pi} & U_{\Pi\Pi} + \lambda\sigma N'' & \sigma N' \\ -1 & -\sigma N' & 0 \end{bmatrix}.
$$

---

[21] Non-Nash behavior allows an agent to anticipate that his optimal action will influence the optimal choices of the other agents.

A sufficient condition for a maximum is that the determinant of H_T be positive, or

$$|H_T| = 2\sigma N' U_{D\Pi} - \lambda \sigma N'' - U_{\Pi\Pi} - (\sigma N')^2$$
$$[U_{DD} + (p_D/p_L)^2 \, U_{LL}] > 0. \qquad (30)$$

Assuming diminishing marginal utility in Π, D, and L makes the last three terms in (30) positive, since $U_{\Pi\Pi}$, U_{DD}, $U_{LL} < 0$ and $-(\sigma N')^2 < 0$. The second term in (30) is dependent on the distribution of $\hat{C}$. For example, a uniform distribution implies a linear function for N and $N'' = 0$. A normal distribution makes N approximately linear and $N'' > 0$, but small. It is, therefore, assumed that this term is zero or insignificant. The sign of the first term depends on $U_{D\Pi}$. If $U_{D\Pi} < 0$, then (30) holds, since $N' < 0$. When $U_{D\Pi} > 0$, (30) holds, provided the first term does not dominate the last three. In the text, both signs are considered.

Separability of the government's utility function is also assumed, where $G(C, \Omega, a_2; D^*) = G(a_2) + G(C, \Omega; D^*)$. Given this simplification, the Hessian matrix associated with equations (14) through (17) is

$$H = \begin{bmatrix} G_{CC} + p^2 G_{a_2 a_2} + \gamma v_{CC} & G_{C\Omega} & pG_{a_2 a_2} & v_C \\ G_{\Omega C} & G_{\Omega\Omega} + \gamma \sigma_u M^- & 0 & -\sigma_u M' \\ pG_{a_2 a_2} + \gamma v_{a_1 C} & 0 & G_{a_2 a_2} + \gamma v_{a_1 a_1} & v_{a_1} \\ v_C & -\sigma_u M' & v_{a_1} & 0 \end{bmatrix}.$$

Sufficient conditions for a maximum require that the determinant of the bottom-right, 3×3 matrix in H be positive and that $|H| < 0$). The 3×3 determinant equals

$$- (\sigma_u M')^2 [G_{a_2 a_2} + \gamma v_{a_1 a_1}] - v_{a_1}^2 [G_{\Omega\Omega} + \gamma \sigma_u M'']. \qquad (31)$$

Assuming diminishing marginal utility, diminishing returns to resources devoted to campaigning ($v_{a_1 a_1} < 0$), and $M'' = 0$ makes (31) unambiguously positive, as required. However, the sign of $|H|$ is ambiguous without further assumptions on functional forms and cross-partial derivatives. For purposes here, it is assumed that $|H| < 0$ and a maximum is attained.

Comparative static results are derived in the usual fashion using Cramer's rule. For example, equation (19) in the text is obtained by forming a column vector of the partial derivatives with respect to p_D of the first-order conditions (6) through (8). After reversing the sign of the vector, it is substituted for the first column in H_T. The determinant of the resulting matrix is then divided by $|H_T|$ to yield equation (19) (see Chiang 1974, Chapter 8).

REFERENCES

Becker, G. S. 1968. Crime and punishment: an economic approach. *Journal of Political Economy* 78: 526–36.

Chiang, A. 1974. *Fundamental methods of mathematical economics*. New York: McGraw Hill.

Corsi, J. R. 1981. Terrorism as a desperate game. *Journal of Conflict Resolution* 25: 47–85.

Downs, A. 1957. *An economic theory of democracy*. New York: Harper and Row.

Ehrlich, I. 1973. Participation in illegitimate activities: A theoretical and empirical investigation. *Journal of Political Economy* 81:521–67.

Hamilton, L. C., and Hamilton, J. D. 1981. Dynamics of terrorism, unpublished manuscript.

Hamlen, W., and Tschirhart, J. T. 1980. Solar energy, public utilities, and economic efficiency. *Southern Economic Journal* 17:318 65.

Gurr, T. R. 1979. Some characteristics of political terrorism in the 1960s. In *The politics of terrorism*, ed. M. Stohl, New York: Marcel Dekker.

Heineke, J. M. 1975. A note on modeling the criminal choice problem. *Journal of Economic Theory* 10: 113–16.

Jenkins, B., Johnson, J., and Ronfeldt, D. 1977. Numbered lives: some statistical observations from 77 international hostage episodes. Santa Monica, Calif.: Rand Corporation.

Laqueur, W., ed. 1978. *The terrorism reader: a historical anthology*. New York: New American Library.

Meyer, R. A. 1975. Monopoly pricing and capacity choice under uncertainty. *American Economic Review* 65:326–37.

Mickolus, E. F. 1976. Negotiating for hostages: A policy dilemma. *Orbis* 19: 1309–25.

—— 1979. Transnational terrorism. In *The politics of terrorism*. ed. M. Stohl. New York: Marcel Dekker.

—— 1980. *Transnational terrorism: a chronology of events, 1968–1979*. Westport, Conn.: Greenwood Press.

Midlarsky, M. I. 1970. Mathematical models of instability and a theory of diffusion. *International Studies Quarterly* 14:60–84.

—— 1978. Analyzing diffusion and contagion effects: the urban disorders of the 1960s. *American Political Science Review* 72: 996–1008.

Midlarsky, M. I., Crenshaw, M. and Yoshida, F. 1980. Why violence spreads. *International Studies Quarterly* 24:262–98.

Mueller, D. C. 1979. *Public choice*. New York: Cambridge University Press.

Olson, M., and Zeckhauser, R. 1966. An economic theory of alliances. *Review of Economics and Statistics* 48:266–79.

Pierre, A. 1976. The politics of international terrorism. *Orbis* 19: 1251–69.

Pyle, D. H., and Turnovsky, S. J. 1971. Risk aversion in chance constrained portfolio selection. *Management Science* 18: 218–25.

Russell, C. A., Banker, L. J., and Miller, B. H. 1979. Out-inventing the terrorist. In *Terrorism: theory and practice.* ed. Y. Alexander et al. Boulder, Colo.: Westview Press.

Sandler, T. 1977. Impurity of defense: an application to the economics of alliances. *Kyklos* 30: 443–60.

—— and Culyer, A. J. 1982. Joint products and multi-jurisdictional spillovers. *Quarterly Journal of Economics* 97:707–16.

—— and Forbes, J. F. 1980. Burden sharing, strategy, and the design of NATO. *Economic Inquiry* 18: 425–44.

—— and Tschirhart, J. T. 1980. The economic theory of clubs: an evaluative survey. *Journal of Economic Literature* 18:1481–1521.

Stohl, M. 1979. Introduction: myths and realities of political terrorism. In *The politics of terrorism*, ed. M. Stohl, New York: Marcel Dekker.

U.S. Central Intelligence Agency. 1981. *Patterns of international terrorism: 1980.* Springfield, Va.: National Technical Information Service.

Zartman, I., ed. 1977. *The negotiation process: theories and applications.* Beverly Hills, Calif.: Sage Publications.

Is Terrorism Evil?

Visual images have a way of cutting through the defense of rhetoric and touching the heart. Most people, when exposed to images of the actual aftermath of violent terrorist attacks on innocent civilians, will react with horror. Despite the undeniably violent history of the human species and the innate tendency for competition for resources, societies have apparently evolved constraints on the amount and types of violence they condone in the name of political goals. Religions often include explicit or implicit codes for sanctioned violence and often classify non-combatants—especially women and children— as morally unacceptable targets. Theories of "just war" accept the need for collective violence under certain conditions, but typically draw bright lines between killing enemy soldiers to escape group annihilation and killing civilians. Setting aside religious, cultural, or intellectual arguments, there seems to be an instinctive abhorrence of brutality against those who are not trying to fight and are much less capable of self-defense. Terrorism—by definition involving attacks on non-combatants—is almost universally condemned as immoral.

Several questions arise. How can terrorists possibly justify their actions? What mode of cognition or emotional state could make a person set aside the nearly universal limits on violence to viciously attack those who are doing them no harm? Are there any circumstances in which such attacks might be justifiable? When states act oppressively and brutalize civilians (either in their own nation or in others) in order to secure political perpetuation or advantage, is that equally morally reprehensible? When, in the course of war, civilians are deliberately targeted to advance a strategic goal (e.g., the bombings of Dresden, Hiroshima, and Nagasaki), are the leaders who order such attacks in the same category of moral culpability as leaders of small non-state political groups who order smaller scale bombings? There are no easy answers to such questions, but the study of the psychology of terrorism is hardly complete unless we try to address the moral dimension.

Reading 24—Wardlaw (1989). Justifications and Means: The Moral Dimensions of State-Sponsored Terrorism

Editors' Comments

"State-sponsored terrorism" might be divided into two types: state support and direction to non-state terrorist groups; and state-committed terrorism, when organs of the state itself such as the military or police attack non-combatants. State-sponsored terrorism tends to get proportionately little attention in the modern dialogues about the psychology of terrorism. In part this might reflect the facts that: (1) the majority of terrorism scholars live in secure, democratic Western nations whose governments arguably commit or sponsor little terrorism; (2) the national and international media tends to focus on highly visible and unexpected attacks by small non-state actors, while it regards longstanding intrastate terrorist campaigns by governments against their own citizens as less noteworthy; and (3) state sponsors are at least one step removed from the action perpetrators. In this paper, Wardlaw draws our attention to the differences in moral frames of reference that confound any simple attempt to demonize non-state actors while permitting states a moral pass.

Discussion Questions

1. Terrorism is defined in the US Code of Federal Regulations as ". . . the unlawful use of force and violence against persons or property to intimidate or coerce a government, the civilian population, or any segment thereof, in furtherance of political or social object-ives" (28 C.F.R. Section 0.85). Wardlaw proposes a somewhat different definition of terrorism. What are the moral implications of the differences in these two definitions?
2. Wardlaw quotes Hans Morgenthau—a political "realist"—as stating that "The state has no right to let its moral disapprobation . . . get in the way of successful political action." What are the advantages or disadvantages for a state that adopts this position?
3. Wardlaw theorizes, "Quite probably, for 'normal' human beings it is psychologically necessary to believe that the cause one is fighting for is just." Might this natural need for self-justifying cognitions help to account for the moral certainty of state and non-state terrorists?
4. This paper cites Coady's tripartite division of the morality of violence. How does state versus non-state terrorism fit into this schema?

Suggested Readings

Arblaster, A. (1977). Terrorism, myth, meaning and morals. *Political studies*, *25*, 413–424.

Coady, C. A. (1985). The morality of terrorism. *Philosophy*, *60*, 50–51.

Primoratz, I. (1997). The morality of terrorism. *Journal of Applied Philosophy*, *14*, 221–233.

Wright, M. (1994). *The moral animal: Why we are the way we are: The new science of evolutionary psychology*. New York: Vintage Books.

Reading 25—Juergensmeyer (2000). Islam's "Neglected Duty"

Editors' Comments

Islam was the dominant religious, cultural, and military force in much of the developing world for centuries. But from the time of the second siege of Vienna (1683) through the defeat of the Ottoman Empire (1923), Islam's prospects for world domination diminished to the point of virtual collapse. According to some interpretations of the holy texts—the Koran and the *Sunna*—this was a tragic interruption in the manifest destiny of political Islam to control the globe. It is difficult to pinpoint the moment when a resurgence of Islamic pride and consciousness became associated with a fast-spreading ideology of militant modern jihad, yet several key texts seem to have played a powerful role in this global trend. One of these is a booklet by Muhammad Ad al-Salam Faraj titled *The neglected duty* (1981). (Another is Sayid Qutb's famous volume, *Milestones* (2005).) In this chapter from his superb book, *Terror in the mind of God*, Marc Juergensmeyer describes his conversations with one of the Islamist terrorists convicted of the 1993 World Trade Center bombing, Mahmud Abouhalima. The author uses this conversation and Abouhalima's striking defense of the morality of terrorism as an introduction to a larger discussion: How do radical Islamists justify the use of violence against civilians? Might some extremists feel morally compelled to attend to their "neglected duty"?

Discussion Questions

1. In this chapter the convicted terrorist Mahmud Abouhalima describes a 17-year period of dissolute life in the West before turning to radical Islam. What psychological mechanisms might link the two periods?
2. Juergensmeyer also interviewed Dr. Abdul Aziz Rantisi, the now deceased Palestinian leader of Hamas. Rantisi asserts that "suicide bombing" is an inappropriate term for the self-chosen martyrdom (*istishaddi*) of his compatriots. How does Rantisi justify the targeting of civilians by the *istishads*?
3. Rantisi states "we are the victims." Israeli civilians could make the same statement. Might embracing the role of "victim" play a part in moral justification of extreme violence?

Suggested Readings

Coady, C. A. J. (2004). Terrorism and innocence. *Journal of Ethics*, *8*, 37–58.

Jansen, J. J. G. (1986). *The neglected duty: The creed of Sadat's assassins and Islamic resurgence in the Middle East*. New York: Macmillan Publishing Company.

Qutb, S. (2005). *Milestones*. New Delhi: Islamic Book Service.

Scheffler, S. (2006). Is terrorism morally distinctive? *Journal of Political Philosophy*, *14*, 1–17.

Justifications and Means: The Moral Dimension of State-Sponsored Terrorism

Grant Wardlaw

While there may seem to many to be little morality in most forms of terrorism, there is no shortage of moralistic language in discussing them. Fulminating against terrorism usually is accompanied by easy reference to moral standards and how their observance is so lacking in those who would practice terrorism. As with all discussions on the subject, however, much of the substance of the argument turns on the definition of "terrorism." All too often the definition is partial or biased or is applied in a partial or biased manner, so that the essence of the argument turns out to be that terrorism is the political violence used by those of whom the labeler disapproves. This essential element of dishonesty, together with a conscious use of the word "terrorism" for strictly propaganda or psychological warfare purposes, ensure that most debate about the morality of terrorism is meaningless, having little to do with morality and much to do with politics.

If this characterization of the debate about the morality of terrorism is valid for the case of rebels, it has even greater force when applied to terrorism carried out by or on behalf of nation states in the pursuit of foreign policy objectives. Rebels may be condemned for their cowardice, their lack of moral scruples, or their murder of innocents; but to many who so condemn them, such behavior is but a reflection of their individual insanity or the gross excesses which accompany alien or absurd political or religious philosophies. That such views either oversimplify or, in some cases, totally misconstrue the motives and the behavior of many terrorists is amply illustrated by other contributions to this volume. Although terrorism is certainly brutal and is sometimes outside the morality of all but the most extreme minority, it is not without a moral dimension—even in the calculation of the terrorists. Most terrorists are neither insane nor immoral. We may condemn their behavior, but we miss some essential elements of the analysis if we ignore the reality that ours is not the only moral frame of reference. While we may like to believe in a universal morality, in fact there are many possible ethical systems, often with very different and sometimes diametrically opposed moral precepts. The realization that this is so ought not to prevent us from condemning behavior that violates our own morality, but may aid us at least to understand why it should occur. In some cases, such understanding will have implications both for preventing future occurrences or for dealing with the present outrage against our code. We must not be cowed by the accusation of some that understanding implies either acceptance or forgiveness. It does not. What it should do, however, is alert us to the need to be consistent in applying our own standards, particularly in applying them to the behavior of friends and allies, and to ourselves. It is this consistency that is missing from most discussions of terrorism. It is a lack that undermines the moral high ground which is sought by all sides of the debate and which reduces the discussion to one characterized by empty moral rhetoric and hypocrisy.

This imbalance is reflected in attitudes to state-sponsored terrorism. If anything, many observers find it even more reprehensible that states should involve themselves in acts of terrorism, especially when they appear not only to support the cause of the terrorists but actually to control their actions. Such observers find it difficult to dismiss the moral failure as being due only to individual pathology or weakness (although others are able to achieve this by seeing the leader of the offending nation as either insane or evil) and conclude that a more serious breach of ethics is committed by virtue of its commission by a state. Here, as in the case of revolutionary terrorism, however, the essence of the debate and the intensity of the outrage expressed turns on the definition of terrorism. Again, it seems that violence in the service of the state (directly or indirectly) is terrorism (and, therefore, reprehensible) if it is used by one's enemies and is something else (and, therefore, necessary and maybe even honorable) if it is used by oneself or one's allies.

Definitional Distinctions

Is there any way out of this moral morass? To the extent that there is, the key will be found in common acceptance of a definition of terrorism. Before one can ask whether or not there are circumstances in which a state might be morally justified in supporting or using terrorism, we must agree upon a definition of terrorism. We may agree with William Casey, the late former Director of the CIA in the United States, when he said that: "In confronting the challenge of international terrorism, the first step is to call things by their proper names, to see clearly and say plainly who the terrorists are, what goals they seek, and which governments support them."[1]

The difficulty is that neither Mr. Casey nor most other senior government officials or national leaders, of any political stripe, are in fact always willing to call things by their proper names. Further, there are many different conceptions of how wide the boundaries of the concept of terrorism should be. Some will argue, for example, that the aerial bombing of civilian populations in warfare is an act of terrorism, while others will contend that terrorism does not encompass military acts in time of declared war.

It is improbable that these confusions, some intentional and some not, will ever be overcome. However, for our analytical purpose we must have some definitional foundation. In this case I draw on a definition I have proposed elsewhere. It differs from those by Rapoport and Gregor above, but it captures, I believe, the essential elements of the phenomenon.

> Political terrorism is the use, or threat of use, of violence by an individual or group, whether acting for or in opposition to established authority, when such action is designed to create extreme anxiety and/or fear-inducing effects in a target group larger than the immediate victims with the purpose of coercing that group into acceding to the political demands of the perpetrators.[2]

The emphasis is on the *effects* of the behavior rather than on the actual *form* of the attack. There are two unique conditions. The first is that the violence committed constitutes an act of terror only when the target group (those being coerced) is distinct from the immediate victims (those being bombed, shot, or held hostage). The second is that the act must create in the target group a condition of extreme anxiety or fear, which is the lever by which pressure is applied (or is intended to be applied) to coerce acquiescence to the terrorist's demands. Thus, an act of violence which is aimed only at a particular immediate victim (be it an individual or group) is not an act of terrorism. The assassination of a head of state aimed solely at removing that person from office is not, therefore, an act of terrorism. A campaign of assassinations of senior police or civil servants, however, designed to coerce the authorities into changing their security policies, for example, would be classified properly as terrorism. On the other hand, a campaign of genocide, which has the objective of removing from existence a particular class of persons, is not an example of terrorism.[3] The confusion arises, I believe, because we fail to distinguish between the words "terror" and "terrorism." Acts which involve terror (and genocide involves the ultimate terror) do not necessarily fall within the category of terrorism as used in the present sense. At the other end of the continuum, being robbed by a violent criminal involves a good degree of terror, but is not an example of terrorism either.

The example of violent robbery also illustrates the importance of the second essential ingredient of terrorism, namely, that the act must cause extra-normal levels of fear and anxiety in the target group. Robbery essentially causes intense fear only in the immediate victim. To the extent that it also causes fear in the community at large (by increasing fear of becoming a victim, for example), it is generalized and not deliberately aimed at forcing some other group (the government, for example) to change a policy or accede to some demands. It is, therefore, not terrorism. Neither, more controversially, is a bombing which does not, in fact, cause fear in the target group, even though it may have been intended to have that effect. The statistics on terrorism are inflated by the inclusion of many acts of violence, such as minor bombings involving no threat to life and minimal damage to property, which do not appear to frighten anybody. Even if the aim is political (for example, some political group claims responsibility and says that it is connected with some cause), it is difficult to see how it can be properly called terrorism if it does not have the consequence of frightening anyone. Similarly, threats to commit violent acts are not acts of terrorism if nobody takes them seriously, if they are not credible, or if they do not create sufficient anxiety to constitute pressure on the putative target group. Applying these restrictions to the definition of terrorism, it seems to me, marks off a phenomenon which is qualitatively different from other forms of violence and gives some coherence to the concept. If applied rigorously (which, of course, they never are, given the politicized use of the term terrorism) these restrictions would reduce

the recorded incidence of terrorism but leave us with a core of seriously disturbing behavior which may conceptually be easier to come to grips with and make moral judgments about.

The other feature of this definition is that it explicitly acknowledges that terrorism may be employed either in the service of the state or in opposition to it. Put another way, it acknowledges the reality that much terrorism is a result of state sponsorship or state control. The definition would allow, therefore, a campaign of aerial bombing of civilian targets by one nation in a state of war with another to be encompassed under the term terrorism (given our acceptance of the notions that terrorism involves extra-normal fear and an aim of coercing a wider audience than the immediate victims into a particular course of action).

We now turn to the issue of the state terror in the international world. Michael Stohl identifies several different forms which I find useful to distinguish.[4] The first is *covert state terrorism*, which is divided into two subtypes; *clandestine state terrorism*, in which the state itself directly participates in acts of terrorism, and *state-sponsored terrorism*, which consists of the state employing other groups to carry out terrorist acts on its behalf. A second basic category is *surrogate terrorism*, again subdivided into two subtypes. *State-supported terrorism* occurs when an interested state supports some third party after it has carried out an act of terrorism that happens to be perceived as being in the interests of the supporting state. *State acquiescence to terrorism* occurs when a state approves or fails to condemn or act against an act of terrorism carried out by a third party. Surrogate terrorism involves what might be called "complicity after the fact" in respect of ordinary crimes and seems to me to imply a different level of moral responsibility than covert state terrorism.

The Moral Dimension

Having defined the phenomenon, we can now turn to the issue of morality. In general terms, the problem is usually put as a question: Are there circumstances in which the use of terrorism is morally justified? In the present case: Are there circumstances in which a state is justified in employing terrorism in pursuit of its own national interests? As other chapters in this book show, there are many people who have asked the first question and have answered, "yes." For such people a number of justifications exist.

The first is that they reject the ethical system of the opponent. This is a serious problem when dealing with terrorists from different cultures. Western values are not universally accepted and we, in our turn, must accept that reality. Although I disagree with the conclusions she draws from it, I agree with the warning sounded by Adda Bozeman when, referring to specifically American values, she writes: "Increasingly American perspectives have become blurred by the assumption that our paramount values are shared by human beings everywhere; and that the United States is therefore justified—even entitled—to insist that the governments of foreign sovereign states (at least the weaker ones) must install these values in their respective societies."[5]

As stated earlier, however, understanding other value systems should not imply acceptance of them when behavior in accord with them offends our morality *and* damages our interests. We must defend both our moral system and our interests, and have a right to do so. What we must do, though, is ensure that our own behavior is in accord with our own stated principles.

In addition, there are two reasons why the problem of rejection of our ethical system may not trouble us greatly. One is that, as far as the behavior of states is concerned, for right or wrong, the system of international relations and laws is based largely on Western European beliefs. That being so, we should be entitled to hold nations to the standards required by those ethical beliefs. The second reason is that we can in many cases reject as fraudulent the terrorist's claim to a different (usually higher) morality. This is particularly relevant in domestic terrorism, but applies also to the behavior of states within the same general cultural tradition. There are many cases in which such a claim by terrorists is merely a justification after the

event rather than a guiding principle and need not be taken seriously.[6]

The second and most important justification for terrorism has its roots in the concept of absolutism. Here, "certain ends of action are assigned an absolute value and are considered worth pursuing no matter what consequences."[7] This is the age-old conundrum of ends versus means. A form of absolutism has found expression in international relations among the so-called realist school of thought. Adherents to this school believe international society to be of a Hobbesian state of nature in which states have both the right and the responsibility to take whatever steps are necessary to guard their own interests (and assume that other states will do likewise). In such a view, the introduction of morality (or in a less extreme reading, of excessive or inconvenient attention to moral concerns) into decision making is foolish, even dangerous, and certainly not necessary. It is seen as akin to "fighting with one's hands tied behind one's back" or "continuing to fight by the rules when one knows that one's adversary has no intention of doing so." The survival of the state is seen as the absolute, so that Hans Morgenthau, a leading realist scholar writes: "The state has no right to let its moral disapproval . . . get in the way of successful political action, itself inspired by the moral principle of national survival."[8]

Another tradition, the Hegelian, approaches the problem not by placing survival of the state as a higher-valued goal, but by specifically absolving the state from moral responsibility. Thus, as Cassirer argues: "Hegel exempted the state from all moral obligations and declared that the rules of morality lose their pretended universality when we proceed from the problems of private life and private conduct to the conduct of states."[9]

There are two major problems with the strict absolutist perspective. The first is that it is a recipe for tyranny. It is, in the extreme, the credo of the powerful who would crush all opposition no matter how just. It is the law of the jungle and, unmodified, cannot serve for the basis of cooperative international relations. The second is that it is, as Kaplan notes, characterized by the sin of total lack of humility. The absolutist "is utterly incapable of asking himself: 'And what if I am wrong?' "[10] Pure absolutism cannot be justified morally unless the pursuit of national interests at any cost is considered an absolute moral good. I do not believe it can be. It follows that terrorism used by a state in pursuance of the absolutist principle also cannot be justified morally.

In recent years there has been a tendency (which I believe misguided) to describe the state's use of terror as "low-intensity warfare."[11] If one accepts this view then we ought to be able to justify it with the same doctrines we use to justify war. But there is an obvious incongruity that raises a question about the plausibility of this characterization as low-intensity warfare in the first place. The "just war" doctrine has two criteria; one refers to our purpose *jus ad bello* and the other to our means *jus in bellum*. We will meet the *jus ad bello* requirement if we act in self-defence and our aim is to restore peace. But there is no way to meet the *jus in bellum* standard just because the rebel or the state terrorist rejects the distinction between combatant and noncombatant, the cardinal moral principle which determines the various limits one may impose on means.[12] It may be true psychologically that a community waives limits when it really believes that its life is at stake, but in a war where there is no such urgency, and this is almost always the case when terror is employed because it is a cheaper weapon, the tendency is for the public to become more concerned with seeing that the *jus in bellum* restrictions are met. Compare the response of the U.S. public to abuses by Americans in World War II with those in Vietnam.

Governments everywhere understand that they cannot say openly that they use terror. This does not stop them from using it upon occasion. *The Document on Terror* may overestimate the degree to which one can conceal culpability. But culpability is often concealed; and states often can call their acts of terror in the international sphere military acts and get away with it. This may give them enormous advantage in the propaganda struggle but does not make their behavior morally correct.[13]

History also warns us to be skeptical about states that claim that justice gives them the right to engage in what we would recognize (by applying my definition) as terrorism. Geoffrey Best, in his comprehensive study of the law of armed conflicts, draws attention to the fact that "justice," when used by states to give moral authority to their prosecution of a war, often is associated with egregious offenses against accepted moral standards. Conviction of righteousness can easily become self-righteousness—the latter becoming the cause of intolerance and excess. In practice, it often seems that it is the most ruthless states that claim to be occupying the moral high ground most vociferously. An excess of self-righteousness seems to be associated with immoderate and inept policies. In the final analysis, the just war defense seems particularly hollow when one realizes the universality of claims to be just cause. Quite probably, for "normal" human beings it is psychologically necessary to believe that the cause one is fighting for is just. As Best concludes:

> The whole fine language about justice in war thus gets dragged through the mire of the battlefield, and is made in practice meaningless; regularly called into use as part of the panoply of emotional self-intoxication so often found necessary . . . to get people fighting furiously, and calculated to cloud judgement about right and wrong.[14]

While Best's concern is with conventional warfare between nations, his points are equally telling with respect to state involvement in terrorism. Such terrorism violates the moral codes by which Western nations seek to condemn "ordinary" (non-state) terrorists and it is insufficient to argue that the claims of such terrorists to a just cause are illegitimate, while the claims in a similar vein made by the state are legitimate merely because they assert them to be so and have superior power and resources to make the argument. There is, of course, no necessary correlation between the loudness and the rightness of a claim. Indeed, if such a correlation exists, it may well be a negative one. This, after all, is what states claim for "ordinary" terrorists. It may be just as aptly applied to themselves.

Moral Equivalence

The claim that there are no innocents among states and that nations of all political or ideological hues, including most Western ones, are involved or have had some state involvement in terrorism is condemned by some as reflecting an inability to discern real moral differences between "good" and "bad" states.[15] Probably the best-known exponent of this view is former U.S. Ambassador to the United nations, Jeane Kirkpatrick.[16] The difficulty with the Kirkpatrick view, apart from its mistakes of fact and overstatement, is that much of what she condemns is not what critics are saying. To claim that the USSR and the United States both have used or sponsored terrorism as foreign policy instruments[17] is not the same as asserting that the two *systems* are morally indistinguishable. Apart from the contentious issue of the relative amounts of such involvement, condemnation of one aspect of a state's behavior does not imply wholesale condemnation of what it stands for. To say that a country uses terrorism as a foreign policy tool is not to say that it is on a moral par with another which does so too if that exhibits many other odious features. If criticism is to be equated with total moral condemnation of a system, it seems to be aimed at deterring people from criticizing. Attack is the best form of defense.

But of course no nation can claim to be morally blameless in international politics, and it seems strange that one of the leading exponents of realist thought should speak as if her country were so. Kirkpatrick, just as she claims her critics to be, is selective in her denunciations of others' wrongs. She condemns the immoral behavior of some nations, yet omits to mention or justifies the same behavior in others. What she fails to acknowledge, however, is the reality that "a democracy can be good and do evil—sometimes even when it is trying to do good."[18] It follows that to condemn our own or a friendly government for indulging in the morally indefensible support of terrorism is not equivalent to saying that its behavior *in toto* is as heinous as another nation whose *system* we find morally repugnant. There are significant moral differences, even when the two nations use the same indefensible tactics. Most importantly, as Zagoria notes in discussing differences between the USSR and the United States: "One such distinction flows from the fact that ours [the USA] is a democratic society in which there is a continuing debate over the proper standards to employ in world affairs; many policies are rejected because they flout our moral standards."[19]

Assessing the Morality of International Terrorism in the Service of the State

It is important to remember in assessing moral claims that terrorism is a means, not an ideology. It is a tactic in the service of some goal (in the present discussion, a foreign or national policy goal). Coady, has pointed out that there are, broadly speaking, three ways of assessing the morality of violence which is viewed as a means to certain ends.[20] The first (the pacifist view) is to reject its use on the grounds that extreme violence of any sort in pursuit of good ends is morally impermissible. This, of course, rejects the morality of warfare *in toto* and would certainly exclude terrorism for moral approval. The second (the utilitarian position) assesses the violence in terms of its efficiency in contributing to the achieving of good ends. The third (a variation in the utilitarian option) examines the violence partly on efficiency grounds, but also in terms of the sort of violence used. The focus in the latter case is on the appropriateness of the target, the proportionality of the behavior and on the existence of extreme forms. Coady terms this the internal viewpoint since the morality of terrorism is judged here not only externally in terms of its consequences.

Coady draws attention to the fact that much of the moral confusion over terrorism arises because "people tend to apply one outlook (the utilitarian) when discussing state violence (especially that of their own state) and another (the internal) when discussing the violence of non-state actors such as revolutionaries."[21]

This dual system leads to inconsistency and hypocrisy. Thus a state may apply the utilitarian standard to its own behavior of intentionally killing noncombatants in a raid on a village carried out in reprisal for an attack on itself and apply the internal standard to the act which initiated the state's response. In the first case, the behavior of deliberately killing women and children is morally sanctioned because of the good ends supposedly served. In the second, the same *behavior* (the intentional killing of women and children) is condemned because of what it involves, even if some believe the cause to be just.

The confusion can be resolved by consistently applying either standard. Applying the utilitarian standard runs the risk of putting no real limits on behavior, since the judgment of efficiency will be subjective and vary greatly according to who is making it. I agree with Coady, however, that the preferable course is the consistent application of the internal standard—which would "object to the technique of terrorism as immoral wherever and whenever it is used or proposed."[22] Essentially the reason for its immorality lies in the fact that the terrorist deliberately fails to distinguish between combatants and noncombatants. In my view, unless one accepts the extreme pacifist position that all violence is immoral, the only morally justifiable target for violence is someone who is directly involved in attacking us or others or in carrying on a gross injustice.[23] I do not accept that the category of "someone" can be enlarged very much past those actually committing the violence or ordering them to do so. Thus, soldiers, policemen, and politicians may in some contexts be viewed as morally legitimate targets of a campaign of violence (for example, if they are part of a repressive regime which tortures and murders to maintain its grip on power). A state may be justified in supporting such violence in such circumstances. It would not be morally defensible to attack those who support those actually committing the injustice. To allow any widening of the category (to include, for example, those who make their weapons, or supply their food, or even support their policies) is to open the floodgates. Any limit placed on the category of guilty past the actual perpetrators (including those who order the crimes) is purely arbitrary and will not be respected by others who would place different bounds. The inevitable consequence is the "There are no innocents" position, or reducing the

equation to "if you are not for me, you are against me." It is essential if we are to place any moral authority behind decisions about appropriateness of targeting to adhere to a strict limit. If we apply the above test, however, it amounts to a justification for revolutionary violence or state support of it, rather than to a justification for terrorism. Attacking those committing direct violence themselves is aimed at removing them directly from the position of being able to so act. The victims are also the targets, thus not meeting our definitional requirement that they be distinguished in the terrorist case. Terrorism remains, therefore, outside of the bounds of morally permissible behavior. It follows that a state, as much as a group or an individual, can claim no moral authority for committing what I would define as terrorism.

Morality versus Reality

There is no moral justification for state involvement in terrorism. Nevertheless there appears to be an increasing use of terrorism in the service of the foreign policy objectives of nations. When it is used by those we oppose, the condemnation is loud. When it is used by ourselves or our friends, we change the labels. It is a reality that states will intervene, with violence if necessary, within their spheres of influence to change conditions which impact (or are considered to impact) upon their national interests. At the general level this is accepted as inevitable and the explanations are not thought to matter much. Thus, as Liska says: "Dating from time immemorial, this [the intervention of major powers in their spheres of influence] is practically an inalienable right. Such actions are routinely clothed in pious rationalizations that do no usually succeed in obfuscating the real reasons behind the intervention."[24]

I believe, however, that the case of terrorism by states as a mode of intervention is a special one. The use of the term has become so emotionally and politically laden and used so skillfully by many nations that it *has* succeeded in obfuscating the real reasons behind many state interventions. Not only that, the renaming of one's own terrorism as something else has often succeeded in convincing the citizens of those states that its use is morally justified. Although its use is manipulated by cynical opportunists, I believe that most politicians have also fallen victim to their own sleight of hand and believe their own moral rationalizations. In addition, scholars have also shrunk from labeling similar behaviors similarly across the international scene and have been unwilling analytically to consider many types of state behavior as terrorism.[25] As a consequence of this self-delusion and deliberate confusion it is difficult to sustain informed debate about the morality of much behavior which should be condemned, because it is simply not accepted as behavior about which severe moral questions arise.[26]

We must accept, too, that the concept of national interest will be used in the future, as in the past, to sweep aside all but the most outstanding moral qualms—and they too will fall victim to necessity in a perceived or actual situation of threat or aggression. Terrorism, in theory at least, is a cost-effective tactic for states to use in some circumstances and an option that appeals to an increasing number of states. Unless it can be uniformly defined and seen for what it is, it is not going to be possible to mobilize effective domestic and international opinion against it. Such agreement on definition is not possible at a global level. Nevertheless, the morally responsible course is to attempt such agreement as it is possible in an effort to delegitimate the tactic. The aim should be "to tear away at the protective clothing that allows agents of the state and the public to ignore the human consequences that state terrorist behavior generates . . . By challenging the behavior and raising public awareness . . . we increase the possibilities of bystanders of the terrorism challenging the behavior. This will contribute to an increase in the response costs that policy makers will have to add to their decision calculus.[27]

A Final Quandary

The reality that states will continue to employ terrorist tactics under whatever name raises a final moral problem we have not considered. It is mentioned here briefly more to allude to its troubling existence than to attempt to resolve it. Indeed, it may in essence be insoluble.

For the policy-maker, there always exists the possibility that terrorism may be a tactic whose use in the international arena in specific cases saves lives, in comparison to its nonuse or to the use of alternative means. Presume for the moment that we can calculate accurately the consequences, in terms of lives lost, of the use of each alternative. Presume further that our state directs a terrorist campaign with the aim of removing a government in power in another state which directly threatens our national interest and that our calculus shows this tactic will result in significantly less loss of life than any of the alternative methods which we could use. Presuming finally that one of the options *will* be used, should our leaders refuse to choose the terrorist option because its use as a tactic is immoral? Would it make any difference to the decision if the lives saved by its use were 10, or 20, or 100 times greater than the next best option? I have earlier alluded to the problem that assigning priority to ends over means always runs the risk of justifying increasingly unjustifiable behavior. But what about extreme situations? The questions are posed thus by Nye:

> At some point, does not integrity become the ultimate egoism of fastidious self-righteousness in which the purity of the self is more important than the lives of countless others? Is it not better to follow a consequentialist approach, admit remorse or regret over the immoral means, but justify the action by the ends? In the domain of international politics, where issues of survival sometimes arise, will not an absolute ethics of being, rather than an ethics of doing, run the additional risk that you will not survive to be?[28]

There can be no formula-based answers to such questions. Perhaps, objectively at least, in the real world occasions demanding the answers will never arise because the alternatives will not be so stark nor the calculations so precise as to allow confident predictions. Nevertheless policy makers will *feel* confronted by such decisions and we must sympathize with their dilemma if they must honestly wrestle with them.

The reality is, then, that decision makers must attend to both rules and consequences. For practical purposes, except in rare circumstances, I believe, the rules are paramount. The rule-based argument I make is that terrorism in the service of the state cannot be defended ethically. We accept this for our foes. We must also accept it for ourselves.

NOTES

1. William J. Casey, "The International Linkages—What Do We Know?" in Uri Ra'anan et al, *Hydra of Carnage* (Lexington: Lexington Books, 1986), p. 5.
2. Grant Wardlaw, *Political Terrorism* (Cambridge: Cambridge University Press, 1982), p. 16.
3. For more discussion on this point see Christopher Mitchell, Michael Stohl, David Carleton, and George A. Lopez, "State Terrorism: Issues of Concept and Measurement," in Michael Stohl and George A. Lopez, eds., *Government Violence and Repression* (Westport, Conn.: Greenwood Press, 1986), pp. 1–25. Aronson's essay in this volume contends that Nazi policy toward the Jews was a case of hostage-taking that went amiss, and thus would by Wardlaw's definition be an instance of state terrorism (editors).
4. Michael Stohl, "States, Terrorism and State Terrorism: The Role of the Superpowers," in Robert Slater and Michael Stohl, eds., *Current Perspectives on International Terrorism* (London and New York: Macmillan and St. Martin's Press, forthcoming).
5. Adda B. Bozeman, "American Policy and the Illusion of Congruent Values," *Strategic Review* (1987), 15(1):12.
6. Determining the validity of the claim may present a serious problem, one whose reputation will inevitably not be accepted by some.
7. Abraham Kaplan, "The Ethics of Terror," in Burr Eichelman, David Soskis, and William Reid, eds., *Terrorism: Interdisciplinary Perspectives* (Washington, D.C.: American Psychiatric Association, 1983), p. 19.
8. Hans J. Morgenthau, *Politics Among Nations*, 5th ed., revised (New York: Knopf, 1978), p. 10.
9. Ernst Cassirer, *The Myth of the State* (New Haven: Yale University Press, 1946), p. 265.
10. Kaplan, p. 20.
11. For expanded discussion of the view that terrorism is a form of warfare see, generally, Ray S. Cline and Yonah Alexander, *Terrorism As State-Sponsored Covert Warfare* (Fairfax, Va: Hero Books, 1986); and Neil C. Livingstone and Terrell E. Arnold, eds., *Fighting Back: Winning the War Against Terrorism* (Lexington: Lexington Books, 1986).
12. See, for example, Michael Walzer, *Just and Unjust Wars* (Harmondsworth: Penguin, 1977) and David C. Rapoport, "The Politics of Atrocity," in Y. Alexander and S. Finger, *Terrorism Interdisciplinary Perspectives* (New York: John Jay, 1977), pp. 46–61.
13. For a discussion of how states have corrupted the language pertaining to terrorism, see my "Terror as an Instrument of Foreign Policy," in *Inside Terrorism*, ed., David C. Rapoport (New York: Columbia University Press, 1982).
14. Geoffrey Best, *Humanity in Warfare* (London: Methuen, 1983), p. 7.
15. For "good," read us and our allies and friends, for "bad," read those who oppose us, our enemies, or those who have ideologies of which we disapprove.
16. See, for example, Jeane Kirkpatrick, "Moral Equivalence and Political Aims," *Society* (March/April 1985), pp. 3–8.
17. As argued, for example, by Stohl, "States."
18. Joseph S. Nye, Jr. "Motives, Means and Consequences," *Society* (March/April 1985), p. 17.
19. Donald S. Zagoria, "Looking for High Ground in Our Backyard," *Society* (March/April 1985), p. 30.
20. C. A. J. Coady, "The Morality of Terrorism," *Philosophy* (1985), 60:50–51.
21. Ibid, p. 56.
22. Ibid, p. 58.
23. Clearly, what constitutes a "gross injustice" is a qualitative decision, but there is no way to avoid that.
24. George Lisk, "The Reagan Doctrine: Monroe and Dulles Reincarnate?" *SAIS Review* (1986), 6(2):84.
25. This point is made by Michael Stohl, "International Dimensions of State Terrorism," in Michael Stohl and George A. Lopez, eds., *The State as Terrorist* (Westport, Conn.: Greenwood Press, 1984), p. 55.
26. At least, those questions which inquire into the legitimacy of the tactic *qua* tactic are missing. There may be questions about the limits of the tactic or the circumstances in which it may be used. The point is that the tactic itself is not ruled out morally because it is not thought of as being terrorism.
27. Stohl, "States."
28. Nye, p. 17.

Islam's "Neglected Duty"

Mark Juergensmeyer

The selection of the American embassies in Kenya and Tanzania as targets on August 7, 1998, for bombings allegedly arranged by Osama bin Laden followed a macabre tradition. Symbols of secular political power were also chosen—perhaps again by bin Laden—when an American military residence hall in Dhahran, Saudi Arabia, was bombed in 1996 and when a truckload of explosives was ignited in the parking garage of New York City's World Trade Center in 1993. Although many of the bombing sites chosen by the Lebanese Amal and Hizbollah movements in the 1980s and 1990s were military, the actions of bin Laden—along with Hamas in Palestine and the al Gamaa-i Islamiya movement in Egypt in the 1990s—were aimed more broadly. They were directed not only at symbols of political and economic power, such as embassies and trade centers, but also at other centers of secular life: residence halls, office buildings, buses, shopping malls, cruise boats, and coffeehouses. In Algeria the inhabitants of whole villages were slaughtered, allegedly by supporters of the Islamic Salvation Front. All of these incidents were assaults on society as a whole.

This series of terrifying events raises a complicated question: why have these three things—religious conviction, hatred of secular society, and the demonstration of power through acts of violence—so frequently coalesced in recent Islamic activist movements? To begin to search for answers to this question, I talked with one of the men convicted of the bombing of the World Trade Center, Mahmud Abouhalima. He was part of a group of Muslims, most of them from Egypt, who lived on the outskirts of New York City in Queens and Jersey City and came together as a paramilitary organization through their commitment to a visionary Muslim ideology articulated by a remarkable leader, Sheik Omar Abdul Rahman.

Mahmud Abouhalima and the World Trade Center Bombing

Mahmud Abouhalima is a strong, tall man whose striking red hair and beard have led some to call him "Mahmud the Red."[1] He was accused but never convicted of being the cab driver for the bungled getaway following the assassination of Rabbi Meir Kahane in 1990. His relationship with the alleged assassin, El Sayyid Nosair, is well established, however, and he is said to have admitted to an investigator that he tried to buy weapons to defend his group against the Jewish Defense League, an American organization founded by Kahane. The man from whom he allegedly attempted to buy the weapons, Wadih el Hage, was a Lebanese Muslim living in Texas who later worked for Osama bin Laden, and who was arrested in September 1998 for being part of the network involved in the bombing of the American embassies in Kenya and Tanzania.[2] Though Abouhalima's

ties to bin Laden are at best obscure, he is well
known for his associations with Sheik Omar Abdul
Rahman and the group responsible for the bombing
of the World Trade Center in 1993, an act for
which Abouhalima himself was charged, tried, and
convicted. When I spoke to him on two occasions
in 1997, he was serving a lifetime sentence at a
federal penitentiary.[3]

According to some accounts of the World Trade
Center blast, Abouhalima was the "mastermind" of
the event, a label of notoriety that is sometimes
also given to his fellow activist, Ramzi Yousef.[4] In
the trial that convicted him in 1994, Abouhalima
was portrayed as crucial to the attack: evidence
was presented that placed him at the site of the
New Jersey warehouse where bomb materials were
collected and assembled, and among the members
of, the group who stopped at a filling station to
refuel the rental truck as it made its final trip to the
World Trade Center parking lot the night before the
explosion. At the time of the blast itself, at noon on
February 26, 1993, some claimed that Abouhalima
was across the street from the towers, looking
expectantly out the window of the classical-music
annex of a record store, J&R Music, disappointed
that the bombing caused such little damage.[5] If
the amount of explosives in the truck had been just
a little larger and the truck placed slightly differently in the basement parking area, it would have
brought down an entire tower—which most likely
would have fallen sideways, destroying the second
tower as well. Instead of six people killed, the
number perished could easily have climbed to two
hundred thousand. It would have included most of
the fifty thousand workers and an equal number of
visitors on site at the World Trade Center on that
fateful day, plus another hundred thousand workers
in the surrounding buildings, which would have
been destroyed if both towers fell. If indeed Abouhalima had expected that sort of disaster, he must
have been disappointed with the relatively modest
explosion that resulted, even though its assault on
the public's consciousness made it one of the most
significant terrorist acts in American history.

The first of two conversations I had with Abouhalima took place in August 1997, when I met with
him by special arrangement in an otherwise empty

visitor's room of the maximum-security prison in
Lompoc, California—which prides itself as "the
new rock," a formidable and secure successor to
Alcatraz. He was brought into the room handcuffed
and accompanied by three guards. Dressed in
green prison garb, Abouhalima's figure was indeed
striking—tall, red-haired, his face freckled—and
his English was fluid and colloquial. He leaned
over as he spoke, often whispering, as if to
reinforce the intimacy and importance of what
he said.

When I talked with him, he was hoping that his
conviction could still be appealed, and for this
reason Abouhalima avoided discussing particulars
related to the trial and to the bombing itself. He
claimed to be innocent of all charges, a point that
he repeated in letters to me in 1998 and 1999.
Moreover, he claimed that he almost never talked
with journalists or scholars for fear of being mis-
quoted or—he said—falsely implicated in the
crimes that put him prison. He specifically denied
the allegations of direct involvement in the World
Trade Center bombing for which he had been
convicted. Abouhalima related to me a dramatic
moment in the trial when the prosecution's sole
witness to his participation in the act—the New
Jersey service station attendant on duty the night
that the truck carrying the explosives was refueled
—was asked to look around the courtroom and
identify the tall, red-headed man he had seen with
the truck at the time. Instead of pointing toward
Abouhalima, the attendant startled the audience by
pointing past him toward one of the jurors, saying
"it was a person like this one."[6] Abouhalima
had reasons, therefore, for thinking that the case
against him was fairly slim, and it was understandable that he did not want to discuss the bombing or
the events surrounding it.

Although restricted in what he felt he could say,
Abouhalima was quite eloquent on the subject that
I wanted to discuss with him—the public role of
Islam and its increasingly political impact. He also
felt free to talk about the subject of terrorism in
general and terrorist incidents of which he was not
accused, including the Oklahoma City federal
building bombing. The trial of Terry Nichols, one
of the defendants in the case, was being conducted

at the time of my second interview with him, and in response to my questions, Abouhalima discussed the progress of the trial and helped me understand why such a bombing might occur.

"It was done for a very, very specific reason," Abouhalima told me, contradicting any impression I might have had that the federal building was bombed for no reason at all, or for the most general of symbolic statements. "They had some certain target, you know, a specific achievement," Abouhalima said, adding that "they wanted to reach the government with the message that we are not tolerating the way that you are dealing with our citizens."[7]

Was the bombing an act of terrorism, I asked him? Abouhalima thought for a moment and then explained that the whole concept was "messed up." The term seemed to be used only for incidents of violence that people didn't like, or rather, Abouhalima explained, for incidents that the media have labeled terrorist.

"What about the United States government?" Abouhalima asked me. "How do they justify their acts of bombings, of killing innocent people, directly or indirectly, openly or secretly? They're killing people everywhere in the world: before, today, and tomorrow. How do you define that?" Then he described what he regarded as the United States' terrorist attitude toward the world. According to Abouhalima, the United States tries to "terrorize nations," to "obliterate their power," and to tell them that they "are nothing" and that they "have to follow us." Abouhalima implied that many forms of international political or economic control could be kinds of terrorism. He also gave specific examples of cases where he felt the United States had used its power to kill people indiscriminately.

"In Japan, for instance," Abouhalima said, referring to the atomic bomb blasts, "through the bombs, you know, that killed more than two hundred thousand people." Perhaps it was just a coincidence, but the number of casualties Abouhalima cited in Hiroshima and Nagasaki was the same number that would have been killed in the World Trade Center blast, according to estimates, if the bombs had been placed differently and both towers brought down as allegedly planned.

Was the Oklahoma City blast a terrorist response to the government's terrorism? "That's what I'm saying," Abouhalima replied. "If they believe, if these guys, whoever they are, did whatever bombing they say they did in Oklahoma City, if they believe that the government unjustifiably killed the people in Waco, then they have their own way to respond. They absolutely have their own way to respond," he repeated for emphasis, indicating that the Oklahoma City bombing "response" was morally justified.

"Yet," I said in an effort to put the event in context, "it killed a lot of innocent people, and ultimately it did not seem to change anything."

"But it's as I said," Abouhalima responded, "at least the government got the message." Moreover, he told me, the only thing that humans can do in response to great injustice is to send a message. Stressing the point that all human efforts are futile and that those who bomb buildings should not expect any immediate, tangible change in the government's policies as a result, Abouhalima said that real change—effective change—"is not is our hands," only "in God's hands."

This led to a general discussion about what he regarded as the natural connection between Islam and political order. Abouhalima said this relationship had been weakened by modern leaders of Islamic countries, such as those in his native Egypt, as a result of the influence of the West in general and the United States in particular. The president of Egypt, for example, was not really Muslim, Abouhalima implied, since he "watered down" Islamic law. Leaders such as President Hosni Mubarak "said yes" to Islamic law and principles, Abouhalima explained, but then turned around and "said yes" to secular ideas as well, especially regarding such matters as family law, education, and financial institutions, where Muslim law prohibits usery.[8] He claimed the character of many contemporary politicians was deceitful: they pretended to be Muslim but in practice followed secular—implicitly Western—codes of conduct.

Mahmud Abouhalima's religious influences began at an early age. He was raised in Kafr al-Dawar, a town in northern Egypt near Alexandria, where he attended a Muslim youth camp. It offered him the "first light for understanding what it is to be a Muslim," Abouhalima said.[9] He took courses at Alexandria University and became increasingly active in Islamic politics, especially the outlawed al Gamaa-i Islamiya, led by Sheik Omar Abdul Rahman.

In 1981, when Abouhalima was 21, he left Egypt—perhaps to escape the watchful eye of the Egyptian internal security forces—and went to Germany on a tourist visa. Egypt's president Anwar Sadat was rounding up Muslim activists at the time, and one week after Abouhalima's departure Sadat was assassinated, allegedly by Abouhalima's former colleagues, supporters of Sheik Omar Abdul Rahman. The sheik himself stood trial, accused of complicity in the act, but was never convicted. During this time Abouhalima was living in Munich, but when the German government tried to deport him in 1982, Abouhalima searched for a way to remain in the country. A rapidly arranged marriage to a somewhat emotionally unstable German nurse living in his apartment building made it possible for Abouhalima to continue his German residency.[10] In 1985 this marriage dissolved and Abouhalima married another German woman, Marianne Weber.

During his initial years in Germany, Abouhalima said, he lived a "life of corruption—girls, drugs, you name it." He went through the outward signs of Islamic reverence—daily prayers, fasting during the month of Ramadan—but he had left the real Islam behind.[11] After a while, he "got bored" with his wayward existence, began reading the Qur'an again, and returned to a committed religious life. At this time his wife, Marianne, who by her own admission had also been living a dissolute life before she married Abouhalima, became a Muslim as well. Soon afterward, in 1985, he and Marianne came to the United States. They settled in New York City, and a three-month visa turned into an extended stay. His renewed interest in Islam was nurtured by a large and active Muslim community centered on Atlantic Avenue in downtown Brooklyn.

"Islam is a mercy," Abouhalima told me, explaining that it rescued the fallen and gave meaning to one's personal life. This was something that he desperately needed when lured by the lifestyle of secular society, first in Germany and then in the

United States. He told a story, a sort of parable, about a lion cub that was raised among sheep. The cub thought he was a sheep until another lion came along and showed him his reflection in a clear pond. That's what his Muslim teachers and his spiritual readings had shown him, Abouhalima said. He was "a Muslim, not a sheep."[12]

Abouhalima seized the opportunity to prove that he was not a sheep in 1988, when he joined the Muslim struggle in Afghanistan. Although he had been earning his income as a New York City taxi driver, Abouhalima was also serving as a volunteer worker at the Alkifah Afghan Refugee Center in Brooklyn. There Afghani refugees told of the Mujahedin's heroic struggle against the Soviet-backed government of Najibullah in their homeland. The center was said to have been funded by Osama bin Laden.[13] Abouhalima admitted to me that he went to Afghanistan during that time (something he had previously denied) but that the was there solely in a nonmilitary "civil" capacity. According to some accounts, however, he was indeed involved in the military struggle and had volunteered for the suicidal task of minesweeping, going in front of the Muslim troops with a long stick to probe the earth for land mines.[14] But even if he had not been involved in any direct military way, I said to Abouhalima, it was a dangerous time to be in that country. Why would he want to risk his life for such a cause? "It is my job," Abouhalima explained, "as a Muslim." He said that he felt he had a mission "to go wherever there is oppression and injustice and fight it."[15]

When he returned, his Afghani service had earned him the admiration of many in his circle of Muslim activists, and according to some accounts he continued to wear his military fatigues and combat boots on Brooklyn's city streets.[16] He became more deeply engaged in Muslim political causes and helped arrange for the leading figure in Egypt's radical Muslim community—Sheik Omar Abdul Rahman—to become established in the United States. The sheik had also been in Afghanistan, and his arrival in July 1990 from the Sudan made significant waves in the militant Muslim community in the New York City area. In fact, he was soon at odds with the man who sponsored his immigration to the United States, Mustafa Shalabi, the leader of the Alkifah Afghan Refugee Center and a friend of Abouhalima. Eventually, however, it became clear that Abouhalima's loyalty in the emerging competition was with the sheik, and when Shalabi was murdered in 1991, Abouhalima was a suspect but was never formally charged. With Shalabi out of the way, the sheik was the unchallenged leader of the New York area's militant Muslim community.

Sheik Omar Abdul Rahman was a blind Islamic scholar who had once been a professor of theology at the prestigious Al Azhar University in Cairo and who was linked with one of Egypt's most revolutionary Islamic movements, al Gamaa-i Islamiya ("the Islamic group"). The sheik was implicated in the assassination of Anwar Sadat and in a series of violent attacks on the government in his native region, the oasis area of Fayoum—charges for which he was eventually acquitted. Suspicions of the sheik's involvement, however, remained. Followers of the sheik were also believed to be responsible for two more killings in Egypt—the murder of Parliament Speaker Rifaat Mahgoub and a secular writer, Farag Foda—and assassination attempts on Prime Minister Hosni Mubarak and the Nobel-prize-winning novelist Naguib Mahfouz. With the government closing in on his group, Sheik Abdul Rahman repaired to the Sudan and eventually made it to New Jersey. He entered the United States presumably by error; officials at the American embassy in Khartoum did not detect his name on a list of those requiring special permission—although some commentators claim that the sheik had been favored by the CIA because of his support for anticommunist rebels in the Afghanistan war and was allowed to enter the United States as a sort of reward.

In the United States, Sheik Abdul Rahman became established in a small mosque called El Salam ("the place of peace") located above a Chinese restaurant in Jersey City, New Jersey. There he preached against the evils of secular society and helped the struggling members of his flock understand why they were oppressed, both in the Middle East and in the United States. He singled out America for special condemnation because it

helped to create the state of Israel, supported the secular Egyptian government, and sent its troops to Kuwait during the Gulf War, all of which the sheik deemed "un-Islamic."[17]

Listening attentively to the words of Sheik Omar Abdul Rahman was a growing circle of mostly male Islamic activists in their thirties who had immigrated to the United States from several Middle Eastern countries. It included Muhammad Salameh, an unemployed Palestinian refugee; Siddig Ali, a Sudanese organizer; Nidal Ayyad, who was trained as a chemical engineer; Ibrahim El-Gabrowny, the president of the Abu Bakr mosque in Brooklyn; his cousin, El Sayyid Nosair, who was imprisoned from charges related to the killing of Meir Kahane; and a man known by various names, including "Ramzi Ahmed Yousef," a Pakistani said to be born in Iraq and raised in Kuwait who had masterminded some of the most imaginative scenarios of recent terrorist history. It also included Abouhalima, who for a time served as the sheik's chauffeur and bodyguard.

I wanted to ask Abouhalima why Muslim activists such as Sheik Abdul Rahman would target the United States as an enemy. Although he did not respond to that question directly—and in fact praised America for its religious freedom, claiming that it was easier for him to be a good Muslim in this country than in Egypt—he did answer indirectly when he talked about how Jewish influence controlled America's news media, financial institutions, and government. In that sense, Abouhalima explained, although the United States claimed to be secular and impartial toward religion, "it is involved in religious politics already."[18]

Abouhalima made it clear that America's involvement in religious politics—its support for the state of Israel and for "enemies of Islam" such as Egypt's Mubarak—is not the result of Christianity. Rather, it was due to America's ideology of secularism, which Abouhalima regards not as neutrality but as hostility toward religion, especially Islam. He cited the U.S. Department of Justice, which he called the "Department of Injustice." I asked him if the United States would be better off if it had a Christian government. "Yes," Abouhalima replied, "at least it would have morals."[19]

Abouhalima's bitterness toward the Justice Department was compounded by its swift prosecution of the case against him and his colleagues in a series of trials. The one that ended on March 4, 1994, focused on the anti-American motives for the assault; it convicted four—Muhammad Salameh, Nidal Ayyad, Ahmad Muhammad Ajaj, and Abouhalima—of bombing the Center and indicted Ramzi Ahmed Yousef as a fugitive in the crime. The second trial, ending on January 17, 1996, convicted nine—including a life sentence for Sheik Omar Abdul Rahman—for their part in what the judge described as a "terrorist conspiracy" of a magnitude comparable with militant fascism and communism.[20] The prosecution offered evidence that the circle of Muslim activists associated with the sheik had intended to blow up not only the World Trade Center but also the United Nations buildings in Manhattan, two New York commuter tunnels under the Hudson River, and the Manhattan headquarters of the FBI.

A third trial, begun on May 13, 1996, focused on the fugitive, who had been captured in Pakistan in a dramatic raid on his Karachi hotel room in February 1995. Yousef, whose real name appeared to be Abdul Basit Mahmoud Abdul Karim, was implicated not only in the New York events but also in a series of terrorist plots, including one aimed at assassinating the pope when he visited the Philippines in 1995 and the so-called Project Bojinka, which, if carried out, would have led to the destruction of eleven large U.S. passenger airplanes over the Pacific Ocean in one momentous day in 1995. The trial ended on September 5, 1996, with Yousef's conviction for conspiracy in the case of the Bojinka plot; in August 1997 Yousef again stood trial in New York City, this time for his part in the bombing of the World Trade Center.

After all of these trials, Abouhalima said, secular America still did not understand him and his colleagues. What, I asked him, was missing? What was it that we did not understand?

"The soul," he said, "the soul of religion, that is what is missing." Without it, Abouhalima said, Western prosecutors, journalists, and scholars like myself "will never understand who I am." He said that he understood the secular West because he had

lived like a Westerner in Germany and in the United States. The seventeen years he had lived in the West, Abouhalima told me, "is a fair amount of time to understand what the hell is going on in the United States and in Europe about secularism or people, you know, who have no religion," He went on to say, "I lived their life, but they didn't live my life, so they will never understand the way I live or the way I think."

Abouhalima compared a life without religion to a pen without ink. "An ink pen," he said, "a pen worth two thousand dollars, gold and everything in it, it's useless if there's no ink in it. That's the thing that gives life," Abouhalima said, drawing out the analogy, "the life in this pen . . . the soul." He finished his point by saying, "the soul, the religion, you know, that's the thing that's revived the whole life. Secularism," he said, looking directly at me, "has none, they have none, you have none."

And as for secular people, I asked, who do not know the life of religion? "They're just moving like dead bodies," Abouhalima said.

Abdul Aziz Rantisi and Hamas Suicide Missions

Although their targets were not as spectacular as the World Trade Center buildings, the series of suicide terrorist attacks in Jerusalem and Tel Aviv conducted in recent years by Muslim activists associated with the radical Palestinian movement Hamas were equally terrifying—just as vicious in their killing of what are traditionally viewed as noncombatants, and just as desperate in their attempts to gain the world's attention for what was perceived by the perpetrators to be a religious as well as a political cause. Like the World Trade Center event; the intended audience included not just those in the immediate vicinity, but all who observed the media reportage and were horrified by it.

To many who witnessed them even at a distance, the horror of the bombings in Jerusalem and Tel Aviv was compounded by the knowledge that the bombers purposefully killed themselves in conducting the acts. Who would do such a thing, and why?

The answers to such questions are best given by those directly involved in them. But because anyone who successfully carries out a suicide bombing is by definition unavailable for interviewing afterward, I found that the next best way of hearing their voices is to watch the videotapes that many of them made the night before the missions. Often crudely photographed, these testimonies were filmed by their Hamas colleagues partly to memorialize the young men and partly to show to other potential volunteers as a kind of recruiting device. These tapes are clandestinely circulated within the Palestinian community in Gaza and the towns on the West Bank. I was privileged to see several that are part of a collection gathered by two American scholars, Anne Marie Oliver and Paul Steinberg, who once lived in Gaza and have written a book on the phenomenon of suicide bombings and the valorization of the young men who committed them.[21]

One of the most moving videotapes in their collection shows a handsome young man, no more than eighteen years old and perhaps less, looking oddly happy as he talked about the sacrifice that he was about to make. Dubbed "the smiling boy" by Oliver and Steinberg, he was videotaped in an outdoor setting beside a rock and a bush, wearing what appears to be a stylish bluejean jacket, his bushy dark hair and grinning face bathed in sunlight. The mission he and his friend would carry out involved plastic explosives, either strapped around his waist or carried in a knapsack, but he was portrayed holding a gun—most likely included in the video to give him a martial demeanor.

"Tomorrow is the day of encounter," the smiling boy said. It was to be "the day of meeting the lord of the Worlds." He went on to say that he and his colleagues would "make our blood cheap for the sake of God, out of love for this homeland and for the sake of the freedom and honor of this people, in order that Palestine remain Islamic, and in order that Hamas remains a torch lighting the roads of all the perplexed and all the tormented and oppressed [and] that Palestine might be liberated."[22]

Another of the volunteers, on a different tape, explained that all people have to die at some time, so one is indeed fortunate to be able to choose one's destiny. He explained that there were those "who fall off their donkeys and die," those "whose donkeys trample them and they die," those who are hit by cars and suffer heart attacks, and "those who fall off the roofs of their houses and die." But, he added, "what a difference there is between one death and another," implying that the choice of martyrdom was a rare opportunity and that he was fortunate to have it. "Truly there is only one death," he said, repeating the words of a famous Muslim martyr, "so let it be on the path of God."[23]

The young men on these tapes look so innocent, so full of life, that the viewer is moved to try somehow to reverse time and stop them from carrying out their deadly missions. Whatever sympathy they engender is superseded, however, by the sense of loss and remorse for the deaths of their victims, who were even more innocent than their attackers. Unlike the smiling boy and his colleagues, they were never given the choice of whether or not to give up their lives for the sake of these violent missions.

On the morning of August 21, 1995, for example, a packed bus carrying students to classes and police officers to their daily assignments was inching its way from stop to stop in a crowded neighborhood of limestone apartment buildings in the northern section of the city of Jerusalem, near the Mt. Scopus campus of Hebrew University. At 7:55 A.M. a lone Arab passenger sitting in the back of the bus— someone very much like the smiling boy— suddenly reached into the handbag he was carrying and detonated a ferociously explosive bomb. It contained what police later estimated to be about ten pounds of the chemical explosive 3-acetone.[24] It was an extraordinary blast instantly incinerating the Arab, a visiting American sitting near him, and three Israelis seated nearby. The force of the explosion ripped open the side of the bus and continued outside, destroying another bus that happened to be traveling alongside. In addition to the five killed, 107 others in the two buses and passing along the street were wounded in the attack.

As I mentioned at the beginning of this book, I happened to be in Israel during those days, presenting a paper on religious violence, and I had visited the Hebrew University campus on Mt. Scopus earlier in the week on a bus that followed the same route as the one marked for disaster. The day before the blast I had been talking with members of the Hamas movement in Gaza, attempting to find answers to my questions about the suicide bombings that had occurred earlier in the year in crowded street corners in Tel Aviv. A little over two years later—after several more suicide bombings had occurred, including the savage attacks in Jerusalem's vegetable market and the Ben Yehuda shopping mall in September 1997—I received an articulate explanation for these missions in a lengthy interview with one of the founders of the Hamas movement, Dr. Abdul Aziz Rantisi.

I met Dr. Rantisi on March 1, 1998, in a village in the southern part of the Gaza Strip that can best be described as only moderately less depressed than the rest of Gaza.[25] Some of Gaza's Mediterranean beaches are quite lovely, but here the streets are dusty and pockmarked, crowded with old buses and donkey carts. Dr. Rantisi's attractive new house was on a small hillside in a suburban area. The driveway was filled with cars, and posters related to Palestinian political issues were plastered on the pillars of the entryway.

I was ushered into a comfortable living room containing a row of couches and overstuffed chairs on one side and several formal-looking chairs on the other, and was offered strong Middle Eastern coffee. It seemed clear to me that the room was meant for meetings. At one end of the room were bookcases and pictures of Rantisi when he was the spokesman for a group of Hamas supporters who had been caught in a no-man's land between Israel and Lebanon in 1992. Next to the bookcases was a sort of shrine with several drawings and pictures of Sheik Ahmed Yassin, the spiritual leader of the Hamas movement, whom I had met years earlier. Sheik Yassin was freed from captivity by the Israeli government in 1997 (and again arrested a few months later). But on the day that I met Rantisi the sheik was in Egypt for medical reasons.

When Dr. Rantisi came into the room, he greeted me cordially. A bespectacled, middle-aged man who spoke excellent English, Rantisi seemed very much the professor and medical doctor he was trained to be, and despite the heat he was nattily

dressed in a business suit with a vest. When I asked him how he wanted to be described, he said, "as a founder of Hamas." Although I was interested in his views on the connection between religion and politics, I told him I wanted to understand their relation to the current situation. It was not long until the conversation had turned to the matter of suicide bombings.

Dr. Rantisi corrected me. I should not call them "suicide bombings," he said. What he preferred was another term, a familiar Arabic word that he wrote out in my notebook in both Arabic and Roman transliteration: *istishhadi*. "It means 'self-chosen martyrdom,'" Rantisi explained, adding that "all Muslims seek to be martyrs." The term one used to describe this act was important, Rantisi went on to say, because it conveyed its significance. "Suicide bomber" implied an impulsive act by a deranged individual. The missions undertaken by the young men in the Hamas cadres, he said, were ones that they deliberately and carefully chose as part of their religious obligation. "We do not order them to do it," Rantisi emphasized, "we simply give permission for them to do it at certain times."[26]

But why, I wanted to know, would Hamas give such permission? Quite aside from the issue of the permissibility of self-martyrdom, there is the matter of targeting noncombatants. Why would Hamas allow a mission in which innocent civilians, including women and children, were the victims in such horrible attacks?

Rantisi answered in military terms, echoing the words that one of his colleagues used in discussing these matters with me in an earlier interview: "We're at war."[27] He added that it was a war not only with the Israeli government but with the whole of Israeli society. This did not mean that Hamas intended to wipe Israel from the face of the earth, he said, although some members of the movement said as much. Rantisi made it clear that he had no animosity toward Jewish culture or religion. "We're not against Jews just because they're Jews," he said.[28] From Rantisi's point of view, Hamas was presently in a state of war with Israel simply because of Israel's stance towards Palestine—especially toward the Hamas concept of an Islamic Palestine. It was Islamic nationalism that Israel wanted to destroy, Rantisi said, claiming political position was buttressed by the attitudes of Israeli society.

For this reason the war between Israel and Hamas was one with no innocent victims. In the beginning, Rantisi said, the military operations of Hamas targeted only soldiers. The movement took "every measure" to stop massacres and to discourage suicide bombings. But two events changed things. One was the attack by Israeli police on Palestinians demonstrating in front of the al-Aqsa mosque near the Dome of the Rock in 1990, and the other was the massacre in Hebron by Dr. Baruch Goldstein in 1994 during the month of Ramadan. Rantisi pointed out that both of these incidents were aimed at mosques, and he thought that Goldstein's attack during Ramadan was not a coincidence. He concluded that these were attacks on Islam as a religion as well as on Palestinians as a people. He was also convinced that despite the Israeli government's denial that it supported the extremist Jews who precipitated the al-Aqsa incident or caused the Hebron massacre, Rantisi was certain that the Israeli military had a hand in them. He pointed out that in Goldstein's attack, Israeli soldiers were standing nearby. Goldstein had befriended them, and he was able to change his rifle magazine clip four times during the incident without being stopped by soldiers.

Rantisi explained that the young Hamas supporters' acts of self-martyrdom—the suicide bombings—were allowed only in response to these and other specific acts of violence from the Israeli side, acts that frequently affected innocent civilians. In that sense they were defensive: "If we did not respond this way," Rantisi explained, "Israelis would keep doing the same thing."

Moreover, he said, the bombings were a moral lesson. They were a way of making innocent Israelis feel the pain that innocent Palestinians had felt. "We want to do the same to Israel as they have done to us," he explained, indicating that just as innocent Muslims had been killed in the Hebron incident and in many other skirmishes during the Israeli-Palestinian tensions, it was necessary for the Israeli people to actually experience the violence

before they could understand what the Palestinians had gone through.

Dr. Rantisi then spoke to me in a manner indicating that his comments were meant not only for me but for the American people he regarded me as representing. "It is important for you to understand," he said, "that we are the victims in this struggle, not the cause of it." He repeated this at the end of my interview, when I asked Rantisi in what way he thought Hamas was misunderstood and what misrepresentations he would like to correct. "You think we are the aggressors," Rantisi said. "That is the number one misunderstanding. We are not: we are the victims."

Rantisi's passionate commitment to the Hamas cause came in large part from his own experience of victimization. "Like most Palestinians," he explained to me, "our family has horrible stories to tell." In his case, one of the stories involved the destruction of his prosperous family's home in a village that was located somewhere between the modern Israeli cities of Tel Aviv and Ashdod. The village, like the family home, was destroyed in the creation of modern Israel. When members of his family struggled against what they regarded as the Israeli occupation of their land, several were killed: Rantisi's uncle, three of his cousins, and his grandfather. In recent years Rantisi witnessed the continued encroachment of Israel into the limited land that Palestinians were allocated. According to Rantisi, one-third of the Gaza Strip is allotted to 1500 Jewish settlers, and the remaining two-thirds to the approximately one million Palestinians crowded there, many as refugees. Such developments have led to frustration. If the Israel government continues to allow settlements to be built, Rantisi said, "we should use all means to stop it."[29]

In such a context, Rantisi said, the actions of self-martyrs are understandable; they are responses. Another Hamas activist, Imad Faluji, had earlier described them as "letters to Israel." They were ways of notifying Israelis that they were engaged in a great confrontation, whether they had been previously aware of it or not, and that their security as a people was "zero."[30] Moreover, Faluji said, these bombings showed that Israel's security "does not lie with Egypt, nor with Libya, nor with Arafat," but "with us."[31]

The notion that Hamas is engaged in a great war with Israel, one with both spiritual and political consequences, was articulated in a similar way by Sheik Ahmad Yassin, the movement's spiritual leader, when I spoke with him at his home in Gaza a number of years ago. Even then the competition between the secular Palestinian Liberation Organization and Hamas was so severe that my taxi driver, a Palestinian from Gaza who was apparently acting on orders from the PLO, took me to the secular movement's unmarked headquarters in Gaza before taking me to Sheik Yassin. I was told that the sheik and his religious nationalism should not be regarded as truly representative of the Palestinian struggle, and it was suggested that I visit an area of Gaza where the PLO was firmly in control—the Jabaliya refugee camp—before visiting the leaders of Hamas. I happily followed this suggestion—although with my PLO-supporting driver at the wheel I had little choice—and only afterward did we proceed to our original destination, Sheik Yassin's modest quarters on a hillside outside Gaza City.

At that time, shortly before he was placed under detention by the Israelis in 1989, Sheik Yassin was living in a motel-like row of rooms that comprised his residence, office, mosque, and meeting rooms. The rooms and the area outside were crowded with a variety of supporters, most of them men in their thirties and forties, who busily talked with one another until the sheik appeared, and then lapsed into respectful silence and crowded into the meeting room. On the wall of the room was the obligatory picture of the Dome of the Rock in Jerusalem and a drawing portraying the Qur'an superimposed on a map: it was drawn with hands extending out of either side of the Holy Book, stretching from Algeria to Indonesia, encompassing the whole of the Muslim world. The drawings indicated two different, though compatible, views of the political significance of Islam—one focusing on a distinctively Palestinian contribution to Muslim culture, the Dome of the Rock, and the other suggesting a transnational Islamic culture that reached from Africa to Southeast Asia.

The sheik's attendants eased an old-fashioned wooden wheelchair out of the private rooms at the end of the building and wheeled the sheik down the veranda to the public meeting room. Suffering from a degenerative nerve condition for most of his life, the sheik had to be lifted from place to place. He sat with difficulty on the carpet in the meeting room, propped up on cushions, and managed the ritual bowing that accompanies Muslim prayers with the greatest of difficulty, tottering back and forth as he uttered the sacred words. After the prayers were completed he gave a short homily to the assembled group, and then, as the group began to disperse, the sheik responded to my questions—translated by one of his aides—about why Islamic militancy was necessary at this moment in history.

"There is a war going on," the sheik explained. Just as Rantisi described it in my interview with him years later, Sheik Yassin implied that the struggle against the Israeli authorities was the expression of a larger, hidden struggle.[32] When I raised the question of why the secular Palestinian movement was not a sufficient agency to carry out this cause, the sheik was careful in his response. Without directly opposing Arafat, he said that the idea of a secular liberation movement for Palestine was profoundly misguided, because there "is no such thing as a secular state in Islam."[33]

This was the position of the Palestinian Muslim Brotherhood, with which the sheik had been associated for many years and which had close ties to the Egyptian movement of the same name. Hamas as a movement began in the late 1980s when the urban, organized strategy of the PLO had floundered and a new struggle emerged from the poorer, rural segments of Palestinian society: the *intifada*, backed by Hamas. The word *hamas* means "zeal" or "enthusiasm," but it is also an acronym for the Arabic phrase that is the formal name of the movement: Harakat al-Muqawama al-Islamiya, or "Islamic Resistance Movement." The term *Hamas* first appeared publicly in a communique circulated in mid-February 1988.[34]

Sheik Yassin and Dr. Rantisi were involved in the movement from the beginning. Both of them—and therefore the movement—had roots in the Muslim Brotherhood, with which Rantisi was associated when he was a medical student in Alexandria in northern Egypt. One of the first communiques issued by the movement described it as "the powerful arm of the Association of Muslim Brothers."[35] Perhaps for this reason, Rantisi chafed at the notion that the Hamas movement was similar to Egypt's radical al Gamaa-i Islamiya, headed by Sheik Omar Abdul Rahman, who was convicted of conspiracy in relation to the World Trade Center bombing. "We are not like al Gamaa-i Islamiya," Rantisi told me, "but like the Muslim Brotherhood. We are legitimate."[36]

This comment indicated that Rantisi was conscious of the criticism that Hamas reflected only a fraction of Palestinian Muslim sentiment, and the most marginal and radical fraction at that. He pointed out that prominent religious figures had been associated with Hamas from the earliest days of the movement. These included Sheik 'Abd al-Aziz 'Odeh and Sheik As'ad Bayud al-Tamimi, a resident of Hebron who was a preacher at the al-Aqsa mosque in Jerusalem, as well as Sheik Ahmed Yassin from Gaza.[37] Yassin, who is described as "a charismatic and influential leader," commanded the Islamic Assembly, which had ties to virtually all the mosques in Gaza. Dr. Rantisi pointed out that the religious legitimacy for the acts of self-martyrdom came from a religious decree—a *fatwa*—issued by a mufti in the Gulf emirates.

In the 1990s Hamas vastly expanded as an organization, and although the heart of the movement still lay in decentralized, local cadres, Hamas developed a fairly sophisticated organizational structure, divided between policy and military wings. Within the latter was a separate organizational structure for the secret cells that recruited and trained the young men who were to become operatives in the missions of self-martyrdom, as Rantisi called them. The men in these cells were seldom known within the wider Palestinian community, and even members of their own families were shocked to discover their involvement, which was often revealed only after the fatal completion of their missions. In a videotape in the collection of Oliver and Steinberg that portrays funeral ceremonies for these young self-martyrs, a group of young men is seen entering the crowd, masked and

carrying rifles. The crowd roars in frenzied approval. These were "living martyrs," those who had already committed themselves to self-martyrdom and were awaiting their call to action.

In some cases, young people were recruited for a suicide bombing mission days before the act was to be carried out; they had no previous affiliation with Hamas and virtually no military training. The explosion at a busy street corner in downtown Tel Aviv in 1995, for example, was carried out by a nineteen-year-old student with a backpack full of explosives. The shy, affable young man had been recruited three days earlier by a Hamas supporter who was asked to find an appropriate volunteer. According to the Hamas organizer and recruiter who was interviewed for a segment on the CBS television program *60 Minutes*, he found someone close at hand: his own cousin, who lived next door.[38]

A study of suicide bombings conducted by Ariel Merari and other scholars related to the Center for the Study of Terrorism and Political Violence at Tel Aviv University indicated that most of the members of the suicide cell of Hamas received from three weeks to several months of training. Based on interviews with friends and family members of thirty three of the thirty four successful perpetrators of Hamas suicide missions in Israel in recent years, the study showed that they were recruited through friendship networks in school, sports, and extended families. They were held to their decision by having to commit to one another in friendship pacts and having to write letters that would be sent to their families after their deaths. Their parents and other immediate family members were kept in the dark about the young men's intentions, but the youths died with the knowledge that all would be rewarded: the dying young man would receive seventy virgins and seventy wives in heaven, and his family would receive a cash payment worth twelve to fifteen thousand U.S. dollars.[39]

Although most Israelis and other non-Palestinians have been aware of the militant side of Hamas through their actions, in Gaza and West Bank towns the peaceful face of Hamas has been more visible. The movement has given support for medical clinics and primary education. Hamas has also provided support for orphans and free food programs and offered cash support to those in need—not only the families of self-martyrs but also those affected by Israeli military assaults on Hamas operatives. When the Israeli government destroyed Palestinian houses as a way of punishing those who supported Hamas's actions, for example, the movement provided the Palestinian families with cash settlements often worth more than the values of the houses.

Some Palestinians have supported Hamas not because they agree completely with its radical platform and actions, but because they believe that Hamas has kept Arafat and the Palestinian Authority on its toes and made the organization stronger than it otherwise would be. "We need Hamas," one student supporter of the movement told me at a seaside cafe in Gaza, adding that the secular Palestinian Authority "compromises too easily." For that reason, he concluded, Hamas is needed as a corrective.[40] He thought that the strength of the movement is in its religious base. Unlike secular organizations, he said, "Hamas won't change over time," because it was "founded on religious principles."

Modern Islamic Justifications for Violence

The religious principles on which Hamas was founded have given the movement credibility and legitimacy, and they have also given it the most important base of power possible: the ability to justify the use of force. But Islam is ambiguous about violence. Like all religions, Islam occasionally allows for force while stressing that the main spiritual goal is one of nonviolence and peace. The Qur'an contains a proscription very much like the biblical injunction "Thou shalt not kill." The Qur'an commands the faithful to "slay not the life that God has made sacred."[41] The very name Islam is cognate to *salam*, the word for peace, and like the Hebrew word *shalom*, to which it is related, it implies a vision of social harmony and spirtual repose.

For this reason, Muslim activists have often reasserted their belief in Islamic nonviolence before defending their use of force. According to Sheik Omar Abdul Rahman in an interview shortly after the bombing of the World Trade Center, a Muslim can "never call for violence," only for "love, forgiveness and tolerance." But he added that "if we are aggressed against, if our land is usurped, we must call for hitting the attacker and the aggressor to put an end to the aggression."[42] In other cases a violent act has been justified as an exception to the rule, as when Muslim supporters of the al-Salam mosque defended the killing of Rabbi Kahane, claiming that this deed did not violate the Qur'an since Kahane was an enemy of Islam.[43] In yet other instances, the use of force has been shown to be consistent with Islamic principles. Iran's Ayatollah Khomeini said he knew of no command "more binding to the Muslim than the command to sacrifice life and property to defend and bolster Islam."[44]

The ayatollah was correct that there are some Islamic tenets that condone struggle and the use of force. In addition to the Qur'an's prohibition against killing, there are Muslim principles that justify it. Violence is required for purposes of punishment, for example, and it is sometimes deemed necessary for defending the faith. In the "world of conflict" (*dar al harb*) outside the Muslim world, force is a means of cultural survival. In such a context, maintaining the purity of religious existence is thought to be a matter of *jihad*, a word that literally means "striving" and is often translated as "holy war."[45] This concept has been used by Muslim warriors to rationalize the expansion of political control into non-Muslim regions. But Islamic law does not allow *jihad* to be used arbitrarily, for personal gain, or to justify forcible conversion to the faith: the only conversions regarded as valid are those that come about nonviolently, through rational suasion and a change of heart.

Even so, Islam has a history of military engagement almost from its beginning. Scarcely a dozen years after the prophet Muhammad received the revelation of the Qur'an in 610, he left his home in Mecca and developed a military stronghold in the nearby town of Medina. Forces loyal to Muhammad instigated a series of raids on Meccan camel caravans, and when the Meccans retaliated, they were roundly defeated by the prophet's soldiers in the Battle of Badr, the first Muslim military victory. Several years of sporadic warfare between the two camps ended in a decisive Muslim victory in the Battle of the Trench. By 630 Muhammad and his Muslims had conquered Mecca and much of western Arabia and had turned the ancient pilgrimage site of the Kaaba into a center for Muslim worship. The caliphs who succeeded the prophet as temporal leaders of the Muslim community after Muhammad's death in 632 expanded both the military control and spiritual influence of Islam, and over the years the extraordinary proliferation of the Islamic community throughout the world has been attributed in no small measure to the success of its military leaders in battle.

The Islamic sanctioning of military force is not indiscriminate, however. Most historical examples have involved the use of force by an established military or governmental power for the purpose of defending the faith. This is a far cry from justifying acts of terrorism, though there were rogue groups of Muslims in the twelfth century—the Nizari branch of Ismaili Islam—who used what might be called terrorism in establishing a small empire based in the north of Persia near the Caspian Sea. Hardly the models of virtuous society, the members of the order were said to have used drugs and were dubbed *hashshashin*—or, in medieval Latin, *assassini*, "drug users." They expanded their political power by infiltrating their opponent's camps and killing their leaders, often by slitting their throats with a knife. Although their empire was short-lived, they left their legacy on the terminology of political terrorism—the word *assassin*— even though most Muslims would regard them as quite peripheral to the mainstream of Islamic tradition.[46]

Present-day religious activists look for more traditional Islamic justifications for the use of violence. Dr. Rantisi and Sheik Yassin, for example, justified the Hamas use of violence based on the Islamic sanction for self-defense. Both Yassin and Rantisi expanded the notion to include the defense of one's dignity and pride as well as one's physical well-being.[47] One of Yassin's colleagues, Sheik 'Abd al-Aziz 'Odeh, explained that the Islamic

intifada differed from the *intifada* waged by secular supporters of the PLO in that the Islamic struggle was a moral struggle as well as a political one, stemming from religious commitment. It was also part of a tradition of Islamic protest against injustice.[48]

This is an interesting idea—that the approval of force for the defense of Islam can be expanded to include struggles against political and social injustice—and it is a relatively new one. Perhaps no writer has had greater influence in extending this concept and reinterpreting the traditional Muslim idea of struggle—*jihad*—than the contemporary Egyptian writer Abd al-Salam Faraj. The author of a remarkably cogent argument for waging war against the political enemies of Islam in the pamphlet *Al-Faridah al-Ghaïbah* ("The Neglected Duty"), Faraj stated more clearly than any other contemporary writer the religious justifications for radical Muslim acts. His booklet was published and first circulated in Cairo in the early 1980s.[49] What is significant about this document is that it grounded the activities of modern Islamic terrorists firmly in Islamic tradition, specifically in the sacred text of the Qur'an and the biographical accounts of the prophet in the Hadith.

Faraj argued that the Qur'an and the Hadith were fundamentally about warfare. The concept of *jihad*, struggle, was meant to be taken literally, not allegorically. According to Faraj, the "duty" that has been profoundly "neglected" is precisely that of *jihad*, and it calls for "fighting, which meant confrontation and blood."[50] Moreover, Faraj regarded anyone who deviates from the moral and social requirements of Islamic law to be targets for *jihad*; these targets include apostates within the Muslim community as well as the expected enemies from without.

Perhaps the most chilling aspect of Faraj's thought is his conclusion that peaceful and legal means for fighting apostasy are inadequate. The true soldier of Islam is allowed to use virtually any means available to achieve a just goal.[51] Deceit, trickery, and violence are specifically mentioned as options available to the desperate soldier.[52] Faraj set some moral limits to the tactics that could be used—for example, innocent bystanders and women are to be avoided, whenever possible, in assassination attempts—but emphasized that the duty to engage in such actions when necessary is incumbent on all true Muslims. The reward for doing so is nothing less than a place in paradise. Such a place was presumably earned by Faraj himself in 1982, after he was tried and executed for his part in the assassination of Anwar Sadat.

This way of thinking, though extreme, was not idiosyncratic to Faraj. He stood in a tradition of radical Islamic political writers reaching back to the beginning of this century and before. Among Sunni Muslims worldwide, the most important radical thinker was Maulana Abu al-Ala Mawdudi, the founder and ideological spokesman for Pakistan's Jamaat-i-Islami religious party.[53] His ideas were echoed by Egypt's most influential writer in the radical Muslim political tradition, Sayyid Qutb. Qutb was born in 1906 and, like Faraj, was executed for his political activities.[54] Although he was not as explicit as Faraj in indicating the techniques of terror that were acceptable to the Islamic warrior, Qutb laid the groundwork for Faraj's understanding of *jihad* as an appropriate response to the advocates of those elements of modernity that seemed to be hostile to Islam.

Specifically, Qutb railed against those who encouraged the cultural, political, and economic domination of the Egyptian government by the West. Qutb spent several years in the United States studying educational administration. This experience only confirmed his impression that American society was essentially racist and that American policy in the Middle East was dictated by Israel and what he regarded as the Jewish lobby in Washington, DC.[55] Alarmed at the degree to which the new government in Egypt was modeled after Western political institutions and influenced by Western values, Qutb, in the early 1950s, advocated a radical return to Islamic values and Muslim law. In *This Religion of Islam*, Qutb argued that the most basic divisions within humanity were religious rather than racial or nationalist, and that religious war was the only form of killing that was morally sanctioned.[56] To Qutb's thinking, the ultimate war was between truth and falsehood, and satanic agents of the latter were to be found well entrenched in the

Egyptian government. It is no wonder that the government found such ideas dangerous. Qutb was put in prison for most of the rest of the 1950s, and a state execution silenced him forever in 1966.

These ideas of Mawdudi, Qutb, and Faraj have been circulated widely throughout the Muslim world through two significant networks: universities and the Muslim clergy. The two networks intersect in the Muslim educational system, especially in the schools and colleges directly supervised by the clergy. It is not surprising, then, that many who have been attracted to paramilitary movements such as the al Gamaa-i Islamiya or Hamas were former students or, like Dr. Rantisi, highly trained professionals.

When I asked Dr. Rantisi which writers he most respected, the first name the Hamas leader mentioned was the founder of modern-day Muslim political activism, Mawdudi.[57] When I posed the same question to Mahmud Abouhalima in the federal penitentiary in Lompoc, at first he gave no specific reply. When I suggested Faraj's name, Abouhalima seemed surprised that I had heard of him, though he corrected my pronunciation. Abouhalima confessed to owning both Arabic and English versions of Faraj's infamous booklet, "The Neglected Duty."

Abouhalima wanted to make certain that I would not use his knowledge of Faraj against him. In Abouhalima's first criminal case, he said, the evidence that he possessed copies of Faraj's book was used to show that he harbored hostile and violent attitudes against the secular government. For that reason, Abouhalima asked me to be careful how I described his attitude toward Faraj. "Do not say 'I was influenced by him,' " Abouhalima instructed me, but rather " 'I respect him.' " Then Abouhalima leaned over, put his head close to mine, and whispered, "but he was right, you know."[58]

NOTES

1. See, for example, Richard Behar, "The Secret Life of Mahmud the Red," *Time*, October 4, 1993, 54–64.
2. Benjamin Weiser, Susan Sachs, and David Kocieniewski, "U.S. Sees Brooklyn Connection to Embassy Bombings," *New York Times*, October 22, 1998, A1.
3. Interview with Mahmud Abouhalima, federal penitentiary,

Lompoc, California, August 19, 1997, and September 30, 1997.

4. Jim Dwyer, David Kocieniewski, Deidre Murphy, and Peg Tyre, *Two Seconds under the World: Terror Comes to America—The Conspiracy behind the World Trade Center Bombing* (New York: Crown, 1994), 192.

5. Dwyer et al., *Two Seconds under the World*, 1–5.

6. Interview with Abouhalima, August 19, 1997. A similar account of what happened in the trial is described in Dwyer et al., *Two Seconds under the World*, 278–79. He repeated his claim of innocence in correspondence to me on May 20, 1999.

7. Interview with Abouhalima, September 30, 1997.

8. Interview with Abouhalima, August 19, 1997. The topic of the relationship between Islam and public order was discussed in both interviews, and clarified in his correspondence to me on May 20, 1999.

9. Interview with Abouhalima, August 19, 1997.

10. Behar, "The Secret Life of Mahmud the Red," p. 58.

11. Interview with Abouhalima, August 19, 1997.

12. Interview with Abouhalima, August 19, 1997.

13. *Newstand*, CNN television news program, December 20, 1998.

14. Dwyer et al., *Two Seconds under the World*, 148. In his correspondence to me on May 20, 1999, Abouhalima underscored the point that he was in Afghanistan solely "for civil purposes."

15. Interview with Abouhalima, August 19, 1997.

16. Dwyer et al., *Two Seconds under the World*, 148; see also Behar, "The Secret Life of Mahmud the Red," 60.

17. Sheik Omar Abdul Rahman, quoted in the British newspaper *The Independent*. Cited in Kim Murphy, "Have the Islamic Militants Turned to a New Battlefront in the U.S.?" *Los Angeles Times*, May 5, 1993, A20.

18. Interview with Abouhalima, August 19, 1997.

19. Interview with Abouhalima, August 19, 1997.

20. Judge Michael B. Mukasey, quoted in John J. Goldman, "Defendants Given 25 Years to Life in N.Y. Terror Plot," *Los Angeles Times*, January 18, 1996, A1.

21. Anne Marie Oliver and Paul Steinberg, *Rehearsals for a Happy Death* (New York: Oxford University Press, forthcoming).

22. Hamas videotape from the collection of Anne Marie Oliver and Paul Steinberg.

23. Hamas videotape from the collection of Anne Marie Oliver and Paul Steinberg. The quotation is from the words of Abdullah Azzam.

24. Lisa Beyer, "Jerusalem Bombing," *New York Times*, August 21, 1995.

25. Interview with Dr. Abdul Aziz Rantisi, Khan Yunis, Gaza, March 1, 1998.

26. Interview with Rantisi, March 1, 1998.

27. Interview with Imad Faluji, journalist and member of the policy wing of Hamas, Gaza, August 19, 1995. Faluji has since left the Hamas movement and joined Arafat's Palestinian Authority.

28. Interview with Rantisi, March 2, 1998.

29. Interview with Rantisi, March 2, 1998.

30. Interview with Faluji, August 19, 1995.

31. Interview with Faluji, August 19, 1995.

32. Interview with Sheik Yassin, January 14, 1989.

33. Interview with Sheik Yassin, January 14, 1989.

34. For an overview of the Hamas movement, see Roger Friedland and Richard Hecht, *To Rule Jerusalem* (Cambridge: Cambridge University Press, 1996), 366–84; and Mark Juergensmeyer, *The New Cold War? Religious Nationalism Confronts the Secular State* (Berkeley: University of California Press, 1993), 69–77.

35. Quoted in Jean-Francois Legrain, "The Islamic Movement and the Intifada," in Jamal R. Nassar and Roger Heacock, eds., *Intifada: Palestine at the Crossroads* (New York: Praeger, 1990), 182.

36. Interview with Rantisi, March 2, 1998.

37. See Elie Rekhess, "The Iranian Impact on the Islamic Jihad Movement in the Gaza Strip," in David Menashvi, ed., *The Iranian Revolution and the Muslim World* (Boulder, CO: Westview Press, 1990). An excerpt from this article, under the title "The Growth of Khomeinism in Gaza," was published in *Jerusalem Post Magazine*, January 26, 1991, 12.

38. Interviews with Hassan Salameh and Mohammad Abulwardi by Bob Simon in "Suicide Bomber," produced by Michael Gavson, aired on *60 Minutes*, October 5, 1997.

39. Interview with Ariel Merari, Center for the Study of Terrorism and Political Violence, Tel Aviv University, March 3, 1998.

40. Interview with Ashraf Yaghi, Gaza, August 19, 1995.

41. *Holy Qur'an*, 6:152.

42. Sheik Omar Abdul Rahman, quoted in James Mann and Robert L. Jackson, "Motive Behind Trade Center Bombing Remains a Mystery," *Los Angeles Times*, March 20, 1993, A16.

43. John Kifner, "Suspect in Kahane Case Is Muslim Born in Egypt," *New York Times*, November 7, 1990, A1.

44. Imam [Ayatollah] Sayyed Ruhollah Mousavi Khomeini, *Collection of Speeches, Position Statements*, Translations on Near East and North Africa no. 1902 (Arlington, VA: Joint Publications Research Service, 1979), 7.

45. See Rudolph Peters, *Islam and Colonialism: The Doctrine of Jihad in Modern History* (The Hague: Mouton, 1979); Richard C. Martin, "Religious Violence in Islam: Towards an Understanding of the Discourse on Jihad in Modern Egypt," in Paul Wilkinson and A. M. Stewart, eds., *Contemporary Research on Terrorism* (Aberdeen: Aberdeen University Press, 1969), 54–71; John Kelsay, *Islam and War: A Study in Comparative Ethics* (Louisville, KY: Westminster/John Knox Press, 1993).

46. See David Rapoport, *Assassination and Terrorism* (Toronto: Canadian Broadcasting Corporation, 1971), 3–4.

47. Interview with Sheik Yassin, January 14, 1989; interview with Dr. Rantisi, March 2, 1998.

48. Interview with Sheik 'Odeh, in *Islam and Palestine*, Leaflet 5 (Limasol, Cyprus, June 1988).

49. It was published in *Al-Ahrar*, an Egyptian newspaper, on December 14, 1981. An English translation, accompanied by an extensive essay about the document, can be found in Johannes J. G. Jansen, *The Neglected Duty: The Creed of Sadat's Assassins and Islamic Resurgence in the Middle East* (New York: Macmillan, 1986). I have also found helpful the analysis of this document by David Rapoport in "Sacred Terror: A Case from Islam," unpublished paper delivered at the 1988 Annual Meeting of the American political Science Association, Washington, DC, September 1–4, 1988. The political implications of the document are discussed in Mohammed Heikal, *Autumn of Fury: The Assassination of Sadat* (London: Andre Deutsch, 1983).

50. Faraj, par. 84, in Jansen, *Neglected Duty*, 199.

51. Faraj, pars. 102 and 109, in Jansen, *Neglected Duty*, 210–11.

52. Faraj, par. 113, in Jansen, *Neglected Duty*, 212–13; see also par. 109, 211.

53. According to an Egyptian scholar who interviewed in prison members of the group responsible for Sadat's assassination, the writings of Mawdudi were "important in shaping the group's ideas." See Saad Eddin Ibrahim, "Islamic Militancy as a Social Movement: The Case of Two Groups in Egypt," in Ali E. Hillal Dessouki, ed., *Islamic Resurgence in the Arab World* (New York: Praeger, 1982), 125.

54. For a discussion of the significance of Sayyid Qutb's life and work, see Martin, "Religious Violence in Islam"; Gilles Kepel, *Muslim Extremism in Egypt: The Prophet and Pharaoh* (Berkeley: University of California Press, 1986), 36–69; Yvonne V. Haddad, "Sayyid Qutb: Ideologue of Islamic Revival," in John L. Esposito, ed., *Voices of Resurgent Islam* (New York: Oxford University Press, 1983); Ronald L. Nettler, *Past Trials and Present Tribulations: A Muslim Fundamentalist's View of the Jews* (New York: Pergamon Press, 1987).

55. Qutb studied in Washington, DC, and California from 1949 to 1951; see Haddad, "Sayyid Qutb," 69.

56. Sayyid Qutb, *This Religion of Islam (Hadha'd-Din)* (Palo Alto, CA: Al-Manar Press, 1967), 87.

57. Interview with Rantisi, March 2, 1998.

58. Interview with Abouhalima, August 19, 1997.

SECTION VIII

How Can Terrorism Be Overcome?

It is important to state, from the outset, that terrorism cannot be "overcome." At this point the reader will have acquired substantial knowledge of the history, diversity, and psychological origins of terrorism. Terrorism is a conflict tactic. Since creating fear by attacking non-combatants seems to have been part of the human conflict repertoire for millennia, it seems unlikely that any effort, policy, or initiative in the foreseeable future will make this tactic go away. Nonetheless, it is entirely legitimate to talk about limiting or reducing the global load of terrorism. Some conflicts, more than others, involve potential or actual terrorist actors who might be accessible to influence. Some potential or actual terrorist actors, more than others, might either be deterred prior to becoming committed to political violence or amenable to change once they have made that commitment. And, as a last resort, some committed terrorists simply must and will be captured or killed. Terrorism is already a serious problem and we know what weapons of mass destruction directed at civilian populations can do. As those with the motivation to kill large groups of civilians for political purposes increasingly acquire biological, chemical, and especially nuclear arms—whether the actors are rogue governments or substate actors—terrorism could morph from a "problem" to a civilization-altering catastrophe.

So what might psychology contribute to the urgent enterprise of limiting the global load? We are not warriors. We are not diplomats. And we may or may not gain sufficient access to the ear of power. Insights from psychological science have an inconsistent track record in moving policy-makers toward wiser, better choices, yet serious social problems have sometimes yielded to advances in psychological knowledge. Earl Warren famously cited research evidence of psychological harm to African-American children associated with "separate but equal" schooling in the Brown v. Board of Education US Supreme Court ruling. Practical gains are being made in education and in public health as psychological findings inform policy. When science is able to make a strong case based on a predominance of the evidence, a tipping point is sometimes reached and political intransigence yields to sense (witness the history of the global warming debate). There are few subjects so important to global security as a better take on the modifiable factors in the genesis of terrorism. As Alan Leschner, Chief Executive Office of the American Academy for the Advancement of Sciences, wrote in 2007: "Sophisticated behavioral analyses are also being applied to many of the most pressing societal issues of our era. Understanding terrorism is among the most timely and challenging" (*Science*, *316*, 953). In this regard, 2008 may represent a watershed moment in the history of intellectual collaboration in the interest of national security. That year, the US government initiated for the first time multi-million dollar Broad Agency Announcements soliciting proposals for rigorous social science research addressing the deep human causes of political violence. Therefore, far from despairing that the so-called war on terrorism will be fought indefinitely without regard for psychological research findings, we should promptly and vigorously move forward toward answering the many empirical questions that arise from our review of the psychology of terrorism. Evidence is our most powerful tool. Good evidence, compellingly presented, will eventually be heard, and may become the critical factor in the efficacy of the long-term struggle against violent extremism.

In this section we will explore recent writings that address the modifiability of terrorism.

Reading 26—Atran (2003). Soft Power and the Psychology of Suicide Bombing

Editors' Comments

Scott Atran is a polymath who has applied his background in anthropology—as well as his rare multidisciplinary instincts—to the problem of terrorism. In this short paper, he explicitly considers a question that has perhaps been implicit from the beginning of this volume: Does a massive military response increase or decrease terrorism? Clearly, since every terrorist campaign occurs under somewhat different historical conditions and strategic issues and involves psychologically unique leaders on both sides, there is no one-size-fits-all answer to this question. But specifically in regard to the polymorphous fundamentalist Islamist campaign against the West, Atran admonishes that current strategic policies may be worse than ineffective.

Discussion Questions

1. Atran cites the International Institute of Strategic Studies report warning that the US-led war in Iraq has focused the energies of al-Qaeda. What evidence does Atran cite?
2. Atran cites a report from the Federal Research Division of the Library of Congress claiming that there is "no psychological attribute or personality distinctive of terrorists." Based on the readings in this book, has methodologically defensible research ever been

done that would justify such a statement? What methodology might determine whether this statement is correct or incorrect?

3. Atran points out that many Islamist extremists are overeducated for the available jobs and argues that "rising aspirations followed by dwindling expectations" generate terrorism. If this is true, what policy initiatives might reduce the risk?

Suggested Readings

Atran, S. (2004). Mishandling suicide terrorism. *The Washington Quarterly, 27*, 67–90.

Atran, S. (2006). The moral logic and growth of suicide terrorism. *The Washington Quarterly, 29*, 127–147.

Blumberg, H. (2002). Understanding and dealing with terrorism: A classification of some contributions from the behavioral and social sciences. *Peace and Conflict: Journal of Peace Psychology, 8*, 3–16.

Hudson, R. A. (1999). *The sociology and psychology of terrorism: Who becomes a terrorist and why?* Washington, DC: Federal Research Division of the Library of Congress. Available at http://www.loc.gov/rr/frd/pdf-files/Soc_Psych_of_Terrorism.pdf

Reading 27—Hafez & Hatfield (2006). Do Targeted Assassinations Work? A Multivariate Analysis of Israel's Controversial Tactic during Al-Aqsa Uprising

Editors' Comments

In the course of the recent *intifadas* (civil uprisings) Israel adopted a policy of "targeted assassinations" to counter the ongoing threat of Palestinian extremist attacks on Israeli civilians. This policy, controversial even in Israel, raises many questions about the best way to respond to and reduce the risk of terrorism. One question is the morality of such assassinations—in essence extra-judicial killings. Another question is the morality of firing missiles into some of the most densely populated areas in the world with the certain knowledge that civilians are often killed by this behavior. Is this "deliberately attacking civilians to achieve political goals" in essence terrorism or does the incidental nature of such collateral death render it less odious? Putting aside moral qualms, the realist asks: Does it work? In this paper, Hafez and Hatfield seek an evidence-based conclusion to that important question.

Discussion Questions

1. This article reviews the literature on the possible benefits of repressive state behaviors in combating terrorism. Four theoretical outcomes are considered. What are they?

2. Hypothesis 1 in this study predicted that repressive attacks by Israel would diminish Palestinian attacks. Did this occur?

3. Hypothesis 2 in this study predicts that repressive behavior by Israel that is viewed as extremely coercive would lead to a backlash. Did that happen?

4. The authors conclude that targeted assassinations might have political benefits independent of any impact on terrorism. What are they? Would one expect those political benefits to be long- or short-lived?

Suggested Readings

Enders, W., & Sandler, S. (2004). What do we know about the substitution effect in transnational terrorism? In A. Silke (Ed.), *Research on terrorism: Trends, achievements, and failures* (pp. 119–137). London: Frank Cass.

Franciso, R. A. (1995). The relationship between coercion and protest: An empirical evaluation in three coercive states. *Journal of Conflict Resolution, 39,* 263–282.

Hafez, M. (2007). *Suicide bombers in Iraq: The strategy and ideology of martyrdom.* Washington, DC: US Institute of Peace Press Books.

Reading 28—Kaplan et al. (2006). What Happened to Suicide Bombings in Israel? Insights from a Terror Stock Model

Editors' Comments

The paper by Kaplan et al. is another look at the Israeli–Palestinian conflict. Like the paper by Hafez and Hatfield, this paper examines, among other issues, the efficacy of targeted assassinations in containing the threat of terrorist attacks. The methodology is somewhat different, and the results are too. Kaplan et al. conceptualize the terrorist enterprise as a warehouse of resources with "stock" (committed bombers) that increases and decreases in response to various internal and external factors. Recruitment increases the stock. Arrests or killings decrease the stock. The question these researchers set out to answer is: How do Israeli counterterrorism behaviors affect the capacity of extremist groups to carry out suicide bombings?

Discussion Questions

1. Kaplan et al. discuss the ability to conduct suicide bombings as a "terror capacity" and the bombers as "stock." Psychologically speaking, what might be the strengths and weaknesses of this model?

2. This paper reports that, from 2001 to 2003, 44 of 75 Israeli "targeted assassinations" killed only militants while 31 of these attacks killed civilians. Despite the high rate of civilian killings, it appears that suicide bombings only increased after (and apparently in response to) killings of militants but not after killings of civilians. How should this be interpreted?

3. The authors find that arresting suspected terrorists was more effective than targeted killings of known terrorists in reducing suicide bombings. How might differences in variables such as (1) proportion of known terrorists killed, (2) ratio of innocent civilians to militants killed in air strikes, (3) number of innocent suspects arrested, or (4) shifts in media scrutiny of these two tactics have altered these results?

Suggested Readings

David, S. R. (2003). Israel's policy of targeted killing. *Ethics and International Affairs*, *17*, 111–126.

Nevin, J. A. (2003). Retaliating against terrorists. *Behavior and Social Issues*, *12*, 109–128.

Nevin, J. A. (2004). Retaliating against terrorists: Erratum, reanalysis, and update. *Behavior and Social Issues*, *13*, 155–159.

Pape, R. A. (2003). The strategic logic of suicide terrorism. *American Political Science Review*, *97*, 343–361.

Soft Power and the Psychology of Suicide Bombing

Scott Atran

The soldiers believed they came that spring to free a part of the Middle East from the tyranny of terrorists and evil men. What amazed them was the warm welcome from Shi'ite Muslims in the south and the Capital. The victors confidently sent in their experts to replace the ousted leadership with locals they considered more "reliable." This soon led to anger and distrust at the "invaders" and their "collaborators." Within a year, a new "terrorist" organization arose from the Shi'ite core to expel the occupiers. It armed itself with a novel type of "smart weapon" that would radically alter the nature of political warfare across the planet – the suicide bomber. That was 1982, when Israel entered Lebanon and Hezbollah (The Party of God) was spawned.

In recent months, Iraqi Shi'ites have joined Sunni insurgents calling for worldwide suicide actions against Americans and their allies. Will history repeat itself on a grander and deadlier scale? The risk increases daily.

Like pounding mercury with a hammer, top-heavy use of massive military force to counter Islamic terrorism only seems to generate more varied and insidious forms of terrorism and broaden support. The London-based International Institute of Strategic Studies reports in its recently released "Strategic Survey 2003/4" that the Iraq conflict has "focused the energies and resources of al-Qaeda and its followers while diluting those of the global counterterrorism coalition." The survey also indicates that massive and direct assault on jihadist networks and their supporters, although effective against traditional armies, has actually benefited al-Qaeda and its associates. Dispersing to many countries, their networks have become more "virtual" and elusive, and much harder to identify and fight. Membership has also become more varied and difficult to profile.

In the first four months of 2004, 60 suicide attackers killed nearly 800 people and wounded thousands. There were first-time suicide attacks in Uzbekistan (by at least 5 female bombers) and in Western Europe (the "no-surrender" suicide explosion by 6 cornered plotters of the Madrid train bombings). In Iraq alone, 30 suicide bombers killed nearly 600 people – a greater number by far than in any single country for any comparable period since the attacks of September 11. Even a casual glance at media outlets and websites sympathetic to al-Qaeda reveals a proliferating jihadist

Scott Atran is a director of research at the National Center for Scientific Research in Paris and Professor of anthropology and psychology at the University of Michigan.

fraternity that takes heart from the fall of Saddam, Iraq's secularist tyrant.[1]

Yet many U.S. and allied leaders continue to persist in their portrayals of Islamic militants as evil misfits and homicidal thugs who hate freedom and thrive only in a moral desert swept by poverty and ignorance. "These killers don't have values," President Bush declared in response to the spreading insurgency in Iraq, "these people hate freedom.[2] And we love freedom. And that's where the clash is." Secretary of State Colin Powell previously told a World Economic Forum that "terrorism really flourishes in areas of poverty, despair and hopelessness."

In fact, study after study finds suicide terrorists and supporters to be more educated and economically well off than surrounding populations. They also tend to be well-adjusted in their families, liked by peers, and – according to interrogators – sincerely compassionate to those they see themselves helping. A report on *The Sociology and Psychology of Terrorism* used by the Central and Defense Intelligence Agencies (CIA and DIA) finds "no psychological attribute or personality distinctive of terrorists."[3] They do not act despairingly out of neediness or hopelessness, as many ordinary suicides do. If they did, they would be denounced as blasphemers and criminals. "He who commits suicide kills himself for his own benefit," warned Sheikh Yusuf Al-Qardawi (a spiritual leader of the Muslim Brotherhood and perhaps the most important religious authority on "martyr actions" for Sunni Islamists around the world), but "he who commits martyrdom sacrifices himself for the sake of his religion and his nation . . . the Mujahid is full of hope."[4] Like the educated and motivated Japanese Kamikaze who romantically described their impending deaths as "cherry petals that fall before bearing fruit," so, too, for the Palestinian shaheed (martyr): "They are youth at the peak of their blooming, who at a certain moment decide to turn their bodies into body parts . . . flowers."[5]

Researchers Basel Saleh and Claude Berrebi independently find that the majority of Palestinian suicide bombers have a college education (versus 15 percent of the population of comparable age) and that less than 15 percent come from poor fam-

ilies (although about one-third of the population lives in poverty).[6] DIA sources who have interrogated al-Qaeda detainees at Guantanamo note that Saudi-born operatives, especially those in leadership positions, are often "educated above reasonable employment level, a surprising number have graduate degrees and come from high-status families." The general pattern was captured in a Singapore Parliamentary report on prisoners from Jemaah Islamiyah, an ally of al-Qaeda: "These men were not ignorant, destitute or disenfranchised. Like many of their counterparts in militant Islamic organizations in the region, they held normal, respectable jobs. Most detainees regarded religion as their most important personal value."[7]

As in nearly all instances of revolutionary terror in history, rising aspirations followed by dwindling expectations – especially regarding personal security and civil liberties – are critical to generating support for terrorism, no matter how rich or educated a person is to begin with. Studies by Princeton economist Alan Krueger and others find no correlation between a nation's per capita income and terrorism, but do find a correlation between a lack of civil liberties, defined by Freedom House, and terrorism.[8] In Iraq, the aspirations that the U.S. invasion initially incited have rapidly dwindled into fearful expectations about the future.

Polls show that Muslims who have expressed support for martyr actions and trust in Bin Laden or the late Hamas leader Sheikh Ahmed Yasin do not as a rule hate democratic freedoms or even Western culture, though many despise American foreign policy, especially in the Middle East. After the 1996 suicide attack against U.S. military housing at Khobar Towers in Saudi Arabia, a Defense Department Science Board report found that: "Historical data show a strong correlation between U.S. involvement in international situations and an increase in terrorist attacks against the United States."[9]

According to the 2004 Freedom House survey of democracy in 47 nations with an Islamic majority, Morocco and Jordan are the Arab states making the most progress towards representative government.[10] But majorities of their people now support suicide bombings as a way of countering the application of military might by America in Iraq and by Israel in Palestine.[11] Survey data from the Pew Research Center reliably show these people favor participation in elected government and decision-making, personal liberty and freedom of expression, educational opportunity and economic choice.[12] Polls by the Iraq Center for Research and Strategic Studies indicate that Iraqi opponents of U.S. occupation, now almost 9 out of every 10 Iraqis (including nearly 6 out of 10 who support radical Shi'ite cleric Moqtada al-Sadr), espouse similar sentiments.[13]

Preempting and preventing terrorism requires that U.S. policymakers make a concerted effort to understand the background conditions as well as the recruitment processes that inspire people to take their own lives in the name of a greater cause. Current political and economic conditions that policymakers are monitoring remain important although not necessarily determinant. Rather, what likely matters more is the promise of redeeming real or imagined historical grievances through a religious (or transcendent ideological) mission that empowers the militarily weak with unexpected force against enemies materially much stronger. This was as true for Jewish Zealots who sacrificed themselves to kill Romans two millennia ago as it is for modern Jihadists.

This doesn't mean negotiating over goals such as al-Qaeda's quest to replace the Western-inspired system of nation-states with a global caliphate. Osama bin Laden and others affiliated with the mission of the World Islamic Front for the Jihad against the Jews and Crusaders seek no compromise, and will probably fight with hard power to the death. For these already committed group members, using hard power is necessary. The tens of millions of people who sympathize with bin Laden, however, are likely open to the promise of soft-power alternatives that most Muslims seem to favor – participatory government, freedom of expression, educational advancement, and economic choice.[14]

Shows of military strength are not the way to end the growing menace of suicide terrorism: witness the failure of Israel's and Russia's coercive efforts to end strings of Palestinian and Chechen suicide bombings. Rather, nations most threatened by suicide terrorism should promote democracy, but be ready to accept "democracy's paradox": representatives who America and its democratic allies don't like, who have different values or ways of doing things, must be accepted as long as this does not generate violence. Democratic self-determination in Palestine, Kashmir and Iraq – or for that matter, Pakistan, Uzbekistan and Saudi Arabia – will more likely reduce terrorism than military and counterinsurgency aid. At the same time, America and its allies need to establish an intense dialogue with Muslim religious and community leaders to reconcile Islamic custom and religious law (*Shari'ah*) with internationally recognized standards for crime and punishment and human rights.

The precondition for such undertaking is to ensure that potential recruits in the Arab and Muslim world feel secure about their personal safety, cultural heritage and participation in political decisions that affect their lives. Although such soft-power efforts may demand more patience than governments under attack or pressure to reform typically tolerate, forbearance is necessary to avoid catastrophic devastation to Iraq, the United States, democracies worldwide, and the future hopes of peoples who aspire to soft empowerment from a free world.

NOTES

1. For example: "Saddam Hussein was an evil tyrant who wreaked havoc and abused his people for many decades. As Muslims we believe wholeheartedly in the miserable ending of all tyrants, including the one who parade today as triumphant victors." From: "What after the Capture of Saddam," December 16, 2003, www.islamonline.net/livedialogue/english/Browse.asp?hGuestID=mYDRef.
2. Cited in Louis Frazza, "Bush Committed to Iraq Hand-over in June," USA Today, April 4, 2004, p.1.
3. "The Sociology and Psychology of Terrorism," Federal Research Division, Library of Congress, Washington, D.C., September 1999, p. 40, www.loc.gov/rr/frd/pdf-files/Soc_Psych_of_Terrorism.pdf.
4. *Al-Ahram Al-Arabi* (Cairo), February 3, 2001.
5. Editorial, *Al-Risala* (*Hamas weekly*), June 7, 2001.
6. Basel Saleh, "Palestinian Violence and the Second Intifada," Paper presented to NATO AWR, "Suicide Terrorism: Strategic Threat and Counterstrategies," Lisbon, Portugal, June 10–14, 2004.

7. "White Paper—The Jemaah Islamiyah Arrests," Ministry of Home Affairs, Singapore, January 9, 2003, http://www2.mha.gov.sg/mha/detailed.jsp?artid=667&type=4&root=0&parent=0&cat= 0&mode=arc.

8. Alan Krueger, Jitka Malecková, "Seeking the roots of terror," *Chronicle of Higher Education*, June 6, 2003, http://chronicle.com/free/v49/i39/39b01001.htm

9. "DoD Responses to Transnational Threats, Vol. 2: DSB Force Protection Panel Report to DSB," U.S. Department of Defense, Washington, D.C., December 1997, p. 8, www.acq.osd.mil/dsb/trans2.pdf.

10. See Martin Walker, "The Democratic Mosaic," *The Wilson Quarterly*, 38(2), Spring 2004.

11. "A Year After Iraq War: Mistrust of America in Europe Ever Higher, Muslim Anger Persists," Pew Research Center Survey Report, March 16, 2004, http://people-press.org/reports/display.php3?ReportID=206.

12. "Views of a Changing World 2003," Pew Research Center Survey Report, June 3, 2003, http://people-press.org/reports/display.php3?ReportID=185.

13. Rouala Khalaf, "Iraq Rebel Cleric Gains Surge in Popularity," *Financial Times*, May, 19, 2004 (reporting on a poll by the Iraq Center for Research and Strategic Studies; – interviews with 1,640 Iraqi adults in Baghdad, Babylon, Diyala, Ramadi, Mousel, Basra and Sulaimaniya, conducted from April 20 to April 27, 2004.).

14. Joseph Nye, *Soft Power: The Means to Success in World Politics* (Public Affairs, New York, 2004).

Do Targeted Assassinations Work? A Multivariate Analysis of Israel's Controversial Tactic during Al-Aqsa Uprising[1]

Mohammed M. Hafez* and Joseph M. Hatfield*

We assess the impact of Israel's targeted assassinations policy on rates of Palestinian violence from September 2000, the beginning of *Al-Aqsa* uprising, through June 2004. Literature concerning the relationship between repression and rebellion suggests four plausible effects of targeted assassinations on insurgents: deterrence, backlash, disruption, and incapacitation. Using differenced and lagged time-series analysis, this article utilizes multiple and logistic regression to evaluate the effect of targeted assassinations on Palestinian violence. It is concluded that targeted assassinations have no significant impact on rates of Palestinian attacks. Targeted assassinations do not decrease rates of Palestinian violence, nor do they increase them, whether in the short or long run. Targeted assassinations may be useful as a political tool to signal a state's determination to punish terrorists and placate an angry public, but there is little evidence that they actually impact the course of an insurgency.

On 22 March 2004, Israeli forces assassinated Sheikh Ahmed Yassin, the founder and spirit- ual leader of the Islamic Resistance Movement (Hamas), as he was returning home from his dawn

*Department of Political Science, University of Missouri— Kansas City, Kansas City, Missouri, USA.

E-mail correspondence is preferred. Authors wish to express their appreciation to the United States Institute of Peace for its generous grant toward this research project.

Address correspondence to Mohammed M. Hafez, Depart- ment of Political Science, University of Missouri—Kansas City, 213 Haag Hall, 5100 Rockhill Road, Kansas City, MO 64110, USA. E-mail: hafezm@umkc.edu prayers at a Gaza mosque. On the night following the assassination, the Israeli daily *Yedioth Ahronoth* conducted a public opinion poll of Israelis to inquire about their views surrounding the assassination. The poll shows that although 60 percent of Israelis support the decision to kill Sheikh Ahmed Yassin, 81 percent expected a surge in retaliatory terrorism following the attack.[2] This belief in the appropriateness of killing a radical leader despite the perceived likelihood of an increase in violent attacks is puzzling, but it may help explain why state leaders might pursue this controversial tactic. But what effect, if any, do targeted assassinations have on cycles of violence? Do targeted assassinations contain, deter, and ultimately lessen rates of violence, or do they intensify anger and increase motivations to attack with more deadly force? Are targeted assassinations effective in combating insurgents and terrorists?

Assessing the impact of targeted assassinations on insurgencies is as difficult as it is important. Theoretically, there is little agreement regarding the logical consequences of repressive measures in general on the strategies and tactical repertoires of insurgent groups. Some observers contend that repression increases the cost of collective action as to make it unlikely (Hibbs 1973; Oberschall 1973; Oliver 1980; Hardin 1982). Others maintain that repression generates additional grievances that motivate further mobilization to punish an "unjust" adversary (Gamson et al. 1982; Goldstein 1983; Olivier 1990, 1991). These two perspectives have largely been challenged on empirical grounds; there are many instances where repression both quells and provokes insurgency (Zimmermann 1980, 1983; Hoover and Kowalewski 1992; Lee et al. 2000; Davenport et al. 2005). Attempts to solve the repression–rebellion puzzle have led some scholars to investigate nonlinear relationships between repression and rebellion, arguing that varying levels of repression—high, medium, or low—are likely to induce mass dissent or hinder it (Gurr 1968, 1970; Feierabend and Feierabend 1972; Snyder and Tilly 1972; Lichbach and Gurr 1981; Muller 1985; Muller and Seligson 1987; Muller and Weede 1990). Others look to the timing of repression in the protest cycle (Snyder 1976;

Tarrow 1989; Costain 1992; and Brockett 1995); its perceived illegitimacy in the context of preexisting networks that could generate micromobilization processes (White 1989; Opp and Roehl 1990; Rasler 1996); the political and institutional context under which it is applied (Gupta et al. 1993); its targets (Mason and Krane 1989) and the consistency of its application in relation to accommodative strategies (Lichbach 1987; Rasler 1996; Moore 1998, 2000; Ginkel and Smith 1999; Ferrara 2003); its impact on mobilization when combined with ethno-political grievances and group coherence (Gurr 1993; Gurr and Moore 1997); the ability of dissidents to adapt to it and unleash backlash mobilization (Francisco 1995, 1996, 2004, 2005); or a combination of these variables (Della Porta 1995; Hafez 2003).

With few exceptions (Gurr 1986; Khawaja 1993; Della Porta 1995; Koopmans 1997; Francisco 2005), much of this literature speaks of repression without specifying its different types (e.g., mass arrests versus massacres, or exile versus targeted assassinations). Nonetheless, this literature provides the theoretical foundations for studying specific tactics of repression to quell insurgency and terrorism. This article explores four plausible hypotheses about the effects of targeted assassinations on rates of Palestinian violence during the *Al-Aqsa* uprising that began in September 2000 and reached its peak in March 2002.

H_1 Targeted assassinations serve as selective disincentives that raise the cost of militancy and deter militant organizations from planning more attacks, thus decreasing rates of Palestinian violence.

H_2 Targeted assassinations enrage militants and produce a backlash effect, increasing levels of Palestinian violence.

H_3 Targeted assassinations deprive militant organizations of valued commanders and force the remaining members to concentrate more on their personal security and less on recruiting and organizing attacks; the disruption effect diminishes the number and success rate of attacks over time.

H_4 Targeted assassinations by themselves are

insufficient predictors of increasing or diminishing Palestinian violence. However, when combined with major military incursions into rebellious towns, they jointly produce a diminishing capacity effect and decrease rates of Palestinian violence, because they target both the resource endowments and personnel of militant groups.

The article investigates rates of Palestinian violence using a multivariate approach to evaluate the significance of targeted assassinations. It utilizes multiple regression for data whose response variable(s) is continuous and binary logistic regression for cases where the response variable is binary. The findings suggest that targeted assassinations have no significant impact on rates of Palestinian violence, even when time lags associated with possible reactive retaliations are taken into account. Contrary to some proponents of targeted assassinations, this analysis indicates that targeted assassinations do not decrease the rates of Palestinian violence, whether in the short or the long run. However, contrary to some critics of targeted assassinations, this analysis shows that targeted assassinations do not increase the rates of Palestinian violence either, whether in the short or the long run. This study does not address the political dimensions of targeted assassinations, especially their potential to signal one's determination to fight back, demonstrate strength to placate an angry public, or as a means for retributive justice. It may well be that the political utility of targeted assassinations is more effective than its military one.

Background

In September 2000, Palestinians embarked on an uprising, commonly referred to as *Al-Aqsa intifada*. This uprising, their second in a little over a decade, came on the heels of a failed peace summit between Palestinians and Israelis and was intended to force Israelis out of the West Bank and Gaza. Unlike the first *intifada*, this uprising quickly turned into a militarized struggle between armed Palestinian factions and Israeli forces. Initially, Palestinian violence was characterized by random shootings at Israeli positions and settlements in the West Bank and Gaza. Toward the end of the second month of the uprising, Palestinian violence became more organized as factions associated with Yasser Arafat's Fatah began to undertake guerrilla-like attacks on Israeli patrols and settlers, whereas the Islamist factions—Hamas and Islamic Jihad—began to organize suicide bombings inside Israel. As the cycle of violence deepened, secular Palestinian factions—Popular Front for the Liberation of Palestine (PFLP) and a new and somewhat shadowy group associated with Fatah, known as Al-Aqsa Martyrs Brigades (AMB)—began to carry out suicide bombings against Israeli civilians.

Many Israelis viewed Palestinian violence as another war against the Jewish state and, consequently, gave their support to the hard-line administration of Ariel Sharon. As suicide bombings persisted, Israel's defense establishment was hard pressed to take measures to reduce the violence. Initially, the Israel Defense Forces (IDF) engaged in a tit-for-tat retaliatory policy aimed at the Palestinian Authority. The latter was accused of inciting—or at least not preventing—violence despite its pledge to do so under the peace and security accords signed between 1993 and 1997. Israeli forces targeted Palestinian security agencies and police stations in pin-point attacks by air and sea. The Israelis also began to impose closures on the territories and restricted the movement of Palestinians from town to town. As violence worsened, Israel became more aggressive in its punishment of Palestinian militants. Targeted assassinations, mass arrests, home demolitions, and expulsions were often used to deter future attacks. In March 2002, following a suicide bombing campaign in which 79 people were killed, 555 were injured, the IDF mobilized its forces in a major takeover of Palestinian cities and towns in an offensive known as Operation Defensive Shield. Since this operation, the Israelis undertook many other incursions in an attempt to capture suspected terrorists and crush the infrastructure of Palestinian militancy.

One of the most controversial measures

taken by Israeli forces has been the targeted assassination of Palestinian military commanders and political leaders. The use of assassinations is not unique to *Al-Aqsa* uprising; Israel has a history of using this method against enemies that have perpetrated violence against its citizenry. Israel waged a campaign of assassinations in retaliation for the Munich Olympic massacre in 1972 by Palestinian terrorists associated with the Black September group (Brophy-Baermann and Conybeare 1994). Some of the more notable episodes of targeted assassinations in recent years has been the fatal shooting of Islamic Jihad leader Fathi Shikaki in Malta in October 1995; the detonation of a booby-trapped mobile phone that killed Hamas's chief bombmaker Yahya Ayyash (the "Engineer") in Gaza in January 1996; and the aborted assassination of Khaled Meshal, one of Hamas's political leaders in Amman, in September 1997.

From November 2000 to June 2004, Israel conducted approximately 151 targeted assassinations. The first assassination was of Hussein Abayyat, a Fatah commander killed on 9 November 2000. Since his liquidation, Israel engaged in some high-profile killings that included Dr. Thabet Thabet, head of Fatah in Tulkarem; Mustafa Zibri (Abu Ali Mustafa), political head of the PFLP; Mahmoud Muhammad Ahmed Shouley (Abu Hnoud), Hamas planner of suicide bombings; Salah Shehadeh, chief commander of Hamas's military wing; Ismail Abu Shanab, one of Hamas's top leaders in its political wing; and Dr. Abdel Aziz al-Rantisi, the number one man in Hamas's political hierarchy following the assassination of Sheikh Ahmed Yassin. Most of the targeted assassinations were conducted by air through the use of Apache helicopters or unmanned drone planes firing laser-guided missiles. Some assassinations relied on the use of jet fighter planes with heavy-load bombs. Other assassinations involved booby-trapping cars or phone booths, or installing land mines along the routes of suspected terrorists. Israelis have also used undercover "Arabized" agents to carry out assassinations from close up. To conduct such sensitive attacks in the heart of Palestinian cities and refugee camps, the IDF relies on an extensive network of local spies and collaborators who can provide just-in-time information on a moving target.

The decision to undertake a targeted killing begins with the Israeli intelligence services. They identify an individual as a major threat to Israel and prepare a detailed report on his past activities. The information is reviewed by IDF commanders and military lawyers and they jointly make a determination if a targeted assassination is warranted. Major General Giora Eiland (IDF) identifies a four-prong criterion to determine when targeted assassinations should be carried out. First, arresting the individual is a near impossibility. Second, the militant must be a high-value target because of his ability to inflict harm on Israelis. Third, the assassination is not likely to involve high civilian casualties. Fourth, the individual is in the process of planning or carrying out an operation; he is a "ticking bomb."[3] When an assassination is deemed necessary, a recommendation is made to the chief of staff, who takes up the matter with the Israeli cabinet to approve or disapprove. Additional approvals may be required by the minister of defense and the Prime Minister if civilian casualties are likely (David 2003, 117).

The debate within Israel over targeted assassinations revolves around four core arguments: legality and legitimacy of assassinations; consequences of assassinations on innocent bystanders; alternative means to fighting terror; and effectiveness of these measures in actually reducing violence (David 2003; Stein 2003; Luft 2003). Many of the claims proffered by proponents of targeted assassinations and their detractors are normative ones that are outside of the scope of this research.[4] However, the debate on the effectiveness of targeted assassinations is an empirical one that can be evaluated through the use of statistical methods. The following sections attempt to determine if targeted assassinations are an effective means to combat violent insurgency.

Hypotheses

The literature on repression and rebellion suggest at least four plausible hypotheses concerning the effects of targeted assassinations on Palestinian violence: deterrence, backlash, disruption, and incapacitation. Each is explored in turn.

H₁ Targeted Assassinations are Selective Disincentives that Produce a Deterrent Effect

A number of studies point out that repression by authorities increases the contenders cost of collective action and serves as a selective disincentive to engage in high-risk activism (Oberschall 1973; Tilly 1978; Oliver 1980; Hardin 1982). Rational actors subject to a set of constraints will calculate costs and benefits of different courses of action and choose the means that are likely to maximize their expected utility, whether individual gains or public goods (Sandler et al. 1983; Mason 1984; Muller and Opp 1986). Cost-benefit calculations are shaped by the importance of the utility being maximized, the probability of group success, and the perceived importance of personal participation to achieving the overall goals of the group (Finkel et al. 1989; Muller et al. 1991). To the extent repression decreases the likelihood of group success or diminishes the ability of individuals to truly make a difference, it will deter others from participating in high-risk activism. As Muller and Weede (1990, 646) explain, "Under a highly repressive regime it is likely that opportunities for collective action of any kind will be low, that the probability of success will be negligible, and that costs will be high. Rational actors who wish to contest policies of a government are likely to think better of it."

Lichbach (1987) gives nuance to this rationalist perspective by focusing on the consistency of repression in relation to accommodative strategies. He maintains that if repression against violent strategies is applied consistently and nonviolent strategies are accommodated, militant groups will substitute violence for nonviolent tactics to avoid the prohibitive costs of violent tactics and seek more efficient and effective means to achieve their aims. Put simply, a consistent repression policy that does not cede concessions to violent strategies only incurs costs to the dissident groups and fails to deliver any meaningful gains to their movement. As a result, violence will diminish over time as groups adapt to a more fruitful strategy. Adaptation may not be immediate due to a learning curve, but violence should decrease in due course.

In addition to consistency, Mason and Krane (1989) argue that the targets of repression matter. Targeting refers to the range of "subversives" encompassed under repressive measures. Do the repressing authorities target only leaders and core activists of the dissident movement, or do they also target supporters, sympathizers, and anyone suspected of involvement with rebellious groups? States that selectively target known militants for suppression and avoid indiscriminate application of repression are likely to reduce mobilization because ordinary people are not drawn into the conflict unwillingly and rank-and-file activists begin to question the ability of their leaders to deliver collective benefits. Selective repression against core militants signals to potential recruits that only "troublemakers" will be punished and, therefore, those who keep their distance will not become victims of repression. Indiscriminate repression, on the other hand, intensifies anger among the public and does not provide guarantees that nonviolent activism will not be repressed. Under these circumstances, supporters and sympathizers may be inclined toward greater risk to mitigate their losses, seek security in militant groups, or inflict revenge.

In the Palestinian–Israeli conflict, the aforementioned literature would hypothesize that a consistent policy of targeted assassinations against known commanders of terrorist cells that recruit, organize, and dispatch attackers against Israeli targets raise the costs of violence and force potential militants to abandon the struggle or, at a minimum, substitute tactics. The expansion of the assassination policy to the political leadership of terrorist groups sends a message that Israel will not accommodate or negotiate with radical groups, thus confirming the futility of violent strategies. Refusal to cede to the major demands of the militant groups—end to the occupation, relinquishing east Jerusalem, halt in settlement construction, and refugees' right of return—while violence persists signals a commitment to not give in to terror. Finally, selectively targeting leaders and commanders of the groups responsible for anti-Israeli violence reduces the likelihood of drawing the broader public into the fray and impresses on potential militants the futility of continuing with violent strategies.

H₂ Targeted Assassinations Produce Backlash, Increasing Violence

Studies by Francisco (1995, 1996) posit the backlash hypothesis: preexisting and mobilized organizations facing extreme coercion will fight back with greater levels of violence. Backlash is defined as massive, swift, and expanding mobilization in response to harsh repression (Francisco 2005). Francisco (2004) argues that acts of severe repression can serve as focal points for backlash mobilization if (a) publicity transmits information of the repressive actions to the wider public; (b) there is continuity in leadership or new leadership arises; and (c) dissidents can offer adaptive strategies that reduce the risk of similar repression in the future. Under these circumstances, repression produces backlash, which is the opposite of what is intended.

In the Palestinian–Israeli conflict, the backlash hypothesis predicts that targeted assassinations will produce an escalation in violence. Targeted assassinations receive immediate and widespread publicity in local and international media, and often spark immediate condemnations and protests from the public. Following an attack, an enraged public gathers at the site of the assassination and within a day, thousands come out for a mass funeral that is covered by the media. Moreover, targeted assassinations rarely remove the entire leadership of militant groups in one fell swoop, thus satisfying Francisco's condition of continuity in leadership. This leadership can take more personal precautions to minimize the risk of targeted assassinations in the future, thus enabling them to mobilize further attacks in retaliation for previous ones. Furthermore, preexisting and mobilized militant organizations facing targeted assassinations are likely to frame targeted assas-

sinations as treacherous and illegitimate acts that demand a commensurate retaliatory response. Tight-knit groups will seek to maintain the internal cohesion of their militant organizations by satisfying their cadres' need to exhibit defiance in the face of oppression. As a result, targeted assassinations are likely to produce a surge in violence and foster conditions that permit for the future recruitment of terrorists.

H₃ Targeted Assassinations Produce a Disruption Effect and Diminish Violence Over Time

Khawaja's (1993) study of repression and Palestinian collective action in the West Bank and Gaza from 1976 to 1985 shows how certain types of repression have a direct impact on the ability of organizations to mobilize collective action. Curfews and home-to-home searches, he argues, disrupt coordination and communication networks, thus making it difficult for the militants to mobilize following rounds of repression. He further argues that medium levels of arrests increased the rate of collective action while mass arrests decreased the rate substantially. The latter is directly linked to disruption of organizational coordination. Khawaja (1993, 67) concludes that "In the absence of organizational mobilization and support, potential activists are more likely to keep their anger and grievance to themselves, fearing retributions by authorities." Khawaja's claims are anchored in the resource mobilization theory, which maintains that grievances alone are insufficient to produce rebellious collective action; groups require a modicum of material resources and organizational capabilities to organize and mobilize aggrieved people (Tilly et al. 1975; McCarthy and Zald 1973, 1977). To the extent repression removes valuable movement resources or makes them difficult to acquire, it disrupts the ability of dissidents to mobilize collective action.

In the case of the Palestinian–Israeli conflict, the resource mobilization perspective implies that targeted assassinations may diminish the number and success rate of attacks in the long run as militant groups suffer the loss of experienced cadres and commanders, and allocate precious resources to secure the remaining leadership. Thus, rather than spend their money, time, and effort on recruiting people, training them, and transporting them to carry out operations, terrorists spend their valued resources on securing safe houses for hiding, alternating vehicles, and communication methods to avoid detection, and restructuring the cells that have been disrupted by assassinations. Moreover, taking out commanders that bear the cognitive load for organizing attacks reduces the quality of future terrorist operations. Bombmaking, recruiting, and intelligence gathering skills are not acquired over night; liquidating persons central to the preparation and planning of operations is a real loss for terror groups and they take a long time to recover. The cumulative effect over time is to reduce levels of violence or, at a minimum, lower the quality and success rate of violent operations against Israeli targets.

H₄ Targeted Assassinations by Themselves Do Not Diminish Levels of Violence Because of the Substitution Effect. However, When Targeted Assassinations are Combined with Military Incursions, They Jointly Produce a Diminishing Capacity Effect and Lessen Violence Over Time

Sandler et al. (1983) and Enders and Sandler (1993, 2004) argue that governments that increase the costs of terrorism through repression, but fail to decrease the flow of resources available to terrorists, will ultimately not succeed in fighting terrorism because of the substitution effect. The latter occurs when terrorists shift from one terror activity (e.g., suicide bombings) to another (e.g., roadside bombs) because counterterrorism policies have made the first activity more difficult to carry out (or increased its relative cost in relation to other terror activities). If the second activity (roadside bombs) can satisfy the same desired goals as the first activity (suicide bombings), and if counterterrorism policies have not sought to increase the relative costs of carrying out the second activity, terrorists will substitute the second, less costly

activity for the first, more costly tactic. As long as counterterrorism policies do not address the *resource endowments* of terror groups, terrorists will adapt to repression policies by substituting tactics to relatively less costly methods. This analysis supplements the resource mobilization theory presented in the third hypothesis by emphasizing the need to deny militant groups the ability to organize collective violence by depriving them of the prerequisite resources and organizational infrastructure for violence. A reduction in one violent tactic does not necessarily mean that the overall rate of violence has diminished.

In the case of the Palestinian–Israeli conflict, the substitution effect suggests that targeted assassinations that remove valuable commanders and cadres without impacting the overall resource endowment of terror groups will result in adaptation, whereby terrorists will alter their tactics to carry out more attacks in the long run. However, targeted assassinations combined with major military incursions that destroy Palestinian bombmaking factories, arrest suspected militants, and destroy weapon-smuggling tunnels not only deprive terror groups of their valuable personnel, they also deprive them of the ability to reconstitute terror cells and diminish their capacity to attack in the future.

Methodology

Data were compiled on violent events between Palestinians and Israelis from 29 September 2000 to 16 June 2004. The data were culled from the quarterly chronologies published in *The Middle East Journal*, which draws from several news sources, including the *Associated Press, BBC, New York Times, Washington Post*, and many other reliable news services. In addition, data were collected from the International Policy Institute for Counter-Terrorism (ICT) in Herzlia, Israel, which keeps detailed records of violent events in the current Palestinian uprising. Data were also collected from Lexus-Nexus searches using as the main sources *Ha'aretz* and *Jerusalem Post*, two daily Israeli papers that are published in English.

Ancillary sources such as *CNN* or *New York Times* chronologies of suicide bombings in Israel, or Israel's Ministry of Foreign Affairs chronologies of Palestinian attacks were used to provide more information on specific events, not as independent sources of data. The following were gathered for the analysis:

- Palestinian violent attacks that materialized (successful attacks), including attack type and group(s) responsible for carrying it out. Violent Palestinian attacks were defined as suicide bombings, non-suicide bombings, sporadic shootings, organized armed infiltrations, rocket attacks, and other forms of lethal violence.
- Palestinian attacks that were in progress but failed to materialize because Israeli forces prevented them (foiled attacks).
- Number of Israelis killed and injured in Palestinian attacks.
- Israeli targeted assassinations that began in November 2000.
- Israeli military incursions that began in October 2000.
- Palestinians killed and injured in Israeli counterterrorism operations.

Three challenges were encountered while collecting this data. First, the authors occasionally found discrepancies in news reports as to the actual date or number of persons killed/injured in an attack. In those instances, they relied on the most conservative estimate or the one that offered the most details about the attack. Undoubtedly, this will not do justice to those excluded from the data, but the authors are not aware of any technique that could avoid this problem. Second, some events were difficult to categorize because of conflicting Palestinian and Israeli claims about what actually happened. For instance, some episodes deemed to be targeted assassinations by Palestinians are contested by Israelis as "workshop accidents"— that is, militants blew themselves up while preparing an attack. When in doubt, these events were excluded from the database. As a result, the aggregate numbers are substantially lower than what Palestinian sources report. These exclusions imply a bias against Palestinian claims. This limita-

tion is recognized, but it is necessary to ensure the reliability of the data. Finally, the data is based on reported events both with regard to Palestinian violence and Israeli liquidations. In such a study unreported attacks are of major importance because they can supply a more comprehensive picture and lead to more accurate (and perhaps different) conclusions. Therefore, the reader is encouraged to view the findings as tentative or pending additional research; the aim is to encourage further study of this topic with a more complete data set in order to confirm, modify, or reject the findings herein.

For all four hypotheses a multivariate approach was used as targeted assassinations constitute one piece of Israel's overall repression strategy. This means that interactions between predictive factors as well as their possible isolated affects were taken into account. Following Box et al. (1978, 496–497) the authors began by using multi-interval differencing of both factor and response variables in order to better stationarize the time-series for regression analysis. Along with differencing techniques, for every model type a weekly response variable lag was tested. The differencing and lag intervals ranged from weekly Lag_0 for real-time models to Lag_4 for the possibility of a four-week lag period between Israeli repression and Palestinian reaction. The authors then looked for interactions and/or collinearity between the predictors. When an interaction was detected the authors included the interaction in the model as a factor in its own right. This inclusion, however, did not take the place of an independent testing of the variables. When factors were found to be collinear, one was removed from the model. When *linear* regression failed to produce a model with significant predictive power, polynomial models (including quadratic and cubic models) were used to attempt a better fit. Statistical significance was tested on a factor basis using the *p*-value for the factor with an alpha level at 0.05 and on a model basis using the model R^2 value. As will be shown later, many factors/models that were found to be statistically significant were determined to have no *practical* explanatory significance. Practical significance for statistically significant factors was determined by a calculation of the ratio of the sequential sum of squares over the total sum of squares. This ratio calculates the percentage of variation in the response variable explained by the factor. Only the models with the highest practical significance are shown at each time lag.

Throughout the investigation the authors found it necessary to include attacks foiled by Israel in the counts for Palestinian violence. Because the study is assessing the ability of targeted assassinations to deter or provoke Palestinian violence, rates of foiled attacks are important to include because a failed attack due to Israeli interception speaks to the ability of Israel to foil, not deter, Palestinian violence. An increase in foiled attacks might substantiate the backlash theory, despite the appearance of calm.

Testing Hypothesis 1

H_1 assumes that repression against violent strategies is applied consistently. Figure 27.1 illustrates

the consistency of repression by Israel over the time-period covered in this study.

Out of the 191 weeks shown earlier, only in 15 weeks did Israel not retaliate against Palestinian attacks, which is less than 8 percent of the time. At each weekly lag period a similarly high percentage of retaliations occurred (see Table 27.1).

It is concluded that Israel's retaliation policy was consistent throughout the uprising, especially in light of the fact that no major concessions were granted to the Palestinians during this time period.

H_1 predicts that the attack success rate (given as the total number of successful attacks/the total number of attacks) for insurgent groups

TABLE 27.1. Israel's Retaliation Rate Following Palestinian Attacks

# Weeks lagged	% Weekly response rate by Israel
1	91
2	93
3	91
4	88

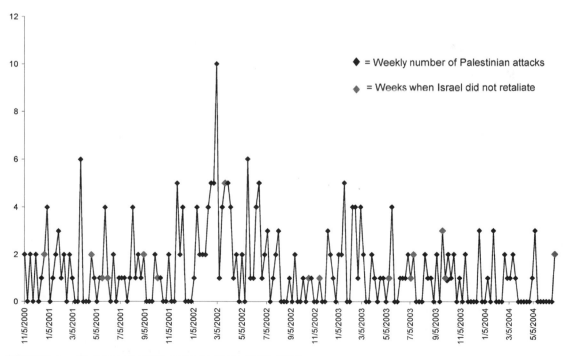

FIGURE 27.1 ■ Consistency of repression by Israel, 2000–2004.

and the type of target affected by the Israeli repression will strongly predict levels of Palestinian violence. Our models for H_1 include the attack success rate and two repression variables intended to measure differing target types. The first repression variable is targeted assassinations, which are more heavily aimed at commanders whereas the second repression variable of major military incursions are less discriminate and more broadly affect insurgent organizations. Table 27.2 provides the most successfully predictive approach found by this study.[5]

The predictive power of this model is relatively low because it explains at best only 21% of the variation in Palestinian violence. Targeted assassinations were not found to be statistically significant. The variable having the highest practical significance is the attack success rate. However modeling it by itself and with other variables did not increase its predictive power beyond 16 percent at a 2-week lag. Interestingly, the attack success rate coefficient is negative, which is the opposite relationship predicted by H_1.

The latter predicts that as the attack success rate diminishes so does the level of Palestinian violence. The analysis has found that as the attack success rate diminishes the rate of Palestinian violence actually increases and vice versa. The analysis has not provided any justification for the relationships asserted by H_1.

Testing Hypothesis 2

H_2 asserts that to the extent that repressive action by Israel is viewed as extreme coercion by Palestinian groups, it will initiate immediate backlash. Two methods were use to separate severe repression, which is more likely to give rise to calls for immediate retaliation, from mild or "normal" repression, which is less likely to produce demands for immediate retaliation. The first is by *aggregate numerical severity*. A repressive act by Israel is determined to be severe if an Israeli repressive act is performed when no Palestinian attack corresponds to it and/or if the ratio of Israeli meas-

TABLE 27.2. Regression Models for Hypothesis 1

Weekly lag	Factors	Regression coefficient	ANOVA SeqSS/TotSS	*p*-value	Model R^2
0	TAs	−0.0596	*	0.752	21.4%
	Mil incursions	0.6629	5.5%	0.000	
	Attack success rate	−2.6424	15.9%	0.000	
	Constant	3.9866	*	0.000	
1	TAs	−0.2517	*	0.234	2.2%
	Mil incursions	0.1432	*	0.472	
	Attack success rate	−0.7487	*	0.122	
	Constant	3.0122	*	0.000	
2	TAs	−0.1111	*	0.571	17.0%
	Mil incursions	0.3357	*	0.070	
	Attack success rate	−2.6957	16.26%	0.000	
	Constant	4.2336	*	0.000	
3	TAs	0.1896	*	0.330	18.2%
	Mil incursions	0.405	2.3%	0.028	
	Attack success rate	−2.6024	15.40%	0.000	
	Constant	3.9495	*	0.000	
4	TAs	0.0104	*	0.958	16.1%
	Mil incursions	0.2533	*	0.173	
	Attack success rate	−2.5955	15.30%	0.000	
	Constant	4.1402	*	0.000	

$a = 0.05$, *where value is not applicable.

ures to Palestinian attacks is >3:1. Otherwise repression is considered "mild." The 3:1 ratio rule has been determined by looking at the distribution of the ratio of Israeli measures to Palestinian attacks during the 191 weeks and finding the point in the histogram presented in Figure 27.2 where normalcy gives way to severity.

The second method is by *victim numerical severity*. Even when a repressive act is not considered numerically severe in the sense calculated earlier, if an attack results in a high loss of life, the act is likely to be seen as extreme. This victim numerical severity also depends on the number of Palestinian attacks over the same time period. If the number of victims suffered by a Palestinian group is very high, but the number of successful attacks carried out by the Palestinian group over this same time period is also very high then it is likely that repression will be seen as less severe than if fewer Palestinian attacks were occurring. Therefore, the numerical severity calculations were normalized by the number of Palestinian attacks over the same time period. A repressive act is thus considered to have caused a severe number of victims when the number of Palestinian victims killed or injured per one successful Palestinian

attack over the same time period is >40. This ratio rule has been determined through an examination of Figure 27.3, which shows the distribution of the ratio over the 191 weeks of the study.

Severe versus mild conditions for the response variable of Palestinian attacks are calculated for clear conclusions about the relationship between factor severity and response severity. Because backlash includes failed attempts as well as actual successful retaliations, attacks foiled by Israel are included in the response variable. Palestinian violence levels are considered severe when the ratio of Palestinian attacks to Israeli measures over the same time period is ≥3:1. Again, see the 191 week distribution of this ratio shown in Figure 27.4 for the dividing point.

A binary logistic regression model is used to assess the predictive power of aggregate numerical severity and victim numerical severity on the severity of Palestinian violence. Table 27.3 provides the most successfully predictive approach.[6]

The goodness-of-fit tests (Pearson, Deviance, and Hosmer-Lemeshow) have an alpha of 0.5 with the null hypothesis being an adequate fit. Thus, there is insufficient evidence for claiming that the models in Table 27.3 do not fit the data adequately.

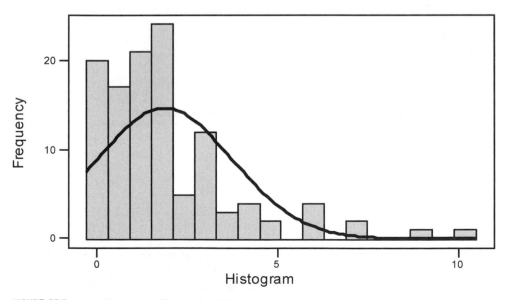

FIGURE 27.2 ■ Israeli measures/Palestinian violence.

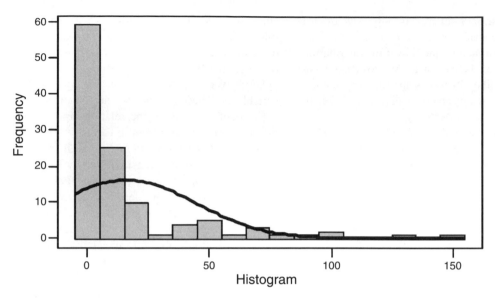

FIGURE 27.3 ■ Palestinian victims/Palestinian violence.

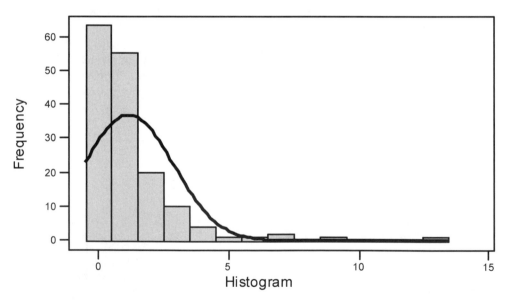

FIGURE 27.4 ■ Binary response for H_2.

The models lack significant predictive ability as the highest coefficient is just 0.45. Furthermore, p-values for regression factors show that movements in the severity of Palestinian violence cannot be predicted by movements in either aggregate numerical severity or victim numerical severity. In particular, targeted assassinations show no promise for either increasing or decreasing the levels of Palestinian violence. No "backlash" is verified by these findings.

TABLE 27.3. Binary Logistic Regression Models for Hypothesis 2

Weekly lag		Severity factors	Regression coefficient	*p*-value	Goodness-of-fit tests	
0		Numerical	−0.9989	0.094	Pearson	0.339
		Victim	0.3073	0.703	Deviance	0.232
		Constant	−2.0697	0.000	Hosmer-Lemeshow	0.511

Model predictive ability

Pairs (%s)				Goodman-Kruskal Gamma	Kendall's Tau-a
Concordant	Discordant	Ties	Somers' D		
41.60%	17.30%	41.10%	0.24	0.41	0.04

Weekly lag		Severity factors	Regression coefficient	*p*-value	Goodness-of-fit tests	
1		Numerical	0.4977	0.347	Pearson	1.00
		Victim	−20.0000	0.998	Deviance	1.00
		Constant	−2.5200	0.000	Hosmer-Lemeshow	1.00

Model predictive ability

Pairs (%s)				Goodman-Kruskal Gamma	Kendall's Tau-a
Concordant	Discordant	Ties	Somers' D		
39.00%	17.10%	43.90%	0.22	0.39	0.03

Weekly lag		Severity factors	Regression coefficient	*p*-value	Goodness-of-fit tests	
2		Numerical	0.2010	0.701	Pearson	0.268
		Victim	−0.5600	0.599	Deviance	0.204
		Constant	−2.4305	0.000	Hosmer-Lemeshow	0.778

Model predictive ability

Pairs (%s)				Goodman-Kruskal Gamma	Kendall's Tau-a
Concordant	Discordant	Ties	Somers' D		
34.60%	23.40%	42.00%	0.11	0.19	0.02

Weekly lag		Severity factors	Regression coefficient	*p*-value	Goodness-of-fit tests	
3		Numerical	1.0754	0.055	Pearson	0.095
		Victim	−0.5960	0.577	Deviance	0.095
		Constant	−2.9300	0.000	Hosmer-Lemeshow	*

Model predictive ability

Pairs (%s)				Goodman-Kruskal Gamma	Kendall's Tau-a
Concordant	Discordant	Ties	Somers' D		
44.10%	16.70%	39.20%	0.27	0.45	0.04

Weekly lag		Severity factors	Regression coefficient	*p*-value	Goodness-of-fit tests

(*Continued overleaf*)

TABLE 27.3. Continued

4		Numerical	0.2035	0.697	Pearson	0.267
		Victim	−0.5730	0.590	Deviance	0.204
		Constant	−2.4187	0.000	Hosmer-Lemeshow	0.778

		Model predictive ability			

Pairs (%s)				Goodman-Kruskal Gamma	Kendall's Tau-a
Concordant	Discordant	Ties	Somers' D		
34.70%	23.30%	42.00%	0.11	0.20	0.02

$a = 0.05$ for p-value and Goodness-of-Fit tests, *where value is not applicable.

Testing Hypothesis 3

H_3 states that repressive measures that disrupt the workings of militant groups will decrease the long-run number and success rate of attacks. Repressive techniques that have a direct impact on the ability of insurgent groups to mobilize collective action will achieve long-term success against violence. Attacks become less frequent because militant groups must concern themselves more and more with internal security and less with training and organizing attacks. Attacks become less successful because repressive measures cause the "bench strength" of the militant organization to decrease as militants spend less time training, gathering intelligence, and organizing attacks and more time protecting themselves.

Certain types of repression are in their nature disruptive. Targeted assassinations dramatically affect the human resources of an insurgent group and create an overall disruptive vacuum that takes time and effort on the part of the affected groups to fill. Military incursions also disrupt violent groups but in a more general way by immersing groups in a repressive environment. The authors include both targeted assassinations and military incursions in the model for the test of H_3.

Another way to determine whether repression is disruptive is by repression severity. As attack levels increase, less long-term planning can be performed, more time is spent on defensive maneuvers, and the overall number and quality of attacks may also decrease. Thus, a factor was

included in the models measuring the severity of Palestinian attack frequencies. A frequency is considered severe when the number of targeted assassinations + military incursions ≥3 and mild otherwise. This number has been derived by looking at a histogram of this sum over the 191 weeks and finding the point in the histogram presented in Figure 27.5 where normalcy gives way to severity.

A descriptive look at the attack success rate over time during the time period under consideration may lead one to believe that repressive techniques by the Israelis are causing a long-run disruption of Palestinian groups and their ability to successfully attack Israel. Indeed, Israel's ability to foil attacks has increased substantially. Figure 27.6 indicates that although variance is high, the success rate of Palestinian attacks has declined substantially over time. Is this decline related to targeted assassinations?

Table 27.4 provides the most successfully predictive approach found for hypothesis 3.[7]

The predictive power of this model is low because it explains at best only 7 percent of the variation in Palestinian violence. Although targeted assassinations are found to be statistically significant they have little practical significance. Except in the very mild case of the Lag_2 model, the factor variables are never significant for the prediction of the attack success rate, thus the decrease in successful attacks due to a disruption by these factors finds no evidence here. The use of targeted assassinations to predict either rates of Palestinian

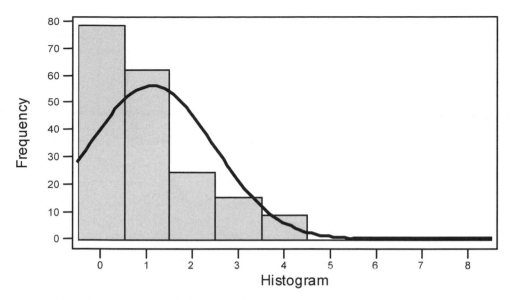

FIGURE 27.5 ■ Assassinations and military incursions.

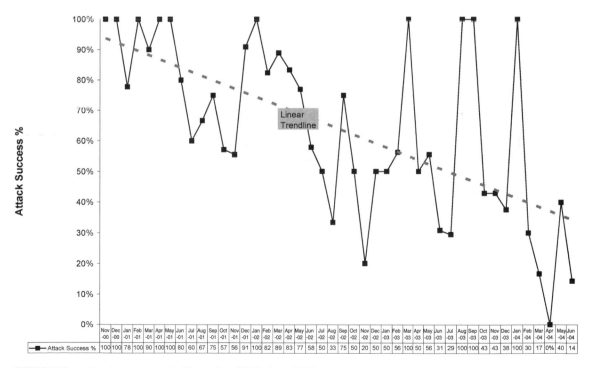

FIGURE 27.6 ■ Attack success rate, November 2000–June 2004.

violence or attack success rates also receives little support from these results. The authors suggest that looking at purely defensive measures such as intelligence collection, barrier building, and increased security measures may shed more light on the decrease in the attack success rate. This suggestion also relates to the results for H_4 and will be elaborated on presently.

TABLE 27.4. Regression Models for Hypothesis 3

Weekly lag	Response	Factors	Regression coefficient	ANOVA SeqSS/ TotSS	p-value	Model R^2
0	Palestinian violence	TAs	0.14448	*	0.607	6.2%
		Mil incursions	0.8288	5.5%	0.001	
		Severe/Mild frequency	−1.0209	*	0.243	
		Constant	2.0145	*	0.000	
	Attack success rate	TAs	0.00005	*	0.999	0.1%
		Mil incursions	0.0013	*	0.973	
		Severe/Mild frequency	0.0344	*	0.800	
		Constant	0.71538	*	0.000	
1	Palestinian violence	TAs	−0.3104	*	0.286	1.0%
		Mil incursions	0.0937	*	0.717	
		Severe/Mild frequency	0.2457	*	0.785	
		Constant	2.4979	*	0.000	
	Attack success rate	TAs	−0.01711	*	0.694	2.3%
		Mil incursions	0.06658	*	0.087	
		Severe/Mild frequency	−0.0956	*	0.478	
		Constant	0.707	*	0.000	
2	Palestinian violence	TAs	0.1823	*	0.531	1.1%
		Mil incursions	0.3723	*	0.152	
		Severe/Mild frequency	−0.8002	*	0.374	
		Constant	2.2167	*	0.000	
	Attack success rate	TAs	−0.09193	0.8%	0.035	3.2%
		Mil incursions	0.00041	*	0.992	
		Severe/Mild frequency	0.2202	*	0.102	
		Constant	0.74131	*	0.000	
3	Palestinian violence	TAs	0.7126	0.5%	0.013	7.0%
		Mil incursions	0.8769	2.4%	0.001	
		Severe/Mild frequency	−2.5011	4.1%	0.005	
		Constant	1.8689	*	0.000	
	Attack success rate	TAs	0.00496	*	0.911	0.1%
		Mil incursions	−0.01088	*	0.782	
		Severe/Mild frequency	0.029	*	0.832	
		Constant	0.71524	*	0.000	
4	Palestinian violence	TAs	0.0149	*	0.959	0.8%
		Mil incursions	0.2043	*	0.434	
		Severe/Mild frequency	0.1523	*	0.866	
		Constant	2.2874	*	0.000	
	Attack success rate	TAs	−0.02842	*	0.522	0.3%
		Mil incursions	−0.00318	*	0.936	
		Severe/Mild frequency	0.0618	*	0.651	
		Constant	0.72481	*	0.000	

$\alpha = 0.05$, *where value is not applicable.

Testing Hypothesis 4

H_4 asserts that only repression that decreases the material and human resources of militant groups will successfully diminish violence over time. Thus targeted assassinations by themselves cannot predict increasing or diminishing Palestinian violence. However, H_4 asserts that when combined with major military incursions into rebellious zones, targeted assassinations and incursions together decrease levels of Palestinian violence, because they diminish the capacity of militant groups by targeting both their resources and personnel. In March 2002, the sudden spike in the number of Israelis killed and injured by Palestinian attacks caused the Israelis to change counterinsurgency methods. The chart in Figure 27.7 illustrates this dramatic increase in the number of Israelis killed or injured during March 2002.

From late March 2002 onward, Israeli forces began coupling targeted assassinations with major military incursions into rebellious Palestinian towns with the intent of striking at the resources, infrastructure, and personnel of militant groups. Although military incursions were used several times prior to March 2002, they were often ad hoc responses to Palestinian violence. In March 2002, the tactic of military incursions became more systematic.

H_4 predicts that the level of Palestinian violence decreases under a policy of combined targeted assassinations and military incursions. Table 27.5 provides the most successfully predictive approaches[8] containing the variables targeted assassinations (TAs), military incursions (MI), or their interaction (TAs*MI).

Table 27.5 illustrates that neither targeted assassinations, military incursions, nor their interaction is a significant predictor of the movements in Palestinian violence. Although targeted assassinations, with their effect on human resources, and military incursions, with their effect on material resources, jointly satisfy the conditions for H_4, the claim that such factors would strongly predict Palestinian violence finds no support from this analysis. The factors are seldom statistically

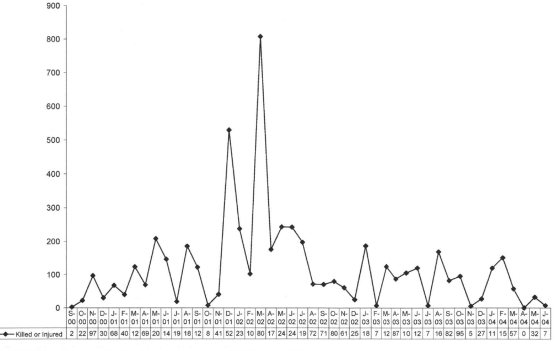

FIGURE 27.7 ■ Israelis killed or injured, November 2000–June 2004.

significant and when they are significant the amount of the movement in Palestinian violence explained by the factors is minimal. Furthermore, regression coefficients for statistically significant factors have the opposite sign as that predicted by H_4. H_4 asserts, for instance, that as the input factor TAs*MI increases Palestinian violence decreases but this analysis shows that as TAs*MI increases so does Palestinian violence. The analysis, therefore, offers no support for the relationships asserted in H_4.

Discussion

The preceding analysis does not substantiate the claim that Israeli targeted assassinations have an effect on the rate of Palestinian attacks. Targeted assassinations do not quell violence, but they do not increase violence either. As a counterinsurgency tactic, their utility is questioned by the findings. Targeted assassinations do not fare much better when combined with military incursions that seek to destroy the resources, personnel, and organizational infrastructure of militant groups.

Expectations of deterrence (H_1) in response to

TABLE 27.5. Regression Models for Hypothesis 4

Weekly lag	Factors	Regression coefficient	ANOVA SeqSS/TotSS	p-value	Model R^2
0	TAs*MI	0.3005	2.1%	0.046	2.1%
	Constant	2.2815	*	0.000	
	TAs	−0.0798	*	0.699	5.5%
	MI	0.6429	5.4%	0.001	
	Constant	2.1043	*	0.000	
	MI	0.6357	5.4%	0.001	5.4%
	Constant	2.0617	*	0.000	
1	TAs*MI	−0.2047	*	0.177	1.0%
	Constant	2.4797	*	0.000	
	TAs	−0.2562	*	0.228	1.0%
	MI	0.1385	*	0.488	
	Constant	2.4761	*	0.000	
2	TAs*MI	−0.0087	*	0.954	0.0%
	Constant	2.4161	*	0.000	
	TAs	0.0058	*	0.978	0.7%
	MI	0.2262	*	0.259	
	Constant	2.2884	*	0.000	
3	TAs*MI	0.2623	*	0.084	1.6%
	Constant	2.3116	*	0.000	
	TAs	0.16	*	0.449	2.8%
	MI	0.4196	2.4%	0.036	
	Constant	2.095	*	0.000	
	MI	0.4332	2.5%	0.029	2.5%
	Constant	2.1822	*	0.000	
4	TAs*MI	0.3624	3.1%	0.017	3.1%
	Constant	2.2844	*	0.000	
	TAs	0.0486	*	0.820	0.8%
	MI	0.2322	*	0.249	
	Constant	2.2735	*	0.000	
	TAs	0.0705	*	0.741	0.1%
	Constant	2.386	*	0.000	
	MI	0.2362	*	0.238	0.8%
	Constant	2.3002	*	0.000	

$\alpha = 0.05$, *where value is not applicable.

targeted assassinations have been rejected outright by this analysis. Despite the targeted nature of Israeli assassinations and the consistency of their application to punish Palestinian militants without ceding any of their demands, violence did not decrease in a statistically significant way. Escalating costs of repression, it appears, have not served as selective disincentives for individual militants. Militants did not substitute violent tactics with nonviolent ones following a consistent repression policy that did not reward militancy with concessions. Despite Israel's persistent use of targeted assassinations and other measures to quell the violence, and despite Israel's determined refusal to concede any of the demands of the Palestinians while violence is taking place, attacks continued virtually unabated. One is hard pressed to find a more consistent repression policy than the one applied by Israel toward militant Palestinian factions. The findings also pose a challenge to the predication that targeted repression deters while indiscriminate repression provokes violence. Public support for suicide bombings against Israelis continued to increase as the insurgency developed. Three years into the insurgency, an October 2003 poll conducted by the Palestinian Center for Policy and Survey Research found that 74.5 percent of Palestinians support suicide bombings. In the period covered by this analysis, September 2000–June 2004, support for suicide bombings never went below 58.6 percent, which was in June 2004.

Expectations of backlash (H_2), which posit harsh repression will result in a massive, swift, and expanding mobilization, are also rejected in the case of targeted assassinations. All three of Francisco's (2004) conditions necessary for backlash—information transmission, continuity in leadership, and adaptive strategies by dissidents—were present. Although Palestinians continued to send attackers against Israeli targets, the rate of attacks did not vary significantly with the application of targeted assassinations to suggest a massive, swift, or expanding campaign of violence. In other words, targeted assassinations did not increase Palestinian terrorism beyond its "natural rate." This finding is consistent with the earlier study by Brophy-

Baermann and Conybeare (1994) that found that retaliation against Palestinian terrorism has no long-term deterrent or escalation effect.

Expectations of disruption (H_3) due to the elimination of organizational experience and valued cadres receive little support in this analysis. Targeted assassinations did indeed remove some of the most capable commanders available for planning and carrying out terrorist attacks, but by themselves they did not impact the number of attacks or the rate of successful attacks as the analysis indicates.

Expectations of diminishing capacity (H_4) implied in Sandler et al. (1983) and Enders and Sandler (1993, 2004) discussion of the need to target the resource endowments of terrorist groups (as opposed to simply increasing the costs of their tactics) is not confirmed, in that none of the predictors asserted in H_4 bear practical predictive significance to Palestinian violence levels.

What, then, explains the decline in the Palestinian attack success rate? Perhaps instead of the focus on offensive repressive strategies, an alternative explanation for this drop may be found in purely defensive measures such as target hardening through placement of security check points in the heart of Palestinian towns; the spread of police and military personnel in crowded public places vulnerable to attack; the building of the security barrier (wall of separation) that began in June 2002; closures of Palestinian towns; better human intelligence on terrorist cells; and growing public precautions against terrorist attacks. All these measures suggest a *diminishing opportunity effect*, whereby terrorists find it difficult to penetrate targets that were previously vulnerable to attack because of purely defensive measures. Targeted assassinations can do little to influence opportunities for violence, unless they target actual "ticking bombs" on their way to conduct an attack.

As was admitted earlier, the ongoing conflict between Israelis and Palestinians does not permit for the exploration of all the available (and yet to be gathered) data on the Palestinian–Israeli cycle of violence. Different coding methods and inclusion of unreported attacks may well alter the findings of this study. Moreover, it is premature to generalize the findings on targeted assassinations without further analysis of the factors that contributed to the decline in the success rate of Palestinian attacks. It would equally be premature to offer policy recommendations to countries currently fighting insurgencies or a war on terrorism with only one case study of targeted assassinations.

Nonetheless, this analysis, taken at face value, raises doubts about the effectiveness of targeted assassinations as a tactic in the arsenal of counter-terrorism measures. Targeted assassinations may signal a determination to fight back the terrorists and exhibit commitment not to succumb to their demands. They may also placate an angry public demanding tough measures to stop the terrorists. Politically, it may not be feasible for governments to fight terrorism by purely defensive measures. Targeted assassinations, however, should not be presented as a proven solution to patterns of political violence and rebellion. While targeted assassinations do not necessarily cause an increase in rates of political violence, it may be more valuable to allocate resources toward investments in defensive technologies to detect and intercept terrorists, harden potential targets that could attract terrorists, expansion of police and security forces in major cities that could be targeted by terrorists in the future, and acquiring human intelligence on known and potential terrorists. Given the controversial nature of targeted assassinations, it may well be that political leaders can jettison this tactic without hindering their overall ability to fight terrorism.

NOTES

1. The datasets utilized by the authors in this article can be made available to any interested party through a written request to: Mohammed M. Hafez, University of Missouri in Kansas City, Department of Political Science, 213 Haag Hall, 5100 Rockhill Road, Kansas City, MO 64110.
2. Molly Moore, "Fear of reprisals casts a pall on Jerusalem: Israelis desert restaurants and buses," *Washington Post*, 24 March 2004.
3. Interview with Frontline (PBS) for a documentary program entitled "Battle for the Holy Land." 4 April 2002.
4. For the full range of moral, ethical, and strategic dilemmas debated by Israelis, see Larry Derfner, "A strategic dilemma," *Jerusalem Post*, 26 October 2001; David B.

Rivkin, Jr., Lee A. Casey, and Darin R. Bartram, "Suicide attacks are war crimes, targeted killings aren't," *Jerusalem Post*, 8 November 2002; David Rudge, "Targeted killing–effective anti-terror or counterproductive?" *Jerusalem Post*, 7 January 2003; Yosef Goell, "Targeted killings and the Left," *Jerusalem Post*, 5 May 2003; Aryeh Dayan, "One day in five, the IDF attempts assassination," *Ha'aretz*, 21 May 2003; Gil Hoffman, "Targeted killings help put pressure on Hamas," *Jerusalem Post*, 17 June 2003; and Tuvia Blumenthal, "Targeted killings can save lives," *Ha'aretz*, 16 March 2004.

5. Pal Violence = $\beta_0 + \beta_1$ Targeted Assassinations + β_2 Military Incursions + β_3 Attack Success Rate + e.
6. G (Severe Pal Violence) = $\beta_0 + \beta_1$ Aggregate Numerical Severity + β_2 Victim Numerical Severity where G = Logit link function mapping the interval (0,1) into the whole real line guaranteeing that the model will produce a predicted probability between 0 and 1.
7. Pal Violence = $\beta_0 + \beta_1$ Targeted Assassinations + β_2 Military Incursions + β_3 Frequency Severity + e AND Attack Success Rate = $\beta_0 + \beta_1$ Targeted Assassinations + β_2 Military Incursions + β_3 Frequency Severity + e.
8. Pal Violence = $\beta_0 + \beta_1$ Targeted Assassinations∗Military Incursions + e AND Pal Violence = $\beta_0 + \beta_1$ Targeted Assassinations + β_2 Military Incursions + e AND Pal Violence = $\beta_0 + \beta_1$ Military Incursions + e.

REFERENCES

Box, G., W. Hunter, and J. Hunter. 1978. *Statistics for Experimenters*, New York: John Wiley & Sons, Inc.

Brockett, Charles D. 1995. "A protest-cycle resolution of the repression/Popular-protest paradox." In *Repertoires and Cycles of Collective Action*, ed. Mark Traugott. New Haven, CT: Duke University Press, pp. 117–144.

Brophy-Baermann, B., and J. A. C. Conybeare. 1994. "Retaliating against terrorism: Rational expectations and the optimality of rules versus discretion." *American Journal of Political Science* 38(1), pp. 196–210.

Costain, Anne N. 1992. *Inviting Women's Rebellion: A Political Process Interpretation of the Women's Movement*, Baltimore: Johns Hopkins University Press.

Davenport, Christian, Carol Mueller, and Hank Johnston. eds. 2005. *Repression and Mobilization*. Minneapolis: Minnesota University Press, pp. 58–84.

David, Steven R. 2003. "Israel's policy of targeted killing." *Ethics and International Affairs* 17(Spring), pp. 111–126.

Della Porta, Donatella. 1995. *Social Movements, Political Violence, and the State: A Comparative Analysis of Italy and Germany*, New York: Cambridge University Press.

Enders, Walter, and Todd Sandler. 1993. "The effectiveness of anti-terrorism policies: A vector-Autoregression-intervention analysis." *American Political Science Review* 87(4), pp. 829–844.

Enders, Walter, and Todd Sandler. 2004 "What do we know

about the substitution effect in transnational terrorism?" In *Research on Terrorism: Trends, Achievements and Failures*. ed. Andrew Silke. London: Frank Cass, pp. 119–137

Feierabend, Ivo K., and Rosalind L. Feierabend. 1972 "Systemic conditions of political aggression: An application of frustration-aggression theory." In *Anger, Violence, and Politics: Theories and Research*, ed. Ivo K. Feierabend et al. Englewood Cliffs, NJ: Prentice-Hall, pp. 136–183.

Ferrara, Federico. 2003. "Why regimes create disorder: Hobbes's dilemma during a Rangoon summer." *Journal of Conflict Resolution* 47, pp. 302–325.

Finkel, Steven E., Edward N. Muller, and Karl-Dieter Opp. 1989. "Personal influence, collective rationality, and mass political action: Evaluating alternative aodels with panel data." *American Political Science Review* 83(March), pp. 885–903.

Francisco, Ronald A. 1995. "The relationship between coercion and protest: An empirical evaluation in three coercive states." *Journal of Conflict Resolution* 39(June), pp. 263–282.

Francisco, Ronald A. 1996. "Coercion and protest: An empirical test in two democratic states." *American Journal of Political Science* 40 (November), pp. 1179–1204.

Francisco, Ronald A. 2004. "After the massacre: Mobilization in the wake of harsh repression." *Mobilization: An International Journal*, 9(2) (June), pp. 107–126.

Francisco, Ronald A. 2005. "The dictator's, dilemma." In *Repression and Mobilization*, eds. Christian Davenport, Carol Mueller, and Hank Johnston. Minneapolis: Minnesota University Press, 58–84.

Gamson, William, Bruce Fireman, and Steven Rytina. 1982. *Encounters with Unjust Authority*, Chicago, IL: Dorsey.

Ginkel, John, and Alastair Smith. 1999. "So you say you want a revolution: A game theoretic explanation of revolution in repressive regimes." *Journal of Conflict Resolution* 43(June), pp. 291–316.

Goldstein, Robert J. 1983. *Political Repression in Nineteenth Century Europe*, London: Croom Helm.

Gupta, Dipak K., Harinder Singh, and Tom Sprague. 1993. "Government coercion of dissidents: Deterrence or provocation?" *Journal of Conflict Resolution* 37(June), pp. 301–339.

Gurr, Ted Robert. 1968. "A causal model of civil strife: A comparative analysis using new indices." *American Political Science Review* 62(December), pp. 1104–1124.

Gurr, Ted Robert. 1970. *Why Men Rebel*, Princeton, NJ: Princeton University Press.

Gurr, Ted Robert. 1986 "Persisting patterns of repression and rebellion: Foundations for a general theory of political coercion." In *Persistent Patterns and Emergent Structures in a Waning Century*, ed. Margaret P. Karns. Westport, CT: Praeger, pp. 149–168.

Gurr, Ted Robert. 1993. "Why minorities rebel: A global analysis of communal mobilization and conflict since 1945." *International Political Science Review* 14, pp. 161–201.

Gurr, Ted Robert, and Will H. Moore. 1997. "Ethnopolitical rebellion: A cross-sectional analysis of the 1980s with risk assessments for the 1990s." *American Journal of Political Science* 41(October), pp. 1079–1103.

Hafez, Mohammed M. 2003. *Why Muslims Rebel: Repression and Resistance in the Islamic World*, Boulder, CO: Lynne Rienner Publishers.

Hardin, Russell. 1982. *Collective Action*, Baltimore, MD: Johns Hopkins University Press.

Hibbs, Douglas A., Jr. 1973. *Mass Political Violence: A Cross-National Causal Analysis*, New York: John Wiley & Sons.

Hoover, Dean, and David Kowalewski. 1992. "Dynamic models of dissent and repression." *Journal of Conflict Resolution* 36, pp. 150–182.

Khawaja, Marwan. 1993. "Repression and popular collective action: Evidence from the West Bank." *Sociological Forum* 8(March), pp. 47–71.

Koopmans, Ruud. 1997. "Dynamics of repression and mobilization: The German extreme right in the 1990s." *Mobilization* 2(September), pp. 149–164.

Lee, Chris, Sandra Maline, and Will H. Moore. 2000 "Coercion and protest: An empirical test revisited." In *Paths to State Repression: Human Rights Violations and Contentious Politics*, ed. Christian Davenport. Boulder, CO: Rowman and Littlefield, pp. 127–147

Lichbach, Mark I. 1987. "Deterrence or escalation? The puzzle of aggregate studies of repression and dissent." *Journal of Conflict Resolution* 31(June), pp. 266–297.

Lichbach, Mark I., and Ted Robert. Gurr. 1981. "The conflict process: A formal model." *Journal of Conflict Resolution* 25, pp. 3–29.

Luft, Gal. 2003. "The logic of Israel's targeted killing." *Middle East Quarterly* 10(1) (Winter), pp. 1–9.

Mason, David T. 1984. "Individual participation in collective racial violence: A rational choice synthesis." *American Political Science Review* 78(4), pp. 1040–1056.

Mason, David T., and Dale A. Krane. 1989. "The political economy of death squads: Towards a theory of the impact of state-sanctioned terror." *International Studies Quarterly* 33, pp. 175–198.

McCarthy, John D., and Mayer Zald. 1973. *The Trend of Social Movements in America: Professionalization and Resource Mobilization*, Morristown, NJ: General Learning.

McCarthy, John D., and Mayer Zald. 1977. "Resource mobilization and social movements: A partial theory." *American Journal of Sociology* 82, pp. 1212–1241.

Moore, Will H. 1998. "Repression and dissent: Substitution, context, and timing." *American Journal of Political Science* 42(July), pp. 851–73.

Moore, Will H. 2000. "The repression of dissent: A substitution model of government coercion." *Journal of Conflict Resolution* 44(February), pp. 107–127.

Muller, Edward N. 1985. "Income inequality, regime repressiveness, and political violence." *American Sociological Review* 50, pp. 47–61.

Muller, Edward N., and Karl-Dieter Opp. 1986. "Rational choice and rebellious collective action." *American Political Science Review* 80(June), pp. 471–487.

Muller, Edward N., and Mitchell A. Seligson. 1987. "Inequality and insurgency." *American Political Science Review* 81, pp. 425–449.

Muller, Edward N., and Erich Weede. 1990. "Cross-national variation in political violence." *Journal of Conflict Resolution* 34(December), pp. 624–651.

Muller, Edward N., Henry A. Dietz, and Steven E. Finkel. 1991. "Discontent and the expected utility of rebellion: The case of Peru." *American Political Science Review* 85(December), pp. 1261–1282.

Oberschall, Anthony R. 1973. *Social Conflict and Social Movements*, Englewood Cliffs, NJ: Prentice-Hall.

Oliver, Pamela. 1980. "Rewards and punishments as selective incentives for collective action." *American Journal of Sociology* 85, pp. 1356–1375.

Olivier, Johan L. 1990. "Causes of ethnic collective action in the Pretoria-Witwatersrand Triangle, 1970 to 1984." *South African Sociological Review* 2, pp. 89–108.

Olivier, Johan L. 1991. "State repression and collective action in South Africa, 1970–1984." *South African Journal of Sociology* 22, pp. 109–117.

Opp, Karl-Dieter, and Wolfgang Roehl. 1990. "Repression, micromobilization and political protest." *Social Forces* 69, pp. 521–547.

Rasler, Karen 1996. "Concessions, repression, and political protest in the Iranian revolution." *American Sociological Review* 61(February), pp. 132–152.

Sandler, Todd, John T. Tschirhart, and Jon Cauley. 1983. "A theoretical analysis of transnational terrorism." *American Political Science Review* 77, pp. 36–54.

Snyder, David. 1976. "Theoretical and methodological problems in the analysis of government coercion and collective violence." *Journal of Political and Military Sociology* 4, pp. 277–293.

Snyder, David, and Charles Tilly. 1972. "Hardship and collective violence in France, 1830–1960." *American Sociological Review* 37, pp. 520–532.

Stein, Yael. 2003. "Response to Israel's policy of targeted killing: By any name illegal and immoral." *Ethics and International Affairs* 17(1), pp. 127–137.

Tarrow, Sidney. 1989. *Democracy and Disorder: Protest and Politics in Italy, 1965–1975*, Oxford: Oxford University Press.

Tilly, Charles 1978. *From Mobilization to Revolution*, Boston, MA: Addison-Wesley.

Tilly, Charles, Louise Tilly, and Richard Tilly. 1975. *The Rebellious Century: 1830–1930*, Cambridge, MA: Harvard University Press.

White, Robert 1989. "From peaceful protest to guerrilla war: Micromobilization of the Provisional Irish Republican Army." *American Journal of Sociology* 94(May), pp. 1277–1302.

Zimmerman, Ekkart 1980 "Macro-comparative a research on political protest." In *Handbook of Political Conflict: Theory and Research*, ed. Ted R. Gurr. New York: Free Press, pp. 167–237.

Zimmermann, Ekkart 1983. *Political Violence, Crises and Revolutions*, Rochester, VT: Schenkman Publishing.

Received August 15, 2005
Accepted August 24, 2005 ■

What Happened to Suicide Bombings in Israel? Insights from a Terror Stock Model

Edward H. Kaplan,* Alex Mintz,** Shaul Mishal,*** and Claudio Samban***

An analysis of three years of suicide bombing data in Israel reveals an increase in such attacks through March 2002 followed by a steep decline through the end of 2003. The authors propose a terror-stock model that treats the suicide bombing attack rate as a function of the number of terrorists available to plan and execute suicide bombings. The intent of Israeli tactics such as targeted killings and preemptive arrests is to reduce the capacity of terror organizations to commit attacks. When fit to the data, this model suggests that the targeted killing of terror suspects sparks estimated recruitment to the terror stock that increases rather than decreases the rate of suicide bombings. Surprisingly, only the deaths of suspected terrorists, and not Palestinian civilians, are associated with such estimated recruitment. Although Israeli actions have reduced the rate of suicide bombings over time, it is preventive arrests rather than targeted killings that seem more responsible for this outcome.

Suicide bombings have emerged as a major method favored by terrorist organizations in recent years (Atran, 2003; Pape, 2003). In Israel, there have been 85 suicide bombings within the 1967 border (the Green Line) during 2001–2003. The suicide bombing rate was not constant over

* Yale School of Management and Yale School of Medicine, New Haven, Connecticut, USA.
** Department of Political Science, Texas A&M University, College Station, Texas, and United Nations Studies, Yale University, New Haven, Connecticut, USA.

*** Department of Political Science, Tel Aviv University, Tel Aviv, Israel.
    Address correspondence to Edward H. Kaplan, Yale School of Management and Yale School of Medicine, Box 208200, New Haven, CT 06520–8200, USA. E-mail: edward.kaplan@yale.edu

these 3 years: there were 8 suicide bombings during the first half of 2001, 13 suicide bombings in March 2002 alone, yet only 17 such bombings in all of 2003, and 3 bombings in the first half of 2004 (Figure 28.1).[1] To prevent suicide bombings, Israel has employed tactical measures such as the targeted killings of terrorist operatives and leaders, intelligence-driven arrests of suspected terrorists, and en route interceptions of suicide bombers at checkpoints or roadblocks. This article develops statistical models that relate Israeli actions to suicide bombing attempts to see if (and how) such tactics plausibly account for the rise and fall of suicide bombings observed in the data.

The modeling approach adopted here is motivated by an earlier article by Keohane and Zeckhauser (2003), who proposed that terrorist activity could be viewed as the "product" of a "stock" of terror. These authors thought broadly of the terror stock as that combination of human, physical, and monetary resources needed to launch terror attacks. Countering terrorism in this framework amounts to reducing the capacity of terrorist organizations to operate via direct assaults on terrorists themselves (a direct "stock-reducing" activity), or by reducing the flow of resources (money, manpower, weapons and so on) to terror groups.

Given the principally human capital expended in suicide bombing operations, this article models suicide bombing attempts as a function of the number of terrorists available for the planning and execution of such attacks, and refers us to this number as the terror stock. The intent of Israeli tactics is to reduce the size of the terror stock, and thus reduce the rate of terror attacks. Although the true number of terrorists cannot be directly observed and must therefore be treated as a latent variable, removals from the terror stock via Israeli tactics such as targeted killings, arrests, en route interception of suicide bombers (to be explained further later), in addition to removals due to suicide bombings themselves can be observed. This leaves the recruitment of terrorists as the key unobservable quantity that must be estimated statistically. A key question is whether Israeli tactics, in addition to directly removing terror operatives, also influence estimated terror recruitment. For example, both Atran (2003) and Pape (2003) have suggested that offensive military action or retaliation against terror organizations conducting suicide bombings are unlikely to succeed. The authors' model affords an opportunity to explore this hypothesis empirically. Finally, even though the size of the terror stock cannot be observed, the authors' models do produce very good estimates of the suicide bombing rate in Israel over time, both within the three years of their study, and also "out-of-sample" during the first four months of 2004, which suggests that the statistical relations uncovered, although not definitive, should be taken seriously.

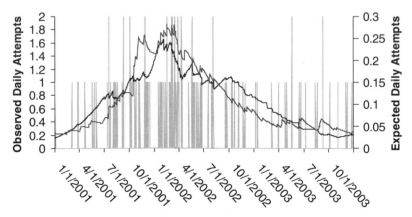

FIGURE 28.1 ■ Observed (gray bars scaled to left axis) and expected daily suicide bombing attempts (constant recruitment model [blue line], on-target hit-dependent recruitment model [red line], both scaled to right axis) in Israel, 2001–2003. (See Color Plate I at end of issue [of *Studies in Conflict and Terrorism*, 28(3)].)

Israeli Tactics and Data Sources

Perhaps Israel's most controversial prevention policy is the targeted killings (or hits) of suspected terrorists within guidelines demanding specific intelligence linking those targeted to impending terror attacks (Harel and Alon, 2002; David, 2003). B'tselem, the Israeli Information Center for Human Rights in the Occupied Territories, has maintained a database reporting the date, location, and names of those killed in such operations since September 2000, distinguishing between the deaths of those targeted and noncombatant civilians.[2] Table 28.1 summarizes the B'tselem data for the years 2001–2003. Although 44 of the reported 75 Israeli hits were "on-target" in that no civilians were killed, 10 hits were "botched" in that only civilians were killed. In the remaining 21 hits, both civilians and those targeted were killed. In total, Israeli hits killed 119 suspected terrorists and 80 civilians over 3 years. The cumulative number of target and civilian deaths over time appears in Figure 28.2.

Israel has also pursued the intelligence-driven capture and arrest of terror suspects by ground forces to prevent suicide bombings. These operations became much more frequent with the launch of Operation Defensive Shield following the suicide bombing that killed 30 and wounded another 140 Israelis at a Passover seder in Netanya on 27 March 2002. The Israel Defense Forces (IDF) does not report individual statistics regarding the number of terror suspects arrested for links to suicide bombings, but does provide monthly counts of "prevented suicide bombings" due to actions of the IDF, the General Security Services, or on occasion due to terrorist errors such as the premature detonation of explosives during bomb preparation.[3] However, in an unusually detailed announcement, the IDF reported the specifics of nine "prevented suicide bombings" during October through December 2003; all cases involved the arrests of terror suspects.[4] The IDF data are therefore interpreted as preventive arrests; the cumulative

TABLE 28.1. Summary of B'tselem Data Describing Israeli Targeted Hits on Suspected Terrorists

Hits killing	Number of hits	Number of civilian deaths	Number of target deaths
Only civilians	10	31	—
Civilians and targeted individuals	21	49	40
Only targeted individuals	44	—	79
Total	75	80	119

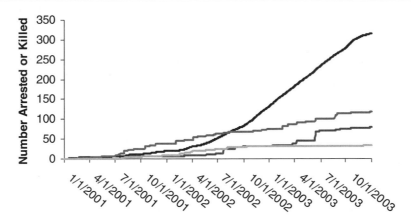

FIGURE 28.2 ■ From 2001–2003, cumulative numbers of: terror suspects arrested in connection with suicide bombings (dark blue); terror suspects killed in targeted hits (pink); Palestinian civilians killed in targeted hits (green); and terrorists intercepted en route to executing suicide bombings (turquoise blue). (See Color Plate II at end of issue [of *Studies in Conflict and Terrorism*, 28(3)].)

number of these events over time also appears in Figure 28.2.

In addition to the 85 suicide bombings that occurred during the study period, a review of Israeli and Palestinian media sources by the authors revealed that Israeli security personnel intercepted an additional 35 terrorists en route to carrying out suicide bombing attacks. Unlike preventive arrests, these publicized interceptions occurred at checkpoints or roadblocks along the route the suicide bomber was traveling (Figure 28.2).[5]

A Terror-Stock Model of Suicide Bombings

As previously discussed, this article views suicide bombings as the product of an underlying stock of terror capacity. This unobserved terror stock is denominated in units of terrorists. Increases in the terror stock thus reflect the recruitment of new terrorists, whereas decreases occur due to Israeli tactical actions or because of suicide bombings themselves. The terror stock in the model is updated daily as

$$s_t = s_{t-1} + r_{t-1} - b_{t-1} - a_{t-1} - h_{t-1} - i_{t-1} \quad (1)$$

where s_t denotes the terror stock at the beginning of day t, r_{t-1} is the number of terrorists recruited on day $t-1$, and b_{t-1}, a_{t-1}, h_{t-1}, and i_{t-1} refer to the number of terrorists removed from the stock on day $t-1$ due to suicide bombings, arrests (taken as the daily average of observed monthly totals), targeted hits, and interceptions, respectively. Given the relatively short time frame of the study, other sources of attrition from terror activity were ignored.

The authors define a suicide bombing attempt as an actual or intercepted suicide bombing (so there are 120 suicide bombing attempts in the data). The occurrence of suicide bombing attempts over time is modeled as a Poisson process with an expected λ_t attempts on day t. This mean level of attempts is linked to the terror stock via the equation

$$\log \lambda_t = \beta_0 + \beta_1 s_t \quad (2)$$

thus a unit decline in the terror stock (whether due to a tactical action or a suicide bombing) implies a $100 \times \beta_1\%$ reduction in the expected number of suicide bombing attempts providing $\beta_1 > 0$.

Table 28.2 reports maximum likelihood parameter estimates and associated standard errors for different versions of the terror-stock model estimated from the observed suicide bombing and prevention tactics data described earlier. The simplest model (column I in Table 28.2) presumes a constant daily recruitment rate (± standard error) estimated to equal 0.52 (±0.02) terrorists per day, or roughly 190 per year. The estimated β_1 value implies that each unit reduction in the terror stock corresponds to a 2.2% (±0.4%) reduction in the expected number of suicide bombing attempts. This model suggests that although reducing the terror stock has the desired effect of lessening the attempted suicide bombing rate (since $\beta_1 > 0$), recruitment replenishes the stock at a rapid rate. For example, the 75 targeted hits recorded in the B'tselem data killed 119 suspected terrorists for an average decrement in the terror stock of 1.6 terrorists per hit, yet at the estimated mean recruitment rate, this stock is restored after only three days.

Figure 28.1 shows observed (gray bars) and estimated daily suicide bombing attempts for the constant recruitment model (blue line). The model is broadly consistent with the observed data: when the estimated mean daily attack rate is high, observed bombing attempts occur with greater frequency (as seen by the clustering of the gray bars in the figure), although when the estimated attack rate is low, observed attempts are fewer and more widely spaced. The model suggests that the terror stock increased rapidly from the start of 2001 through March of 2002. During this time period, Israel pursued targeted killings of terrorist operatives in the West Bank, but as suggested previously, recruitment easily compensated for the resulting losses to the terror stock. With the launch of Operation Defensive Shield, Israel changed its tactics to focus more on arresting those believed to be involved with the planning and execution of suicide bombing missions (Figure 28.2). As is clear from Figure 28.1, this change

TABLE 28.2. Maximum Likelihood Estimation of Alternative Terror-Stock Models

Variable	Constant recruitment per day (I)	Hit-dependent recruitment (II)	Differential hit-dependent recruitment (III)	On-target hit-dependent recruitment (IV)	Differential death-dependent recruitment (V)
Constant	−3.714 (0.433)	−3.263 (0.456)	−3.260 (0.462)	−3.379 (0.342)	−3.206 (0.488)
Terror stock	0.022 (0.004)	0.018 (0.004)	0.012 (0.006)	0.016 (0.002)	0.024 (0.007)
Constant recruiting rate	0.518 (0.019)	−0.014 (0.235)	−0.187 (0.431)	—	0.095 (0.165)
Hit-dependent recruiting rate	—	7.591 (3.264)	—	—	—
Botched hit-dependent recruiting rate	—	—	−9.004 (18.139)	—	—
On-target hit-dependent recruiting rate	—	—	13.089 (8.559)	8.626 (0.419)	—
Civilian death-dependent recruiting rate	—	—	—	—	0.979 (0.682)
Terror suspect death-dependent recruiting rate	—	—	—	—	3.059 (1.394)
Log likelihood	−366.1	−361.0	−360.1	−360.4	−361.9
Estimated total recruitment	567	554	556	561	547

Cell entries report parameter estimates (standard errors) for the different recruitment models. Also reported is the log-likelihood and estimated total recruitment associated with each model. The log-likelihood function maximized is $\sum_{t=1}^{1095} ((b_t + i_t) \log \lambda_t - \lambda_t)$ where $b_t + i_t$ and λ_t are the observed and expected (via the terror-stock model) number of suicide bombing attempts on day t.

in tactics appears to have led to a reduction in suicide bombing attempts over the rest of 2002 and 2003.

The results of the constant recruitment model suggest that although Israel's policy of targeted hits failed to control suicide bombings, arresting terror suspects has met with greater success. Why might this be the case? Is it possible that the apparent failure of targeted hits to control suicide bombings is because such hits were too infrequent to have a meaningful impact on the terror stock relative to ongoing recruitment? Alternatively, as has been argued (Atran, 2003; Pape, 2003), are targeted killings counterproductive in that such hits motivate the recruitment of terrorists, in which case hits would serve to increase rather than decrease the terror stock? To explore these questions, the authors allowed the terror stock recruitment rate on day t to depend on hits at time t in accord with the formula

$$r_t = a_0 + a_1 x_t \qquad (3)$$

where x_t is the number of targeted hits executed by the IDF on day t, while a_0 and a_1 are parameters to be estimated. These parameters have natural interpretations: a_0 is the base daily recruitment rate irrespective of hits, whereas a_1 is the incremental number of new terror recruits in response to a hit. If hits serve to motivate recruitment, then a_1 will be positive; alternatively if hits deter recruitment, then a_1 would be negative. If a_1 equals zero, the constant recruitment discussed previously is obtained.[6]

The results from this analysis are shown in column II of Table 28.2. This hit-dependent recruitment model provides a significantly better statistical fit to the data than the constant recruitment model (likelihood-ratio $\chi^2 = 10.2$, $p = 0.0014$). The impact of a unit decrement in the terror stock is an estimated 1.8% (±0.4%) reduction in the expected suicide bombing attack rate, an effect similar to that estimated in the constant recruitment model. However, the estimated dependence of recruiting on hits is strong: each hit increases the terror stock by an estimated 7.6 (±3.3) recruits. Furthermore, the estimated base recruitment rate is not statistically different from zero, suggesting that hits account for all increases to the terror stock. Indeed, both the constant and hit-dependent recruitment models estimate similar total increases to the terror stock over the three years of the study (565 and 555, respectively), but the specific timing of recruitment differs—1 recruit every 2 days in the constant model versus 7.6 recruits following each targeted hit in the second model.

Although the analysis thus far has established a strong, positive statistical association between targeted hits and suicide bombing attempts via terror stock recruitment, is it plausible to treat this association as causal? Suppose that in a given month, terrorists select four different days on which to attempt suicide bombings in Israeli cities, but that Israeli intelligence agents obtain precise information regarding these plans. Suppose further that upon learning of these plans, Israeli authorities order targeted hits to prevent the bombings, but that only two hits are successful in doing so. At the end of the month, data would report that there were hits on four days, that there were suicide bombings following two of these hits, and that there were no suicide bombings on any other days. A statistical analysis of these data would suggest that hits were positively associated with suicide bombings, even though hits actually cut the number of suicide bombings in half. Might the present analysis suffer from a similar bias?

The B'tselem data provide an opportunity to address this concern. Although there were 75 hits carried out by the IDF, not all of these hits were successful in striking the intended targets. As shown in Table 28.1, 10 of these hits were botched in that only civilians were killed, whereas in the other 65 hits at least 1 of those targeted was killed. If the positive association between suicide bombing attempts and (via recruiting) targeted hits estimated in this analysis is an artifact of the timing of hits intended to disrupt bombings, this effect should be much stronger for botched hits that failed to kill those targeted than for on-target hits, and thus detectable in the data.

To test this proposition, the authors allowed the recruitment rate to depend differentially on botched versus on-target hits as

$$r_t = a_0 + a_1 x_t^B + a_2 x_t^T \qquad (4)$$

where x_t^B and x_t^T are the number of botched and on-target hits recorded in the B'tselem data on day t. The results are shown in column III of Table 28.2. First, distinguishing between botched and targeted hits does not improve the statistical fit of the model beyond our earlier hit-based recruitment model, which provides evidence against a differential effect of botched versus on-target hits on recruitment. Second, the estimated parameter values distinguishing the effects of botched versus on-target hits are inconsistent with the timing-artifact theory. Although the estimated effect of on-target hits is to increase the terror stock by 13.1 (±8.6) recruits per hit, botched hits are estimated to reduce the terror stock by 9 (±18) recruits per hit.

Not only do these results argue against the timing-artifact theory; they also suggest that although on-target hits motivate recruitment to the terror stock, botched hits fail to do so. Might it be that on-target hits alone account statistically for all of the increases to the terror stock? To investigate, the authors forced $a_0 = a_1 = 0$ in Equation (4) and reestimated the remaining three parameters. The results are shown in column IV of Table 28.2. The estimated effect of a unit reduction in the terror stock is a 1.6% (±0.2%) reduction in the daily attempted bombing rate, whereas each on-target hit is associated with 8.6 (±0.4) additions to the terror stock. Because 1.8 terror suspects are killed per on-target hit, this model suggests that on average, the terror stock increases by 6.8 for each on-target hit. These results are conditional on having forced $a_0 = a_1 = 0$, but Table 28.2 shows that the hypothesis cannot be rejected that only on-target hits spark recruitment.[7] Recruitment was also modeled as a function of the number of suspected terrorists and civilians killed (as opposed to the number of on-target and botched hits in Equation (4)), and found that although the terror stock responds to the deaths of terror suspects, there is no statistically significant effect of civilian deaths on recruitment (column V of Table 28.2), again refuting the timing-artifact theory.

The authors explored additional terror-stock model formulations allowing recruitment to depend on preventive arrests and successful suicide bombings in addition to targeted hits and preventive arrests (results not shown). They also investigated the effect of border closings and Israel's security fence: although there is evidence that border closings serve to facilitate preventive arrests, and that the security fence is protective in those locations where it exists (Figure 28.3),[8] none of these formulations change the results of the parsimonious on-target hit recruitment model (column IV of Table 28.2).

The daily expected number of suicide bombing attempts under the on-target hit recruitment model is shown in Figure 28.1 (red line).[9] Recalling that 35 out of 120 suicide bombing attempts were intercepted en route, successful suicide bombings can be predicted from this model by multiplying the estimated daily number of attempts by 85/120. The cumulative numbers of observed and modeled suicide bombings in Israel from 2001 through 2003 are shown in Figure 28.4. Data available on hits and preventive arrests through the end of April 2004 enable a further check on the reasonability of this model. There were an additional three suicide bombings in Israel during these four months. Using the parameters estimated from the 2001–2003 data, the model also predicts an additional three successful suicide bombings through the end of April 2004.

Discussion

This analysis suggests that preventive arrests, as opposed to the targeted killings of suspected terrorists, are responsible for the dramatic reduction in suicide bombings inside Israel since March 2002. Although on-target hits might remove an immediate terrorist threat, the present analysis suggests that such actions actually increase the terror stock via hit-dependent recruitment. It might be argued that because ground operations leading to preventive arrests place Israeli soldiers at great risk,

missile strikes against terrorists are a safer tactic, but again the analysis suggests a flaw in this reasoning: even if hits reduce risks to Israeli soldiers, hits increase the expected suicide bombing rate due to the impact of hit-dependent recruiting on the terror stock, in turn increasing suicide bombing risks to the Israeli public at large.

Preventive arrests hold a further advantage over targeted hits. Thinking of terror organizations as networks (Krebs, 2001; Farley, 2003), targeted killings serve only to knock out individual nodes (terrorists). Arrests enable the interrogation of terror suspects, which could lead to the discovery of links to more nodes in the terror network. It is difficult to interrogate the target of a successful missile strike. That the B'tselem data suggest that hits targeting terrorists have killed two civilians for every three suspected terrorist deaths (Table 28.1) further adds to the arguments against the use of targeted hits. The authors also discovered that, surprisingly, it is the killing of terror suspects, and not Palestinian civilians, that appears to spark estimated recruitment to the terror stock. One interpretation of this result is that the terror organizations do not care about civilian lives, and are only motivated to recruit and retaliate when their organizations are threatened. An alternative interpretation is that when Israeli-targeted hits go awry and many civilians are killed, terror organizations strategically choose to cease operations for a short time period, granting Palestinian leaders sympathetic attention from the media, world governments, and international bodies such as the United Nations.

To the authors' knowledge, this study provides the first empirical support for previous suggestions that offensive military measures are unlikely to prove effective against suicide bombings (Atran, 2003; Pape, 2003). To the extent that the Israeli experience generalizes to other countries facing suicide bombing threats such as Afghanistan, Iraq, Russia, or Sri Lanka, investing in intelligence that leads to preventive arrests stands a better chance of success. The key tactical question in preventing suicide bombings is how to reduce the terror stock without inadvertently replenishing it and unduly harming civilians. Israel continues to rely on targeted killings, but this analysis suggests such hits

Suicide Bombings in Hadera-Netanya

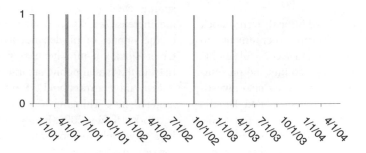

Suicide Bombings in Tel Aviv Area

Suicide Bombings in Jerusalem

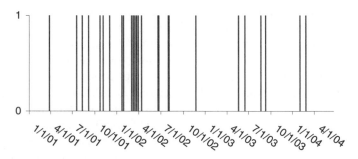

FIGURE 28.3 ■ Observed suicide bombings in areas now protected (Hadera-Netanya) and unprotected (Tel Aviv, Jerusalem) by Israel's security fence.

are counterproductive. Arresting suspected terrorists appears to reduce suicide bombings without inducing the recruitment of additional terrorists, and likely delivers intelligence information leading to further life-saving reductions in the terror stock.

NOTES

1. Data describing suicide bombings in Israel are available online from Israel's Ministry of Foreign Affairs (http://www.mfa.gov.il/mfa/terrorism-%20obstacle20to%20peace/palestinian%20terror%20since%202000/) and the Inter-

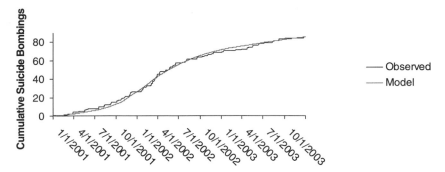

FIGURE 28.4 ■ Observed (blue) and expected (pink) cumulative suicide bombings in Israel, 2001–2003. Expected values derive from the on-target hit-dependent recruitment model (Table 28.2, column IV) adjusted for interceptions as explained in the text. (See Color Plate III at end of issue [of *Studies in Conflict and Terrorism*, 28(3)].)

national Policy Institute for Counter Terrorism's terror attack database (http://www.ict.org.il/arab_isr/arab-isr_frame.htm).

2. These data are available on-line from B'tselem (http://www.betselem.org/Hebrew/Statistics/Fatalities_Lists/Extrajudicial_Executions.asp; in Hebrew).

3. These data are available online from the Israel Defense Forces (http://www1.idf.il/dover/site/mainpage.asp?sl=EN&id=22&docid=16703).

4. This announcement is available online from the Israel Defense Forces (http://www1.idf.il/dover/site/mainpage.asp?clr=1&sl=HE&id=7&docid=26412; in Hebrew).

5. Numerous additional variables, including the terror organization sponsoring the attack, the origin and destination of each bomber, and whether there was a terror alert at the time of the attack have been assembled into a database for all suicide bombings and publicized interceptions in Israel during 2001–2003 (Mintz, A., Mishal, S., and Samban, C. 2004. "Suicide bombings in Israel." Available from the authors).

6. The authors also explored models where recruitment was allowed to depend on past hits via the formula $r_t = a_0 + a_1 \sum_{j=0}^{t} \theta^{t-j} x_j$ with θ restricted to fall between 0 and 1. Setting $\theta = 1$ makes recruitment depend on cumulative hits to date, whereas setting $\theta = 0$ forces recruitment to depend only on current hits as in Equation (3); intermediate values of θ allow past hits to influence current recruitment but with geometrically decreasing weight. It was found that setting $\theta = 0$ produced the best statistical fit to the data, thus the authors' comments are restricted to such formulations.

7. Because the on-target hit-dependent model is a special case of Equation (4) with $a_0 = a_1 = 0$, it can be tested whether restricting recruiting to depend only on on-target hits significantly worsens the fit of the model. Comparing the log-likelihoods in columns III and IV of Table 28.2, the 0.3 point change in the log-likelihood is not sufficient to reject the hypothesis that only on-target hits matter ($\chi^2 = 0.6$, $p = 0.74$).

8. The authors obtained the dates on which Israel's borders with the West Bank were sealed from the Spokesman's Office of Israel's Ministry of Defense, and investigated whether suicide bombing attempts differed by closure versus non-closure days controlling for targeted hits and preventive arrests via the terror-stock model. Although there was no significant effect of border closures within this analysis (results not shown), the authors note that the number of preventive arrests is significantly higher during closure periods. Specifically, during 196 border closure days there were 81 preventive arrests, a rate of 150.8 per year. During the remaining 899 non-closure days there were 232 preventive arrests, a rate of 94.2 per year. This difference is highly significant, and suggests that border closures serve to facilitate operations intended to apprehend terrorists.

In July 2002, Israel began constructing a security fence with the intent of preventing terrorist infiltrations into Israel from the West Bank. By the end of 2003, however, only about one-fourth of this fence was completely operational. Having obtained the completion dates of individual fence segments from the Head of Israel's Seam Line Project, the authors investigated whether the cumulative number of kilometers completed was predictive of attempted suicide bombings, again controlling for hits and preventive arrests via the terror-stock model. Although there was no significant effect within this framework (results not shown), simply examining the locations of successful suicide bombings over time suggests that there has been a shift in the locations of successful bombings away from those areas now protected by the fence, as shown in Figure 28.3. Hadera and Netanya are located along the Mediterranean coast, and were the first major cities to be fully protected by completed sections of the security fence. By contrast, neither Tel Aviv nor Jerusalem are fully protected as the fence has yet to be completed across access routes from the West Bank to those cities.

9. Goodness-of-fit tests show that the on-target hit-dependent model provides a satisfactory match to the data (Pearson $\chi^2 = 20.8$ ($p = 0.1433$); likelihood-ratio $\chi^2 = 18.6$ ($p =$

0.2324); 15 degrees of freedom after grouping to achieve expected cell counts of at least 5).

REFERENCES

Atran, S. 2003. "Genesis of suicide terrorism." *Science*, 299, pp. 1534–1539.

David, S. R. 2003. "Israel's policy of targeted killing." *Ethics and International Affairs*, 17, pp. 111–126.

Farley, J. D. 2003. "Breaking Al Qaeda cells: A mathematical analysis of counterterrorism options (a guide for risk assessment and decision making)." *Studies in Conflict & Terrorism*, 26, pp. 399–411.

Harel, A., and Alon, G. 2002. "IDF lawyers set 'conditions' for assassination policy." Ha'aretz, 4 February 2002. Available at (http://www.haaretzdaily.com/hasen/pages/ShArt.jhtml?itemNo=125404).

Keohane, N. O., and Zeckhauser, R. J. 2003. "The ecology of terror defense." *Journal of Risk and Uncertainty*, 26, pp. 201–229.

Krebs, V. E. 2001. "Mapping networks of terrorist cells." *Connections*, 24, pp. 43–52.

Pape, R. A. 2003. "The strategic logic of suicide terrorism." *American Political Science Review*, 97, pp. 343–361.

Received August 20, 2004
Accepted September 20, 2004 ■

Author Index

Abdollahi, A., 293
Abrams, D., 254
Abu-Amr, Z., 131, 132, 137
Abu-Nasr, D., 128
Abu Toameh, K., 131
Achen, C.H., 218
Achenbach, T.M., 62
Adamie, L., 12, 14
Adams, L.J., 69
Aiken, L.S., 217, 290
Akhtar, S., 72, 75
Albert, S., 343
Alexander, M.G., 255
Alexander, Y., 66, 68, 356, 413
Allport, G., 151
Alon, G., 469
Alon, H., 354
Al-Qaradhawi, Y., 150
al-Shaqaqi, F., 174
Alvarez, M.E., 166, 168
al-Zahhar, M., 175
Amos, J., 378
Anand, V.S., 15
Anders Strindberg, N.T., 65, 78
Anderson, N.B., 69
Andriolo, K., 188
Angrist, J., 207
Arblaster, A., 31
Arce, D.G., 64, 65
Armstead, C.A., 69
Armstrong, K., 67, 76
Arndt, J., 283, 292, 293, 294, 295
Arnold, T.E., 413
Aronson, E., 343, 411
Art, R.J., 170
Ashley, K., 319
Atash, N., 40
Aten, B., 225
Atkinson, S., 214, 381
Atran, S., 37, 47, 62, 67, 152, 153, 467, 468, 471, 473

August, M., 59, 60
Aveni, A.F., 308
Avrich, P., 15, 376
Axell, A., 147
Axelrod, R., 153
Ayers, B., 319
Azam, J.-P., 63, 65

Back, K.W., 340
Badey, T.J., 56
Baghdadi, J., 59, 60
Bainbridge, W.S., 311, 337, 338, 339, 340
Bakr, A., 173
Baldwin, D.A., 380
Baldwin, M.W., 283
Ballif-Spanvill, B., 56, 77
Bandura, A., 67, 325
Banker, L.J., 383, 385, 398
Barb, K.H., 308
Barber, B.K., 62, 151
Bargh, J.A., 36, 50
Barko, A., 44
Barlow, S.H., 56, 77
Barnard, C.I., 130
Barnes, J.A., 309
Baron, R.M., 261
Baron, R.S., 341
Barr, C.W., 127
Bartram, D.R., 448
Bassiouni, M.C., 337
Baumann, M., 30
Bazerman, M., 153
Bearden, M., 163
Beck, N., 222
Becker, E., 283
Becker, G., 150, 203, 386, 387
Becker, J., 333, 334
Begin, M., 31, 71
Behar, R., 419, 422
Bem, D.J., 343

Benario, S., 9
Bennet, J., 69
Benson, M., 229
Ben-Yishai, R., 136, 138, 139
Bergensen, E., 11
Berkowitz, L., 38
Berrebi, C., 38
Best, G., 413
Beyer, L., 425
Billig, M., 68
Billig, O., 307, 333, 334, 335, 336
Bird, F., 339
Birum, C., 69
Bishop, G.D., 342
Björgo, T., 243
Blomberg, S.B., 223
Bloom, M., 160, 172
Blumenthal, T., 448
Boix, C., 168
Böllinger, L., 71, 72, 104, 333, 334, 335
Borah, L.A., 64
Boustany, N., 30
Bowen, B.D., 257
Bowen, R., 66
Box, G., 452
Bozeman, A.B., 412
Braden, M., 339, 340
Brannan, D.W., 65, 78
Branscombe, N.R., 254
Braungart, M.M., 235
Braungart, R.G., 235
Brehm, J.W., 351
Brennan, G., 14
Breus, M., 292
Brewer, M.B., 254, 256, 265
Brock, S., 355
Brock, T.C., 355
Brockett, C.D., 446
Brody, G.H., 69
Brooks, A., 76
Brooks, D., 65, 151
Brophy-Baermann, B., 65, 448, 463
Brown, G.L., 28
Brown, P.A., 60
Brown, R., 256, 341
Bruce, S., 311
Brumfiel, G., 78
Bruno, F., 28, 59, 60, 102, 103
Bryant, E.T., 40, 74
Brynen, R., 187
Buck, A., 76
Budner, S., 74
Bultena, G.L., 308
Bunney, W.G., Jr., 28
Burnstein, E., 341
Burt, R.S., 309
Burtsev, V., 12
Buruma, I., 46, 47, 269

Cacioppo, J.T., 40, 355

Calvert, G., 324
Cameron, A.C., 218
Canetti, D., 69, 74
Carey, B., 59
Carleton, D., 411
Carmichael, S., 322
Caro, J., 234
Carr, C., 42, 43
Carr, E.H., 9
Carroll, L., 95
Carter, A., 327, 328, 329
Caselli, G., 314
Casey, R.D., 310
Casey, W.J., 410
Cassirer, E., 412
Cauley, J., 64, 449, 451, 463
Chaiken, S., 153
Chammah, A.M., 64
Chapin, D., 148
Chatel, D., 289, 291
Chatterjee, S., 219
Cheibub, J.A., 166, 168
Chiang, A., 389, 402
Chirol, V., 15
Chivers, A., 151
Chomsky, N., 145, 270
Chun, W.Y., 36
Classens, D., 104
Clark, E.T., 338
Clark, L.A., 285
Clark, R., 58, 59, 69, 105, 149, 239, 334
Clayton, C.J., 56, 77
Cline, R.S., 413
Clutterbuck, R., 160
Clutton-Brock, T.H., 76
Coady, C.A.J., 414, 415
Cohen, F., 283, 284, 292, 293, 295
Cohn, S.J.D., 24
Collier, P., 209
Collins, L., 355
Colomer, J.M., 217
Confino, M., 31
Contorreggi, C.S., 40, 74
Conybeare, J.A.C., 65, 448, 463
Cook, A., 293
Coombs, G., 310
Cooper, H.H.A., 24, 28, 29, 62, 63, 101, 103, 337
Corbett, M., 69
Cordes, B., 331, 336, 337, 347
Corrado, R.R., 28, 64, 72, 78, 96, 97, 98, 99
Corsi, J.R., 383, 384, 385, 386, 397
Costain, A.N., 446
Cox, R., 66
Crayton, J.W., 71, 72, 76
Crenshaw, M., 31, 45, 60, 63, 64, 65, 66, 67, 69, 71, 77, 78, 97,
    102, 105, 130, 159, 162, 213, 319, 326, 329, 330, 332, 333,
    334, 335, 336, 337, 373, 384, 386
Cronin, P.M., 170
Crozier, B., 67
Culyer, A.J., 401

Cutrona, C.E., 69

Dahl, R.A., 213
Dahl, R.E., 75
Daniels, S., 325
Danizewski, J., 67
Davenport, C., 446
David, H., 12
David, S.R., 448, 469
Davidson, K., 323
Davies, J.C., 68, 348
Dayan, A., 448
De Figueiredo, R., 172
de Graaf, J., 337
Deininger, K., 225
della Porta, D., 63, 77, 307, 308, 314, 446
Demaris, O., 333, 334, 335
DeMause, L., 79
DeNardo, J., 48, 371, 373, 375, 377
Denny, L.M., 40, 61, 63, 64, 69, 77
de Quervain, D.J.-F., 76
Derfner, L., 448
Deutsch, A., 338, 339
Deutsch, K.W., 64
Deutsch, M., 341
Devine, P.E., 73, 353
DeYoung, K., 277
Dickey, C., 186
Dietz, H.E., 449
Dixon, W.J., 217
Dohrn, B., 319
Dollard, J., 68
Doob, L.W., 68
Dorsch, C.C., 45
Douglass, W.A., 79
Dovidio, J.F., 265
Downs, A., 386
Droppleman, P., 76
Dublin, L., 189
Duckitt, J., 69
Dugard, J., 42
Dumont, L., 270
Dunning, D., 45
du Plessis, I., 69
Durkheim, E., 186, 187, 193
Dworetzky, J.P., 96
Dwyer, J., 420, 422

Eagly, A., 153
Edelbrock, C., 62
Edelman, M., 327
Edler Baumann, C., 160
Ehrlich, I., 386, 387
Eisen, S.V., 96
Eisenstadt, D., 283
el Sarraj, E., 72, 76
Elliott, P., 161
Ellsburg, D., 379
Enders, W., 56, 65, 203, 213, 219, 224, 225, 451, 463
Ergil, D., 188

Erickson, B.H., 310
Ericson, E.E., Jr., 324
Erikson, E., 71
Eriksson, M., 225
Ernst, M., 40, 74
Eslerm, P.F., 65, 78
Esposito, J., 284
Eubank, W.L., 58, 59, 70, 77, 211, 212, 213, 217
Evans, M., 229
Eyerman, J., 211, 212, 213, 214, 217
Ezekiel, R., 150

Fairbank, J.A., 69
Fanon, F., 69, 71
Faour, M., 257
Farley, J.D., 473
Fearon, J., 209, 215
Feger, H., 104
Fehr, E., 76
Feierabend, I.K., 446
Feierabend, R.L., 446
Feldmann, T.B., 96, 98, 100
Feldner, F., 127
Ferejohn, J., 64, 66
Ferracuti, F., 28, 36, 48, 59, 60, 63, 64, 71, 78, 102, 103, 104, 105, 328, 349
Ferrara, F., 446
Festinger, L., 336, 340, 343
Figner, V.N., 13, 378
Finkel, S.E., 449
Fireman, B., 446
Fischbacher, U., 76
Fishbach, A., 36
Fleming, P., 189
Florian, V., 282, 293
Foley, C., 31
Forbes, J.F., 399
Francisco, R., 446, 450, 463
Franklin, J., 27
Fraser, S.C., 343
Frazza, L., 442
Freedman, J.L., 343, 355
Freud, S., 71, 79
Fried, R., 72
Friedland, N., 38, 55, 66, 68, 76, 77, 337, 351, 357
Friedman, R., 36, 45, 294, 428
Friedman, T., 29, 30, 150, 152
Frolenko, M., 11
Fromkin, D., 349
Fromm, E., 283

Gabbard, G.O., 70, 71
Gaertner, S.L., 265
Galanter, M., 338, 339
Gamson, W.A., 373, 446
Ganor, B., 42, 137, 138, 186, 188, 189, 191
Garner, R., 308
Gates, S., 223
Gazzaniga, M.S., 74
George, A., 159, 168

Georges-Abeyie, D.E., 332
Gerard, H., 341
Gerlach, L.P., 308
Gibbons, E.F., Jr., 97
Gilbert, D., 324
Gilbert, S.J., 342, 343
Gillespie, J., 151
Ginkel, J., 446
Glaser, J., 205, 288, 289, 295
Gleditsch, N.P., 223, 225
Goell, Y., 448
Gold, S.N., 63
Goldberg, J., 125, 132, 136
Golden, C.J., 40, 74
Goldenberg, J.L., 283, 287, 289, 292
Golder, M., 217
Goldman, E., 14
Goldman, J.J., 424
Goldstein, R.J., 446
Golec, A., 48
Gollwitzer, P.M., 36, 50
Goodwin, F.K., 28
Gopal, P., 15
Gottlieb, R., 324
Grady, K., 355
Grant, S.J., 40, 74
Grathwohl, L., 318, 320
Green, D., 205
Greenberg, J., 162, 254, 282, 283, 284, 285, 287, 289, 291, 292, 293, 295, 296
Greene, W.H., 222
Gross, F., 9
Grossman, D., 65
Guillaume, J., 10
Gunaratna, G., 56
Gunaratna, R., 48, 49, 188
Gupta, D.K., 446
Gurr, T., 38, 41, 68, 348, 383, 385, 386, 446

Haas, R.G., 355
Haber, A., 323
Habermas, J., 318
Hacker, F.J., 62, 75, 77, 348
Haddad, Y.V., 432
Hadi, A.S., 219
Hafez, M.M., 446
Hager, R., Jr., 41
Halevi, Y.K., 138
Halloran, M.J., 288
Hamad, G., 59, 60
Hamilton, C.V., 322
Hamilton, J.D., 384
Hamilton, L.C., 384
Hamilton, W., 153
Hamlen, W., 387
Handelsman, M., 343
Handler, J.S., 59
Harbinson, H.J., 103
Hardin, R., 446, 449
Hardyck, J.A., 339, 340

Hare, R.D., 97
Harel, A., 139, 469
Harihara, M., 282, 288
Harmon, C.C., 68
Harmon-Jones, E., 283
Haroun, A.M., 78
Harris, T., 355
Harrison, M., 343
Hasisi, B., 68
Hassan, N., 59, 62, 123, 125, 127, 137, 138, 151, 204
Hassel, C., 98, 100, 101
Havens, M.C., 9
Hayden, T., 318, 321, 323
Hecht, R., 428
Heikal, M., 431
Heiman, R.J., 39
Heine, S.J., 282, 288
Heineke, J.M., 386
Henry, P.J., 39, 255, 256, 257, 263, 264, 270, 277
Heskin, K., 28, 63, 103, 333, 342
Hess, G.D., 223
Heston, A., 225
Hibbs, D.A., Jr., 189, 446
Higgins, T., 40
Hildermeier, M., 14
Hillenbrand, C., 47
Hine, V.H., 308
Hinkle, S., 256
Hirschman, A.O., 308
Hoagland, J., 377
Hodgins, S., 97
Hoeffler, A., 209
Hoffer, E., 77
Hoffman, B., 41, 42, 56, 57, 65, 76, 131, 158, 285, 331, 333, 336, 337, 347
Hoffman, G., 448
Hoffman, R.P., 42
Hogarth, R., 64, 66
Hogg, M.A., 254
Holmes, J.G., 293
Homans, G.C., 308
Hoover, D., 446
Horgan, J., 37, 56, 63
Horowitz, M., 167
Hosenball, M., 186
Hovland, C., 205
Hroub, K., 167
Hubbard, D.G., 27, 60, 72, 102
Huber, J.D., 215, 217
Huddy, L., 254
Hughes, M., 308
Hunter, J., 452
Hunter, R., 12
Hunter, W., 452
Huntington, S.P., 168, 269, 284, 348
Hussien, S.A., 270
Hutchings, B., 40, 74
Hutchinson, M.C., 332, 333, 334

Ibrahim, S.E., 432

Ignatieff, M., 285
Ignatius, D., 46
Inbar, E., 173
Israeli, R., 186
Ivanski, A.I., 15
Iviansky, Z., 25, 307

Jaber, H., 137
Jackson, R.L., 430
Jacobs, H., 319, 320
Jacobs, J., 319
Jacobson, P., 129
Jäger, H., 60, 63, 72, 75, 104
Jaggers, K., 217, 225
Jai, J.J., 150
Jaime, O., 228
Jansen, J.J.G., 431
Jefferson, P., 205
Jenkins, B., 56, 78, 158, 161, 331, 336, 337, 347, 348, 350, 356, 357, 383, 386, 394, 395
Jensen, R.B., 44
Jervis, R., 169
Jodice, D., 189
Johns, M., 283, 289, 292
Johnson, C., 348
Johnson, J., 383, 386, 394, 395
Johnson, K., 187
Johnson, M., 186
Johnson, P.W., 96, 98, 100
Johnston, H., 446
Jonas, E., 283
Jones, J., 319
Jongman, A.J., 42, 96, 97, 104, 160
Jöreskog, K.G., 272
Josephus, 24
Joshi, M., 186
Jost, J.T., 288, 289, 295
Juergensmeyer, M., 75, 76, 125, 127, 129, 130, 428

Kadi, L., 31
Kandel, E., 40, 74
Kaplan, A., 326, 412, 413
Kaplan, E., 47
Kappen, D., 254
Kashima, E.S., 288
Katz, J., 222
Kaufmann, C.D., 177
Kellen, K., 75, 327, 331, 336, 337, 347, 348
Keller, B., 203
Kelley, J., 127, 136
Kelly, R.J., 67
Kelman, H.C., 265
Kelsay, J., 430
Keniston, K., 312
Kenny, D.A., 261
Keohane, N.O., 468
Kepel, G., 67, 432
Khalaf, R., 443
Khaled, L., 371
Khawaja, M., 446, 450

Kimes, A.S., 40, 74
King, D.W., 69
Kirgegaard-Sorenson, L., 40, 74
Kirkpatrick, J., 414
Kitayama, S., 39
Klandermans, B., 314
Klein, A., 59, 60
Knop, J., 40, 74
Knutson, B., 76
Knutson, J.N., 307, 319, 326, 329, 333
Kocieniewski, D., 419, 420, 422
Kohlberg, L., 44
Kohut, H., 71, 72
Koopmans, R., 446
Kopkind, A., 323
Kornhauser, W., 308
Kowalewski, D., 446
Kramer, M., 168, 170, 171
Kramer, N., 158
Krane, D.A., 446, 449
Krause, R.M., 64
Kravshinsky, S., 378
Krebs, V.E., 473
Kroes, R., 328
Kropotkin, P., 10, 25, 31
Krosnick, J.A., 257
Krueger, A.B., 37, 38, 60, 68, 69, 150, 442
Kruglanski, A.W., 36, 40, 45, 47, 48, 50, 288, 289, 295
Krupskaya, N., 18
Kupperman, R.H., 355
Kushner, H., 136, 137, 186
Kuznets, S., 205
Kydd, A., 172

Laabs, D., 59
Laitin, D.D., 38, 209, 215, 239
Lake, D.A., 41
Landau, M.J., 283, 289, 292, 293
Lander, L.E., 68
Landes, W., 203
Lapan, H.E., 64, 65
Lapierre, D., 355
Laqueur, W., 26, 30, 38, 56, 65, 68, 75, 78, 97, 104, 124, 158, 331, 332, 333, 334, 335, 337
Lasch, C., 29, 99, 102
Laschi, R., 27
Lasswell, H.D., 310
Lebow, R.N., 169
Lee, C., 446
Legrain, J.-F., 429
Lehman-Wilzig, S.N., 189
Leiden, C., 9
Lelyveld, J., 126
Lepisto, E.M., 69
Levin, S., 39, 254, 255, 256, 257, 258, 263, 264, 265, 270, 277
Levine, S., 75, 76
Levitt, M., 134
Lewis, B., 25, 146, 148, 158, 269
Lezak, M.D., 74
Li, Q., 212, 214, 217, 218, 223, 225

Lichbach, M.I., 446, 449
Lifton, R.J., 73, 283, 285
Light, D., Jr., 327
Limongi, F., 166
Linton, R., 337
Lipset, S., 348
Lisk, G., 415
Little, C.B., 337
Livingstone, N.C., 307, 413
Lluch, E., 239
Lofland, J., 308, 337, 338
Lombroso, C., 14, 27
London, E.D., 40, 74
Long, G., 319
Long, J.S., 217
Loo, C.M., 69
Lopez, G.A., 411
Luft, G., 448
Lynch, C., 152
Lynd, S., 322
Lyon, D., 283, 285
Lyons, H.A., 103

MacCrimmon, K., 64, 66
Machina, M.J., 64, 66
Machtinger, H., 319
MacLeod, S., 59, 60
MacStiofain, S., 376
Mahmood, C.K., 79
Maitron, J., 378
Makovsky, D., 173
Malakoff, D., 148
Maleckova, J., 37, 60, 68, 69, 150, 442
Maline, S., 446
Malle, B.F., 258, 277
Mann, J., 430
March, J.G., 371
Margalit, A., 46, 47, 269
Marighella, C., 31, 67, 378
Markham, J.M., 26
Markus, H.R., 39
Marlowe, L., 125
Marsella, A., 42
Marshall, M.G., 217, 225
Marshall, T., 67
Martens, A., 283, 289, 292
Martin, R.C., 430, 432
Marton, K., 75
Mason, D.T., 446, 449
Mathey, M., 282
Maxfield, M., 283, 295
Maya, M.L., 68
McCarthy, J.D., 450
McCauley, C., 37, 41, 43, 341, 342
McCoy, S.K., 287
McDermott, T., 59
McGregor, I., 293
McGuire, M., 376
McGuire, W.J., 355
McNeilly, M.D., 69

McPhail, C., 310
Mednick, S.A., 40, 74
Mellen, J., 319
Meloy, J.R., 76
Melucci, A., 308
Merari, A., 38, 55, 60, 61, 63, 66, 68, 74, 76, 122, 123, 137, 138, 150, 158, 168, 186, 188, 351, 429
Mesulam, M.-M., 74
Meyer, R.A., 387
Mickolus, E., 70, 216, 350, 383, 384, 385, 386, 393, 394, 395, 399, 401
Midlarsky, M.I., 329, 373, 384, 386
Mikulincer, M., 282, 293
Milburn, T.W., 64, 66
Miles, M., 323
Milgram, S., 148, 342, 343, 344
Miller, B.H., 59, 209, 307, 332, 333, 336, 383, 385, 398
Miller, D., 310
Miller, N.E., 68
Miller, W.H., 76
Millon, T., 99, 100, 101
Mills, J., 355
Mintz, A., 47, 470
Mishal, K., 175
Mishal, S., 47, 131, 164, 470
Mitchell, C., 411
Moghadam, A., 122, 188
Monti, D.J., 348
Moore, M., 446
Moore, W.H., 446
Moran, S., 331, 336, 337, 347
Morf, G., 29, 72, 102
Morgan, R., 229
Morgenstern, O., 64, 66
Morgenthau, H.J., 412
Morozov, N., 9, 16, 19, 31
Morris, H., 129
Moscovici, S., 341, 342
Mowrer, W., 68
Moxon-Browne, E., 352
Mueller, C., 446
Mueller, D.C., 386
Muller, E.N., 329, 348, 371, 446, 449
Murdock, J.M., 216
Murphy, D., 420, 422
Murphy, K., 423
Murry, V.M., 69
Mustafa, N., 59, 60
Myers, D., 341, 342

Neff, D., 208
Neidhardt, F., 104
Netanyahu, B., 355, 356
Neto, F., 69
Nettler, R.L., 432
Neumayer, E., 223
Newell, D.A., 373
Newhouse, J., 337
Niebuhr, R., 161
Niiya, Y., 282, 288

Noffsinger, S., 62
Nusse, A., 167
Nye, J., 14, 416, 443

Oberschall, A., 308, 311, 446, 449
O'Brien, C.C., 29, 374
O'Brien, J.P., 322
Ochsmann, R., 282
Ogilvie, D.M., 284
Oliver, A.M., 425
Oliver, P., 446, 449
Olivier, J.L., 446
Olson, M., Jr., 308, 399
Olsson, P.A., 71
O'Neill, R., 158
Oots, K.L., 329
Opp, K.D., 371, 446, 449
O'Sullivan, A., 140

Paine, L., 103
Palazzi, A.H., 123
Palombarini, G., 312
Papageorgis, D., 355
Pape, R., 37, 38, 46, 158, 159, 162, 163, 165, 166, 168, 467, 468, 471, 473
Parker, G.A., 76
Paz, R., 41, 123, 125, 126, 128
Pearce, K.I., 28, 62, 63, 99, 101
Pearlstein, R.M,, 71, 79, 99
Pedahzur, A., 59, 64, 68, 69, 74
Pepitone, A., 343
Perliger, A., 59, 64
Peters, G.B., 189
Peters, R., 430
Petrocik, J.R., 265
Pettit, G.S., 75, 79
Petty, R., 40, 355
Pfefferbaum, B., 45
Phillips, C., 308
Pieper, C.F., 69
Pierre, A., 383
Pierro, A., 40
Pilsudski, J., 17
Pinard, M., 308
Pinkas, A., 173
Pizzorno, A., 308, 313
Pobog-Malinowski, W., 17
Podesta, D., 30
Podhoretz, N., 356
Ponterotto, J.G., 69
Ponton, L.E., 75
Post, J.M., 40, 56, 59, 61, 63, 64, 69, 72, 76, 77, 97, 99, 104, 105, 130, 158, 168, 326, 329, 333, 335, 336, 337
Powell, G.B., Jr., 216, 217
Pratto, F., 38, 39, 68, 254, 255, 256, 257, 258, 263, 264, 270, 277
Pribyleva Korba, A.P., 13
Price, B., 219
Pryor, F.L., 205
Przeworski, A., 166, 168

Pyle, D.H., 392
Pyszczynski, T., 254, 282, 283, 284, 285, 287, 289, 291, 292, 293, 295, 296

Quattrone, G.A., 96
Quayle, E., 40, 67, 68, 69, 71, 74, 97
Qutb, S., 432

Rabin, Y., 174
Rabinowitz, J., 254
Rabkin, J., 338, 339
Rabkin, R., 338, 339
Rafalko, R.J., 73, 353
Rageh, R., 278
Raine, A., 97
Rank, O., 283
Raper, A., 204, 205
Rapoport, A., 64
Rapoport, D.C., 24, 25, 41, 44, 66, 126, 158, 161, 327, 328, 413, 431
Rasch, W., 28, 6, 77, 103
Rasler, K., 446
Reagan, R., 170
Rees, M., 59, 60
Reich, W., 25, 50, 56, 57, 63, 72, 77, 78, 160
Reimer, B., 339
Reinares, F., 228
Reiter, D., 167
Rekhess, E., 429
Resnick, P.J., 62
Reynal-Querol, M., 216, 217
Rhode, D., 151
Rich, A., 205
Rieber, R.W., 67
Riecken, H.W., 340
Riemer, W.J., 187
Rivkin, D.B., Jr., 448
Robbins, T., 319
Roberts, A., 64, 66
Robins, R.S., 72
Robinson, E.L., 69
Rochford, E.B., 308
Roehl, W., 446
Rogers, D.L., 308
Rogers, W.H., 218
Ronfeldt, D., 31, 383, 386, 394, 395
Roots, C.A., 326
Rosato, S., 168
Rosenberg, D., 71
Rosenberg, R., 40, 74
Rosenblatt, A., 283, 285
Rosenhan, D.L., 96
Ross, J.I., 211, 213, 214
Ross, L., 149
Rotella, S., 77
Roth, A., 64, 66
Routledge, C., 293
Rubin, E., 186
Rubin, J.Z., 337
Ruch, L.O., 69

Rudd, M., 319
Rudge, D., 448
Rummel, R.J., 43
Russell, C.A., 59, 209, 307, 336, 383, 385, 398
Russell, C.V., 332, 333
Ryan, H., 57, 76, 77
Rytina, S., 446

Sachs, S., 419
Sageman, M., 37, 38, 39, 49, 59, 61, 67, 68, 72, 73, 76, 77
Said, E., 257, 271, 278
Saleh, B., 442
Salvioni, D., 334
Samban, C., 47, 470
Sanders, G.S., 341
Sandler, T., 56, 64, 65, 203, 212, 213, 214, 216, 219, 224, 225, 381, 398, 399, 400, 401, 449, 451, 463
Saper, B., 67, 75
Sater, W., 31, 331, 336, 337, 347
Satterfield, J.M., 40, 74
Sauvagnargues, P., 171
Savarkar, D.K.V., 15
Savio, M., 323
Schachter, S., 340, 341
Schalk, P., 163
Schaub, D., 212, 214, 217, 218, 223, 225
Schbley, A.H., 65, 188
Schellhammer, M., 76
Schelling, T., 159, 379
Schiff, Z., 120, 128, 129, 134
Schimel, J., 292, 295
Schlesinger, L.B., 76
Schmemann, S., 134
Schmid, A.P., 42, 56, 68, 69, 96, 97, 104, 160, 189, 213, 214, 331, 337, 347, 349
Schmidtchen, G., 28, 60, 63, 72, 75, 104
Schmitt, K.M., 9
Schmitt, M.T., 254
Schnyder, U., 76
Schück, H., 11
Schulsinger, F., 40, 74
Schultz, R., 56
Schwartz, S.H., 256
Schweitzer, G.E., 45
Schweitzer, Y., 185, 186, 188
Sciolino, E., 152, 166
Scott, G.E.J., 97
Scott, J.C., 270
Scott, M.L., 40, 74
Scurfield, R.M., 69
Sears, D.O., 355
Sears, R.R., 68, 205
Seaver, B., 263
Segal, H., 208
Sela, A., 131, 164
Seligson, M.A., 446
Serge, V., 14
Shafritz, J.M., 97
Shah, J.Y., 36, 40, 45
Shaked, R., 126

Shallah, R., 175
Shaw, E.D., 71, 104
Shay, S., 188
Shikaki, K., 41, 42, 47, 48, 49, 167
Shternberg, L., 16
Sidanius, J., 38, 39, 68, 74, 254, 255, 256, 257, 258, 263, 264, 265, 270, 277
Silke, A., 37, 38, 41, 63, 69, 97
Simon, L., 283, 289, 291, 292
Simon, R., 229
Simons, R.L., 69
Sinclair, S., 265
Singh, H., 446
Sirriyeh, H., 187
Skolnick, J.H., 324
Sleeth-Keppler, D., 36
Slovic, P., 64, 66
Smalley, S., 71
Smelser, N., 329, 338
Smith, A., 446
Smith, B.L., 310
Snow, D.A., 308
Snyder, D., 446
Sohlman, R., 11
Sollenberg, M., 225
Solomon, S., 254, 282, 283, 284, 285, 287, 289, 291, 292, 293, 295, 296
Sörbom, D., 271
Soskis, D., 79
Spencer, S.J., 293
Spiegel, J., 327
Spiegel, S., 40
Spiridovich, A., 12
Sprague, T., 446
Sprinzak, E., 36, 40, 43, 61, 63, 64, 69, 77, 158, 159, 186, 318, 321, 324, 328, 330
Spurgeon, L., 40, 74
Squire, L., 225
Stack, S., 187
Stallworth, L.M., 258, 277
Stark, R., 308, 311, 337, 338, 339, 340
Stein, Y., 448
Steinberg, P., 425
Stephanson, A., 334
Stern, J., 37, 38, 48, 56, 57, 76, 77, 130, 210, 285
Stern, S., 319, 320
Stillinger, C., 149
St. John, P., 160
Stohl, M., 189, 383, 386, 411, 414, 416
Stoner, J.A.F., 341
Strand, H., 225
Strentz, T., 59
Streudfert, S., 40
Struch, N., 256
Suedfeld, P., 40
Sulloway, F.J., 288, 289, 295
Süllwold, L., 28, 60, 63, 72, 75, 98, 99, 100, 104
Summers, R., 225
Sunder, M., 127
Sutherland, E.H., 337

Tajfel, H., 254
Tappis, S., 319
Tarnovsky, V., 16
Tarrow, S., 314, 315, 446
Taylor, C., 189
Taylor, M., 40, 57, 62, 63, 67, 68, 69, 71, 74, 76, 77, 97, 209
Taylor, S., 187
Telhami, S., 43
Tellegen, A., 285
Tenny, G., 324
Teodori, M., 320, 322
Tetlock, P., 40
Thaler, R., 64, 66
Theodoulou, M., 175
Thomas, S., 76
Thomas, T., 317
Thompson, E., 40
Thompson, J.L.P., 335, 344
Tilly, C., 329, 374, 446, 449, 450
Tilly, L., 374, 450
Tilly, R., 374, 450
Tori, C.D., 40, 74
Traub, S.H., 337
Treyer, V., 76
Trivedi, P.K., 218
Tschirhart, J.T., 64, 214, 381, 387, 398, 400, 401, 449, 451, 463
Tuchman, B.W., 161
Turco, R.M., 98, 100
Turk, A.T., 348
Turner, J., 254
Turnovsky, S.J., 392
Tyre, P., 420, 422

Ungar, M., 68
Utsey, S.O., 69

Van Belle, D., 219
van den Bos, K., 293
Vanhanen, T., 216, 217
van Laar, C., 265
Varenne, H., 12
Varma, S.K., 15
Velvel, L.R., 324
Ventura, A., 312
Verba, S., 310
Victoroff, J., 37, 38, 40
Vinokur, A., 341
Vizetelly, E.A., 14
Volk, S.S., 15
Volkan, V.D., 76
von Baeyer-Kaette, W., 104
Von Drehle, D., 148
von Neumann, J., 64, 66

Waddell, L., 71
Wagner, C., 69
Waldmann, P., 242

Walker, M., 442
Wallenstein, P., 225
Wallerstein, R.S., 70, 71
Wallis, R., 311
Walsh, E.J., 308, 311
Walter, B.F., 172
Walzer, M., 413
Wardlaw, G., 56, 337, 410, 411
Warland, R.H., 308, 311
Waterman, H., 371, 376
Watman, K.H., 64, 66
Watson, D., 285
Waxmonski, J., 292, 295
Webster, D., 40
Weede, E., 446, 449
Weerapana, A., 223
Weigele, T.C., 329
Weinberg, L., 58, 59, 64, 70, 77, 211, 212, 213, 217
Weingast, B.R., 172
Weisberg, H.F., 257
Weiser, B., 419
Wesley, R., 283
West, L.J., 27
West, S.G., 217, 290
Whitaker, B., 69
White, R., 446
Whittaker, D.J., 65
Wicklund, R.A., 288, 295
Wieviorka, M., 62, 66, 78
Wilkinson, P., 9, 97, 104, 215, 350
Wilkinson, T., 60, 120
Williams, R.L., 218
Wilson, J.Q., 130, 308, 376
Wilson, M.A., 64, 78
Witte, R., 243
Wohlstetter, R., 380
Wood, M., 308
Wright, F., 329
Wright, P., 329

Ya'ari, E., 128, 129
Yoshida, F., 329, 373, 384, 386
Young, J., 151
Young, L.-C., 187, 188

Zagoria, D.S., 414
Zald, M.N., 308, 450
Zamoyski, A., 69
Zanna, M.P., 293
Zartman, I., 383
Zavalloni, M., 341, 342
Zawodny, J.K., 335
Zeckhauser, R., 399, 448
Zimbardo, P., 355
Zimmermann, E., 446
Zuckerman, M., 40, 75
Zulaika, J., 79

Subject Index

Abayyat, Hussein, 448
Abbas, Mahmoud, 47
Abel, Rudolf, 364
Abouhalima, Mahmud, 407, 419–24, 432
Absolutism, 13, 16, 17, 73, 412–13
Absolutist/apocalyptic theory, 7, 72–4
Abu Sayyaf group, 58
Acetylcholine, 27
Achille Lauro, 335
Achilles, 76
Action directe, 13
Action mobilization, 314
Afghanistan, 154n13, 163n3, 181, 209, 272, 282, 361–2, 364, 422–3, 473
African National Congress (ANC), 65, 331
Ajaj, Ahmad Muhammad, 424
Al-Aqsa intifada *see* Intifada, second
Al-Aqsa Martyrs Brigades, 59, 134, 143n88, 162, 181–2, 192, 193, 443, 447
Al-Aqsa mosque attack, 1990, 427
Al-Turabi, Hassan, 362
Al Qaeda, 40, 49, 61, 65, 71, 117, 147, 150–4, 155n27, 158, 163, 165, 166, 169, 171, 177, 178, 181, 188, 209, 284, 361–5, 441, 442, 443
Al-Qardawi, Sheikh Yusuf, 442
Al-Qassam Brigades *see* Izz a-Din al-Qassam
Al-Sadr, Moqtada, 443
Al-Shaqaqi, Fathi *see* Shiqaqi, Fathi
Al-Tamimi, Sheik Asad Bayud, 429
Al-Turabi, Hassan, 364
Al-Zahar, Mahmud, 164, 175
Al-Zawahiri, Ayman, 61, 362
Alexander II, 11, 15
Algeria, 182, 233, 248, 319, 332, 333, 349, 350, 362, 419, 428
Ali, Siddig, 423
Alice in Wonderland, 95–6, 106
Amal, 61, 419
American military, 166, 170, 176, 177n6, 178, 281–2
American Revolution, 328

Americans, 39, 44, 147, 148, 162, 163, 248, 250, 254, 255, 257, 292
    African, 69, 202, 295, 436
    Latino, 254
Anarchism, 3–4, 9–10, 13–18, 25, 44, 46, 59, 146, 161, 202, 331, 348, 375–6, 378
Anarchist International, Italian Federation of, 10
Angola, 44
Anticolonial movements, 37, 39, 71
Antidominance reaction, 264–5, 269–78
Antisocial personality disorder, 62, 88, 98–9, 100
Antiterrorism, 39, 215, 228, 271, 272, 274
Apartheid, 65, 299
Arab countries, 52n36, 139, 167, 233, 255–6
Arab identification, 248, 253, 256–65
Arabs, 129, 138, 154n8, 207, 248, 249, 255–7, 263–5, 269–70, 276–7, 361
    Core, 39
    Israeli, 254
    Maghreb, 39
Arafat, Yasser, 49, 58, 59, 133, 162, 206, 428, 430, 447
Argentina, 26, 332, 334, 335, 348
Armée de Libération Nationale (ALN), 334
"Armed deed, the," 10
Armed Fighting Formations (Formazioni Armate Combattenti), 309
Armed Proletarians for Communism (Proletari Armati per il Comunismo), 309
Armenia, 335
Armenian Secret Army for the Liberation of Armenia, 332
Asahara, Shoko, 57, 58
ASALA, 26
Assassination, 146, 331, 351, 385, 386, 393, 410, 432, 448;
    see also Targeted assassinations
    anarchist, 12, 14
    "Golden Age of," 44
    in Judea, 24
    "lone wolf," 14
    political, 9, 11, 13–14, 16, 347
    research on, 19n1

Assassins, the, 24, 186, 431
Atomic bomb, 13, 18, 44, 147
Atta, Mohamed, 59, 117, 196, 362, 367
Attribution theory, 96
Aum Shinrikyo, 73, 285
Australia, 284, 399
Authoritarianism, 39, 40, 50, 75, 215, 333, 374
Autonomia Operaia (Workers Autonomy), 313
Axis I disorders, 7, 62–3
Axis II disorders, 62–3
"Axis of Evil," 284, 294
Ayyad, Nidal, 423, 424
Ayyash, Yihye, 131, 448
Azev, Evno, 15
Azzam, Abdullah, 110

Baader, Andreas, 101, 103, 335
Baader-Meinhof Group *see* Red Army Faction
Bakr, Ahmed, 173
Bali bombing, 2002, 363
Barricades, 380–1, 385, 386, 395
Bashir, Abu Bakar, 363
Begin, Menachem, 52n42, 58, 71
bezmotivnyi terror, 14, 25
Bin Laden, Osama, 46, 58, 65, 117, 162, 166, 196, 207, 272,
    278, 362, 364, 419, 420, 422, 442, 443
Biological weapons, 3, 33, 435
Bishop, Charles, 71
Black liberation movement, 322
Black Panthers, 325
Black September, 377, 395, 448
Black Tigers, 188
Bologna bombing, 1980, 351
Bolsheviks, 10, 25
Borderline personality disorder, 104, 105
Bosnian Muslims, 151, 263
Bourgeoisie, 12, 14, 15, 19n3, 25, 319
Brain function, 27, 74, 76
Brazil, 378
Bresca, Gaetano, 14
Brigate Comuniste (Communist Brigades), 313
Brousse, Paul, 10
Buddhists, 339
Burtsev, Vladimir, 12
Bush, George W., 44, 148, 149, 177n6, 201, 283–5, 293, 294,
    295, 442

Calvert, Gregory, 324
Cambodia, 146, 350
Camp David, 111, 391
Canada, 38, 41, 332, 399
Capitalism, 12
Car bombs, 44
"Carlos the Jackal," 58
Carter, Jimmy, 391
Casablanca bombings, 2003, 364
Casey, William, 410
Castro, Fidel, 110, 376
Catarain, María D. González (Yoyes), 232
Censorship, 187, 189, 213, 374

Central Intelligence Agency (CIA), 162n3, 209, 361, 443
Charismatics, 339
Chechens, 299, 363
Chechnya, 63, 159, 164, 165, 166, 181, 443
Chemical weapons, 3, 291, 435
Chernov, Viktor, 12
"Cheshire-Cat thinking," 88, 95–6, 98, 101–2, 106
China, 399
Christianity, 76
Circoli del Proletariato Giovanile, 312
Civil disobedience, 206
Civil liberties, 44, 166, 212, 214–15, 223–4
Civil wars, 209, 215
"Clash of civilizations," 249, 256, 269–78, 284
Club theory, 398–401
Cognitive capacity, 74, 80, 81
Cognitive style, 74, 80
Cognitive theories, 7, 74–5, 358
Cold War, 154n16, 201, 320
Collateral damage, 47
Collectivism, 7, 70, 77, 87, 112–13, 372
Collettivi Operai (Workers Collectives), 312
Collettivo di Via dei Volsci, 313
Colombia, 26, 57, 70, 160, 348
Combat Organization, 374
Comitati Comunisti, 311
Comitati di Base (Rank and File Committees), 312
Commando forces, 138, 383, 384, 398–401
Communism, 205, 311, 321, 424
Communist Attack Division (*Reparti Comunisti d'Attacco*), 309
Communist Fighting Formations (*Formazioni Comuniste
    Combattenti*), 309
Comparative statics, 385–6, 392–7
Concentration camps, 13, 18
Conflict of legitimacy, 302, 326, 327–8, 330
Consensus mobilization, 314
Contras, 146
"Corporate capitalism," 324
Counterculture, 319, 327
Counterdominance orientation, 248, 254, 259, 263, 265
Counterinsurgency, 146, 154n4, 443, 461, 462
Counter-Reformation, 147
Counter-terror, 18
Counterterrorism, 39, 47, 56, 78, 79–80, 213, 248, 351, 354,
    355, 357, 438, 441, 451, 452
    morality of, 44, 437
    strategies of, 56
Crime, 15, 97, 149–50, 203, 328, 331
Criminals, 12, 27, 97, 244, 386
Criminology, 76, 348, 386
Crisis of confidence, 302, 326, 327
Crisis of legitimacy, 328–30
Crisis management, 387, 399, 402
Crusades, 47, 76, 146
Cuba, 350, 376
Cults, 72, 73, 285, 303, 331, 337–40
Cultural anthropology, 70
Cultural worldviews, 254, 281–3, 288, 294, 296
Culture, 66, 70
Czar of Russia, 12, 13, 378

Dalai Lama, the, 149
"Days of Rage," 318
Death wish, 29, 36
Defense Intelligence Agency (DIA), 442
Degayev, Sergey, 15
Dehumanization, 1
Democratic Front for the Liberation of Palestine (DFLP), 109
Democratic participation, 216–20, 222–3
Demographic separation, 177–8
Depression, 62, 333
"Direct action," 9
Direct Action (France), 26
Dissonance theory, 343
Dohrn, Bernardine, 319, 320
Dolphinarium attack, 42, 128, 206
Dresden bombing, 405
Durkheim, Emile, 64, 88, 93, 185, 186–7, 193
Dynamite, 10, 11, 12, 20n26, 25, 33, 376

Eban, Abba, 377
Ego, 71, 72
Egypt, 39, 59, 117, 138, 182, 186, 361–3, 398, 419, 421–3, 428, 429, 432
Egyptian Islamic Group (EIG), 61
Egyptian Islamic Jihad (EIJ), 61
Eiland, Major General Giora, 448
Ejercito Revolucionario del Pueblo (ERP; People's Revolutionary Army), 332, 381
El-Gabrowny, Ibrahim, 423
el Hage, Wadih, 419
El Salvador, 351
Elisabeth, Empress, 14
Endorphins, 27
Ensslin, Gudrun, 103
Eretz Israel, 65
Erhard Seminars Training (EST), 339
Ethnic profiling, 47, 153
Ethniki Organosis Kyprion Agoniston (EOKA), 52n36, 350
Ethnocentrism, 74–5
Euskadi Ta Askatasuna (ETA), 26, 37, 58, 59, 63, 69, 97, 105, 196, 198, 227–45, 247, 332–4, 336, 374
Euskera (Basque language), 230, 232, 233, 235, 237, 239–41, 245
Eusko Gaztedi (EGI), 235
Existential psychology, 73, 281–3, 288–9, 292, 294, 295, 304, 352
Explosives, 10, 11, 12, 19n10, 20n26, 25, 33, 375, 386, 420
nuclear, 3, 30, 34, 176, 289, 291, 334, 435
Extreme military intervention, support for, 39, 281–2, 284, 288–92, 294, 295

Faluji, Imad, 427
Family activism, 110
Faraj, Abd al-Salam, 431–2
Fascism, 378, 424
Fascists, Italian, 26
Fatah, 30n23, 59, 61, 89, 109, 113, 116, 117, 124, 127, 130–3, 135, 136, 143n88, 162, 272, 377, 447, 448
Fatwas, 162, 362, 429
Fenians, the, 376

Ferdinand, Archduke Franz, 9
Feudalism, 12
Fighting Communist Cells, the, 26
Figner, Vera, 378
First Amendment, 324
First World War, 9, 374
"Focalism," 44
Foda, Farag, 423
"Foot in the door" effect, 343
For Communism (Per il comunismo), 309
Fraga, Manuel, 234
France, 13, 14, 26, 38, 59, 92, 145, 147, 165, 167, 170, 178, 229, 238, 363, 380, 398
Francoism, 228, 235, 237, 240, 243–4
"Free riders," 368, 372, 398, 399, 401
Free speech, 15, 211
Free Speech Movement, 323
FRELIMO, 350
French Resistance, 145, 202
French Revolution, 68, 146, 328, 372
Freud, Sigmund, 71, 79
Frolenko, Mikhail, 11
Front de Libération Nationale (FLN), 52n36, 63, 332, 333, 334, 349, 350
Front de Libération du Quebec (FLQ), 41, 72, 332, 335
Front Line (Prima Linea), 309, 310
Frustration–aggression hypothesis, 7, 38, 68, 196, 205, 348–9
Fundamental attribution error, 40, 74, 79, 81, 148

Gamaa-i Islamiya, 419, 422, 423, 429, 432
Game theory, 7, 64–5, 369, 380, 386
Gamma-aminobutyric acid (GABA), 27–8
Gangsterism, 14, 15
Gaza, 38, 41, 48, 49, 60, 62, 69, 125, 126, 128–9, 132, 135, 136, 138, 139, 150, 151, 152, 157, 158, 159, 162, 164, 166, 167, 171–4, 176, 178, 182, 193, 203–4, 206–8, 270, 425–8, 445, 447, 448, 450
Gemayel, Bashir, 147
Genocide, 43, 411
Germany, 13, 26, 32, 38, 39, 162, 202, 205, 333, 348, 349, 378, 398, 422
"Global war on terror," 43, 45
Globalization, 55, 68, 212, 223
Goering, Hermann, 96
Goldman, Emma, 14
Goldstein, Baruch, 42, 161n1, 427
Government constraint, 217–20, 222–4
Government model, 390–2
Great Depression, 205
Greece, 52n36, 399
Group behavior, 1, 40, 70, 73, 78, 112, 300
Group dynamics, 40–2, 73, 77, 78, 80–1, 112, 336, 340–2, 344, 364
Group equality, desire for, 253, 255, 258, 261–4
Group identification, 253–5, 331
Group process theories, 7, 67, 76–7, 81
Groupe Salafiste pour la Prédication et le Combat (GSPC), 61
"Groupthink," 320, 322, 324, 336
Guantanamo Bay, 442
Guatemala, 154n4

Guerrilla warfare, 26, 331, 376, 379
Guevara, Che, 110, 321
Guilt, 13, 333
Guipúzcoa, 238–9, 244
Gulf War, 126, 423
Guzman, Abimail, 40

Habash, George, 377
Hadith, 126, 137, 431
Halal laws, 363
Hamas, 41, 48–9, 59, 61, 67–8, 69, 89, 109, 113, 114, 115, 117,
    123, 124, 126, 127, 128, 130–3, 135, 136, 143n88, 147,
    154, 164–73, 175, 180–2, 185, 188, 193, 204, 247, 256,
    258, 259, 272, 276, 419, 424–30, 445, 448
Hare Krishnas, 339
Harkat al-Ansar, 151
Hashishiyun, 24, 186, 431
Hate crimes, 150, 202, 204–6
    definition of, 204
Hayden, Tom, 318, 321, 322, 324
Haymarket affair, 12
Hebron Massacre, 1994, 42, 161n1, 171, 427
Hegel, G.W.F., 412
Henry, Emile, 15, 25
Herri Batasuna, 230
Hess, Rudolf, 96
Hezbollah, 28, 40, 41, 48–9, 60, 61, 63, 65, 89, 109, 110, 147,
    150, 165, 169, 170–1, 175, 188, 208, 247, 256, 258, 259,
    272, 364, 419, 441
Hijacking, 44, 60, 65, 160, 331, 333, 376, 379, 381, 385, 386,
    393, 395, 397
Hiroshima, 44, 153, 405, 421
Hitler, Adolf, 37, 58
Hizballah see Hezbollah
Holy Inquisition, 148
Homosexuals, 205
Hostages, 11, 12, 44, 160, 354, 372–3, 379, 386, 393, 395
Huks, the, 319
Humiliation–revenge theory, 7, 76, 99, 122
Hunger strikes, 161n2

Identity theory, 71, 72
Ideology, 9, 46
Illégalistes, 14, 17
India, 9, 10, 15, 20n26, 120, 158, 165, 167, 181
Indian revolutionary movement, 15, 20n26
"Individual terror," 4, 7, 9, 13, 14, 16, 18, 19n2, 25
Individualism, 7, 70
Indonesia, 59, 153, 363, 398, 428
Insanity, 62–4, 67
Intelligentsia, 15, 16, 20n33
Intergroup enmity, 1
Internet, 41, 44, 189, 365
Intifada, 299, 431, 437
    First, 62, 111, 113, 127–8, 150–1, 173, 175, 207, 208, 428,
        447
    Second, 41, 47, 119, 120, 125, 129, 131, 133–4, 136, 139,
        151, 152, 164, 171, 175, 190, 192, 193, 206–8, 445, 447–8
Iran, 26, 27–8, 39, 41, 146, 154n13, 217, 284, 289, 292–5, 350
    Shah of, 65

Iran–Iraq war, 163n3
Iranian hostage crisis, 391, 397
Iraq, 28, 52n36, 57, 73, 162, 168, 203, 251, 256, 270, 282, 283,
    292, 364, 441, 443, 473
Iraqi embassy attack, Beirut, 147, 182
Ireland, 344, 373
Irgun (IZL), 26, 52n42, 65, 75, 352
Irish Free State, 65
Irish National Liberation Army, 335
Irish Republican Army (IRA), 26, 30n23, 58, 63, 65, 67, 69, 97,
    103, 161, 209, 247, 332–3, 334–6, 341, 344, 349, 352, 374,
    376, 388
Islam, 24–5, 41, 113, 125, 126, 130, 148, 151, 154n13, 162, 188,
    270, 284, 295, 407, 422, 427, 430–2
    fundamentalist, 147, 158, 284, 436
    Ismaili, 431
    vs Judaism, 125
    and military engagement, 430–1
    Nizari branch of, 431
    and political order, 421, 428, 431
    public role of, 420
    radical, 39, 67–8, 117, 124, 125, 139, 147, 149, 407
    Shia, 24, 147, 188
    Sunni, 147, 442
Islamic Jihad see Palestinian Islamic Jihad
Islamic militancy, 428, 442
Islamic Order of Assassins, 146
Islamic Salvation Front, 419
Islamists, 123–4, 136, 147, 166, 305, 361, 407, 423, 428, 436,
    442
    Apocalyptic, 48
    Utopian, 48
Israel, 30n24, 48, 61, 90, 92, 109, 111, 117n1, 119, 120, 124,
    125, 128, 135, 140, 150, 152, 158, 159, 164, 167–73, 176,
    185, 189–90, 208, 254, 256, 272, 276, 351, 356, 383, 398,
    399, 423, 424–7, 432, 441, 443, 463, 468
Israeli Defense Forces (IDF), 47, 61, 76, 112, 113, 115, 126,
    127, 128, 131, 136, 157, 170, 172, 175, 176, 178, 193, 203,
    248, 427, 430, 447, 448, 461, 469, 472
Israeli–Palestinian conflict, 69, 119–40, 147, 153, 155n44, 164,
    165, 180–2, 185, 196, 206, 256, 272, 276, 373, 424–7, 437,
    443, 447–64, 467–75
    casualties of, 120, 180–2, 437, 438
Israelis, 11, 21n34, 29, 38, 42, 47, 48, 49, 69, 70, 74–5, 111–15,
    124, 125, 126, 131–3, 136, 140, 173, 299, 351, 352, 357,
    395, 428, 437, 447, 461
Istishad, 64
Italian Communist Party, 311
Italy, 13, 26, 27, 36, 38, 44, 52n36, 92, 160, 209, 300, 307, 314,
    333, 335, 374, 376, 398
Izz a-Din al-Qassam, 61, 109, 112, 113, 115, 125, 131–2, 136,
    142n64, 204

Jacobins, 146
Jakarta Marriott bombing, 2003, 363
"Jam joints," 343
Jamaat-i-Islami, 432
Japan, 42, 44, 59, 103, 146, 176, 285, 325, 335
Japanese Red Army, 209, 398n16
Jarrah, Ziad, 59

Jemaah Islamiyah, 61, 151, 155n35, 363, 442
Jerusalem Brigades (Al-Quds), 132, 152
Jewish Defense League, 419
Jewish settlements, 48, 427
Jewish Underground, 208
Jews, 24, 73, 115, 117, 125, 128, 140, 173, 205, 208, 254, 348, 350, 417n3, 426–7, 432, 443
Jihad, 46, 47, 49, 67, 111, 114, 115, 124–5, 127, 364, 407, 431–2, 441, 443
  meanings of, 124, 430
  "national," 128
Jordan, 131, 171, 175, 442
Judaism, 125, 363
"Just war," 405

Kaczynski, Theodore ("Unabomber"), 43, 66, 247, 363
Kahane, Rabbi Meir, 419, 423, 430
Kamikaze, 146–7, 153, 442
Karim, Abdel, 162
Kashmir, 61, 145, 159, 164, 165, 166, 181, 443
Kenya, 181, 349, 350, 419
Kerry, John, 284, 295
Khadr, Ahmed Saeed, 363
Khaled, Leila, 333
Khalef, Salah (Abu lyad), 377
Khobar Towers attack, Saudi Arabia, 442
Khomeini, Ayatollah, 27–8, 125, 146, 147, 430
Kidnapping, 44, 65, 146, 331, 336, 349, 375, 376, 379–81, 385
Kim Dae Jong, 149
Kirkpatrick, Jeane, 414
Klein, Melanie, 72
Kohut, Heinz, 71
Koran, 111, 113, 115, 125, 126, 407, 422, 428, 430, 431
Korea, 337
Koresh, David, 58
Kravchinsky, Stepniak, 18–19
Kropotkin, Peter, 10, 25
Kumaratunga, Chandrika, 171
Kurdish Workers' Party (PKK), 40, 165, 169, 177, 181, 188
Kurds, 157, 159, 164, 165, 166, 168, 299
Kuwait, 28, 39, 178, 182, 423

Lackawanna Six, 364
Land and Freedom Party, 15, 17, 19n8
Laos, 350
Laporte, Pierre, 335
Lebanese Christians, 255–9, 270–8
Lebanese identification, 258–65
Lebanon, 26, 28, 29, 48–9, 60, 61, 65, 67, 120, 152, 158, 159, 164, 165, 166, 170, 175, 176, 178–9, 182, 186, 188, 208, 209, 253, 255–6, 270–8, 349, 381, 399, 426, 441
  Southern, 48, 174, 175, 176, 178–9, 182
Lehi, 11, 21n34
Lenin, Vladimir Ilyich, 15, 18, 146, 244
Leninism, 157, 158, 319, 320, 330, 348
Liberation Tigers of Tamil Ealem (LTTE), 63, 157, 158, 162, 165, 169, 170–1, 181, 188
Libya, 52n36, 217, 428
Linea di Condotta, 314
Lo Muscio Brigade (Brigata Lo Muscio), 309

Lombroso, Cesare, 19n20, 27
London bombings, 2005, 36, 44
Lotta Continua (Continuous Struggle), 311–12
"Low-intensity warfare," 413
Luciani, Luigi, 14
Lydda airport massacre, 103
Lynchings, 202, 204–5

M-19, 26, 348
Ma'alot attack, 1974, 15, 354
Mac Stiofain, Sean, 376
Madhi, Sheikh Ibrahim, 125
Madrasas, 67, 82, 152, 210, 305
Madrid bombings, 2004, 36, 44, 364, 365, 441
Mahfouz, Naguib, 423
Mahgoub, Rifaat, 423
Mahler, Horst, 334, 335
Maidan, Ibrahim, 155n35
Majoritarian system, 216–17, 220, 222
Makawi, Mohammed Ibrahim, 362
Malvo, Lee, 43
Mandela, Nelson, 57, 58
Manson, Charles, 320
Maoism, 323, 328, 348
Marighella, Carlos, 46, 67, 333, 337, 378
Martyrdom, 29, 39, 49, 65, 66, 67, 90, 114, 116, 122–7, 130, 136, 137–40, 147, 150, 153, 163, 174, 186, 281–2, 284–7, 291–2, 294, 372n3, 425–7, 429–30, 442
  and prospect of paradise, 126, 127, 186, 187, 429, 432
Martyrdom cells, 138, 146, 150–1
Marx, Karl, 244, 321
Marxism, 59, 157, 158, 323–4, 329, 340, 373
Mau-Mau, 349, 350
Mawdudi, Maulana Abu al-Ala, 432
Mazen, Abu, 53n84
McVeigh, Timothy, 163, 209
Meinhof, Ulrike, 58, 103, 333, 334, 335
Meir, Golda, 377
Mensheviks, 10
Meshal, Khaled, 448
Messianic leaders, 58, 73
Middle-ear defects, 102
Mikhailov, Alexander, 13
Milgram, Stanley, 148, 303, 342–4
Militants, 20n33, 52n42, 244, 245, 300, 449
  ETA, 227–45
  far-left, 109
  female, 229–33, 245
  German, 63, 75, 77
  Islamic, 364, 442
  Italian, 63, 77, 307–14
  male, 230–3, 244
  Palestinian, 204, 208, 447, 449–52, 458, 463
Military-industrial complex, 322
Milosevic, Slobodan, 58
Mish'al, Khalid, 175
"Misplaced idealism," 64
Mississippi Freedom and Democratic Party, 322
Mobilization potential, 314
Montoneros, 26, 332, 334, 348

Moral dilemmas, 43–5
Moral equivalence, 414
Moro Islamic Liberation Front, 61
Morocco, 363, 442
Morozov, Nikolai, 16, 18–19
Mortality salience, 250, 281–95
   and American students, 250
   and Iranian students, 250
Most, Johann, 12
Mountbatten, Lord Louis, 335
Moussaoui, Habib Zacarias, 61
Mozambique, 350
Mubarak, Hosni, 361, 421, 423
Muhammad (the Prophet), 110, 126, 305, 362,
   430–1
Muhammad, John, 43
Mujahedin, 61, 77, 422, 442
Munich bombing, 1980, 351
Munich Olympic massacre, 1972, 448
Muslim activists, 422–4, 430
Muslim Brotherhood, 110, 113, 442
Muslim countries, 270
Muslim dietary laws, 363
Muslim identification, 248
Muslims, 247, 284, 363–4, 424, 431–2, 443
   fundamentalist, 49
   Lebanese, 256–7, 270–8
   Shi'a, 65, 67, 257, 348, 441
   Sunni, 73, 257, 348, 432, 441
Mutually assured destruction, 154n16

Nagasaki, 44, 153, 406, 421
Narcissism theory, 71–2, 73, 98, 99–101, 104
Narcissistic personality disorder, 99, 101, 104
Narcissistic rage, 72
Narodnaya Volya, 9–10, 11, 13, 15–17, 25, 26, 334,
   376
Nash, John, 367
Nasserallah, Sayyed Hassan, 46
National cultural theory, 7, 70
National Islamic Front, 362
National Liberation Army (Colombia), 160
National liberation struggles, 9, 16, 25
   in Armenia, 25
   in the Balkans, 9, 16, 17, 25, 52n36
   in India, 9
   in Ireland, 9, 16, 17, 25
   in Poland, 9, 16–17
Nationalism, 4, 228
   Basque, 228–9, 233–4, 238
   Islamic, 278, 427–8
   Palestinian, 128
Nazis, 26, 32, 37, 96, 145, 202, 417n3
Nazzal, Muhammad, 175
Negotiation models, 384–7
Neofascism, 329, 348, 374
Neo-nazis, 245, 348
"Neo-partisan warfare," 10, 16
Neuroimaging, 76
"New Barbarism," 319–20

New Left, 325, 329
   in Italy, 311–12
   in the USA, 317, 321–4
Nicaragua, 44, 146, 350
Nichols, Terry, 420
Nidal, Abu, 26, 30n24, 57, 58
Nitroglycerine, 11, 19n10
Nixon, Richard, 372
Nobel, Alfred, 11
Nonviolence, 321, 323, 412, 430, 449, 463
Norepinephrine, 27
North Korea, 289
Northern Ireland, 29, 41, 103, 333, 349, 351, 352, 374
Nosair, El Sayyid, 419, 423
Novelty-seeking theory, 7, 75, 80
Nuclear weapons, 3, 30, 34, 176, 289, 291, 334, 435
"Nuclei," the, 309
Nuclei Armati Proletari, 313

Obedience studies, 303, 331, 342–4
Object relations, 71, 72
Ocalan, Abdullah, 40
Odeh, Sheik Abd al-Aziz, 429, 431
Okamoto, Kozo, 103, 104
Okinawa, Battle of, 146
Oklahoma City federal building bombing, 420–1
Omar, Mullah, 364
Onishi, Takijiro, 146
Operation Defensive Shield, 140, 142n63, 447, 469, 470
Oppression, 6, 13, 16, 17, 32, 36, 38, 40, 43, 49–50, 68, 69, 93,
   247, 405, 422, 450
Oppression theory, 7, 69
Orange Volunteers, 160–1
Oslo Accords, 171–2, 174
Ottoman Empire, 407

Pacifism, 414–15
Pakistan, 67, 70, 120, 152, 154n13, 158, 163n3, 182, 210, 362,
   424, 432, 443
Palestine, 147, 150, 153, 154n8, n13, 164, 165, 167, 172, 174,
   175, 196, 350, 352, 419, 425–7, 443
Palestine Liberation Organization (PLO), 133, 164, 172, 173,
   351, 357, 388, 428, 431
Palestinian Authority, 47, 53n84, 128, 130, 131, 174, 175, 206,
   430, 447
Palestinian Islamic Jihad (PIJ), 41, 59, 61, 89, 109, 117, 120,
   123, 124, 126, 127, 131–3, 135, 136, 143n88, 147, 168–71,
   173–5, 181–2, 188, 193, 204, 256, 258, 259, 272, 277, 447,
   448
Palestinian–Israeli conflict *see* Israeli–Palestinian conflict
Palestinian Liberation Front, 319
Palestinian Muslim Brotherhood, 132, 428
Palestinian police force, 172
Palestinian Territories, 69
Palestinians, 26, 27, 30n23, 37, 38, 41, 42, 44, 47, 48, 67, 77, 93,
   113–14, 116, 119, 120, 124–31, 138–40, 150, 151, 154n8,
   161, 167, 170, 174, 187, 206, 247, 269, 332, 437, 463
Panama, 120
Paranoia, 7, 37, 61, 73, 98
Paranoia theory, 71, 72–3

Paranoid personality disorder, 88, 100–1
Paranoid-schizoid position, 72
Parnell, Charles Stewart, 373
Parsons, Albert, 12
Parti Quebecois, 41
Partido Nacionalista Vasco (PNV), 235–6
Partisan warfare, 17
Patriot Act, 289, 290–1
Peñalva, Belén González, 233
People's Liberation Army, 209
Permanent terrorist revolution, 16
"Permissive society," 71
Perovskaya, Sofia, 17
Personality disorders, 62
Peru, 332, 377
Philippines, the, 319
Pilsudski, Josef, 10, 20n28, n33
Pistoleros, 14
PKK see Kurdish Workers' Party
Poisonous gas, 44, 285
Pol Pot, 146
Polish Socialist Party, 10, 15
Popular Front for the Liberation of Palestine (PFLP), 26, 109,
    120, 135, 136, 182, 256, 258, 259, 272, 332, 333, 372, 378,
    395, 398n16, 448
Port Huron Statement, 320, 321, 322
Potere Operaio (Worker Power), 311–12
Powell, Colin, 442
Powers, Gary, 364
Press freedom, 211, 214, 219, 222, 224
Prima Linea, 374
Progressive Labor party (PLP), 323
Project Bojinka, 424
Projection, 71, 72
Proletarian Armed Groups (Nuclei Armati Proletari), 308–9
Propaganda, 137, 140, 149, 152, 308, 364, 374, 384, 385,
    387n5, 388, 409
"Propaganda by the deed," 4, 9, 10–11, 14, 18, 25, 378
Proportional representation, 216–17, 220, 222
Psychiatry, 56, 61, 96, 348, 363
Psychoanalysis, 62, 70–4
Psychological identification, 264
Psychological war, 337, 349–50, 409
Psychology, 23, 34, 56, 77–8, 96, 300, 348, 371, 372n3, 413,
    435–6
    conflict, 1
    forensic, 76
    group, 33, 76, 106, 319n13, 326
    means-end, 35, 46, 48–50
    nonpsychoanalytic approaches to, 67, 74–6
    political, 56, 75
    psychoanalytic approaches to, 67, 70–4
    social, 169, 300, 303, 331–44, 347–58
Psychology of terrorism, 1–2, 4, 7, 23–4, 26, 32–4, 36, 49, 56–7,
    60, 62, 78–80, 96, 300, 301, 329, 331–44, 347–58, 371–2,
    436, 442
    theories of, 7, 70–6
Psychosis, 62
Public choice, 386
"Pyramid model," 41

Quran see Koran
Qutb, Sayyid, 361, 407, 432

Rabin, Yitzhak, 169, 173, 174
Racism, 74, 243, 320, 432, 436
Radicalization, 147, 152, 300, 321, 326, 330
Rahman, Sheik Omar Abdul, 419, 420, 422–3, 430
Rantisi, Abdul Aziz, 76, 127, 128, 426–9, 431, 432, 448
Raspe, Jan-Carl, 103
"Rational-actor" models, 383–6, 398–402, 449
Rational choice theory, 7, 62, 64–7, 150, 152, 155n33, 372
Ravachol, 14
Reagan, Ronald, 169, 170
"Realist" school of thought, 412
Reality testing, 62, 73, 80
Rebellion, act of, 14
Red Army Faction, 26, 37, 39, 40, 41, 63, 97, 100, 161, 209,
    247, 325, 332–6, 340, 341, 372, 374, 378
Red Brigades (Brigate Rose), 26, 36, 41, 48, 59, 97, 160, 247,
    308, 325, 332, 334, 374
Red Guerrilla (Guerriglia Rossa), 309
"Red Terror," 9
Regime change, 212, 218
Regime durability, 217–20, 225
Reign of Terror, 146
Relative deprivation theory, 7, 62, 68–9
Religious fundamentalism, 56, 67, 123, 147, 148, 191
Religious identification, 256–7, 272, 274, 278n5
Repression, 10, 25, 34, 215, 244, 315, 374–5, 377–9, 415,
    449–55, 458, 461, 463
    and rebellion, 10, 178, 445, 446, 452
Reprise individuelle, 9, 14
Resource mobilization theory, 450, 451
Ressam, Ahmed, 363
Revenge, 30, 47, 49, 76, 81, 99, 101, 122, 126–7, 139, 140, 336
Revolutionary Armed Forces of Colombia (FARC), 161
Revolutionary Cells (Germany), 348
Revolutionary Communist Movement (Movimento Comunista
    Rivoluziona, rio), 309
Rhodesia, 299, 350, 353
Riaño, Idoia López, 233
Right-wing extremism, 28, 75
Robespierre, Maximilien, 146, 202
Roosevelt, Theodore, 44
Rosso, 311
Rudolph, Erik, 43
Russia, 9–12, 14, 15, 17, 18, 20n26, n33, 25, 27, 146, 158, 166,
    167, 181, 202, 299, 374, 443, 473
"Russian method," 15
Russian Revolution, 9, 18, 68, 146
Russian revolutionary movement, 15, 25, 374, 378
Russian social democracy, 18
Russian terrorist movement, 17, 146, 332, 373, 374

Sadat, Ahmed, 136
Sadat, Anwar, 361, 422, 423, 432
Saddam Hussein, 126, 443n1
Salafis, 36–8, 49, 59, 61, 305, 361–2, 365
Salame, Hassan, 117n1
Salameh, Muhammad, 423, 424

Saudi Arabia, 39, 59, 64, 117, 158, 164, 165, 166, 177n6, 256, 270, 272, 362, 363, 377, 419, 442, 443
Savio, Mario, 323
Savoy Hotel attack, Tel Aviv, 1975, 354
Schizophrenia, 62
   paranoid, 66
Schleyer, Hans-Martin, 334
Scientologists, 339
Second of June movement, 349
Second World War, 42, 65, 147, 162, 176, 202, 353, 413
Self-immolation, 161n2
Self psychology, 71
"Sentiment pool," 41
Senza Tregua, 311
September 11 attacks, 2001, 36, 37, 44, 56, 59, 65, 117, 152, 163, 177, 206, 207, 248, 253–60, 262–6, 269–78, 282, 288, 289, 291, 292, 361, 364, 367, 441
Serge, Victor, 14, 17
Serotonin, 27–8
Shabiba, 110
Shalabi, Mustafa, 423
Shallah, Sheikh Ramadan, 132, 175
Shamir, Yitshak, 75
Shanab, Ismail Abu, 448
Shari'ah, 443
Sharon, Ariel, 134, 447
Shehadeh, Salah, 448
Shining Path (Sendero Luminoso), 26, 40, 332, 377
Shiqaqi, Fathi, 147, 174, 448
Shouley, Mahmoud Muhammad Ahmed (Abu Hnoud), 448
Shternberg, Lev, 16
Sicarii, 5, 24, 146, 186
Singapore, 151, 153, 442
Sinn Fein, 48, 374
Skyjacking see Hijacking
Social comparison theory, 341–3
Social Democratic Party (Germany), 334
Social destabilization theories, 348
Social dominance orientation (SDO), 248, 253–66
Social dominance theory, 248, 254, 263
Social identity theory, 7, 254, 265
Social learning theory, 7, 67–8
Social networks, 239, 300, 308, 309, 338, 361
Social revolution, 4, 13, 15
Social Revolutionaries, 10, 12
Socialism, 10, 46
Socialist German Student Society, 334
Sociological theories, 67–70
Sociopathy, 62–4
Socio-political struggle, 13
Soft power, 443
South Africa, 57, 299, 375
Southern Lebanese Army, 178–9
Soviet-Afghan War, 147, 163n3, 361, 422–3
Soviet Union, 32, 34, 38, 52n36, 414
Spain, 13, 14, 38, 196, 228, 229, 234, 238, 240, 244, 245
Sri Lanka, 120, 157, 159, 162, 164, 166, 167, 170–1, 176, 179–80, 181, 186, 188, 299, 473
Stalemate equilibrium, 397
Stalin, Joseph, 19n3, 37

Stern Gang (LHI), 26, 352
Strategic choice theory, 7, 64–5, 81, 372
Structural sociology, 300
Student Nonviolent Coordinating Committee (SNCC), 321, 323
Students for a Democratic Society (SDS), 301, 318, 319, 320–5
Sudan, 209, 362, 364, 377, 423
Suicidal acts, 14
Suicide, 103, 114, 124, 147, 158, 367, 424
   altruistic, 64, 88, 93, 185, 186–8, 191–3
   anomic, 187
   egoistic, 187
   fatalistic, 88, 93, 185, 186–8, 192
   "fatalistic altruistic," 186
Suicide terrorism, 29, 37, 44, 47, 49, 59, 61–2, 76, 77, 87–8, 90, 91, 92, 93, 111, 114–15, 117, 119, 120–40, 141n5, n6, 145–54, 157–82, 185–94, 281–2, 284, 424–7, 429, 438, 441, 447, 451–2, 463, 467–75
   apparent success of, 170–1
   concessions to, 177
   cult of, 126
   data on, 120, 121–2
   definition of, 161
   against democracies, 167–8
   and dignity/humiliation, 127
   and economic factors, 128–9, 139, 148, 186, 192, 204, 223
   and education, 148, 189–91, 209, 442
   and expected sexual benefits, 127
   and family, 126, 140, 203–4
   and humiliation, 122, 127
   indoctrination for, 120, 122, 130, 137–8, 140
   limits of, 175–8
   logic of, 92, 160–8
   media coverage of, 130–1, 146
   motivation for, 76, 120, 122, 123–9, 139, 158, 186, 425
   and nationalism, 127, 139, 166–7
   opposition to, 48
   organizational aspects of, 120, 122, 130–9, 188
   planning and execution of, 138
   prevention of, 152, 160, 176–8, 443
   psychological aspects of, 130
   and psychopathology, 145, 148, 333
   recruitment for, 122, 130, 136–7, 145, 186, 467–8, 470–4
   and religion, 123–4, 139, 188, 294
   and socialization, 188
   sociological aspects of, 129–30, 158–9, 188, 189–93, 442
   statistics on, 131–5, 163, 165, 174n5, 178–82, 190–2, 467–8
   and status after death, 126, 127, 186, 187, 429
   stereotypes of, 204, 285
   strategic, 159, 224
   support for, 77, 130, 163, 463
   and target selection, 139, 162, 164, 168
   "terror stock" model of, 467, 470–3
   terrorists' assessment of, 168–75
   timing of, 164–6
   training for, 120, 122, 130, 137–8, 140
   two-phase model of, 122–3
   understanding, 120, 155n33
   weapon procurement for, 138
   by women, 59, 189
Sun Myung Moon, Reverend, 337

Sungkar, Abdullah, 363
Sunna, 407
Superego, 63
Symbionese Liberation Army, 26, 349
Syndicalism, 12
  revolutionary, 9, 15
Syria, 52n36, 154n13, 289
"Systematic assassination," 9

Tablighi Janaat, 49
Taliban, 147, 154, 177
Tamil Tigers *see* Liberation Tigers of Tamil Ealem
Tamils, 26, 166, 171, 299
Tanzania, 120, 181
Tanzim, the, 134, 136
Targeted assassinations, 47, 272, 437, 438, 445–64, 467,
    469–74
  arguments regarding, 448
  and "backlash" effect, 446, 450, 453–6, 463
  as disincentive to militancy, 445, 446, 449–50, 462–3
  and disruption effect, 445, 446, 450–1, 458–60
  effects of, 47, 445, 446–7, 451, 462
  and incapacitation effect, 445, 446–7, 451, 461
  statistics on, 448, 453, 459, 469
Tarnovsky, V., 16
Tate, Sharon, 320
Technology, 9, 11, 12
Tell, Wilhelm, 19
Terror management theory (TMT), 248, 282–5, 287–9, 292,
    294, 295
"Terror stock," 47, 438, 468
  model of, 467, 470–3
Terrorism, 7, 20n33, 23–6, 35–6, 55, 70, 77, 96, 130, 149, 154,
    158, 203, 206, 211–12, 248, 270, 285, 299, 300, 319,
    325–6, 330, 331, 350, 352–7, 363, 373, 376–82, 383, 405,
    431, 435, 442, 446; *see also* Suicide terrorism; Terrorist
    groups; Terrorists
  and absolutist thinking, 71
  aims and objectives of, 11, 336–7, 378
  Algerian, 52n36
  alternatives to, 47
  American, 59, 332
  anarchist, 3–4, 9, 13
  arbitrary, 15
  attractiveness of, 373
  and authoritarianism, 39, 40, 50, 75, 212
  Balkan, 52n36
  and belief systems, 46
  biological model of, 27, 36, 78
  and brain chemistry, 27–8
  catastrophic, 48
  clandestine state, 411
  and cognitive style, 40
  and collectivism, 39–40, 50
  conditions for, 373–6
  contagion model of, 305, 373, 384, 386–7
  contributing factors to, 38–40, 50
  cost–benefit analysis of, 368, 377–9
  and country size, 218, 219
  covert state, 411

and criminality, 328
Cypriot, 52n36
definition of, 1, 3, 12, 23, 42–3, 56, 97, 145–6, 160–1, 201–2,
    347, 385, 409, 410–11, 421
and democracy, 196–7, 211–25
demonstrative, 160–1
destructive, 160–1
discarding of, 34
discouraging, 47, 81, 210, 349
as "disease," 36
domestic, 347–8, 353, 412
and economic factors, 68–9, 207, 209–10
and education, 38, 48, 60, 61, 91, 150, 201, 203, 207, 208–10,
    305
and foreign aid, 201
funding of, 336, 375
and gender, 198, 228–34, 332
goals of, 17–18, 24
and group dynamics, 40, 42
history of, 5, 24, 33
and identity, 71, 111
ideological, 25, 325–30, 350–1
ideology of, 4, 6, 336
inhibiting, 398, 399, 401–2
and insanity, 63, 64, 67
insurgent, 97
international, 34, 347, 349, 410
Iranian, 332
Islamist, 29, 60–2, 67, 441–2
in Italy, 307
Japanese, 332
justification of, 412
left-wing, 26, 46, 63, 70, 72, 75, 308, 333, 348
legitimation of, 46, 89
logic of, 2, 92, 367–8, 371–82
media coverage of, 44, 219, 356, 421
and mental illness, 28, 37, 63, 97, 103, 326, 386, 409
military response to, 436, 441, 443
modeling of, 79, 81, 224, 384, 386–95, 454, 468
and money, 29n23
morality of, 11, 43–5, 406, 407, 408, 411–17
and mortality salience, 39, 40
motivation for, 196, 371, 382
multifinality of, 47
and narcissism, 7, 29, 37, 50, 61, 71–2, 73, 88, 98, 99–101,
    104
nationalist, 26–7, 56, 63, 69, 70, 81, 97, 100, 348
negotiation models of, 384–92
New Left, 329
opponents of, 10
and other violence, 4
overcoming, 2, 92, 435
Palestinian, 47, 52n36, 61, 64, 90, 116–17, 332, 335, 351,
    395, 463
and personality, 28–9, 37, 49–50, 57, 60–1, 77, 78, 98, 104–5,
    303, 307, 348, 363, 442
and petty crime, 61
and poverty, 6, 36, 37–8, 40, 49–50, 60, 68–9, 91, 149–50,
    152, 186, 195, 201–10, 442
prediction of responses to, 353–5

promotion of, 67–8
and prosociality, 64, 80
as psychological warfare, 349–50, 409
psychology of, 1–2, 4, 7, 23–4, 26, 32–4, 36, 49, 56–7, 60, 62,
    70–6, 78–80, 96, 300, 301, 329, 331–44, 347–58, 371–2,
    436, 442
psychopathology of, 7, 28, 37, 49, 62, 88, 95, 96–7, 101, 104,
    307, 333, 409
and psychopathy, 37, 62–3, 98–9, 101
public attitudes to, 350–7
and rationality, 367–8, 371–4, 449
reasons for, 1, 31, 81–2, 154, 348, 362, 373, 377
reasons for becoming involved in, 1, 29–30, 38, 61, 63, 66,
    67, 75, 87, 97, 110, 229, 234–5, 300, 308–12
and relative deprivation, 38
religion-oriented, 27, 46, 57, 61, 69, 70, 81, 123–4, 154,
    285
and remorse, 61, 113, 115
research on, 4, 5, 7, 19n1, 33–4, 56, 60–4, 77–81, 87, 96–7,
    102–3, 148, 150, 309, 325, 348, 361, 386, 436
and revenge, 126–7
revolutionary, 9, 13, 56, 63, 378, 442
rewards of, 30n23, 33
right-wing, 57, 69, 333
and right-wing authoritarianism, 39
root causes of, 37, 46, 50, 349, 362
Russian, 11–12, 18, 46, 332, 373
Salafi, 36, 37, 38, 49, 59, 61, 305, 361–2, 365
and sensation seeking, 40, 50
separatist, 57, 63, 69, 70, 81, 97, 100, 348
significance of act of, 10
single-issue, 57
social revolutionary, 57
and socioeconomic factors, 195, 227–8
and sociopathy, 64, 99, 103
state(-sponsored), 5, 32, 33, 42–3, 50, 57, 68, 146, 202, 406,
    410–17, 435
state acquiescence to, 411
state-supported, 411
statistics on, 43, 163, 347–9, 385, 411
stereotypes of, 130, 382
strategy of, 371–3
substate, 5, 32, 33, 57, 65, 146, 202, 406, 413, 435
successful, 65, 304, 336, 349, 350, 354, 386
support for, 2, 39, 41, 47, 49, 51n36, 61, 67, 69, 110, 161,
    195, 206–7, 247–8, 253–66, 272, 282, 284–8, 335, 350,
    375, 377, 379
surrogate, 411
"syndrome" approach to, 6, 35–42, 49–50
targets of, 4, 11, 15, 70, 375
and "terror," 411
"tool" approach to, 6, 35–6, 43–5, 49, 50
transnational, 57, 61, 67, 197, 203, 209, 211–25, 383–403
Turkish, 332
typology of, 56–8, 66, 98, 386
understanding, 3, 50, 56, 303
unified theory of, 80
Uruguayan, 332
users of, 48–9
varieties of, 4, 5, 349

Terrorist groups, 2, 5, 16, 26–33, 36, 41, 49–50, 57, 59, 63, 64,
    71, 74, 82, 97–8, 105, 147–8, 159, 162, 167, 169, 172, 203,
    212–13, 215, 219, 259, 274, 299, 307–8, 310–15, 331–7,
    340–1, 348, 364, 393, 395
  conflict within, 334–6
  cooperation among, 393, 398
  group extremity shift in, 340–2
  individual extremity shift in, 342–4
  resource endowments of, 447, 451, 463
  rewards of membership of, 336
Terrorist model, 387–90, 393–6
"Terrorist personality," 28, 37, 42, 333, 348
"Terrorist revolution," 16
"Terroristic warfare," 10, 15, 16–17
Terrorists, 13, 23–4, 27, 36, 72, 75, 101, 109, 117, 303, 330,
    364, 368, 374–5, 378–82, 446
  abnormality of, 98–9, 102–4, 106
  Algerian, 337
  "anarchic ideologue," 332, 334
  biographies of, 361
  cognition in, 74–5
  demographic characteristics of, 7, 37, 59, 61, 209, 227–8,
    332–3
  families of, 110, 113, 114, 116, 117, 126, 231, 237, 305, 336,
    364
  German, 71, 104, 332, 337, 398n16
  hierarchy of, 114
  as individuals, 332–3
  Irish, 71
  Islamist, 59, 109, 110–14
  Italian, 28, 102, 310, 313
  left-wing, 46, 58, 59, 60, 69, 102, 105
  "lone wolf," 247, 363
  "nationalist-separatist," 332, 334–5
  negotiation with, 23, 49, 75, 82, 96, 105, 153, 164–6, 170,
    172–5, 177, 206, 272, 313, 349, 369, 376, 381, 383, 384
  Palestinian, 52n36, 53n84, 59, 89, 116, 161, 175, 186, 190,
    195, 332, 335, 395, 398n16, 448
  political careers of, 311–12
  political identities of, 312–14
  preventing people from becoming, 91, 148, 443
  psychology of, 23, 57, 70–6, 105
  psychosocial data on, 57–62
  punishment of, 47, 113, 167, 445
  recruitment of, 113, 307–15, 336–40, 438, 443, 450, 451
  religious fundamentalist, 109
  right-wing, 58, 59, 60, 102
  secular, 109, 110–12, 116, 154, 158
  social-network analysis of, 361
  socialization of, 36, 78, 113, 186, 188, 192, 243, 312–14, 340
  sociological characteristics of, 7, 227, 242, 245, 332–3,
    362–3
Thabet Thabet, 448
Theory of mind, 1
Thinning of forces, 399–400
Totalitarianism, 13, 18, 187, 195, 245, 321
Trojan War, 76
Troop thickening, 400–1
Trotskyism, 328, 348
Truman, Harry, 44

Tupamaros, 26, 319, 325, 332, 333
Turgenev, Ivan, 17
Turkey, 120, 157, 158, 159, 164, 165, 166, 167, 168, 177, 181, 182, 186, 188, 299, 333, 351
Tutu, Desmond, 149
TWA hijacking, 1985, 331, 335
28th of March Brigade (Brigata 28 Marzo), 309
Tyranny, 15, 16, 17, 25, 412

Umberto I, 13–14, 19n19
Unconscious, the, 70–1, 73
Underground press, 18
Unification Church, 303, 337–9
United Red Army, 335
United States of America, 14, 34, 39, 46, 92, 124, 153, 158, 167, 169, 170, 176–8, 181, 193, 205, 217, 248, 254, 269–70, 281, 283, 285–9, 292–5, 301, 321, 349, 361–5, 383, 398, 414, 421–4, 432, 443
    anarchism in, 9, 13–14
    as "Great Satan," 284, 294
    political extremism in, 26
    terrorism in, 58, 59; see also Weathermen
Uruguay, 26, 319, 325, 332
US embassy attack, Beirut, 1983, 158, 349
US embassy bombings, East Africa, 1998, 361, 362, 419
US embassy takeover, Tehran, 1979, 391, 397
US Marines, bombing of Beirut barracks of, 1983, 375
Uzbekistan, 441, 443

Vaillant, August, 12
Vandals, 319
Venezuela, 332
Victimization, 99, 128, 151, 427
    sense of, 87, 112, 152
Vienna, second siege of, 407
Vietnam War, 162, 301, 317, 318, 322, 329, 334, 413
Violence, 23, 26, 41, 42, 65, 67, 88, 96, 97, 99–101, 111, 112, 146, 151, 204, 263, 285, 291, 293, 300, 302, 303, 321, 331, 347, 371, 373, 377, 405, 407, 410, 415, 419, 427, 431, 443, 449–54, 456, 458
    "age of," 9
    cycles of, 296, 301, 446
    inhibitions against, 1, 294, 295, 344, 373, 376
    justification of, 407, 415, 430–2
    morality of, 414
    Palestinian, 445, 446–7, 449, 452–6, 458, 460–2

political, 1, 6, 60, 69, 75, 77, 189, 194, 202–3, 304, 305, 319, 321, 324–5, 331, 374n10, 409, 464
    reasons for, 68, 74
    research on, 148, 194
    revolutionary, 9, 13, 15, 375, 415
Visigoths, 319

Waco siege, 421
Waite, Terry, 381
"War on Terror," 43, 152, 213, 256, 294, 436
Warner, John, 148
Weapons
    biological, 3, 33, 435
    chemical, 3, 291, 435
    of mass destruction, 44, 56, 109–10, 111, 115, 117, 435
    nuclear, 3, 30, 34, 176, 289, 291, 334, 435
"Weather Bureau," 317, 319, 320
"Weather collectives," 320
Weathermen, 26, 36, 39, 40, 41, 301–2, 317–30, 341, 372
West Bank, the, 38, 41, 48, 49, 60, 62, 125, 128–9, 132, 135, 136, 150, 152, 157, 158, 159, 162, 164, 166, 167, 172–6, 178, 193, 203–4, 206–8, 270, 447, 450, 475n8
Wiesel, Elie, 149
"Women's Militia," 317
World Islamic Front for the Jihad against the Jews and Crusaders, 443
World Trade Center bombing, 1993, 407, 419–21, 424, 429, 430, 432

Xenophobia, 75, 243, 245

Yassin, Sheikh Ahmed, 170, 171, 426, 428, 431, 442, 445, 448
Yemen, 158, 181
Yousef, Ramzi, 420, 424
Yugoslavia, former, 263, 265

ZANU, 353
ZAPU, 353
Zasulich, Vera, 52n41
Zealots, 5, 24, 36, 146, 443
Ze'evi, Rehavam, 136
Zhelyabov, Andrey, 15, 17
Zibri, Mustafa (Abu Ali Mustafa), 448
Zicher, Stephen, 318
Zionism, 114, 116, 127, 128, 140, 175, 352
Zionist Organization of America, 372